# Child Psychotherapy

# Child Psychotherapy

## PRACTICE AND THEORY

MARY R. HAWORTH, Editor

JASON ARONSON INC.
*Northvale, New Jersey*
*London*

**THE MASTER WORK SERIES**

**First softcover edition 1994**



**Library of Congress Cataloging-in-Publication Data**

ISBN: 1-56821-265-8
Library of Congress Catalog Card Number: 94-71315

Manufactured in the United States of America. Jason Aronson Inc. offers books and cassettes. For information and catalog write to Jason Aronson Inc., 230 Livingston Street, Northvale, New Jersey 07647.

# Preface

THE PRESENT volume was planned as a book in child psychotherapy for use by students and practitioners of clinical psychology, child psychiatry, and social work. Many significant writings in this field have appeared as articles in journals representing various disciplines, and each of the existing books on the subject presents only one point of view. An effort has been made to assemble representative selections from differing approaches to child therapy and to arrange them so as to cover the various aspects of the therapeutic process. Regardless of school or theory, all treatment plans involve an initial and a final session; the therapist–child interaction in the intervening hours will necessarily encompass resistance, transference, and countertransference; reflections and/or interpretations will be made; and the problem of limits will need to be faced. Such are the issues to be treated. Whenever possible, contrasting methods or points of view are presented.

Few therapists strictly adhere to one theoretical orientation or school of therapy. But it is important that a therapist develop a general philosophy of therapy and that he function consistently within his chosen framework. To achieve such a philosophy, he must have given thought to, and been continually concerned with, the general problems and situations that will arise in any therapeutic relationship. It is assumed that the reader is familiar with the fields of personality dynamics and childhood psychopathology and that he has acquired a groundwork in therapeutic processes including experience with adult patients. However, students often find that work with children raises issues and technical problems which never occurred in their contacts with adults.

Since this book is intended as an orientation in the field of child therapy, the selections are mainly concerned with the individual treatment of the neurotic child in the five-to-twelve–year age range. It is felt that problems in handling the psychotic child, the adolescent, the very young child, and the group therapy situation are best mastered after experience with a middle-age range and with the milder disorders. Some of the procedures discussed would need to be modified or avoided when working with the seriously disturbed child. The editor's introductory sections will raise issues and point out problems. Questions will be asked, rather than answered, in order to stimulate further consideration before the situations are actually encountered in the playroom. From the various points of view represented by the different authors, the reader is invited to select those aspects which he can assimilate most comfortably into his own emerging frame of reference.

Part I consists of general theoretical considerations, such as the meaning of play in the life of the child and adult, the description of several therapeutic orientations, the question of diagnosis prior to therapy, and the selection of appropriate techniques. Part II is concerned with structuring the therapy situation for the parent and the child, whereas Part III covers the processes encountered in the course of therapy—resistance, transference, interpretation, and termination. Part IV is designed to aid the therapist in understanding the symbolic significance of the child's activities, play themes, and artistic productions. Part V is again concerned with theoretical issues, such as the assessment of progress, research, and the therapist–supervisor relationship.

It is recognized that one cannot teach a step-by-step method of therapy and that the student cannot expect to learn how to "do" therapy from books. Freud best describes the learner's dilemma:

> He who hopes to learn the fine art of the game of chess from books will soon discover that only the opening and closing moves of the game admit of exhaustive systematic description, and that the endless variety of the moves which develop from the opening defies description; the gap left in the instructions can only be filled in by the zealous study of games fought out by master-hands. The rules which can be laid down for the practical application of psychoanalysis in treatment are subject to similar limitations.[1]

Erikson cautions the novice against becoming engrossed in theoretical details and missing the real essence of therapy. Viewing his clinical descriptions as an analytical instrument, he states:

> But to learn to know the properties and the range of an instrument is one thing—to learn to use it unself-consciously and firmly, another. It is good to be explicit for the sake of training; for the sake of therapy, it is necessary to act with intuitive regard for implied probabilities and possibilities. The scientific world wants to know *why* we are so sure to be on the right track; the patients only *that* we are sure.[2]

---

[1] Sigmund Freud, "Further Recommendations in the Technique of Psycho-Analysis [1913]," in *Collected Papers* (New York: Basic Books, 1959), II, 342.

[2] Erik H. Erikson, "Studies in the Interpretation of Play: I. Clinical Observation of Play Disruption in Young Children," *Genetic Psychology Monographs*, XXII (1940), 557–671, p. 667. *See also* Chapter 13, this volume.

Many of the selections concern more than one topic; consequently, problems have arisen in placement. To avoid cutting and segmenting, selections have been placed where the bulk of their content fits. Their other pertinent aspects are referred to in the editor's chapter introductions. In order to produce a cohesive, comprehensible collection, parts of certain selections have been deleted. Where this is done, it is indicated by ellipses. In general, case material has been omitted to conserve space, except where it is basic to the discussion. There is no intent to minimize the value of case material; in fact, a beginning therapist should be encouraged to read the case descriptions scattered throughout the literature.

Also in the interest of cohesiveness, the references for the selections have been gathered at the ends of chapters. Only references mentioned in text are included.

It may be of interest to point out that, of the 43 sources used, all but five have been published within the past twenty years (since 1944), thus attesting to the still-nascent state of this area of therapy.

Appreciation is extended to all the authors who agreed to let their writings be reproduced and to the publishers for granting permission to do so. Specific notations appear in the Acknowledgments section.

Mary R. Haworth

# Contents

PART ONE

# THEORETICAL CONSIDERATIONS

❀ CHAPTER ONE

# The Meaning of Play

MANY THEORIES of play have been proposed, from Plato to current psychologists and philosophers. But the use of play as a therapeutic medium with young children is a recent approach. Erikson, in a chapter entitled, "Toys and Reasons," an excerpt of which is presented here, treats play as an ego function, examines the role of play in adulthood, and suggests that Freud was the first to recognize the therapeutic possibilities of play for the child. Erikson sees play as the child's means of achieving mastery over traumatic experiences and suggests fresh approaches for understanding the meaning of play to the child.

In the second selection, Amster outlines several purposes served by the use of play techniques: an aid in diagnostic understanding; a substitute for verbal methods; and a medium for working through defenses, handling anxieties, and symbolically relieving tensions. As therapy progresses, play can help the child develop new skills, creative outlets, and avenues of sublimation for use outside the therapy situation.

## ❀ *Toys and Reasons*

ERIK H. ERIKSON

What is play—and what is it not? Let us consult language and then return to children. The sunlight playing on the waves qualifies for the attribute "playful" because it faithfully remains within the rules of the game. It does not really mingle and interfere with the chemical world of the waves. It demands from them only that they be good sports and agree to an intermingling of patterns. These patterns change with effortless rapidity and with a repetitiveness which promises pleasing phenomena within a predictable range without ever creating the same configuration twice.

When man plays he must intermingle with the laws of things and people in a similarly uninvolved and light fashion. He must do something which he has chosen to do without being compelled by urgent interests or impelled by strong passion; he must feel entertained and free of any fear or hope of serious consequences. He is on vacation from reality, or, as is most commonly emphasized, he does not work. It is this opposition to work which gives play a number of connotations. One of these is "mere fun"—whether it is hard to do or not. As Mark Twain commented, "constructing artificial flowers . . . is work, while climbing the Mont Blanc is only amusement." In Puritan times and places, however, mere fun always connoted sin; the Quakers warned that you must "gather the flowers of pleasure in the fields of duty." Men of equally puritan mind could permit play only because they believed that to find "relief from moral activity is in itself a moral necessity." Poets, however, place the emphasis elsewhere: "Man is perfectly human only when he plays," said Schiller. Thus play is a borderline phenomenon to a number of human activities, and, in its own playful way, it tries to elude definition.

It is true that even the most strenuous and dangerous play is by definition not work, i.e., does not produce commodities. Where it does, it "goes professional." But this fact, from the start, makes the comparison of adult and child's play somewhat senseless, for the adult is a commodity-producing and commodity-exchanging animal, whereas the child is only preparing to become one. To the working adult, play is re-creation. It permits a periodical stepping out from those forms of defined limitation which are his reality.

Take gravity: to juggle, to jump, or to climb adds unused dimensions to the awareness of our body. Play here gives a sense of divine leeway, of excess space.

Take time: in trifling, in dallying, we lazily thumb our noses at this, our slave-driver. Where every minute counts, playfulness vanishes. This puts competitive sports on the borderline of play, they seem to make concessions to the pressure of space and time, only to defeat this very pressure by a fraction of a yard or of a second.

Take fate and causality, which have determined who and what we are and where. In games of chance we re-establish equality before fate and secure a virgin chance to every player willing to observe a few rules which, if compared to the rules of reality, seem arbitrary and senseless. Yet they are magically convincing, like the reality of a dream, and they demand absolute compliance. Let a player forget that such play must remain his free choice, let him become possessed by the demon of gambling, and playfulness vanishes again. He is a gambler, not a player.

Take social reality and our defined cubicles in it. In play-acting we can be what in life we could not or would not be. But, as the play-actor begins to believe in his impersonation, he comes closer to a state of hysteria, if not worse; while if he tries, for purposes of gain, to make others believe in his "role," he becomes an impostor.

Take our bodily drives. The bulk of the nation's advertising effort exploits our wish to play with necessity, to make us believe, for example, that to inhale and to eat are not pleasurable necessities, but a fanciful game with ever-new and sensuous nuances. Where the need for these nuances becomes compulsive, it creates a general state of mild addiction and gluttony which ceases to transmit a sense of abundance and, in fact, produces an undercurrent of discontent.

Last but not least, in love life we describe as sex play the random activities preceding the final act which permit the partners to choose body part, intensity, and tempo ("what, and with which, and to whom," as the limerick has it). Sex play ends when the final act begins, narrowing choice and giving rein to "nature." Where one of the preparatory random acts becomes compelling enough to completely replace the final act, playfulness vanishes and perversion—or inhibition—begins.

This list of playful situations in a variety of human endeavors indicates the narrow area within which our ego can feel superior to the confinement of space and time and to the definitiveness of social reality—free from the compulsions of conscience and from impulsions of irrationality. Only within these limitations, then, can man feel at one with his ego; no wonder he feels "only human when he plays." But this presupposes one more most decisive condition: he must play rarely and work most of the time. He must have a defined role in society. Playboys and gamblers are both envied and resented by the working man. We like to see them exposed or ridiculed, or we put them to worse than work by forcing them to live in luxurious cages.

The playing child, then, poses a problem: whoever does not work shall not play. Therefore, to be tolerant of the child's play the adult must invent theories which show either that childhood play is really work or that it does not count. The most popular theory and the easiest on the observer is that the child is *nobody yet* and that the nonsense of his play reflects it. Scientists have tried to find other explanations for the freaks of childish play by considering them representative of the fact that childhood is neither here nor there. According to Spencer, play uses up surplus energy in the young of a number of mammalians who do not need to feed or protect themselves because their parents do it for them. However, Spencer noticed that, wherever circumstances permit play, tendencies are "simulated" which are "unusually ready to act, unusually ready to have their correlative feelings aroused." Early psychoanalysis added to this the "cathartic" theory, according to which play has a definite function in the growing being in that it permits him to work off past emotions and to find imaginary relief for past frustrations.

In order to evaluate these theories, let us turn to the game of another, a younger boy. He lived near another mighty river, the Danube, and his play was recorded by another great psychologist, Sigmund Freud (1937), who wrote:

> Without the intention of making a comprehensive study of these phenomena, I availed myself of an opportunity which offered of elucidating the first game invented by himself of a boy eighteen months old. It was more than a casual observation, for I lived for some weeks under the same roof as the child and his parents, and it was a considerable time before the meaning of his puzzling and continually repeated performance became clear to me.
>
> The child was in no respect forward in his intellectual development; . . . but he made himself understood by his parents and the maidservant and had a good reputation for behaving "properly." He did not disturb his parents at night; he scrupulously obeyed orders about not touching various objects and not going into certain rooms; and above all he never cried when his mother went out and left him for hours together, although the tie to his mother was a very close one: she had not only nourished him herself, but had cared for him and brought him up without any outside help. Occasionally, however, this well-behaved child evinced the troublesome habit of flinging into the corner of the room or under the bed all the little things he could lay his hands on, so that to gather up his toys was often no light task. He accompanied this by an expression of interest and gratification, emitting a loud, long-drawn-out "O-o-o-oh" which, in the judgment of the mother (one that coincided with my own), was not an interjection but meant "go away" [*fort*]. I saw at last that this was a game and that the child used all his toys only to play "being gone" [*fort sein*] with them. One day I made an observation that confirmed my view. The child had a wooden reel with a piece of string wound round it. It never occurred to him, for example, to drag this after him on the floor and so play horse and cart with it, but he kept throwing it with considerable skill, held by the string, over the side of his little draped cot, so that the reel disappeared into it, then said his significant "O-o-o-oh" and drew the reel by the string out of the cot again, greeting its reappearance with a joyful *Da* ["there"]. This was therefore the complete game, disappearance and return, the first act being the only one generally observed by the onlookers and the one untiringly repeated by the child as a game for its own sake, although the greater pleasure unquestionably attached to the second act. . . . This interpretation was fully established by a further observation. One day when the mother had been out for some hours, she was greeted on her return by the information "Baby o-o-o-oh," which at first remained unintelligible. It soon proved that, during his long, lonely hours, he had found a method of bringing about his own disappearance. He had discovered his reflection in the long mirror which nearly reached to the ground and had then crouched down in front of it, so that the reflection was *fort*.

To understand what Freud saw in this game, we must note that at the time he was interested in (and, in fact, writing about) the strange phenomenon of the "repetition compulsion," i.e., the need to re-enact painful experiences in words or acts. We have all experienced the occasional need of talking incessantly about a painful event (an insult, a quarrel, or an operation) which one might be expected to want to forget. We know of traumatized individuals who, instead of finding recovery in sleep, are repeatedly awakened by dreams in which they re-experience the original trauma. We also suspect that it is not so innocently accidental that some people make the same mistakes over and over again; that they "coincidentally" and in utter blindness marry the same kind of impossible partner from whom they have just been divorced; or that a series of analogous accidents and mishaps always must happen just to *them*. In all of these cases, so Freud concluded, the individual unconsciously arranges for variations of an original theme which he has not learned either to overcome or to live with; he tries to master a situation which in its original form had been too much for him by meeting it repeatedly and of his own accord.

As Freud was writing about this, he became aware of the solitary play described and of the fact that the frequency of the main theme (something or somebody disappears and comes back) corresponded to the intensity of the life experience reflected, namely, the mother's leaving in the morning and her return at night.

This dramatization takes place in the play sphere. Utilizing his mastery over objects, the child can arrange them in such a way that they permit him to imagine that he is master of his life predicament as well. For, when the mother had left him, she had removed herself from the sphere of his cries and demands; and she had come back only when it happened to suit her. In his game, however, the little boy has the mother by a string. He makes her go away, even throws her away, and then makes her come back at his pleasure. He has, as Freud put it, "turned passivity into activity"; he plays at doing something that was in reality done to him.

Freud mentions three items which may guide us in a further social evaluation of this game. First, the child threw the object away. Freud sees in this a possible expression of revenge—"If you don't want to stay with me, I don't want you"—and thus an additional gain in active mastery by an apparent growth of emotional autonomy. In his second play act, however, the child goes further. He abandons the object altogether and, with the use of a full-length mirror, plays "going away" from himself and returning to himself. He is now both the person who is being left and the person who leaves. He has become master by incorporating not only the person who, in life, is beyond his control, but the whole situation, with *both* its partners.

This is as far as Freud goes with his interpretation. But we may make a point of the fact that the child greets the returning mother with the information that he has learned to "go away" from himself. For the game alone, as reported by Freud, could be the beginning of an increasing tendency on the child's part to take life experiences into a solitary corner and to rectify them in fantasy, and only in fantasy. Let us assume that, at the mother's return, the child were to show complete indifference, extending his revenge to the life situation and indicating that he, indeed, can now take care of himself, that he does not need her. This often happens after the mother's first excursions: she rushes back, eager to embrace her child, only to be met by a bland face. She may then feel rejected and turn against or away from the unloving child, who is thus easily made to feel that the vengeance in the game of throwing away and his subsequent boast has hit its mark too well, that he has indeed made the mother go away, whereas he has only tried to recover from being abandoned by her. Thus the basic problem of being left and leaving would not be improved by its solution in solitary play. Our little boy, however, told his mother of his play, and we may assume that she, far from being offended, demonstrated interest and maybe even pride in his ingenuity. He was then better off all around. He had adjusted to a difficult situation, he had learned to manipulate new objects, and he had received social recognition for his method.

But does the child's play—so a frequent question goes—always "mean" something personal and sinister? What if ten children, in horse-and-buggy days, begin to play with reels on strings, pulling them behind themselves and playing horsie? Must it mean anything to one of them over and beyond what it seems to mean to all?

As we have said already, children, if traumatized, choose for their dramatizations play material which is available in their culture and manageable at their age. What is available depends on the cultural circumstances and is therefore common to all children who share these circumstances. Ben's[1] today do not play steamboat, but use bicycles as more tangible objects of coordination—which does not prevent them from imagining, on the way to school or the grocery, that they are flying through the air and machine-gunning the enemy or that they are the Lone Ranger himself on a glorious Silver. What is manageable, however, depends on the child's powers of coordination and therefore is shared only by those who have reached a certain level of maturation. What has a common meaning to all the children in a community (i.e., the idea of having a reel and string represent a living thing on a leash) may have a special meaning to some (i.e., all those who have just learned to manipulate reel and string and may thus be ready to enter a new sphere of participation and communal symbolization). Yet all of this may have, in addition, a unique meaning to individual children who have lost a person or an animal and therefore endow the game with a particular significance. What these children "have by the string" is not just any animal; it is the personification of a particular, a significant, and a lost animal—or person. To evaluate play, the observer must, of course, have an idea of what all the children of a given age in a given community are apt to play. Only thus can he decide whether the unique meaning transcends the common meaning. To understand the unique meaning itself requires careful observation, not only of the play's content and form, but also

[1] Erikson is referring to pages of his chapter in which he discusses Mark Twain's scene in which Tom Sawyer is whitewashing the fence and Ben Rogers approaches, impersonating a steamboat.

of accompanying words and visible affects, especially those which lead to . . . "play disruption."

In order to approach the problem of anxiety in play, let us consider the activity of building and destroying a tower. Many a mother thinks that her little son is in a "destructive stage" or even has a "destructive personality" because, after building a big, big tower, the boy cannot follow her advice to leave the tower for Daddy to see, but instead *must* kick it and make it collapse. The almost manic pleasure with which children watch the collapse in a second of the product of long play labor has puzzled many, especially since the child does not appreciate it at all if his tower falls by accident or by a helpful uncle's hand. He, the builder, must destroy it himself. This game, I should think, arises from the not-so-distant experience of sudden falls at the very time when standing upright on wobbly legs afforded a new and fascinating perspective on existence. The child who consequently learns to *make* a tower "stand up" enjoys causing the same tower to waver and collapse; in addition to the active mastery over a previously passive event, it makes one feel stronger to know that there is somebody weaker, and towers, unlike little sisters, can't cry and call Mummy. But, since it is the child's still-precarious mastery over space which is thus to be demonstrated, it is understandable that watching somebody else kick one's tower may make the child see himself in the tower rather than in the kicker; all fun evaporates. Circus clowns later take over when they obligingly fall all over the place from mere ineptness and yet continue to challenge gravity and causality with ever-renewed innocence; there are, then, even big people who are funnier, dumber, and wobblier. Some children, however, who find themselves too much identified with the clown cannot stand his downfalls; to them they are "not funny." This example throws light on the beginning of many an anxiety in childhood, where anxiety around the child's attempt at ego mastery finds unwelcome "support" from adults who treat him roughly or amuse him with exercises which he likes only if and when he himself has initiated them.

The child's play begins with and centers on his own body. This we shall call "autocosmic play." It begins before we notice it as play and consists at first in the exploration by repetition of sensual perceptions, of kinesthetic sensations, of vocalizations, etc. Next, the child plays with available persons and things. He may playfully cry to see what wave length would serve best to make the mother reappear, or he may indulge in experimental excursions on her body and on the protrusions and orifices of her face. This is the child's first geography, and the basic maps acquired in such interplay with the mother no doubt remain guides for the ego's first orientation in the "world." Here we call as a witness Santayana (1936):

> . . . Far, far in a dim past, as if it had been in another world or in a pre-natal condition, Oliver remembered the long-denied privilege of sitting in his mother's lap. It had been such a refuge of safety, of softness, of vantage. You

> were carried and you were enveloped in an amplitude of sure protection, like a king on his throne, with his faithful bodyguard many ranks deep about him; and the landscape beyond, with its messengers and its motley episodes, became the most entertaining of spectacles, where everything was unexpected and exciting, yet where nothing could go wrong; as if your mother herself had been telling you a story, and these pictures were only the illustrations to it which painted themselves in your listening mind.

The "microsphere"—i.e., the small world of manageable toys—is a harbor which the child establishes, to return to when he needs to overhaul his ego. But the thing-world has its own laws: it may resist reconstruction, or it may simply break to pieces; it may prove to belong to somebody else and be subject to confiscation by superiors. Often the microsphere seduces the child into an unguarded expression of dangerous themes and attitudes which arouse anxiety and lead to sudden play disruption. This is the counterpart in waking life of the anxiety dream; it can keep children from trying to play just as the fear of night terror can keep them from going to sleep. If thus frightened or disappointed in the microsphere, the child may regress into the autosphere—daydreaming, thumb-sucking, masturbating. On the other hand, if the first use of the thing-world is successful and is guided properly, the pleasure of mastering toy things becomes associated with the mastery of the traumata which were projected on them and with the prestige gained through such mastery.

Finally, at nursery-school age, playfulness reaches into the "macrosphere," the world shared with others. First these others are treated as things, are inspected, run into, or forced to "be horsie." Learning is necessary in order to discover what potential play content can be admitted only to fantasy or only to autocosmic play, what content can be successfully represented only in the microcosmic world of toys and things, and what content can be shared with others and forced upon them.

As this is learned, each sphere is endowed with its own sense of reality and mastery. For quite a while, then, solitary play remains an indispensable harbor for the overhauling of shattered emotions after periods of rough going in the social seas. This and the fact that a child can be counted upon to bring into the solitary play arranged for him whatever aspect of his ego has been ruffled most form the fundamental condition for our diagnostic reliance on "play therapy," which will be discussed next.

What is infantile play, then? We saw that it is not the equivalent of adult play, that it is not recreation. The playing adult steps sideward into another reality; the playing child advances forward to new stages of mastery. I propose the theory that the child's play is the infantile form of the human ability to deal with experience by creating model situations and to master reality by experiment and planning. It is in certain phases of his work that the adult projects past experience into dimensions which seem manageable. In the laboratory, on the stage, and on the drawing board, he relives the past and thus relieves left-over affects; in reconstructing the model situation, he redeems his failures and strengthens his hopes. He anticipates the future from the point of view of a corrected and shared past.

No thinker can do more, and no playing child less. As William Blake puts it: "The child's toys and the old man's reasons are the fruits of the two seasons."

Modern play therapy is based on the observation that a child made insecure by a secret hate against or fear of the natural protectors of his play in family and neighborhood seems able to use the protective sanction of an understanding adult to regain some play peace. Grandmothers and favorite aunts may have played that role in the past; its professional elaboration of today is the play therapist. The most obvious condition is that the child has the toys and the adult for himself and that sibling rivalry, parental nagging, or any kind of sudden interruption does not disturb the unfolding of his play intentions, whatever they may be. For to "play it out" is the most natural self-healing measure childhood affords. . . .

# *Differential Uses of Play in Treatment of Young Children*

FANNY AMSTER

The play activity of a child, his natural medium for self-expression, has stimulated much thought, experimentation, and conclusions as to the ways in which play can be used in treatment of children. We are all aware of the many psychoanalytic contributions on play technique and of how we caseworkers, in our usual adaptive manner, take over psychoanalytic contributions. We must keep in mind that the differences in the psychoanalyst's and the caseworker's use of play are inherent in the differences in training, orientation, understanding, experience, and skill. In other words, the caseworker's use of play in treatment is basically an adaptation.

In my experience as a caseworker, I have attempted to develop some understanding of what play means to a child. I have tried to integrate such understanding with my casework training, the agency's function, the child as a person, and the problems he presents. Through the composite of this awareness and integration, I have attempted to evolve applicable uses of play in the treatment of children.

As have others, I, too, have found play to have many meanings and values to a child. Essentially, play is an activity a child comprehends and in which he is comfortable, an integral part of his world, his method of communication, his medium of exchange, and his means of testing, partly incorporating and mastering external realities.

A child, to whom a formal interview situation can be an uncomfortable experience, can feel more at ease when he finds play materials which are known entities to him. Provision of play materials means the provision of a medium, a natural means of communication through which the child's problems may be expressed more readily and the treatment be more likely to succeed.

In treatment of children, play is always a medium of exchange, and it is comparable to words, the adult's medium of exchange. It is not a therapy in itself any more than words can be. All therapies require a therapeutic relationship and a medium of exchange. The purpose of the play activity determines its role and importance in treatment. *Therefore, play as a medium differs from play as a technique even as words differ from any purposive use of them. Play is a technique when it is used in treatment for definite diagnostic and therapeutic purposes.*

I have found various adaptations of play activity to be useful in the treatment of children. These adaptations have differential purposes and values and varying roles for the therapist. In what follows, I shall attempt to define, illustrate, and examine six uses of play through excerpts of case material. Although I recognize that the use of excerpts isolates a technique from its total context in a case and necessitates the omission of pertinent data, I believe that only by the method of using excerpts of case material can these uses of play be defined clearly within limited space.

As these uses of play are delineated, each excerpt of case material will be examined for the diagnostic and therapeutic aspects. None of these uses are mutually exclusive. More than one use of play is usually necessary in the total treatment of a child, and all uses have both diagnostic and therapeutic values. The conscious direction of the play activity gives it purpose, meaning, and value in treatment.

Play can be used for diagnostic understanding of the child, supplementing the historical material. We can observe the child's capacity to relate himself to others, his distractibility, his rigidity, his areas of preoccupation, his areas of inhibition, the direction of his aggression, his perception of people, his wishes, and his perception of himself. In the play, his behavior, ideas, feelings, and expressions help our understanding of his problem and how he sees it.

MARTHA, age nine, is referred because she wrote an impassioned love note to a boy in school. She is a stout, meticulously dressed girl who walks with her arms far away from her body. In play, she tries to keep clean, avoids using her hands, and refers to paints as "dirty." She squirms as I begin modeling in clay, vehemently insists that I model fully dressed figures, prudishly says she dislikes people without clothes, and furtively peers at some undressed dolls in the room.

In this play activity, Martha reveals her aversion to dirt, discomfort about her sex curiosity, a strong desire to peep, efforts to cloak her interest in nudity, and the possibility of masturbation.

ELLEN, age nine, is an unusually polite, compliant child who speaks like an old woman resigned to her many burdens. To help her feel like a child, I suggest we play, and she selects drawing, but uncomfortably asks for suggestions. When I comment that her ideas are important and that she draw what she wants, Ellen sits with pencil poised in mid-air while she frowns and radiates mental struggle. After several minutes, she draws an unimaginative, precise picture, a copy of one she recently made in school.

In this play activity, Ellen reveals inhibitions of play and thought and inability to act like a child.

LAWRENCE, age six, elder of two children, is referred for spitting on people. For several interviews, he draws large figures of women with exaggerated breasts and then scribbles over and spits on them. As he annihilates these figures, he boasts of his strength and, with mischievous glances at me, carefully accumulates a quantity of spit. He alternates the drawings of women with drawings of trees laden with fruit. He makes many demands, snatches what he wants, and insists that I should not see other boys. I limit the amount of materials he can use and give him toys when he does not demand them.

In his play activity, Lawrence shows capacity for relationship and reveals that to him women have large sources of satisfaction; that his spitting provides gratification and retaliation; that fruit probably symbolizes substitutive gratification; that destructiveness makes him feel weak; and that he seeks support and strength through boasting, snatching, and through demands for material gratification and for the only place in the affections of a mother substitute.

These children, cited as illustrations of the use of play for diagnostic understanding, derived some therapeutic values in their individual play activity. Martha achieved some release through a sharing activity with an adult who tolerated her interests and accepted her feelings. Ellen could feel more like a child, learned she was expected to be a child with ideas and imagination, and shared an activity with an adult to whom her ideas and wishes were important. Lawrence secured release of his feelings and shared an experience with an adult whose attitude and handling were different.

Play can be used to establish a working relationship. This use of play is helpful with the young child who lacks the adult's facility for verbal self-expression and with the older child who shows resistance or inability to articulate.

BERTHA, age ten, is referred by her mother, who asks for "lectures" and complains of the girl's temper tantrums. In the interview, Bertha, with stolid expression, seems overtly compliant but guarded in her limited responses. She is startled and nonplussed when I inquire about her interests and blurts out that she likes to draw. I provide the materials, and she draws what she labels as an "ideal girl." We discuss the "ideal girl" whom Bertha vests with an appearance which is the antithesis of her own. When I comment about Bertha's aptitude for drawing, she tearfully blurts out that her family thinks her drawings are babyish. She is surprised by my recognition of her feelings.

In this situation, the therapist provides materials in which Bertha is interested, meets her passive aggression by doing the unexpected, encourages her interests, and identifies with her feelings about her family. Bertha sees she is accepted as a person, releases feeling about her family, has a sharing experience with an adult different from others she knows, and establishes a working relationship with the therapist. Two focal areas of treatment are presented: Bertha's perception of herself as contrasted with the "ideal girl" and Bertha's feelings about her family's attitude toward her and her interests.

JEANNETTE, age nine, is referred for her hostile behavior toward her younger siblings and for refusal to permit her mother out of her sight. History material reveals she has suffered alternate overindulgence and cruel punishment from her father, rejection by her mother, and many traumatic hospitalizations. At the first interview, with a fearful expression in her eyes and rigidity in her body, Jeannette eyes me apprehensively, but slowly enters the room when she sees the play material. For several interviews, she models animals in clay or draws stilted landscapes, keeps her head lowered, and speaks to herself in whispers. Gradually, she permits me to assist her, and I confine my comments to the play activity and to her real abilities. When Jeannette achieves the first therapeutic objective of thawing out, she confides that now she is sure I will not send her away as her mother threatened.

In this situation, the therapist provides play material from which the child can select and through which she can safely express herself, remains passive until invited to share, confines comments to play activity and to the child's abilities, helps the child thaw out, and prepares the child for a relationship. Jeannette slowly releases some tension through her activity, slowly permits the activity to become a sharing one, feels encouraged to again extend herself as a person and to expect warmth from an adult, learns that all adults are not punitive like her mother, feels the therapist is her ally, and establishes a working relationship with the therapist.

ARTHUR, age five, is referred for extreme stubbornness and refusal to speak. In the interview, he stands as far from me as possible and only shakes his head in response to my overtures. I seat myself, begin to model clay figures, and whisper to myself. Arthur edges toward me, peers over my shoulder, and, exasperated, shouts: "What you say?" He grabs some clay and chatters in a husky, flat voice.

In this situation, the therapist ignores the boy's method of avoiding participation, initiates play activity which piques the boy's curiosity and stimulates his desire to participate, whispers to further pique his curiosity and to secure his interest. Arthur begins to speak, surrenders some negativism as he learns to share activity with another person, recognizes that his refusal to speak can block him from pleasure, and establishes a working relationship with the therapist.

These children provided through their individual play activity some additional diagnostic understanding. Bertha revealed her stolidity and limited responses to be defenses against "lectures" and punishment and that she was unaccustomed to any acceptance or interest in her or her feelings. Jeannette's apprehensiveness, inability to share, and whispering to herself revealed her fear of attack and her ways of protecting herself. Arthur showed that his stubbornness and refusal to speak helped him secure attention.

Play can be used to break through a child's way of playing in his daily life and his defenses against anxiety. This use is helpful as an additional way of treating distortions in a child's way of playing.

> Morris, age seven, feels inadequate, and his mother reports that in his games with other children, he emphasizes winning. In one interview, he brings a game of tickets and insists I play with him. When he thinks he is losing the game, he immediately changes the rules. I comment about his way of playing, and we discuss his concern about his strength. Several interviews later, his mother reports that, in his street games, Morris enjoys a game even when he does not win.

Jeannette, Lawrence, and Ellen were also helped through this use of play. Jeannette's protectiveness made it necessary for her to emphasize rules; cleanliness; and tiny, precise production in her play activity. During treatment I encouraged her, through my attitude and participation, to change rules, to smear with paints, and to draw large figures. As the motivations for her protectiveness are worked out, the play activity concurrently helps her learn that she can play in a different way. Lawrence, who snatched everything, learns through the play activity that he must accept limitations and that, when he does not demand, he secures gratification. Ellen showns inhibition of play and thought. In treatment I encourage her to express, develop, and strengthen her own ideas. I stimulate her interest in drawing and in making up stories. Through this play activity, she tests out and learns that self-assertion results in recognition and approbation instead of danger as she feared.

With these children, who had distorted ways of playing, the therapist provides material, opportunities, and encouragement which break through the child's distorted way of playing and his defenses against anxiety. Each child, through the play activity, receives help in developing ways of handling himself which are valuable to him as a child and which will help him as an adult.

Play can be used to help a child verbalize certain conscious material and the associated feelings. This use is helpful when a child blocks in discussing certain material and an impasse in treatment is created.

> STANLEY, age ten, doggedly refuses to discuss his encopresis and his mother's attitude toward him. Since he is interested in building with blocks, I suggest he build a house. He builds one, but omits the bathroom. We discuss what such omission might mean to the imaginary family who lives in the house. Stanley then builds an ornate bathroom, but places it outside the house. We discuss this in terms of the inconvenience to the family. The boy comments that he dislikes the simple bathroom in his home. Later, he relates that he soils himself, that his mother punishes him by whipping and by rubbing his feces on his face, that he gets even because she has to wash his trousers. We discuss the pleasurable aspects of his soiling and whether, through his "getting even," he can achieve the escape he wants from his mother's domination.

In this situation, the therapist uses material in which the boy is interested at this point in treatment; initiates a general play situation and permits the boy to fill in the details; discusses his omission of a reality; makes interpretive remarks geared to the content of the play; and, later, when the boy makes his own associations, the therapist makes interpretations which point up the symptomatic nature of his soiling and which fit this into his general problem. The boy is helped to verbalize material which represents failure, punishment, and retaliation; secures release of his feelings; surrenders some of his negativism; gradually accepts the reality of bathrooms; verbalizes his role in his relationship to his mother; and is helped to doubt the effectiveness of his method. Some of his discomfort is alleviated, and an impasse in treatment is worked out.

> LEON, age seven, who was referred for refusal to attend school, denies any concern as to what his mother and I discuss, yet he always stands outside my door when I am interviewing his mother. In an interview with him, I initiate a play situation with three dolls which are designated as a boy, his mother, and myself. Leon quickly uses chains of paper clips to outline the floor plan of my office and the small outside foyer and uses strips of paper for the office furniture. As he moves the dolls around, he talks freely: "I am standing outside. I can't hear. I smack you down 'cause I can't hear what you tell my mother. I can't smack her down—she's my mother." He acts out and verbalizes what happens from the time he and his mother arrive for their appointments: "We come in. We ask for you. You tell me, 'Come in.' You ask questions. Then you say, 'Time is up. I want to see your mother.' I say, 'Oh, yeh?' I knock you down. I go home with my mother. Now it is next week. We come here. . . ." Leon demonstrates and verbalizes this scene three times, and the intensity of his feelings diminishes. He then starts the same scene but shows that he permits the mother to come into my office and that he accompanies her. He shows that I tell him to go outside and says: "I go out. I try to open the door but you

won't let me. I listen. I can't hear." He quickly draws two figures, designates them as him and me, and says I am shooting and killing him. I recognize his fearfulness, his concern about what will happen to him, and his feeling that I am mean because I limit his desire to control. Leon now draws me a valentine, then decides it is too good for me and that he will keep it.

In this situation, the therapist initiates a general play situation and permits the boy to fill in the details; allows him to continue the play activity until the intensity of his feelings diminishes; and, after the boy has expressed his hostility and fearfulness, the therapist verbalizes his feelings and his wishes. Leon secures release of his feelings of exclusion and fearfulness, feels omnipotent and retaliatory in his play, reduces the intensity of his feelings through the repetitive play, recognizes the unreality of the power he desires, verbalizes guardedly his hostility toward his mother while he uses the therapist as a substitutive foil for her, and expresses mixed feelings for the therapist. Some of his discomfort in the therapeutic relationship has been alleviated, and the barrier in treatment has been removed.

These children provided in their play activity some additional diagnostic understanding. Stanley revealed his desire to maintain infantile behavior and ability to carry his negativism to the point of denying the existence of bathrooms. Leon revealed his desire to maintain infantile omnipotence, his resentment at limitations which were set on his efforts to control and which heightened his feeling of helplessness, and his expectation of annihilation for his behavior.

Play can be used to help a child act out unconscious material and to relieve the accompanying tension. This cathartic use of play deals with symbolic material which has dangerous significance to the child. The therapist must be aware of how much release in play the particular child can tolerate without panic and must be aware of the kind of participation and interpretation in which to engage.

Morton, age seven, is referred for a sudden onset of sleeplessness. He anxiously relates that Max is the name of the neighborhood bully who beat him severely. He slowly writes out: "Max is a triple based [bastard]" and walks restlessly about the room as he shows me how well he can bounce a ball. He quickly accepts my suggestion that we make up a story about a little boy and a big boy. I draw the stick figures while Morton tells the story. He relates that the little boy meets the big boy who beats the little boy until the little boy loses his nose and legs. The little boy manages to escape by running home on his hands. The little boy is disappointed because his mother does not kiss him. A doctor makes the little boy well. The second scene shows the little boy challenging the big boy to fight. This time Morton and I decide the little boy has grown and has muscles. In the fight the little boy knocks off the bully's nose, legs, and arms. The last scene shows the big boy, covered with bandages, confined to his bed and weeping. A doctor is preparing painful remedies, and the little boy who is standing outside the bedroom window is laughing heartily.

In subsequent interviews, Morton acts out through stories and jokes various dangers which overtake small boys and how these boys emerge victorious. After this play activity, Morton spontaneously relates that he and Max are friends and share activities. His mother reports that Morton is now able to sleep.

In this situation, the therapist initiates a general play situation in which the boy can act out his fear and relieve his tension, permits the boy to fill in the details of the play activity, participates in a manner which helps the boy work out his feelings, and interprets only through activity geared to the content of the play. Morton acts out his fear of injury by stronger males, his feeling of weakness, and his desire for strength and retaliation. He becomes less anxious and develops strength through the repetitive play. In his daily life, he forms a friendship on equal terms with a stronger male whom he formerly feared and avoided. He regains his ability to sleep. This boy contributed through play activity additional diagnostic understanding. He revealed his feeling of weakness, desire for consolation from his mother, concern about injury, and his need to feel strong.

Play can be used to develop a child's play interests which he can carry over into his daily life and which will strengthen him for his future life. This use of play has particular importance because of the correlation between the play and work capacities of an individual.

MAURICE, age nine, who has many phobias, is unable to participate in any activity with other children. When, during treatment, he becomes less phobic, he expresses an interest in baseball, but feels inadequate because he cannot throw a ball. I plan several interviews in which Maurice can spend some of the time in the use of a ring-toss game which develops his skill in throwing. Subsequently, he reports that he is playing ball in the street with other children.

JOSEPHINE, age eight, was referred for her voracious thumb-sucking. In one interview she complains that nobody chooses her for games of jumping rope. She feels she would spoil the games because she does not know how "to run in." Since this child needs to compete socially with children her age, I feel it is important for her to learn this activity. I teach her, by revolving a pencil in large circles into which she runs and jumps, how to time the "running in." In a later interview, she reports how well she can jump rope.

With these children, the therapist provides material, opportunities, and encouragement in order that each child may use the interview situation as a place to test himself out as a person and to mobilize his strength for his current and future life. Each child develops sources for current gratification and capacity for future accomplishments.

The examination of these uses of play reveals that, in each use, irrespective of the specific purpose, both diagnostic and therapeutic values are present. Since we can learn more about any child through his play activity, all uses of play add to our diagnostic understanding. Since all play helps a child to share himself and, in varying degree, to re-enact, relive, and release, all play has some therapeutic value. The therapist's role, which includes the tolerant attitude permissive within realistic limitations, depends on the purpose of the play and the child's use of the relationship. The therapist may be part of a room, part of a symbolic representation, or a person. The therapist's role and significance can change many times during the play activity. One generalization of applicable importance is: in all uses of play, diagnostic understanding of the dynamics of a child's personality determines the kind of material selected for the particular child and the kind and degree of the therapist's verbal and motor activity.

As stated above, the limited space led to the plan of using excerpts of case material to illustrate these adaptations of play. The use of excerpts not only removed material from its total context in a case, but necessitated the omission of data which would offer a comprehensive understanding of each child and of the interpretations of the specific case material. With these points in mind, this paper might be viewed as a limited outline of ways in which play can be used in casework treatment of a child. In this outline I have attempted to indicate that the caseworker's role, including participation, limitation, and interpretation, is only analogous to that of the psychoanalyst.

In conclusion, several basic points should be emphasized. Play activity, irrespective of how we want to use it, must be recognized always as a complex, distorted assortment of the child's conscious and unconscious expressions. The therapeutic relationship is basic whether we use the medium of words or the medium of play activity in treatment. The purposive, conscious use of play determines when and how it is interwoven with the therapeutic relationship in our effort to provide a meaningful therapeutic growth experience for our young clients. Treatment of a child includes more than the use of a technique. Total treatment of a child's difficulties also involves the handling and treatment of all factors in his life situation which have contributed to his problem.

## REFERENCES

Freud, S. A *general selection*. J. Rickman (Ed.) London: The Hogarth Press, 1937.

Santayana, G. *The last puritan*. New York: Charles Scribner's Sons, 1936.

❀ CHAPTER TWO

# Varieties of Play Techniques

WOLTMANN'S ARTICLE has been chosen to place play therapy in its historical setting. His introductory comments present various definitions and theories of play and the uses of play in child therapy. He discusses different "schools" or methods of treatment, giving their respective theoretical positions and basic working approaches. For more detailed discussion of any particular play technique the reader is referred to the bibliography at the close of this chapter.

## ❀ *Concepts of Play Therapy Techniques*

ADOLF G. WOLTMANN

Numerous papers, articles, and monographs have appeared in our journal and elsewhere in which play therapy and play techniques have been theoretically evaluated, treated as adjuncts to the analysis of case material, and discussed with regard to the merits of special techniques and materials.

Attempts have been made to select specific methods of play therapy for particular behavior disorders in children; various phases have been investigated with regard to the application of special materials, time factors in terms of length of treatment periods, the effect of antecedent frustration on projective play, and the reflection of the family constellation through doll play. These represent a few of the areas that have come under research scrutiny. Studies have been made concerning attitudes which play methods have evoked in children with regard to parental figures, siblings, and environmental awareness. The expression of aggression through play techniques has been recorded. Some contributions have stressed the diagnostic value of play therapy; others have investigated therapeutic gains; still others have concerned themselves with configurational aspects; and special studies have told us how the average or "normal" child handles play materials at various ages.

Play therapy is a comparatively new field in the treatment of behavior disorders. Only sixteen years ago at the Orthopsychiatric meeting more questions were raised than could be answered. Now there is a large body of interrelated as well as isolated knowledge. The 1938 discussion was much concerned with the legitimacy of the use of the term "play therapy," and the inherent values of play techniques were perhaps insufficiently stressed. We have come a long way since then; today, play therapy and a variety of special play techniques have come to be accepted methods in treatment.

The applications, modifications, concepts, and practices of play therapy and the use of materials are now numerous. Although this may sound confusing, it nevertheless is a healthy sign of development. It demonstrates what Lowrey (1948, p. 692) said when summarizing trends in therapy: ". . . that our approach to the study and treatment of behavior problems must be many-sided, our therapeutic armamentarium must be richly and variously stocked, that we must individualize rather than categorize when it comes to the complex problems of personal and social adjustment, and that our syntheses must be adequate to indicate what to treat, when to treat, and how to treat, maintaining flexibility throughout."

It has been said that wherever there is strong light, there also is a black shadow. The dark side of the play-technique situation is that relevant knowledge, information, and scientific reports are spread throughout numerous books and journals instead of being available in one comprehensive presentation. It is hoped that before long this will be remedied.

In this paper, at the risk of being called presumptuous, I shall attempt to survey play therapy and various play techniques with the aim of indicating what they have in common. The historical and conceptual developmental trends will be sketched briefly and the relative value of researches discussed.

A few basic points should be presented first. With regard to the play of children, I follow Margaret Lowenfeld's definition of play. This, she says, applies to all activities of children "that are spontaneous and self-generating, that are ends in themselves, and that are unrelated to 'lessons' or to the normal physiological needs of the child" (Lowenfeld, 1935). It would follow that the spontaneous and self-generated activities of the child enable him to conceptualize, to structure, and to bring to tangible levels of activity his experiences and the feelings with which he invests them. Play, in this meaning, furnishes the child with opportunities to "act out" situations which are disturbing, conflicting, and confusing to him. The small child especially lacks semantic fluency; since the development of his apperceptive processes is in a state of growing, not to say "groping," flux, various types of play materials seem to be ideally suited for the expression of his feelings and attitudes.

Lowrey (1939, p. 697) states: "The therapeutic effects of the play, however, are, for the most part, secondary to the therapeutic value of the relationship which it facilitates and the insight it affords to the therapist regarding the child's inner problems." There is a great deal of truth in this statement. Yet the child himself gets a great deal of satisfaction out of being able to play what he wants and how he wants. Watching the child and his play activities, and trying to decipher the real meaning of his activities, is a sign of mature, professional responsibility. But we often forget to appreciate thoroughly the child's position. Therapy, in any shape or form, is a two-way street. The child's ability to structure a play situation and to "live out" many of his inner feelings, vague perceptions, and conflicts has a decided cathartic value for him, even though the real meaning of a particular play situation may not be immediately clear to the therapist. Psychoanalysis with adults furnishes many examples of this kind, as when a dream defies immediate understanding on the part of the analyst, but nevertheless the patient experiences an inner feeling of relief.

A good example of how play activities by a child, without the interference or cooperation of the therapist, can lead to a cathartic climax is the case of Billy. This seven-year-old boy was referred for therapy because he constantly showed negativistic attitudes toward his parents, especially toward his mother. He was not getting along with other children, bullied them, and was very aggressive toward his brother, who was two years younger. When first seen, Billy refused to speak and openly resented the therapist and his efforts. After exploring various play possibilities, he settled down to a play pattern which lasted for five sessions. Having dumped all the toys on the floor, Billy picked out a toy jeep which he vigorously pushed through the heap of toys on the floor. The toys hit by the jeep went flying through the playroom until all were scattered. He would then pick up the toys, reassemble them into a heap in the middle of the room and start all over. My attempts to enter into his play were met with hostile silence. At the beginning of the sixth session, Billy spontaneously spoke to me about the power of the jeep, which could "knock out the whole world." From then on, it was possible to direct his attention to his problem of aggression and to ascertain whom he was attacking and why he felt this way.

Certainly a relationship developed between Billy and myself which enabled him to play out what he wanted as he wished. I learned later on that Billy could play this way because he was first victorious in being able to push me away and to keep me, the adult, out of his activities. My permissiveness lessened his fear of adult disapproval and possible punishment. The point raised by Lowrey with regard to the understanding the therapist gains about the inner problems of the child also applies. However, this point must be emphasized: Billy himself experienced a tremendous catharsis by his activities before he was able to tackle his problem of aggression (in which sibling rivalry played only a minor part) in a more directed and organized manner.

Billy's case has strengthened my belief that free play in and of itself has decided cathartic value, over and above the therapeutic implications ascribed to it by the therapist.

We have learned to regard the play activities of children as nonverbal forms of expression, a sort of specific language for the child. It sounds almost ridiculous to restate what is obvious and self-understood, by reminding ourselves that in therapy with children we have selected an activity natural to the child, namely, his ability to play. Yet this is no more ridiculous than the reminder that we all have temperatures, which for the greater part are normal. The physician becomes concerned only when there are deviations and fluctuations in our body heat. Similarly, the therapist becomes concerned when the child's play activities reveal deviations or show unusual features. This is possible only if the therapist understands the meaning of the, for the most part, nonverbal expressions and is able to realize for himself and then indicate to the child the hidden meanings of particular play activity or activities.

The ever-growing literature on play therapy and play techniques is ample proof that we try in many different ways to understand and evaluate this special language of the child. Regardless of the school of thought to which we belong, we seem to agree on the simple but basic assumption that the structuring of toy material leads to configurations which have psychological roots. These in turn are conditioned by the age, previous experiences, intelligence, physical and social maturity, and other abilities of the child who produces play constellations. These play configurations are projections if we see them in the formulation of Lawrence K. Frank. He defines projections as expressions of innermost thoughts, drives, and motivations which are handled and structured in such way that they reflect and express a person's private, idiosyncratic meanings, not what an experimenter has arbitrarily decided beforehand should constitute a proper response. Frank (1948) does not underrate the importance of interpretation, but he underlines the fact that "it is important to recognize that what a subject does in a projective situation may be directly expressing his private world and characteristic personality processes."

To equate play therapy and play techniques with projective methods or techniques may sound surprising. We have been accustomed to think of projective methods and techniques primarily as diagnostic aids. The work of Bellak, Pasquarelli, and Braverman (1949) has shown that a diagnostic projective instrument such as the Thematic Apperception Test can be purposefully utilized in therapy. Whether play activities of children are used therapeutically, or diagnostically as play interviews, or become the topic of research, they must be regarded as projections of the inner life, since we must assume that personality is dynamic. A further assumption is that

> behavior is functional and reflects the compromise between the internal structure of the personality and the demands of a given external situation. The assumption of a personality structure further postulates that one deals here with

> depth phenomena. Readily observable behavior is only a surface manifestation, while many layers and facets of the personality are anchored in the unconscious. Since personality forms a "whole" or "totality," unconscious drives and motivations are related to observable surface phenomena. This allows for the formulation of inferences from the overt observation to the latent structure and content. (Woltmann, 1952)

The adult uses language for expression, but the child needs the representations of configurational reality. In working out a specific situation, the play pattern takes place within a specific setting. The essential elements are visible and form the tangible background against which actions take place. This is directly related to the child's developmental level, in which conceptual abstractions are mostly absent and play activities are only nominally invested with introspection. They usually represent an attempt of the child either to understand, to master, or to clarify his own position in relationship to the world around him. Erikson (1940) regards play activities in children as their microcosm through which they deal with the macrocosm of the adult world. Lowenfeld (1935) has a similar view when she says that the play of children is the expression of the child's relationship to the world. She adds that "no theory of play is possible which is not also a theory which will cover the whole of a child's relation to life," and concludes that play serves the child's need for making contact with the environment. Other aspects of play activities of children are summarized by her as follows:

> Play serves the bridge between the child's consciousness and his emotional experiences, and so fulfills the role that conversation, introspection, philosophy, and religion have for the adult. Play represents to the child the externalized expression of his emotional life, and in this aspect, serves for the child the function taken by art in adult life.

Inherent in play activity is the make-believe element. A child cannot drive a car, fly an airplane, or go into outer space. Reversal of roles in the parent–child or teacher–pupil relationships can be achieved by the child only in a play situation. Overt expressions of hostility, of aggression, and of the desire to punish are not tolerated by the adult world, but are possible for the child in play; such activities are not less real to the child, or less cathartic. The make-believe element eliminates guilt feelings which would appear if action could result in real harm and damage and enables the child to be victorious over forces otherwise above his reach and capacity.

Lauretta Bender[a] stated several years ago that one could do play therapy with children living near the Equator by using sand, stones, and palm leaves; snow and pieces of ice could serve the same purpose in arctic regions, provided all such materials had structural and conceptual meanings for the chil-

[a] Personal communication.

dren involved. In other words, specific selection of play material is less important than consideration of the child's need and his ability to structure and to endow the materials with conceptual and functional content. It is also equally important for the therapist to give the child a certain leeway, by letting the child select toys or engage in activities to his liking. The skilled therapist will easily gain helpful clues from the play activities. Some therapists have complained that they must work with only a few available toys, while others find it difficult to accept the fact that children coming for treatment will overlook a well-stocked playroom and engage in play activities of their own, disregarding the wealth of available materials. Children at times literally wade through heaps of toys and ask for more; others become overwhelmed and complain that there are too many toys. It is not the abundance or absence of toys which is important in play therapy; most significant are the alertness and skill of the therapist.

Margaret Lowenfeld (1939) writes: "Toys to children are like the culinary implements to the kitchen. Every kitchen has them and also has the elements of food. It is what the cook does with these implements and food elements that determine the dish." So for the context of this paper—children play and use toys of various types and sizes for their activities, and the outcome depends on how these are used and combined. Therefore, when we speak of play therapy and play techniques, it should be remembered that play activities of children are primary and that the use, interpretation, and therapeutic management of a technique depends upon the training, temperament, and inclination of the therapist. The preparation of food, plain or fancy, is done to nourish and strengthen the body. The activity here is secondary to the goal of nourishment. Play therapy should first and foremost be concerned with assisting the young patient to achieve release from troublesome symptoms.

Children are referred for treatment for many reasons. Therapy always starts from a nucleus of complaints which imply that something has gone wrong in the child. Treatment reveals that children have some faculty for relationship, even though such disclosures are not always verbal but are more likely in configural play, the activities representing projections. Methodology depends largely upon the conceptual frame of reference of the therapist. This may be child analysis or modifications of psychoanalytic technique such as release or active therapy. The frame of reference may comprise the tenets of individual psychology or follow the concepts of nondirective therapy. Treatment may concentrate primarily on deciphering of the symbolic meanings of play patterns, or it may evaluate their configurational aspects. All these theoretical concepts and methods have in common the fact that they are designed to help children with difficulties. This common bond unites all of us who are actively engaged in therapy for children.

The following brief survey of the evolution of play therapy mentions some of the more important contributions. Critical remarks should not be taken as an attempt to minimize any method; rather there is an attempt to clarify certain concepts in the effort to establish a general frame of reference.

Freud, through his investigations, made possible the treatment of behavior disorders in adults which, up to his time, had defied understanding. Because he worked little with children, it is therefore creditable that he was able to reconstruct, from work with adults, psychological developments in infancy and childhood. His intuitive feeling for the child and his play activities is well stated in his paper on "The Relation of the Poet to Daydreaming [1908]" (1953). He wrote:

> We ought to look in the child for the first traces of imaginative activity. The child's best loved and most absorbing occupation is play. Perhaps we may say that every child at play behaves like an imaginative writer, in that he creates a world of his own or, more truly, he arranges the things of his world and orders it in a new way that pleases him better. It would be incorrect to say that he does not take his world seriously; on the contrary, he takes his play very seriously and expends a great deal of emotion on it. The opposite of play is not serious occupation, but reality. Notwithstanding the large affective cathexis of his play world, the child distinguishes it perfectly from reality; only he likes to borrow the objects and circumstances that he imagines from the tangible and real world. It is only this linking of it to reality that still distinguishes a child's "play" from "daydreaming." (Freud, 1953, pp. 173–174)

Unfortunately, Freud did not develop these thoughts further. In *Beyond the Pleasure Principle* (1922), he comes to the conclusion that play activities in children are conditioned by repetitions in order to master inner and outer unpleasant experience. This notion of regarding the child's play only as a form of repetition still permeates psychoanalytic thinking and is stressed by Robert Waelder (1933) in his formulation of a psychoanalytic theory of play.

Ruth C. Cohn, in her course on "Psychoanalytic Childhood Theories" at the National Psychological Association Institute for Psychoanalysis, stresses the point that, for historical reasons, psychoanalytic childhood theories emphasize regressive rather than progressive phenomena. The word *drive*, however, implies the progressive element as its major function. Psychoanalysis, in stressing phenomena such as birth trauma and the desire to return to the womb, has neglected the important counterpart, that of breaking out of the confining cage.

Play activities, in Cohn's theory, can be seen as progressive and regressive trends. Progressive trends show the desire to go forward, to discover, and to take in the world. Regressive trends are well expressed in Freud's "repetition compulsion"—the compulsion to regress to and to replay traumatic events. Yet even in the primarily regressive phenomenon of repetition compulsion, there is still transparent the progressive element of curative intent. The child's primary job is to grow; his main tool, play, is therefore in the service of progressive trends.

Shifting from theory to practical application, we find four women, three of whom have made lasting contributions to play therapy. Hertha von Hug-Hellmuth (1921) mentions the importance of play activities in the treatment of a young girl, but adds nothing further. The contributions of the other three women—Melanie Klein, Anna Freud, and Margaret Lowenfeld—are well known.

Melanie Klein (1932), assuming that the character of a child is like that of an adult, fashioned her treatment of children in much the same way as an adult analysis. Since children do not or cannot use the method of free association, she substituted free play. She regarded the child's play as symbolic representation of unconscious content and interpreted it as such directly to the child. She also postulated that the superego is already in the infant's psyche and felt that the aim in child analysis was to protect the budding ego from an overwhelming, domineering superego. She further assumed that transference neurosis does take place in children. Since parents represent external elements or sources of the superego, they were eliminated from the treatment scene and their reports on the child's previous history were ignored.

Anna Freud's approach (1928) differs in many respects from that of M. Klein. Anna Freud carefully compares the analysis of an adult with that of a child. She agrees with Klein in the uselessness of free association with children, but rejects the notion that transference neurosis develops because the original love objects, the parents, are still actively in the situation. They are not fantasy objects which can be transferred to the analyst. An adult usually comes to analysis on his own behalf, but the child is usually not aware of difficulties and is brought to therapy. A. Freud also believes that the superego of children is not yet detached from real external objects. Helping the child to accept the growing demands of the superego calls for educational rather than for analytical measures. Direct interpretation is used sparingly, and valuable information about current happenings in the child's life is obtained through contact with the parents.

Margaret Lowenfeld (1939) seems to be the first worker in the field of play therapy to pay attention to the form principles, or configurational aspects, of the child's play. She uses trays filled with sand; against such a realistic background children place toys and build realistic, though miniature, worlds. Whereas M. Klein and A. Freud are primarily concerned with the content of a given play activity, M. Lowenfeld combines content with realistic forms. Although she borrows psychoanalytic concepts, she rejects the psychoanalytic orientation of child therapy, particularly Klein's application, on the ground that the child analyst brings to work with children " . . . an already formed outline of a doctrine concerning the structure of the mental and emotional life of children which is implicitly accepted." Lowenfeld sees the task of psychotherapy as that of making contact with the whole of the patient's mind, " . . . not only by intuition but by direct and conscious knowledge and understanding of the laws of the mind." She speaks of her "world games" as instruments " . . . with which a child can demonstrate his own emotional and mental state without the necessary intervention of an adult either by transference or interpretation, and which will allow of a record being made of such a demonstration."

Lowenfeld's rebellion against the dominance of seeking for and interpreting symbols in the play content along psychoanalytical lines led her to stress reality form factors. Bender and Schilder (1936) go further by focusing on form principles in the play of children.

> Spontaneous play in children is essentially a means of investigation and experimentation in the laws of nature and human relationships. . . . Physical properties of the play object as well as the laws of gravity are also played with by the child. By investigating these properties through patterns and motives the child is quickly led to aggressive and destructive play in which rhythm and repetition play a part. The emotional problems and the formal problems cannot be completely separated. The child's experimentation with form and configuration is an expression of his tendency to come to a better handling of objects by action. By trial and error the child comes to an insight into the structure of objects.

These authors state that such experimentation includes general spatial qualities of objects, momentum and push, as well as lines, series, and groups. They believe that the play of the child is determined by the motor and perceptual patterns of the organism, and that form principles, evidenced in play, reflect the general plan of psychophysiological orientation.

Erikson (1940) is the mediator between extreme points of view by trying to combine spatial configurations and psychoanalytic or, as he calls it, therapeutic interpretation. In clear and concise language he describes the necessary steps by which the therapist arrives at an understanding of the specific meaning of a play situation. He begins with common sense descriptions of what happens before the observer's eyes. These crude observations are then ordered into a "morpho-analytic description" which emphasizes the configurations manifested in four areas of behavior. The affective sphere covers the child's manifest emotional interest in and withdrawal from the object of behavior. Verbalized content and acted-out themes belong to the ideational realm. Configurations in the three-dimensional sphere refer to the development of spatial factors. Finally, verbal aspects of the play are evidenced by modes of expressions, by the voice and manner of speech in terms of pitch and rhythm. From all this the therapist attempts an approximation of what he sees and hears. Then the therapist forms an " . . . impression ['it was as if . . . '] and associates past impressions, previous observations on the child in question, data communicated to him by his parents, etc." The therapist also reflects on latent possibilities and especially hopes there is some agreement between what is played out before the observer and what the child is said to have done elsewhere.

> His observational and reflective reactions lead the observer to various interpretational hints. A symbolic equation or metaphor may make it possible to recognize a play as alluding to and standing for an otherwise manifestly avoided item [person, object, or idea]. A play arrangement may prove to represent a specific effort on the part of the child to rearrange "in effigy" his psychological position in an experienced or expected danger situation. Such an arrangement usually corresponds to the child's defense mechanism. If these hints survive the shifting process of further observation and investigation, they will sooner or later grow together and create a conviction and an image in the observer's mind in the form of a reconstruction of a genetic sequence or of a dynamic configuration pertaining to the patient's inner and outer history. (Erikson, 1940)

Interpretation takes place when the therapist, at a time which he deems to be right, conveys parts of these reconstructions to the child.

The basic assumptions of nondirective therapy and its application to play therapy differ fundamentally from the approaches mentioned so far. Axline (1947) states: "Non-directive therapy [formulated by Carl Rogers] is based upon the assumption that the individual has within himself not only the ability to solve his own problems satisfactorily, but also this growth impulse that makes mature behavior more satisfying than immature behavior." Nondirective play therapy, in the light of this definition, is " . . . an opportunity that is offered to the child to experience growth under the most favorable conditions."

Melanie Klein sees the child in danger of being frustrated, inhibited, emotionally strangled and dwarfed by a strong and domineering superego. Nondirective therapists, on the other hand, firmly believe in the child's capacity for self-determination and respect the child's ability as a thinking, independent, and constructive human being. In nondirective play therapy the child is allowed and actually encouraged to use materials as a means to express freely what he wants; the therapist does not direct the play in any way. According to Axline (1947), the child playing freely and without direction " . . . is expressing his personality. He is experiencing a period of independent thought and action. He is releasing the feelings and attitudes that have been pushing to get out into the open."

Six main approaches have been briefly mentioned. All of these, and many more which could not be surveyed within the limitations of this presentation, lead toward and converge at a common point—the troubled child in need of help. Without minimizing the importance of the pros and cons inherent in all these methods, concepts, and approaches, without favoring this or that approach, with full knowledge of the claims staked out for each technique, and knowing the criticism stated against each method in favor of another, it must be repeated that all approaches were designed to guide and to help children, though this collective goal is often lost sight of in the scuffle for advantage and position.

Direct treatment of the child has been excellently described by Gerard

(1948). Lowrey (1948) included the child guidance movement in his adequate survey of the field of orthopsychiatric treatment. Important contributions have been made by Allen (1942), Conn (1948), Despert (1940), Fries (1937), Gitelson (1938), D. M. Levy (1939), Solomon (1938, 1948, 1951), and Woltmann (1951). Discussions about general and specific aspects of play therapy are found in the publications of Anderson and Anderson (1951), Bell (1948), Bender (1952), Bender and Woltmann (1941), Traill (1945), and Woltmann (1952).

Relevant researches in the field of play therapy have been summarized by me (1952). I found that all these studies were based on data collected during comparatively brief contacts with children. The studies were carried out primarily with supposedly normal children and therefore have no direct application to therapy. Indirectly, however, they are of value because of the need for norms against which we can compare. Although many of these reports contain valuable observations, they all suffer in that only specific segments were singled out for scientific consideration. Total or global approaches to the child's personality (even for the supposedly normal) have not been adequately studied.

The greatest barrier to the establishment of universally valid conclusions and inferences, drawn from the child's configurational and ideological handling and structuring of play materials, is that there is a lack of correlation between methods of collecting data and those used for evaluation.

> We forget that projective methods were developed because our previous psychological methods failed us in the deeper understanding of personality structures. We try to validate and to look for reliability by using the same tools and methods which had blocked a basic understanding of the intricacies of human behavior and motivation. Our present statistical methods set up general hypothetical norms against which the individual is measured and compared. Projective methods aim to understand a person's own private, idiosyncratic personality structure, which differs from one person to the next. We know how to elicit material, but as yet we have not found a sound approach toward the so-called "scientific" handling of this material. (Woltmann, 1952, p. 286)

A presentation of this kind may sound confusing because it shuttles back and forth between approaches, questions concerning therapy, and configurational aspects. This is unavoidable, since the field has grown so large in a short time. Sometimes "play," at others "therapy," has been stressed. Differing ideological approaches have led to distinct labels. What may confuse is only an attempt to sort out ideas of play therapy, so that methods and techniques which promise further growth may develop and result in better ways of restoring peace, harmony, and happiness to the troubled child. In order to achieve this, one must not only pay attention to the ideas and methods to be used, but also to the soil in which growth is to take place.

This means that we must know more about children and their play activities at various ages, in order to arrive at more comprehensive appraisals of what is to be called normal and what is to be regarded as abnormal in the play presentations of children. There are hopeful beginnings. Attention is called to *Life and Ways of the Two-Year-Old* by Woodcock (1937) and to *Life and Ways of the Seven to Eight-Year-Old* by Biber and others (1942). These studies, carried out at the Bank Street College of Education in New York, give as complete as possible a picture of how children behave at these ages and how development occurs. Research workers as well as therapists will find a wealth of information here.

Last but not least, mention must be made of the excellent studies carried out in private and public kindergartens in New York City by Hartley, Frank, and Goldenson (1952a, 1952b). They state:

> The importance of creative activities and play opportunity in pre-school and early school settings is recognized more and more by workers in many areas of human development. . . . What is perhaps not so frequently emphasized is the great plasticity of the young during these years, their instant response to environmental impacts, their relative freedom from compartmentalization and their consequent readiness to benefit from favorable experiences and to assimilate these into their growing concept of self. Likewise it has not been fully recognized that while the young child is undergoing many of the trial and error experiences that are crucial for his mental health, he needs an "educational therapy" designed to help him with his difficulties and conflicts while they are still in process. This, like treatment for mental and emotional battle casualties just behind the front lines, may prevent their fixation and permanent damage. (1952a, pp. 4–5)

As Erikson (1940) says: "The child uses play to make up for defeats, sufferings and frustrations, especially those resulting from a technically and culturally limited use of language. . . . If we can establish the language of play with its various cultural and age dialects we may be able to approach the problem why it is that certain children live undamaged through what seem to be neurotic episodes and how early neurotic children have indicated that they have reached a deadlock."

## REFERENCES

Allen, F. H. *Psychotherapy with children.* New York: Norton, 1942.

Anderson, H. H., and Anderson, Gladys L. (Eds.) *An introduction to projective techniques.* New York: Prentice-Hall, 1951.

Axline, Virginia M. *Play therapy.* Boston: Houghton Mifflin, 1947.

Bell, J. E. *Projective techniques.* New York: Longmans, Green, 1948.

Bellak, L., Pasquarelli, B., and Braverman, S. The use of the Thematic Apperception Test in psychotherapy. *J. Nerv. Ment. Dis.*, 1949, **110**, 51–65.

Bender, Lauretta. *Child psychiatric techniques.* Springfield, Ill.: Charles C Thomas, 1952.

Bender, Lauretta, and Schilder, P. Form as a principle in the play of children. *J. Genet. Psychol.*, 1936, **49**, 254–261.

Bender, Lauretta, and Woltmann, A. G. Play and psychotherapy. *Nerv. Child*, 1941, **1**, 17–42.

Biber, Barbara, Murphy, Lois B., Woodcock, Louise P., and Black, Irma S. *Life and ways of the seven to eight-year-old.* New York: Basic Books, 1942.

Conn, J. H. The play interview: an investigative and therapeutic procedure. *Nerv. Child*, 1948, **7**, 257–286.

Despert, J. Louise. A method for the study of personality reactions in preschool children by means of analysis of their play. *J. Psychol.*, 1940, **9**, 17–29.

Erikson, E. H. Studies in the interpretation of play. *Genet. Psychol. Monogr.*, 1940, **22**, 557–671.

Frank, L. K. *Projective methods.* Springfield, Ill.: Charles C Thomas, 1948.

Freud, Anna. Introduction to the technique of child analysis. *Nerv. Ment. Dis. Monogr.*, 1928, No. 48.

Freud, S. The relation of the poet to daydreaming (1908). In *Collected papers.* London: Hogarth Press, 1953. Vol. IV.

Freud, S. *Beyond the pleasure principle.* London: Psychoanalytic Press, 1922.

Fries, Margaret E. Play technique in the analysis of young children. *Psychoanal. Rev.*, 1937, **24**, 233–245.

Gerard, Margaret W. Direct treatment of the child. In L. G. Lowrey and V. Sloane (Eds.), *Orthopsychiatry, 1923–1948.* New York: American Orthopsychiatric Association, 1948. Pp. 494–523.

Gitelson, M. Clinical experience with play therapy. *Am. J. Orthopsychiat.*, 1938, **8**, 466–478.

Hartley, Ruth E., Frank, L. K., and Goldenson, R. M. *Understanding children's play.* New York: Columbia Univer. Press, 1952a.

Hartley, Ruth E., Frank, L. K., and Goldenson, R. M. *New experiences for children.* New York: Columbia Univer. Press, 1952b.

Hug-Hellmuth, Hertha von. On the technique of child analysis. *Int. J. Psychoanal.*, 1921, **2**, 294–295.

Klein, Melanie. *The psychoanalysis of children.* London: Hogarth Press, 1932.

Levy, D. M. Release therapy. *Am. J. Orthopsychiat.*, 1939, **9**, 713–736.

Lowenfeld, Margaret. *Play in childhood.* London: Gollanez, 1935.

Lowenfeld, Margaret. The world pictures of children. *Brit. J. Med. Psychol.*, 1939, **18**, 65–101.

Lowrey, L. G. Trends in therapy. *Am. J. Orthopsychiat.*, 1939, **9**, 669–706.

Lowrey, L. G. Orthopsychiatric treatment. In L. G. Lowrey and V. Sloane (Eds.), *Orthopsychiatry, 1923–1948.* New York: American Orthopsychiatric Association, 1948. Pp. 524–549.

Solomon, J. C. Active play therapy. *Am. J. Orthopsychiat.*, 1938, **8**, 479–498.

Solomon, J. C. Trends in orthopsychiatric therapy: play techniques. *Am. J. Orthopsychiat.*, 1948, **18**, 402–413.

Solomon, J. C. Therapeutic use of play. In H. H. and G. L. Anderson (Eds.), *An introduction to projective techniques.* New York: Prentice-Hall, 1951. Pp. 639–661.

Traill, P. M. An account of Lowenfeld technique in a child guidance clinic, with a survey of therapeutic play techniques in Great Britain and U.S.A. *J. Ment. Sci.*, 1945, **91**, 43–78.

Waelder, R. The psychoanalytic theory of play. *Psychoanal. Quart.*, 1933, **2**, 208–224.

Woltmann, A. G. The use of puppetry as a projective method in therapy. In H. H. and G. L. Anderson (Eds.), *An introduction to projective techniques.* New York: Prentice-Hall, 1951. Pp. 606–638.

Woltmann, A. G. Play and related techniques. In D. Brower and L. E. Abt (Eds.), *Progress in clinical psychology.* New York: Grune & Stratton, 1952. Pp. 278–289.

Woodcock, Louise P. *Life and ways of the two-year-old.* New York: Basic Books, 1941.

❀ CHAPTER THREE

# Diagnosis and Choice of Therapeutic Approach

THE QUESTION in this chapter is whether any one type of therapy can be applied, without modification, to all children and all kinds of problems. To say each child is unique would be a cliché. Does it follow that no one therapeutic technique could be expected to serve all children? Related and relevant questions are as follows: What is the place of the diagnostic interview? Should the therapist be acquainted with the child's referral problem, the psychological findings, and diagnostic appraisal? Would such knowledge tend to influence the therapist to "remake" the child, attack the symptoms, and become too intent on achieving preconceived goals? What is the therapist's value orientation, and should this be imposed on the patient?

The Axline excerpt presents the client-centered belief that there is a forward-moving growth process and drive toward self-realization in all persons and that the individual should be completely accepted as he is at the present moment. Consequently, prior diagnostic evaluation becomes unnecessary and no attempt should be made to remodel the child in the therapist's image or to fit the therapist's goals. In contrast to this point of view, Rabinovitch strongly advocates careful diagnostic evaluation prior to treatment, as a basis for selecting the appropriate type of psychotherapy. He stresses the importance of biological and psychodynamic evaluations *and* the integration of these findings with an understanding of family relationships. He discusses the major categories of psychiatric problems in childhood (brain damage, schizophrenia, conduct disorders, and so forth) and suggests the most appropriate approach for each type of disturbance.

Whereas Rabinovitch addresses his discussion to broad diagnostic categories, McClure elaborates on three "reaction types" found in maladjusted children: hysterical, obsessional, and labile. She discusses each in terms of the varying strengths of superego, ego, and id impulses and suggests variations in technique for the treatment of each disorder. For a further elaboration of her approach and its extension to schizophrenic children, the reader is referred to J. C. Solomon, "Therapeutic Use of Play."[1]

There has been no attempt in this volume to cover the treatment of psychotic children. The selection by Escalona, dealing with this topic, is included to point out the effects of two differing approaches to a particular diagnostic syndrome. A further reason for including this selection is that it provides an excellent picture of the reactions of the psychotic child, in contrast to the neurotic, and so should help the beginning therapist be alert to signs and symptoms should they become evident in the child he is treating.

Rexford discusses the specific problems of therapy with antisocial children, the tasks and goals involved, and the reasons why approaches that are successful with the neurotic child cannot be employed, at least in the early stages.

# Nondirective Therapy

VIRGINIA M. AXLINE

. . . Nondirective therapy is based upon the assumption that the individual has within himself, not only the ability to solve his own problems satisfactorily, but also a growth impulse that makes mature behavior more satisfying than immature behavior.

---

[1] J. C. Solomon, "Therapeutic Use of Play," in *An Introduction to Projective Techniques,* Harold H. and Gladys L. Anderson, eds. (New York: Prentice-Hall, 1951), p. 639–661.

This type of therapy starts where the individual is and bases the process on the present configuration, allowing for change from minute to minute during the therapeutic contact, if it should occur that rapidly, the rate depending upon the reorganization of the individual's accumulated experiences, attitudes, thoughts, and feelings to bring about insight, which is a prerequisite of successful therapy.

Nondirective therapy grants the individual the permissiveness to be himself; it accepts that self completely, without evaluation or pressure to change; it recognizes and clarifies the expressed emotionalized attitudes by a reflection of what the client has expressed; and, by the very process of nondirective therapy, it offers the individual the opportunity to be himself, to learn to know himself, to chart his own course openly and aboveboard—to rotate the kaleidoscope, so to speak, so that he may form a more satisfactory design for living.

. . . Nondirective play therapy . . . may be described as an opportunity that is offered to the child to experience growth under the most favorable conditions. Since play is his natural medium for self-expression, the child is given the opportunity to play out his accumulated feelings of tension, frustration, insecurity, aggression, fear, bewilderment, confusion.

By playing out these feelings, he brings them to the surface, gets them out in the open, faces them, learns to control them, or abandons them. When he has achieved emotional relaxation, he begins to realize the power within himself to be an individual in his own right, to think for himself, to make his own decisions, to become psychologically more mature, and, by so doing, to realize selfhood.

The play-therapy room is good growing ground. In the security of this room where the *child* is the most important person, where he is in command of the situation and of himself, where no one tells him what to do, no one criticizes what he does, no one nags, or suggests, or goads him on, or pries into his private world, he suddenly feels that *here* he can unfold his wings; he can look squarely at himself, for he is accepted completely; he can test out his ideas; he can express himself fully; for this is *his* world, and he no longer has to compete with such other forces as adult authority or rival contemporaries or situations where he is a human pawn in a game between bickering parents, or where he is the butt of someone else's frustrations and aggressions. He is an individual in his own right. He is treated with dignity and respect. He can say anything that he feels like saying—and he is accepted completely. He can play with the toys in any way that he likes to—and he is accepted completely. He can hate and he can love and he can be as indifferent as the Great Stone Face—and he is still accepted completely. He can be as fast as a whirlwind or as slow as molasses in January—and he is neither restrained nor hurried.

It is a unique experience for a child suddenly to find adult suggestions, mandates, rebukes, restraints, criticisms, disapprovals, support, intrusions gone. They are all replaced by complete acceptance and permissiveness to be himself.

No wonder the child, during his first play contact, often expresses bewilderment. What is this all about? He is suspicious. He is curious. All his life there has been someone to help him live his life. There may even have been someone who was determined to live his life for him. Suddenly this interference is gone, and he is no longer living in the shadow of someone who looms larger than he on his horizon. He is out in the sun, and the only shadows are the ones which he himself wishes to cast.

It is a challenge. And something deep within the child responds to this clearly-felt challenge to *be*—to exercise this power of life within himself, to give it direction, to become more purposeful and decisive and individual.

He tries it out—gingerly at first—then, as he feels the permissiveness and security in the situation, he sets forth more boldly to explore the possibilities of this arrangement. He is no longer blocked by exterior forces, and so the drive within him for growth has no barriers to go around. The psychological resistance that he has formerly met is gone.

The presence of an accepting, understanding, friendly therapist in the playroom gives him a sense of security. The limitations, few as they are, add to this feeling of security and reality. The participation of the therapist during the therapy contact also reinforces the child's feeling of security. The therapist is sensitive to what the child is feeling and expressing through his play and verbalization. She reflects these expressed, emotionalized attitudes back to him in such a way as to help him understand himself a little better. She respects the child and his ability to stand on his own two feet and to become a more mature and independent individual if he is given an opportunity to do so. In addition to helping the child gain a better understanding of himself by the reflection of his emotionalized attitudes, the therapist also conveys to him the feeling that she is understanding him and accepting him at all times regardless of what he says or does. Thus, the therapist gives him the courage to go deeper and deeper into his innermost world and bring out into the open his real self.

To the child, therapy is indeed a challenge to this drive within him that is constantly striving for realization. It is a challenge that has never been ignored in the writer's experience with children. The speed at which they utilize this opportunity varies with the individual, but the fact that varying degrees of growth do take place during a play-therapy experience has been demonstrated many times.

To the therapist, it is an opportunity to test out the hypothesis that, given a chance, the child can and does become more mature, more positive in his attitudes, and more constructive in the way he expresses this inner drive.

The writer believes that it is the same inner drive toward self-realization, maturity, fulfillment, and independence that also creates those conditions which we call maladjustment, which seems to be either an aggressive determination on the part of the child to be himself by one means or another or a strong resistance to the blocking of his complete self-expression. . . .

Since the element of complete acceptance of the child seems to be of such vital importance, it is worth a more penetrating study. Acceptance of what? The answer seems to be that it is acceptance of the child and a firm belief that the child is capable of self-determination. It seems to be a respect for the child's ability to be a thinking, independent, constructive human being.

Acceptance seems also to imply an understanding of that never-ceasing drive toward complete self-realization—or complete fulfillment of himself as an individual that is psychologically freed, so that he can function at his maximum capacity. An adjusted person seems to be an individual who does not encounter too many obstacles in his path and who has been given the opportunity to become free and independent in his own right. The maladjusted person seems to be the one who, by some means or other, is denied the right to achieve this without a struggle. Examination of the records indicates this again and again. Sometimes the individual is rejected and brushed aside. Sometimes he is smothered by supportive care that makes it difficult for him to break through the barrier. It seems as though the individuals would not manifest the behavior symptoms that they do unless they were striving to achieve individual status. The ways in which they attempt to do this are varied and many, but there always seems to be some manifestation of the individual's resistance to the blocking of his maturity and independence. Even the dominated child who becomes rigidly dependent seems to be achieving a controlling independence in that way. The "babied" child, who refuses to learn to read when sent to school, at first glance seems to be fighting independence and maturity. It could be that it is the most effective way that he has discovered to control the situation and is therefore a satisfaction to him because it is an expression of his power to direct and individualize himself. This is a very controversial hypothesis and is presented as an interpretation of the play-therapy records' primary manifestation—that of growth within the individual at all times, unfolding sometimes in an unbelievably short time, but always present in greater or lesser degree.

Many cases seem to prove that the only need of the individual is the need to be unshackled, to be freed, to be permitted to expand into a complete self without a frustrating and warping struggle to satisfy this inner drive. This does not mean that he becomes so self-centered that the rest of the world ceases to exist for him. It means that he achieves the freedom to fulfill this inner drive naturally, without its becoming necessary to make it the central issue of his whole existence and to channel all of his energies into an onslaught against the barriers that are preventing his maturity and that turn the individual's attention inward.

When this inner drive is satisfied naturally and constantly—because growth is a continuous process as long as there is life—it is an outgoing thing.

The individual is achieving physical maturity and must achieve psychological maturity in order to strike a balance.

Just as an individual utilizes increasing physical independence to extend the boundaries of his physical capacities, so he uses the increasing psychological independence to extend the boundaries of his mental capacities.

The child who can run can go farther than the baby who can only crawl. The child who has learned to talk can communicate more effectively than the baby who can only coo and gurgle. With maturity comes the expansion of the individual to encompass the world as far as he can incorporate it in his scheme of life. And so it is, all through life. The child who is psychologically freed can achieve far more in a creative and constructive manner than can the individual who spends all his energies in a frustrating, tense battle to achieve this freedom and status as an individual.

He *will be* an individual. If he cannot achieve it by a legitimate way, then he will get it by some substitute action. Thus, the child has tantrums, teases, sulks, daydreams, fights, and tries to shock others by his behavior. Teachers have many times said, when trying to "manage" a show-off, "Give him a legitimate reason to show off. Let him take a part in a play. Give him some responsibility in the classroom!"—and have used other such devices to meet the child's need to be recognized as a person of value. Similarly, during the play-therapy hour the child is given the opportunity to realize this power within himself to be himself.

The toys implement the process because they are definitely the child's medium of expression. They are the materials that are generally conceded to be the child's property. His free play is an expression of what he *wants* to do. He can order this world of his. That is why the nondirective therapist does not direct the play in any way. The therapist renders unto the child what is the child's—in this case the toys and the undirected use of them. When he plays freely and without direction, he is expressing his personality. He is experiencing a period of independent thought and action. He is releasing the feelings and attitudes that have been pushing to get out into the open.

That is why it does not seem to be necessary for the child to be aware that he has a problem before he can benefit by the therapy session. Many a child has utilized the therapy experience and has emerged from the experience with visible signs of more mature attitudes and behavior and still has not been aware that it was any more than a free-play period.

Nondirective play therapy is not meant to be a means of substituting one type of behavior that is considered more desirable by adult standards for another "less desirable" type. It is not an attempt to impose upon the child the voice of authority that says, "*You* have a problem. *I* want you to correct it." When that happens, the child meets it with resistance—either active or passive. He does not want to be made over. Above all things he strives to be himself. Behavior patterns that are not of his own choice are flimsy things that are not worth the time and effort required to force them upon him.

The type of therapy which we are describing is based upon a positive theory of the individual's ability. It is not limiting to any individual's growth. It is outgoing. It starts where the individual *is* and lets that individual go as far as he is able to go. That is why there are no diagnostic interviews before therapy. Regardless of symptomatic behavior, the individual is met by the therapist where he is. That is why interpretation is ruled out as far as it is possible to do so. What has happened in the past is past history. Since the dynamics of life are constantly changing the relativity of things, a past experience is colored by the interactions of life and is also constantly changing. Anything that attempts to shackle the individual's growth is a blocking experience. Taking the therapy back into the individual's past history rules out the possibility that he has grown in the meantime, and, consequently, the past no longer has the same significance that it formerly had. Probing questions are also ruled out for this same reason. The individual will select the things that to him are most important *when he is ready to do so.* When the non-directive therapist says that the therapy is client-centered, he really means it, because, to him, the client is the source of living power that directs the growth from within himself.

During a play-therapy experience, that sort of relationship is established between the therapist and the child that makes it possible for the child to reveal his real self to the therapist; and, having had it accepted—and, by that very acceptance, having grown a bit in self-confidence—he is more able to extend the frontiers of his personality expression.

The child lives in a world of his own, and very few adults really understand him. There is such a rush and pressure in modern times that it is difficult for a child to establish the intimate, delicate relationship with the adult that is necessary to enable him to lay bare his innermost secret life. Too many people are tempted to exploit his personality, and so he defends his identity. He keeps himself apart, reveling in the things that to him are so vastly important and interesting. . . .

# *An Evaluation of Present Trends in Psychotherapy with Children*

RALPH D. RABINOVITCH

These are difficult times to assess progress in the social sciences; pessimism is the inevitable trend of the times, and this is particularly apparent in the attitudes of social scientists. In the field, in general, there are many notes of troubled introspection and discouragement. Constructive motivation is dampened by tension and fear. Against this background the recent literature is pervaded by statements of anxiety and concern about the world for our children (Rabinovitch & Dubo, 1952). Some writers try to be encouraging, but subtle Jeremiahs insert themselves. Typical is Weston La Barre's reassurance regarding the permanency of the American family: "We shall have the family so long as human beings are around." This is reassuring, but La Barre hastens to add this sobering postscript: "Our major concern is literally whether or not there will be human beings around." (1951, p. 55)

Notwithstanding these broad concerns there has been in recent years growing evidence in the field of child psychiatry of a constructive interest in evaluating critically both theory and practice. One might say that child psychiatry has come of age and feels mature enough to tolerate introspection and self-examination. We find in our literature of recent years growing concern with practical problems of diagnosis and treatment and diminishing emphasis on purely theoretical speculation. One can sense the recognition of the need to eschew fantasy in favor of objectivity and ritual in favor of service. There is an expressed need to define more precisely basic psychopathology of childhood and to adapt treatment methods to the realities at hand (Bender, 1947).

This brings us to the first major trend in psychotherapy with children, the recognition that careful diagnosis on both a biological and a psychodynamic level must precede treatment. For some years there has been what one might call an antidiagnostic feeling in psychiatry. This developed historically as a reaction to an earlier tendency to be concerned primarily with nosology, or classification per se. The idea that we must treat the whole child evolved, and attempts at diagnosis were viewed as threats to the concept of the child as a whole. Deploring diagnosis, therapists attempted to treat children as children and not as children with specific problems. This would have been fine if it were not for the fact that diagnosis so often provides the key to treatment. Today the tide is turning, and we are recognizing that we can still treat children as children and at the same time understand their specific disturbances in terms of both biological and psychodynamic reality. This issue of diagnosis is not an academic one but is intensely practical and directly related to therapy. Several years ago, Lawson Lowrey (1950, p. 676) commented pointedly on this problem: "a most inappropriate type of treatment may be established on the basis of some common symptom with disastrous results for the patient and for the therapist." Lowrey added:

> There is danger of jumping headlong into therapy, and in recent years I have been puzzled by what seems to be a tendency to treat first, and then inquire afterward what was the matter. I have also been bothered by the appearance of a tendency to think that one can be a therapist without having undergone some fairly adequate training in the background procedure of determining what is to be treated, and how one is to treat it. (1950, p. 676)

A similar point of view is expressed by David Levy in his 1951 academic lecture before the American Psychiatric Association. Levy reviews the historical background of child psychiatry in America and is alarmed by what he calls "an anti-diagnostic attitude" prevalent in some clinics. He points out (Levy, 1951) that psychotherapy, like any other treatment method, involves of necessity "diagnostic and prognostic study." . . . Nathan Ackerman (1953) in an outstanding contribution expressed similar views:

> While the accretion of scientific knowledge does not yet permit a comprehensive statement of diagnostic and etiological principles, we are, nevertheless, firmly on the road to discerning some of the basic concepts needed for this task. . . . Child therapists sometimes pursue the treatment of the child without a clearly defined clinical diagnosis, and without a dynamic appraisal of the total functioning of the child's personality. Only too often therapy is conducted in a setting that reflects a cloudy conceptualization of the dynamic operations of personality. Too often therapists treat without knowing what they treat. . . . Equally regrettable is the related tendency of child therapists to learn a stereotyped set of therapeutic techniques and apply them indiscriminately to all child patients alike. This is a form of therapy utterly lacking in specificity. It is more like the practice of magic medicine than modern child psychiatry.

Our recent literature contains many references of this type with statements by some of our most experienced and distinguished clinicians deploring the tendency to cast aside the responsibility for clinical diagnosis and taking issue with those who suggest that diagnosis serves as a deterrent to effective therapy. This stress, then, on the importance of diagnosis as the first step in establishing a treatment program represents, I believe, the major current trend. I would like to emphasize that we are not interested in diagnosis per se but in the use of diagnostic insights in our practical treatment work.

There are two aspects of diagnosis that must concern us: first, an attempt to appreciate the child's biological status, the level of his innate adaptive capacity, and the quality of his neurological integration; second, the child's reaction to patterns of relationship and identification opportunities and to life experience—in summary, the psychodynamics at play. We have an incomplete understanding of any child unless we have insight into both these aspects of his personality. The symptomatology of the disturbed child stems from deficiencies or pathology in the total personality; interrelationships between the biological and the psychodynamic factors can be seen in many clinical problems. The brain-injured child, for example, can be expected to manifest difficulties in impulse control, hyperactivity, and reactive anxiety with poor social adaptability. But the ultimate prognosis will, in many cases, depend primarily on the quality of the child's earlier and present relationships; where the mother can meet the child's increased dependency needs and, through support and giving, help to establish more integrated patterns of response, the prognosis may be good; where there is rejection by the mother and lack of opportunity for dependency, the prognosis, in a case with equal pathology, is poor. Similarly, in childhood schizophrenia, the prognosis is by no means dependent on the psychotic process alone, but in many cases on the capacity of the family to identify with the child's difficulties and to provide a therapeutic milieu.

Recognizing the presence of a neurotic patterning overlying other pathology we must, at the same time, avoid the temptation to explain the total picture on the basis of the psychodynamics alone. We see, for example, many children, showing a retarded level in psychometric testing, in whom the psychodynamics might suggest an adequate cause for neurotic blocking. This by no means rules out primary mental deficiency; both conditions, primary mental deficiency and neurosis, frequently occur together. We often see neurotic children who, in addition, present severe reading difficulties. This does not mean that the reading disability itself can be considered a neurotically determined symptom. Some may interpret the convulsive movements of the epileptic as evidence of regressive trends with a drive to return to the fetal state, but the origin of idiopathic epilepsy remains a primary disturbance in electrocortical physiology, the cause of which is still unknown. Lauretta Bender (1949, p. 411), referring to analogous cases, summarizes the situation well: "A dynamic interrelation may describe the psychological problem, but still does not touch the cause."

I have stressed at some length the need for a clinical orientation in terms of biological, psychopathological, and psychodynamic evaluations because I believe that many of our failures in therapy occur because we have had inadequate insight into the total realities of the individual case. A consideration of some specific diagnostic groups may serve to bring into practical focus some of these remarks.

Grossly neglected children constitute a surprisingly high percentage of cases referred for treatment. These children, living in conditions of severe deprivation, under circumstances that of themselves preclude normal development, find their way to the psychiatric clinic when the community finds them disturbing. That there are virtually uncivilized children wandering about our large cities is shown too clearly in some of our referrals. From the research standpoint, these cases can be of extreme interest, providing us with ample if anachronous opportunities to repeat the historic experiments carried out by Itard in 1799 with the Wild Boy of Aveyron. But the treatment of these children is primarily a challenge to our resources for social and educational retraining; direct interpretative psychotherapy cannot meet their needs. The paucity of suitable benign institutional placement opportunities for the neglected child who cannot fit into a foster home is, I am sure, a chronic source of concern to placement workers.

Research in mental deficiency has provided increasing insight into the necessity for recognizing mental retardation as a symptom and never as a diagnostic entity in itself. When testing indicates deficiency it must be determined whether the cause is endogenous or exogenous, whether the problem stems from a primary biological lack or deviation, or whether it is secondary to another difficulty such as brain damage, mental illness, or neurotically determined blocking. Our program of handling and treatment will depend upon the nature of the basic disturbance when the problem stems from exogenous factors, and treatment may be effective in raising the level of intellectual functioning and the child's total adjustment. Although some recent research has raised high and exorbitant hopes for effective treatment of primary retardation, we still have essentially only special education to offer these children. Too often, on the basis of a therapist's misguided hopes, well motivated as these may be, they are exposed to prolonged psychotherapy with an illusory goal, and in the end the patient and his family suffer all the more. Whether or not the child of borderline intelligence or with mild retardation is able to adapt to community living depends primarily upon two factors: first, the ability of families to understand and accept the situation—and here casework has an important role to play; second, special educational opportunities in a regular school to allow for training within realistic limits of the child's capacities. Fernald's recommendations for special classes for retarded children, which he put into practice as far back as 1896, have still to be implemented in many of our communities, although progress is now being made in this direction.

As our diagnostic insights are sharpened through research, we are recognizing an increasingly larger number of children who present evidence of brain damage stemming from intrauterine factors, birth trauma, anoxia at birth, encephalitis, or posttraumatic states. When the encephalopathy has not seriously impaired intellectual functioning the child's problem is often unrecognized, and this large group is frequently neglected. The brain-injured child must deal with difficulties in impulse control and in the patterning of his motor behavior; he makes great efforts to adapt to group situations, but because of the nature of his illness, he tends to respond impulsively to each environmental stimulus. Thus average family living or a routine school situation is often overstimulating and leads to reactive behavior difficulties. Along with special education much support and special handling in the home are required, and unless the diagnosis is established, an inappropriate psychotherapy may be attempted that sometimes overstimulates and increases problems. The recognition of these children, interpretation of their difficulties to parents and teachers, and special opportunities for their schooling and appropriate psychotherapy are important needs in this large treatment area.

One of our most challenging treatment problems is presented by the child with schizophrenia. Through the work of Bender (1947a), Kanner (1949), Despert (1951), Putnam, Rank, and Kaplan (1951), and others, we have come to recognize more definitively the clinical entity of childhood schizophrenia; it occurs probably much more commonly than previously believed. The core of the problem is the child's dysidentity, or his inability to establish ego boundaries and clear-cut appreciation of the limits and realities of his perceptual experiences and the world about him. This same lack of clarity pervades his interpersonal relationships, and he appears remote and unrelated.

The problem in therapy is to help the child establish clear-cut identities, develop ego boundaries, and, in so doing, be able to enter into closer relationships. The techniques are specialized, and we are just beginning to develop them. Tragic as these cases are, recent research suggests that the prognosis is by no means uniformly poor; where the family and the school can be taught to appreciate his special problems and to identify his inner needs and where an opportunity for appropriate direct psychotherapy is provided, the schizophrenic child may be helped to maintain a community adjustment. As in so many problem areas, the chief criterion is often the family's attitude and capacity to deal with the child, and here again casework has a major role to play.

One group of children, whom we are called upon particularly urgently to treat, are, I believe, virtually untreatable; it is paradoxical that there is no disorder in children in which the psychogenesis is more clearly known. These are the affectionless personalities or psychopathic personalities, or those with psychopathic conduct disorders, or whatever name you choose to use. Through the work of Levy (1937), Lowrey (1940), Goldfarb (1943), Bender (1947b), Spitz (1951), and others, we have come to recognize a specific psychogenetic cause for this disorder, and our understanding of these children has taught us much about the physiological needs of infants and about the primary sources of superego or social awareness (Rabinovitch, 1952). In many of these cases the child has been institutionalized in infancy, spending his first year, or perhaps two or three years, in a hospital or institution crib, receiving almost no mothering and having no continuity of relationship with a mother figure. In other cases, the child at home has been exposed to an institution-like experience—which, unfortunately, is quite possible. The result is gross impairment in capacity to establish later relationships. When we see these children at the age of eight or perhaps ten years, they show a startling lack of anxiety or guilt and have a shallowness of inner life and capacity for intrapsychic conflict. Direct psychotherapy is usually ineffective because the child does not establish a relationship through which he can be treated. These are, in fact, perhaps the most tragic of all the children we see, for, while the condition is virtually untreatable, it is totally preventable. While in later years benign institutionalization for children may be not only nontraumatic but therapeutic, it is always disastrous when it occurs in infancy. There are other important implications for social work in these findings, principally that all neglected or abandoned infants be placed in foster homes as close to the time of birth as possible; here they can have the stimulation and gratification through mothering that alone can lead to normal personality growth and that serve as the matrix for all later depth relationships.

There is another very large and neglected group of children who ultimately become the concern of the child psychiatrist, but whose problem is primarily educational. These are the children with specific educational difficulties, particularly reading problems. It has been estimated that more than 10 per cent of children in the public schools do not learn to read adequately in the regular classroom situation. Our own feeling about this problem is that it usually represents a developmental lag, which is related to as yet poorly-defined aspects of neural integration (Kennard, Rabinovitch, & Wexler, 1952); but whatever our views regarding etiology, we must recognize the fact that our culture imposes an extremely heavy burden on this group of nonreaders or poor readers. Inevitable school failure, feelings of inadequacy, and inability to tolerate pressures frequently brought to bear at home and at school account for the severe degree of emotional disturbance we so often see in these children. We have probably tended to underestimate the importance of this problem as a factor in emotional disturbance and delinquency. We have ample clinical evidence to suggest that we cannot wait for these children to outgrow their difficulty. Reactive patterns of negativism and emotional block make retraining difficult when the disability has been neglected in the early school years. I believe it is an important responsibility for our schools to spot these children and to provide them with opportunities for remedial work before secondary neurotic patterns develop. Without adequate attention to specific needs, based on a full diagnostic assessment, nonspecific psychotherapy is again usually ineffective. . . .

# *Reaction Types in Maladjusted Children*

AGNES G. McCLURE

## ***Basic Principles of Play Therapy***

Behavior disorders, habit disorders, nervous disorders, and intellectual disorders, if of true psychological origin, arise from a conflict which may be partly or wholly unconscious. True therapy should result in an integration of the emotions, intelligence, and will, which produces harmonious psychosomatic function. To achieve such a result the therapist must be prepared: (a) to make contact with the child's unconscious; (b) to split the ambivalence; (c) to participate in the guilt released (the latter, an essential distinction between the role of play therapist and that of analyst); (d) to probe no deeper into the unconscious than is necessary for therapy; and (e) to foster a reconstruction of the personality on its own lines, i.e., true to its basic reaction type with the adjustment achieved through therapeutic integration.

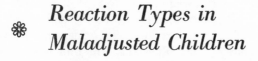

### *Diagnosis of the Source of Conflict*

Diagnosis should be based on material from (a) the psychiatrist's and psychologist's interviews with the child and (b) history obtained by, and experiences of, the social worker.

Maladjusted children may be grouped into types: (1) hysteric: those with an exaggerated emotional response which tends to evoke an emotional response in others; (2) obsessional: those with apparently very little emotional response and that mainly concerned with things rather than people. This tends to evoke an unemotional response from others; (3) labile: those with a spontaneous and quick emotional response which becomes satisfied by its own expression.

To put it slightly differently, one might say that the labile deals with his emotion as it arises, violently or gently as the case may be; the hysteric seems to seek and strive for answering emotion in others; the obsessional strives to avoid his own emotion and that of others.

The basic reaction type supplies one element only in the personality configuration. It is modified from the beginning of life by its interaction with two different sets of factors. Its interaction with one of these has effects which are predictable within limits. Its interaction with the other in the present state of knowledge is not predictable.

Different intelligence levels mean different learning capacities from infancy and consequently a wider or narrower field of experience in which the basic reaction type will operate—the borderline intelligence in a labile type easily produces the delinquent; the high intelligence in the labile type produces the leader and will seldom be a case for child guidance. The intelligent hysteric more often encounters difficulties than the dull hysteric since the demands of the former are more difficult to satisfy. The obsessional of average intelligence is less likely to make a satisfactory adjustment than the dull or bright obsessional.

The third element in the personality configuration is supplied by the environment, and, in all cases save the hypothetical one of the infant, that must have two aspects: (1) the historic aspect, consisting of the successive modifications which have existed in time and which constitute the socio-emotional history of the individual; (2) its immediate aspect in socioemotional relationships of the moment. This information should come from the social history and should give a clear picture of an organism interacting with its environment physically in terms of health; emotionally in terms of relationships; behaviorally from the point of view of actions and speech at home and school among playmates and adults; intellectually in terms of the acquisition of the normal knowledge and skills.

The two sets of information, obtained from interview with the child and from interview with the parent or other adult guardian, need careful consideration in their relation to one another before the therapy can begin. To take an example, the mother may complain that the boy wanders and is unreliable in all errands and duties just like his father; yet the boy may enjoy school and a boys' club by his own report, with no complaint of failure there in routine. Such discrepancy might significantly point to further investigation of the mother's attitude to father and son.

The conflict which has resulted in overt difficulties, sufficient to bring the child to the clinic, issues from the interaction of all those factors, reaction type, intellectual level, and socioemotional environment. The conflict probably has its roots in all three factors and consequently there is more than one focal point in the problem. The basic reaction type of the child will help to determine which aspect of the problem will be most responsive to therapy.

## *Indications for Treatment*

The historic aspect of the environmental factor is more important for therapy with the hysteric than it is in the case of the labile or the obsessional. The relief of the pressure of past guilt and frustration will help in obtaining insight into the present and a more detached attitude to reality. This is equally true for the young five-year-old hysteric and for the adolescent. With obsessionals, the focal point to which relief can best be applied frequently lies in immediate environmental conditions such as trauma of a recent death or separation. In obsessionals of high intelligence the focal point at which therapy can most successfully begin may lie in the inadequacy of intellectual outlets involving creativity. The integration of intellect with the still primitive and undeveloped emotions is a primary aim in the therapy of all obsessional children. The obsessional is the one type with an awareness of the future which can be turned to therapeutic value. The labile lives completely in the present, unlike the hysteric whose reactions are rooted in the past.

Translating into Freudian terms (S. Freud, 1953), one might differentiate among the hysteric with strong superego and primitive urges but an unintegrated ego; the obsessional with strong ego and superego while the primitive urges remain violent, undeveloped, and unintegrated; the labile with strong primitive urges and ego but a lack of development and integration with the superego.

The unconscious of the hysteric has a "snapshot" quality, throwing up emotions of violence and short duration in which the interactions of the superego and primitive urges are clearly seen. There is ejection, i.e., the bodying forth of a primitive urge to kill or to love, followed by guilt. The pressure of the superego on this guilt is followed by a fresh ejection of the polarized primitive urge—love succeeding hate and hate, love in cycles—a continual flux, a sequence of touch and go.

Primitive urges are essentially impulses and, at their primitive level, must issue in movement, however directed (A. Freud, 1937). Where the superego and the primitive urges act, as in the hysteric, without a mediating ego, the rigid control of the superego acts as a violent brake on the impulses. This brake fails from time to time and the impulses escape with renewed force. So the hysteric is shuttled to and fro between his unassimilated past and his unrealized future as bodied in the demands of the superego. The maladjusted hysteric can rarely find "now," the situation that is really before him, the point of stillness and balance in adjustment to the situation actually presented to him. The hysteric's first need is an external stabilizing force, which the therapist can provide, remaining unshaken through the rising storms of emotion and guilt. The effect of play therapy on a child of this kind, especially if the child is under seven, will often be to produce a temporary intensification of the violence of this flux. In children whose symptom is temper tantrums, weeping, behavior difficulties such as spitting, obscenity, and destructiveness, an intensification of the symptom after the beginning of treatment is an aid in differential diagnosis from the behavior difficulties of the labile and is an indication for different treatment. With the hysteric, repressive measures, save where there is real danger to life, are contraindicated. The stability and lack of emotional response in the therapist help the hysteric child to make his first contact with reality and to prove that the environment is, after all, not emotionally charged. With the labile, restrictive measures are called for, with the supporting sanction from the therapist that such behavior will earn dislike and loss of his friendship. Here, for the labile, comes the first understanding of the role to be performed eventually by his own superego.

Having established some contact for the hysteric with reality through the therapist's own stability, the therapist must next find, in the historic emotional environment, the emotional obstruction which first disorientated the child's reactions.

The child's creative play should give indications of where this lies. Such indications can be construed in conjunction with facts of the social history, such as nearness in age of a sibling, temperamental coldness of a parent, etc., to give direct clues for interpretation of his own situation to the child.

With the obsessional, the onset of the symptoms frequently coincides with some additional strain in the immediate environment such as the illness or departure from home of a parent. Such a situation naturally calls for the expression of feeling; but for the obsessional all expression of feeling is difficult. The feeling side remains primitive and quite out of touch with the ego and superego. His attitude is within its own limits, rational and matter of fact and, in the case of the intelligent obsessional, excessively intellectual.

The primitive urges, denied all ordinary outlets in show of feeling, issue as apparently rational acts such as touching or counting certain articles. Here bodily movement is involved, which is a partial substitute for the expression of primitive impulses.

The approach to the unconscious of such a child is difficult as he frequently resists therapy and maintains both in words and in attitude that he is in no need of help. Children with tics sometimes belong to the obsessional type and sometimes to the hysteric. Those of the latter are fairly readily discriminated since they respond readily to contact with the therapist.

The aim of therapy with the obsessional is best directed toward creativity. Fantasy here is heavily chained by the superego; but if fantasies of punishment can be reached, then later the question of what or who is punished can be explored through painting, play, interest in fiction, films, etc. From this will come the first contact with the child's feelings. Interpretation should be used as little as possible at the verbal level with the obsessional. Since words are intellectual, the likelihood is that the interpretation itself will be used to reinforce the system of the superego and further control the primitive urges. Most therapists have encountered the adult obsessional who can talk as much correct psychology as they can themselves, and this can also be seen in adolescents.

Along with the release of fantasy must come creativity, which should be subtly encouraged, even if it seems to have no direct bearing on the problem. Creativity arises from primitive impulses and has its roots in the flux which the obsessional's ego and superego are unable to tolerate. When the obsessional has experienced pleasure from creativity, e.g., from the typical activity of map-making, he has already moved a step from the characteristic feeling tone of his obsession, which is generally anxiety or superficial indifference.

With the hysteric the therapist's first role is to act as a stabilizing force. With the obsessional, he must provide the dynamics. The therapist's own combination of detachment with free-flowing and unexaggerated feeling is most valuable here—his appreciation and enjoyment of the obsessional's achievement in play or painting, his calm commiseration of misfortunes in the same field, all combine to lessen the anxiety.

Sooner or later the primitive impulse of extreme aggression will emerge and this must be accepted with overt reassurance. It is at this point that verbal interpretation is helpful. This should not be of a systematic or intellectual kind, but contain a feeling response that gives the child the assurance that his guilt is not unique. By this means the ego, deformed by the extreme pressure of the superego, is enlarged and the child is brought into a better contact with reality. The child's own feeling cannot be thrown into a void; and toward the obsessional, the therapist needs a warmer manner than toward any other type of child.

Much therapy with the labile can be done at a positive and extroverted level. Any access to the unconscious in paintings and play should be used to give the child insight into restraint of primitive impulses. Much can be done with such children at an extroverted reality level, and they are particularly responsive to group treatment. They can obtain considerable help if their loyalty and interest can be attached to a youth organization during treatment. The rules and demands of attendance at such a group can be of aid in fostering the superego if the child has come to the point, under the guidance of the therapist, where he wishes to be accepted by his fellows.

***Conclusions***

(1) Maladjusted children may be grouped according to reaction type.

(2) Such grouping enables the therapist to distinguish between different conditions involving the same symptoms.

(3) The general aim of therapy will be the same in all cases; but the particular aim will vary according to the type to which the child belongs.

(4) The methods of therapy and the optimum attitude of the therapist will vary according to the type receiving therapy.

# *Some Considerations Regarding Psychotherapy with Psychotic Children*

SIBYLLE ESCALONA

When a relatively new group of clinical phenomena becomes prominent in his experience, the clinician is impelled to review the extent of his knowledge in the area in question. The following comments are the result of such a re-evaluation of some of the assumptions which underlie much of our psychotherapeutic work with severely disorganized children. No striking successes will be reported, nor new treatment ideas advanced. The aim is merely to integrate certain clinical observations with established modes of thinking in the field of psychotherapy generally. The only conclusions that may be anticipated, therefore, are a series of question marks.

Our thinking about treatment and the goals of therapy is largely determined by our convictions regarding the etiology and nature of the condition to be treated. Hence, it will be necessary to briefly describe the type of illness here to be referred to as "psychosis of childhood." The very term, "psychosis of childhood," is disapproved by many who feel that no maladjustment in childhood can be so diagnosed in the absence of certain classical signs and symptoms which serve as criteria for a diagnosis of psychosis in maturity. Whatever term one decides to use—and childhood psychosis may be taken as an abbreviation for "grossly atypical development" or for "severe disintegration of personality"—we have an only too vivid mental picture of the type of child to whom these and similar terms are applied. Several varieties of (in this sense) psychotic children have been described in the literature within recent years. Among the better-known publications are those by Kanner (1943, 1944, 1946),

Bender (1942, 1947a), Bradley (1941), and Schumacher (1946). In spite of the semantic confusion in this area, certain descriptive criteria have emerged which characterize the various disorders of childhood which may be grouped together under the heading of childhood psychosis.

During the last four years, seventeen children between the ages of five and sixteen years were diagnosed as suffering from a psychosis of childhood by the Children's Division of the Menninger Clinic. All of these children were free from organic pathology within the limits of validity set by clinical neurological and physical examinations including routine laboratory work, EEG, and skull X-ray. Upon survey of the entire group of cases, the following characteristics seem outstanding:

(1) Wherever an adequate early history could be obtained it was noted that the development of these severely disturbed children has been atypical and irregular since earliest infancy. The deviant development need not be in the direction of retardation; in some instances there was a precocity of development in certain areas and retardation in others. (Some of these children, for instance, walked early and showed generally advanced neuromuscular development and motor control but were seriously retarded in speech or some other area.) Also, not infrequently, certain developmental achievements were gained at an approximately normal time but were lost again, or else developmental progress in a certain sphere was arrested at a given point whereas in other areas this was not the case. For instance, several of the children learned to speak quite early only to lapse into prolonged periods of mutism later on. One learned to walk at thirteen months, but returned to more primitive modes of locomotion during the second year of life and had to learn to walk upright all over again. Mental functioning, inasmuch as this could be ascertained at the time of examination, varied from a generally retarded level to very superior intelligence functioning, but in all cases it appeared to be uneven with spot-like areas of accomplishment way above and way below what would appear to be the basic or most representative level of mental functioning for the particular child.[a]

(2) Wherever the life histories of severely disorganized children were given adequate scrutiny, it was noted that disturbances in the earliest and most basic interpersonal relationships were present. Early feeding difficulties, resistance to weaning, traumatic toilet training, difficulties over physical restraint, sleeping disturbances—all the familiar landmarks of infantile maladjustment—cropped up with monotonous regularity. Furthermore, most of the mothers or other persons in close contact with these children, spontaneously commented that there was something puzzling and "different" about these children from a very early age on. Mothers felt that they never knew

[a] This is more-or-less a matter of definition since children who show other psychotic-like features but give the characteristic picture of essential feeblemindedness (to psychological testing) are grouped under a different diagnostic category, namely, "mental deficiency and psychosis."

what to expect, that they lacked a sense of intimacy and close rapport which they had known with their other children. One gains the impression that either remoteness or an exceptionally high degree of irritability (or both) in the child prevented a close interdependent relationship between mother and child in many of these instances.

This is one of the points at which we wish to call attention to a possible source of error in our thinking about the nature of this illness and hence about the appropriate therapeutic approach. From experience with nonpsychotic children it is well known that behavior deviations of the kind just enumerated are often produced by parental attitudes. Hence, it is easy to assume that in these severely disturbed children, maternal rejection is at the root of the trouble. Yet, the more one studies the early life history of psychotic children, the more one is impressed with the atypical and pathological reaction of the children to perfectly ordinary maternal attitudes and to the inevitable daily routines. A baby who will not eat when food is offered, who cries when he is expected to sleep, who is incessantly active or pathologically lethargic, who reacts with panicky resistance to routine procedures such as bathing or being dressed, and who rarely provides for the mother the emotional gratification that comes from having the baby respond to her positively, cannot help but be upsetting to even the most loving mother. Finding the usual methods of baby care unsuccessful with their atypical children, these mothers will, of course, "try everything" and thus go to extremes in both strictness and indulgence. They will seek and receive contradictory advice and act on much of it, and when we come along to take a developmental history, it is found that the child has been managed inconsistently. After years of more-or-less unsuccessful attempts to manage the child effectively, feelings of ambivalence and guilt must of necessity develop in mothers of such children, and the presence of such maternal attitudes is apt to lead the therapist to think of the disturbed mother–child relationship as the cause of the child's illness. It seems possible to the writer that we may sometimes be confusing end-results with causes. Therapeutic programs might at times be modified if these early developmental disturbances were regarded as arising in large measure from the pathology within the child rather than from parental attitudes per se. With this assumption the disturbed mother–child relationship will still be regarded as an important etiological factor in that it creates an unfavorable psychological atmosphere in the home, but will be viewed as a by-product of the total maladjustment picture.

(3) Turning from characteristic features of the developmental history in cases of childhood psychosis to the condition as seen when such children are brought to the attention of psychiatrists and psychologists, one may say that they present a large variety of behavior pictures which in all cases lead to a generalized and far-reaching inadequacy on the part of the child. This inadequacy, whatever form it took, made it impossible for these children to cope with whatever life situations are ordinarily appropriate at a given age and

under given environmental circumstances. More specifically, the following phenomena were frequently encountered:

(a) Speech disorders, ranging from near mutism to peculiar, bizarre, deviantly structured speech often including neologisms.

(b) Deviant thought processes including circular and autistic logic. The peculiar type of reasoning encountered among these children is most readily discernible on a battery of psychological tests but is also apparent in clinical examination if an effort is made to investigate this area of mental functioning.

(c) Bizarre preoccupations and unusual interests which may or may not be accompanied by special ability in the area of preoccupation. Among these children we have often seen a peculiar fascination with machinery (sometimes narrowed down to one type, such as fans or telephones); one child was interested principally in skin and thought content as well as fantasies centered on differences between various kinds of skin, etc.; one child was obsessed with spatial relationships such as inside–outside, upsidedown, etc.; and some children focused their interest, almost to the exclusion of anything else, on oddly selected topics such as magic, frogs, circuses, marine life, etc.

(d) All of these children showed extraordinarily low frustration tolerance, amounting to a kind of hypersensitivity, which experiences any delay or impediment, however small, as intense frustration and may lead to rage reactions or autistic withdrawal.

(e) Characteristically these children showed excessive fantasying of an irrealistic kind which permits conscious awareness and open expression of material which ordinarily remains unconscious and which can be elicited from neurotic or normal children only with difficulty.[b] Often these children showed a genuine inability to distinguish between fantasy and real experience, leading to glaring misinterpretation of reality situations and occasionally to definitely crystallized delusions.

(f) Learning ability may be intact, but fail to function in normal school situations because of the child's inability to maintain social relationships and accept restriction. (Some of our patients expelled from school as feebleminded made up the work equivalent to several grades in one year of private tutoring.) On the other hand, there may be learning disabilities seemingly arising from a lack of integrative capacity and a lack of motivation rather than from a lack of ability.

If this descriptive summary is representative, what are the implications for appropriate treatment programs? It goes without saying that in cases of this type, as well as in any therapeutic work with children, treatment programs must be a total educative effort whether it includes twenty-four-hour planning in an institution or whether it includes guidance of the family in planning for the child. The issues we wish to discuss here, however, have to do with what goes on in the therapeutic sessions.

---

[b] We have been impressed with the predominance of cannibalistic fantasies, but, of course, all other types of fantasies may also occur.

On the basis of clinical experience with the more usual types of psychiatric disorders in childhood our general approach may be described as follows: We assume that what has been done to a human being can be undone. Thus we believe that if a maladjusted child can experience—in his relation to the therapist—some of the gratifications and the sense of continuity and stability which he lacked in his earlier life, if he can be helped to remember and understand events which were traumatic to him, and if his misconceptions about human affairs can be interpreted in terms of his needs, then normal processes of ego development can be resumed, and the object of psychotherapy will have been achieved. Therapeutic endeavors, therefore, are directed at permitting the expression of previously unconscious material, fantasies are seen as meaningful and interpreted in the context of the child's reality experiences, and the relationship between affects and their source, as well as between symptoms and their deeper meaning, is explored.

Endless hours have been spent by qualified therapists in treating psychotic children on the basis of these axioms, often with discouraging results. It has occurred to us that, although the symptoms of these children are just as meaningful psychologically and as amenable to interpretation as is the case with neurotic children, the immediate aim (and possibly the ultimate aim) of psychotherapy with psychotic children might be almost the opposite from the one we are accustomed to using with neurotic children. If the type of therapy just described may be referred to as "expressive," the alternate type might be called "suppressive." Suppressive psychotherapy proceeds from a recognition of the fact that psychotic children, by definition as it were, show extreme weakness in ego functioning and at times a disintegrative process appears to interfere with ego development. Hence, these children have failed to repress psychic experience which normally should be unconscious so that their spontaneous verbalization of conscious content resembles the dreams of other children; and the play of psychotic children during initial interviews is often much like the play material obtained from neurotic children who have been in therapy for many months. If the ego is judged to be too weak to assimilate and reconcile the impulses, needs, and conflicts actually present, it is conceivable to plan in the direction of protecting the ego from the impact of instinctual forces. Thus therapy would be directed at discouraging the expression and acting-out of fantasies, and providing as much gratification as possible in more realistic pursuits, and at strengthening reality testing by all possible means. Both suppressive and expressive psychotherapy have in common, of course, that they work primarily through the relationship between child and therapist. (In suppressive therapy, however, the relationship itself would rarely become the subject of analysis. In fact, as far as we can see, this type of psychotherapeutic relationship with a child is possible only if a positive transference can be maintained.) [c]

[c] Technically this can often be accomplished by limiting transference interpretations to rather superficial ones on negative aspects of the transference. Positive transference phenomena are then accepted at face value and thus maintained.

As one follows the progress of a series of psychotic children in treatment of either of these two varieties, one cannot help receiving the impression that neither approach is entirely successful in the sense of bringing about improvement which will be maintained after cessation of treatment. In the following, we shall briefly summarize the characteristic responses of psychotic children to the two types of treatment under the conditions prevailing at our clinic.

Given a sufficiently long time in which to do so, the psychotic children of whom we know all were able to form a strong dependent relationship with their therapist. In fact some became so dependent that a therapist's absence, for any reason, or a change in therapists were major traumatic events causing serious sudden relapses into modes of behavior characteristic of the child during earlier phases of the illness.

The children who received what we have called an expressive type of psychotherapy have demonstrated, on occasion, an almost uncanny ability to understand their own behavior, even offering spontaneous interpretations which, as far as could be ascertained, were keen and accurate statements of fact. For instance, one seven-year-old girl, suffering from a life-long maladjustment, judged to be of psychotic degree at age six, who later developed a clear schizophrenic syndrome, was able to work through her very severe eating difficulties in treatment. Through the verbalization of fantasies and dreams and endless hours of role play, she became convinced that food is not fecal matter and resumed eating in satisfactory amounts. However, in spite of a strong attachment to the therapist, and although the content of therapeutic sessions was by no means limited to this topic, her general behavior remained relatively unaltered. Fearfulness, infantile speech and motor patterns, periods of inexplicable excitement, excessive openly expressed fantasies of a bizarre nature, and other overtly psychotic features continued to be present.

Another child, a schizophrenic boy whose treatment began during his tenth year and who at age twelve showed definite signs of deterioration, surprised us not only by his extreme dependence upon the therapist (he used to say in a manner far from bland, "You have to be here so I can be happy"), but by flashes of rare insight. This withdrawn, deluded child, who gave the appearance of feeblemindedness and was out of contact with his environment much of the time, said on one occasion when he discussed the reasons for his institutionalization with the therapist, "Nobody can really help me. I don't like anybody, not even my mother. Doctor——(mentioning his previous therapist) liked me and tried to help me, and you like me but you can't help me. I don't love anyone, I want to kill everybody." Immediately afterward he lapsed into rambling incoherent talk centering on one of his longstanding preoccupations and never mentioned the matter again. It is of interest that the matter of this child's capacity for affection had not been mentioned to him previously. This boy, like several others, aroused deceptive hopes in his therapist by apparent good clinical improvement contingent upon daily contact with the therapist. He gave up much of his fantasy life, or at least no longer expressed it openly, he resumed school work and entered into friendly contacts with children and adults—all accomplishments of which he had been thought incapable. The important point here is, however, that a short separation from the therapist caused a complete relapse and that he at no time developed even a minimum of tolerance for any frustration whatsoever.

These examples are meant to be representative of a good many more and tend to show that even overtly psychotic children are capable of developing a meaningful relationship to a therapist, of showing temporary clinical improvement due to such a relationship, and of verbalizing and affectively experiencing insight. Yet (with one possible exception) in our experience, such improvements are not maintained, nor does treatment set in motion the autonomous functions of growth and development as it does in neurotic children. It is as though, to use an analogy, psychotic children could be held above water by the therapist's support, whereas nonpsychotic children can be taught to swim by their own efforts.

The response of psychotic children to a suppressive type of psychotherapy, as far as we have been able to observe, has been somewhat different but not necessarily more encouraging. In the case of the little girl mentioned previously, for instance, the type of therapy was changed after one year, in view of the fact that while a specific symptom disappeared, her total development seemed to continue in its pathological course. She saw another therapist, the same number of hours per week, for several years. After initial difficulty in connection with the change in therapists she developed an equally intensive relationship with the new person, but the content of the sessions, although they still took the form of play, changed to an emphasis on the immediate reality situation. This girl, gradually, showed marked clinical improvement in that she lost her infantile mannerisms, became able to associate with her peers, accomplished school work in keeping with standards for her age (though this was done by private tutoring), and hardly ever spoke in the excited, irrational manner previously characteristic of her. However, psychological tests as well as psychiatric interviews of the usual permissive type, showed that the psychotic process continued undiminished. The bizarre fantasies could easily be elicited though they were no longer volunteered, thought patterns continued autistic and schizophrenic-like, and her capacity for genuine affective rapport continued very poor—although she went through the motions of ordinary social interaction.

A very similar series of changes was noted in a boy, age eight, when treatment was initiated, in whose case therapy was of the suppressive type to begin with and went on for a number of years. At age eight he was flighty, rambling and incoherent in speech, expressed bizarre ideas, had many fears, was unable to relate himself to anyone, lost bowel and bladder control whenever excited, and generally presented the picture of a totally deviant inadequate child. Very gradually, almost all of the overtly striking symptoms disappeared. His speech, when listened to closely, was still rambling and disjointed. Since the content had become innocuous where it used to be bizarre, however, this was rarely noted by the casual observer. Disturbances in elimination control had been overcome, as had most of his fears, and his violent aggressive outbursts were replaced by generalized mischievousness. So favorable an impression did this child make after some years of treatment that placement in a school for normal children was considered. Yet, here again, re-examination showed that the illness had merely gone underground, so to speak, and actually had reached a more advanced stage. Neither rational thought nor adequate reality testing were possible for him, a positive attachment to people was lacking, and the most extraordinary fantasies could readily be elicited—they were merely held in check.

These examples of observations, chosen from a somewhat larger group, if verified by the clinical experience of others, suggest certain cautions and problems for further investigation in regard to the treatment of psychotic children. The following summarizing statements are offered very tentatively as a basis for further discussion and in no sense as conclusions:

(1) Illness of psychotic degree occurring in early childhood is associated with severe developmental irregularities beginning at earliest infancy, as well as with profound disturbances in the relationship between the child and his parents. It is suggested that maternal feelings of ambivalence, guilt, etc. and the resultant inconsistent and apparently punitive management of the child may often arise in consequence of the child's atypical behavior. Therefore, it cannot be assumed that the child's illness was largely caused by an unfavorable psychological milieu.

(2) Two principally different therapeutic approaches to the psychotic child have been mentioned, both of which are consistent with established psychodynamic concepts of personality development and psychopathology. Both expressive and suppressive psychotherapy, provided they are maintained for a long time and embedded in an adequate total treatment program, have resulted in clinical improvement in some instances. The main difference in the response of psychotic children to these two modes of treatment appears to be that expressive therapy may work through and really "cure" specific symptoms. It may also bring about temporary all-over improvement which, however, is not maintained. The functioning of the entire personality, however, is not altered significantly.

Suppressive psychotherapy may bring about clinical improvement, principally in the direction of increased controls and conformity. The underlying psychotic process remains untouched, however, limiting the most favorable outcome of such therapy to a pseudoadjustment on the part of the child.

(3) The response of psychotic children to therapy is often such as would justify an optimistic prognosis in neurotic children. In severely disturbed children under our observation, the occurrence of insight, development of a transference situation, and clinical improvement in direct response to therapeutic work, all were present, yet the treatment failed to result in ultimate

improvement. This suggests that criteria by which the success of treatment is measured may have to be modified in regard to psychotic children.

(4) Adequate therapeutic measures, in cases of childhood psychosis, can be developed—if at all—only if the nature and causes of these conditions can be understood much more fully than they are at present.

# *Antisocial Young Children and Their Families*[2]

EVEOLEEN N. REXFORD

. . . Our experiences at the Thom Clinic with the psychotherapy of antisocial young children (now numbering approximately 175, including Kurt Rose's original group) permit us to draw certain conclusions about therapeutic methods with these children. Our therapy with early delinquents is based upon the understanding that these children suffer from maturational defects of varying degrees of severity; the extent of modification of the techniques used with neurotic children depends upon our diagnostic appraisal of the level of the child's ego and superego functioning. It should be emphasized that the approach and techniques used are those of child psychotherapy and not of child analysis.

Those children who suffered a primary emotional and physical deprivation during infancy are the most traumatized and most difficult to treat because of their very limited capacity for object relations and their tenuous reality grasp. Their acting-out expresses forbidden impulses which they cannot or will not control because of poorly developed ego defenses and a lack of inner discipline. They show a marked intolerance for anxiety and for frustration, and their aggressive outbursts often express their perception of anyone who denies or thwarts them as an enemy. They cannot tolerate delay of satisfactions for reality reasons and demand immediate gratification of their wishes. Their life experiences and intimate relationships have yielded them no confidence that their needs will be met and they expect and provoke deprivation and hostility at every turn. Denial, projection, and withdrawal are their principal mechanisms of defense which are replaced only very slowly

[2] Earlier portions of this chapter discuss the original treatment studies begun in 1947 by Kurt Rose with forty-eight children between the ages of six and ten years. All had been referred to the Thom Clinic for aggressive, destructive behavior of at least two years' duration. Clinical diagnoses varied from psychoneurosis with antisocial trends to psychosis with aggressive and destructive behavior. The majority resembled Friedlander's description of the "antisocial character disorder."

in treatment by more mature defenses. They are isolated individuals, rejecting and rejected repeatedly by everyone with whom they come in contact. While they come regularly to the clinic from the beginning, their distrust of the therapist is profound and their testing of him prolonged and ingenious. Their narcissism finds expression in many of their delinquent acts which have an obvious exhibitionistic and omnipotent coloring. These children suffer from very disturbed relationships with their parents. In some instances, the obvious vicarious satisfaction the parent gains from his child's delinquent acts encourages the lack of control and contributes to the feeble motivation for discipline. Conscious and/or unconscious severe rejection by the mother and a close tie to a sadistic father appear to foster strong sadomasochistic fantasies to which the child reacts in terms of kill or be killed. The child may be dominated by his fantasies with an intensity which seems almost delusional in character, and his behavior may be viewed as an obvious attempt to protect himself from danger. Many of the homes from which these children come are characterized by a lack of ethical standards and a flagrant defiance of authority in any form. The developmental history of these children mirrors the depriving emotional and physical milieu; at each stage of psychosexual development, disturbances are reported—in feeding, in toilet training, in socializing, and in learning.

Another group of early delinquents represents a paler and less serious edition of the first because they suffered emotional and/or reality deprivation at a later stage in their development. The birth of a sibling with withdrawal of affection by an immature mother incapable of loving more than one child at a time, departure of father from the home because of imprisonment, a commitment, death or desertion, serious illness with a long hospitalization are events that for a number of children appear to interfere drastically with their previously relatively normal development. They have a greater capacity for a trusting relationship with an adult, their defenses are less infantile, and their conflicts more on the neurotic level.

In a third group, the delinquent behavior appears to be the direct expression of a specific neurotic conflict, or of a strong identification with a particular emotional disturbance in a parent. A few of our children belong to a fourth group in that their aggressive and antisocial behavior represents a relatively transient stage of development readily worked out in psychotherapy.

The basis for therapy in each instance is the establishing of a trusting, confident relationship with an adult who is aware of the needs of the child. The task of therapy involves (1) the promotion of object relations, (2) the strengthening of useful ego defenses, (3) the encouragement of suitable identifications, and (4) the modification of superego functioning.

It is obviously the first group which presents the most difficult technical problems for psychotherapists. The task of building a working relationship with a child whose way of relating to others is predominantly hostile and whose image of the interchange between human beings is so colored both by his unrewarding life experiences and his sadomasochistic fantasies has frequently proved insoluble in the child guidance clinic or casework agency. For this reason, a brief description of crucial elements in the early stage of the therapy may be helpful to other clinicians.

In the initial phases of psychiatric treatment, which may last from one to two years, the therapist must be prepared to tolerate overt physical and verbal hostile outbursts which may be extreme and persistent and may recur later at times of rising anxiety. He must be patient and permissive without being masochistic and indulgent; at the same time, he needs to be able to set definite limits, to avoid both injuries to others and undue property destruction without being punitive to the child. The child needs to learn that the therapist can protect himself and the child from the latter's aggressive, destructive outbursts, which are so very frightening to the patient. We believe that failures in therapy with delinquents often occur precisely because the permissiveness adequate for treatment of the neurotic child does not provide the stimulus to inner control vital for the delinquent. The therapist must make clear from the beginning that he does not approve of, or side with, the child's unacceptable behavior, although he is not punitive or moralistic in his attitude. The child will test him out in every conceivable manner, looking for weaknesses in the therapist's standards, trying to prove that he, too, steals, cheats, or lies when it is to his advantage. The child will impose on the therapist's patience and sympathy, certain that the affection and tolerance will fail if the adult is tried sufficiently. The therapist must be scrupulously honest with him, consistent in attitude, and mindful of reality as well as of the child's inner needs.

The combination of emotional acceptance and presentation of definite behavior standards enables the therapist to contribute to the child's inner control while making some restitution for the emotional deprivation the child has suffered. During this relation-building phase, which may last many months, the child is strengthened by learning about his problems and other people's difficulties. His misconceptions are clarified, his isolation relieved, and sublimations are encouraged. Therapy is a new emotional experience and an orientation toward reality and away from destructive fantasy life. As the acting-out diminishes, more mature patterns of behavior develop and neurotic conflicts and fantasies emerge which become the focus of the therapy. The more mature the child is emotionally, the more predominant the neurotic elements in his delinquency; as the very infantile child matures in therapy, neurotic difficulties play a larger part in his problems.

There are other significant differences in the techniques required during the relation-building phase, for instance, the importance of gifts from the therapist of actual food, drink, and small articles. These children's instinctual cravings are very strong, and it is extremely difficult for them to understand and appreciate the symbolic gifts of the therapeutic situation, to a far greater extent than is true of the neurotic child. In several instances, Kurt Rose gave a regular allowance to boys who stole persistently and to others he gave the guns, knives, or jewelry which the children had been stealing persistently from stores. In each instance, the gifts were indicated by the therapeutic situation and were used purposefully both to make restitution to the deprived child and to remove him from the reality dangers of actual thefts. It must be faced that the boys may regard such gifts as seductions or bribes, and precise clarification of the reasons for the gifts has been helpful in dealing with this complication.

Impulsive aggressive children are usually overactive and react to the suggestion of restraint with anxiety, restlessness, and destructive outbursts. They may find it impossible during the relation-building phase to remain in the playroom so that regular trips are a necessary part of the therapy pattern. The therapist must obviously develop the technique of utilizing the locale and the experiences of the trip for clarification of the boy's problems and anxieties. As Rose (1951, p. 843) observed,

> Where we followed them out on the street, we did not simply exchange the restrictive and threatening clinic setting for the freer atmosphere of the open air; we were not just buying ice cream at the drugstore; we were always on the track of the unconscious forces which were responsible for the selection of the locale or of the activities and even of the specific choice of food. We followed them into church, where Frank lit candles for his deceased criminal father; we accompanied Billy into the department store where he unconsciously repeated his first public theft, committed three years earlier, by taking a gun; we watched Walter's contorted facial expression when we walked toward a collection of pocket knives at Sears Roebuck. Inner forces had driven this boy to steal fifteen knives previously. We noticed John's greedy intent to steal candy from the corner drugstore.

John first told Rose of his frightening homosexual experiences after he had seen a reproduction of Blake's "Adam and Eve"—Eve with the snake's head in her mouth—at the Museum of Fine Arts. At the museum also, Tony began to tell his therapist of his fears of death when he returned repeatedly to the exhibit of Egyptian mummies.

It is evident that "relationship therapy" alone is not adequate to deal with these suspicious, anxious, and acting-out children. Their way of relating to others is predominantly hostile, and their ego defenses against their wishes and fears are of such a primitive nature that clarification and interpretation of their feelings and anxieties must accompany each step in the therapeutic process. Such interpretations are more effective if couched in as direct and primitive a verbal form as these children experience their thoughts and fears.

The impressions gained from other Thom Clinic therapists working with similar children corroborates the findings in Rose's progress notes regarding his forty-eight children that weekly psychoanalytic psychotherapy carried over several years' duration can lead to significant changes in the child's behavior and psychopathology. The child develops a more trusting attitude toward adults through his confidence in his therapist and identifies in varying degrees with the latter's behavior and standards. His image of the outer world as a totally hostile and dangerous milieu gives way to a more realistic appraisal of the intent and behavior of others, and his own need for hostile action is greatly diminished. Insatiable oral cravings and fears of total annihilation or abandonment become greatly modified, and he gains some perception of the role his own destructive wishes and behavior play in what happens to him. His longings for warm affectionate relationships come to his awareness, and he can reach out cautiously to adults other than his therapist for support and understanding.

In all of the boys who progressed markedly in treatment, a consistent finding has been the modification of the predominantly hostile image of the mother with the appearance of a more oedipal type of attachment to her. Repeatedly, the boy's strong identification with a criminal, psychotic, or highly inadequate father has proved a strong barrier to further working-out of the boy's oedipal conflicts. When the father was dead or permanently absent from the home, the therapist was apt to be more successful in promoting the boy's identification with a different kind of father figure which made it possible for the child to progress further in resolving his oedipal conflicts.

The development of more mature ego defenses such as reaction formations, repressions, and sublimations leads to a curbing of the antisocial behavior, but the status of the treated children in the original treatment group on follow-up points to the defects in character structure which remained: the predominantly narcissistic orientation, the paucity of solid object relations, the few skills and achievements possible for most of the boys, and the generally restricted nature of their personalities.

The curbing of the antisocial pattern is an achievement in itself, but if we are to aim for a more mature and self-reliant personality in the treated child, our Thom Clinic experiences raise important questions. Would it be possible to achieve further changes in character structure by the continuation of therapy for longer periods? Would therapeutic sessions two or three times weekly bring the desired results? Or do we have to conclude that the ambitious redistribution and transformation of instinctual forces we seek can take place only in psychoanalysis? The possibilities of a residential total treatment program are very attractive but the experiences of the Redl group (Goodrich and Boomer, 1958; Redl and Wineman, 1951) both in Detroit and at Bethesda illustrate both the technical difficulties and the great expense of such a program. As our attention has turned more persistently to the emotional milieu in which these children are brought up, another question emerges, namely, if it is possible to find a way to work with the parents to modify the emotional climate of the home, would this support enable the child to move toward a more optimal level of adaptation? . . .

## REFERENCES

ACKERMAN, N. H. Psychiatric disorders in children: diagnosis and etiology in our time. In P. H. HOCH and G. ZUBIN (Eds.), *Current problems in psychiatric diagnosis*. New York: Grune & Stratton, 1953. Pp. 205–230.

BENDER, LAURETTA. Childhood schizophrenia. *Nerv. Child*, 1942, **1**, 138–140.

BENDER, LAURETTA. Childhood schizophrenia. *Am. J. Orthopsychiat.*, 1947a, **27**, 40–56.

BENDER, LAURETTA. Psychopathic conduct disorders in children. In R. M. LINDNER (Ed.), *A handbook of correctional psychology*. New York: Philosophical Library, 1947b. Pp. 360–377.

BENDER, LAURETTA. Psychological problems of children with organic brain disease. *Am. J. Orthopsychiat.*, 1949, **19**, 404–415.

BRADLEY, C. *Schizophrenia in childhood*. New York: Macmillan, 1941.

DESPERT, J. LOUISE. Some considerations relating to the genesis of autistic behavior in children. *Am. J. Orthopsychiat.*, 1951, **21**, 335–350.

FREUD, ANNA. *The ego and the mechanisms of defence*. London: Hogarth Press, 1937.

FREUD, S. The predisposition to obsessional neurosis (1913). *Collected papers*. London: Hogarth Press, 1953. Vol. II.

GOLDFARB, W. Infant rearing and problem behavior. *Am. J. Orthopsychiat.*, 1943, **23**, 249–265.

GOODRICH, D. W., and BOOMER, D. S. Some concepts about therapeutic interventions with hyperaggressive children: part I. *Soc. Casewk.*, 1958, **39**, 207–213.

KANNER, L. Autistic disturbances of affective contact. *Nerv. Child*, 1943, **2**, 217–250.

KANNER, L. Early infantile autism. *J. Pediat.*, 1944, **25**, 211–217.

KANNER, L. Irrelevant and metaphorical language in early infantile autism. *Am. J. Psychiat.*, 1946, **103**, 242–246.

KANNER, L. Problems of nosology and psychodynamics of early infantile autism. *Am. J. Orthopsychiat.*, 1949, **19**, 416–426.

KENNARD, MARGARET, RABINOVITCH, R. D., and WEXLER, D. The abnormal electroencephalogram as related to reading disability in children with disorders of behavior. *Canad. med Ass. J.*, 1952, **67**, 330–333.

LA BARRE, W. Appraising today's pressures on family living. *Soc. Casewk.*, 1951, **32**, 51–57.

LEVY, D. M. Primary affect hunger. *Am. J. Psychiat.*, 1937, **94**, 643–652.

LEVY, D. M. Critical evaluation of the present state of child psychiatry. *Am. J. Psychiat.*, 1951, **108**, 481–494.

LOWREY, L. G. Personality distortion and early institutional care. *Am. J. Orthopsychiat.*, 1940, **10**, 576–585.

LOWREY, L. G. Symposium: training in the field of Orthopsychiatry. *Am. J. Orthopsychiat.*, 1950, **20**, 674–678.

PUTNAM, MARIAN. C., RANK, BEATA, and KAPLAN, S. Notes on John I.: a case of primal depression in an infant. In *Psychoanalytic study of the child*. New York: International Univer. Press, 1951, **6**, 35–58.

RABINOVITCH, R. D. Observations on the differential study of severely disturbed children. *Am. J. Orthopsychiat.*, 1952, **22**, 230–238.

RABINOVITCH, R. D., and DUBO, SARA. Child psychiatry. In E. A. SPIEGEL (Ed.), *Progress in neurology and psychiatry*. New York: Grune & Stratton, 1952, **7**, 465–479.

REDL, F., and WINEMAN, D. *Children who hate*. Glencoe, Ill.: The Free Press, 1951.

ROSE, K. E. Personality structure and therapeutic manipulation of a young offender. *Am. J. Orthopsychiat.*, 1951, **21**, 838–844.

SCHUMACHER, H. Schizophrenia in children. *Ohio State med. J.*, 1946, **42**, 1248–1254.

SPITZ, R. A. Hospitalism. In *Psychoanalytic study of the child*. New York: International Univer. Press, 1951, **2**, 113–117.

PART TWO

# STRUCTURE

❀ CHAPTER FOUR

# Orientation and Involvement of the Parents

THE MAIN issues of this chapter relate to whether parents should undergo treatment, whether the same therapist should treat parent and child, and, if two therapists are involved, how much communication should take place between them. These questions directly lead to the crucial issue of the confidentiality of the sessions and its implications for the child and the parent. The reactions that may be anticipated from mothers when their children enter therapy and the need for careful orientation of the parents with regard to the entire therapeutic process are also discussed.

Various combinations of the therapist–parent–child triad are considered in the selections that follow; unfortunately, there is no discussion of the trend toward family therapy, in which the therapist sees two or more family members, including the child patient, simultaneously. The pros and cons of each combination of assignments need to be evaluated in the light of the specific case. Questions, such as the following, need to be answered: Does the degree of severity of the child's illness affect the choice of treatment combination? Would some arrangements be more, or less, suitable with psychotic and neurotic constellations? Is the age of the child or the level of anticipated uncovering a crucial factor? Does the therapeutic orientation arbitrarily determine the choice?

The question of confidentiality becomes important in any

but total family therapy. Each of the selections contributes to this subject, while Ross's article is devoted exclusively to various aspects of the problem. He describes the feelings the child must have toward being brought to therapy and suggests reasons for the child's suspicions of the adults involved.

The need to consider the parents' role is discussed by Ross and Burlingham. Included are considerations of the guilt and concern of the parents at having produced a disturbed child, their jealousy of the therapist and unconscious maneuvers to sabotage treatment, and their assumption that they will be kept as minutely informed as if the child's illness were of a medical nature. Further situations to be anticipated are the parents' urge to question the child as to his therapy activities or to ask the therapist, in front of the child, for an account of behavior or progress. Since the child will receive most of his initial orientation and attitudes toward therapy from his parents, how can they be helped in presenting the situation to the child? Each of the selections offers suggestions for suitable explanations and for preparing the parent for his own problem in separating from the child.

Further questions are briefly posed in the articles that follow; they warrant serious consideration by the therapist. If the father cannot be actively engaged in treatment, what contacts should be made with him, and by whom? To what extent should the school become involved? What problems may arise if the person who initially diagnosed the child subsequently becomes his therapist or if the person who interpreted the diagnostic findings to the parents is assigned as therapist to one or both of them?

Training clinics have an additional problem in ensuring dissemination of uniform explanations of therapy to the parents, since this may become the responsibility of various students in training. Clinics often prepare a memo which includes a description of the play-therapy process and suggestions and instructions for the parents. It is not intended that this be read or given to the parents, but that the clinician communicate the main points during the interpretive interview.

AN EXPLANATION OF PLAY THERAPY

Some children experience difficulties in making adjustments. Play therapy provides an opportunity for them to work through these problems in a permissive situation. Adults find relief in talking over their difficulties with an understanding therapist. Usually children cannot express their thoughts and feelings in words, but can find release through various forms of play.

Since a child's fears and anxieties have been built up during his past experiences with persons close to him—parents, teachers, brothers and sisters—he has very little opportunity to explore and examine these feelings in either the home or school situation. Play therapy can offer him a unique relationship with an objective and accepting adult who is not in a position to "use" any of his disclosures for or against him in any way.

In order to ensure the privacy of this arrangement, it is essential that the child not feel any necessity to give an accounting of the events that occur in the playroom. This should be viewed as his own private hour with the therapist. For this reason, parents are asked to refrain from questioning the child as to his activities, or from asking him how he likes it, if he had a good time, and so forth. Occasionally, the child may bring home a drawing, painting, or other object he has made. As these may often have a hidden meaning of which even the child is not aware, it is best (1) not to question him as to what it represents; (2) not to praise it as a "masterpiece"; (3) not to criticize it or make suggestions for its technical improvement. If he offers it to you, accept it casually and without much comment.

In bringing the child for the first session, he can be told that he will be coming to the clinic each week to play with ——————in the playroom, that there are a lot of toys there which he can play with in any way that he wishes. If he questions further as to reasons for coming, he can be told that it seems to help children to have someone that they can talk to and play with all alone.

As children often want to use paints or clay or other messy materials, it is suggested that they wear old clothes that will not be hurt.

# ❀ Child Analysis and the Mother

DOROTHY T. BURLINGHAM

There are certain difficulties which arise in the analysis of a child that are not encountered in the analysis of an independent, nonpsychotic adult. There is, for instance, the child's relative inability to express himself in words and his frequent use of other means of communication. Furthermore, the child's emotional relationship to the analyst is complicated by many factors, among them his natural attachment to and dependence upon his parents. In turn, his dependence upon his parents forces the analyst to keep the child's parents in a favorable attitude toward the analysis. It is this last problem which will be the chief topic of this paper. To maintain the sympathy and the cooperation of the parents throughout the entire analysis of a child is a difficult and trying problem; and yet, if one does not succeed in this, the analysis moves inevitably to an abrupt and premature interruption. In this paper we will talk chiefly of mothers, because it is almost exclusively with them that the analyst must deal.

There are two kinds of mothers; those who are completely ignorant of analysis and those who know something about it and who perhaps have themselves been analyzed. Those who are informed about analysis are, at first, easier to deal with, for they understand the analytical process. Nevertheless, it is inevitable that difficulties should arise, for the analyst's suggestions often conflict with the mother's unconscious needs. Mothers who are in analysis at the same time as their children will often unwittingly allow their attitudes toward their own analyses to influence their behavior toward the analyses of their children. Those who know little or nothing of analysis cannot help making difficulties, no matter how hard they try not to. Mothers in general, therefore, have to be dealt with as part of the treatment. They must be appealed to, and their interest must be gained. The analyst must find out just how much of her child's analysis the mother can stand. Upon her ability in this direction may depend the success of the whole treatment.

A mother can make countless small difficulties for the analyst. Thus, she may not see that the child comes punctually to the hour and may often let him miss a session without any adequate reason. She may make derogatory remarks about analysis in general or about the child's analysis in the presence of the child and may treat it all as a jest. Or, on the other hand, she may expect miracles and anticipate that the child's difficulties will vanish as soon as analysis begins. Or, during analysis, the analyst may with great difficulty bring the child to a better understanding of his mother; and the mother may then at the first opportunity act in such a way that everything that the analyst has explained to the child must seem like nonsense. For instance, the analyst may have to prove to the child that his mother really loves him, and the mother may just at that moment treat him in an unusually harsh manner. Or if the child has become freer in his attachment to his mother so that he can turn to other people as well, the mother may react with intense jealousy. The analyst may ask the mother to behave in a certain manner toward the child, and the mother may not be able to carry out this suggestion or else may so overdo it that it cannot have the desired effect.

The analyst must therefore consider the mother as part of the little patient's environment. Even before one has seen the child, one knows that the parents have had a large share in forming the neurosis. Whether the parents are narrowminded and "conservative" or broadminded and open to outside influences makes a difference, not merely because of their overt behavior toward the child, but even more because of their own inner tensions. Therefore, it is necessary to keep in mind the parents' attitude toward religion. A mother may cling to her religion not as a faith alone, but as a vitally necessary solution of her own problems; she may, therefore, wish to foster it in the child by every means in her power. In the same way, a mother's attitude toward sex and the strictness of her own upbringing are reflected in the way she trains her child. It is hard for her to give up ideas about sex that were instilled in her when she was a child and that she has maintained ever since. The mother has surely had her own difficulties and peculiarities and out of them, without help, she has had to form her own character and work out her own adjustments as best she may. She will cling to these solutions defiantly and desperately; and they in turn are bound to play a large part in the formation of the child's character.

The power of unconscious forces is especially marked in its interplay between parent and child. It is so subtle and uncanny that it seems at times to approach the supernatural. The analyst knows this and knows that this quality is more marked in some people than in others and that if it is found in a child it must be taken into account as an unknown quantity that will bring many uncertainties into the analysis. Therefore, when the analyst first comes in contact with a mother there are many things to be watched and to be kept in mind. One must wonder in what way the mother cares for her child, whether the child is not an outlet for very complex feelings, and how these feelings will play into the changes that the analysis will bring about in that child. One wonders whether the mother will cooperate and if she will be amenable to the analyst's influence and will yield to guidance, so that in the end she will help to continue the growth which the analysis made possible. Or, on the other hand, is this perhaps a mother who cannot be influenced and who at the first difficulty will turn against the analyst?

On the other hand, let us consider the mother who brings her child to an analyst for treatment. Usually this step is taken only after every other measure has been tried. She comes to the analyst because she cannot cope with her child alone and is much relieved to find someone who will help her. Nevertheless, once the analysis is under way she may become astonished and frightened when her desire to have the symptoms removed is not all that is achieved by the analysis. She sees all sorts of things being taken into account that she would much prefer to have left out. She sees the child suddenly behaving in a quite altered manner and even treating her differently. She feels herself being dragged into the analysis. Her relationship toward her child, her actions and behavior toward him, what she says to him and how she says it, her moods and her tempers—everything is studied from the analytical angle. That is bad enough, but when she realizes that her whole private life is also being brought in, she naturally feels abused. She can understand why all that concerns the child is necessary material for the analyst, but when it comes to her private life—that seems to her to be going one step too far. She will not stand for it and struggles against it. Naturally she feels injured, criticized, misunderstood. Furthermore, she feels jealous even of the attention which is now being given to her child. It was she who suffered from her child's behavior, and now it is her child who gets all the sympathy and help. She, who was most affected by his difficulties, now not only is not being considered, but an even more difficult situation is being made for her. Moreover, she feels her child loving someone else more than herself, turning to someone else with all his troubles as he did before to her. It does not make it easier for her to realize that this person really does understand her child better than she does. She feels humiliated. And then, added to all of this, the child begins to look at her, his mother, with newly opened eyes, even criticizing her —her actions, her very thoughts; and she knows that her child finds sympathy in all of this with his new-found friend, the analyst. Is it astonishing that the mother resents the analyst's efforts? Is it strange that analysts often lose cases just because parents can not stand the analysis and suddenly break off the treatment?

Analysts have tried to meet this situation in several ways. Some ignore the parents and confine themselves purely to the child, interpreting his unconscious expressions and the transference relationship. They leave out all of the child's daily life and his reactions to his surroundings, except that which comes into the hour as necessary material. They prefer not to know the parents nor to have them report on the child. Some prefer, when it is possible, to remove the child from his parents and to place him in more impersonal surroundings during the analysis and to return him to his parents to adjust as best he can when he has completed his analysis. Still others try to take in the child and his surroundings, his parents and his reactions to them as a part of the analytical treatment. They try not only to show the child his reactions to his parents, but also to take the parents with them through the analysis, showing them step by step what they are trying to accomplish with the child and giving them an insight into the child's troubles so that they can change certain outer and inner conditions which tend to increase the child's neurosis. Their hope is that, as the personality of the child is freed through the analysis, the parents will then be enabled to guide the child away from the neurosis instead of repeating the old mistakes.

There are difficulties in each of these three methods. One cannot carry through an analytical treatment without the parents' consent, because they can break off the analysis at any moment, they can disturb it, and, when the analysis is completed, they can make it impossible for the child to make use of the freedom he has just acquired. When an adult has successfully completed an analysis, he knows what to do with his released potentialities; but a child, just because he is a child, still has to be guided and helped and given opportunities to use these released powers. In the development of a child, this is a part of his normal education.

When one examines the three methods and takes into account the drawbacks and advantages of each, one must bear in mind the further development of the child. Where the analyst ignores the parents, according to the first method suggested, how will the child behave during his analysis, and how will he adjust to his environment at the close of the treatment? There is no question but that to ignore the parents makes the situation much easier for the analyst. At best, he has enough difficulties to cope with. Why should he add one more to the others? If he is able, through his treatment, to uncover the child's unconscious and to interpret it to him and to understand the mechanism of his actions and thoughts, will the child not lose his symptoms? Why should he take the trouble to understand the mother who will only make difficulties for him and, should he not succeed with her, probably cause him to lose his patient? He risks more if he tries to win the mother than if he completely ignores her. Let us see, however, how the child is after he has been treated in this manner. When one talks to him he can recite to you at length all the conscious and unconscious reasons for all his actions and where they come from; but, if one watches him in his surroundings, he seems like a ship at sea. He has no connection with reality. He cannot use his newly acquired understanding of himself to adjust to reality, even if he has lost his symptoms. His world is changed for him only so far as his symptoms interfered with his ability to meet it; but his environment, the atmosphere which was conducive to the formation of his neurosis, has not changed. He still has the same situations to fight against even though he can meet them less neurotically. He cannot try out new lines of thought and action; he is still tied to the old difficulties—perhaps not in the same way, but they are still absorbing his energy.

If, according to the second method, one takes a child away from his parents and puts him into another home for the duration of the analysis, he will at first have much fewer difficulties there; but after a certain length of time the child will transfer the difficulties that he had at home to the new setting. Again one has the choice of one of the two methods, either to try to gain the cooperation of the foster parents or to ignore them. Nevertheless, there may be certain advantages in transplanting the child into a new home. The child's own parents may be so neurotic that an analysis at home would be impossible. Or, from the very beginning, one may realize that the parents could not stand the child's analysis and would make it impossible. The child, in his new home, might not have such neurotic adults to deal with, nor would they necessarily react to him with the neurotic intensity of his own parents. For the analyst, it is surely easier to understand the child's neurosis in this less complicated home. The child can, as he becomes freer through his analysis, adjust more easily to his new parents. He can see the part that he has played and often the part his parents played in forming his neurosis. Here, in his foster home, he can become better adjusted to his environment. But, when the child at the close of his analysis returns to his own home he finds it very difficult to adjust there. He has felt so contented in this less neurotic atmosphere that he cannot adjust himself to the old situation. One often hears of a child begging to be sent away to school because he feels his home problems too difficult to meet. He cannot stand being put back into the home of his neurosis. Children who have lost their symptoms in their adopted homes often produce them again immediately after returning to their own homes.

The third method, that is, to try to gain the cooperation of the parents in the treatment, is by far the most difficult. It is, for the duration of the analysis, an added complication. One knows from the very beginning that one is carrying not only the child's difficulties but the parents' as well. The mother is bound to bring in her jealousy, her criticism, and her hurt feelings. One cannot forget her for a moment, for one has really come between her and her child. Even though this is only for a short time, she feels that she must protect her rights.

One has means, however, with which to meet this difficult situation. Obviously one must give the mother something to make up for her loss. The analyst must show her that he is interested not only in the child but also in the mother. She must be encouraged to join in the treatment of her child. She must feel that any information she brings about her child is important. She must be urged to observe everything the child does at home, not only in his general activities, but in his relation to her. She must feel that she too is taking part in a piece of research work, so that her interest is awakened. Then she will bring in material about herself, making comparisons between herself and her child, and finally taking as great an interest in the analysis as the analyst himself. In the study of her child, her own natural interest in herself is approached, for her child is often an image of herself, and her interest in her child is indirectly an interest in her own personality. There is another important trait that the analyst can count on for help in their relationship, namely, the mother's feeling of guilt toward the child. A mother almost always feels that she could have done more for her child. She quickly calls to mind all of the occasions on which she has made mistakes with him and turns to the analyst for help in undoing the harm which she has done. By means of these two approaches one can usually reach a mother, keep her from harming the analysis, and even gain her assistance during the treatment.

At the same time that the analyst is winning the mother's cooperation in this way, he must initiate her into each phase of the child's analysis in order that she may not be unprepared or too shocked by each step of the analysis through which the child has to go. If she is told of each improvement, she can help the child make use of his new freedom. As the end of the analysis draws near, the analyst should feel that there is someone who is adequately prepared to resume the parental role in the emotional life of the child, which the analyst had partly usurped. This, of course, should be a gradual process continuing throughout the terminal phases of the treatment.

Perhaps this consideration of the three methods of dealing with the mother during a child's analysis will enable us to decide on the best method of introducing the mother to the subject. We see both the analyst's difficulties and the mother's. The analyst wants to start his treatment and to have it proceed without interruption. The mother wants the analyst to start the treatment, but naturally she resolves in the back of her mind that, if she finds that she does not like what is going on, if it does not seem to help the child, or (as we can add ourselves) if she cannot stand the strain, she will simply take the child away. She does not realize that to start a treatment and break it off might be harmful. How then should the analyst proceed? Should he decide which method he should use only after having seen the mother a few times? This would seem to be the sensible thing to do; but the difficulty is that, if he starts with one method, he must usually continue it. Should the analyst introduce the mother to her child's analysis as one introduces an adult into his own analysis, telling all the difficulties that lie in the way? Should he enumerate the child's difficulties, his possible reactions to the treatment, his probable bad behavior at home? Should he mention the necessity of enlightening the child concerning religion, babies, sex, masturbation, and intercourse? Should he prepare her for the turning of her child's affection to the analyst and for her own probable reaction of jealousy and hate? Should he tell her of the necessity of bringing all that concerns her private life into the analysis—everything she says, does, and feels—and of her inevitable self-protective impulse? How many mothers would put their children into analysis if the analyst told them all of these facts? Or should one first give the mother a few weeks in which to get used to the analysis and to the analyst and then tell her of the difficulties that await her? Would this increase the chance that she would keep her child in analysis? Should one tell the mother only a few of the difficulties at first and prepare her step by step as the difficulties appear, hoping to be able to carry her along as her interest in the analysis and her confidence in the analyst grows? Or are there some cases which, no matter how suitable the child is for analysis, must be refused at once, because it is evident from the start that the mother's resistance to analysis is too strong to stand the treatment? Or should one tell the mother, in such a case, that it is impossible to analyze the child in his home and that, if she wants an analysis for him, she must put him in another home for the duration of the treatment? . . .

## Work with the Parents

LYDIA JACKSON
AND KATHLEEN M. TODD

### *Importance of the Social Worker's Part*

The success of the child's treatment depends partly on the interest which the parents, particularly the mother, take in his ultimate cure. It is the task of the social worker to ensure parental cooperation not only in the earlier stages, but throughout a long treatment, in some cases running into many months. The "problem" child's parents themselves very often have problems, and in order to be fully equipped to deal with them, the social worker must have a special training, psychological and psychiatric.

The reader might wonder why an intermediary between the therapist and the parents is needed. Why should not the therapist interview the parents himself? There is a practical disadvantage in such a scheme; if the mother herself accompanies the child for regular treatment, the child would have to wait while she is seen, or vice versa. The alternative is for the mother to pay two visits weekly to the clinic, which not many can manage. The therapist, of course, sees one or both parents when the child is brought for consultation and arranges occasional interviews afterward at the parents' wish; to see parent and child together, too, is of supreme value for a diagnostic assessment of their effect upon each other, and this is always done, at least during the physical examination. Experience has shown, however, that it is prejudicial to the success of treatment for the therapist to be in open communication with the parent, least of all that he should see the parent every time the child comes to the clinic. This holds particularly for long-treatment cases.

The reasons for this need some elaboration. In the majority of children needing treatment, the relationship between the child and his parents is in some way unsatisfactory. Even if superficially it appears to be good, there are undercurrents of anxiety or irritation in the parents which communicate themselves to the child. When he is brought for treatment, therefore, the child is likely to fear a conspiracy on the part of the adults against himself;

he feels that he is coming to treatment because he is not like other children, and in the beginning his attitude to the therapist is often apprehensive, suspicious, or hostile. The therapist's first task is to remove this defense, which is often a reflection of the child's attitude to the whole adult world; only then can he win the child's confidence. When the child has given his confidence—either in words or in play—by showing himself as he is with his real emotions and impulses, he is naturally anxious that his confidence should not be betrayed. It seems true that, because of his love for his mother and the fear of losing her affection, the neurotic child tends to conceal his real self from her more than from anyone else. One is not surprised then that, during the child's treatment, mothers commonly complain, "He won't tell me what he does at the clinic."

Children, no less than adults, have their reticences, and most of them cherish a private life which should be respected by adults. This private life includes the child's personal imagery and fantasy, often vivid and highly individual, and it is out of this rich store that he builds up his personality—in great measure alone and without the intervention of adults. If he allows the therapist a peep into this world, he does so on the tacit assumption that no one else should be let into the secret or through his intuitive appreciation that here is someone who will not betray him.

When, however, the therapist sees the parent without the child, the child naturally and rightly assumes that he is going to be discussed. The mother, he knows, will tell the "doctor" about his misdeeds and transgressions. Will the therapist, too, betray him to his mother and will they together range themselves against him? There is little doubt that some such thoughts, however vague, pass through the child's mind when he sees the therapist shutting himself off in company with the parent, for the majority of children show marked disturbance when the parents are thus interviewed. One small boy, with a mother who could never forgive herself if she omitted one detail, kept knocking on the door during the interview. In the end he could contain himself no longer, rushed in, and burst into tears, saying, "My mother always likes talking and now she is going to talk to you and use up all my time."

Some children object even to the parent's being interviewed by a person other than the therapist, but obviously in communication with him. An intelligent boy of five, seeing his mother walk off with a social worker as he was being taken to the playroom, remarked meditatively: "I wonder what my Mummie talks to that lady about for so long? What do you think she says to her? I suppose she tells her what I've been up to."

Yet, it is obviously necessary for the therapist to know how the effects of treatment are reflected in the child's everyday behavior and in his home circle. It is also necessary in the interests of both parents and child that, as treatment proceeds, the parent should be influenced in such a way as to make the child's recovery speedier and smoother. With younger children especially, the parent's handling of behavior can be decisive in bringing about an improvement or in delaying it indefinitely. In fact, some child psychiatrists (John Bowlby) think that treatment of young children is not likely to be successful unless the mother can be influenced at the same time in a desired direction. Therefore, the therapist treating the child must be in constant touch with the parent, but, in view of the specific relationship between the child and the therapist, this communication must be indirect. Because of her early and intimate relationship with the child, the mother rather than the father tends to be the focal point in social treatment. This does not, however, mean that the influence of the father and his point of view are ignored, but only that for practical purposes it is, as a rule, the mother's responsibility to come for weekly interviews to the clinic, while the father is seen when it is both practicable and necessary for a wider appreciation of the family relationships.

The psychiatric social worker thus plays her part as a liaison officer between the child's therapist and his parents. She interviews the parent at the clinic. She visits the child's home before he is seen at the clinic and records as full a social and personal history as it is possible to obtain. She also visits the school and supplements her knowledge of the child's character and behavior by the report of his teachers; further visits of course are paid to the school for the exchange of additional information, especially if there are scholastic problems superadded. . . .

### *Explanation to the Parent of the Meaning of Treatment*

The parent naturally wants to know what the child's treatment means, what are its aims, and in what way it is likely to affect his behavior at home or at school. Many parents seeing the toys in the consulting-room are interested to know how toys and "play" can be an aid in disentangling his problems. Every mother wishes her child to conform to a reasonable extent to his social milieu, but there are many who do not understand that a too rigid adherence to outer codes at too early an age may be crippling to the later development of his individuality. The "too good" child is often misinterpreted and overvalued by parents and teachers alike, who fail to see in "model" behavior seeds of certain types of neurosis.

The task of explaining to the mother that many things the child does are not "naughty" but occur naturally in the development of every child falls to the lot of the social worker. She also has to prepare the mother for the changes which are likely to take place in the child's attitude toward herself and other members of the family. Parents coming to the clinic expect a speedy improvement, not only in symptoms but in general behavior as well, and have to be warned that the child may become more, rather than less, aggressive, noisy, or overactive on the way to final adaptation. During this phase, the previously "overgood" child is particularly in need of tolerance and understanding from his parents. When parents expect an immediate improvement, they are unprepared for the disappointment they may feel if this does not happen. They must be told that psychological changes are as slow and subtle as physical ones, that they become obvious only over a long period of time, and that it is difficult to hurry treatment if one hopes for a lasting cure.

While some parents tend to be pessimistic about the outcome of treatment, impatient with its slowness, and adversely critical of psychological methods, others go to the opposite extreme and regard the child as "cured" whenever there is a slight improvement in symptoms. The social worker's task in such cases is to modify their enthusiasm, to indicate that such miraculous "cures" are often deceptive, and to warn them that a relapse is to be expected when a change for the better has been too sudden. Even when the improvement has been gradual and steady, some parents wish to discontinue treatment because they are satisfied with the results already achieved and cannot see the value and meaning of further attendance at the clinic; this occurs, for instance, when a bed-wetting child has become dry for a few weeks or a stammering child can at last be understood. Even once-weekly visits are a burden to a busy mother, and unless she comes to regard the clinic as a valuable social and educative contact, she often anticipates too eagerly the termination of treatment. The difference between amelioration of symptoms and fundamental alteration of a disturbed personality has to be explained, making it clear to her that the gains must be consolidated and the "cure" made certain before a decision concerning the end of treatment can be made.

Throughout treatment the child's confidences to the therapist should be respected, for the success of treatment can be greatly prejudiced by injudicious discussion of the play or talk of his interviews. This point is illustrated by the following incident related to one of the writers by the child concerned in it. The story was told by a very intelligent delinquent girl of eleven who had attended for treatment in another clinic and had been told by her therapist that "nothing she said of a personal nature would go out of the room." She noticed, however, that the therapist was writing notes during the interview. That made her suspicious, and on one occasion she took a peep at the notes. From that time on she refused to cooperate in treatment. In the child's own words, "She has written down everything I told her—from now on she'll have nothing from me." The girl felt that she would be betrayed to some authority or other, and treatment had to be discontinued.

It is the parent who is himself a prey to conflict who cannot bear that the child should possess a private life of his own; parents of this type find it disappointing when the details of treatment interviews are withheld from them. To help the mother to accept the child's right to his reserves deepens her understanding of human values; it allays any jealousy, conscious or unconscious, she may have of another adult, in this instance the therapist, to whom her child gives his trust; and it makes the child free to confide more in his therapist. Without this explanation and the development of parental objectivity, treatment may become impossible, for the child would build up defenses against "cure," as even young children can, while the mother goes on probing to know what happens at his interviews.

The mother's unconscious antagonism to the therapist's influence on the child would especially complicate his task of inducing the child to give up his neurotic defenses. These, as analytical writers have shown (A. Freud, 1937; Adler, 1918), serve the purpose of protecting the individual from inner dangers, created by his own conflicts and often imaginary or greatly exaggerated. These "defenses" have to be abandoned, for the protection they give is mainly illusory; their chief effect is to constrict the free development of personality, to fence the individual in, and thus bind and impoverish him spiritually. . . .

# *Confidentiality in Child Guidance Treatment*

ALAN O. ROSS

The confidentiality of psychotherapeutic interviews is a well-established and generally accepted principle. Inherited from medicine on its ethical basis, practical considerations have made it a virtual *sine qua non* in psychiatry. Without the assurance that his communications will be held in the strictest confidence, no patient would feel free to divulge the highly personal material which needs to be verbalized if treatment is to be effective. In the psychotherapy of adults, the therapist will usually assure his patient during the first interview of the confidential nature of treatment. In the rare case where it may appear therapeutically necessary to diverge from this principle, the conscientious therapist will attempt to obtain the patient's specific concurrence before revealing material obtained during treatment to an outsider. This rare instance where confidentiality thus becomes relative instead of remaining absolute is usually one involving an acute danger to the life of the patient or of others.

The concept of absolute confidentiality also becomes slightly modified when treatment takes place not in individual practice but in a clinic or training setting where the need to discuss case material with supervisors or other members of the clinic staff brings third parties indirectly into the therapist–patient relationship. In a clinic, these third parties also include clerical personnel responsible for record-keeping and the confidential relationship thus obtains between the patient and "the Clinic"as a professional institution. The primary ethical responsibility for confidentiality rests at all times with the therapist. Whenever treatment takes place under these circumstances, the patient should be made aware that the principle of confidentiality is being extended to include other, indirectly involved individuals.

The practical need for assuring the patient of the confidentiality of his communications, important in the treatment of adults, becomes crucial in the treatment of children. Most children, and particularly those being treated for emotional disturbances, have had important experiences which they entrusted to or shared with one adult, who promptly revealed the information to another, to the embarrassment and chagrin of the child. A neighbor, observing the child in some "forbidden" activity and rushing to tell his mother; mother telling father of the child's misdeeds; or parents sharing a laugh over something "funny" the child said or did are frequent childhood experiences. Often, too, a child may have worked up courage to make known to his mother an important question or a confidential experience, only to have the mother share the material with the father or another adult in the most casual manner. From such situations many children generalize that adults cannot be trusted, and when a therapist first enters the picture he is usually viewed as just another adult, in alliance against the child.

The initial experience in a child-guidance-clinic contact tends to reinforce this idea, which is compounded by generalizations stemming from visits to the pediatrician or family physician. The parents usually contact the clinic before bringing in the child, who then comes to a place which is strange to him but familiar to his parent. In most instances, the parents are unable to prepare the child adequately for his visit to the clinic, for no matter how well preparation was rehearsed with the parents during the initial contact it frequently becomes distorted or omitted entirely because of the parents' own anxiety and conflict about the visit.

The child, arriving at the clinic anxious and confused, has nothing but his own generalizations about doctors and adults by which to order this new experience conceptually. Being responsible for bringing the child to the clinic and having obvious familiarity with the physical layout and the receptionist, the mother is viewed by the child as having "the inside track" in the clinic—apparently being in conspiracy with all the other adults inhabiting the place. Assuming that the child is first undergoing an evaluation, as is usual at most clinics, he will at this point be seen by an adult who will either want to "play and talk" with him or give him psychological tests. It is unlikely that this contact will do much to change the attitude with which the child came to the clinic. He will undoubtedly assume (and usually correctly) that the "doctor" talked to his mother before he saw the child, thus getting her side of the story, and that he is going to talk to her again afterward to tell her what he "found out" about the child. Everything that happens would appear to be for the mother and against the child.

As said above, confidentiality cannot be absolute in a child guidance clinic because information received from the patient must be shared with other staff members. The team approach in which mother and child are treated by different individuals requires that the two therapists involved in a given case frequently and regularly exchange information relevant to that particular family. This exchange of information may be oral or written (through the medium of the case record); and it may take place in an informal discussion between the two therapists or in the setting of a staff conference, where the information is shared with yet other professional persons. This is a modification of absolute confidentiality, discussed earlier, and the patient is entitled to know that this condition obtains and that it is in the best interest of treatment progress. The adult members of a family in treatment will usually accept this relatively easily, and if any doubts about the confidential nature of communications should later on disrupt the treatment relationship, they can be worked through like any other resistance mechanism.

In the case of the child, however, the situation is somewhat complicated, for he may be expected to find it more difficult to conceptualize the nature of the therapeutic-team operation. If, following evaluation, the child is taken into treatment, the therapist will have to establish a relationship of confidence and trust within which treatment can become possible. This task is complicated by the child's attitude of not trusting adults in general and the people at the clinic in particular. Again, as at the time of the first contact, the child is brought to the clinic by the mother, and although she is not in the same room, her physical presence in the building continues to make the child suspect that she will find out anything he may do or say. The question of confidentiality of the relationship thus becomes of paramount importance. The therapist will want to explore the child's feelings and thoughts about his coming to the clinic during the first treatment sessions. He will want to discuss what sort of a place the clinic is, what will and what will not happen to the child, and what he can and cannot do. As part of this general introduction to treatment, the question of confidentiality should be taken up, but what and how should the child be told about it?

A statement such as "Everything you do and say in your hour with me is strictly between the two of us and I won't tell your mother about it" is obviously incomplete, but anything more than this raises a great many problems. If one adds "While you are playing and talking with me, your mother will be talking to her social worker, and the social worker and I will be talking with each other from time to time so that we can all help you better," one tends to lend support to the child's initial suspicion that his mother will hear about what he says and does in his treatment session. It would thus be necessary to add a specific assurance that neither the therapist nor the mother's worker will tell the mother anything about what goes on in the child's hours. Unfortunately, even this extended statement fails to cover every potential situation. What if the therapist becomes convinced that a child is serious about a threat to commit suicide or that a five-year-old actually plans to run away from home? Most therapists would feel obliged to inform the mother or another responsible adult so that this potential danger can be averted. At the same time, they would probably inform the child of their intention of doing so, trying to obtain the child's agreement but taking the required step with or without his concurrence. Does this mean that one should refer to such a contingency at the time confidentiality is taken up at the beginning of the child's treatment? One might say that one won't inform the mother of anything the child does or says unless one had first talked to the child about one's intentions. This is an innocuous enough statement for most adults, but a child with limited abstract ability and only a vague concept of the future might easily find this confusing. He may well attend solely to that part of the statement referring to telling the mother, using it to confirm his suspicion and disregarding the qualifying clause altogether. It would thus seem best to keep the statement in its simplest form at the beginning of treatment, adding modifications at a later time when a relationship has been established and any resulting confusion can be more readily resolved.

The problem of assuring the child of the confidentiality of his therapeutic sessions seems complicated enough even in situations where therapists sincerely have no intention of communciating the child's material to the mother except in the most crucial situations involving the child's safety. While most therapists subscribe to this concept of confidentiality, some advocate a further modification which might be called "limited confidentiality." Faced with the apparent lack of progress and productivity in the child's sessions and stymied in their indirect attempts to focus on an area in which they know the child to be holding back, they are sometimes inclined to directly introduce material obtained from the mother's hours in order to elicit movement on the part of the child. At the same time, they will usually insist that nothing the child produces shall be transmitted to the mother. The principle involved has sometimes been referred to as "one-way communication" and introduces a critical complication. Limited confidentiality requires that one announce to the mother at the beginning of treatment that some of the material she brings to her worker will be used by the child's therapist in his treatment of the child. Since the time element does not make it feasible to obtain the mother's consent each time some of her material is to be used in this manner, the decision as to what is and what is not to be treated confidentially must, of necessity, be left to the child therapist's discretion and thus becomes arbitrary. If this were not so, at least two weeks would pass under a conventional once-a-week treatment schedule before the child's therapist could utilize a specific piece of information.

An example will help to clarify this: In a given week the mother tells her worker that the child has begun to refuse to go to school. In conference following this session, the child's therapist learns of this and decides that he would like to use this fact with the child, who has failed to mention it himself. The worker would now have to clear this with the mother in the subsequent week and to transmit the mother's reply to the therapist, who then raises the issue with the child in the third week.

The first problem arising from acceptance of limited confidentiality as a working principle has to do with the mother's reaction. Even though she may accept the rationale that this approach is therapeutically advantageous, the realization that some of the things she reveals to her worker are going to find their way to the child in some form or other may well result in her being less than frank in her treatment session. Not only may she fear that the child, in turn, might wish to talk about a topic with her before she is ready to accept such discussion without embarrassment or uneasiness, but she may also fear that the child might reveal to outsiders or the father something she does not wish to become known. Because of these concerns, many mothers will shy away from revealing sensitive material unless they are fully convinced that the information will remain, if not with the worker, then at least among the professional clinic staff.

The second, and it would seem more serious, complication arises out of the child's awareness that he can find out some of the things his mother talks about in her sessions. This makes it very difficult to convince a disturbed child that communication of this nature really goes in only one direction. If he can find out things his mother says to her worker, how can he be sure that his mother will not also find out things he tells his therapist? A complicated statement, such as "Your mother will not find out what you say or do in your hours, but sometimes, when I think it will help you, I will introduce in your hours with me things your mother tells her social worker," cannot possibly be very convincing, no matter how simplified the wording. The realization that therapy material is carried back and forth plays into and tends to confirm the child's suspicion that the therapist cannot be trusted and may well represent a major obstacle to treatment progress. It is highly probable that the apparent advantage gained by using the mother's material in the child's hours is vitiated by the reinforcement this lends to both the mother's and the child's resistances. For this reason, it would seem advisable to carry out treatment in a setting where only information the child himself feels free to introduce is used in his treatment sessions.

A different aspect of the problem of confidentiality is that involving direct contact between the child's therapist and the mother. In the individual practice of psychotherapy, it is generally accepted usage that the therapist either occasionally or regularly interviews one of the child's parents. The fact that treatment can be carried out under these circumstances would seem to demonstrate that this approach does not make treatment impossible, but one of the reasons the child-guidance-team approach was evolved is that such contact makes treatment more difficult because it interferes with the therapist–child relationship in many cases. That this is being recognized by therapists in individual practice is demonstrated by the recent trend of having social workers, charged with the responsibility of maintaining contact with parents, collaborate with private practitioners. In spite of the obvious advantages the team approach lends in the separation of treatment functions and the concomitant greater ease with which the child can be convinced of the trustworthiness of his therapist, there exists an occasional urge on the part of some child therapists to short-circuit the team and talk directly with the mother. When this urge becomes translated into action, it demonstrates a lack of confidence in the team partner who is thus shunted aside and a failure to appreciate and accept the principle of the team approach. In addition, it tends to disrupt the social worker's treatment of the mother; but worse than these, it jeopardizes the relationship between therapist and child. Knowing, as he ought to, that his therapist talks to his mother, the child cannot but assume that he is the topic of discussion and to fear that his therapist will not only divulge information obtained from him but also hear the mother's version of his behavior outside the clinic. Avoiding the treatment-disrupting reaction which must follow this reasoning on the part of the child seems well worth relying on the social worker for interpreting to and gathering relevant information from the mother.

The therapist's urge for direct communication with the mother has its counterpart in the mother's desire to talk directly to the child's therapist. It was pointed out earlier that the child comes to the clinic with certain preconceptions carried over from his experience with pediatricians and other physicians. It must be remembered that the mother, too, tries to order the new and threatening experience of coming to a child guidance clinic in terms of something she is familiar with and thus tends to generalize from taking the child to a pediatrician to taking him to a "psychiatric doctor." In all the old situations, she has known the physician examined the child, nearly always in her presence, and then told her of his findings and recommendations. In a child guidance clinic, however, she is suddenly excluded from the "examination" and has the recommendations interpreted to her by someone who has never talked to the child. Many mothers will react to this exclusion with resentment and a negative attitude toward the interpretations of the clinic's findings. If the recommendations are unwelcome and threatening, as statements of the child's disturbance and need for treatment invariably are, the mother may well refuse to accept them and fail to follow through on any treatment plan offered.

To avoid this reaction, many clinics are making it a practice to have the person who saw the child during diagnostic study join the mother's worker in interpreting the results of an evaluation. This not only places the weight of the doctor's prestige behind the statements made but it also enables the mother to ask specific questions of the person who has first-hand familiarity with the child. While this practice has undoubted advantages, it should be remembered that if the individual who saw the child during study is assigned the case for therapy, this direct contact with the mother may place him at a handicap in establishing a treatment relationship. For the child must feel that the only reason the therapist talks with him again is to "find out more things" in order to communicate them to the mother. The advantages gained from direct interpretation to the mother should always be weighed against the possible disadvantages such contact represents in the treatment situation.

Unfortunately, the disadvantages are not confined to the initial phase of treatment. Having once had direct contact with the child's therapist, the mother may expect that she can continue to talk to him directly. As pointed out earlier, any contact between the child's therapist and the mother during treatment is deleterious to the therapist's relationship with the child, but as treatment takes its slow and lengthy course many mothers will continue to want to know "what the doctor found out." This is why some mothers will try to buttonhole the therapist in the waiting room to ask him "how Johnny is doing." The mother's worker must be constantly aware of her patient's need to know what progress, if any, is being made with the child, so that she can interpret therapeutic principles to her and satisfy her legitimate desire to know what is going on. This means that the nature of treatment, in general, and the practice of the team approach, in particular, must be brought up again and again, and any attempt on the part of the mother to communicate directly with her child's therapist should be viewed not only as a failure to make this interpretation meaningful and acceptable but also as an indication of a weakness in the worker–patient relationship.

Unable to learn from the child's therapist "what he found out" and not satisfied with the worker's generalized statements about treatment progress, some mothers will attempt to elicit from the child information about the content of his hours with his therapist. This "pumping" frequently occurs soon after the hour, usually on the way home from the clinic and takes the form of such questions as "What did you and your doctor talk about today?" or "What did you do today?" While these queries would seem to reflect only casual interest (parents often ask their children what they did in school that day), they have a deeper meaning and can seriously hamper treatment progress. Such inquiries may indicate that the mother cannot permit the child to be close to anyone but her, so that her questions are attempts to insinuate herself into the child–therapist relationship. Again, "pumping" may reflect the mother's concern that the child will "tell on her," will reveal aspects of her life or of her relationship to the child about which she feels guilty. By asking him questions, she may unconsciously be trying to sabotage the child's treatment, and this is exactly the result that these questions tend to bring about. Knowing that after each hour he may have to "report" to the mother on what he did or said, the child will soon censor his productions, the effect being the same as if the treatment hour were conducted with the mother present in the room.

Whenever either the child's or the mother's therapist discovers that the mother tries to "pump" the child in this manner, it will have to be taken up with the mother in order to try to have her desist. It may, in fact, be desirable to cover this point with all parents in one of the first treatment hours, possibly at the time the topic of confidentiality of interview content is dealt with, since many parents find it difficult to understand that the child is entitled to the privacy of his treatment hours and even more difficult to accept their exclusion from the therapist–child relationship.

Child guidance treatment is a costly procedure due to the duplication of professional services, nearly every case involving at least two staff members. This expenditure of money and time has proved worthwhile because it provides both parent and child with his own therapist, thus avoiding the treatment-retarding complications which often result when both members of a family are treated by the same person. Therapists in individual practice, who have to work with both parent and child, have to deal with these complications during treatment, thus spending valuable time on a problem which therapy itself creates and which the team approach is ideally suited to avoid. From the point of view here represented, this major advantage of the team approach over individual practice is vitiated when contacts between child therapist and parent are permitted or when the principle of limited confidentiality is accepted.

It would therefore seem generally best to forego the questionable benefits of limited confidentiality, operating instead within a framework where nothing either parent or child reveals in his hours is directly introduced into the other's treatment and where contact between the child's therapist and the parent is held to an absolute minimum. In this manner, optimal use can be made of the unique opportunities the child-guidance-team approach presents for the treatment of emotional disturbances of children.

# *Introducing the Child to the Therapeutic Situation*

J. LOUISE DESPERT

... In the initial phase of treatment, much depends on the degree of wisdom shown by family and psychiatrist in bringing the child to treatment. Some children have been threatened with psychiatric treatment and hospitalization because of their "bad" behavior; others were led to believe that they were visiting a teacher or a friend of the family. The father of a very disturbed girl of ten years introduced the writer as "a business associate." (He was an accountant.) He had planned the whole approach in his own way, even after indicating his willingness to follow suggestions carefully discussed at the first interview with both parents; it thus became evident that he had no intention at any time to carry them out. The father said he had come to "say just a few words" to his business associate and was going to leave the child "for a few minutes, while I'm going on an errand." The physician would not take any part in the deception, and the father later insisted that it was this lack of cooperation which had caused the child to be upset and resistive. While such attitudes are very revealing of habitual techniques used by parents in the handling of their children, they are so damaging to the first contact as to make further contact difficult, if not impossible.

Since the child almost never asks to be taken to a psychiatrist, it is up to the therapist and the parents to pave the way for the anticipated experience. Frequently, the parents have given thought to the matter, some have had a tentative talk with their child, most parents ask for suggestions. After the anamnesis has been taken, the patient's complaint, as interpreted by his environment, is more-or-less clearly delineated. In particular, it is then known what specific manifestations have been openly mentioned and discussed in the family. The stress at this point is on the child's *awareness* of his symptoms, rather than their severity. A child may be more distressed by the fact that he "cannot make friends" than by the concomitants of associability and poor reality contact or by his avowed fears rather than his aggressive, antisocial behavior.

Thus, the parents are advised to start from whatever specific complaint has been brought up on previous occasions and explain to the child that he can be helped and that, in order to achieve this end, they plan to take him to a man (or woman) whose job is to do precisely that—help children with such problems. In the older age group, there is no reason for not referring to the anticipated visit as a visit to a psychiatrist, even if the reference aroused some resistance. In the face of the discomfort experienced by the child, any step taken toward alleviation is frequently welcomed. In the lower age group, however, the very mention of a doctor—and especially an unfamiliar one—may bring on such a severe reaction in an anxious child, that it is preferable first to let him become acquainted with the therapist; during the first interview, the question is raised, "Do you know my name? . . . Dr. ———." By this time, he has learned a good deal about the new category of experience. The young child frequently expresses it in very revealing spontaneous comments, such as "You're a funny doctor . . . a different kind of a doctor . . . a doctor that doesn't give you needles . . . how come you don't examine me?" etc., all of which provide additional opportunities to make clear the therapist's function.

Another point relating to the first interview is the separation from the parent, generally the mother, who brings the child. It is clearly indicated beforehand that only one parent is to come, as separation is thus more easily achieved; in a total experience of several hundred first interviews there have been a few instances of two parents, alone or together with one or two siblings, and even in one case, his whole family accompanied a patient, despite earlier recommendations; while such occurrences are highly significant of the family as a whole, they are quite destructive. A separation which lingers, with additional hugs and "one more word before I leave you" comments on the part of the parents, is a poor introduction to therapy, and is best avoided through a thorough discussion of its devastating effects on the child at the time of anamnesis-taking. The child feels the more insecure about the strange setup as his parent manifests more reluctance to leave him there.

Although, in the early stages of child-guidance practice, parents and child were frequently seen together by the therapist, this approach is not common now. Play therapy precludes the presence and participation of the parents in the situation. In the writer's experience, there have been only a few exceptions to this rule, when it was thought advisable not to attempt the separation; in the several cases, the child was very young and acutely disturbed. One of them was treated for a number of months with the mother in the playroom, a fact which added complexity to the therapeutic situation as it required a constant unobtrusive interpretation to the mother of the child's behavior, as well as reassurance regarding its most severe manifestations.

In recent years, the technique has been adopted by the writer to ask that the child be left at the office, with the mother returning later to pick him up, rather than waiting in an adjoining room. This change was prompted by the anxiety of some children, about their mother being within hearing distance, especially those in the middle and older age groups (approximately six years and above). This was not actually the case, since there were two intervening doors as they had been informed, but they wanted to know further if the doors were locked or if their mother could listen. In the case of the younger children, the close proximity of their mother led them to request more frequent visits to her than was possible to handle. So, for all age groups, it has been found that the complete removal of the mother from the setup works out better when straightforwardly presented to the child, even at the cost of arousing a little more anxiety at the initial interview. It is made clear to the younger children that their mother is available and can be reached if they feel the need to see her before their time is up, but very few children have availed themselves of the opportunity. . . .

As regards the question of communication between parents and therapist, the parents are advised not to send notes via the children (a common practice, if it were not checked), as the latter usually want to know *re* the content, as a rule not meant for his perusal. The children are also informed that the therapist, at intervals, sees their parents (if that is to be the case); it is explained that whatever *understanding* doctor and child have gained regarding the child's difficulties can be passed on to his parents. Stated in simple terms, the communication is accepted by most children.

Another aspect of communication deserves to be mentioned briefly; almost universally, children choose not to let anything transpire of what is going on in the playroom. As a matter of routine, following the first interview, the parents are asked what the child reported about his first visit. The parents usually express their disappointment that the patient was willing to say so little, even when they questioned him (some of them show unwanted persistence in this respect and may thus arouse antagonism in the child). The query serves two purposes: one is to ascertain the child's reaction, expressed to his close environment and also to demonstrate to the parents that the child's reticence expresses his own choice, although it is also psychologically sound, a point which is thus brought up for discussion. This reticence toward the visits and their content is noted, not only in relation to the parents, but also toward other relatives and friends. It has been possible for nearly two years to conduct the simultaneous treatment of two first cousins, though they were closely associated in their family life, without either of them telling the other of the experience. An interesting incident took place when the therapist's name was mentioned accidentally by a teacher in the midst of her group. One boy was under treatment, a girl had been discharged several months earlier. The girl began to refer to "a friend" of hers who had been "treated there." The boy reported the many details she gave regarding the therapist and the setup, not suspecting that the girl might have been the patient; both children were eleven years old. Similarly, when siblings are simultaneously or successively treated, each may be very inquisitive about the other, but refuse to divulge his experience in the office. Even very young children show this tendency, indicating that the segregation of emotional experiences is manifested very early in the psychological economy of the personality.

The child must be assured that his "secrets" are protected, even as the understanding gained through their coming-out is to be imparted to his parents. Throughout the period of treatment the therapist must sift what can be emotionally accepted by the parents, what they can handle without setting off neurotic explosions; their new knowledge of the patient's inner feelings may, at intervals, act destructively in their own relation to the child. The time at which one or the two parents should be referred for treatment is often determined by the neurotic parent's reaction to the child's progress in therapy. This indeed may bring up feelings of anxiety and hostility in the parents, which need clarification and resolution if adjustment in the family is to be successful.

## REFERENCES

Adler, A. *The neurotic constitution.* London: Kegan Paul, Trench, Trubner & Co., Ltd., 1918.

Freud, Anna. *The ego and the mechanisms of defence.* London: Hogarth Press, 1937.

❀ CHAPTER FIVE

# The Initial Session

THE THEORETICAL differences between the non-directive and dynamic orientations are clear in the discussions of the first session. Of primary importance to the client-centered therapist is the early establishment of a relationship; inept or inconsistent handling of the initial session can delay or prevent the relationship from being formed. For example, if the first session has been structured in such a way that the child sees the therapist as a representative of the parents, as one more authority figure, and as the one who makes the decisions and directs the games, subsequent efforts to shift to a client-centered approach would indeed be difficult.

While the establishment of rapport and the relationship with the child is recognized as valuable in the dynamically oriented therapies, the content of the child's activities is also seen as a crucial aspect of the first session. Quite often the child seems to utilize this hour to present an outline of his problems via the toys he chooses and his manner of using them. In other instances he may literally "choose his weapons." Hellersberg,[1] in discussing the initial phase of therapy, states: "The touching of sand, the terse fingering of a book while probably studying the therapist, the throwing down of some puppets, any initial action, however arbitrary it may appear, should be considered as significant as the first dream brought to the initial analytical session in adult therapy."

---

[1] Elisabeth F. Hellersberg, "Child's Growth in Play Therapy," *American Journal of Psychotherapy*, IX (1955), 484–502, p. 485. See also Chapter 9 of this volume.

The child's maneuvers may be so subtle that the impact would be lost to any but a perceptive therapist; the toys the child discards or handles briefly may be the ones later used as his media for working through his deepest concerns; casual expressions, offhand gestures, and tentative questions may reveal the sources of his difficulties. One child, who later spent many sessions working through problems of looking and seeing and primal scene experiences, had walked backward down the hall to his first play session, as if afraid of seeing. Soon after entering the room he spied a bandaid and impulsively slapped it onto his forehead, only to tear it off in a panic because "it makes my eyes water and I can't see." Another highly anxious child previewed, in his first session, the content of many subsequent hours of search for the source of babies and conflict between acceptance of his adoptive mother and longing for his real mother. His concerns about boundaries and his own identity were evident as he laid out blocks in the sand to be "property markers" and "name markers." This was a desert town (his adoptive mother could have no children of her own), the blocks became "water lines"; "water is free" and "we don't need much water." Finally, he pounded on his pipe line and said, "This will hit the water at the *center* place."

Technical questions that come to the fore in any consideration of the initial session involve: (1) the mechanics of getting a reluctant child into the playroom (How should the therapist greet the child? What happens if the child refuses to accompany the therapist? Should the parent ever go with the child? Should the playroom be kept as a sanctuary for child and therapist?); (2) initial structuring to the child (How does one explain therapy to the young patient, or need it be explained? How far should one go in emphasizing the permissiveness of this new situation?); (3) answering the child's questions as to why he is coming (Should this be in general terms, or should the therapist mention the specific referral problem? Should the question be turned back for the child to answer? Should the therapist bring up the subject, directly or indirectly, if the child does not do so?).

In the selections that follow, the relationship-oriented viewpoints are presented first, starting with Axline's outline of basic principles and followed by her suggestions for handling various problems encountered in the initial session. Allen's excerpts stress the impact of this new experience on the child and the role of the therapist in facilitating the establishment of a therapeutic relationship. The brief selection from Moustakas was chosen to illustrate specific responses which the therapist might use in the initial structuring of therapy.

In describing the dynamic approach Erikson pictures the situation as it must appear to the child and stresses the importance of the child's "sign language" as expressed in his choice and use of toys. He emphasizes the necessity for observing the sequence of activities in which the child engages.[2] In the last selection, Despert gives several play episodes to illustrate her thesis that the events of the initial session will provide clues to the nature and extent of the child's problem.

# *The Eight Basic Principles*

VIRGINIA M. AXLINE

The basic principles which guide the therapist in all nondirective therapeutic contacts are very simple, but they are great in their possibilities when followed sincerely, consistently, and intelligently by the therapist.

The principles are as follows:

(1) The therapist must develop a warm, friendly relationship with the child, in which good rapport is established as soon as possible.

(2) The therapist accepts the child exactly as he is.

(3) The therapist establishes a feeling of permissiveness in the relationship so that the child feels free to express his feelings completely.

(4) The therapist is alert to recognize the *feelings* the child is expressing and reflects those feelings back to him in such a manner that he gains insight into his behavior.

(5) The therapist maintains a deep respect for the child's ability to solve

[2] The phenomenon of play disruption, which is discussed in Chapter 13 with later sections of Erikson's monograph, is also illustrated by the case material presented here.

his own problems if given an opportunity to do so. The responsibility to make choices and to institute change is the child's.

(6) The therapist does not attempt to direct the child's actions or conversation in any manner. The child leads the way; the therapist follows.

(7) The therapist does not attempt to hurry the therapy along. It is a gradual process and is recognized as such by the therapist.

(8) The therapist establishes only those limitations that are necessary to anchor the therapy to the world of reality and to make the child aware of his responsibility in the relationship.

The therapist realizes that nondirective therapy is not a panacea. She admits that, like all things, it, too, has its limitations, but accumulating experience indicates that the implications of this type of therapy are a challenge and an inspiration to those who are concerned with the problems of adjustment.

When a child comes for play therapy, it is usually because some adult has either brought or sent him to the clinic for treatment. He enters into this unique experience just as he enters all new experiences—either with enthusiasm, fear, caution, resistance or any other manner that is typical of the way he reacts to new situations. The initial contact is of great importance for the success of the therapy. It is during this contact that the stage is set, so to speak. The structuring is demonstrated to the child, not merely by words, but by the relationship that is established between the therapist and the child.

The word "structuring" is used, in this instance, to mean the building-up of the relationship according to the foregoing principles, so that the child understands the nature of the therapy contacts and is thus able to use them fully. Structuring is not a casual thing, but a carefully planned method of introducing the child to this medium of self-expression which brings with it release of feelings and attendant insight. It is not a verbal explanation of what this is all about, but [is demonstrated] by establishing the relationship.

The relationship that is created between the therapist and the child is the deciding factor in the success or failure of the therapy. It is not an easy relationship to establish. The therapist must put forth a sincere effort to understand the child, to constantly check her responses against the basic principles, and to evaluate her work with each case so that she, too, grows in her understanding of the dynamics of human behavior.

# ❁ *Establishing Rapport*

VIRGINIA M. AXLINE

The therapist meets the child for the first time. She is beginning the initial contact. Structuring has begun. What does she do? A smile is usually an indication of warmth and friendliness. A few words of greeting should establish rapport. So the therapist goes up to the child and smilingly says, "Good afternoon, Johnny. I'm glad to see you. Did you like that Mickey Mouse over there on the table?" Now Johnny should smile back and say, "Yes, he's funny." He might. But the very fact that Johnny has been recommended for play therapy is an indication that he might not act "according to Hoyle." He might very likely turn his back on the therapist. Then what? The rapport-seeking therapist is not easily discouraged. "Would you like to come over to the playroom with me and see all the nice toys?" "No." "Oh, come on, Johnny. There are paints and clay and toy soldiers. You like toy soldiers, don't you?" "No. And I don't want to come!" says Johnny.

The therapist might well pause here. In fact, she should have paused, perhaps, before she spoke. What about those basic principles which she is trying to convey to Johnny? She is trying to establish a warm and friendly relationship, but she is sacrificing some of the other principles. She is not accepting Johnny as he is. She is not reflecting his feelings. He said that he did not want to go with the therapist and see all the toys. Apparently, this therapist has not yet started to let the child take the responsibility to make choices. "Lots of children come up here and they like our playroom," says the persistent therapist. "We've got a big doll house and a whole family of dolls." She looks appealingly at Johnny. He steals a glance at her. She is trying to make him act like other children. She is coaxing him. She is warm and friendly enough, goodness knows, but at what expense. Johnny, who is resenting her more and more, begins to whine. "I don't wanta. Mamma, I don't wanta!" Mamma becomes active. "Now, Johnny, you go with the nice lady. She has lots of toys for you to play with." Johnny begins to whimper. "I don't wanta. I wanta go home." "Now, Johnny," says Mamma, "I am ashamed of you. Here this nice lady is offering you a whole room of playthings to play with and you act like this. The lady won't like you!" Mamma will enter into the structuring if the therapist doesn't look out. "The lady won't like you" isn't a particularly good basis for establishing a therapeutic relationship.

What on earth should she do? Should she pick up the child and carry him over to the playroom and, when he howls his protests, reflect his feelings back to him?—"You are angry because I picked you up and carried you over here. You don't like to be treated that way." That would get him into the playroom.

However, all therapists are not Amazons and all problem children are not light-weights!

Perhaps she had better try getting him into the playroom under his own power. She might say, "Hello, Johnny. I'm glad to see you. Do you like the Mickey Mouse over there on the table?" Johnny turns his back. "Oh! You just don't feel like talking to me now. *You* don't *know* me." The therapist watches the tone of her voice. It must not sound like a reproof. But the therapist mustn't forget Mamma. She might say, "Johnny, look at the lady when she talks to you." Johnny whines, "I don't wanta. I wanta go home." Then the therapist says, "You don't want to have anything to do with me. You want to go back home. The playroom is over here if you want to look in before you make up your mind to go home." She leads the way. Mamma follows. Johnny tags along reluctantly. Then the therapist has an inspiration. "You had an appointment to talk to Mr. X, didn't you, Mrs. Johnny?" "Yes, I did," Mrs. Johnny says. "Well," says the therapist, "if Johnny doesn't want to stay in the playroom with me and play, he may wait in the waiting room for you." "Yes, Johnny," says Mamma, "would you rather wait in the waiting room? I'll be gone an hour." "I wanta go with you!" says Johnny tearfully. "You can't go with her, Johnny. She must talk to Mr. X alone. It will be either the waiting room or the playroom. It's up to you." More tears, and Johnny creeps into the playroom. Getting him there is half the battle.

The therapist must be ready for the mamma who is not so cooperative—the one who has made her Johnny so dependent. She will want to go into the playroom with Johnny. What will the therapist do about that? Will she take the mother along, thinking that the therapy contacts will never materialize unless she makes that concession? Will she say, "Only children are allowed in the playroom, Johnny; your mother will wait for you; she won't go away and leave you"? Johnny cries. "Johnny doesn't want to leave his mother," says the therapist. "He is afraid to come into the playroom by himself." Mamma rushes in with reassurance. Johnny edges toward the playroom. The door is closed. Mamma waits outside.

Suppose Mamma wasn't ready to be separated from Johnny? Could there be much hope for therapy? There have been occasions wherein the mother went into the playroom and sat there during the play contacts and Johnny's willingness to let Mamma leave was considered a sign of progress. If it became an issue of Mamma's sitting through the play sessions or no play contacts, what should the therapist do? It seems that the therapist must permit Mamma to stay if she follows the basic principles. In fact, she might be able to clarify a good many of the feelings between Mamma and Johnny by having them both in the playroom. This is an untried theory, but it seems to have possibilities if it is the only way out. Mamma, at least, might gain some insight if the therapist handled the situation skillfully. Johnny might act out his complete dependence upon his mother by constantly asking her to do this or that for him. The therapist, alert for the attitudes and feelings, might catch some of them—"Johnny wants Mother to show him how to play with the doll. Johnny wants Mother to tell him what to do next." She may even be able to reflect back some of Mamma's feelings. Perhaps Mamma is volunteering the suggestions to Johnny—"Don't do that, Johnny; play with it this way." The therapist might help Mamma gain a little insight by saying to her, "You don't think Johnny could figure that out by himself. You like to tell him everything to do." However, such an experiment is not advocated for beginning therapists.

It is pleasant to note that most children go into the playroom readily. It becomes a source of great satisfaction to them. There is no serious problem involved in establishing a warm and friendly relationship with the children who go willingly with the therapist.

It might be well to voice the warning that the therapist can unwittingly inject subtle influence into the relationship in an effort to gain rapport. For example, the therapist says to a cooperative client, "My, what a nice big boy you are! Want to come over to the playroom and play? There are paints and clay and all sorts of toys." Once inside the room, perhaps he starts to paint, and he says to the therapist, "I can't paint so good." And she answers, "Why, I think that is a fine picture. And you did it all by yourself! And you don't think it is so good." Finally she reflects the attitude the child expressed, but it is so discounted by the time she gets around to it that it doesn't do much good.

Then there is the case in which two brothers, aged four and five, were having a play-therapy session. One boy was painting and accidentally spilled some paint. He got the paint rag and wiped up the paint. The therapist said, "Bobby is careful. He wiped up the paint that he spilled." From then on, the contact became a display of how careful both boys were and the stock comment was, "Look, I'm being careful. See? I'm being careful." Finally, they identified the therapist—"Look, *teacher*, I'm being so careful!" Unintentionally, the therapist had directed the behavior of the boys. Praise for actions committed in the playroom is not conducive to therapy.

The beginning therapist might examine the case of six-year-old Oscar. He was brought to the therapist by his mother. The father had been killed when Oscar was two years old. On the day the father was killed, Oscar came down with a bad case of measles. Oscar was sent out of town to a relative. The mother had a nervous breakdown and was in the hospital for three months. Finally, when she recovered her health sufficiently to go back to work as a private secretary, she took Oscar back into her home and hired a woman to take care of him. The woman was not satisfactory, and others came and went at surprisingly short intervals. Oscar had no sense of security at all. Some of the helpers mistreated him. He became one of the most maladjusted children imaginable. He was aggressive, belligerent, negative, insecure, defiant, dependent. He was a masterpiece of conflicting feelings. His mother, erratic and nervous, brought him to the psychologist. This is an excerpt from the initial contact.

MOTHER: This is Oscar. Heaven only knows what you can do with him! But here he is.

THERAPIST: Would you like to come over to the playroom with me?

OSCAR: NO! Shet up! (*Yells.*)

MOTHER (*Also yelling.*): Oscar! Now you be polite. Stop that sass!

OSCAR (*Louder than ever.*): No! No! No!

MOTHER: Well, you are! What do you think I brought you up here for? The ride?

OSCAR (*Whimpering.*): I don't wanta!

The beginning therapist asks herself at this point, "Now what? Cajole him into the playroom?"—"We have such nice toys over in the playroom. You're such a nice big boy now. You come with me, and I'll show you what there is to play with." That is not accepting Oscar exactly as he is. He doesn't want to come. Or should she say, with a note of regret in her voice, "Your mother brought you all the way up here and you don't want to come into the playroom with me"? That is a reflection of feeling, but it also carries subtle condemnation. There is an implied "My, aren't you an ungrateful little brute!" If the therapist wants to reflect his feeling only, what should she say?—"You don't want to come with me." The therapist tries that.

THERAPIST: You don't want to come with me.

OSCAR: NO! (*Makes face at therapist and folds up fists.*) Shet up!

MOTHER: If you don't go over there, I'll leave you here forever.

OSCAR (*Attaching self to mother, whimpering.*): Don't leave me. Don't leave me. (*Sobs hysterically.*)

THERAPIST: Oscar is scared when Mother threatens to leave him here.

[This is a recognition of Oscar's feeling, but condemnation of Mother, who flares up.]

MOTHER: Well, I've got to do something. Honest to God, Oscar, if you don't shut up and go with this lady, I *will* leave you! Or *give* you away!

OSCAR: You wait for me? (*Pitifully.*) You be here when I come back.

MOTHER: Of course I will—if you behave.

OSCAR (*Transferring death-like grip from mother's skirt to therapist's skirt.*): You wait?

THERAPIST: You want Mother to promise you that she will wait.

OSCAR: You promise?

MOTHER: I promise!

(*Therapist and Oscar go into the playroom. Therapist starts to close the door.*)

OSCAR (*Screaming.*): Don't shet the door! Don't shet the door! (*Tears roll down his cheeks.*)

THERAPIST: You don't want me to shut the door. You're afraid to stay here with me if we shut the door.

This is recognition of his feeling. He looks up, amazed, and then nods his head. Now what? Does the therapist, after recognizing his feeling, disregard it and say, "But when we come in here we shut the door," and convince herself that this is a valuable limitation? What purpose would that serve? To point up the fact that we recognize feeling, but ignore it. Is she accepting Oscar exactly as he is—fear of closed doors and all? Is she showing the child what she means by letting him make the choices and lead the way? Is she establishing an atmosphere of permissiveness to express his true feelings? Is she maintaining a deep respect for the child? It seems that she is forsaking all these principles if she closes the door. So what does she say?

THERAPIST: You don't want me to shut the door. You're afraid to stay here with me if I shut the door. Very well. We'll leave the door open and you close the door when you feel like it.

[This leaves the responsibility up to Oscar. It is up to him to make the choice. Oscar looks around the playroom. As he thaws out, he becomes aggressive.]

OSCAR: I'll bust up everything in here!

What about limitations? Should the therapist say, "You can play with the toys in here any way you want to, but you can't bust them up," or, "Other children use these toys, too, so you can't bust them up"? That is not responding to Oscar's expressed *feeling*. That is succumbing to the trap of responding to content rather than feeling back of content.

THERAPIST: You're feeling tough now.

OSCAR (*Glaring at therapist.*): I'll bust you up, too.

THERAPIST: You're still feeling tough.

OSCAR: I'll . . . (*Suddenly laughs.*) I'll . . . (*He wanders around the playroom and picks up the toy telephone.*) What's this?

This is another challenge to the therapist. Shall she say, "You wonder what that is?" or, "It is a telephone"? It seems more conducive to progress in this session to answer the simple question rather than make an issue out of it.

THERAPIST: It is a toy telephone.

OSCAR: I'll bust it up, too.

THERAPIST: You want to bust up the telephone, too.

OSCAR (*Smiling like a little angel.*): Yeah, I just love to tear up things and bust people.

THERAPIST: You like to bust up things and hurt people.

OSCAR (*Calmly.*): Yeah. Oh, look. Dishes. I'll play house. (*Begins to set the table, then picks up the telephone. Talking into telephone.*) Hello. Is that you, Mary? Oh, I'm home. I'm getting supper. (*Aside to therapist.*) I am getting supper, ain't I?

THERAPIST: You're getting supper.

OSCAR (*Back to telephone.*): Yeah, I'm getting supper. What we having? (*The tone of voice implies that Mary is asking him and he is repeating it. He turns to the therapist.*) What we having?

THERAPIST: You want me to tell you what we are having for supper?

OSCAR: Yeah. Tell me quick.

Should the therapist quickly speak up with the menu? Or should she say, "What would you like," or, "You do want me to tell you, don't you"? A menu would seem to carry on the play a little more expediently. The therapist quickly names some food. Oscar repeats it word for word over the telephone.

OSCAR: What? You want to know have we got a doll house here? (*Aside to therapist.*) Have we got a doll house?

(*The doll house is quite obviously there.*)

THERAPIST: We've got a doll house.

OSCAR: Have we got toy soldiers?

(*Repeats this in aside to therapist, who answers, "We've got toy soldiers."*)

Oscar continues this itemizing of all the toys in the playroom. The therapist responds to each aside question. What is Oscar trying to do? Of course he knows the answers to his questions. Then why does he continue to ask the therapist if what he sees before him is there? How else could Oscar establish rapport with the therapist? It seems that that is what he is trying to do. After he asks about everything in sight, he says over the telephone:

OSCAR: You want to know will I kiss the lady? (*Then to the therapist.*) Will I kiss you, lady?

The therapist remembers the caution against too much display of affection that might smother out the therapy. Should she say, "You would like to kiss me," or should she follow along on this, too?

THERAPIST: You want to know will you kiss the lady?

OSCAR (*Grinning.*): I will.

He comes over and very gently kisses the therapist's hand; then, probably thinking of his old self, he rushes over and grabs the hammer and begins to pound on the peg-board set. The door is still open. Here is another challenge to the therapist. What about that door? The noise is terrific. Should she close it while he is busily pounding? Should she direct his attention to it and ask him if he thought he should close it? Should she keep faith with the little fellow and wait for someone who is bothered by the noise to come over and see that it is stopped? In this particular incident, no one was apparently bothered by the noise, and it did not become necessary to close the door. However, if someone had come, it seems that it would have been a necessary part of the therapy to inform Oscar that the noise was bothering other people and that either the door must be closed or the noise stopped and to let him make the choice, being alert to reflect all the feelings he expressed at this point. It would be an injection of reality that would create this limitation to the permissiveness of the therapy situation. The following week Oscar closed the door voluntarily when he entered the playroom with the therapist. Had he not done so, the therapist would have waited until he did make the move to decide the issue himself. To suggest it would have been an attempt to hurry things along. The voluntary closing of the door might indicate a certain amount of progress in establishing the relationship. It seems to be a gesture of confidence toward the therapist as well as an indication of growth on the part of Oscar toward a new independence and an ability to make choices.

# *The Beginning Phase of Therapy*

FREDERICK H. ALLEN

. . . The understanding and direction a therapist brings to the beginning hours of treatment, in relation to the child's first reactions, in no small measure determine the outcome of the case. It is important, therefore, to gain a clear understanding of what happens in the first interviews and of the more noteworthy factors that influence the child's responses. Hence, this . . . will be devoted to a discussion of the dynamics of the beginning interviews.

Certain influences are already at work that invest with significance the child's reactions before he arrives for the first appointment. Usually, one or both parents have come alone to the clinic to discuss the troublesome situation. An enhanced awareness of their own part in the difficulty and of their participation in a plan of working results from this initial interview which does not include the child. The parents, by taking this first step toward solution of a problem that involves both themselves and the child, may get immediate relief, or, as sometimes occurs, they may be thrown into more uncertainty. Whatever the response, it is soon clear that this first step is of prime importance for them.[a]

As a next step in treatment, parent and child come together. Sometimes the parents have prepared the child with a frank discussion of their reasons for bringing him to the clinic and have indicated that all of them need help for

[a] For fuller discussion of the significance of the parent's step in seeking help and the part the parent has in the therapeutic process, see Almena Dawley, "Interrelated Movement of Parent and Child in Therapy with Children," *American Journal of Orthopsychiatry*, IX (1939), No. 4, pp. 748–754.

their mutual difficulties. Other children are told nothing but are just brought. Others may be told about the "nice person who plays with little children." Some may be fooled in more evasive ways, and many are told: "I am taking you to a man who makes children behave." Irrespective of the explanations given, the fact that the troubled child is having to face a new situation will leave him wondering and anxious about what is going to happen to him. That is inevitable. The child himself has not been the one originally to seek help, and being brought into active participation in the experience now crystallizes for him two important implications. One is that he needs to be changed. Irrespective of whether the preparation has been clear-cut or evasive, there is in this step the implication that change is necessary. The second and more subtle implication is that the child is to have a part in the procedures designed to help him with his difficulties. The very fact that he is given his own separate appointment with the therapist implies that he has something to do with his own growth, that, as he has been a participant in the creation of the problem, he now can be a participant in effecting change.

The important thing here is that the actions and attitudes of the adults concerned seeking help with the child and the responses of the child that are brought into play by this step give particular significance to the first interviews with both parent and child. They arrive at the clinic together for their first appointment but go separately to their interviews with therapist and caseworker. At the end of the interview, they meet again and leave the clinic together. This may seem like a routine procedure and, in itself, to be of no particular meaning. But the responses that frequently appear may be dramatized expressions of the problem which has necessitated this step. The fear aroused in the child and the anxiety of a parent, who trusts her child to another person and allows him to go with that new person without the support of her presence, is not incidental behavior requiring only a reassuring tone or word from the therapist. These are reactions that precipitate the therapist into the very heart of the child's emotional turmoil.

The child is embarked on an experience which awakens feelings he must immediately come to terms with. He may be afraid, or may be angry or defiant, or he may be just passive and indifferent. Whatever the behavior, the fact that he is responding with his own feelings and in his own way makes him, from the very outset, a participant in an experience that will revolve and develop around his feelings. He is immediately placed in the center of a relationship that is significant because of its uniqueness. It is unique because he finds a person who is able to accept him just as he is. If he is angry, he can be helped to experience the full surge of that feeling. If he is fearful, the child has the support of a person who can understand his need to be afraid and who does not immediately try to reassure him in order to take that feeling away. He comes expecting to be changed and ready to fight or protect himself against the power of this strange, unknown person. Instead, he finds a person who is interested in him as he is.

These are points which were emphasized in the preceding chapter. We now see their practical illustration in the beginning therapeutic hours of a child who has been in trouble with himself and others and who is brought for help by his parents, who frequently start treatment with the same mixture of feelings he has. Irrespective of what the therapist does, children respond with feelings closely related to the difficulties they present. These will vary as widely as the types of problems and kinds of individuals who seek help. They occur at the very start, irrespective of what the therapist does, since up to the moment of first coming together the therapist seems to the child a specter or a god, or a threatening and alien force with unknown potentialities. In that first impact the therapist now becomes a reality.

The degree to which the immediate behavior of the child is utilized in this beginning phase is influenced by the particular therapeutic approach. Only as these responses are understood in relation to the whole therapeutic process, and not as being merely preliminary to the therapy that will follow, can they be utilized for the growth-inducing values inherent in them. If the fears activated by the separating nature of this first step are seen as barriers to the establishment of a relationship, to be removed in order to reach other and "deeper" sources of fear, then the therapist will necessarily take more active steps to reassure the child and work toward the building of a positive "transference." Similarly, the therapist who holds that the antagonism and anger stirred in the child by coming for help are barriers to the establishment of a therapeutic relationship will strive as quickly as possible to change this response in order to inveigle himself into the child's confidence.[b]

When the emphasis in these early interviews is on the therapist's activity with the goal of drawing the child into a therapeutic relation, the child's immediate reactions have a secondary place and are often interpreted as resistance. The point of view presented here . . . is the opposite of this. The child's immediate responses are the center of the therapist's interest. To help the child bring to this relationship his own feelings will be the immediate goal of the therapist. A child who can do this in his first hour may begin to find his capacity to express feeling, while at the same time making a connection with the therapist with his own emotional responses. This is an important step. There is no need at this point to delve into the hidden or original sources of the fear that may be stirred when the immediate situation brings the child face to face with fear and with the necessity to organize his own resources around that feeling. The therapist provides support for the child in his efforts to deal with the reality of this new experience. In doing this, he enters into a significant and growth-inducing relationship with the child, a relationship which has a beginning and an end, with an intermediate period of self-testing and self-discovery.

[b] For an excellent discussion of this use of the first interviews see Anna Freud, "Introduction to the Technique of Child Analysis," *Nervous and Mental Disease Monograph*, Series 48 (New York: Nervous & Mental Disease Publishing Co., 1928), Ch. I.

The emphasis here is on the experience itself and not on the particular content of the experience. How the child uses this relationship is of more importance than what he says. A child may start by a frank statement of some of his difficulties and talk freely about what he thinks is the cause of them. The therapist naturally is interested in what he has to say and may encourage him to talk as freely as he will. But his major concern must be with what the child is doing with the therapist and the therapy[c] through talking and with a sensitiveness to whatever uses the child is making of this. A child who talks with apparent ease about his difficulties may be pushing the responsibility for doing something about them entirely onto the shoulders of the therapist. His statement of them may be his first challenge to the person who is supposed to have the power to change him. Conversely, this early discussion of his difficulties may indicate the child's beginning readiness to do something about them. The therapist must be aware of the various uses the child will make of him and must maintain, at the same time, his own integrity, which establishes a differentiating foundation for the entire experience.

The therapist must know and believe that whatever a child does or says in these initial hours has meanings that are influenced and determined by the fact that the therapist is there with him in the room. He may talk about his gangs, about his dislike of school, how good or how mean everyone is to him, or he may plunge into play with the toys he chooses. Whatever he does or says conveys, to a considerable degree, his feelings about the immediate situation. Failure to know or believe this can lead a therapist into many blind alleys. . . .

Beginning where the child actually is and dealing directly and immediately with his feelings, rather than with his problem behavior and its causes, give an immediate impetus and meaning to the therapeutic process. The child is taken for what he is and is not squeezed into any theoretical scheme nor cajoled into giving up any particular "secrets" or content. Whatever form the child's feelings may take, angry or fearful, happy or sad, aggressive or placating, talkative or silent, "cooperative" or "uncooperative," they engage the therapist's immediate interest because these are the indicators of a troubled child floundering around to find a way of adapting himself to the world in which he lives. The child is accepted as having, within himself, the potentiality for achieving a new inner balance as he is helped to find value in a living relationship. Thus the therapist enters at once into a significant relationship with the child and becomes a growth-inducing influence throughout the steps that follow.

These beginning hours with the child must be understood as an integral part of a therapeutic process and not as preliminary to it. They are as much a part of therapy as dawn is a part of the day. Any therapeutic philosophy which fails to catch the significance of this and neglects to utilize the feeling re-

[c] In connection with this point I want to emphasize . . . that therapy is a precipitated growth experience, not apart from but akin to life.

sponses aroused in the child by starting a new experience will miss the opportunity to give this new experience immediate significance in terms of the turmoil that requires therapy. If these early responses are seen as preparatory, it implies that therapy is regarded as springing from the therapist and from what he says and does. If therapy, however, is viewed as a child-centered experience, then whatever reactions the child brings can be used to aid the child in achieving a new sense of himself. This can never occur in isolation. It must occur as a living experience. It is that which begins in a variety of ways, in these first hours with a child who, because he is confused and troubled, is brought for help.

# ❀ *Structuring the Relationship*

CLARK E. MOUSTAKAS

. . . During the early phases of therapy, structuring is an important process. The child is introduced to the playroom, and the permissive nature of the situation is conveyed to him. Through the structuring statements of the therapist, the child gains an understanding of the therapeutic relationship and the nature of his freedom and responsibility.

The therapist may use expressions such as the following: "In here you are free to do what you want"; "I would rather know what your opinion is"; "This is your time and place"; "What you say here is between us—not anyone else's affair"; "I can't decide for you, the only thing that matters is that you decide for yourself"; "You want me to tell you what to do, and I say it's up to you to decide"; "You want me to do that for you, but here you do things for yourself"; "This is your project, I cannot manage it for you"; "You must see it through"; "I understand. It's not easy to work it. Perhaps I can help by giving you a start. Then I think you can finish on your own." The therapist may offer information, or point out possibilities the child has not seen, or even offer help when it is absolutely necessary, but his constant attitude is that the child can use his capacities and skills and can take full responsibility for his actions and decisions. The structuring statements aid the child in becoming aware of himself, in facing his inner conflicts, and in working through painful, negative self-attitudes. They give recognition to the child's self and help him to come to terms with himself and to bring to expression his own real feelings, thoughts, choices, and wishes. . . .

# The Initial Situation and Its Alternatives

ERIK H. ERIKSON

Every psychotherapist has certain vague expectations in regard to what a disturbed child entering his room for the first time may be expecting of him and may do. Against this generalized picture, the behavior of a single child stands out in its dramatic individuality.

Our young patient usually arrives hand in hand with his mother. He can be expected to have made a mental note of the fact that our office is in a "hospital-like" institution. On entering the waiting room he finds a friendly secretary and is then invited into an inner room about half of which (signified by "adult furniture") is set aside for the therapist's plainly nonmedical business, the other half (signified by floor space and an array of ordinary toys) for a child's play. He is told sooner or later that he is expected to let his mother withdraw to the waiting room and to allow the connecting door to be closed; the therapist and the toys are then to be at his disposal.

This situation confronts the young patient with a maze of conflicting possibilities. We would like to describe it as consisting of several overlapping fields of ambiguity which are created by the child's relation to mother, therapist, toys, and inner conflict.

There is first of all his mother. He may hold on to her hand or body, insist on staying with her in the waiting room, demand that the door remain open, or stubbornly remain near the door which has closed between her and him. If he does this, the situation is for him still related mainly to one goal, his mother, and through her the way home from a vague danger. This idea, however, is rarely unequivocally pleasant. Our small patient usually has reached a deadlock with his mother, who cannot understand why he does not "simply drop" his problem; while the home atmosphere, in which he, in most cases, has been subjected to varying educational methods, has become charged with unsolved conflicts. Thus, frightened as he may be, he feels attracted by the doctor possibilities, the second field and one which offers possible escape from the unbearable pressure of the domestic situation. Something which the mother or somebody else has said usually has created a slight hope in the child that the therapist may be a person who understands the conditions and the tempo in which a symptom of fear can be gradually abandoned without giving place to chaos within or more trouble without. Many a child has learned also to expect that he will be able to play for time by repeating to this new therapist what has satisfied the old ones. On the other hand the therapist has been called a "doctor" and the medical implications of the surroundings add to the mere strangeness of the situation and create the expectation in the child that some kind of surprise attack is to be made on his physical or moral inviolacy. The mother, with the best intentions, often transfers the negative aspects of the "mother field" into the field of doctor possibilities; she insists, for example, on reporting in the child's presence latest developments, on admonishing, or even threatening him, or on trying to secure the therapist's promise of diagnosis and advice. Literally and psychologically, therefore, the mother has to be referred to the waiting room; the child must feel that time has another quality in the doctor sphere, in which, paradoxically, there is no hurry about getting well.

In the meantime, a third ambiguous field has competed with mother and therapist in dominating the child's expectancies, namely the toys. For the child they open another haven, in which space too has another quality, and the therapist usually is quite glad to resign for a while in favor of this quasifree sphere. Indeed, "what would we do without toys," has become a common exclamation now that we have relaxed our efforts to ignore this most natural tool. The toys evoke in the child that remainder of playful explorativeness which his neurosis and the present doctor situation has not been able to submerge; and once he has started to select and manipulate, we can be sure that the temptation to play and to be the unquestioned and inviolable master in a microcosmic sphere will be great. However, we again see the child manifest hesitation. He has experienced too often the fact that the imagined omnipotence in the toy world only makes him feel his impotence the more keenly when he is suddenly interrupted. Playfulness does not rule until (and then only as long as) pressing purposes and fears have lost their compelling power. Thus the child often begins to play with hesitation, with selection, with one eye on the therapist or the door—but he begins to play.

Peace seems to reign. The mother is comfortably seated in the waiting room and has promised "not to go away"; the doctor has been diagnosed as a person who will not make surprise attacks on one's bodily or moral reserve; the toys, sure not to question or to admonish, promise a time of "unpurposeful" play.

However, it is at this point that the most dangerous field of ambiguity; namely, the child's reluctance to confess and his need to communicate his conflict, takes possession of the peaceful situation. Whatever it is that drives the child—an urge to get rid of some past or to prepare himself for some future, or both—the everpresent gestalt of the life task which has proved too much for him appears in the metaphoric representation of the microsphere. It is here that our "sign-reading" sets in and that the tools which Freud gave us become indispensable; for they make us realize that in the playful arrangement which the child is driven to superimpose on the inventory of toys we offer him, he offers us an outline of the "inner maze" in which he is caught. Our small patients either show an anxious care in excluding this or that toy from their play or they work themselves toward a borderline where they themselves suddenly find their own doings unsafe, not permissible, unworkable, or unsatisfactory to the point of extreme discomfort. They cannot go on playing in peace—a phenomenon which we shall call "play disruption."

I shall give a brief example of the place of such a play disruption in the four fields of ambiguity, governed as they are by the changing valences of the parent who is present, the therapist, the toys, and the shadow of inner conflict.

A girl of four still withstands toilet training. When put on the toilet, she seems unable to "let go"; later she soils her bed. Recently she was knocked down by an automobile; this has increased her inaccessibility and her pale stubbornness. (As is obvious from her utterances at home, a small neighborhood dog is, at the moment, important in her fantasy life. It is female like herself, and not housebroken, and recently was knocked down by an automobile too; but unlike herself, it is frequently beaten for soiling, was badly hurt in the accident [it lost a leg]. This little dog apparently represents to her all that "is coming to her.")

Very pale, the little girl has finally left her mother in the waiting room. She stands near the door of my room, sucking her finger, neither willing to play nor wanting to go back to her mother. I try to help her by outlining with some blocks a few rooms on the floor (an approach I use only on rare occasions). A little girl lies in a bed, and a woman stands in the middle of the bedroom from which a door leads into a bathroom. There is a garage with a car and a man. After a while the little girl suddenly warms up, approaches with flushed cheeks and kicks the woman doll so that it falls over, closes the bathroom door, and goes to the toy shelf to get three shiny red cars for the man in the garage. May we say she expresses a dislike for what must mean, to her, a mother in front of the little girl's bed and for the demand of the open bathroom door and that she shows a readiness to give whatever the cars mean to the man (father). At this point, however, she bursts into tears and anxiously asks, "Where is my mummy?" In panicky haste she takes three red pencils from my desk and runs out of the room to present them to her mother. Then she sits down beside her, pale and rigid, determined not to return to me. (The mother wants to give back the pencils, but she is told that the child is free to return them another time.)

The patient has scarcely reached home when she seems to feel guilty about having taken my pencils and shows signs of despair at not being able to bring them back until the next day. However, when the time for her next hour has arrived, she sits in the waiting room clutching the pencils in one hand, some unknown object in the other. She refuses to come with me. After a while it becomes noticeable that she has soiled herself. When she is picked up to be led to the bathroom, the pencils fall to the floor and with them a little toy dog, one of whose legs has been broken off.

If we undertake to interpret this example properly, we would be led to consider in detail the patterns of guilt-feeling in this child: Having manifested aggression toward the woman in the play setup, she experienced the fear of the possible loss of her mother's love; in hurrying to bring her an equivalent of what she had given to the man in the play, she happened to snatch objects which belonged to me, thus provoking a situation which would again ask for acts of rectification and which would imply an element of desire for punishment. (As if under compulsion to do or to allude to that which brings punishment, she held on to my property, brought the toy dog with a damage identical with her dog friend's injury, and soiled in my room—transferring a "symptom" for which she had never been punished in a way either quantitatively or qualitatively equal to the hostility it expressed, as subsequently became apparent.)

What interests us here first of all is the traffic between the fields outlined above and the play disruption's place in them. The little girl, moderately sure that her mother would not leave and somewhat loosened by the playful way in which the therapist approached her problem, got as far as to say in the language of play signs that she did not like the idea of the lady standing there near the open bathroom door but was willing to give the reddest cars to the man, when she must have experienced what Adam did when he heard God's voice: "Adam, where art thou?" Her play suddenly seemed all-visible in the mother-field, and she went to atone for her deed not, however, without stealing my pencils and thus innocently establishing a new goal in the doctor sphere. The trip home again increased the stubbornness against mother and bathroom demands and, consequently, the importance of the goal she had established in my sphere. The next day, back in my office and faced with the necessity and possibility of making everything come out even, she is caught by emotional paralysis and her symptom expresses for her what she did not dare to express in her play; namely, the inability "to give" to an ambivalently loved person.

It is this very inability which in this case called for analysis and re-education. However, we shall have to resist the temptation to describe the little girl's treatment at this point. Instead we concentrate on some further aspects of the described play situation.

We may call the toy scene on the floor "microcosmic," i.e., an arrangement of small objects in such a way that their configuration signifies a configuration of conflicting forces in the child's life, in this case the child's retentive attitude toward her mother and her generous attitude toward the father. That the woman in the play really signified her mother (and that the man, perhaps, already indicated a father transference on the therapist) became plain when the microcosmic play was disrupted, and she tried to rearrange another sphere in such a way that it represented a reversal of the "guilty" microcosmic configuration; she gave to her mother—and robbed me. Such rearrangement of the child's relationship to the real persons or the life-sized objects present in the therapeutic situation we shall designate as "macrocosmic." In this case the traffic from what we shall call, for short, the "microsphere" to the "macrosphere" implied a play disruption which, of course, is not always necessarily the case. Such a shift can take place as a playful expansion, perhaps with a transition from solitary play to a game, especially if another person is induced to play a role in the desired macrocosmic arrangement. (Using, for example, with an omnipotent gesture, a chair for a horse to ride on and to order about, would be the macrocosmic play equivalent to the microcosmic form of making a toy rider hop along the floor.)

Beside the microcosmic and macrocosmic "spheres" of representation we can discern an autocosmic one: *the sphere of dramatization by means of an interplay of body parts and organ systems.* The little girl's soiling belongs here: it was a *symptom in the autosphere.* There is also "autocosmic play," i.e., the original play in the growing world of the child's expanding body consciousness and the mutual enchantment of its parts. . . .

# *Using the First Interview as a Basis for Therapeutic Planning*

J. LOUISE DESPERT

It is of practical importance to ascertain the nature of the therapeutic problem as soon as possible and evaluate approximately the duration of treatment. As a rule, the first interview gives enough insight into the nature of the conflict to be a decisive one, as regards future plans; this, provided certain areas are searched, more-or-less systematically, by utilizing the words, gestures, feeling tones, and other expressions demonstrated during the first contact. First memories, dreams, early fears, past and present family relationships are brought to light, not in answer to direct questions regarding these particular points, but through the interpretation of the child's spontaneous activities in the playroom.

Again, one is impressed with the infinite variety of patterns shown by the patients, in spite of which a common characteristic is found in all cases, namely that the first interview gives the needed clue to the child's conflict, whether the medium is a reported dream, a first drawing, an early memory, or a spontaneous bit of play. To illustrate the point, several cases are briefly quoted:

> A boy of twelve years four months was brought to treatment shortly after it was discovered that he used women's underwear, preferably his mother's, in the performance of sexual activities (at least the family surmised), which had considerably disturbed the people in his close environment. It was suspected that the activities had taken place over a period of months, possibly years;

the informants—the mother and her (female) cousin—did not know what the activities were but feared that they might involve the younger sister. They were only sure that their underwear disappeared in large numbers, later to be found soiled, torn, often in inaccessible hidden spots, and that the boy would "get frantic" if he could not secure the feminine apparel; to this end, once, he had broken into the garage and broken the trunk lock of a visiting female relation. He was a boy of superior intelligence, the older of two children in a family of high economic status. His sister was three years younger. His father had committed suicide when he was seven-and-one-half years old, and a maternal female cousin had then moved, literally, into his father's bed. The mother was a psychopathic individual and a chronic alcoholic. Marital relations had been poor, and the mother-relation to her cousin was strongly suggestive of homosexual adjustment. The first interview illuminated the dynamics in this case with no delay; the boy was not interested in toys, his first drawing showed a "volcano and smoke," with the smoke in the shape of a spermatozoon, head upward, a short distance above the crater of the volcano. He was freely communicative, but in a superficial way, until asked about early memories. He recalled his father's death, recalled in particular having been confused by the conflicting explanations given and by the avowed contempt of his mother for her husband's family. He recalled very little regarding his sister's birth, but one memory was quite vivid in his mind; this first memory became the clue to his transvestitism. As reconstructed later, through the identity of the nurse, and the description of the house, both of which he gave with accuracy, the experience recalled had taken place when he was less than two years old. His mother had left on a long trip, he was standing in his crib, crying, when the nurse put his mother's girdle on him, he stopped crying, and felt "funny" (obviously referring to erection). He had sought the repetition of this experience, intermittently, following this episode. At times of stress, he put on feminine underclothes, three to six samples of each item, and masturbated while fantasying that he was his mother or some attractive woman resembling her. The first memory, promptly brought up, presented a multifold interest in that the specific details recalled ("the thin nurse, not the fat one . . . the one who beat me, etc.") set the time of the episode accurately, although no one in the family was in a position to have known of its occurrence.

The record of another patient illustrates a different introduction to therapy.

This was a boy of eight years and two months, at the time of admission. He was brought to treatment because of asociability, emotional immaturity, and schizophrenia-like behavior, in which fantasy and reality were often confused. He was extremely fearful, did not let his mother out of his sight, did not engage in any play with other children and had, as a realistic life-companion, a huge Teddy bear with whom he slept, whom he addressed as a living person, etc.; on the other hand, he fought constantly with his only sibling, a younger brother. His IQ was over 150, and he attended a class for exceptional children where he had considerable difficulties owing to his daydreaming and poor contact. He was an omnivorous reader, selecting classics and "books of knowledge," which he absorbed at top speed during any hour he was free from school. A verbal child, he talked freely during the first interview, although he was manifestly anxious. In a high-pitched voice and with blunted affect, he talked mostly about imaginary characters, some of them taken from radio programs and comic strips. Looking the toys over, he expressed his contempt for "that baby stuff," but kept glancing sideways at some of the dolls. Reassured that boys also played with the dolls sometimes, he selected two large dolls, a girl and a baby, and began a play theme which was very revealing. He used the baby's diaper as a flowing cape tied at the neck, calling this doll "Superman," and the other doll "Lois," both well known comics characters. His story, however, differed from the Superman story; over and over, Superman and Lois "fought" in violent physical attacks upon one another, then lay side by side on the floor. "They're tired, they're going to sleep." When first asked regarding Lois, he had stated that she was "his girl friend" (Superman's). The symbolism of the play was so clearly evocative of the primal scene and a child's reaction to it that after he had laid the dolls down once more, a comment was made to the effect that they behaved more like man and wife than boy and girl friend. Besides, what were they fighting about? It was not long before the boy referred to his own parents in a puzzled, questioning way. Later, upon checking with the mother, it was learned that several years prior to admission, and before the brother's birth (which would make his age as under four years), the patient had once come to the parents' room, at night, and witnessed sexual intercourse. At least, they now surmised that he had been there for some time when first seen; he had stood in the doorway, "like in a trance"; the mother had brought him back to his bed, and no one had ever referred to the episode, then or afterward.

A third case which presents differences from the two cases referred to above, was also different from the large majority of neurotic children seen in that the child stepped directly into the area of conflict on his first contact with therapy.

This was an only child, a boy of eight years and four months, who was referred for severe anxiety manifestations, refusing to go out on the street, alone or accompanied; "he was petrified." He also had reading and spelling difficulties, in spite of superior intelligence and satisfactory achievements in other subjects. Nightmares had marked the onset of anxiety manifestations at six years, following a performance of Hansel and Gretel. He had become increasingly difficult to manage owing to his fears and inhibitions. Both parents were neurotic: the father, a compulsive individual, was undergoing psychoanalytic treatment, and the mother, insecure, vague, circumstantial, had been under psychiatric treatment, intermittently, for several years. As later developments confirmed, the child's conflict was in the nature of castration anxiety and in the first contact presented itself with little symbolization or complexity of expression. The boy drew "a lady and a man," both armless; then, when asked if he knew why he came to see the therapist, he said that people, men and women, "come when my father and mother are away at night" (fears which prevented him to sleep), that he had nightmares, dreamed of "drunken men and crazy men," then added, "will you please tell me the difference between a drunken and a crazy man?" He said he'd feel easier if he "only could know the difference in the street." A drunken man might come, kidnap him, and kill him or "do worse things than that"; this, he would not elaborate upon, but, as he talked, he rammed one plane inside another and said, "they're going under each other." The association with the drunken man was clearly brought out when he said that he did not actually know any drunken man, "except my father but he never got drunk."

Sometimes, a child, although seemingly interested in the play setup and the toys, gives the clue to his emotional problem through his behavior rather than his use of the toys.

An only child, a girl of four and one-half years, very precocious, was brought to treatment because of anxiety, clinging to her mother, and feeding difficulties. The parents were divorced, and she lived with her mother, who had been under analysis for nearly two years. When she gave the history, it became apparent that she was acutely hallucinating (she had placed a screen between the child's bed and her own, fearing she might harm the child, as she saw her rising from her crib, in mid-air). The father, passive, effeminate, immature, had been under analysis himself for several months at the time of admission. Although the mother appeared frail and the child was well able to walk, she carried the little girl to the office, hugging her passionately and holding on tightly to her. The child was upset, screamed, stamped her feet, but the absence of tears was striking. After her mother had left (this was not as difficult for the child as had at first been assumed), she stood in the middle of the room, sucking her thumb, making obvious efforts not to seem interested in the toys, though at intervals she made forward motions toward the shelves. "No, I don't want to do anything. . . ." She was afraid to get involved with the strange person and the strange setup. When the therapist took two beds from the shelves to make a bedroom arrangement, the child volunteered that she had "only one bed," and that she had "scary dreams . . . a man kills a girl . . . and lions to eat her. . . ." She then made significant statements regarding her actual unhappy experience. "I want my daddy and my mommy together again . . . sometimes, I'm alone . . . no daddy, no mummy. . . ." Throughout her treatment of several months duration, in weekly visits, she chose the type of direct play which involved almost no toy equipment. There was considerable body contact—climbing over the physician or on her lap; at intervals being quite aggressive toward her. She assigned definite roles to her (father, mother, child), with complimentary identifications for her own part, so the play patterns were varied and showed great fluidity. Her selection was the more conspicuous as she was a young child, and one who had had considerable opportunity for play with toys (in nursery school and with young cousins who were frequent companions). Her anxiety, her ambivalent attitudes toward both parents were largely resolved; on the other hand, while the home situation was to a great extent clarified, it could hardly be made happier, especially as the mother, early in the treatment, had to be hospitalized.

Material from the few cases referred to above was selected and may be sufficient to give some conception of the diversity of reactions shown, even if only the first interview is considered. Examples could be multiplied, they would only further emphasize the high degree of individuality and differentiation encountered in play therapy with children.

CHAPTER SIX

# Special Situations

SITUATIONS ARISE in the course of therapy with children which may catch the beginning therapist "off guard," unless he previously has given some thought to possible ways of handling them. In most cases the situation, if recognized rather than ignored or treated as inconsequential, can be used to further the progress of therapy. The questions raised in this chapter are closely associated with the general issue of structuring and will reappear many times in the course of any therapy.[1]

The selections by Klein, Ross, and Ginott contribute views of relevant issues, but few crystallized answers to the questions raised can be found in the literature. The reason for this is that each therapist must answer them in a way which is consistent with his philosophical framework. It is important that he consider these problems and not ignore their possible therapeutic importance.

Issues which may arise in connection with the playroom and the use of toys and equipment are as follows: If several playrooms are available, should the same room be used each time? Should all sessions be held indoors? What are the advantages or disadvantages of going for walks and playing outdoors? What may be the result of therapist and/or child making repeated trips out of the room for toys or materials? Would the child's reactions differ depending on whether the room is immaculately neat, casually disarranged, or in utter confusion? Is it important that the condition remain

[1] The subject of limits and related issues involved in handling aggressive acts will be covered in Chapter 7.

the same from session to session? If some semblance of neatness is preferred, should the toys always be in the same general location? Are there any therapeutic reasons for putting an "occupied" sign on the door when the room is in use? If one-way mirrors and microphones are visible, how will the child's questions be answered? How can his real concern that his parents are watching or listening be allayed?

If a toy such as Bobo is usually available, what effect will be produced if it is deflated when the child arrives? What if the child breaks a toy? If he wants to replace it, should he be permitted to do so? Should the toy be immediately replaced by the clinic? Should the toy be replaced rather than repaired? What are the dynamics involved in all aspects of broken toys? Klein suggests that each child's toys be kept in a separate box or drawer. What are the advantages or disadvantages of such a plan? May toys be taken home and returned the next session? Should any piece of equipment —paper, balloons, cookies—be considered "expendable" and given to the child? If so, should any limit on quantity be set? Who should clean up the playroom—the child, the therapist, or custodial service? What therapeutic implications are involved?

Another group of questions relates to therapist–child interactions with respect to play activities. These should be considered in the light of their meaning to the child and their effect on the total therapy process. Should one praise the child's products and efforts? Should specific skills in crafts or games be "taught"? To what extent, if any, should the therapist enter into the child's play?[2] Is the kind of play involved an important consideration (e.g., checkers versus cops and robbers)? Is the amount of initiative required and taken by the adult relevant to the issue?

What if the child brings books from home for himself or the therapist to read or his own toys to play with during the hour? What if he insists on setting up school-type activities and exercises? What are the advantages and disadvantages of letting the child take his drawings, clay products, and craft objects home? Is the privacy of the therapy hour violated by this practice? What should be done if the child sneaks small

---

[2] Ross and Ginott present contrasting views on this subject.

toys into his pockets, regardless of whether he is aware that the therapist has observed his action? Should the therapist accept gifts from the child—not only small items, such as candy, as discussed by Ginott, but Christmas presents? Should the therapist give birthday, Christmas, or "farewell" gifts to the child?

The following questions are concerned with the role of the therapist. What special problems are involved if the diagnostician becomes the child's therapist? Should the child be encouraged or permitted to call the therapist by his first name? How does one handle the child's questions about the therapist's personal life?[3] Why is the child so concerned? Is there a different significance to such questions if they occur early in therapy or closer to termination?

How can questions of religion and sex be answered therapeutically? How should the therapist react to obscene language and comments indicative of prejudice and bigotry?[4]

If one decides to take notes, what may be the child's reaction and how can it be handled? Should the therapist refrain from smoking, as recommended by Ginott? Should the child (and therapist) be discouraged from wearing good clothes? What may be the repercussions if the child does spill paint on his clothes or ruin them in other ways?

Many subtle, as well as obvious, reactions arise when the child realizes that other children are using the room and that his therapist is seeing other children. Should efforts be made to avoid this issue? In what ways will the child express his awareness? How can they be handled to further therapy? This raises related questions as to the advisability of decorating the playroom with paintings done by other patients or of leaving block constructions, craft items, sand box creations, or paint-smeared toys for the next child to see.

Some children develop violent reactions to invisible authority figures who govern the institution and determine its policies: "I'll mess the room so *they* will have to clean it up"; "I'll break this and the owner of the building will wonder who did it"; "If I take all the cookies, the president of the

---

[3] Ginott and Ross contribute their views on this matter.

[4] See Ross in this area.

clinic will be mad." What is being conveyed by such comments and how should they be treated?

The closing of each session presents technical questions. If physical arrangements make it feasible, is it best for the child to return alone to the waiting room? If the therapist accompanies him, should discussion of therapy situations be continued in the hall or should a definite effort be made to change to a casual form of relating? What complications may arise as therapist and parent meet in the waiting room?

Many issues of structuring appeared in Billy's third therapy session. Not all children are as open in expressing their concerns, but the therapist can be certain that at least some of these questions will be troubling his young client.

> Soon after entering the room, Billy pointed to the hanging microphones: "Those look like tape recorders—they use something like that in wars." He noticed another child's drawing on the blackboard and a toy arrangement in the sandbox: "Somebody's been careless here; sometimes *they* come in to arrange things." He painted a picture then washed the paint off his hands: "So mother won't know what I did. If dynamite blasts from a bullet, mother would know that." He was mad that "somebody" had not hung up the towel. Later on, he asked if there were other playrooms in the building. He pointed to two large closed storage cabinets: "Now I know what mikes are, and I have to know about those boxes." He then took an airplane to a table and said to the therapist, "Now let's get better acquainted." He brought over a water pistol "to squirt if somebody comes in," and carried on an imaginary phone conversation, relaying the messages to the therapist: "*They* think I've gone nuts because I'm in here"; and "*They're* telling us we have ten minutes left, but we only have five minutes; we'll get out faster." He wanted to take several balloons home with him and was limited to two: "I could sneak balloons and *they* wouldn't know." He selected two, then hid the others behind some toys: "I have to hide these, I'm not sure if they'll still be there next time." Before leaving the room, to reassure himself and possibly because not all of his questions had been adequately handled by his beginning therapist, he compulsively lined up all the toys he had been using along the edge of the table.

If each question or area of concern had been answered to his satisfaction, would he have needed to pose so many?

# ❋ *The Psychoanalytic Play Technique*

MELANIE KLEIN

. . . I have described how the use of the toys, which I kept especially for the child patient in the box in which I first brought them, proved essential for her analysis. This experience, as well as others, helped me to decide which toys are most suitable for the psychoanalytic play technique. They are mainly: little wooden men and women, usually in two sizes; cars; wheelbarrows; swings; trains; airplanes; animals; trees; bricks; houses; fences; paper; scissors; a not too sharp knife; pencils; chalks or paints; glue; balls and marbles; plasticine; and string. The small sizes of such toys, their number and variety, enable the child to express a wide range of fantasies and experiences. It is important for this purpose that the toys should be nonmechanical and that the human figures, varying only in color and size, should not indicate any particular occupation. Their very simplicity enables the child to use them in many different situations, actual or fantasied, according to the material coming up in his play. The fact that the child can thus simultaneously present a variety of experiences and situations also makes it possible for us to arrive at a more coherent picture of the workings of his mind.

In keeping with the simplicity of the toys, the equipment of the playroom is very simple. It should not contain anything except what is needed for the psychoanalysis. It has a washable floor, running water, a table, a few chairs, a little sofa, some cushions, and a chest of drawers. Each child's playthings are kept locked in one particular drawer, and he therefore knows that his toys and his play with them, which is the equivalent of the adult's associations, will only be known to the psychoanalyst and to himself. The box in which I first introduced the toys . . . turned out to be the prototype of the individual drawer, which is part of the private and intimate relation between analyst and patient, characteristic of the psychoanalytic transference situation.

I do not suggest that the psychoanalytic play technique depends entirely on this particular selection of play material. In any case, children often spontaneously bring their own toys, and the play with them enters as a matter of course into the analytic work. But I believe that on the whole the toys provided by the psychoanalyst should be of the type I have described, that is to say, simple, small, and nonmechanical.

Toys, however, are not the only requisites for a play analysis. I have already mentioned the running water. Many of the child's activities are at times carried out round the basin which is equipped with one or two small bowls, tumblers, and spoons. There are other occupations, such as drawing and painting, cutting-out, writing, and repairing of broken toys. At times, the child plays games in which he allots roles to the psychoanalyst and himself, for instance, playing shop, doctor and patient, school, or mother and child. In such games, he often takes the part of the adult, thereby not only expressing his wish to reverse the roles, but also demonstrating how he feels the parents or other people in authority behave toward him or *should* behave. Sometimes he gives vent to his aggressiveness and resentment by being sadistic, in the role of parent, toward the child, represented by the psychoanalyst. The principle of interpretation remains the same whether the fantasies are presented by toys or by dramatization. For, whatever the material used, it is essential that the psychoanalytic principles underlying the technique be applied. I have elsewhere (Klein, 1927; 1929; 1932) given instances both of play with toys and of the games described above.

Aggressiveness is expressed in various ways in the child's play, either directly or indirectly. Often a toy is broken or, when the child is more aggressive, attacks are made with knife or scissors on the table or on pieces of wood; water or paint is splashed about, and the room generally becomes a battlefield. It is essential to enable the child to bring out his aggressiveness, but what counts most is to understand why at this particular moment in the transference situation destructive impulses come up and to observe their consequences in the child's mind. Feelings of guilt may very soon follow after the child has broken, for instance, a little figure. Such guilt refers not only to the actual damage done, but to what the toy stands for in the child's unconscious, e.g., a little brother or sister, or a parent. The interpretation has, therefore, to deal with these deeper levels as well. Sometimes, we can gather from the child's behavior toward the psychoanalyst that not only guilt but also persecutory anxiety has been the sequel to his destructive impulses and that he is afraid of retaliation.

I have usually been able to convey to the child that I would not tolerate physical attacks on myself. This attitude not only protects the psychoanalyst, but is of importance for the analysis as well. For such assaults, if not kept within bounds, are apt to stir up excessive guilt and persecutory anxiety in the child and therefore add to the difficulties of the treatment. I have sometimes been asked by what method I prevented physical attacks, and I think the answer is that I was very careful not to inhibit the child's aggressive *fantasies;* in fact he was given opportunity to act them out in other ways, including verbal attacks on myself. Moreover, I did not show disapproval or annoyance at the child's aggressive desires and was usually able to interpret their deeper motives in time and thus to keep the situation under control. This was not always so; with some psychotic children I occasionally found it difficult to protect myself against their aggressiveness.

I found that the child's attitude toward a toy he has damaged is very revealing. He often puts aside such a toy, representing for instance a sibling or a parent, and ignores it for a time. This indicates dislike of the damaged object, due to the persecutory fear that the attacked person (represented by the toy) has become retaliatory and dangerous. The sense of persecution may be so strong that it covers up feelings of guilt and depression which are also aroused by the damage done. Or guilt and depression may be so strong that they lead to a reinforcing of persecutory feelings. However, one day the child may search in his drawer for the damaged toy. This suggests that by then the psychoanalyst has been able to diminish persecutory feelings, thus making it possible for the sense of guilt and the urge to make reparation to be experienced. When this happens we can also notice that a change in the child's relation to the particular sibling for whom the toy stood, or in his relations in general, has occurred; and this confirms that persecutory anxiety has diminished and that, together with the sense of guilt and the wish to make reparation, feelings of love, which had been impaired by excessive anxiety, have come to the fore. With another child, or with the same child at a later stage of the psychoanalysis, guilt and the wish to repair may follow very soon after the act of aggression, and tenderness toward the brother or sister, damaged in fantasy, may become apparent. The importance of such changes for character formation and relations to other people, as well as for mental stability, cannot be overrated.

It is an essential part of the interpretative work that it should keep in step with fluctuations between love and hatred, between happiness and satisfaction on the one hand and persecutory anxiety and depression on the other. This implies that the psychoanalyst should not show disapproval of the child's having broken a toy; he should not, however, encourage the child to express his aggressiveness, nor suggest to him that the toy could be mended. In other words, he should enable the child to experience his emotions and fantasies as they come up. It was always part of my technique not to use educational or moral influence, but to keep to the psychoanalytic procedure only, which —in a nutshell—consists in understanding the patient's mind and in conveying to him what goes on in it. . . .

## *Techniques of Therapy*

ALAN O. ROSS

. . . Once the therapist has structured the situation for the child, he will find that some children will be able to enter play activity immediately and without direct assistance, while others need considerable help. Depending on the manifest needs of the child, the therapist should either take a passive, observing role or an active, participating one. Though one may wish to help the child verbalize that he finds the unstructured nature of the situation a little "scary," it is important not to let his discomfort become so acute that the experience takes on negative valence. As Solomon (1948) has observed, passivity can be carried to the danger point. If the child cannot decide on any activity at all and refuses to follow the invitation to explore the available toys, the therapist may wish to suggest that they explore the room together, in the extreme case giving the child a more structured choice of two or three activities from which to pick one. Under the approach here described, it is rarely, if ever, necessary for the therapist to propose a specific game, and this should be avoided since by doing so he assumes the role of the dominating adult, paving the way for the child's generalizations from other adults to the therapist.

The therapist must attempt to establish himself in the role of an interested, understanding, helpful adult to whom the child and his concerns are of primary importance. He has to be a reasonable, nonpunitive, consistent figure who, while going along with the child's wishes, is able to adhere to clearly defined limits in a consistent fashion. In order to play this role, the therapist and his approach must be flexible enough to permit him to enter actively into the child's games, if the child indicates that this is what he wants, or to remain passively on the sidelines without trying to impel the child in directions in which he is not ready to move. Again, it is important to remember that a lot of meaningful material is being produced, and many significant experiences are being absorbed by the child even when *nothing* appears to be happening. One's need to produce tangible results must not make one attempt to dominate the situation. Given a therapeutic setting, the recuperative powers of the patient's ego will bring conflictual material to the surface where the therapist, always alert to significant cues, can use it to help the child understand his feelings and handle his conflicts. Remembering the various forms—dramatic, symbolic, and social—in which play activity can bring emotional difficulties to expression, the therapist must stand ready to label or interpret such expression to the child at the appropriate time, thus utilizing play to introduce and facilitate discussion on a verbal level. If he feels that his patient is not ready for such discussion or if he fails to recognize a cue in time, because of his necessarily sincere involvement in play activity, he can rest assured that, if the material thus expressed is at all significant, it will come out again in a different context at a later time, provided the therapist has done nothing to discourage such expression. The latter can occur when the therapist, instead of merely joining the child's activity at the child's explicit or implicit invitation, assumes a guiding role, interfering with the child's expression by giving it a different direction, thereby "changing the subject" and indicating that the particular form of expression the child has chosen is undesirable. Activity must not turn into dominance, passivity must not imply disinterest, and neither constant activity nor constant passivity can be the mode of participation for every patient or, in fact, for any patient all of the time. The skilled therapist must adapt his behavior to the specific needs of the child at any particular phase of treatment.

Some children may be most comfortable in engaging in a specific activity if the therapist is busy with a parallel function. Thus, a patient may decide to do fingerpainting and hand the therapist a piece of paper of his own. In a situation of this nature, the therapist must guard against dictating the content of the painting by having his production serve as a model for the child to copy. The child who asks his therapist to make a fingerpainting of his own is looking for explicit permission to use the medium with its smearing implications and the therapist can be the model in this respect, demonstrating that it is all right to use the whole hand and not just the tip of one finger, but he should not usurp leadership in the creative expression to which the medium is to be put. Playing along with, not playing ahead of, the child is the important feature. If the child paints a snake because he is copying the therapist's snake, the therapist's needs and not the child's conflicts are finding expression.

A child's specific questions and requests often create special problems for which experience with adult therapy gives little preparation. Asking questions is the child's way of evaluating and exploring reality, and inquiries addressed to the therapist frequently have the same function. Take, for example, the question, "Do you have children of your own?" If, as in adult therapy, one responds to this with, "I wonder why you ask?" one will, more often than not, receive the answer, "Because I want to know," which is, indeed, the reason why the child has asked. An adult asking a similar question may be expressing negativism, transference, hostility, or resistance. A child often asks because, as a child, he has to try and find his place in the world by discovering what the world is like and who belongs where and to whom. Deflecting his question by interpreting the unconscious reasons for asking it (such as sibling rivalry) can inhibit further questioning by demonstrating to the child that his therapist is not interested in the things which concern him most. A realistic question deserves a realistic answer, particularly since the child therapist must help the child not only with his unconscious conflicts but also with his ego development. Before answering a question, however, one must give the child an opportunity to express his fantasies and wishes. The first response to the question about the therapist's children might thus be, "How would you like it to be?"; and if the child later repeats his original question, trying to check his fantasies against reality, a factual reply is indicated. The classical requirement of the therapist's anonymity, of his being a blank screen for the patient's projections, must be greatly modified in the play therapy of children; one cannot long remain anonymous if one joins in a game of "cops and robbers"!

Questions of a religious nature are often among the most difficult to answer. Where therapist and child have different religious backgrounds and values, the therapist must be careful not to bring his own views into conflict with those of the child's parents. Instead of immediately answering a question dealing, for example, with the creation of man, it is well to find out the child's version and who told him about it. One may then want to explore what doubts, if any, the child has about this version, a procedure which frequently reveals conflicting sources of information in the child's background. Finally, the therapist may wish to point out that different people believe in different stories, telling, if the child asks for it, his own version in a straightforward, unemotional manner.

Questions about sex should be handled in a similar manner. Here again it is desirable to explore the child's fantasies and the source and nature of his own knowledge. If, as frequently happens, the child has inadequate, incomplete, or inaccurate information originating with his parents, it is best to explain that his parents, at the time they told him, may have thought that he was not old enough to understand but that the therapist, knowing that the child is old enough, will tell him how these things really are. It is important that the caseworker of the child's parents has previously told them that, when the issue arises, the therapist will discuss questions of sex with the child and that he will do so in a frank manner. Unless parents have been prepared for this, they can become greatly embarrassed and upset to the point of withdrawing the child from treatment when they discover from something the child tells them that the therapist has been discussing such "awful" things with their offspring.

The child's request for sexual information may be either expressed or implied, and in either case the therapist must be prepared to supply adequate answers without overloading the child with facts or taking the topic beyond the immediately relevant. The child's own names for the various anatomic organs and functions should be ascertained, substituting, where necessary, the "grown-up" word for it. Particular care must be taken to help the child distinguish between organs where semantic confusions might contribute to primitive fantasies and distortions. Many children with fantasies about oral impregnation have been told that babies grow in the mother's stomach, and the confusion between feces and fetuses often stems from inadequate differential labeling of anus and vagina. Proper labeling is an important aspect of providing sexual information, and drawing simple sketches or showing pictures from a book can greatly facilitate the discussion. Depending on the child's individual concerns, his first questions to his therapist may be either about insemination or parturition. Discussion should be limited to whichever aspect the child is interested in, leaving the other until such time as the child is ready to inquire about it.

A specific problem which often arises in the course of therapy is the child patient's request to be permitted to take a toy home with him. Such a demand has different meanings for different children and may even differ in its implications for the same child at different times during treatment. The underprivileged, deprived child may be seeking to supplement his meager belongings with toys from the playroom; the child who is acting out a sibling problem may wish to deprive other patients of a particularly desirable toy; the child who sees therapy as a very positive experience may wish to symbolically take part of the experience home; the child who fears rejection may wish to make certain that he *has* to come back next time to return the borrowed toy, or, following an aggressive act, he may wish to test the therapist's continued affection by soliciting a present from him. Whatever the meaning of the request, the therapist must be able to utilize it to further treatment by making an adequate interpretation or an appropriate response. Generally, it is best to limit the taking home of objects to those things which the child has made during the treatment session, such as paintings, plaster of Paris moldings, or cardboard and paper constructions. Beyond these items, one should set and consistently adhere to a reality limit, pointing out that the toys will still be there the next time the child comes and that he can play with them in the playroom whenever he wants to. If one fails to set this limit, one may not only reinforce a child's neurotic behavior but one can also encounter an acute problem should the next patient find *his* favorite toy missing. Some therapists find it helpful to keep a supply of candy on hand since the symbolic meaning of "eating together" helps some children to establish a relationship more quickly, while with others a piece of candy can act as an acceptable substitute for the toy they want to take home. Eventually, of course, successful therapy should obviate these oral rewards, but until that stage is reached an occasional apple or stick of chewing gum can have great value. . . .

# *Problems in the Playroom*

HAIM G. GINOTT

## *Children's Interviewing Techniques*

Children get to know the therapist through tricky interviewing techniques of their own. They probe the therapist ingeniously, and, in an amazingly brief time, they learn more about the therapist than he does about them. Their most common initial approach to the therapist is to ask him questions that seem rather puzzling to an adult. The child picks up a toy and says, "What is this?" The therapist may answer with a question—"What is it?" The child will reply, "A gun." He will then pick up another toy and ask, "What is this?" The therapist will say, "What is it?" The child will reply, "It's a boat." This duet may go on throughout the first session.

What is the purpose of this peculiar conversation? This stylized talk is to children what discussing the weather is to newly acquainted adults: an opportunity to scrutinize each other before delving into more intimate material.

Johnny, aged eight, spends almost half of his first session questioning the therapist about the use of the toys in the playroom. He then switches to more subtle methods of investigation. He starts writing the word "playroom" on the board, but he spells it "pleyroom." He turns to the therapist and says, "Is this the right spelling?" This is not a simple request for information. Johnny, with an IQ of 130, may or may not have known how to spell "playroom." But what he really wants to know is the therapist's attitude toward misspellers. Understanding this, the therapist does not rush to give the "right" spelling. He does not assume the conventional role of a teacher. Instead, he says, "In here you can spell any way you want to."

But Johnny is not convinced, and he gives the therapist another test. He writes an arithmetic problem on the board and makes a mistake in simple addition. He asks the therapist to check the answers for him. Again the therapist is careful not to fall into the conventional role that Johnny has cast for him. He says, "In here you can add any way you want to."

Johnny learns a great deal from his spelling and arithmetic exercises. He learns that the clinic is a unique place, that the playroom is not a school, and that the therapist is not a teacher.

Next Johnny picks up a splintered plastic car and asks in a righteous tone, "Who broke the car?" What he really wants to know is what happened to the boy who broke the car. Understanding the question, the therapist gives a reassuring answer—"Sometimes toys get broken. It happens."

Johnny gets quite a bit of information with his car question. He learns that this grownup does not get angry easily, even when toys are broken, and that there is no need to be overcautious or to walk a tightrope in the playroom.

Next Johnny says, "My teacher gave me a spanking." The therapist does not ask him for further factual details but says softly, "It must have hurt your feelings and made you good and mad, too." There is a mile-wide smile on Johnny's face as he replies with a very long "Yeah-h-hh." Johnny's interviewing skill has again proved valuable. He has learned that the therapist does not blame children for school troubles and that he can talk to him without being lectured.

Finally Johnny says, "You have so many closets in here. What do you have in them?" The therapist answers, "You want to look and see?" Again Johnny obtains very pertinent information; it is all right to be curious in the playroom without being reminded that curiosity killed the cat. By responding to the hidden meanings of the questions, the therapist not only conveys deep understanding to the child but helps him to get a clearer picture of the therapist and the therapy situation.

### *The Therapist's Language*

The therapist must exercise great caution in formulating responses to the child's communications. In his mirroring of feelings, the therapist should usually repeat the symbols used by the child. When a child points to the family dolls and says, "She hates the boy," the therapist should not identify the symbols, transparent as they may be. He should not say, "Mother hates you" or "Mother hates the boy." He should reflect the statement prudently—"She hates the boy" or "She hates him." The child should be the one to assume the responsibility for naming the objects of his feelings.

There are occasions, however, when the therapist must avoid using the child's symbols. When a child makes obscene or offensive remarks, the therapist should not sanction such expressions by including them in his own speech. For instance, when a child says, "My brother is a louse," the therapist should reply, "That's what you think of him" or "You don't like your brother," omitting the offensive expressions. The therapist should also avoid repeating unacceptable racial slurs. When a child says, "I don't play with niggers," the therapist may reply, "You don't play with them" or "You don't like them." He should never give sanction to bigotry by his own use of unacceptable terms.

The therapist should pay careful attention to children's reactions to his reflections. Some children like their words sounded back to them without any change, like an echo. The following excerpts will serve as illustrations:

JIMMY: I like the color blue.
THERAPIST: You prefer blue.
JIMMY: I didn't say "prefer"; I said I like blue.
THERAPIST: Oh, you like blue.
JIMMY: That's better.

JIMMY: I don't paint well.
THERAPIST: You don't think you can paint?
JIMMY: I can paint. I just can't paint well.

Other children soon become aware of the therapist's technique of mirroring feelings, and they may be annoyed by it. They say, "Why do you always say what I say?" or "I knew you were going to say that." When this happens, it is time to change techniques. The therapist should reflect the child's feelings in his own words. For instance, when a child says, "I want to go out," the therapist will reply, "Oh, that's what you want to do." When the child relates some incident, the therapist will say, "That's what happened" or "That's what you think of it," etc.

## *To Play or Not to Play: The Therapist's Dilemma*

One of the controversial issues to be determined in advance by every play therapist is whether or not to participate *with* a child in his play and games. Children frequently try to involve the therapist in playing tick-tack-toe, checkers, or ball.

Therapists who believe in playing with children have two different rationales. Some do so because they believe in acting the part of an ideal parent. They are impressed with the role of parental cruelty in the etiology of childhood neurosis, and they aim to neutralize the ill effects of early unkindness with a second edition of motherly love. They believe that, in order to get well, children need not only interpretations and insight but also the kind of warmth and tenderness refused to them in infancy. They maintain that such human kindness can be supplied best by a therapist who is a loving participant and not just a permissive observer. These therapists do not hesitate to participate actively in children's games and consider such activities a logical part of their "parental" role.

Other therapists play with child clients in order to induce regression and eliminate resistance to therapy. They attempt to win the child's confidence by eliminating the traditional distance between adult and child. They intentionally devalue their adult status by participating in playroom activities on a child's level; they may sit on the floor, take part in the child's play, and compete with the child in rivalrous games. All this is done in the hope of overcoming resistance to therapy.

The writer believes that therapy is retarded when the therapist participates with the child in play activities, either as "parent" or "playmate." The unique therapeutic role can be best carried out when the play therapist maintains a nonplaying relationship with the child, thus assuring that the session is strictly the child's hour.

There are few advantages and many disadvantages in playing with children. The main disadvantage is that it enables the child to exploit the adult mercilessly. The child starts the session with an innocent, "Let's throw the ball to each other" and ends by sitting comfortably in the therapist's chair while the adult is running and retrieving balls.

If the child wants to play ball, he may throw it at the wall or to group mates. If he wants to play tick-tack-toe, the therapist may say, "You choose for me and for you, and I'll watch." If he starts shooting darts and requests or demands that the therapist retrieve them, he may be told softly, "You get them if you want to." Otherwise, the therapy hour may turn into a running race in which most of the running will be done by the therapist. Such sessions may arouse annoyance and antagonism in the therapist toward the child. The therapist does not like the hourly runaround, and the child knows it. As one child commented to his therapist, "You don't like to do this, but you have to because you are paid." The therapist feebly defended himself with, "I do it because I like you," but the child was not convinced.

In fact, such sessions do not create warmth in the therapist or security in the child. There can be little healing value in allowing a child to manipulate an adult. Effective therapy must be based on mutual respect between the child and the therapist, without the therapist's ever abdicating his adult therapeutic role. . . .

## *Some Commonsense Don'ts*

*No Tuxedos.* Napoleon is credited with the saying that he who goes into a battle should not wear his best pants because they would interfere with his military zeal. This advice pertains also to child therapists. A play therapist should not come to the playroom dressed in his best suit. The anxiety and effort entailed in keeping clothes clean will interfere with the therapist's ability to maintain free-floating attention.

*No Smoking.* The therapist should refrain from smoking in the playroom. The possible symbolic meanings of striking a match, lighting a fire, and holding a cigarette in the mouth should not be overlooked. Also, the children may come from homes in which smoking is synonymous with sin. The therapist should not introduce unnecessary conflicts of values. And perhaps the most important reason against playroom smoking is that during therapy the therapist should be neither occupied nor preoccupied with his own pleasures.

*No Gifts.* Some children bring an arsenal of chocolates, chewing gum, and candy to the playroom, and they offer it generously to the therapist. It is advisable not to accept gifts from children, especially during the first sessions. The therapist may say, "Thank you, but you keep it. I don't feel like having gum." If the child offers his painting or clay work to the therapist, the therapist should acknowledge it by saying neutrally, "You want me to have it." He will then let the child put the painting wherever he wants—in the therapist's hands, out on the table, or in the closet.

*No Autobiography.* Infrequently the therapist will encounter children who try to interview him directly, as though taking his case history. They do not hesitate to ask many personal questions of the most intimate nature. It is not necessary for the therapist to give the children a detailed autobiography. The therapist may reflect the fact that the child wonders about him and wants to get to know him better. Frequently such a response will stop this inquisition. The therapist's responses to specific questions should be truthful, short, and general. Thus:

CHILD: Where do you come from?
THERAPIST: From up north.
CHILD: Where do you live?
THERAPIST: In town.

## *Who Cleans the Playroom?*

It is inadvisable to make the child clean up the playroom at the end of the play hour. Such a demand may seem too authoritarian to a child and may inhibit his free play. It may also give the rebellious child an opportunity to dirty the walls, the furniture, and the therapist's clothes, all in the name of careful cleaning. Another disadvantage is that it puts the therapist in an evaluative role of judging the child's cleanup performance. Nor should the therapist subtly encourage children to clean up the playroom. Statements such as "I see you are careful to put toys away after you use them" may boomerang. Axline (1947, p. 81)[5] tells of a young child in group therapy who spilled some paint and wiped it up. The therapist said: "Bobby is careful; he wiped up the paint that he spilled." From that moment on, the therapy hour turned into a competition between the boys to show the therapist how careful they could be. The therapist himself does not clean the playroom during the session, except to remove dangerous objects. If a bottle is broken accidentally, the therapist may comment, "The bottle broke" and then proceed to remove the broken glass or sweep the floor.

It is essential that the therapist should not be the one to clean up the playroom, session after session. A maid should do it. A therapist can be much more accepting of sandstorms and smeary messes when he knows that someone else will sweep the floors and tackle the toys. It is not an easy task to keep the playroom in order, especially in a community clinic where the playroom is used almost continuously for both individual and group therapy. The playroom must be rearranged before each appointment so that the activities of children will not be influenced by the playroom arrangements of preceding sessions. The playroom is a miniature world to the child, and the neatly arranged playroom symbolizes that the world can be orderly. The playroom must be neat in the beginning of each session, with the floor swept, broken toys removed, paints and clay in working order, and the nursing bottles sterilized and refilled. This job requires the services of a professional maid. The therapist should be able to rest in the interlude between sessions and meditate about life outside the playroom. . . .

## REFERENCES

AXLINE, VIRGINIA. *Play therapy*. Boston: Houghton Mifflin, 1947.

KLEIN, MELANIE. Criminal tendencies in normal children. *Brit. J. med Psychol.*, 1927, **7**, 177–192.

KLEIN, MELANIE. Personification in the play of children. *Internat. J. Psa.*, 1929, **10**, 193–204.

KLEIN, MELANIE. *The psychoanalysis of children*. London: Hogarth Press, 1932.

SOLOMON, J. C. Play technique. *Amer. J. Orthopsychiat.*, 1948, **18**, 402–413.

[5] See Chapter 5, p. 97, of this book for Axline's discussion.

## CHAPTER SEVEN

# Limits and the Handling of Aggression

THE PROBLEM of limits raises specific questions of what, when, where, and how. Most therapists would agree that children should not be permitted to injure either themselves or the therapist or to destroy property at will. But, given these basic postulates, the kind and degree are legion, and each therapist will need to consider what his interpretation of injury and damage will be. The question arises as to whether the therapist should clearly specify limits in advance or wait until a *verboten* act is underway.

Should situations that might require limits be kept to a minimum, or do children seek until they find an activity that will need to be restricted? Conversely, is it possible to have too many limits? Should we become concerned about a child who never tries to see how far he can go?

The actual words used in stating a prohibition may become significant in conveying a sense of impartiality, security, personal pique, impulsive authoritarianism, or uncertainty on the part of the therapist. Below are similar ways in which a limit against shooting the therapist could be stated, yet each conveys a different attitude and perspective.

I don't think we'd better do that.
I can't let you do that.
There's a rule you can't do that.
No shooting at people.
You must not do that.

You can't do that.
You can shoot at the target, but not at me.
We can't do that.

If a limit is defied, then what should be done? Should the child ever be dismissed from the room?[1] If one decides to remove the child, just how is this carried out? Is the child put into the hall for the other clinic personnel to handle, or does the therapist accompany the child back to the waiting room? In either case, what will happen next?

These questions have been asked in terms of procedural techniques. But it cannot be stressed too strongly that even after a course of action has been decided on the situation remains extremely important from the therapeutic standpoint. Why is the child "testing the limits"? What are his feelings and reactions to being restrained? What other emotional associations are being activated? Whom does the therapist symbolically become? How can the child be helped to gain insight into the emotions that are exploding? And how is the therapist handling his own feelings at this point?

While a discussion of limits considers reasons for and ways of restricting and binding the expression of aggressive impulses, consideration also needs to be given to the therapeutic handling of the allowable aggression. Various articles throughout this volume include pertinent material, but none take this subject as their main focus. Consequently, more space is devoted to the topic at this point. Assuming that suitable limits will be decided on and imposed when necessary, two points are still crucial to the handling of aggression: What is the meaning of the aggressive act to the child? To what extent should the therapist participate in the aggression?

Should we infer, if a child engages in aggressive shooting, beating up Bobo, biting the toys, and burying soldiers in the sand, that this is always a symbolic representation of his hostile wishes toward others? Cannot such activities also represent the child's fear of being the object of aggression, his panic at prospects of annihilation, his need to suffer, or the working-through of past traumas and the attempted

---

[1] The two selections by Bixler and Ginott present opposing views on this question.

mastery of fears? How can we determine whether aggressive acts represent the desire to punish or the need to be punished? Is the child identifying with the attacker or with the victim in these play representations? Or is the play a condensed symbol incorporating active *and* passive components of the aggression? Interpretations or reflections may entirely miss the mark if the therapist's assumptions are not correct; and the patient may withdraw under the added threat of misunderstanding on the part of the adult.

Sometimes children are more obvious in attacking themselves—aiming a dart at the ceiling so that it bounces back on them, shooting at their reflections in the mirror, or shooting quite directly at their stomachs and hands. Here again, adequate interpretation of the need for this particular behavior at this particular time seems important.

Will reflections of the child's active aggressive feelings reinforce aggressive behavior or allow for catharsis? Is the wording of these reflections important? For example, if a child is shooting at parent doll figures, is there any difference in effect if we say, "You like to kill them," "You really want to kill them," or "Sometimes you get so mad you just feel like shooting everybody." Should the therapist spontaneously, or if invited, shoot at these parent figures along with the patient? What if the child has set up opposing camps of cowboys and Indians and wants the therapist to shoot for one side?

And finally, what happens when the therapist allows himself to get caught in the trap of shooting at the child? The child's requests always sound so innocuous—a simple game of cops and robbers with the dart guns or throwing ping pong balls or water balloons—and he begs and insists he really wants the therapist to participate. Careful analysis of the sequence of events preceding this request may give clues to the deeper aspects of the game. What would being shot at by the therapist represent to the child? Why is he wanting to pit himself against the stronger adult? Is there some reason for the child, at this moment, to need to defeat the therapist or to be "punished" by him?

As important as observation of the play episodes leading to an aggressive act is awareness of the sequelae of behavior and affect subsequent to the event. Murphy and Krall,[2] in a discussion of children's free play, suggest using a "process analysis" much as in Rorschach interpretation. With specific reference to aggression they state, "The process analysis tells us what the child is doing with his play—whether a discharge of aggression is followed by relaxation and constructive activity, by peace-making efforts and restoration, by fear of retaliation, by guilt, or just by more and more aggression." The skillful therapist will be alert to the particular affects that follow each aggressive episode and communicate some of this awareness to the child.

# ❀ *Limits Are Therapy*

RAY H. BIXLER

Restriction of behavior is one of the few universal elements in therapy. Limits have a role in all treatment methods, whether the client is adult or child, withdrawn or aggressive. It may be this very universality which accounts for the scanty material available in the literature. Obvious differences in therapy are sufficiently stimulating and threatening to hold our attention in spite of the fact that problems common to all therapies are being resolved at an equally rudimentary level. The role of limits on behavior may be more important than our current interest in them would indicate.

In the play interview the therapist will encounter children who refuse to accept the limits, who kick the therapist, mar his wall, and throw his desk calendar on the floor in spite of verbalized limits and clarified feelings. The literature reveals few suggestions for dealing with this phase of play therapy. Allen (1942) emphasizes the essential role of limits and stresses their importance, but omits discussion of what he does when limits are broken. Axline (1947, pp. 132–133) acknowledges that limits are broken.

> Now, what about the child who breaks the limitation? Suppose he aims the block at the window and, although his feeling is recognized and he is told not to throw it there, he does so anyway. Usually the recognition of his feeling

---

[2] Lois B. Murphy and Vita Krall, "Free Play as a Projective Tool," in *Projective Techniques with Children*, Albert I. Rabin and Mary R. Haworth, eds. (New York: Grune & Stratton, Inc., 1960), pp. 290–304, p. 298.

> is sufficient to bring down the block; but suppose this time it doesn't. The therapist should be alert to the possibility that he may not put the block down. She should try to prevent the throwing of the block if she can do so without engaging in a physical battle with the child. But if the block should go through the window, what then? Should she lecture the child? Put him out of the playroom? Or act as though she really didn't care? Such a situation would be a real challenge to the therapist. She could not temporarily shelve her basic principles. She would not reject the child because he disobeyed her. She would stay right there with her reflection of feelings. "It was important to you to throw it anyway. You wanted to show me that you *would* throw it."

Again the therapist cannot help but wonder what else to do with a child who is going to attack him or permanently mar furnishings unless there is "physical battle."

The most effective method for each therapist in dealing with limits or any other problem he encounters in the interview is probably that method with which he is most comfortable. Believing this to be true, there is, nevertheless, value in understanding the approach of others. This paper is concerned with the theory and practice of limits in therapy with children. Special emphasis is placed upon the problem of refusal to accept limits with accompanying illustrations.

## *Limits Are Necessary*

Most therapists assume that limits are essential. Verbal expression and much of other behavior may be free of regimentation, but the rights, property, and physical well-being of others must be protected. Some therapists limit verbal activity by indirect means, others protest against this, but almost all therapists set limits upon the *range* of *nonverbal* activity.

The obvious value of limits in the orderly operation of the clinic is only one of several functions that limits may serve. The therapist who protects his person and property from physical aggression has an opportunity to feel accepting of the child. The potential loss of personal possessions or the experience of physical discomfort seemingly would create pressures which operate against real acceptance of the child and his attitudes.

There may be another and even more important role in controlling behavior. The child who is allowed remarkable freedom in most of his activity but is rigidly controlled in specific areas seems to differentiate between the therapeutic experience and other relationships. Rather than giving free expression to his attitudes at home, school, or church, he seems to conform to the accepted mores of the environment of the moment. This has been observed in interview and environmental (institutional) therapy with amazing regularity. To the best of this writer's knowledge this is not equally true of children who are experiencing a passive therapy (no limits). This tentative hypothesis would seem worthy of further evaluation and may be amenable to clinical research of relatively exacting nature.

### *Limits Should Be Minimal in Number*

Consensus seems to indicate a minimal number of limits. If the therapist is free to plan his play-therapy room for that purpose alone, many limits become unnecessary. The presence of a desk with desk set, telephone, clock, papers, books, and desk drawers necessitates setting of numerous limits in order to protect property. The same is true for overstuffed chairs and other pieces of furniture which are desirable for adult interviewing. The writer has found it necessary to set limits most frequently on destruction of items associated with his desk. This condition is undesirable because of the numerous limits it places on the child as well as the previously mentioned pressures created in the therapist by potential loss of personal possessions. A playroom such as Axline describes (1947, Ch. 3) minimizes these dangers without eliminating the therapeutic functions of limits.

### *Basic Limits*

Basic limits set by any therapist will tend to differ. In therapy with the writer children are not supposed to: (1) destroy any property or facilities in the room other than play equipment; (2) attack the therapist in any physical sense; (3) stay beyond the time limit of the interview; (4) remove toys from the playroom; (5) throw toys or other material out of the window.

In addition to these rigid limits the therapist employs some relative limits which are invoked rarely and necessitated by the room in which he works. It is necessary to inhibit noise which interferes with therapeutic interviews in other offices and to keep the child from pouring excessive amounts of water on the floor, which is not leak proof. An example of the first limit and the only time it has been invoked was with a group of two children who were pushing a chair and table across the floor. Here the limit was invoked by two other staff members who found that verbal contacts were impossible in their own offices. Sound proofing, a first floor office, and isolation of the playroom from other interviewing offices would minimize these limits.

### *Relative versus Rigid Limits*

Wherever possible it seems desirable to use well-defined limits. Both the child and therapist can achieve greater comfort when confronted with concrete demarcation between acceptable and unacceptable behavior. Such limits are easier to distinguish and are less apt to lead to insecurity on the part of the therapist. For example, there is a clear distinction between hitting the therapist and not hitting him, but the vague transition point between hitting so as to do no harm and hitting to do harm places both therapist and child in tenuous positions. Wherever degree of activity is a consideration in setting limits, therapy may suffer because the nature of demarcation is such as to place both child and therapist in the position of making decisions without criteria. It would appear preferable to limit a child's throwing a ball at the window, splashing water on the therapist, and playing with the articles on his desk on an all-or-none basis, rather than on a basis of the degree of harm to person or things involved.

No matter how hard one may try, it is unlikely that he can remove all relative limits. If for no other reason, the therapist will see many of his "rigid" limits melt before the uncanny ability of the maladjusted child. With consummate ease he manages to place himself squarely on the line of demarcation between acceptable and unacceptable behavior. What extent the therapist may go in setting rigid limits will be determined in part by his own comfort with intangible limits. Undoubtedly some therapists work more easily with a "You can hit me, but not hard," orientation than does this therapist.

### *When Limits Are Established*

There seems to be little or no disagreement upon the optimal time to establish limits. Few therapists set limits prior to the child's attempt to define them. Not until the child threatens to break a limit is he confronted with the request that he refrain from so doing. This avoids a lengthy and incomplete dissertation by the therapist at the onset of treatment. A preliminary discussion of limits is apparently more disturbing to therapists than suddenly confronting the child with specific limitations upon his behavior.

There seems to be ample justification for this point of view. It is impossible for the therapist to outline all limits that will have to be set with any child before the therapeutic relationship develops. Even if this were possible, the relationship would probably be retarded by a "You can do this and that, *but*. . . ." orientation. Furthermore, the initiative for developing the play sessions would be taken from the child by even the most nonauthoritative therapist.

As a result, the child learns what he is permitted to do as he explores and tests the relationship with the therapist. If the latter is oriented primarily to attitudes expressed rather than the content of the child's behavior, any negative potential which could accrue from unexpected limitations seems to be minimized.

### *Mechanics of Setting Limits*

With experience the therapist develops a meaningful system of dealing with behavior which exceeds his acceptable limits. It seems desirable to graduate therapeutic reactions to such behavior. The following steps may be used successfully: (1) reflecting the desire or attitude of the child; (2) verbal expression of the limit; and finally (3) control by physical means of the child's behavior. For example, a child might be angry at the therapist and want to hit him because the therapist will not let the child take a doll home with him. The gradation of limits might take place in some manner similar to the following hypothetical example.

THERAPIST [1]: You're mad at me because I won't let you take the dolly. You want to hit me because you're mad.

[To many children this is sufficient. Acceptance of their desire seems to eliminate need for the act itself.]

CHILD [1]: (*Hits at therapist, who wards off blow if possible.*)

THERAPIST [2]: You're awfully mad at me and want to hurt me. It's all right to be mad at me but you're not supposed to hit me.

[The vast majority of children stop at this point.]

CHILD [2]: (*Tries to kick or hit therapist, who tries to protect self.*)

THERAPIST [3]: If you hit me again you'll have to leave the room for today. You want to hurt me because you're awfully mad at me. If you do hit me you'll have to leave for today.

CHILD [3]: (*Hits at therapist again.*)

[When limits reach the stage of Therapist (3) for the first time, the child almost always challenges this limit. In ensuing interviews it rarely happens that he will do so again.]

THERAPIST [3]: You'll have to leave for today, John. (*Stands up and opens door.*) I'll see you next week—you're awfully mad at me because I won't let you do some of the things you want to do.[a]

At this point the child almost always leaves the room. Only two times in five years has the writer been forced into picking the child up and placing him outside the room. Several children, one of whom is discussed later (Marvin), have continued their attacks in the outer office to the point where it has been necessary to hold them at arm's length.

Perhaps the most significant factor in maintaining the all important therapeutic attitude of acceptance is simply that the therapist receives very little punishment and the time involved is not excessive. Under these conditions it is quite possible to feel acceptance of the child and his attitudes while rejecting a phase of his behavior. If the therapist were to be under the influence of continual attack over a period of time in one interview, he would have to be a very strong personality to keep from rejecting the child and behaving in a puni-

[a] Warning the child that he may be removed from the office may seem like threatening him. There seems to be a very real and clear-cut distinction between threatening and the procedure suggested here. The therapist is not punitive in attitude and he carries out exactly what he says he will do. When he fails to invoke this limit he actually invites more aggressive antisocial acts. The writer is indebted to Virginia H. Bixler, Director of the Vince A. Day Center, for considerable help in clarifying the role of limits in therapy. Opportunity to observe group treatment of aggressive children at the Center has played a major role in the development of this thesis.

tive manner. Even if this were possible, it seems undesirable to allow broken limits, especially where they involve antisocial acts.

The fact that children frequently leave the office with a sense of relief when involved in the third stage of limitations lends credence to the generally held belief that children do want to have their aggressive behavior controlled. This is further substantiated by accompanying positive changes in the child's behavior at home and in his respect for limits in therapy. Clinical experience seems to indicate that *rigid* adherence to behavioral limits accompanied by an acceptance of the attitudes which motivate this behavior serves as the crux of therapy with many aggressive children.

## *Cases of Pat and Marvin*

The following excerpts were taken from play-therapy contacts the writer has had with very aggressive children. They were selected because therapy was "mussy" in spots, thus highlighting the effectiveness of sound limits when they were invoked and because they illustrate many of the extreme problems involved in setting limits.

The first is the case of Patrick Moriarity, ten years old. He was referred to M.P.I. because of uncontrolled aggression in and out of the classroom. He had been expelled from school. In his initial contacts (the record starts with the fifth interview) his aggression was verbal or directed at the toys. In order to partially compensate for the lack of verbatim notes, comments regarding the process of setting limits are added.

> *5-9-47* Pat was very mad at me. He came in and kicked the ball and then with a gleam in his eyes looked around the room. He made several comments about the use of various objects in the room as weapons to be used against me. I mentioned that he was awfully mad at me and thinking up a number of ideas that would hurt me. He acknowledged this. Shortly after this it was necessary to limit his attempt to pour water on the calendar. He spent most of his time today trying to make me mad in one way or another, although it was occasionally interspersed with friendly discussion. He pinched my nose at one point and hit me at another.

It is apparent that Pat broke several limits in this interview. The therapist recognized his hostility and set the limits, but other than defending himself in a physical sense did not invoke limits to make Pat stop his aggression. It may have been desirable to have set and invoked the limit of leaving the office.

> *5-13-47* He started out again today to try to make me mad. First he threw the nipple out of the window, then poured the water out of the nursing bottle. He started to pour it on the table. I limited him. This intensified his trying to make me mad. He got very angry at me because I didn't get mad, but all during this he readily accepted the limits that I set. When I told him it was time to clean up, he made a few moves to do so but did not finish. He asked me what

I would do if he didn't clean up. I told him that that was something I would have to clean up after he left if he didn't do it. That made him quite happy and I recognized his joy at my having to clean up the messes he made.

*5-16-47* In the initial part of the period today there was a marked change in Pat's behavior. It was largely constructive. He talked about, instead of demonstrating, his aggressiveness. After awhile, however, he took the nipple off the bottle, threatened to throw it out and I set a limit on him at this point. He then threw the pegs on the floor. After this episode he started to play and talk in a friendly, constructive way. I mentioned that sometimes he was mad and wanted to make me mad, and sometimes he wanted to play and talk with me. During the rest of the period his antagonism increased, but at no time today did it approach what it has been in the past. This is somewhat difficult to evaluate at this stage in therapy.

The therapist is obviously confused. Speculation about the significance of an attitude of confusion on the part of the therapist leads to the question, "Is what ensues in later contacts a result only of the child's maladjustment, or does the therapist, because of his own uncertainty, create a subtle stimulus pattern which intensifies the youngster's reactions?"

*5-20-47* Pat was very angry. As he came down the hall he struck me from behind and threw himself around in the room when he came in. He took the nursing bottle and tried to break it. His attempts to break it were not very wholehearted at first, pounding it against the radiator easily for quite a period of time. I recognized that he wanted to break it and yet in some ways was a little afraid to do so. At this point he broke it. I said, "You wanted to show me that you weren't afraid. You also wanted very much to make me mad." He was pretty upset about breaking it. I recognized this and told him that he was supposed to clean it up. He began to do so and did quite a bit of the cleaning up. He got angry with me, however, much more so at this point when I didn't get mad because he broke the bottle. He was very hostile and spun my chair around. He quieted down. He asked about my writing and I told him. This upset him, too, and he didn't believe it. I recognized his feeling that I probably was giving it to other people to read. He went to the table, turned his back to me, and spent a long time there, growling. He turned to me and said, "Why do you write to yourself?" I said, "You don't believe I write these things just for myself—you feel pretty sure that I give them to somebody else to read." He responded, "Yeah, I bet you do." He talked about eating me up and other savory forms of getting rid of me. I mentioned that he was awfully mad at me and wished he could get rid of me, that he was pretty unhappy because I didn't let him do some of the things he wanted to do. At this point he came over and hit me. The time was about up and I told him it was time to clean up the water on the floor, and he asked me what I would do if he didn't. I told him, "Nothing." He said, "Who would clean it up?" I said, "I would." He threw the rag on the floor. I mentioned that it was a lot of fun to think that I would be the one who would have to clean up any mess that he left. He was pleased by this and then gradually became more angry again—apparently because I didn't get angry.

Note the intense frustration Pat experiences in his relationship with the therapist. This may be due to Pat's inability to control the therapist's emotional reactions and to the therapist's fuzzy reaction to Pat's struggle with limits.

> *5-23-47* Pat checked on the things he had done last time to see if they were still the way they were and looked outside to see if the nipple was there and at the back of the doll to see if it were still broken. He played quietly at the sink for awhile, then he came over to me and hit me on the head. I limited this behavior and mentioned that he was still pretty angry at me. He went over to the sink again where he played for quite awhile—then he came to me for help with opening the gun. I mentioned that he was having a lot of fun playing. He was very intent on his work and a moment later I mentioned that sometimes he liked to do things to make me mad and other times he just liked to play. He played a little while longer and then came over and tried to throw water on me. When I limited him he returned and dropped the gun behind the radiator. He played quietly for quite awhile. It was apparent that he was trying to destroy the doll. He was trying to tear or hurt it, and when I recognized this at the time when our time was just about up he suddenly flew into a very intense rage and attacked me. He has become more and more frustrated because he has been unable to make me mad.

Note that the therapist seems to feel that Pat's frustration is due solely to his inability to anger the therapist.

> *5-29-47* Pat came into the room and immediately became aggressive. He tried to destroy the doll and was unable to. He poured water on the floor from the nursing bottle and when he began to fill it up the second time to throw it on the floor, I told him that he could throw two bottles of water on the floor but no more; that if he poured more, he would have to leave the room. He dumped the second bottle and immediately filled it up and started to pour a third. He left readily when I invoked the limit.

This seems long overdue. Invoking of the limit was consummated while the therapist was still calm and able to accept Pat's attitudes. In the next interview Pat's mother reported marked improvement for the first time.

> *6-4-47* Pat refused to come in and hung around the door for ten or fifteen minutes. As soon as he came in he threw the ball out of the window. I warned him and then he threw a doll out and I sent him from the room again.

Again the limit was invoked quickly. This approach to therapy appears to be far removed from what is considered good counseling. Ensuing interviews and the change in behavior reported by Pat's mother would indicate that therapy is taking place.

> *6-11-47* He was mad today. He didn't know why or at whom and was able to say so. He spent most of his time talking in a friendly way with me. There were

only two mildly aggressive acts during the period. He worked awfully hard to be good during the period, and I recognized this. I said that in many ways he wanted to be good and it was pretty hard to be good. This is encouraging in light of the improvement that has taken place outside of interviews. It may be an indication that we are drawing near a close in this treatment situation.

The improvement noted at home appears for the first time in the play interviews. This is not a dramatic example of the role of limits in therapy, rather it is typical. The child as well as the adult receives much security from external control of his antisocial acts.

*6-20-47* Pat was much better today. His only aggressive act during the whole period was to tear my blotter and drop it on the floor. I asked him when he thought he would want to stop coming to see me, and he was not able to answer this question at this point, saying, "I don't know."

Since this interview there has been no significant trouble at school or at home. Visiting teachers report that his behavior is exemplary. His mother called up the first week of school this fall because the principal did not want to admit him. He has been admitted and is a "changed boy." Undoubtedly more forthright limits in the earlier contacts would have brought this change about sooner. At this date, May, 1948, he still retains this level of adjustment.

*6-27-47* Today Pat was very constructive in his behavior. No aggressive acts toward me were apparent. He expressed some feeling about coming in, and I brought up the question of whether or not he wanted to continue. He thought at first he would like to come in three times, then he changed it to one time and finally to two times. He and I went in and spoke to Mrs. Wood and his mother about it and they decided they would come in for two half-hour appointments.

*7-11-47* Pat was somewhat uncomfortable today, and I brought up the fact that he would be seeing me one more time and he growled "Yeah." I said, "Maybe you would be happier if this were the last time." He looked at me and smiled and said, "Yes." So I called Mrs. Wood to see if it would be possible to make it the last time as far as Pat's mother was concerned. She felt it would be and I told Pat, who felt very good about this. There was no evidence of hostility today. He was somewhat troubled, found it a little difficult to break with me, but at the same time maintained the improvement that he has demonstrated in the last few interviews.

Marvin was five years old. His aggressive and infantile behavior had caused a nursery school and later a kindergarten to expel him. He threw numerous temper tantrums, especially in public places. He was very fearful and used his fear to control his mother. Several contacts had preceded the first described here. These had been in the presence of his mother. (Fearful children usually can give up their parents in one or two interviews. By letting the parents come with the child if he so desires, the trauma of separation is avoided by starting at the level which is feasible for the child. Marvin was unable to make this transition. An intermediate stage was initiated to let his mother see a psychiatric social worker. He was told he could come in to see me if he desired.)

*2-19-47* As soon as I came to the waiting room, Marvin shouted, "I'm not going with that old stinker Bixler." I said, "You're not going to have anything to do with me. You're awfully mad at me." He did not come into my office at all during the period, but as they got ready to leave I came out and he started calling me all sorts of names. This was more in a teasing rather than angry fashion, and I mentioned that sometimes he got awfully mad at me and wanted to call me names, and at other times it was fun to tease me by calling me names. He continued this for some time, calling me an old stinker, a pooh-pooh, a Mr. Grease, and other names. Twice he kicked my foot and several times made as if to hit or kick me on the shin. After I went back to my office he came back to it twice, stuck his head around, and yelled that I was an old stinker. The second time I said "Hi," and he shouted "Mind your own business." After he was fully dressed to leave, he and his mother came back because he wanted to say good-by to me. He stepped completely into the office and said, "Good-by, you old mind-your-own business" and shouted as he went down the hall that I was an old pooh-pooh.

Setting and controlling limits in an outer office is difficult. Where a child continues his attack it would usually seem better to separate from him at the door of the play-therapy room.

*3-4-47* Last week Marvin refused to come to the room and called me names when I was in the waiting room, expressing this more in a mingled anger and teasing than pure anger. About midway through our period I came out and told him that if he would like to come into the office he could come. Otherwise I was going down for coffee. He said he didn't want to see me so I went on out. He did apparently come to the office later on while I was out and was disappointed. His mother had told me at the initial part of the contact that Marvin was very anxious to come today.

Contact on *3-4-47*. When I went out to get Marvin he shouted, "I'm not going in your office today." He called me an "old stinker" and several other names. I mentioned that he was awfully mad at me and didn't want to have anything to do with me; that he could come down later if he wanted to and I would be in the room. As I went to the office he followed me a short distance and stopped short of the door. He then came to the door, peeked around it, and screamed at the top of his voice. I mentioned that he was afraid to come in, yet he wanted to come in—he couldn't decide whether to do so or not. He rushed out of the room again. He returned to the door, screamed in anger, came in and pounded on the peg board. He hit my foot at this point. I mentioned that he was afraid of me and mad at me, but that he must not hit me. He went back and hit the pounding board some more.

I mentioned that he was awfully afraid and mad and when he was like that he felt like making a lot of noise. He rushed out of the room again into Mrs. Wood's (psychiatric social worker) office, then out of there and back very quickly. He started to pound, looked at me, expressing both anger and fear, which I recognized. "You B.M.", he shouted. "When you're mad at me you feel like calling me names." "You ham. I'll smash you in the jaw." I mentioned that he was awfully mad at me and would like to hurt me, and yet he was afraid of me, too. He pounded on the peg board and counted in a shout "1, 2, 3," and so on up to ten. I mentioned that it helped to make a lot of noise when he felt like he did. He said, "Shut up. None of your business," and rushed over and hit me. I again limited him.

He went to the chair on the other side of the room and said, "I can hit you if I want to." I mentioned that he wanted to hit me and yet was afraid of me. He came over and swung the mallet very close to my face and I jumped. He smiled. I mentioned that it was fun to scare me and that he was glad he could do it. He threatened time and time again to hit me at this point. I recognized his desire to scare me and at one point mentioned that he was afraid of me and wanted to make me afraid of him. He called me a snot, and then "You little snot." "You're mad at me and like to call me names because you'd like to have me get mad at you." He then rushed over and kicked me and rushed out of the room again. He returned very shortly and continued threatening me with the mallet. These threats were handled again by recognition of the anger and fear he felt.

The time was about up and I told him. "I'm glad it is." He asked me several questions at this point about the toys and then returned to his pounding, saying without any provocation, "Mind your own business, you old snot." I mentioned that he was awfully angry at me because I talked to him, and at times he got angry because I didn't. "You little snot. If you don't keep quiet, you little do-something, I'll crack your head open." When the time was up he found it very hard to leave the room.

Note that, as in Pat's case, the therapist allows limits on aggressive behavior to be broken time and time again without removing the child from the room.

The mother broke off contacts. A period of six-and-one-half months elapsed. His mother returned two weeks before school started because she was afraid he would be expelled from school. She wanted him straightened out "in time for school." In order to be of as much help as possible, Marvin was seen daily for two weeks and three times the first week of school. His fear of the play situation made it impossible at first for him to come to the room without his mother.

8-20-47 Marvin was full of intense hostility. He would come into the room only because his mother came with him, threw water around the room, and very shortly after he came into the room I had set several limits and finally had to tell him if he didn't stop throwing water on the floor I would have to send him out. He continued, and I sent him out.

Maybe the therapist has learned something from his previous experience.

*8-21-47* Marvin came in and spent the first part of the period having his mother read out of a comic book; then he played for a while. His play was very aggressive as it had been in the previous interview, throwing the water, etc. When I set limits about having to leave the room if he continued, he stopped. There was much less antagonism today, but the antagonism was intense.

Note the rapidity with which Marvin has altered his reaction to limits.

Summary *8-22-47* through *9-5-47*. Marvin continued his aggressiveness through this period, though there have been marked changes for the better. During the next seven interviews he was able to come to my office only once by himself—that was a day when his mother had an appointment with Mrs. Wood. The last three interviews he has been able to come in by himself and play. In this period, he was excluded from the room several times because of failure to meet limits, but this has diminished so that the play is much less aggressive and he meets limits much better. He continued to throw water around the room several times and to destroy things on my desk. This, too, has diminished considerably. During the last three interviews much of the time has been spent in play, rather than expressing hostility toward me. His attitude has changed from one of complete hostility to a very ambivalent attitude toward me, coming close to me many times, talking to me about things, even playing with me and asking me to do things for him. I notified him that I was going on vacation and that we would see each other three more times, and kept that up through this period.

The day of the last interview, near the end of it, he said, "Please call my Mommy and ask if I can't go to her, or if she won't come to me." He was very upset, and I called her and arrangements were made. During the last three days it was not necessary to lock the door of the room in which his mother was in order to keep him out. At first when he separated himself from his mother he would run two or three times to see her, to see if she was there, and then return to me. The last few days he has been able to stay away from the room and not run to her, the last day being the only exception and at this point instead of running to her he asked me to get her. At the conclusion of each interview he has tried to kick me. At the conclusion of the final interview on September fifth he kicked me twice, and the second time it was with sufficient vigor so that it hurt me. He kicked at me again. This time I threw my foot up to protect my shin, and he kicked his shin against my heavy shoe, which put a large scratch on his leg. It hurt him considerably and threw him into a temper tantrum. Considering the fact that this was the end of our interviews for a period of time, it seemed most desirable to be with him as he worked through this temper tantrum. After all, he was not seeing me for three weeks and I had just hurt him, which might give him a real basis for feeling rejected. The temper tantrum took place in Mrs. Wood's office, where he screamed and yelled and threw himself around. He wanted me to leave the office and was very insistent that I would. I recognized his feelings and worked with him on this. Gradually the temper tantrum receded and he began to get control of himself. There were a few sporadic outbursts after the first one, but they, too, diminished; and

> finally with a grin on his face he said, "I'm going down to his office and pull his chair out of the room." This had been a limit which had been set in the interview and was one way of getting even with me. I recognized this desire and he rushed down to the office, pulled the chair out, put it back in, and for the next two or three minutes he tried to struggle to take the chair out of the office. I mentioned that it made him happy to try to get even with me, that he was awfully disappointed and unhappy because I had hurt him and he wanted to get back at me because of that. He seemed to be in good control of himself when he left and seemed to have worked out much of it. He was quite unhappy and sad. He was terribly sad because I was leaving and was awfully mad and unhappy because I had hurt him; yet much of the extreme tension around it had been relaxed and he was in much better control of himself.

The improvement in Marvin's behavior is faltering but marked. Marvin had actually "drawn blood" in two spots on the therapist's shin bones. Had the therapist and child separated at the office door, Marvin's injury as well as the punishment the therapist took could have been avoided. Marvin made a very good adjustment to school. The only complaint was that he did not sing when the other children sang. Six weeks elapsed between this and the following interview.

> *10-15-47* Marvin has made almost unbelievable progress. The first twenty minutes it was not necessary to set any limits. He was quite unhappy. I recognized this and he agreed to it. He gradually changed his unhappiness to anger and in the extremes of his anger expressed it by pounding very hard on the pounding board and screaming and yelling. He became exceedingly wild but remained within the limits of the situation, never attacking me or the permanent fixtures of the room during this period. His words became unintelligible as he shouted and screamed and pounded. Suddenly he stopped and took the nursing bottle. He began to squirt some on the floor and the wall and the windows, then he took the ball and threw it hard. I mentioned that he was awfully angry and that it made him feel good to be able to pound and yell and throw things. At this point his play took on an even more constructive aspect and he returned to his pounding without the previous fervor. I mentioned that sometimes when he was mad he tried to hurt other people and make them mad and other times he just pounded and yelled when he was mad. He pounded a little bit and then became quite quiet during the rest of the period, playing without any expression of hostility whatsoever. I wouldn't be surprised but that we are beginning to reach the conclusion of treatment.

Here we begin to see the closing phases of treatment. Marvin's mother again stopped treatment at this point. He maintained this level of adjustment until the end of the school strike in March, 1948. Apparently the school provided some support. His mother and father are seriously maladjusted and the mother made very little progress. She has now returned for treatment and the therapist's relationship with Marvin is again very shaky.

### *Limits with Adults*

The reaction of children to limits, although better known and understood, is in all likelihood no different than that of adults. The staff at the Minnesota Psychiatric Institute has been trying to evaluate (clinically) the potential role of limits with adults. Although the number of cases is small and the experience too limited to be more than provocative, it would appear that limits may have a significant therapeutic role with:

(1) Hysterical clients who "faint," or engage in other histrionics so as to interfere with the efficiency of the office. (Restriction of such behavior or discontinuance of contacts.)

(2) Clients who seek treatment from numerous staff members, including secretaries, at odd moments and between scheduled appointments. (Setting of limit to relationship with one staff member.)

(3) Clients who fail to make progress over a period of several months but tenaciously continue contacts. (Setting limit to the remaining number of appointments. We have used a limit of ten or fifteen more interviews. Results have been very encouraging and would suggest experimentation on a much wider basis.)

### *Conclusion*

The use of limits with adults and children seems to be most effective when the therapist's attitude is nonpunitive. It is possible to be accepting of the client's feeling or need to commit antisocial acts without permitting him to carry these feelings into action within the interview. Limits within a punitive structure apparently inhibit rather than reorient behavior.

The experiences related here indicate that limits may be of greater therapeutic value than our current interest implies.

### *Summary*

The value of limits in therapy has been minimized in the current directive-nondirective arguments. The therapist may find that the more precise his limits and the more quickly they are invoked, the easier it is for him to use them therapeutically. That limits are therapeutic is illustrated by two examples with very aggressive children. It may be that the use of limits on behavior in therapy is equally as important as acceptance of the attitudes which provoke behavior.

# The Theory and Practice of "Therapeutic Intervention" in Child Treatment

HAIM G. GINOTT

The literature reveals basic differences of opinion about the implication of permissiveness and the application of limits in child treatment. Some leading therapists (Rosenthal, 1956; Schiffer, 1952; Slavson, 1943) consider unconditional permissiveness and unrestrained acting-out the primary requisites for effective child therapy. They strongly object to the imposition of prescribed limits by the therapist and see in it a dangerous technique that undermines the very foundation of the therapeutic relationship. They maintain that no predetermined set of limits can ever be applied in psychotherapy because "therapeutic intervention"[a] must always be based on insight into the needs of the individual child and must vary accordingly.

Other leading therapists feel that "the role of limits may be more important than our current interest in them would indicate" (Bixler, 1949, p. 1), that "limitations . . . are set up as a prerequisite to satisfactory therapy" (Axline, 1947, p. 131), and that "without limits there would be no therapy" (Moustakas, 1953, p. 15).

The difference between the two schools of thought is succinctly summarized in their definitions of permissiveness. According to the one approach, "Permissiveness means the acceptance of all behavior as it appears in the [therapy] group, be it aggressive, hostile, destructive, sadistic, masochistic, etc., without reproof, censure or restriction on the part of the therapist" (Schiffer, 1952, p. 256). To be sure, the therapist does not sanction such behavior; he only permits it.

According to the other approach, permissiveness means the acceptance of all *symbolic* behavior as it appears in therapy, be it destructive or constructive, without censure or restriction. All feelings, fantasies, thoughts, wishes, passions, dreams, and desires, regardless of their content, are accepted, respected, and allowed expression through words and play. Direct acting-out of destructive behavior is not permitted; when it occurs, the therapist intervenes and redirects it into symbolic outlets.

These formulations of permissiveness touch on issues that strike at the very core of one's therapeutic concept and conduct. In the absence of objective research evidence, these are not issues that one therapist or one school of therapy can decide for another. At the present stage of knowledge, psychotherapists acting upon and reporting on different hypotheses will need to state

[a] This term was coined by S. R. Slavson in a personal communication.

their orientation, describe their practice, glean evidence from their experience, and present it for scientific evaluation.

This [paper] . . . aims to provide a rationale for the use of limits in play therapy, to discuss various limits conducive to effective therapy, and to suggest techniques of limit-setting as well as methods of dealing with limit-breaking.

The following six statements are proposed as a rationale for the use of limits in individual and group play therapy.

(*1*) *Limits Direct Catharsis into Symbolic Channels.* One of the aims of therapeutic limits is to promote release through symbolic means. The unfulfillable nature of some of the children's desires makes the setting of limits on direct acting-out unavoidable. Certain acts, such as murder, incest, thievery, and vandalism are absolutely forbidden in our society. Such acts may not be performed in therapy either, except in effigy. Symbolic release enables children to channel even incestuous and destructive urges into harmless outlets and to develop sublimations compatible with social demands and mores. Thus a child with oedipal entanglements may undress, hug, kiss, and make love to a mother doll. Obviously he may not act so toward his mother or his therapist. By setting limits, the therapist helps the child to change his object choice while allowing him gratification of sex interests through socially acceptable channels of playing, painting, modeling, puppetry, and discussion.

A child who is angry with his father can stab or shoot a father doll. The aggressive child may symbolically destroy his parents, teachers, and therapist over and over again in his play and games and learn from his own experience that his impulses do not actually kill anybody. The neurotic child may discover that his inner impulses can be discharged into the playroom without dooming him, thus learning that his desires are not fatal and need not be so rigidly inhibited.

(2) *Limits Enable the Therapist to Maintain Attitudes of Acceptance, Empathy, and Regard for the Child Client throughout the Therapy Contacts.* It is reasonable to assume that a therapist cannot remain emotionally accepting and empathic when the child attacks him, pulls his hair, paints his forehead, tears his shirt, or breaks his glasses. Such activities must be prohibited to prevent the arousal of anger and anxiety in the therapist himself. The ability of any person to tolerate aggressive attacks is not unlimited. The invoking of limits prevents the therapist from exceeding his own capacity for tolerance and enables him to remain consistently unperturbed and tranquil. To retain his role as ego ideal and identification model, the therapist must not come too close to the brink of his endurance. If the therapist questions his ability to stay calm and accepting when the child scatters mud all over the playroom, he should limit the spilling to the sandbox or to one corner of the room. If the therapist cannot tolerate the child's painting of walls, he should limit the painting to paper or toys.

It must be stressed that therapeutic controls always apply to behavior, never to words. A therapist may set necessary limits on undesirable behavior, provided that he is permitting verbal and play outlets for the expression of feelings. If the therapist cannot tolerate the children's conversation or finds it necessary to limit the symbolic content of their play, then it is unlikely that therapeutic gains will accrue. (This point is discussed more fully in another part of the [paper].)

(3) *Limits Assure the Physical Safety of the Children and the Therapist in the Playroom.* Several common sense health and safety limits must be set in the course of play therapy. Children may not drink polluted water, hang out of the window, or set themselves afire. They also may not endanger the life or health of the therapist; they are not allowed to throw sand in his eyes, cough in his face, or dent his cortex with a mallet. For his own safety, then, the therapist may not be attacked physically. Other important reasons for this prohibition will be discussed later.

(4) *Limits Strengthen Ego Controls.* Many young children present behavior problems characterized by an inability to cope with socially unacceptable inner impulses. The aim of therapy with these children is not the relaxation of superego functions but the tightening of ego controls. By setting limits and invoking prohibitions the therapist becomes the external authority figure whose values, it is hoped, the child will absorb through identification and introjection. Without limits, therapy may only delay self-regulation, encourage narcissism, and lead to a false sense of omnipotence. By encountering limits on some actions in an accepting atmosphere, the child learns to distinguish between wishes and deeds without negative consequences. He learns that he may feel all his feelings but may not act as he pleases. By accepting the child's feelings and preventing his undesirable acts, the therapist reduces the child's guilt and at the same time turns his wishes in the direction of reality controls. Thus the child comes to accept and control impulses without excessive guilt.

(5) *Some Limits Are Set for Reasons of Law, Ethics, and Social Acceptability.* Children may not sexually play with each other in the playroom because, among other reasons, it is socially unacceptable and against the law. A child may not deliberately defecate in the sandbox or urinate on the floor, because it is socially unacceptable. A child may utter "smutty" words in the playroom to his heart's content, but he may not yell profanities at passers-by or at the secretarial staff, again because it is socially unacceptable.

(6) *Some Limits Are Set because of Budgetary Considerations.* Some limits are set simply because of realistic monetary considerations. A child may not destroy expensive toys because they are expensive and clinics usually have limited budgets. Thus Bobo, the costly clown, cannot be hit with a sharp instrument; it is only "for boxing."

## *Therapeutic Limits and Parental Restrictions*

There is a vast difference between therapeutic limits and parental restrictions. In disciplining a child, parents and teachers generally focus on *stopping* undesirable actions, not on liquidating the negative feelings motivating these actions. The child is usually neither helped to bring out his troubled feelings nor provided with safe channels for catharsis. The restrictions are frequently set in the midst of angry arguing and are often punitive and inconsistent. More often than not the child is left with the sad conclusion that not only his deeds but also his feelings and wishes are disapproved of.

Therapeutic limits help the child deal both with his feelings and actions. The therapist permits all verbal and symbolic expression of feelings but limits and redirects undesirable acts. The limits are always set in a manner that preserves the child's self-respect. The limits are never punitive, arbitrary, or capricious. They are treatment-motivated and are applied without anger or violence. The child is not rejected or shamed for resenting the prohibitions. His objections to the limits and his wish to break them are recognized and respected, and harmless channels for expressing his feelings are provided.

When limits are employed therapeutically, they may lead to voluntary acceptance by the child of the need to inhibit antisocial wishes. In this sense limits are conducive to the development of self-discipline; through identification with the therapist and the values he personifies, the child achieves greater powers of self-regulation and self-command.

## *The Techniques of Limit-setting*

Both in therapy and in life, children need a clear definition of acceptable and unacceptable behavior. They feel safer when they know the boundaries of permissible action. Therefore, limits should be delineated in a manner that leaves no doubt in the child's mind as to what constitutes unacceptable conduct in the playroom. It is preferable that limits be total rather than conditional. There is a clear distinction, for instance, between splashing and not splashing water on the therapist. However, a limit that states, "you may splash me as long as you don't wet me too much," is inviting a deluge of trouble. Such a vague statement leaves the child without a clear criterion for making decisions.

Limits should be stated in a friendly but firm manner. Children do not readily accept restrictions invoked with a halting and hesitant mien. When presented clumsily, limits may become a challenge to children, evoking a battle of wills and focusing therapy on restrictions rather than relationships.

Limits must be presented in a manner that minimizes the arousal of resentment in the children. The very process of limit-setting should convey a spirit of nonpunitive and helpful authority. There are different ways of phrasing specific limits. At times the following four-step sequence may prove helpful: (1) The therapist recognizes the child's feelings or wishes and helps him to express them as they are. (2) He states clearly the limit on a specific act. (3) He points out other channels through which the feelings or wishes can be expressed. (4) He helps the child bring out feelings of resentment that are bound to arise when restrictions are invoked.

This approach is illustrated in the following play-therapy sequence: Johnny, age nine, wanted very much to take a gun home and made his desire known.

JOHNNY: I'm going to take this gun with me.

THERAPIST: It's easy to see, Johnny, that you like the gun and would like to take it home.

JOHNNY: Yes, I would. Can I?

THERAPIST: The rule of the playroom is that *all* the toys have to stay in here. But you may have the gun whenever you come to the playroom.

JOHNNY: I don't like the rule.

THERAPIST: You wish there weren't such a rule.

JOHNNY: I wish the rule was that you can take all the toys home.

THERAPIST: Such a rule you would really like?

JOHNNY (*Smiling.*): Yeah, but then you wouldn't have a playroom.

It is not always necessary or feasible to phrase the limit in the above pattern. At times it is more effective to state the limit first and reflect feelings later. When a child is about to fire a dart gun or throw a block at him, the therapist might say—and he had better speak quickly—"Not at me—at the toys." He will do well to point to the toys in order to distract the child from himself. He might then reflect the child's wish to shoot at him and perhaps suggest to the child some harmless ways of expressing anger; e.g., "You may draw my face on the blackboard and shoot at it, or you may write my name on Bobo and punch it."

Limits should be phrased in a language that does not constitute a challenge to a child's self-respect. Limits are heeded better when stated succinctly and impersonally. "Time is up for today" is more readily accepted than "*Your* time is up and you must leave now." "No shooting at each other" is obeyed more willingly than "*You* must not shoot at Johnny." Whenever possible, limits should be stated in the passive rather than the active. "Walls are not for painting," is accepted with less resistance than "You must not paint the walls." "Toys are not for breaking," is better received than "You may not break toys."

At times limits may be set nonverbally. When a child "plays" the xylophone with a hammer, the therapist may hand him drumsticks and take away the hammer. This can be accomplished without a word, just with a smile. The child may not even be aware that a limit has been invoked. The therapist may even be thanked for providing the appropriate tools.

### *Situational Limits*

The materials and toys as well as the physical setting of the playroom should be so planned that they exert a "limiting" influence on children. Undesirable behavior can be prevented by removing in advance objects used for inappropriate acting-out. Sharp or pointed toys should be taken out of the playroom before a session with aggressive children. Fingerpaint should not be given to overactive children; it overstimulates them and invites smearing of each other and the walls. Toys should be sturdy and hard to break. Windows, lights, and one-way vision glass should be protected with wire mesh. Floors must be waterproofed and walls readily repaintable. Office desks with stuffed drawers, overdecorated chairs, telephones, and personal books have no place in a playroom; their protection necessitates the setting of too many limits and interferes with the therapist's ability to maintain "free-floating attention."

It is advisable that the playroom be sound-proofed and isolated from clinic offices so that play therapy will not interfere with the other activities of the agency.

## *Limits Conducive to Effective Therapy*

*A Time Limit.* A time limit is always necessary in child therapy. A play therapy session usually lasts fifty minutes. The therapist tells the child of the time limit and toward the end of the session reminds him that he has only a few minutes left to play. The therapist will say, "There are only five minutes more before time is up." He may also give the child a one-minute reminder. At the end of the hour the therapist will get up and say, "Time is up for today." With young children he may add, "Now we go out." The therapist should adhere to the time limit consistently. He should not prolong the session even if the child brings out "significant material." The child gains security from the predictability of the therapy hour.

*Toys May Not Be Taken Out of the Playroom.* Sooner or later children want to take toys home. They may want to borrow, exchange, or buy playroom toys. A limit should be set stating that "all the toys must stay in the playroom." Toys may not be taken home, or to the waiting room, or to the bathroom. If the child wants to show a specific toy to his mother, he may invite her to see it in the playroom. However, children are allowed to take home any painting or clay sculpture made by them during the session. The limit on taking toys home pertains also to broken toys. They, too, may not be removed from the playroom by the child. The reason is obvious: too many toys would be broken for the purpose of taking them home. What is the rationale for not allowing children to take toys home? Besides obvious budgetary considerations, there is a therapeutic reason for not giving toys to patients: the relationship between therapist and child should be based on emotional, not material sharing.

*Breakage.* Children are not permitted to break room equipment or expensive toys. They may not pierce the rubber clown with a sharp instrument. They may not break the window or throw sand in the air conditioner. Their wish will be recognized but a limit invoked. The therapist may say, for example, "You would like to cut Bobo to pieces but he is not for breaking.

He is for punching" or "The air conditioner is not part of the play material. It is part of the equipment of the room."

*Physical Attacks upon the Therapist.* Child-therapy literature shows general consent about the necessity of prohibiting physical attacks on the therapist. Both analytic and client-centered therapists do not believe that physical attacks are helpful either to the therapist or to the child. The rationale for this prohibition is as follows: (1) It assures the physical safety of the therapist. As Dorfman (1951, p. 258) puts it, "It saves wear and tear on fragile therapists." (2) It saves the child from guilt, anxiety and the fear of retaliation. (3) It allows the therapist to remain emotionally accepting of the child.

Some therapists (Slavson, 1952, p. 294) allow young children of preschool age to attack them physically. They interpret to the children the reason for the attack. Other therapists modify this limit to state, "You may hit me a little, but you can't really hurt me."

The writer believes that the limit against hitting the therapist should not be modified under any circumstances. There can be little therapeutic value in permitting a child to attack an adult. Effective therapy must be based on mutual respect between the child and therapist, with the therapist never abdicating his adult role. Allowing a child to dominate the relationship arouses too many insoluble problems both for the therapist and the child, and it anchors therapy outside the world of reality. Telling a child that he may "hit but not hurt," the therapist is asking him to make a too fine distinction. Such a vague limit does not contribute to the security of the child or the peace of mind of the therapist. The child is irresistibly challenged to test out the prohibition and establish the "just noticeable difference" between hitting playfully and hurting seriously.

*Physical Attacks among Children.* While most therapists agree that physical aggression toward the therapist must be prohibited, there are conflicting theories regarding the value of setting limits on physical attacks among children. Despert (1945, p. 223) believes that children, especially young ones, should be allowed to fight in the playroom. According to her, symbolic acting-out through toys provides children "only a limited means of release." The prohibition of physical attacks may seem to the child as "equivalent to censorship—the type of which is often the basis of his own problem."

Slavson (1943, p. 160), on the other hand, believes that children, especially young ones, need external restraint when they are over-aggressive. "Unless the children are checked by someone outside themselves their aggression gains momentum and increases in intensity."

Some therapists allow aggressive fights but keep them under control by serving as referee. Axline (1947, p. 137) is against this practice because "It tends to involve the therapist in a role that calls for assumption of authority and judgment which might at times appear as partiality to a certain member or members of the group." Axline believes that "the ruling out of physical attacks should be one of the limitations of group therapy."

In the opinion of the writer, there is little healing benefit in allowing children to attack each other physically. Besides the obvious danger of serious injury, such attacks merely serve to displace aggression from original sibling to substitute sibling. It is more therapeutic to channel aggressive impulses through symbolic actions against inflated clowns and family dolls and into rivalrous target-shooting and other sublimatory competitive games.

## *When Should Limits Be Presented?*

There are conflicting opinions regarding the optimal time of introducing limits. Some therapists believe that limits should be stated at the onset of treatment because children may feel betrayed and disappointed when confronted with limits unexpectedly. That this is true of some children can be seen from the following play-therapy extract.

> When Eleanor, age thirteen, first encountered a limit she became quite upset and voiced her disappointment openly. She said, "There isn't a place in the world without restrictions. Even this place has some. I thought that here we could do anything we wanted. Now I see that even here there is no freedom. I am disappointed because I wish there was one place in the world without any restrictions at all."

Many therapists, including the writer, are of the opinion that limits should not be mentioned before the need for them arises. There seems to be little advantage in starting therapy by invoking prohibitions on actions that may never occur. There are some disadvantages to this practice. The listing of limits may serve as a challenge to aggressive children and as catharsis-deterrent to submissive ones.

> When Tommy, age eight, first entered the playroom, he was told by his therapist, "You may play with the toys any way you want to but you may not hit me or break toys." Tommy became quite upset and he said, "Oh, no sir, I'd never think of hitting you." Tommy hardly touched a toy during the next few sessions.

## *When Limits Are Broken*

Child-therapy writers, with one or two exceptions, do not acknowledge the obvious fact that limits are sometimes broken by child patients. Few suggestions can be found in the literature for dealing with this phase of therapy. Even writers who emphasize the vital role of therapeutic limits omit specific discussion of what is to be done when a limit is broken.

In dealing with limits-breaking, Axline stresses the therapist's need to remain accepting of the child. Even when a child breaks a limit, the therapist should "stay right there with her reflection of feelings." Axline recommends that the therapist try to prevent the breaking of a limit "if she can do so without engaging in a physical battle with the child."

The question is, what is to be done when the child does engage in a physical battle with the therapist? Some therapists (Bixler, 1949; Moustakas, 1953) suggest that after an initial warning, the therapist should terminate the session and put the child out of the playroom.

This writer objects to expelling a child from the playroom regardless of his transgression. Besides conveying rejection, ejecting a child is a dramatic way of telling him that he can defeat adults. This admission of failure on the part of the adult is of no benefit to the child. It may well prove to him the suspicion that he is hopeless and helpless; since he can defeat all adults, no one remains to help him. No blanket recommendation can be made on how to deal with the child's aggression, since the therapeutic reaction will depend on the meaning of the child's specific action. Some aggressive children cannot accept the therapist and his friendly overtures because they have never recognized or accepted any external authority. These children may need an experience of submission to an adult who is firm, just, and strong.

When Joel, age nine, insisted on throwing a chair at the therapist in spite of verbalized limits and reflected feelings, the therapist got up and said calmly, "I am bigger and stronger than you." The boy put down the chair and started cursing the therapist, who helped him *verbalize* his choking anger.

It must be added that this method of limiting aggression should be applied only in specific cases when other means have failed to achieve results. However, when a child has a false sense of omnipotence, expressed in neurotic defiance, submission to the authority of an adult may be clinically indicated and may prove helpful.

Another method used successfully by some therapists is to transfer a very defiant child from individual to group therapy. An aggressive child who insists on attacking the therapist and on breaking limits may be put in a group of older children. Usually, instead of continuing his defiance, such a child will seek the therapist's friendship as a protection against the actual or anticipated aggression of the other children. The older groupmates frequently are able to convey more directly and more potently than the therapist that limits must be observed. The following play-therapy sequence from an article by the author (Ginott, 1958, p. 416) will serve as an illustration.

> Nine-year-old George resented bitterly the few limitations set in the playroom as part of therapy. He claimed to be "superman" and seemed intent on destroying the toys, damaging the room, and attacking the therapist. When George was transferred from individual therapy into a group of older boys, he tried to continue his aggressive pattern. However, in the group, "superman" George met some rival "supermen."
>
> When George threw a wooden block at ten-year-old David, the boy looked at him with surprise and in a very convincing voice, he echoed one of the playroom limitations. "This is not for throwing," he said, "only rubber toys are for

throwing." When George deliberately shot a dart at his face, David became angry. He took hold of George, shook him and said, "Look, the playroom is for playing, not for hurting. This is the law in here."

"I'm above the law," said George, "I'm superman." "Shake," said David, extending his hand, "I'm superman too." "I'm super-superman," answered George. "And I'm super, super, superman," retorted David. The boys burst out in a loud laughter. The therapist said, "Both of you are supermen and above the law?" "No," answered George, "nobody here is superman and nobody is above the law."

## *A Different View on Limits*

Dorfman (1951, p. 262) reports that a number of client-centered therapists use only one criterion for therapeutic intervention: they only limit activities that interfere with their ability to remain emotionally accepting of the child. Some of these therapists allow the child almost complete control over the therapy situation; the children may paint the therapist's face, take toys home, urinate on the floor, leave the playroom at will, miss sessions, or terminate treatment.

Again it must be stated that thus far there have been no published research studies on the comparative effectiveness of different practices of limit-setting. As therapists with different rationales and orientations report the result of their experimentations, the more fruitful treatment technique will become evident.

## *Summary*

This article proposes a rationale for the use of limits in child-centered play therapy, discusses various limits conducive to effective therapy, and suggests several techniques of limit-setting as well as methods of dealing with limit-breaking.

## REFERENCES

Allen, F. H. *Psychotherapy with children.* New York: Norton, 1942.

Axline, Virginia M. *Play therapy.* Boston: Houghton Mifflin, 1947.

Bixler, R. H. Limits are therapy. *J. consult. Psychol.*, 1949, **13**, 1–11.

Despert, J. Louise. Play analysis in research and therapy. In N. D. C. Lewis and B. L. Pacella (Eds.), *Modern trends in child psychiatry.* New York: International Univer. Press, 1945. Pp. 219–255.

Dorfman, Elaine. Play therapy. In C. R. Rogers (Ed.), *Client-centered therapy.* Boston: Houghton Mifflin, 1951. Pp. 235–277.

Ginott, H. G. Play-group therapy: A theoretical framework. *Int. J. group Psychother.*, 1958, **8**, 410–418.

Moustakas, C. E. *Children in play therapy.* New York: McGraw-Hill, 1953.

Rogers, C. R. *The clinical treatment of the problem child.* Boston: Houghton Mifflin, 1939.

Rogers, C. R. *Counseling and psychotherapy*. Boston: Houghton Mifflin, 1942.

Rosenthal, L. Child guidance. In S. R. Slavson (Ed.), *The fields of group psychotherapy*. New York: International Univer. Press, 1956. Pp. 215–232.

Schiffer, M. Permissiveness versus sanction in activity group therapy. *Int. J. group Psychother.*, 1952, **2**, 255–261.

Slavson, S. R. *An introduction to group therapy*. New York: Commonwealth Fund, 1943.

Slavson, S. R. *Child psychotherapy*. New York: Columbia Univer. Press, 1952.

CHAPTER EIGHT

# The Meaning of Time

According to Taft, time can be seen as one form of limit, as it marks the beginning and end of every hour and every relationship. The way a child handles the time limits of the therapy hour reflects his reactions to all limiting experiences.

How should we respond to the child who wants to leave early or who asks to stay beyond his hour? In the latter case he may not ask in words, but develop innumerable delaying tactics. Should these be ignored or recognized and handled for what they represent? Should the child be permitted to return to the therapy room after his hour is ended? What is the meaning of time to the clock-watcher who, although not asking to leave early, counts the remaining minutes at regular intervals? Is he afraid his mother will leave without him? Is he wishing the hour were longer? Is he anxious to leave, but fearful of expressing the wish openly? Or is this an expression of his general compulsive concern with minutiae?

Most therapists try to warn the child five or ten minutes before the hour is up and this often precipitates a flood of activity. Does this reaction represent frustration at having to leave "so soon"? Or has the child been reluctant to give expression to certain feelings and then finally "lets go" with the realization that time is passing?

Should the hour be extended if the child was late in arriving? Does it make a difference if the child, or the mother, was responsible for the late arrival? What if the therapist is the one who is late? One student therapist was unavoidably delayed for two consecutive sessions with a ten-year-old boy. The third week the therapist was careful to be on time, but the boy had arrived even earlier and was looking at a magazine in the waiting room. He pointedly ignored the therapist until he had turned every page. How can this situation be turned to therapeutic advantage? The therapist who is repeatedly late to therapy or supervisory sessions might well ponder the meaning of time and the dynamics underlying his own reluctance to become involved.

Questions so far have related to problems within the single hour. Others arise with respect to changes in the day of the week—to suit the mother's convenience, the child's school or outside activities, or the therapist's schedule; cancellation by patient or therapist, with or without prior notification; and vacation arrangements. Ross treats some of these aspects in a selection which also covers problems in termination and so is placed in Chapter 14.

## *The Time Element in Therapy*

JESSIE TAFT

. . . Whatever takes place between worker and client of a therapeutic nature must be present in some degree in the single contact if it is ever to be there. If there is no therapeutic understanding and use of one interview, many interviews equally barren will not help. In the single interview, if that is all I allow myself to count upon, if I am willing to take that one hour in and for itself, there is no time to hide behind material, no time to explore the past or future. I myself am the remedy at this moment if there is any, and I can no longer escape my responsibility, not for the client but for myself and my role in the situation. Here is just one hour to be lived through as it goes, one hour of present immediate relationship, however limited, with another human being who has brought himself to the point of asking for help. If somehow this single contact proves to have value for the applicant, how does it happen? What in the nature of my functioning permits this hour to be called therapeutic at least qualitatively?

Perhaps one reason we find it difficult to analyze what takes place in the short contact, is that here we are brought face to face with a present from which it is hard to escape and which in consequence carries symbolically and really our own personal pattern as it relates to time and the self-limitation which is involved in its acceptance. Not only is the client limited by this brief period of time, not only is he facing the possibility of being turned out too soon or kept on after he is ready to go, but I also am forced to admit my limited function as therapist, dependent as I am upon his right to go when he must or to deprive me of a second opportunity no matter how willing I may be to continue the contact, no matter how much he may need the help I have to give from an objective standpoint. My only control, which is not easy to exercise, is my control over myself in the present hour if I can bring myself to the point of a reasonable degree of acceptance of that hour with all of its shortcomings. The fact that our personal reaction to time gives a clear picture of the real nature of our resistance to taking full responsibility for therapeutic casework, makes it necessary at this point to consider time and its relation to therapy more philosophically.

Time represents more vividly than any other category the necessity of accepting limitation as well as the inability to do so, and symbolizes therefore the whole problem of living. The reaction of each individual to limited or unlimited time betrays his deepest and most fundamental life pattern, his relation to growth process itself, to beginnings and endings, to being born and to dying. As a child I remember struggling with the horror of infinite space, but the passing of time was even more unbearable. I can remember my gratitude for Christmas, because at least presents remained, something lasted beyond the moment. There was deep depression in adolescence over the realization of this flow of time. Why go to a party since tomorrow it will be over and done with? Why experience at all, since nothing can be held? On the other hand, there is equal fear of being permanently caught in any state or process. Fear of being bored is perhaps its most intellectualized form, panic in the face of a physical trap or snare its most overwhelming and instinctive expression. As living beings we are geared to movement and growth, to achieving something new, leaving the outworn behind and going on to a next stage. Hence we do not like a goal that can never be reached nor yet a goal that is final, a goal beyond which we cannot go. In terms of this primary double fear of the static and of the endlessly moving, the individual is always trying to maintain a balance and frequently fails because of too great fear either of changing or of never being able to change again. To put it very simply, perhaps the human problem is no more than this: If one cannot live forever is it worthwhile to live at all?

We see this problem and this double fear reflected in every slightest human experience from birth to death and consequently also in the caseworker's as well as the client's attitude toward the long or the short contact. Whether or not she can face the reality of either, depends on whether life to her can be accepted on the terms under which it can be obtained, that is, as a changing, finite, limited affair, to be seized at the moment if at all. The basis for believing that life can be thus accepted, beyond the fact that all of us do more-or-less accept it if we continue to exist, lies in this: that we are, after all, part and parcel of the life process; that we do naturally abhor not only ending but also never ending; that we not only fear change but the unchanging. Time and change, dying and being born, are inner as well as outer realities if fear of external violence or compulsion does not play too great a part. Life is ambivalent but so are we, "born and bred in the briar patch." And on this fact rests the whole possibility of therapy. We cannot change the fundamental biological and pyschological conditions of living for others, nor for ourselves, but somewhere within each individual is this same life process which can go on for and of itself, if the fear which has become excessive primarily in birth and the earlier experiences can be decreased in quantity sufficiently to permit the inherent normal ambivalence to function and hence to provide its own checks and balances. Time in itself is a purely arbitrary category of man's invention, but since it is a projection of his innermost being, it represents so truly his inherent psychological conflict, that to be able to accept it, to learn to admit its likeness to one's very self, its perfect adaptation to one's deepest and most contradictory impulses, is already to be healed, as far as healing is possible or applicable, since in accepting time, one accepts the self and life with their inevitable defects and limitations. This does not mean a passive resignation but a willingness to live, work, and create as mortals within the confines of the finite. . . .

Since death is so much more final and compelling than any time limit man can set and difficult to take into the self, so complete an experience is seldom granted, but the principle is the same and however strange it may seem, all endings, all partings, being more-or-less shadowed with the fear of death, become important and fearful out of all proportion because their value is symbolic. Perhaps the ending of a long-time therapeutic relationship, agreed to by the patient from the beginning, takes on more of this compelling quality than any other situation where threat of death is entirely absent; hence its therapeutic worth, which consists primarily in this fear-reducing heightening of the value of the present and the releasing discovery that an ending willed or accepted by the individual himself is birth no less than death, creation no less than annihilation.

So literally true even in the slightest situations is this description of our relation to time and particularly to a time limit that in any therapeutic interview where in coming the individual admits a need for assistance, it is possible to see the operation of this person's particular pattern, his own way of reacting to time or if you like to the life problem itself. This one is at your door fifteen minutes too soon, the other keeps you waiting, or perhaps fails to turn up at all. The very one who makes you wait at the beginning of the hour may be equally loath to go at the end and leaves you to be responsible for getting him out. The other who comes before you are ready is on edge to be gone before the time you have allotted to him is up. Neither can bear the hour as it is, with limits set by the other, even though he has agreed to them beforehand. The one makes you bear the burden of his lateness and his lingering, the other tries to bear too much, both his own responsibility and yours depriving himself of what is his, and you of the chance to contribute what you have already assigned for his use in terms of time. And so it goes, for every individual a slightly different pattern but with the same motivation which is so deeply symptomatic of the individual's problem that one might fairly define relationship therapy as a process in which the individual finally learns to utilize the allotted hour from beginning to end without undue fear, resistance, resentment, or greediness. When he can take it and also leave it without denying its value, without trying to escape it completely or keep it forever because of this very value, insofar as he has learned to live, to accept this fragment of time in and for itself, and, strange as it may seem, if he can live this hour, he has in his grasp the secret of all hours, he has conquered life and time for the moment and in principle.

Here then in the simplest of terms is a real criterion for therapy, an inner norm which can operate from the moment the person enters your office to the moment at which he departs more-or-less finally, whether he comes once or a hundred times. It is a goal which is always relative, which will never be completely attained, yet is solved in every single hour to some degree, however slight, if the client really wants help and I offer a contact in which limitation is accepted and acted upon, at least for myself. If I believe that one hour has value, even if no other follows; if I admit the client's right to go as well as to come and see his efforts and resistances in both directions even when he cannot; if I maintain at the same time my own rights in time as well as my responsibility and limitations and respect his necessity to work out his own way of meeting a limit even when it involves opposition to mine as it must, then I have provided the essentials of a therapeutic situation. If with this personal readiness, I combine self-conscious skill and ability to utilize the elements which make for therapy, the client may if he choose, in greater or lesser degree, learn to bear this limited situation which, as he finally comes to realize, is imposed by himself as truly as by me, by his own human nature, no less than mine, or if you like, by the nature of the life process itself. . . .

PART THREE

# PROCESS

CHAPTER NINE

# Developmental Phases of Play

AS INDICATED in the quotation from Freud in the preface, the actual process of therapy can only be learned through practice; the theoretical principles can be expounded and the possible stumbling blocks pointed out in advance, but each therapy situation is a unique experience which takes place as the child and therapist live through each hour together.

By way of introduction to discussions of different facets of the therapeutic process, attention will first be focused on the developmental stages of play characteristic of all children. As Fraiberg[1] has stated elsewhere:

> In direct treatment of the child—or in therapeutic work with the child—if we like, our objective is to bring the child up to the level of development appropriate for his age. This means of course that our therapy is geared to the psychosexual development of the child and our objective can be no greater than his growth potential for this period. This means, further, that a theoretical knowledge of the psychosexual development of children, and the developmental tasks and conflicts which come with each stage, are an indispensable part of the worker's equipment. To achieve this task one may have to go deeply into the childhood neurosis, or one may go into it superficially. This depends not on arbitrary rules—or territorial mandates —but on the requirements of the individual case.

The disturbed child may become fixated at one stage or level or may regress to earlier infantile levels. Often, thera-

[1] Selma H. Fraiberg, "Application of Psychoanalytic Principles in Casework Practice with Children," *Quarterly Journal of Child Behavior*, III (1951), 175–197, 250–275, p. 250.

peutic progress can be measured by the extent to which the child relives and "outgrows" each of the earlier phases until he reaches the stage appropriate to his current maturational level.

Hellersberg stresses the ego aspects which accompany each of the libidinal stages and describes the therapist's role in facilitating progress from one level to the next.[2]

Peller's selection gives detailed discussion of the age-stages of play, the dynamic and libidinal aspects of each stage, the toys and materials most typically used, the social aspects, and the secondary gains for each phase.[3] She emphasizes, as does Hellersberg, the important role of the ego in the play of all periods and the operation of defense mechanisms as the child matures. Peller's discussion of postoedipal play and games is one of the few comprehensive treatments to be found in the literature with respect to this aspect of the latency period.

# *Child's Growth in Play Therapy*

ELISABETH F. HELLERSBERG

## *Functional and Physical Aspects Needed for Discussion*

It is a valid assumption that every serious problem causes an arrest of the child's growth process and that therapy aims to revive this process in an accelerated form (Allen, 1942; Whitaker, 1953). This is possible only when the functional and physical needs, as well as the mental and emotional ones, are understood and satisfied. By stressing some physical, developmental aspects of child therapy, it may be possible to broaden the understanding of the curative process beyond the description of the influence the therapist alone exerts. In the past, the strong emphasis on libido development has overshadowed the observation of the ego functions which characterize the child's changing psychophysical needs. These needs are expressed in his play activities, in his relationship to the place of treatment and to the objects presented to him, as well

---

[2] In the original paper, Hellersberg has illustrated her points with case material and demonstrated the functions served by the specific play patterns of each child discussed.

[3] For further elaboration and illustrations of some of the points made in Peller's selection, see Lili E. Peller, "Libidinal Phases, Ego Development, and Play," *Psychoanalytic Study of the Child*, IX (1954), 178–198.

as in his relationship to the therapist. By play he makes or regains contact with the world, and thus he tests and re-experiences his ego boundaries and ego strength. To understand the full meaning of play therapy for the child's total growth, more attention should be paid to the sensory and, particularly, tactile explorations of the child, his motor activity, and even occasional devotion to movements which appear nonsensical. The child's absorption in various games or building projects is also important. Each of these activities, properly observed, will broaden the understanding and deepen the interpretation of the therapeutic process.

What is said in the following is, therefore, not a new way of treating the child patient, but another way of evaluating and describing the established mode of treatment. By this emphasis on physical and developmental happenings, this paper wants to stimulate similar observations in therapy. The author aims at a more effective use of the psychoanalytic discoveries and believes that, for a child's therapeutic progress, the verbalized interpretations of his problems appear of minor importance (Allen, 1942; Whitaker, 1953), but essential is a therapist's enlightened and alert responsiveness to every single movement of the child in a very physical sense. For the neurotic child, the therapeutic method is different from that chosen to help the ego-weak or schizoid child. In this paper only the first is under study, leaving the observations of the schizoid child to a later publication.

### *Initial Phase of Therapy*

To illustrate what I mean, let me begin with the initial phase of therapy and focus on the physical and functional aspects of its setting. The child has been in trouble before he comes for therapy; at least, he has noticed other adults' concern. Frequently, the child expects the therapist to be one of these eager, but unsuccessful people whose disapproval he has earned, people who tried in vain to change or to reform him (Allen, 1942; Despert, 1945). In order to counteract such anticipations, his first entrance into the playroom should assure him of minimal interference on the part of the therapist. In an unobtrusive way the latter explains to the child that there are many things at his disposal which he can use as he likes. He gives the child ample time to approach the situation so that the patient does not feel intruded upon by a new adult. Whatever his age he should be exposed to toys or materials suitable for different developmental stages. Offering a variety and giving the child freedom for discovery, one rarely fails to produce a positive response. The child finds a new place where his troubles are forgotten and where he can explore his own suppressed needs. Such needs automatically come to life sooner or later. The touching of sand, the tense fingering of a book while probably studying the therapist, the throwing down of some puppets—any initial action, however arbitrary it may appear, should be considered as significant as the first dream brought to the initial analytical session in adult therapy. The less the child's first movements are influenced by the therapist, the more they may be interpreted as first steps to health and normal functioning. At this phase the therapist helps most, not by discussing the child's problems, but by fully identifying with the child and approving any move expressing his needs. Thus the therapist becomes the nurturing agent to gratify these needs by means of what the playroom offers. In this way, the first play hours become comparable to the first weeks of an infant's life. We may assume that the patient's capacity to accept human relationship is only latent. This capacity grows indirectly within the child, after he first discovers his own needs and searches for their satisfaction. If he finds something he enjoys touching or handling, he will have a positive and pleasant reaction. No demands are made upon him, and just "having a good time" turns, almost without fail, into liking the agent who grants the security for this new experience. Thus, the basis for trust and confidence in an interpersonal relationship is laid. The child must come to the realization that the therapeutic session is the time to reveal hidden and repressed needs and that he will have opportunity to pursue their gratification. By discovering his suppressed needs the patient becomes able to recapture those phases of his former development which he has not fully assimilated in his present, incomplete state of maturing. Such growth will be possible only if the therapist promotes a state of genuine spontaneity in the child and tries to maintain this state as far as possible. It is a common truth that without spontaneity no life develops, no growth can be secured (Allen, 1942; Meyer, 1948; Whitaker, 1953). How to create or maintain a spontaneous spirit in a child is the very problem with which we are dealing. It is not merely one conflict from which the child is suffering, it is the total personality of the child which must be brought to full responsiveness.

## *Various Activities Point to Various Developmental Needs*

A frequently observed need is the sensory one, particularly a tactile contact with the material world. The child explores the surface, the texture of things, and also its properties. From the tactile he proceeds to the use of other senses, of taste, smell, sight, and hearing. Another basic need is the child's rediscovery of space, the relationship of his own body shape and capacity to the physical world and its spatial condition. A third definite phase in the child's therapeutic activity is shown by his urge to master something, to create or construct a miniature world or to utilize some material such as clay, paint, wood, erector set, and so on in order to make them yield to an idea. He wishes to build a town, a pioneer fortress, or to make boats, guns, houses, airplanes, etc. These different types of child activities correspond to stages recognized by psychoanalytic doctrine as major phases of libidinal development in childhood: namely, the sensory, related to the oral phase, and the motor, to the anal phase. The child's wish to master engages his total organization just as does the genital phase (Erikson, 1950).

To supplement the libidinal viewpoint, I wish to throw light on the corresponding phases in the child's ego development during therapy. It is desirable for the therapist to recognize such phases, to understand their dynamic significance, and in reporting or interpreting therapy to give each incident and activity full credit. Later, in the case material, I shall demonstrate that these phases are not separated when dealing with a child beyond four years, but are intermingled in many parts of the actual, as well as the therapeutic growth process. Exploring matter is, for instance, not only the need of a one- to two-year-old child. It never ends in human life. Yet I maintain that such exploration bears particular meaning when it occurs in the sequence of the therapeutic hour. This is due to the fact that in the permissive atmosphere with the encouragement of an unknown, protective person, the therapist, inner urges of the child are revived and set in motion. Automatically, they serve the tendency of growth which is dormant in every living organism (Allen, 1942; Whitaker, 1953). On this assumption, it is possible to recognize the child's activities as manifestations of different stages in their rudimentary form and to regard each movement as instinctively and developmentally conditioned. The sequence of various manipulations, fully observed and understood, will reveal the whole breadth and uniqueness of the child's striving for new growth.

We could make better use of our therapeutic observations if all aspects of the child's normal development were better defined so that they could be brought closer to clinical consideration. However, as long as these two disciplines—the clinical and developmental theories of childhood—have not yet found a theoretical synthesis, a presentation like this must remain hypothetical (Hartmann, 1950).

## *Sensory–Tactile, Exploratory Needs*

When the child first explores his therapy room, one often observes his search for sensory–tactile contact with this new world. How important such contacts are can be learned by watching normal children. They continuously test out a new environment to satisfy their curiosity. In doing so they gain familiarity with their surroundings which contributes to their security. These are vital experiences which problem children need to repeat. Due to pressure from the outside, exerted by misunderstanding adults or due to inner conditions which have hampered the child's alert curiosity in the past, many of our problem children have not had this opportunity. Freedom in tactile exploration is, in our understanding, the most concrete means to gain security in the playroom world. By exploring in therapy, the child recaptures early primitive satisfactions. He finds a new link between himself and the surroundings, which, for the first time, answer fully to his desires. If, by these means, his mental curiosity and his need for object relation are satisfied, the playroom or the play hour becomes his own in a very important sense of the word. The relationship to the therapist as an agent who provides this gratification is then beyond any question. It is in this first phase that we can compare the development of affection through gratification of needs with the smiling infant after his hunger is stilled. Any interference at this phase by probing into the problems of the child or making him talk about his difficulty only delays the process. . . .

## *Muscular–Motor Needs*

The next physical need we will discuss is the child's urge for moving and discovering his body in relation to the space around him. In some movements we observe a one- to three-year-old child's urge to find his own body boundaries. He squeezes himself into small closets, cuddles on a shelf after he removes the toys, jumps on the couch bouncing up and down, proudly noticing how big he is and that he can jump from the couch without falling. Other children want to test their energies. For instance, a five-year-old child grabs a saw and tries to test his strength by cutting wood. Another one wants to drive nails in a board. No concrete or definite idea of what they wish to produce inspires these activities. They just feel good when their muscular efforts make an impression upon the substance. This pleasurable experience is, no doubt, a form of tension release. It also serves as a testing-out of their body form and capacities and brings to children the awareness of their physical and mental selves. . . .

## *Motor Constriction as Related to Compulsive Neurosis*

We stress the need for such body release action in child therapy in order to re-create the flexibility lost in the former years and to help the child regain fluidity and spontaneity, the basis of all growth.

The study and interpretation of such release by movement is particularly valuable in neurotic conditions which in adults are often diagnosed as obsessive or compulsive, but which also appear in younger children . . . to a milder degree. These symptoms are easily traceable to the attitudes of parents who, too early, set unusually high standards, thwarting the child's need for self-expression and self-enjoyment. Parents' restrictions of body activity are most crucial in the period between one and three. When practicing toilet training, such parents demand from the child too much inner control; when confining him in playpens or exerting anxious supervision over all his actions, they deprive the child of vitally needed motions such as toddling, creeping, climbing, etc. His needs conflict with his parents' concept of his safety or with their exaggerated ideas about what is clean or dirty, good or bad. To shield himself against outer pressures and continuous demands, the child acquires a cramped control. This gradually affects his whole psychophysical system and may later lead to that compulsive neurotic character structure in adults whose analytical treatment is a most arduous one. Often the patient requires years of therapy to bring back to him some of the freedom and spontaneity he lost in early years. By contrast, it seems easy to open up the chance for release action in children, a fact which places the child therapist in a very favorable position. Providing and channelizing freedom of action has a multiple meaning. First, the patient rids himself of some tension. When he mobilizes his needs for body activity he soon discovers a new Body-Self. This leads automatically to serious groping for new values in judging not only his Body-Self but also his rights and needs in relation to his environment. . . .

Often, the therapist becomes directly instrumental in leading the child to search for new values about himself. If he encourages the child's desire for free body movement and physical outlets, the therapeutic relationship becomes something more than merely nurturing and permissive. The child's action may endanger his health and safety, and the therapist naturally gives warning. The child becomes able to understand the therapist's protective attitude as a confirmation that the latter identifies with his infantile need to find outlets, but nevertheless does not wish to see the patient harmed. This makes the patient susceptible to reasoning. He discovers on a less infantile level what his growing interests really are. He comprehends that he has to take responsibility for himself. This shift in the patient provides the basis for searching his own standard, for finding self-chosen controls and limitations in his behavior. Thus, the process of voluntary self-control, destroying the faulty superego forces, first begins on a completely physical level. After the child's body constrictions and his oppositional defenses are released, he becomes susceptible to new experiences. The child's contacts with the outer world widen, and he acquires new conceptions of reality, less laden with fear. Gradually, as the child's anxiety symptoms and defenses disappear, he discovers and also identifies himself with the needs of other children outside the playroom. In fact, it is the protective and free atmosphere which enables the child to develop new trust and confidence, first in the therapist, then in his own peers and adults. The symptomatology of the compulsive neurotic is here understood in relation to the child's early confinement in space and the prohibition and control of his body activities, which extend automatically to the eliminatory function and give this type of neurosis its name. . . .

## *Representational and Constructive Play as Related to Elementary Physical Needs*

The sensory, tactile, and motor activities comprise the regressive needs expressed in play. A more complex aspect of child's play is usually characterized by imaginative or projective activity. He builds in life size or in miniature a representation of his own understanding of the environment by playing with dolls, miniature objects, or puppets. Sometimes he transforms the whole playroom into his house, street, or school, and often he re-enacts adult roles he has observed: his mother, teacher, the milkman, mailman, etc. (Erikson, 1950). Developmentally speaking, this play serves as a means for the child to explore and understand the social world around him in relation to himself. It also allows him to project the emotional handicaps which have impaired his human relationships. Hence, this sort of play is highly important for diagnostic as well as therapeutic purposes. Yet, to the author's understanding, any sort of social conflict must be understood also in relation to earlier frustrations, like those expressed in sensory and muscular motor needs. It is a truism that all social problems have their origin in infancy. In fact, in any therapy one can observe not only the child's social conflicts, but also his need for physical regression, interspersed, as the child indulges in his representational and imaginative projection. . . . The earlier residues of elementary needs are emphasized, not because we believe that the physical developmental aspects of ego growth are more important than the libidinal ones, but because we see in the physical activities the beginning of the new growth process, a means to mobilize the child's social and libidinal development.

The construction of toys or other objects is the fourth category of child's play activity we shall discuss here. When the child employs a work bench and uses tools, he is mastering material and creating a replica of what he has seen in the adult world (Erikson, 1950). In such construction, the child not only imitates an adult world as in the representational activity; he becomes identified with a grown-up person who produces his own objects. This is "work" and not merely play. He proves himself in his physical and also mental qualities. I mentioned before that representational and constructive play activities may well be compared to the genital phase of libidinal development. This point becomes particularly significant, when we observe the assimilation of earlier infantile drives in this constructive effort of producing an object by satisfying tactile and motor needs or when the child projects his social world in a spatial reality around him. If the early ego stages which produced the sensory and motor needs are not fully consummated, the child's attempts toward constructive or projective activities are in vain. He obviously has not reached the developmental stage of mastering his genital phase. He pretends to build something, but he does not succeed. Often he squanders the material by mishandling it, or he is completely unrealistic in applying his energies or his reasoning. He cannot judge his capacity in relation to the idea he has in mind, nor can he choose or organize the proper material. The playful creation of a miniature world may be the first step to this object-building tendency, if one considers both activities in terms of the effects on ego growth. The construction of objects, fully accomplished by the child, gives him a great feeling of independence and mastery. From this viewpoint the comparison of the neurotic child here described with the schizoid personality is especially fruitful. . . .

### *The Role of the Therapist*

By giving the above-developed aspects greater weight, the role of the therapist can be somewhat redefined. We mentioned already his nurturing attitude when he encourages the child to discover his needs and search for gratification. It is the nursing mother who promotes the first contact with reality. Tackling various objects while exploring the room, trying out some activity, enriches the child with new concrete experiences. The situation becomes more realistic when the therapist warns the child of some discomfort if he thoughtlessly pursues his aim. The warning must be in such a form that the child still realizes the full identification of the therapist with his own interests. At the same time the patient is motivated to search for more subtle gratifications. As child therapist one often encounters situations where one wishes to have the patient insured for possible physical damages. Yet, in many years of this kind of practice, no child ever got harmed. On the contrary, many children showed an awakening sense of responsibility combined with their awareness of the physical realities. The more spontaneity is developed for any activity, the easier it is for the therapist to check destructive tendencies either toward themselves, toward people, or toward play material. In this way the therapist moves toward the role of a conscious agent and mediator between the child and the world outside the playroom.

Here again, something happens which can be compared with the development from infancy to later childhood. At first, the nurturing parent is liked for his need gratification; later he becomes the representative of a group beyond the narrow confines of the two-way exchange of sympathy. The parent bridges this step by showing the child the positive gain he will make when meeting friends and moving in the realms of neighbors who also accept him. In therapy, likewise, the narcissistic self-demands change into something new, namely, the child's desire for mutuality and social give-and-take. . . . Nurturing then, is no longer necessary. Cautioning to safeguard material or the interests of other people proves to the child that the therapist is identified, not only with the patient's needs, but also with the rules and requirements of a world outside the play hour. The proper timing of such a hint to the reality beyond the play hour is a very important point. While the therapy progresses, the question arises whether the child can take such suggestions or not. . . . From this point of view also, it must be stressed that the treatment of the neurotic child differs essentially from that of the schizoid child. The latter's reality-testing is the main object of therapy, while for the neurotic child our aim is to reduce or remodel his defenses. The neurotic child must learn to reconcile his pleasure drives with his obligations toward a wider world, and the therapist must be the agent to accomplish this. When he first confirms the child's right to self-expression, he gradually makes the child choose his own way of limiting and controlling his impulses. The patient becomes able to develop a more subtle desire for satisfaction when he feels accepted by the therapist first, and then he strives to be accepted by the outer world beyond the playroom.

In this last phase, the freedom of the child's own expressiveness is merged with the child's chosen self-control. When his social responses have improved and he gains the rewards of being accepted in his environment, the therapist can well, retrospectively, point out the meaning of these play hours, relative to the concrete conflict in which the child found himself. Now he is able to understand his former problems, and he will also understand that the purpose of all the fun and freedom he has experienced was a means to help him express what he was never able to express before. His new, voluntary adjustment to his environment was what he wanted more than just some "good times" in the play hours. It is easy to give the child the feeling that he himself chose this new order and social adaptation, just as an adult realizes that his therapy is actually a self-educating process, after his inner needs have been fully realized. This explains why the child, in his regained self-respect and self-confidence, finds it so easy to leave the therapist. There is hardly any good-by. The child now feels as good about not coming to the play therapy as he formerly felt eager to come. His urges and strivings are again turned toward the larger world of his home, friends, and school. His spontaneity is regained, and thus, he can now utilize anything that is offered him for further growth. His contacts with people and the outer world have been re-established.

# *Libidinal Development as Reflected in Play*

LILI E. PELLER

We can think of childhood as a sequence of libidinal phases, each one dominated by one main attachment and each characterized by one area of greatest sensitivity where gratifications and deprivations are felt most. In each period fantasies arise denying the most keenly felt limitations or deprivations and leading into play activities which help the child to come to terms with his central conflicts.

Each new phase brings a shift to different joys and sorrows. The old ties, the former areas of conflict and apprehension do not disappear, but they yield the center of the stage.

A child's play not only reflects his libidinal but also his ego development, e.g., his body skill; his experience; his level of reasoning, of differentiation, and integration; and his abilities for social give and take.

Before we go on with our attempts to uncover the elements woven into a child's play, let us listen to a warning: for many years the major part of the child's day is spent in play; there are so many varieties of it, some in full dress and some in glimpses—obviously there is such an abundant opportunity for interpretations that the danger is to "find" too much or to align play activities which have a high discharge value with those which are shallow and transitory. Unless specifically stated, we consider here only play activities which are highly meaningful to the players. Indicative are the child's facial expression, the number of repetitions, the degree of obliviousness of his environment, his willingness to surmount obstacles, etc. (The construction of a rating scale of play interest is feasible and might be helpful to future observers.)

We will present some of the main features of play characteristic for successive libidinal stages. While the child attains more mature levels of action and cherishes his recent acquisitions, there is also a continual homecoming to earlier gratifications.

## *Narcissistic Play*

In the earliest months the playing infant appears interested in the parts of his body, in their functions and their products. Gratifications and their counterparts—deprivations—stay in the immediate neighborhood of body needs. Earliest interest in toys is largely derived from body interest. In the manipulation of a toy, the movements of the child's fists, legs, and voice seem repeated, varied, and amplified.

In the long solitary play with fingers, or toes, or any small object that strays into the child's cradle, in the babbling monologues, the functioning per se seems to yield pleasure ("functional pleasure") and comfort and to support fantasies of grandeur or of functioning with perfect ease. Remember that gratifications as well as frustrations are not yet accompanied by words or symbols.

## *Preoedipal Play*

Even before this type of play comes to full bloom, an attachment is formed to the early mother figure, which is the source of all the good and all the bad that flows into the child's life. At a very early age she is perceived as a person —provided she behaves like a person. (If a confusing group of people caters to the distressed infant or if the mother acts like an automaton—the attachment will be delayed or impaired.)

Naturally the child's play revolves around this all-important attachment. The child's main concern is her leaving him—and all mothers are absent at times—even the most devoted mother goes to the next room or looks after the other members of the family. The main vulnerability of this period can be expressed by "My mother can abandon me" or "My mother can do with me as she pleases." In his play the child tries to conquer his fears by turning the tables: "I'm the one who *sends* Mother away, I am the one who *brings* her back!" The baby pulls a sheet over his face—"Mother is gone"—and with great glee and laughter pulls the sheet down again: "Mother is back." The peek-a-boo game initiated by the mother, but eagerly picked up by the healthy infant, is played in all parts of the globe—many languages have an endearing term for it.

The baby also has to go through tedious daily routines, to sit still to be dressed and combed; he is bathed, fed, and put to bed and has no say about it. Our ideas about body care and cleanliness are completely outside his understanding—thus all that is done to him is experienced either as caress or assault, and more often as the latter. So here too his helping formula is "I'll do to others what has happened to me," and he tries to bestow some mothering on anyone or anything that will take it. Teddies and dolls, or a puppy dog, are carried around, fed, put to sleep, or brushed and wiped.

Excellent examples for maternal play can be found in "Infants without Families" (A. Freud and Burlingham, 1944). Here, in the group of toddlers, the children tried to mother one another. Actually any advantage of size, skill, or position was used to victimize another child. According to Ruth Brunswick (1940) the mothering of the mother herself is the ultimate goal.

In all play a passive experience is turned into an active one, but in preoedipal play this turning of the tables is most obvious and can be best observed. Young boys have the same need as young girls to play out the various aspects of maternal care. Through this play they do not slip into a feminine role, although some later forms of doll play are distinctly feminine. The young boy making his first crude attempts at mothering a doll or a teddy might be exposed to ridicule. I am under the impression that the little boy in our American culture has to prove his masculinity in no uncertain terms and earlier than in the "old" countries. Being caught at "girls' play" is a greater threat for him. Those who plan for the child's play—parents and educators—need an awareness of both the attitude of our society and of the needs of the toddler boy.

## *Oedipal Play*

Once the child overcomes his utter helplessness and is able to walk and talk, he develops attachments to both his parents. But this growth of his social orbit is not the decisive feature of the new phase; it is the different role he assumes toward those whom he loves. In the preoedipal phase he wanted his mother to be present all the time, to cater to his physical needs all the time. Now, in the oedipal phase, he forms ties of love, envy, and admiration to both his parents, and he wants to be taken as their equal. These feelings are of great intensity, they alternate and are partly incompatible with one another. There would be conflict even if the outer world would not sharply curb some of his desires. Inner conflict characterizes this period. . . . Early play reflected the simplicity and the directness of his needs, in the play content (leaving and returning, body care), in the meagerness of the plot (tit for tat invariably), in the paucity of roles (mother and child, giver and recipient). And what might be called the style of his play mirrored the fact that he was insatiable; his play consisted of innumerable repetitions with few variations. The play-indulging adult who introduces variations in order to alleviate his own boredom often enough meets resistance.

For good contrast we may look a couple of years ahead and watch how colorful and varied his play is then. But before we do this, a few words about the general trends of development. By and large, the child's ego development proceeds in an orderly, one-directional fashion—the child takes one step after the other; but in his libidinal development there is a contrapuntal element which was not seen in preanalytic times. The child seems to jump from one rather extreme position to another and adopts the middle of the road only afterward. Thus, successive periods may show greater divergence than those which lie further apart. For instance, there are some similarities between preoedipal play and latency play—like repetitiveness, rigidity of form—while oedipal play has fluidity and endless change which makes it unpredictable. Or, the superego of early latency knows no compromise and no exception to the rule and order while behavior in late latency and in the late oedipal period are more similar to one another. In the preoedipal phase, the child was keenly aware of his smallness and helplessness and overrated the mother's power, while sexual differences were hardly noted. The reverse is true for the oedipal phase. There is awareness of the sexual roles (with gross errors which have biological reasons and thus will return even if corrected by a well-intentioned parent), but there is, on and off, a complete blindness to the age difference between himself and his parents. Time and again the child fantasies or acts as if he were his parents' full-fledged partner. Behavior of this kind leads invariably to a rude awakening, but playing adult roles does not lead to such a downfall.

This then represents the focal vulnerability of the oedipal period: to be excluded from the pleasures of the grownups. The core of his fantasies can be phrased as, "I can do what any grownup can. I am big." He assumes impressive masculine (or feminine) roles (ship captain, lion tamer, king, doctor, or nurse, fairy, teacher), or he masters small replicas of adult tools and possessions, or he creates things (using building blocks, or paints and clay, or words for their sound or story value). His earlier dealings with the same materials were manipulative, dabbling, with many shifts in focus, in interest and resembling more primary processes.[a]

---

[a] The criticism might be voiced that developments which are characteristic for children in our Western culture are presented as if they were to be found everywhere. In more primitive cultures, children's imaginative play is far less imaginative as the child is drawn into the adults' pursuits at an earlier age, as he lives with adults whose life is more narrowly defined, etc. Yet basically the same types of play exist.

A few words about the style. In its fully developed form this play shows successive stages, possibly a climax. There is a great variety of plots, themes, roles, emotions, and there are unforeseen developments; and thus every hour of play differs from the one preceding or following it. There is an air of triumph, of felicity and lightheartedness in this play which is remembered with nostalgia not only by those who write their childhood memories, but in glimpses by all of us. Even where amnesia covers most of childhood, scenes of play are remembered with an amazing wealth of details. The apparent innocence of these scenes makes them suitable as screen memories. Many statements found in psychological literature about "play" are correct for oedipal play only—not for the play activities characterizing other phases.

Things drawn into narcissistic play are experienced as body parts or body extensions. In preoedipal play the child begins to use simple tools, in oedipal play insignia and "props" appear. Because the play structure is so different in the three phases, an identical object used in play may assume a completely different meaning.

Earliest play is solitary. In the next phase the fantasy is still a private production, but in its content it is social, i.e., it encompasses others. Its execution may be either solitary or between mother and child; other children seemingly drawn into play are really puppets. Their response is not ploughed back into the play, it falls by the wayside as does the far greater part of the world we adults live in. In oedipal play, the fantasy may be social in its *origin* (several children putting their heads together). It is usually social by way of *content*, dealing with several people in various roles, and the execution may be either solitary (e.g., a child plays alone with dolls or toy soldiers) or social (several children playing together). However, contact between coplayers is loose. It can be lost, and the players may never know the difference.

## *Postoedipal Play*

In games—the next and last group we are going to discuss—a close rapport between the players is vital. Each one must stay within his role and support the roles of his coplayers; otherwise the game cannot be carried on.

These remarks about the social interplay indicate the progress from (1) play which is purely idiomatic to (2) an activity which can encompass others as objects to (3) one which can be shared by several subjects and where theme and content are communicable, and finally to (4) play forms which are predicated on step-by-step communication and mutual understanding.

A few words about this last phase of childhood. It is the postoedipal phase, and the child's attachments to his playmates gain in importance, while his anxiety is focused on his superego and superego representatives. He feels anxiety when he has to face them alone or when his own superego is dissatisfied with him. Hence the compensating fantasy, "There are many of us —we are alike, we belong to one group" or "We observed the rules to the letter." The young child always liked his own performance, but the latency child is critical of himself and may feel uneasy and unhappy over his achievement. This makes him vulnerable and evokes the wishful fantasy, "I can go back and start all over again as many times as it pleases me."

These fantasies already indicate most of the essential features of games: a loyal group of brothers plays together, the actions of one player dovetail with those of his coplayers. The plot is meager and—much in contrast to the preceding period—plot, roles, and insignia are traditional and stereotyped. Two groups or two individuals as commanders of phantom armies (checkers, cards, chess figures, domino bones, etc.) compete with one another according to strict rules and in a narrowly defined field. Elements of luck count far more in some games than in others. Chess represents one extreme, since luck is almost excluded, and the so-called hazard games the other, since skill or proficiency are of little avail. (Incidentally, the real gambler does not play, he acts out an inner compulsion. Phenomenologically, the element of choice is absent.)

But elements of chance enter into most games and make for the unforeseen developments which in national and international contests may grip the attention of huge crowds. It is incorrect to think of the spectators as passive. Obviously, they are not taking part with their muscles; but if watching a game would be entirely passive then the knowledge of the game would not be a prerequisite for enjoyable watching. We do not mean to be facetious with the following comparison: just as familiarity with the intricacies of music will enhance the pleasure of listening to a Beethoven symphony, so will knowledge of the finer points in baseball augment the pleasure and the emotional response of the spectators.

In another context, Kris (1952) develops the idea that a certain optimal distance is essential for the appreciation of a piece of art, a play, or a painting. If this distance shrinks, art enjoyment is reduced to a banal literal attitude—the art product is mistaken for a piece of reality; but if the distance widens, the art lover becomes a critic.

It is interesting that for the participants in games similar concepts also have validity. In the case of "underdistance," the player will try to win at all cost even using "unfair" play, whereas with an attitude of "overdistance," there will not be any infringement of rules, but neither will there be any ardor to win. In art as well as in games emotions may be aroused too much or too little.

In most respects the course of a game is narrowly defined, much in contrast to oedipal play, and the formal elements are essential parts of games. Ontologically speaking, formal elements appear for the first time in games. Oversimplifying, we might even say that oedipal play is defined by its content, games by their formal elements.

One purpose of oedipal play is to telescope time, to have the future now, while in games the emphasis is on the possibility to start again and again—the formal structure of games making this possible. In the deepest strata, oedipal play denies the fact that the child is excluded from the adult's genital life, from intercourse with a partner as well as from the creation of progeny. In the deepest strata, games deny the fact that time is ticking away, irreversibly. They attempt to deny death.

The contrast between the play forms of the two phases can be expressed in still a different way. In oedipal play the tale, the plot, is spun at the spurt of the moment. It is an "à la carte" production and for this reason gives relief in a period when the child's acts are unpremeditated and his emotions of joy and disappointment flare up and change suddenly.

The favorite games of latency have a plot which is codified. Games channelize homosexuality, i.e., they provide outlets which are sanctioned by society and which keep it from assuming dangerous proportions. Games do the same for aggressive drives and possibly for masochistic tendencies. The players identify with one another; they even identify with their adversaries (yes—the opposing team consists of opponents, not of enemies). They see their ego ideal in their playmates, or in their leader, or in nationally famous players, and as long as they play in the same game, they partake in this ego ideal, and this lessens the pressure of the superego. Being a Baltimore Oriole fan may be an essential part of a boy's group identity. Games thus provide gratification, but as they are prefabricated, run in traditional molds, the player remains rather anonymous and unexposed—to himself and to the others.

So far we spoke of the play of children and of the adolescents' games. Do adults not play? They certainly do and possibly more so in our time than in former days, the superficial reason being that more people have increasingly greater leisure. However, the deeper reason is that more people are engaged in work which is neither challenging nor rewarding per se.

In our economy the number of routine jobs increases. There are more and more occupations which neither demand nor offer a possibility for libidinal investment. More and more adults—young and old—turn to play to obtain narcissistic gratifications which their work does not yield. Play, hobbies, collections, and games assume a tremendous importance for their libidinal economy.

To the best of my knowledge, no psychoanalytic study of the play activities of adults exists, but I would venture the thought that we find the same basic types of play in their world. The libidinal core providing the leitmotiv fantasy remains, while the growth of the ego works radical changes in the play activity itself. To indicate just a few forms of adult play: there are the so-called hobbies—an almost infinite variety of pastimes in which the range of libidinal investment runs from dilly-dallying to passion. The name seems derived from "hobbyhorse."[b] A hobbyhorse was, before the motorcar's arrival, the main toy of little boys, providing masculine pride besides its play value and

[b] In German, *Steckenpferd* also has these two meanings.

adult approved zonal gratification. The boy's play with his hobbyhorse belonged to narcissistic play (the paraphrasing or aggrandizing of body parts or functions), and today's hobbies belong in the same group. The body play of infants is a private affair in all aspects, while the adult's hobby is solitary in its libidinal core, but socialized in its ego aspects. Fellow hobbyists share and enhance their pleasure through many channels, like journals, exhibitions, conventions. In any case, even for the secluded collector, his interest is communicable—whether he chooses to do so or not.

The excessive pride and care often lavished upon the hobby equipment is an inheritance from the beloved body parts (or functions or products) which this equipment once replaced and which it unconsciously still signifies (A devoted fisherman may spend hours shining and arraying his rod, his reel, his flies, etc.). The skill and the intelligence invested in hobbies or collections reflect ego qualities.

The keeping of pets may be a remote reflection of the preoedipal tie, the tie between two beings, of whom one is inarticulate, helpless and direct in his body wants and body gratifications, while the other one appears omnipotent. The pet's little stunts prove both how clever he is and how good the rapport between animal and trainer. There are other avocations reminiscent of preoedipal relations, but with a different distribution of roles.

In the vast realms of art we may see adult counterparts of oedipal play. (I have mentioned before that in oedipal play the emphasis is on content; in games, on formal elements. For true art, a successful marriage of formal elements and content seems to be a prerequisite.)

While all the earlier mentioned groups of play undergo such radical metamorphosis, postoedipal play, e.g., games, changes comparatively little. When the mature ego embodies a deep and unconscious libidal fantasy in a play activity, the resulting structure differs, almost beyond recognition, from the play forms of infant and child. After the decline of the oedipus complex, the foundations of the ego are here to stay, and games, like other postoedipal addenda to the personality, change slowly and almost imperceptibly from decade to decade.

These remarks about the play of adults are too general and too sketchy to be more than suggestive. A study of the play activities of adults, an area of growing importance for our mental balance today, remains to be done.

## REFERENCES

Allen, F. H. *Psychotherapy with children.* New York: W. W. Norton & Co., 1942.

Brunswick, R. M. The preoedipal phase of libido development. *Psychoanal. Quart.*, 1940, **9**, 293–319.

Despert, J. Louise. Play analysis in research and therapy. In N. D. C. Lewis and B. L. Pacella (Eds.), *Modern trends in child psychiatry.* New York: International Univer. Press, 1945. Pp. 219–255.

ERIKSON, E. H. *Childhood and society.* New York: W. W. Norton & Co., 1950.

FREUD, ANNA. *The psychoanalytical treatment of children.* London: Imago, 1946.

FREUD, ANNA, and BURLINGHAM, DOROTHY T. *Infants without families.* New York: International Univer. Press, 1944.

HARTMANN, H. Psychoanalysis and developmental psychology. In *The psychoanalytic study of the child.* Vol. V. New York: International Univer. Press, 1950.

KRIS, E. *Psychoanalytic explorations in art.* New York: International Univer. Press, 1952.

MEYER, A. Spontaneity. In *The commonsense psychiatry of Dr. Adolf Meyer.* New York: McGraw-Hill, 1948.

PIAGET, JEAN. *The construction of reality in the child.* New York: Basic Books, 1954.

PELLER, LILI E. Models of children's play. *Ment. Hyg.*, 1952, **36**, 66–83.

WHITAKER, C. A., and MALONE, T. *The roots of psychotherapy.* New York: Blakiston, 1953.

❀ CHAPTER TEN

# Resistance

IT IS ASSUMED that the readers of this volume are familiar with the concepts of resistance, transference, and countertransference. The readings have been selected, not to define these processes, but to point out their unique aspects in work with young patients. Obviously, one can hardly discuss resistance without touching on transference, and transference and countertransference cannot be handled in isolation. Consequently, the placement of articles in the next three chapters is somewhat arbitrary; they have been assigned to the chapter where the bulk of their content seems to fit most appropriately.

Resistance usually becomes apparent in the initial or early sessions, or it may be well under way before the child reaches the clinic. Procedural methods for lessening the amount of resistance in the initial session were discussed in Chapter 5. Here the emphasis will be on the handling of resistance as a psychotherapeutic phenomenon.

Markowitz discusses some of the underlying reasons for resistance, particularly in the early sessions, with respect to personality dynamics and transference potentials. He suggests that the therapist may appear formidable to the child, who consequently will fear exposure of his "bad" self and will view the first interpretations as a further threat.

Anna Freud points out that resistance represents the ego's defense against liberation of instinctual impulses. She discusses symptom formation and the protective role served by the various defense mechanisms. Since the same type of defenses will be used against the affects derived from the impulses and the impulses themselves, she finds it particularly useful in working with children to first interpret the transformations of the affects. For further illustration of this point of view, the reader is referred to Berta Bornstein's article "On Latency."[1]

Taft's selection is presented without the actual therapy notes which preceded it, but it is hoped that her references to the case material will sufficiently orient the reader so that he can follow her theoretical formulations on the handling of the resistance. Much of Taft's philosophy concerning limits, transference, countertransference, and termination is also contained in this selection.

## *The Nature of the Child's Initial Resistances to Psychotherapy*

JOEL MARKOWITZ

The first vehicle of contact between caseworker and psychiatrist in a child's life may be in their dealing mutually with his resistances to psychotherapy. It is especially the child requiring help from both disciplines who will be most fearful of both. Inevitably he will try to use each as a weapon against the other.

Any disagreement he can find between the two will confirm his resistances and increase his fear. Since the resistances themselves may first provide the major issues in both relationships, it is important that the psychiatrist and caseworker agree upon the dynamics involved. Where agreement exists, each "parent" essentially confirms the findings of the other, and the agreement itself reassures the child. Both relationships benefit, and the child's prognosis may improve inestimably.

For the past two years the author has worked with many children prepared for psychotherapy by caseworkers at the Pleasantville Cottage School, a residential treatment center. This paper presents the findings regarding some of the determinants of the resistances they encountered. There are several qualities characteristic of the psychic make-up of the child—as opposed to that of the adult—which are responsible for the child's initially more fright-

[1] Berta Bornstein, "On Latency," *Psychoanalytic Study of the Child,* VI (1951), 279–285.

ened and more resistive approach to psychotherapy. The child is, in reality, inferior to adults in size, strength, and knowledge. These real differences tend to exaggerate the fantasied differences. They may also provide a "valid" focus for the child's anxieties and may be used by the child as a façade behind which to hide his fantasies.

The child is afraid of adults to some degree. He is less aware than is the adult of the many "civilized" aspects of our society and is more aware of difficulties in controlling his impulses. In that he is less sophisticated, he is less aware of the structure and controls of our society; in that his ego is still weak, he is unaware of the degree of control the adult ego has achieved over its impulses.

> Man, my cottage father is big! He could crush me with one hand. I'm keeping out of his way. I'd hate to be around when he loses his temper. . . . He'll kill me one day. Sure, I'm scared, he's bigger than me. . . . What chance does a little kid have? You're all on his side.

Through the above circumstances plus projection, therefore, the child, more than the adult, tends to see himself as a small, weak animal in a jungle setting, surrounded by far stronger and more able animals in league against him.

The child is to some degree afraid of his parents. The superego of the child is different from that of the adult. It is more primitive in that the ego of the child is more primitive and the child's concepts are, therefore, more primitive. We have all seen how frequently—e.g., in the absence of a father—the child's concept of father is far more exaggerated and frightening than in situations where even a brutal father is present. Reality, even when frightening, is rarely as frightening as the fantasies of a child, especially of a disturbed child. I mention the superego because it results partly from the most important early identifications with adults and represents, therefore, the earliest conceptualizations of adults. We must remember that the superego serves the function of orientation, not only regarding the standards of the parents but regarding the parents themselves. The child is generally at a disadvantage as compared with the adult patient, therefore, because his concepts of parent, authority, the adult world, punishment, and so on tend to be more primitive and therefore more exaggerated and frightening.

These factors will, of course, influence the child's reaction to a psychiatrist. There are other factors, however, which are more specifically related to psychiatry. The adult patient has had frequent intellectual exposure to psychiatry through many media in our sophisticated society. He has developed some intellectual awareness of the techniques and even of the rationale of the psychiatrist. The child has not had these reassurances and his fantasies are unmodified by intellectual awareness. These fantasies are sometimes revealed in initial interviews by remarks such as, "Can you read my mind . . . ? I don't want you to hypnotize me . . . to change my mind about religion. . . . Do you ever operate on the brain . . . ?" These remarks, from nonpsychotic children, would be consistent with much more serious psychopathology in adults, of course.

## *Child Is More "Magical"*

These remarks suggest another difference between the child and the adult patient. The child is, in general, more "magical" than is the adult. Chronologically he is closer to primary process thinking, to prelogical reasoning. He is less familiar with adult logic and understands it less well than does the adult. As his peers are similarly oriented, he derives less support from his contacts than is available to the adult patient.

We must constantly keep in mind the remarkable lack of sophistication of the child. He has been brought up in contact with only one conceptual frame of reference, that of his parents, and he believes without question that this is not only the *true* frame of reference (reality) but the only one. The vocabulary of his frame of reference consists mainly of "value terms," which are essentially emotionally reinforced short cuts to discipline. The "good" terms apply to conformity and bring some reward; the "bad" terms apply to rebellion and, according to the experience of the child, result in punishment by an angry parent. There are no "neutral" terms. That a child may break a rule and suffer the consequences without being "bad" is a concept beyond the child's experience. The implication has always been that "bad behavior" has derived directly from "badness" in the child, and the punishment is aimed at the primary badness in the child in an effort to eradicate it.

> I'm no good, never was. I wish you could cut it out of my brain. I've always been different from other kids. . . . Send me to Bellevue; I need shock treatments.

The conceptual frame of reference of the home was "primitive" in a pure sense—separations were not established between various concepts: e.g., the dynamics of the child, the child's behavior, the reality consequences of this behavior, the attitude of the adult world toward this behavior (as opposed, for example, to the attitude of the adult world toward the child), and so forth. Such separations are outside of the child's experience, and it is with difficulty that we can teach the child that such separations exist. Attempts to establish such separations in the child's concepts are at first considered sophistry and are distrusted; the child may become even more frightened that his crimes are so terrible that the psychiatrist must attempt to deny them. The psychiatrist may therefore be seen at first as another disciplinarian who is perhaps less honest and more verbal than previous ones.

Why a disciplinarian? The psychiatrist is obviously a representative of the adult world which the child has become convinced is in league against him.

The psychiatrist has been enlisted in what is evidently a final effort to "control" the child. The child deduces that the psychiatrist must be, therefore, more powerful and thus more dangerous than previous adults. The child has heard that the psychiatrist is equipped with more frightening devices than any previously used, such as hypnosis, brain surgery, electroshock devices, medications. Since all previous efforts of the adult world seemed directed toward forcing the child to conform, the child deduces rather logically that this must be an even more heroic attempt. And, especially if this particular child sees conformity as a loss of his ego, of identity, an annihilation of individuality, the psychiatrist may appear to be the ultimate enemy, the devouring parent.

> You're just like the others—everything I do is wrong. . . . It's your job to prove I'm wrong. . . . Why must I do everything your way and think like you do? Why don't you send me to Bellevue and have it over with?

The child knows that the psychiatrist is only rarely enlisted "against" children and then only when the child is especially "bad" (uncontrollable, crazy, dangerous). Frequently the child attempts desperately to deny that he is in this class

> I don't need you . . . I'm not crazy. . . . There's nothing wrong with me . . . I'm controlling myself better now. . . .

and may make a great effort to hide all evidence of the problem. To belong to the "worst" class of children is to anticipate the worst punishment (castration, incarceration, brain surgery, shock treatments). It is, I believe, impossible to eliminate this concept early in therapy with many children.

Let us assume, however, that the child can be induced to enter the psychiatrist's office and that some communication is established. The mystery regarding the psychiatrist deepens. Apparently there is to be no frontal attack, at least not at this time. Perhaps the approach is more subtle, more indirect; perhaps the psychiatrist attempts to get the child to lower his guard before striking. If he isn't a disciplinarian, then what does he do? By testing more-or-less cautiously, the child discovers that the psychiatrist is not a different type of social worker, exerts no direct influence on the child's life, and has no contact with his parents. A possibility which invariably comes to mind and, because of some validity, is never quite dispelled, is that a function of the psychiatrist is to elicit information which will be permanently recorded and which ultimately will be used to control the child. This consideration may severely limit the child's productivity, especially early in therapy.

> You think I'll tell you? I'm not so dumb. Next thing my social worker will know and I'll be in trouble. . . . I've been to psychiatrists before and they got nothing out of me.

The child is invariably told by someone that "talking will help." Although he has strong needs for attention, understanding, and sympathy, his predominant attitudes are resistive. He feels that (1) his problems are too serious to be solved by talking (this is, of course, valid); (2) the benefit he will derive does not warrant the danger of exposing the great degree of his badness, weakness, and so forth to his adult enemies; and (3) he must, therefore, distrust and guard against his need to "talk." The child—especially the more intellectual child—learns also, early in therapy, that material which seems innocuous to himself may be meaningful to his therapist. This frightening concept may constrict his productivity to so great a degree that therapy may become impossible.

But suppose that, through the dedication and skill of the therapist and the intensity of the child's inner pressures and environmental influences, the child "enters therapy," that is, invests emotionally to a degree compatible with meaningful experiences. In the course of time, the first interpretation is made.

### Resistance to Interpretation

I have always been impressed by the relatively considerable resistance of the patient to the first interpretation—regardless of the content—and can only conclude that the resistance is to interpretation per se. One factor is certainly that to the child, as to the adult patient, an interpretation is a criticism. As discussed before, all previous comments on his behavior were made in "value terms," and the child is unaware that "objective criticism" exists. Since behavior can be only "good" or "bad," it follows that any behavior which should be changed is "bad." And since the child is organically identified with his behavior, his self-esteem and survival depend upon the label identifying his behavior. Part of a child's reaction to an interpretation will correspond, therefore, to his reaction to criticism of himself in value terms. An interpretation, therefore, is always to some degree a judgment of "badness," and the child, to some degree, always feels compelled to defend himself against this annihilating judgment. Of course, had the child been conditioned differently, had he not been so closely identified with the disruptive element within him, he would be less resistant to accepting the aid of a therapist in discovering and eliminating it.

There is another source of resistance to an interpretation. I believe that this is a factor in any interpretation. It may always contribute to the anxiety and "excitement" following an interpretation. It is extremely primitive and is, for obvious reasons, more evident in children and adults to whom orientation is of greater importance. It is that an interpretation implies a distortion in the patient's conceptual frame of reference and points, therefore, to defective ego-functioning.

> He [his previous psychiatrist] was nuts. What I say to my social worker has nothing to do with my mother. Did he think I'm crazy and don't know the difference between my social worker and my mother.

We can theorize that the ego is always somewhat afraid of pressures from the id, that secondary process thinking is always threatened by primary process tendencies, and so on in that the latter constitutes the primary danger to the integrity of the former. I invoke these deep causes in attempting to explain my belief that everyone is somewhat threatened by the idea that, since our conceptual frames of reference are subjectively derived (not objectively, as most people wish to believe), they all contain distortions (i.e., at best they only approximate reality), and no two are identical. It would be reassuring to most people to believe that their pictures of the world are accurate. We have always attempted to reassure ourselves that conceptual distortions occur only in a class apart, in people who are "crazy," who have "lost their minds."

Those patients who are most concerned by the considerable distortions in their conceptual frames of reference are most terrified by further evidence of differences between their concepts and those of the group. They may constantly attempt to deny any disorientation regarding the group standards and may desperately cling to evidences of relative agreement regarding superficial reality, especially those aspects of reality which are measurable. The constant "testing" of the severely disturbed child and much of his obsessive and compulsive activity may in part derive from attempts at orientation on the group frame of reference.

It is unfortunate that this child must be introduced to the concept of the subjective origin of our conceptual frames of reference and the universality of variations among them at a moment when this concept is most threatening to his feeling secure. We must remember that he enters the psychiatrist's office believing that he is in battle with a world that is attempting, by punishment or threat, to force him to conform. He has been able to deal with the world thus far, perhaps, through constant reaction to and orientation on certain superficial aspects of reality; he has limited his anxiety mainly by intellectually reassuring himself regarding his ego strengths. The adult world has sent him to the psychiatrist as a last resort. At least one of the reasons for the frequency and emphasis by the child of his fear that hypnosis, surgery, or drugs will be used is that these seem to be heroic measures to force conformity when the individual has been resistant to conforming. The psychiatrist in making an interpretation reinforces this concept. The child feels that the psychiatrist, perhaps before resorting to organic methods to influence the child's mind, is attempting intellectually to cast doubt on his ability to judge reality—is trying to convince him "how crazy he is," so that, in order to survive, he will depend on the concepts of society and conform.

> All right, so I'm nuts, I don't know what I'm doing. Now are you satisfied? Now that you've proved it, you can lock me up.

Most previous behavior toward the child seems to reinforce this fantasy. It is legitimate for the child to question the fact that he has never been previously introduced to the concept that subjective distortions are universal. If universal and normal, why was he never told of it before? Why are his friends not told of it?

> Maybe so, but it's funny, Doc, that you're the only guy who thinks like this. . . .

And how can the psychiatrist possibly be his friend? When he is so frightened and in need of reassurance, it is the psychiatrist who tries to convince him that he "misinterprets . . . distorts reality"—is "crazy." Under such circumstances, of course, vigorous resistance develops. The interpretation is rejected as sophistry—"Psychiatry is crap"—or worse—"The psychiatrist is nuts,"—and the child may actively attempt to avoid further investigation into his conceptual frame of reference, since this can at best result in further revelations of "insanity" which can somehow be used to control (castrate, annihilate, incarcerate) him.

Of course, the child is fighting not the psychiatrist but his own needs, perhaps the most basic and compelling being his need to surrender his identity and become completely passive. From this "womb-need" derives his unconscious need to be swallowed by a parent. The child's unconscious ego, confusing fantasy and reality, sees this as a real threat to survival and will react to dependency, being influenced or controlled, and even such "swallowing" processes as identification as endangering his identity.

In this regard, the interpretation is seen as a magical negation of identity-elements, a pruning of nonconforming (individualizing) characteristics in order to facilitate swallowing him. This is more frightening to children, in general, than to adults because of the child's more oral developmental level, his greater dependency needs, his constant seduction toward dependency by his environment, and the flimsier self-concept which he has little confidence in maintaining against a strong "swallowing force."

Now, attempts are always made, of course, by our social workers to prepare the child for his first psychiatric contact, and the importance of this preparation is constantly stressed. But how does one prepare a child for psychotherapy on an emergency basis? The most effectively reassuring type of approach I have encountered suggests that the psychiatrist will teach or help the child to better *control* himself. More accurate attempts to explain psychotherapy must imply that the psychiatrist will help the child to *understand* why he is unhappy, why he is behaving as he is, and so on. This is, of course, far from reassuring to the child; it is precisely what the child most wants to avoid. The unconscious motivation for the neurotic or antisocial behavior of the child, behavior which is usually far more frightening to the child himself than to his environment, is most frequently to avoid becoming conscious of his fantasies and dynamics; the closer they are to consciousness, the more desperate the child may become in attempting to avoid seeing them. Without a very much more extensive preparation than time will usually allow, therefore, an attempt to prepare a child honestly for psychotherapy may be quite frightening.

### Conclusion

I believe that these difficulties in preparing a child for psychotherapy are generally underestimated, as is their significance, and that this is one important factor that makes psychotherapy with children frequently so difficult. It is also a factor in the many failures to induce a child to enter and remain in therapy. In more cases than we are usually aware, I believe, these difficulties are never resolved and constitute hidden obstructions limiting the progress of therapy. Certainly the task of the psychiatrist is complicated; in attempting to induce the child to enter therapy, to keep the child in therapy, to prepare the child for therapy, to educate the child regarding basic facts about himself and the world, he must broaden his psychotherapeutic role beyond its optimum range, must be more active than is desirable for psychotherapy, and must be active in areas not specifically his specialty. He pays for these complications in the difficulties he encounters in later transforming the relationship into a more specifically psychotherapeutic one, in attempting to become more passive and increase the activity of the child, for instance. Most important, in that he must initially be more than a psychiatrist to a child, the transference relationship is confused and more difficult later to delineate and analyze.

# *The Ego's Defensive Operations Considered as an Object of Analysis*

ANNA FREUD

### The Relation of the Ego to the Analytic Method

The tedious and detailed theoretical discussions . . . may for practical purposes be summed up in a few simple sentences. It is the task of the analyst to bring into consciousness that which is unconscious, no matter to which psychic institution it belongs. He directs his attention equally and objectively to the unconscious elements in all three institutions. To put it in another way, when he sets about the work of enlightenment he takes his stand at a point equidistant from the id, the ego, and the superego.

Unfortunately, however, the clear objectivity of this relation is clouded by various circumstances. The analyst's absence of bias is not reciprocated; the different institutions react to his efforts in different ways. We know that the id impulses have of themselves no inclination to remain unconscious. They naturally tend upward and are perpetually striving to make their way into consciousness and so to achieve gratification or at least to send up derivatives to the surface of consciousness. As I have shown, the analyst's work follows the same direction as, and reinforces, this upward tendency. Thus, to the repressed elements in the id he appears in the light of a helper and liberator.

With the ego and the superego the case is different. Insofar as the ego institutions have endeavored to restrain the id impulse by methods of their own, the analyst comes on the scene as a disturber of the peace. In the course of his work, he abolishes repressions which have been laboriously achieved and destroys compromise formations whose effect, indeed, was pathological but whose form was perfectly ego-syntonic. The analyst's aim in bringing the unconscious into consciousness and the efforts of the ego institutions to master the instinctual life are contrary to one another. Hence, except insofar as the patient's insight into his illness determines matters otherwise, the ego institutions regard the analyst's purpose as a menace.

. . . [W]e shall describe the ego's relation to the work of analysis as threefold. In exercising the faculty of self-observation, . . . the ego makes common cause with the analyst; its capacities in this direction are at his service, and it transmits to him a picture of the other institutions, drawn from such of their derivatives as make their way into its territory. The ego is antagonistic to the analysis in that it is unreliable and biased in its self-observation and, while conscientiously registering and passing on certain facts, falsifies and rejects others and prevents them from coming to light—a procedure wholly contrary to the methods of analytic research, which insist on seeing everything that emerges, without discrimination. Finally, the ego is itself the object of analysis, in that the defensive operations in which it is perpetually engaged are carried on unconsciously and can be brought into consciousness only at a considerable expenditure of effort, very much like the unconscious activity of any of the prohibited instinctual impulses.

## *Defense against Instinct, Manifesting Itself as Resistance*

. . . I [have] tried for the purposes of this study to draw a theoretical distinction between the analysis of the id and that of the ego, which in our practical work are inseparably bound up with one another. The result of this attempt is simply to corroborate afresh the conclusion to which experience has led us, that in analysis all the material which assists us to analyze the ego makes its appearance in the form of resistance to the analysis of the id. The facts are so self-evident that explanation seems almost superfluous. The ego becomes active in the analysis whenever it desires by means of a counteraction to prevent an inroad by the id. Since it is the aim of the analytic method to enable ideational representatives of repressed instincts to enter consciousness, i.e., to encourage these inroads by the id, the ego's defensive operations against such representatives automatically assume the character of active resistance to analysis. And since, further, the analyst uses his personal influence to secure the observance of the fundamental rule which enables such ideas to emerge in the patient's free associations, the defense set up by the ego against the instincts takes the form of direct opposition to the analyst himself. Hostility to the analyst and a strengthening of the measures designed to prevent the id impulses from emerging coincide automatically. When, at certain moments in the analysis, the defense is withdrawn and instinctual representatives can make their appearance unhindered, in the form of free associations, the relation of the ego to the analyst is relieved of disturbance from this quarter.

There are, of course, many possible forms of resistance in analysis beside this particular type. As well as the so-called ego resistances there are, as we know, the transference resistances, which are differently constituted, and also those opposing forces, so hard to overcome in analysis, which have their source in the repetition compulsion. Thus we cannot say that every resistance is the result of a defensive measure on the part of the ego. But every such defense against the id, if set up during analysis, can be detected only in the form of resistance to the analyst's work. Analysis of ego resistances gives us a good opportunity of observing and bringing into consciousness the ego's unconscious defensive operations in full swing.

## *Defense against Affects*

We have other opportunities beside those provided by the clashes between ego and instinct for a close observation of the activities of the former. The ego is in conflict not only with those id derivatives which try to make their way into its territory in order to gain access to consciousness and to obtain gratification. It defends itself no less energetically and actively against the affects associated with these instinctual impulses. When repudiating the claims of instinct, its first task must always be to come to terms with these affects. Love, longing, jealousy, mortification, pain, and mourning accompany sexual wishes, hatred, anger, and rage the impulses of aggression; if the instinctual demands with which they are associated are to be warded off, these affects must submit to all the various measures to which the ego resorts in its efforts to master them, i.e., they must undergo metamorphosis. Whenever transformation of an affect occurs, whether in analysis or outside it, the ego has been at work and we have an opportunity of studying its operations. We know that the fate of the affect associated with an instinctual demand is not simply identical with that of its ideational representative. Obviously, however, one and the same ego can have at its disposal only a limited number of possible means of defense. At particular periods in life and according to its own specific structure, the individual ego selects now one defensive method now another—it may be repression, displacement, reversal, etc.; and these it can employ both in its conflict with the instincts and in its defense against the liberation of affect. If we know how a particular patient seeks to defend himself against the emergence of his instinctual impulses, i.e., what is the nature of his habitual ego resistances, we can form an idea of his probable attitude toward his own unwelcome affects. If, in another patient, particular forms of affect transformation are strongly in evidence, such as complete suppression of emotion, denial, etc., we shall not be surprised if he adopts the same methods of defense against his instinctual impulses and his free associations. It is the same ego, and in all its conflicts it is more-or-less consistent in using every means which it has at its command.

## *Permanent Defense Phenomena*

Another field in which the ego's defensive operations may be studied is that of the phenomena to which Wilhelm Reich (1935) refers in his remarks on "the consistent analysis of resistance."[a] Bodily attitudes such as stiffness and rigidity, personal peculiarities such as a fixed smile, contemptuous, ironical, and arrogant behavior—all these are residues of very vigorous defensive processes in the past, which have become dissociated from their original situations (conflicts with instincts or affects) and have developed into permanent character traits, the "armor-plating of character" (*Charakterpanzerung*, as Reich calls it). When in analysis we succeed in tracing these residues to their historical source, they recover their mobility and cease to block by their fixation our access to the defensive operations upon which the ego is at the moment actively engaged. Since these modes of defense have become permanent, we cannot now bring their emergence and disappearance into relation with the emergence and disappearance of instinctual demands and affects from within or with the occurrence and cessation of situations of temptation and affective stimuli from without. Hence their analysis is a peculiarly laborious process. I am sure that we are justified in placing them in the foreground only when we can detect no trace at all of a present conflict between ego, instinct, and affect. And I am equally sure that there is no justification for restricting the term "analysis of resistance" to the analysis of these particular phenomena, for it should apply to that of all resistances.

## *Symptom Formation*

Analysis of the resistances of the ego, of its defensive measures against the instincts and of the transformations undergone by the affects reveals and brings into consciousness in a living flow the same methods of defense as meet our eyes in a state of petrification when we analyze the permanent "armor-plating of character." We come across them, on a larger scale and again, in a state of fixation, when we study the formation of neurotic symptoms. For the part played by the ego in the formation of those compromises which we call symptoms consists in the unvarying use of a special method of defense when confronted with a particular instinctual demand and the repetition of exactly the same procedure every time that demand recurs in its stereotyped form. We know (S. Freud, 1936; A. Freud, 1946, p. 46) that there is a regular connection

[a] *Konsequente Widerstandsanalyse.*

between particular neuroses and special modes of defense, as, for instance, between hysteria and repression or between obsessional neurosis and the processes of isolation and undoing. We find the same constant connection between neurosis and defense mechanism when we study the modes of defense which a patient employs against his affects and the form of resistance adopted by his ego. The attitude of a particular individual toward his free associations in analysis and the manner in which, when left to himself, he masters the demands of his instincts and wards off unwelcome affects enable us to deduce a priori the nature of his symptom formation. On the other hand, the study of the latter enables us to infer a posteriori what is the structure of his resistances and of his defense against his affects and instincts. We are most familiar with this parallelism in the case of hysteria and obsessional neurosis, where it is especially apparent between the formation of the patient's symptoms and the form assumed by his resistances. The symptom formation of hysterical patients in their conflict with their instincts is based primarily on repression; they exclude from consciousness the ideational representatives of their sexual impulses. The form of their resistance to free association is analogous. Associations which put the ego on its defense are simply dismissed. All that the patient finds is a blank in consciousness. He becomes silent, that is to say, the same interruption occurs in the flow of his associations as took place in his instinctual processes during the formation of his symptoms. On the other hand, we learn that the mode of defense adopted in symptom formation by the ego of the obsessional neurotic is that of isolation. It simply removes the instinctual impulses from their context, while retaining them in consciousness. Accordingly, the resistance of such patients takes a different form. The obsessional patient does not fall silent; he speaks, even when in a state of resistance. But he severs the links between his associations and isolates ideas from affects when he is speaking, so that his associations seem as meaningless on a small scale as his obsessional symptoms on a large scale.

## *Analytic Technique and the Defense against Instincts and Affects*

A young girl came to me to be analyzed on account of states of acute anxiety, which were interfering with her daily life and preventing her regular attendance at school. Although she came because her mother urged her to do so, she showed no unwillingness to tell me about her life both in the past and in the present. Her attitude toward me was friendly and frank, but I noticed that in all her communications she carefully avoided making any allusion to her symptom. She never mentioned anxiety attacks which took place between the analytic sessions. If I myself insisted on bringing her symptom into the analysis or gave interpretations of her anxiety which were based on unmistakable indications in her associations, her friendly attitude changed. On every such occasion the result was a volley of contemptuous and mocking remarks. The attempt to find a connection between the patient's attitude and her relation to her mother was completely unsuccessful. Both in consciousness and in the unconscious that relation was entirely different. In these repeated outbursts of contempt and ridicule the analyst found herself at a loss and the patient was, for the time being, inaccessible to further analysis. As the analysis went deeper, however, we found that these affects did not represent a transference reaction in the true sense of the term and were not connected with the analytic situation at all. They indicated the patient's customary attitude toward herself whenever emotions of tenderness, longing, or anxiety were about to emerge in her affective life. The more powerfully the affect forced itself upon her, the more vehemently and scathingly did she ridicule herself. The analyst drew down these defensive reactions upon herself only secondarily, because she was encouraging the demands of the patient's anxiety to be worked over in consciousness. The interpretation of the content of the anxiety, even when this could be correctly inferred from other communications, could have no result so long as every approach to the affect only intensified her defensive reaction. It was impossible to make that content conscious until we had brought into consciousness and so rendered inoperative the patient's method of defending herself against her affects by contemptuous disparagement—a process which had become automatic in every department of her life. Historically this mode of defense by means of ridicule and scorn was explained by her identification of herself with her dead father, who used to try to train the little girl in self-control by making mocking remarks when she gave way to some emotional outburst. The method had become stereotyped through her memory of her father, whom she had loved dearly. The technique necessary in order to understand this case was to begin with the analysis of the patient's defense against her affects and to go on to the elucidation of her resistance in the transference. Then, and then only, was it possible to proceed to the analysis of her anxiety itself and of its antecedents.

From the technical standpoint this parallelism between a patient's defense against his instincts and against his affects, his symptom formation and his resistance, is of great importance, especially in child analysis. The most obvious defect in our technique when analyzing children is the absence of free association. To do without this is very difficult and that not only because it is through the ideational representatives of a patient's instincts, emerging in his free associations, that we learned most about his id. After all, there are other means of obtaining information about the id impulses. The dreams and daydreams of children, the activity of their fantasy in play, their drawings, and so forth reveal their id tendencies in a more undisguised and accessible form than is usual in adults, and in analysis they can almost take the place of the emergence of id derivatives in free association. But, when we dispense with the fundamental rule of analysis, the conflict over its observance also disappears, and it is from that conflict that we derive our knowledge of the ego resistances when we are analyzing adults—our knowledge, that is to say, of the ego's defensive operations against the id derivatives. There is, therefore, a risk that child analysis may yield a wealth of information about the id but a meager knowledge of the infantile ego.

In the play technique advocated by the English school for the analysis of little children, the lack of free association is made good in the most direct way. These analysts hold that a child's play is equivalent to the associations of adults, and they make use of his games for purposes of interpretation in just the same way. The free flow of associations corresponds to the undisturbed progress of the games; interruptions and inhibitions in play are equated with the breaks in free association. It follows that, if we analyze the interruption to play, we discover that it represents a defensive measure on the part of the ego, comparable to resistance in free association.

If for theoretical reasons, as, for instance, because we feel some hesitation in pressing the interpretation of symbols to its extreme limits, we cannot accept this complete equation between free association and play, we must try to substitute some new technical methods in child analysis to assist us in our investigation of the ego. I believe that analysis of the transformations undergone by the child's affects may fill the gap. The affective life of children is less complicated and more transparent than that of adults; we can observe what it is which evokes the affects of the former, whether inside or outside the analytic situation. A child sees more attention paid to another than to himself; now, we say, he will inevitably feel jealousy and mortification. A long cherished wish is fulfilled: the fulfillment must certainly give him joy. He expects to be punished: he experiences anxiety. Some anticipated and promised pleasure is suddenly deferred or refused: the result is sure to be a sense of disappointment, etc. We expect children normally to react to these particular occurrences with these specific affects. But, contrary to expectation, observation may show us a very different picture. For instance, a child may exhibit indifference when we should have looked for disappointment, exuberant high spirits instead of mortification, excessive tenderness instead of jealousy. In all these cases, something has happened to disturb the normal process: the ego has intervened and has caused the affect to be transformed. The analysis and bringing into consciousness of the specific form of this defense against affect—whether it be reversal, displacement, or complete repression—teaches us something of the particular technique adopted by the ego of the child in question and, just like the analysis of resistance, enables us to infer his attitude to his instincts and the nature of his symptom formation. It is therefore a fact of peculiar importance in child analysis that, in observing the affective processes, we are largely independent of the child's voluntary cooperation and his truthfulness or untruthfulness in what he tells us. His affects betray themselves against his will.

The following is an illustration of what I have just said. A certain little boy used to have fits of military enthusiasm whenever there was any occasion for castration anxiety; he would put on a uniform and equip himself with a toy sword and other weapons. After observing him on several such occasions, I guessed that he was turning his anxiety into its opposite, namely, into aggressiveness. From that time I had no difficulty in deducing that castration anxiety lay behind all his fits of aggressive behavior. Moreover I was not surprised to discover that he was an obsessional neurotic, i.e., that there was in his instinctual life a tendency to turn unwelcome impulses into their opposite. One little girl appeared to have no reaction at all to situations of disappointment. All that could be observed was a quivering of one corner of her mouth. She betrayed thereby the capacity of her ego to get rid of unwelcome psychic processes and to replace them by physical ones. In this case, we should not be surprised to find that the patient tended to react hysterically in the conflict with her instinctual life. Another girl, still in the latency period, had succeeded in so completely repressing her envy of her little brother's penis—an affect by which her life was entirely dominated—that even in analysis it was exceptionally difficult to detect any traces of it. All that the analyst could observe was that, whenever she had occasion to envy or be jealous of her brother, she began to play a curious imaginary game, in which she herself enacted the part of a magician, who had the power of transforming and otherwise influencing the whole world by his gestures. This child was converting envy into its opposite, into an overinsistence on her own magical powers, by means of which she avoided the painful insight into what she supposed to be her physical inferiority. Her ego made use of the defense mechanism of reversal, a kind of reaction formation against the affect, at the same time betraying its obsessional attitude toward the instinct. Once this was realized, it was easy for the analyst to deduce the presence of penis envy whenever the game of magic recurred. We see, then, that what we acquire by applying this principle is simply a kind of technique for the translation of the defensive utterances of the ego, and this method corresponds almost exactly to the resolution of the ego resistances as they occur in free association. Our purpose is the same as in the analysis of resistance. The more completely we succeed in bringing both the resistance and the defense against affects into consciousness and so rendering them inoperative, the more rapidly shall we advance to an understanding of the id.

## *Theoretical Implications*[2]

JESSIE TAFT

... Resistance, too, is evident enough here on every page but it is never handled by interpretation nor is any attempt made to break it. Rather it is met, as far as possible, frankly and without denial or counterresist-

---

2 In previous sections, Taft has presented therapy notes from the case of Helen, a seven-year-old girl referred for persistent tearing of her clothes and refusal to go to school. There were sixteen sessions, covering a span of two months.

ance in feeling, even when its practical execution must be checked, and with a real appreciation of its inevitability and positive value as an expression of the child's will, however negatively put.

Perhaps the feature of difference most conspicuously present is the emphasis on time. This came about not so much through my Rankian principles as because the ending was set in advance by practical considerations. Certainly in working with an adult no such arbitrary arrangement would be planned by me although it might happen. But in this case I was really glad of the protection of a predetermined limit which I tried quite consciously with the use of suggestion to put in terms of Helen's vacation rather than my own. However, I am convinced that the suggestion was as acceptable to her as to me, and if she had shown genuine unreadiness to take it, I was quite prepared to announce my own vacation well in advance and to work through the more intense resistance and resentment which this would probably have occasioned.

Perhaps the aspect which surprised me as much as it may have surprised the reader is the way in which Helen herself seizes upon every limitation or alteration in time and makes it the bone of contention between us. An adult will react, too, just as promptly, though less openly, to the time elements but one does not expect a child to be so aware. Possibly my own interest in time in this particular case increased her sensitivity to it. Be that as it may, the picture is true in spite of its unusual emphasis. Time—the time of the individual hour, the number of hours per week, the total number of weeks—represents, in its different spans, units of experience in which life is accepted, if at all, as it goes on the painful terms of giving up, of separation, of reluctant admission that it is possible and, if guilt is not too strong, even desirable, to go on to the new experience, however precious that which is left behind.

Perhaps just this way of looking at time and the series of endings, of separations of which analysis, like life, is made up, may bring out the difference in the Rankian understanding and use of the transference, so much feared by the lay person. You will find in this material clear evidence of the growing positive feeling, expressed shyly in such phrases as, "I love you and you love me." (Note that she will not carry full responsibility for the emotion but makes me share it.) My response is first of all to accept her feeling simply, ignoring her reference to mine, and second, to bring out the equally real negative feelings which she is not so ready to admit but which are easier to bear in the presence of the positive and actually strengthen them. If I emphasize the positive at the time she is expressing it, it will throw her back again into the negative. The fact that I can carry the negative side leaves her free to feel the positive to the full. In no case do I try to deny the love emotions or to belittle them, but only to balance them with the inevitable opposite which Helen is expressing in action anyway while denying it consciously.

Transference, like resistance, is accepted for what it is, a stage in the growth process, in the taking over of the own will into the self. It is the point at which the will is yielded up to the other, is worshiped, if you please, in the other and kept in abeyance in the self. Inevitably, as inevitably as life goes on of its own impulse, this transference projection will flow back into the positive will of the patient and be acknowledged as his, unless the vanity of the analyst or his own inability to let himself be abandoned, increases the guilt of the patient so that he cannot admit his own will and the desire to be free. From Rank's point of view, there need be no anxiety about fixation on the analyst, or about breaking up the transference, if one believes in life and growth and individuality. All one need to do is to look to one's own emotions and see that they do not interfere with the struggle of the patient to find himself. The more positive and conscious the emotion he feels for the analysis or the analyst at the end, the more sure one may be that the actual dependence is over. Conscious feeling measures the degree of the giving-up, indicates the abandonment of the effort to possess the other, in favor of the will to be oneself, to go on. One truly loves only what one leaves.

There is something very touching about the fact that life is true to itself even in a child of seven. Despite my experience with adults and my own analysis, somehow I could not believe that a child would be able to bear the leaving of a situation which can take on such meaning as the analytic relationship. My fear expressed itself as it naturally would ambivalently: first, would a child find anything in this type of analysis to compensate for the deprivations, and, second, if it did, could it give up what it had found. In other words, I was afraid either that nothing would happen or that too much would happen, a common enough fear with all of us. Apparently my fear for the child was nothing but my doubt of myself projected, the possibility that I might not be able to bear the child's transference or his withdrawal. It is evident to me now that the child, like the adult, can save himself, can adapt himself to whatever time is at his disposal, can select and use what he needs, go as deep as it is safe to go under the circumstances and no deeper, provided only the analyst is able to see what the child is doing, to bear it, and to be willing to let the child conquer, to have it, finally, his way.

This brings me back to what is after all the only essential in analysis, to speak statistically, the bare bones of the process stripped of all content, whether it be drawn from past, present, or future, and this is the meeting of two wills—in this case, the actual clash with the child, the living, immediately present action and reaction of her will upon mine, which constitutes whatever of reality, therapeutic or otherwise, there may be in the relationship.

Nothing is more obvious than the will conflict which Helen sets up from the first moment of her resistance to going with me to the final leave-taking and her reluctance to say good-by. The initial hesitation and fear, which I overcome by direct pressure, are followed at once as fast as she gains courage by a great variety of methods of attack, ways of trying out my strength and testing her own negatively; for instance, her persistent efforts from the beginning almost to the bitter end to find something which she can force me to let her take home. It is not so much a matter of wanting the things she takes, she doubtless destroys or loses them almost at once, but of enjoying the process, the conflict itself. If I gave her everything she asked for, she would only go on to find the forbidden object. She is looking for an external limit, for someone who has the strength to stand up to her but who will not turn upon her destructively. Like all the rest of the world, she longs to find that rock upon which she may safely lean, but to be free also to leave it when she gets ready. It takes a great deal of testing-out—many attacks upon me—to get to the point where she feels her own will safe enough from my encroachment to yield it up in the transference emotion of the sixth and seventh hours. Even here aggressiveness is only suspended momentarily, her behavior is still a challenge, now intended more to arouse feeling in me, to make me the one to care rather than to get the better of me externally. The battle continues to the very end as it must but the admission of herself, her own intentions, and feelings grows more constant and free. "I won't do it really, I'm only fooling you." "Everything I do is to fool you." This kind of frankness becomes quite the rule. Her dislike of my writing, which is present from the beginning but is very indirect at first and apparent only in her increased attempts to gain my attention or prevent me from using the pencil by borrowing it, finally breaks out into an explosive, "Stop that writing," and an admission that it makes her mad. The clash over the ink which comes along in the second half of the relationship has a totally different character from that of earlier encounters. We are now able to be humorous, to assert and accept each other's difference. She allows for my dislike of spilled ink; I enjoy her breaking the letter of the law when the ink dries up enough to make it possible to play with it. A certain tolerance has come into our relationship as well as a mutual understanding. Perhaps this is what she is trying to express in the tenth hour when she says, "You think what I think."

This movement which so obviously takes place as the relationship develops, chiefly in terms of Helen's attitude but secondarily of mine too, results from the nature of the analytic situation, the only situation in life where one is allowed to project to the limit without the interference of counterprojection. Because I do not fight Helen back, do not try to conquer her but see and admit the nature of the negative feelings which naturally arise when her efforts to conquer me come to naught, she is forced for lack of anything to oppose, to fall back upon other aspects of herself, and slowly, with many denials, withdrawals, and negative interludes, she begins to project the positive will, the possessive attitudes. Now she tries to control me through her positive interest instead of the negative. As Santa Claus, she gives me the presents I have refused her; she makes me come to see her in play even if I won't in reality; she is the teacher, I am the pupil who is to be corrected. Yet underlying this play world in which she controls me is always the reality of time and place as well as my separateness which continually throws back upon the self of the child even the most positive projection. Gradually, however, so much of herself both positive and negative has been expressed and accepted without interference that now she is somewhat released from the drive to defeat or dominate the other and can take it back partially into herself with new recognition and tenderness for the person who has permitted the projections and a guilt for the dawning impulse to leave the restraining though satisfying conditions under which she has begun to chafe.

It is interesting to see that after the ninth and tenth hours in which she comes to a climax of aggressive possession of me and the situation with wild play and the spilling of water over the blotter, there follows in the eleventh hour just what one would expect—the climax of guilt feeling and the overt expression of anxiety. Repentance and uneasiness regarding her treatment of the blotter are almost the only signs and admissions of fear during the entire time, except her reference to being scared in the last hour, while the confession of her sin of clothes-tearing in terms of the reformed doll baby is also the only time when the behavior for which she was brought to clinic is spontaneously mentioned.

It is at this point that my traditional morality and pedagogical responsibility for the young overcome the analyst, and I am caught in the net of content to the extent of trying to teach her something about the folly of tearing one's own clothes. Analytically, I should realize that she brings up the tearing of clothes as symbolically as she might any tale from her past or dream of the night before to carry her present feeling of guilt which arises not from any actual tearing but from the change in relation to me. She is guilty for what she has done to me, for the freedom of will she has exercised in the situation, for the fact that she has let herself go so far in yielding to another, and still more for the realization that underneath she is already feeling the impulse to go. With Helen, clothes-tearing is the cardinal sin of the local situation, not lying, stealing, or sex as with many children, and she brings it in at the moment when she is most aware of guilt to express her present feeling in the analytic situation. That she resents my taking advantage of her to preach is clearly evidenced in her rising from the chair and attacking the doll so viciously. I come to in time to accept this feeling at least, for what it is, an attack upon me, a justifiable resentment for my lack of understanding.

Perhaps what brings the relationship to so sharp a climax at this point, is my deliberate reference in the ninth hour to the close of school and the fact that she will want to stop coming sometime. This she denies stoutly at first but when I persist, "But you may not always want to come," she says reluctantly as if the truth came out in spite of her, "No, not always." This admission naturally brings about its own denial as a reaction, an aggressive taking possession of the next hour with the simultaneous expression of hate and tenderness, a desire to hurt, to get even, combined with positive emotion, "You always make me happy . . . make me feel nice." The eleventh hour then, naturally produces the full confession of the ambivalent will and the determination to use it constructively at least for that hour: "I'm going to work, not play at all, but see how much I can draw" which expresses, as with adults, the need for a social justification of will. In this very hour, she herself refers to the closing of school and by the twelfth hour is almost willing to admit both her love and her readiness to go in one breath. . . .

## REFERENCES

FREUD, ANNA. *The ego and the mechanisms of defense.* New York: International Univer. Press, 1946.

FREUD, S. *Inhibitions, symptoms, and anxiety* (1926). London: Hogarth Press, 1936.

REICH, W. *Charakteranalyse, Technik, und Grundlagen für studierende und praktizierende Analytiker.* Vienna: Author, 1933, 1934.

❀ CHAPTER ELEVEN

# Transference

ANY DISCUSSION of transference in the positive sense necessarily involves consideration of the opposite side of the coin—negative transference—which in turn implies resistance. Consequently, the discussion in this and the previous chapter overlap with respect to content.

The transference situation in the treatment of children is generally regarded as differing from the transference neurosis of the adult patient. The child is still living with, and closely tied to, his parents who are the original objects around which the neurotic conflicts and symptoms developed in the first place.

In a paper antedating the one reproduced in this chapter, Fraiberg[1] emphasizes that the therapist only shares with the parents the child's feelings of affection, dependence, and aggression. She also points out that the child's symptoms are not displaced from the original objects but, rather, are "extended into" the therapeutic situation. The therapist may be seen as a dangerous person who could expose the child to intolerable anxiety. The child, in resisting the threatened liberation of impulses, will employ the same defenses against therapy that he formerly used against the affects. In the current paper, Fraiberg continues these themes through a descriptive account of the course of therapy with a destructive and aggressive little boy. Transference fantasies and reactions were repeatedly in evidence and accompanied by periods of marked resistance.

[1] Selma H. Fraiberg, "Clinical Notes on the Nature of Transference in Child Analysis," *Psychoanalytic Study of the Child,* VI (1951), 286–306.

Frankl and Hellman develop the concept of the "therapeutic alliance" (as differentiated from the transference neurosis) which involves, on the patient's part, the desire to be helped, the ability to tolerate anxiety, and the capacity to establish relationships. The therapist strives to maintain a supportive role and to let the child know that his feelings are understood. Ego functions are reinforced and reality-testing emphasized, e.g., the child is helped to a recognition that although hostile fantasies can be projected onto the analyst, this same analyst also retains his basic function as a representative of the real world. The establishment of a therapeutic alliance is seen as essential to reassure the child and to provide support during periods of resistance and negative transference.

# *Technical Aspects of the Analysis of a Child with a Severe Behavior Disorder*

SELMA FRAIBERG

From the earliest days of child analysis, the treatment of the child with behavior problems has been regarded as a special problem. The child who acted out his inner conflicts and whose behavior obtained satisfactions for him was not, strictly speaking, analyzable. In order to make this child analyzable, our earliest techniques were directed toward bringing about an internalization of the conflict, we "created a neurosis," in effect. The analyst actively intervened to bring about restriction of the behavior, to reduce the gratification obtained through direct discharge of impulses, and sometimes deliberately created anxiety in the child in order to give him an incentive to curtail his acting and to motivate him in analysis.

In the intervening years, the mutually enriching progress of child analysis and ego psychology has brought about many changes in child analytic techniques. As Anna Freud has pointed out, many of the differences between the method of adult analysis and that of child analysis have begun to fade. Now, speaking generally of child analysis, we try as far as possible to relieve the analyst of educational functions and active interference in order not to obscure or distort the transference. As our knowledge of defense has expanded, we are able to employ interpretation for certain analytic objectives where once we would have been obliged to intervene or prohibit.

There remains the special problem of the child with behavior problems, but he, too, has been the beneficiary of new insights and progress in child analysis. We have greatly enlarged our understanding of the defensive aspects of certain types of behavior and are in a position to use analytic means to bring about a restriction of acting that in earlier days required intervention. Analysis of behavior as defense against anxiety may bring about the desirable analytic cooperation in a child. When the child himself has learned to regard his behavior as a defense the analysis can examine the complex structure of the behavior, which almost invariably reveals a phobia of massive proportions at the core of the disorder. The readiness to transfer both id impulses and defense, which is characteristic of the child with behavior problems, can be employed to advantage in the analysis of transference resistances.

There remain, of course, those occasions when a child bent on destruction can close out the analyst's interpretations and oblige us to restrict or prohibit. I should not wish to minimize the practical problems of dealing with many severely disturbed children with behavior problems. However, the advantages are all on the side of the analytic measures for dealing with acting. When we must intervene out of practical necessity, we almost always pay a price and we learn nothing new about the significance of the behavior. If, on the other hand, we can handle the behavior analytically, we have the double advantage of restoring the child's control and of obtaining valuable insight and new progress in the analysis.

In the case example that follows, I shall attempt to describe the resistances encountered in the analytic treatment of a severely disturbed boy and the technical problems that I encountered. The treatment extended over a three-and-one-half-year period and was brought to a very satisfactory conclusion.

Roger began his analysis with me at the age of four. His parents had finally been reduced to complete helplessness in coping with his behavior problems. He was obstinate, negative, and relentlessly goading. He would seize upon any trivial point to challenge his parents and finally provoke them to anger and a spanking. At three, he had once thrown his nursery school group into chaos by claiming that he was God and he could make everybody do what he said. His parents described destructive orgies in which he would run about the house in a giddy fashion, kicking doors, smashing objects, and giggling in a peculiarly joyless way. He showed no signs of remorse for any of his behavior.

His nursery school teachers and I felt that we could not assess his intelligence. He appeared to be at least normal, possibly bright normal. In the chaos of Roger's four-year-old personality none of us had been able to catch a glimpse of an extraordinary intelligence that revealed itself after better integration of the personality was achieved.

Roger's parents dated their conflicts with him back to the second year. Roger's first year, according to the parents, had been uneventful. There were no problems in feeding; his health had been excellent. Speech and motor development appeared to have been accelerated. As the outlines of the history filled in during the three years of analysis I could reconstruct the second year along these lines: almost as soon as Roger became active he came into conflict with his mother. The contest between mother and toddler became the model for the later relationship; every wish of the mother had to be negated.

The parents at that time were very much preoccupied with their own conflicts in marriage and were contemplating divorce. Roger was the unplanned-for second baby. A sister, Judy, who figured prominently in Roger's analysis, was two years older than he. The unwanted baby made divorce more difficult now. At a time when the mother's hostility toward her husband was at its height, the little boy became the object of a good measure of her destructive feelings toward males. The children were witnesses to the verbal battles between the parents, and at night they could easily overhear the parental quarrels in the bedroom next to the room they shared. Roger had witnessed his mother's destructive rages on many occasions. On one occasion she had literally smashed a piece of furniture to bits. We had good reason to believe that one of the motives in Roger's destructive behavior was an early identification with the dangerous and destructive mother. The mother herself began analysis a year before I began to work with Roger, and at the time the parents consulted me the family had acquired more stability and the mother had acquired far better control of herself.

A contest between mother and child over bowel training began in Roger's second year and continued until he was nearly four. Roger soiled himself and refused to use the toilet. According to the mother, when she finally "put her foot down" the soiling ceased.

The parents had found no effective means of discipline for Roger. He was spanked often in parental rage and helplessness, but there was no conviction on the part of either parent that spanking served any purpose in controlling his behavior.

Roger's father was harassed, resigned, and deeply wounded as a husband and a father. He, too, was drawn into conflict with his son. Roger's successful challenging of his father's authority further devalued him as a man, and he found himself impelled against his better judgment to take up the challenge and use physical force to subdue this relentless opponent, aged four.

In the early analytic observations of Roger I obtained a fair picture of his typical behavior problems. Almost from the beginning he transferred his provocative behavior to the analytic sessions. He gleefully smeared chocolate over my furniture, smashed the furniture of the doll house, tore up books and magazines, and ran up and down the halls of the apartment house banging on doors and annoying other tenants. When my words could not reach him, I tried on two occasions to hold his hands to prevent him from destroying objects. This was a mistake. The first time he kicked me savagely and ran out of the room. The second time he giggled with excitement and tried to press himself against me. When I quietly withdrew he renewed his antics, now challenging me to punish him.

I knew that I could not influence him until I achieved a relationship with him, but here, too, Roger presented special problems. He could relate only through negating strenuously. When I invited him into my office at the beginning of the session he would refuse obstinately. If I quietly ignored him and entered my office alone, pretending to work at my desk, he would come barging triumphantly in five or ten minutes later under the illusion that he was disturbing me. If he became destructive and I asked him to leave the room and come back when he could control himself, he would obstinately refuse to leave. Interpretations directed to his fear of me or his expectations of punishment fell upon deaf ears. He could negate interpretations, too.

In the early interviews, he paraded around with a paper cigarette in his mouth, boasting that he was a daddy and that he was stronger than his daddy. He confided, with much giggling, that he would sometimes get up at night and get into his mother's bed. He played out his obsessive interest in parental activities in games with the dolls. The dolls wrestled together, they made noises, and regularly the play ended with a car wreck or an explosion.

There was little point in handling any of this material analytically. It is only useful to describe this material in order to show the naked and undisguised character of these communications. Much more significant is the fact that all this material emerged without any manifest anxiety or guilt.

There is no doubt that at this time Roger's behavior achieved certain satisfactions for him and that as long as these satisfactions existed there would be little motive for him to cooperate in his treatment. During the early weeks of treatment I was able to help Roger's parents understand one of the motives in his behavior, the relentless provocation of punishment. I enlisted their cooperation in giving up the spankings and we discussed other means of discipline. Much time was devoted to a re-education of the parents in this area, strengthening the positive ties to the child and enabling the parents to employ their relationship in a more effective discipline in which parental approval and disapproval might carry the necessary weight.

In the meantime, I began to deal analytically with Roger and used every good opportunity to help him see how his behavior was a defense against anxiety. When anxiety began to break through at home and in the analytic sessions, I am sure that this first success was due as much to the parents and their change of discipline as to the analytic interpretations.

I mark the real beginning of Roger's analytic treatment as the day on which Roger announced, "I'm afraid at night. A man chases me." And when I asked about the dream and the man who chased him he said forlornly, "I don't want to tell you. It's somebody in my family."

And then in the sequence that followed I could see very clearly one of the patterns in Roger's behavior. He could not tell me what he feared from the man but immediately translated the thought into action. He became a burglar in his play, breaking into the doll house, then deliberately broke one of the andirons of the fireplace in the doll house. Suddenly he was off on one of his destructive orgies, breaking crayons, pencils, doll furniture, everything at hand. And there was no affect now; the anxiety that had briefly shown itself at the beginning of the hour had vanished. There was only the pixie Roger, gleefully destroying objects and closing me out. But now we could understand the pattern. In the moment that castration anxiety emerged in association to the dream, he acted out the dream, reversing the active and passive roles. In the dream he was passive and in great danger; in re-enacting the dream he became active, he performed the symbolic destructive act. By identifying with the aggressor and by switching from passive to active, he did not need to experience anxiety. Now we can understand why Roger was capable of performing aggressive and destructive acts without any manifest anxiety. And now we were in a position to deal with the behavior as defense.

As soon as I was able to show Roger how his behavior was a defense against anxiety we had the means to bring about some control of the behavior and I was able to bring him into a therapeutic relationship. Often I could prevent a destructive orgy or his wild running around the room by the suggestion, "Now we know that something is making you afraid inside. Let's talk about it so I can help you." And when Roger began to understand that talking about his fears relieved them, the initial resistances to treatment began to dissolve. I was struck by the fact that the transference now had the same character as the transference obtained in phobic cases. He was strongly dependent upon me, he needed me as an ally against danger.

Meantime, too, the picture at home began to change. There was considerably less acting and less need to provoke the parents, and the parents began to catch glimpses of the terror and helplessness of the child which gave them a new perspective on his behavior. With diminution of the acting, Roger became a more gratifying child to his family; his parents began to respond with some warmth and found qualities in him that were easy to overlook earlier. With greater satisfactions at home Roger had additional strong incentive to work on his problems with me.

Yet, I do not wish to give the impression that the communication of fears and the accessibility of his fantasies made Roger's analysis easier than any other. During the first two years of analysis we had a flood of material around the themes of castration, primal-scene observations, masturbation, and sex play with his sister Judy. He could tell me, in so many words, that he feared that the faceless man in his recurrent terror dream would cut off his penis with a butcher knife. He could tell me that he thought mothers and daddies mutilated each other in intercourse. But the affect that accompanied these communications was thin and dilute, and I soon began to realize that isolation of affect played a very significant role in Roger's disturbance.

When we now turned our attention in analysis to the defenses against affects I encountered the most formidable resistance. It was difficult to explain to a little boy, now five and one-half, who was cooperating most earnestly in treatment, that it was really the feelings that were most important and that it was the feelings inside that were causing all the trouble. Only gradually was Roger able to appreciate that when he put the ideas in one place and the feelings in another he got no real relief from talking. As anxiety began to emerge in small quantities, Roger's suffering made me see why the defenses were so strong.

During a period in which we were dealing with sex play and his obsessive concern with the female genitalia, he complained of dizziness in his hours. And for several hours he would begin each session with the ritual statement, "I am always the same Roger whether I come here or whether I'm home." During tense moments in the hour he would suddenly cry out, "I'm always the same Roger!" When I inquired about this he would say, "I *have* to say it. I *have* to say it!" It was clear that at such times he experienced feelings of depersonalization and that the formidable defenses against anxiety had been erected to protect the ego against loss of identity. During the same period he played a repetitious game with the doll house which he called "catastrophe." The game always began with innocuous doll play in which the doll family had dinner, looked at television, etc. Then the family would go to bed. Suddenly a "hurricane" or "tornado" would come up. Roger would throw all the doll furniture down the doll-house stairs or pile it in heaps on the floor of the doll house. Once he said there was a big explosion and he ran to call "The Red Cross" to come and rescue the people. "Oh, is this fun!" he would say, laughing in a singularly joyless way. And then, suddenly, in the midst of one of these games he turned pale, complained of dizziness and the "funny feeling" which I understood to be feelings of depersonalization.

The emergence of primal-scene memories was accompanied by an obssessive interest in his sister's and mother's genitalia; during this period his castration anxiety was so intense that it produced frequent episodes of depersonalization. Sometimes, during the same period, he would desperately clutch his penis which he understood, too, represented his fear that something could happen to his penis. As anxiety began to emerge more and more in our sessions, each of his characteristic defenses was brought into play. Sometimes in the same hour he would revert to identification with the aggressor; and if this was pointed out to him, he would inhibit the acting but almost immediately isolate anxiety. At other times he would simply take flight. During several sessions, he would stop in the midst of a dream analysis or play and cry out, "Oh, the feelings are coming, the feelings are coming," and run out of the room or run into a closet and close the door. He would return later, pale and tired. He understood fully now what tremendous anxiety there was within him and once, after much suffering, he said to me with marvelous wisdom, "I want to get it all out, but it will have to come out little by little, won't it?"

All the evidence pointed to the fact that the defenses against anxiety and guilt feelings were closely connected with masturbation fantasies. He was able to talk about masturbation and his fears of damage to the penis. He was also perfectly willing to communicate his fantasies to me, and I knew that certain of these were masturbation fantasies. But if I attempted to bring together the masturbation and the masturbation fantasies for analysis, I met the most determined resistance. In one of these fantasies, for example, he was a great inventor, greater, he said, than Edison. He had a secret invention, a rocket that could surpass anything invented to date. For a period of several weeks his mother reported that she could not get Roger up in the morning. He would lie in bed for an hour apparently masturbating. Roger's version of his reluctance to get up in the morning was that he was too busy thinking about his invention which, in a certain sense, was quite true. When it finally seemed necessary for me to bring together the fantasy and the masturbation for analysis, he began to act up in his session, ran around the room in giddy fashion and sang, "cuckoo, cuckoo, cuckoo," over and over, hitting himself on the head. "You're making me cuckoo with all that talk," he yelled. On the following day he was somewhat subdued and regretted his antics of the day before. When I now tried to link up the antics with his anxiety about the invention fantasy he closed me out securely. "I've decided not to talk about my inventions any more," he said. And he explained prudently, "If someone knows about it, then they'd want to copy it, and I don't have a copyright yet."

Now I began to understand one of the functions of isolation as a defense in Roger's case. The masturbation and the attendant fantasies needed to be maintained in isolation from each other. If he acknowledged that they belonged together, he would suffer anxiety and guilt. At the same time isolation of the ideational content from the act served to maintain the affects in isolation. Now, too, it became clear that there was a close connection between the behavior disorder and the masturbation fantasies. There was some evidence that at certain times his masturbation fantasies became too exciting to him; at such times he would abandon masturbation and act out his fantasies. (Here the mechanism is identical with the one described by Anna Freud [1949].) During the period that the boy inventor, Roger, declined to bring his inventions in for analysis, he was both coy and seductive with his mother and mercilessly challenging of his father's authority, finally bringing his father's wrath down upon him one weekend.

A good part of the three and one-half years of Roger's analysis was devoted to analysis of the defenses against affects. In child language I succeeded in helping him see how he put feelings and ideas in separate compartments and how this was his biggest problem.

Perhaps it would be useful now to examine in a little more detail a segment of the analysis in which the analysis of the transference brought us a very good part of the way toward successful resolution of these conflicts.

At this time Roger was six and one-half years old.[a] This period of analysis coincides with the period I had earlier described in which Roger had shown

[a] In order to explain Roger's ability to spell and do simple arithmetic in the sequence that follows, I should mention that Roger was in the second grade at this time, following advancement from nursery school to the first grade at the age of five.

the most determined resistances against the analysis of his masturbation fantasies.

This sequence begins with a daydream that Roger reported to me with dread and loathing. It precedes by one analytic hour a night terror and its accompanying daydream, in which the analysis reveals common themes. Roger confessed with great reluctance that there was something he just could not tell me. He didn't think he could ever tell me, he said, but maybe it wouldn't be necessary. If he could figure it out himself, it might solve the problem and he wouldn't need to tell me. When I explained to him that the big problems could not be solved unless we had all the parts, he made a heroic struggle and there followed this extraordinary sequence:

> "I think I can tell you. I think it's coming. Wait a minute. I'll have to go into the closet to think." While I waited, baffled, he ran into the closet, and presently I heard a queer, melancholy, atonal song, something like an infant's ah-ah-ah-ah "singing" when he rocks himself in bed. Then in the same singsong Roger began to tell me. "If my mo-ther and my fa-ther had to go away for a lo-ong, lo-ong time. That's the first part. Now give me time so I can tell you the next part. . . ." There was a pause, then Roger burst out of the closet. "I can't say it. I just can't." I tried to help him to tell me. With help he managed to say, "Well, someone would come to live with me." "Who would that be?" "I can't say it." And finally, spelling, "a g-i-r-l." "Now the rest I can't tell you right out. I'll tell it to you backwards and you'll have to figure it out. I'll give you a clue. If I said, 'eight' that would mean 'sixteen or seventeen' so, I'll say a girl of eight." I: "Does that mean that someone, a girl of sixteen or seventeen, would come to live with you?" "Don't say it! Don't say it!" "But Roger, what makes you so scared and ashamed in all this?" "I don't know." "Is this a daydream?" "Yes." "What happens next?" "That's what I don't know either. Whenever I get to that part I get stuck and it's just blank. . . . My mother and father are dead, see [first time he had used this word instead of "going away"]. And then this g-i-r-l comes to live with me and she is you know how old." I tried to get at his feelings. If he has to spell, it must mean that there are some thoughts in connection with all this that make him ashamed. He agreed. He doesn't know what it is.

In the next hour Roger reported "a night dream" and "a daydream." When he woke up that morning after the "night dream" he had a daydream while he was lying in bed. I should mention that he did not tell me the daydream until some time after reporting the night dream. I shall report them together here, only in order to organize the material better for study.

> *The nightdream.* There was a witch with Judy and it seemed they were fighting on one side against me and my boy friends on the other. Then in the next scene me and Judy and my mother and father were trying to dissolve a powder that would make a mask like a witch's.
>
> *The daydream.* I'm in a boat with a girl, a girl about sixteen or seventeen. The boat has wheels on it so it can go on land or water.

I had taught Roger to analyze his dreams through what we called "The What Pops into Your Mind Game." When I now invited Roger to tell me what popped into his mind, he could only report an obsessive thought, "This is crazy; this is crazy." We had already encountered the obsessive thought on a number of occasions and understood that it served the purpose of blocking all other associations and had the significance of repudiating analysis and of disbelieving the evidence of analysis. When I asked for details of the dream he described the witch quite exactly, giving particular emphasis to the fact that the witch wore a Halloween mask. Now I proposed that the witch's mask might represent his wish to disguise, that the witch represented someone he knew whom he did not wish to know in the dream. Instantly he said, "I think the witch was you! And then it pops into my mind that you have a secret about me and Judy has a secret about me!"

In the next hour he remembered a forgotten detail of the dream. "It takes place on the porch. There's the witch and Judy and me. The witch has a needle or a pin or something and she dropped it on the floor. I was going to reach for it when Judy grabbed it and gave it to the witch." He goes on, "And that makes me think that you or Judy could play a trick on me. Judy used to play tricks on me. She used to say there was a burglar in the house and make me come into bed with her. But there was no burglar. . . ." Now I reminded him that it was through such a trick that Judy used to get him to play games in bed with her, the secret games that they used to think were like the things grownups did. Roger said, "That must be it!"

In associating to the dream detail in which Judy "grabbed at" the needle that the witch lost we found another connection with the sex games in which Judy would "grab at" Roger's penis, half playfully, half maliciously. The almost explicit meaning of Judy's behavior toward Roger's penis had been well understood by Roger. This was an old game and when Judy was younger she was outspoken in her wish to take Roger's penis and make it her own. Now Roger understood that in the dream and its attendant anxiety he feared that Judy could take his penis. The detail in which the witch had lost her needle led us back to material in which Roger had earlier related his fantasies about the woman with a penis.

At one point I reminded Roger that the scary dream of the witch had occurred on the night of the day that he had told about the daydream of the "sixteen- or seventeen-year-old girl" who came to live with him. I asked if there could be a connection. Now Roger remembered the daydream of the girl in the amphibian boat, a variation of the earlier daydream that took place on the morning after the dream. But he did not want to talk about it. "Do I have to?" he asked with dread in his voice. I asked him to try. He struggled with the narration again, and I saw that once again he needed to spell "girl" and avoided the age of the girl. He could not remember how the daydream ended —"because my mother came to get me out of bed or something." (I was sure now that this was one of his morning masturbatory fantasies. There had been renewed difficulty at home in getting Roger out of bed, and his mother would come upon him openly masturbating.) Once, in the narration when he began his complicated game of disguising and reversing the numbers in the age of the girl, I asked, "Are you sure the girl was sixteen or seventeen?" Roger looked up sadly, as if he already knew the answer. "You guessed right the first time when I first told you the daydream." (From the number code I had first guessed Judy or me. He had denied it.) "What was the right guess?" "It was you." But it was not only I. In the complicated code he had worked out sixteen was the double of eight, which was Judy's age, and the double of seventeen was thirty-four, my age at the time, which he knew. Roger, who knew the doubles of numbers very well (and had an almost obsessive preoccupation with doubling numbers) had nicely condensed Judy's age and my age. I now helped Roger make the connection between his guilty feelings and my identity in the daydream. I suggested, too, that this must have something to do with Judy and the secrets with her in the old days. I drew his attention to the way in which he had first told me the daydream of the girl sixteen or seventeen, in a number code and with spelling. A code and secret words and spelling had been part of the secret games with Judy, too, and had the function of warding off guilty feelings.

How had the sex games with Judy been drawn into the transference? It seems to me that my analytic encouragement to talk about the forbidden games with Judy had made me, in the child's fantasy, the seducer, or the partner in "forbidden games," as Judy had been in reality. The games with Judy had been given up for nearly a year, and I have good reason to believe had survived in masturbatory fantasies of a sadomasochistic character. As the analysis at this point had begun to investigate the masturbatory fantasies, the analyst became the dangerous seducer and the fantasies were transferred to the person of the analyst and in turn made use of the analyst in elaboration of content. To Roger, I only explained at this point that the daydreams about me seemed to be a way of remembering the games with Judy and the fears and guilty feelings that went with them. I explained that if we understood the feelings that came out toward me in this way, we would have a way of solving the problems inside.

The transference fantasy and its accompanying guilt feelings made it possible for the first time to show Roger the full strength of his guilt feelings and to help him see how much guilt had attached itself to the old games with Judy. Yet as soon as we identified the guilt feelings, Roger succeeded in isolating them again. The serial daydream of the girl in the amphibian boat continued and now, from many clues, I began to understand how isolation of the guilt feelings served pleasure. I now understood better than before how Roger had engaged in sex play with Judy without apparent guilt. As long as he maintained the guilt feelings in isolation he could enjoy the games. In the masturbation fantasy, he succeeded in isolating guilt and anxiety in order to enjoy the fantasy. Roger had already had a lot of experience in analysis in seeing how he "moved his guilty conscience into the wrong departments," and now it remained to show him how guilty feelings can be moved into other departments so that they will not get in the way of enjoying certain thoughts or games. Roger accepted this interpretation and then, characteristically, followed this session with a period of acting.

In the next session, he was sulky and petulant, whined incessantly for a cookie, and I had none that day. He began throwing objects around the room in the monotonous driven fashion I had seen many times before. He would not discuss his behavior with me and several times walked out of the room. In the following hour, he continued to sulk and refused to talk about the wild behavior of the previous hour. When I asked what happened to make him move his guilty conscience into another department, he said, "Oh that's easy. I know the answer to that. I moved my guilty conscience so you won't find it." And then, suddenly intrigued by a thought, "Maybe it's like the witch again. Maybe I'm afraid you'll take it away from me." Then, "I figured out something else. You know who I think the witch was in my dream? My mother! That's who it was. And you and Judy and my father all wrapped up together. Maybe inside I'm afraid that you would play a trick on me. You know. Like someone would offer you a cookie if you did something, and then they wouldn't give it to you. . . . Oh! There's the cookie, yesterday. A trick. Something that witches do. And that must be why I thought of the Musicians of Bremen Dream when I first told you the Witch Dream. A trick, see. And robbers."

Now I made a suggestion. I reminded him that it is said that witches have a magic, that they can change things. Roger came up with, "Witches could change you into anything they wanted to. Oh! Oh! And *you're* trying to change me. Well you *are* in a way. Trying to make me better." I reminded him now of fears we had discussed earlier, fears of being changed into a girl. Roger said, "*That's* it. Maybe *inside* in the dream I thought the witch could change me and my boy friends into girls. We were fighting the witch and Judy in the dream. And wait a minute . . . that fits into the part of the dream where we're trying to dissolve a powder to make the witch's mask. . . . See magic again and changing something into something else. Oh! Oh! I see another connector. The daydreams. The part where I'm in a boat with the girl, the boat with wheels so it can go on the water or on land." What connections did he see here? Roger: "Why the changing over, of course. The boat can change over for land or water. . . . I wish I could remember the other dream, the one I had last night. But it was all chopped up in little pieces and I can't remember any part of it. . . . All chopped up! Oh! Oh! That's what witches are supposed to do too. They could chop you up into little pieces. Witches could kill you! That must be what I'm afraid of. And steal. Maybe inside I thought the witch could steal my penis and give it to Judy."

All of this expert analysis had been achieved without any display of affect. He had turned it into an intellectual exercise. Now Roger stopped and congratulated himself. "Don't you think I'm doing good today? I'm surprised myself at how good I can think when I don't try to. Now we're getting a lot of connectors." I said that this was good, but there was one very important connection that we didn't see here. Where were the feelings that would go with all of this? If a boy was so afraid of such terrible things, we would expect to see the feelings too. Roger took this in soberly. Then, surprisingly, he said that he thought he had better tell me another part of the daydream that he had not been able to tell me before (i.e., concerning the daydream of the girl in the amphibian boat). He started to tell me and a look of misery came over his face. He had to force himself to get the first words out. "In the daydream, I have a stick and it . . . it . . . has nails at the end of it." He couldn't finish the sentence. "I'll have to spell. To poke the g-i-r-l with." When I asked about this he was in agony again. "I don't want to say it. It's like what the needle in the dream was." And then, gathering courage, said, "like a penis, you know."

Now he stopped. He begged off from further work in this hour. Could we please talk about something else? I said, he could talk about anything else he wanted. The farthest thing from his problems he could think of. Roger said, "O.K." And then, "But you know what. I keep coming back to the same thing anyway. Then I think about Leila. Did I ever tell you about Leila? Well . . . well. . . . It's about some games we played. You know the funny little penis girls have. Well . . . I have to spell L-O-O-K." I said, "Look." Roger: "Don't say it. Don't say it!" I told him that the spelling would not help us. This was the way he was hiding his feelings, but the feelings were very important to us. Roger said, miserably, "All right. I won't spell." He exerted a great effort. "We looked at each other." I asked, "How do you feel right now?" Roger said: "Sick in the head again." I told him I thought this was where his feelings were trying to come out. And he said, "That's my guilty conscience again."

At this point we began to experience increased resistance in analysis and a new period of acting. His behavior at home which had been much improved for some time now reverted to old patterns. He was tirelessly negative and provocative with his mother. Every one of the most ordinary demands that a parent might make was encountered with stubborn refusal. When I began to see some of this behavior in transference reactions I could show Roger that at such times he behaved as if he were in terrible danger. When grownups said something *had* to be done, he went to pieces. It was as if he were afraid that by doing what they wished they might get some kind of control over him and put him in danger, like a witch who could get power over someone.

Roger was immediately struck by this. "That's it. And the witch in my dream was my mother, too! But I know that my mother wouldn't hurt me so why do I do it?" I encouraged him to associate to this idea and he came up with "Witches can change you. . . . Maybe *inside* I wish I could have a little penis like a girl." He looked surprised himself when this statement came out.

"I don't know why I said that. I just said it." When I inquired about the feelings in connection with such an idea a look of agony came over his face. And then he cried out, "Oh, the feeling is coming, the feeling is coming! Talk about something else. *Right* away." And then he began to talk quickly about trivial things, banishing the feelings in a few seconds.

The negativism toward mother continued, and Roger himself seemed baffled by his behavior at home. He said, "I know that my mother and my father aren't witches or ghosts, but I act like they were." He was reminded of the witch dream again.

In one hour he was suddenly struck by the fact that everything his mother asked him to do made him want to do the opposite. I remarked on his fear of women and girls. At this point he buried his head in a pillow. Then suddenly he brought a rabbit's foot out of his pocket. He asked if I knew the joke about the rabbit. "What does a rabbit hate to have most?" Answer: "A rabbit's foot." He began to fondle the rabbit's foot. He liked its feel, he said. This reminded him of Tumpis, his Teddy bear with whom he sleeps each night. (Tumpis had a prominent place in the analysis. He was properly a fetish.) I drew the analogy between the rabbit's foot and Tumpis, pointing out that both made him feel safe. I suggested that as long as he had Tumpis close to himself he might feel that he was not in danger of losing a part of himself, a penis perhaps. He started to say with surprise, "That's it! That's what Tumpis means." And then he cried out in pain, "My foot hurts! My foot hurts!" (This was an old hysterical symptom that had come up frequently in analysis.) He hugged his foot in misery. "I wish I could cut it off. So it wouldn't hurt. And if I didn't have it *then it couldn't hurt*. It would be nice not to have a foot. Cut off both of them."

I reminded him that we already had seen how the anxiety around the foot was displaced from the penis and could now make an essential point. We could connect this to his earlier statement about the wish to be a girl, that is, if one were a girl, one would not need to be afraid that something could happen to the penis because there wouldn't be any to lose. Roger said, "Yes." And then, in a suffering voice, he said, "Oh, I wanted to say 'No' so you wouldn't guess, but I made myself say 'Yes.' Wasn't that good of me?"

Later in this hour we returned to the conflict with mother and his own statement that everything mother wanted him to do made him want to do the opposite. I told him that it occurred to me that he was afraid that if he did what mother wanted he would become like his mother, that is, he would be like a girl. He did not agree, and it was not until I was able to handle this in the transference some months later that this insight was achieved.

Along with dread of castration, oedipal longings for mother were revived during this period. Roger had already discovered his mother behind the transference fantasies of the analyst as witch and the girl in the amphibian boat. Now as we reworked the daydream and the night dream with this new insight, he suffered agonies. He could not bring himself to give associations;

his tongue just could not utter them. He would hide his face or alternatively become impudent and revive his provocative behavior. Once, he succeeded in telling me one of his shameful thoughts in connection with the girl in the amphibian boat, and he did it through spelling. "That I want *all* my mother's l-o-v-e." When I brought his attention to the spelling as a defense against guilt feelings, he could only nod, miserably. When we consider the depth and the intensity of Roger's guilt feelings as they came out in this period of analysis, it is impressive to remember the earliest period of analysis when Roger could bring out undisguised oedipal fantasies without a trace of guilt or anxiety. All this had been achieved through the most elaborate defenses against affect.

In the weeks that followed, much of the material centered around dread of the female genitalia. Observations of his sister and his little girl friend came into the analysis again, now with strong anxiety. He could not rid himself of the conviction that girls and women do have a penis hidden somewhere—"Even though I know better." In the resistance, I encountered an interesting specimen of disbelief which occasionally attached itself to my interpretations or the merits of analysis itself. Clearly, he had to hold on to his belief in the woman's penis in order to defend against his own castration fears. His sister was frequently cited to me as an authority on all kinds of subjects, and eventually we were able to discover how she became an authority on anatomical differences between the sexes. She had told Roger that girls had something much better than boys hidden inside their vaginas. He was glad to believe her.

Tumpis, Roger's Teddy bear, finally became our most valuable tool in this phase of analysis. Tumpis was properly speaking a fetish and, as I mentioned earlier, Roger had already seen that Tumpis was a reassurance to him against the danger of loss. On a few previous occasions, Roger had brought Tumpis himself to see me in the hope that Tumpis could tell us something about his problems. As we might expect, Tumpis proved to be very resistant to analysis. Then on one occasion during this period when I had reason to believe I might get cooperation from Roger, I proposed that we try an experiment. I asked Roger (who still took Tumpis to bed with him) if he would be willing to put Tumpis in another room for a few nights in order to help us understand a problem. I told him that he could certainly take Tumpis back at the end of the experiment if he still needed him. The experiment was not immediately successful. There seemed to be some increase in anxiety, but no specific content that could demonstrate the role of Tumpis. At the end of the two-day period Roger did not ask to have Tumpis back, although he knew he could have him back if he needed him. And then one day he brought in what he called "a horrible dream."

> He was coasting on a sled down a steep hill with Tumpis sitting in front of him. They crash into a tree. Next thing he knows they have landed on a big toboggan and go coasting down on this one.

He did not want to discuss the dream. It was too horrible. I tried to help him out by reminding him of his analytic hour in which he had told me about the sex games with his girl friend, Leila. There had been considerable feeling, something close to panic as he told me about how Leila and he looked at each other and as he was reminded of "the little hole" of girls. He agreed. But then, instead of continuing associations, he fell back upon acting. He began roaming restlessly around the room, "I want *something!*" he kept saying. Would I give him something—a pad of paper, a pencil, a paper clip, *anything*, but he must have *something*. I interpreted the acting as a defense against anxiety which finally persuaded him to sit down and analyze the dream.

He associated the first accident to his fear of damage to his penis. Then his associations led to the disappearance of grasshoppers that he had been saving in a jar, then observations of Leila, as if something has "disappeared." Then he came forth brilliantly with the solution—"Maybe inside I thought a girl had one and lost it and then got a bigger one later on." (The sled is exchanged in the dream for the toboggan.) The "I want *something*," which we may take as an association to the dream, had the same significance as the fetish, Tumpis, the illusory penis of the woman that protects him against his castration fears.

The analysis of the fetish and the surrender of the fetish (which was permanent) had the effect of liberating a large quantity of affect. For a time we had anxiety, guilt, and hostility erupting in unpredictable fashion in the analytic hours and often without content. In the resistance we had the affects, and the ideational content was now isolated. He wandered restlessly around the room, complaining of funny feelings, of feeling afraid and not knowing what he was afraid of, or feeling crazy.

From clues I gathered that there was anxiety about masturbation, and when I tentatively suggested this possibility he exploded with me. He denied that he masturbated "any more," and then finally admitted that he did "sometimes." I suspected, of course, that his resistance had to do with masturbatory fantasies and encouraged him to tell me. There were more denials and then with much suffering he told me only this much, that it was the old daydream about me, the girl in the amphibian boat. He refused to give me details.

Now he reverted to the old provocative behavior in his sessions with me. He was negative, obstinate, and used any trifle as an excuse to try to engage me in arguments. Only later when I saw this behavior in a sequence I realized that this behavior had the significance for him of "fighting" with me; it was an attempt to engage me in a verbal wrestling match. This behavior culminated in a piece of acting at home that finally revealed the meaning of the whole period of resistance.

One evening he went on a rampage at home, goading his mother until her patience was exhausted and they both wound up yelling at each other. At one point during this evening both his parents were in their room, and Roger locked them in. He refused to let them out for nearly an hour.

This time Roger really exceeded himself and when he arrived for his hour the next day he was tormented with guilt. As we analyzed this piece of acting, he brought out his fantasy with much suffering. He said that he wanted to see what his parents would do. When I asked for his fantasies of what they might do, he blurted out that he had forgotten everything I had ever told him about what parents do to make babies. He begged me to tell him again. I told him that this would not help, that it was much more important to find out what he thought and what the feelings were, since it was the feelings that prevented him from remembering. Now he became furious with me. He became very aggressive, yelled at me, knocked over a desk ornament, threw pillows around, and finally ran out of the room. With great difficulty I got him to return to the room and sit down with me to analyze the acting. Then I was able to show him how his acting was a way of telling me, that he was trying to fight with me, and that this must be his idea, deep inside of him, of what the parents do. He must think it was something like fighting.

This was by no means a new insight for Roger. We had worked with his sadomasochistic fantasies of parental intercourse throughout the analysis. Primal-scene memories had emerged in a terror dream a year earlier in analysis. A dream which Roger called "The Musicians of Bremen Dream" had occupied months of analysis, and Roger recalled overhearing parental quarrels at night and the sounds of intercourse. But now we were able to tie up the primal-scene observations with his own castration fears, and Roger could see how his observations had confirmed for him his belief that the woman tried to castrate the man. This also provided one of the last important links in the "night dream–daydream" sequence of the witch and the girl in the amphibian boat, his fear that his incestuous longings would lead to castration by the mother. But now, too, we could find an important motive in Roger's behavior problems. The fighting with his mother represented the acting-out of an incestuous fantasy that incorporated a sadomasochistic conception of intercourse. Once again the behavior originated in a masturbation fantasy.

The analysis of this material had a dramatic effect. This ended the period of acting-out, and it was also the last period of acting outside of the analysis that we experienced. Roger's behavior, which had steadily improved through the three years of analysis that preceded these events, now became so much better that his parents began to ask if he was not ready to terminate analysis. There was scarcely a trace of the old provocative behavior, and all the slow gains of analysis seemed to consolidate in the months that followed.

But in the analysis itself I now encountered new resistances. First of all, he insisted he was all well and no longer needed analysis. He was irritable and whiny with me and often exploded in anger over the most trivial things. When I tried to show him that this anger toward me was, in itself, a reason for working further in analysis, he countered shrewdly by pointing out that he was much better every place but here in analysis and if he quit analysis, there would be no reason to be angry at me and no problems.

The content of this period was so chaotic that I had difficulty for a while in sorting out the many themes and their implications in transference. First of all I could detect in certain fantasies passive longings toward the father. These fantasies had emerged in various forms earlier in the analysis, most prominently in the form of a kidnaping fantasy. There was a bad man who would take little boys into the woods and play with their penises. (This had first appeared two years ago when his parents had warned him about playing in the woods near the house and, following a kidnaping scare in the community, had warned him against going off with strangers.) Our earlier analysis of the kidnaping fantasies had centered primarily in his wish to be loved by his father and his fantasy that his father would love him better as a girl.

A second theme in this disordered period was anality. There was a terror dream in which "a witch" and "a toilet" led him to recall his old fear of toilets and the association that the witch "wanted to steal me." Further analysis of the dream connected the fear of losing feces and fear of castration.

Meantime, too, it would be entirely correct to say that Roger at certain times in this analytic period behaved just like a two-year-old. He would litter my office with scraps of paper and gleefully empty the wastebasket on the floor. He recited a large collection of chants and songs about garbage cans, toilets, and feces. He was stubborn, negative, and completely unreachable at times. There were other times when he was charming and reasonable and sometimes announced himself at the door by saying, "Well, the old Roger is back today!" If on such occasions one reminded him of the other Roger who had torn up the place the day before, he assumed an attitude of amused and clinical detachment toward his alter ego. He was not interested in analyzing him.

For five months we had these visitations from "the other Roger" who, it strikes me, had marked resemblances to the Roger I had known at an earlier stage of analysis. At home and at school there were no complaints. He was progressing very well; he was a satisfaction to his parents and a joy to his teachers. His parents could see no reason for continuing the analysis, and I am sure that if they had not had so much confidence in analysis, they would have withdrawn him or pressed me to terminate. Roger himself could point to his good behavior at home and at school and argued strenuously against continuing this unprofitable business. In short, we had a behavior in analysis that might justifiably be called a transference neurosis. The analysis of this period proved to be very profitable and finally illuminated the origins of Roger's character disorder in striking fashion.

During these five months of acting in the analysis we were still able to make use of dreams and acting in a slow and laborious investigation and reconstruction of a period in early childhood before I knew him. The first important communication came through a dream.

> He was in a movie—lost in the dark—trying to find his way to the candy counter. Then he is eating a chocolate bar, "the round kind with nuts in it."

The insight must have dawned upon him almost as soon as he finished telling me the dream, because he suddenly became restless, began to wander around aimlessly, and positively refused to give associations. I suggested that there were feelings of shame in connection with it. He nodded, and now the familiar look of suffering came on his face. He could not say it, he told me. In the end I had to help him out, and he was relieved when I asked him if the candy bar reminded him of a bowel movement. He looked as if he were about to gag and then said, "That's it, but I couldn't say it." I was able to show him how something was remembered in the dream, something that belonged to a time when he was very small. I commented particularly on the feeling of shame that attached itself to this experience and suggested that this experience and others like it might account for the very great shame that we have seen in Roger for so long, a shame that got itself attached to all sorts of things later on.

During one period of acting I became impressed that much of his provocative behavior and his stubbornness and messiness finally obliged me to become firm and to "put my foot down"; and when I did so, calling a halt to his behavior, he looked as if this was just exactly what he had wanted. When I mentally reviewed this behavior with his anal preoccupations, I was very certain that this pattern exactly corresponded to the picture I had obtained in the early history. Roger had soiled until he was nearly four years old, and his mother had been completely unsuccessful in trying to train him. When she finally "put her foot down," according to the record, he became trained within a very short time. But from the transference reactions and content of dreams I could also understand that Roger had not been simply defiant during this period. He had been afraid to use the toilet. He was afraid of the noise of the toilet and afraid of falling in. And in the witch dream reported earlier he had equated loss of feces with castration. I was able to help Roger see how his behavior during this period was a way of remembering important things that had happened to him when he was very little and began to reconstruct from behavior and dreams the critical second and third years.

Then I learned from Roger's mother that she had observed a return of anal masturbation which we had not seen for some time in analysis. Roger could not bring himself to tell me this, and finally his mother and I decided that she should tell Roger that she knew about this and she would like to discuss this with me unless Roger thought he could tell me himself. He preferred to have mother tell me, and I was now free to bring this up with him. He was actually quite relieved to have me know. And now I learned that he had surrendered phallic masturbation "because I don't like it when my penis gets hard—it doesn't feel good." When I pointed out that this pleasure in the anus is a kind of pleasure that very small boys feel, and I did not understand why he had gone back to this, he said very intelligently, "Well, I think it's because we've been talking about when I was a little boy and I've been remembering it, so I got to doing it again."

The anal masturbation was accompanied by fantasies of "what it would be like to be a girl." He equated the anus with "the hole that girls have." The old kidnaping fantasies were revived now and could be analyzed more fully. The idea of passive surrender to a man was exciting to him. His identification with his sister came out in fantasies and even in a brief period of acting-out in which he persuaded his sister once again to let him look at her genitals. There was a terror dream during this period in which there were robbers in the house and a radio announcer said in a loud voice, "All boys are going to have their a-s-s cut off!" (He spelled "a-s-s.") He was scared and began to run away and then woke up. We were finally able to establish that he had renounced phallic masturbation out of anxiety once again, that he felt it was dangerous to be a boy and safer to be a girl, and yet when he fantasied being a girl this was a terrifying thought for him, too.

I now began to understand the origins of the active–passive conflicts that played such a prominent role in his behavior disorder. The danger of passive surrender to the mother was succeeded by the danger of passive surrender to the father. To "give in" was to invite castration. But there was also a more primitive defense in operation here, a good example, I think, of Anna Freud's (1952) "negativism and emotional surrender." In the transference during this period I was able to observe the negativistic patterns with a quality of urgency and necessity that I think was very close to that which had earlier been characteristic of his behavior at home. My summary of this period and of the analytic insights gained does not do justice to the labor of working through the resistances encountered every inch of the way.

For a time every help that I tried to offer him, every insight was first encountered with the most obstinate negation. The nature of the resistance was partially obscured by material that suggested that he disbelieved analysis because it deprived him of the illusion that women had a penis. (For a time he returned to his earlier authority, his sister Judy, who offered him her own consoling theory that she had "something better inside.") But when we cleared this area once again the desperate negativism still remained and at last I was reminded that I had once seen this in a very specific way in relation to the mother. It was the fear that to be in accord with, to agree with, the mother, to comply with her wishes, would demand the surrender of his own identity, would compel him to become one with his mother. (I had heard Anna Freud's paper nearly a year earlier, and it had illuminated Roger's case for me.)

When I now began to draw Roger's attention to his negativism in transference I suggested an anxiety behind the behavior. I suggested that he behaved as if he were afraid that if he agreed with me he would somehow not be Roger. I proposed that there might be some connection between his old fears of "not being Roger" and the negativism that we saw in transference. He, of course, negated the interpretation strenuously. Yet it became a useful measure, and on several occasions during this difficult period it was often enough just to say, good-humoredly, "You don't have to be afraid to agree with me. You'll still be Roger!" and he would laugh and relax.

This period culminated in the presentation of a most interesting gift to the analyst. Roger was very much absorbed in scientific projects at school, and when he was not hating me or throwing trash around my office, he sometimes spent part of his hour describing his scientific experiments and his scientific ambitions. He was collecting specimens of bread mold during this period. I did not, of course, make any interpretations regarding the anal significance of his new hobby, and as far as possible I had always tried not to interfere with sublimations that were being formed. I was privately amused and sympathetic with the dilemma of his mother who now had to put up with little dishes of bread mold all around the house in a way that was reminiscent of a period long ago when she had to put up with little deposits of feces around the house. In analysis, I listened with attention to his scientific conversation. I was not myself interested in bread mold, and I must have overdone my simulated interest. Following one climactic hour in which Roger had put on an infantile display and dumped the contents of the wastebasket on the floor and begged to be released from this horrible prison that was analysis, he came in for his next hour beaming with shy happiness. He had a package in his hands, clumsily wrapped and tied with ribbon. "I have a present for you," he said. I opened it and found a specimen of bread mold. "It's a very unusual strain," he said proudly.

A good part of the material of this period helped us to reconstruct Roger's earliest conflicts with his mother, and Roger was able to see that a part of his life that he could not remember in words was remembered through his dreams and his behavior during this period. The difficult work of this period finally brought about a very satisfactory resolution of the transference resistances, and Roger terminated his analysis at the end of approximately three-and-one-half years.

I was able to follow Roger's progress for five years while I remained in the same city. He sustained all of his gains. He had become a gratifying child to his parents and presented no problems that they could not handle themselves during these years. His schoolwork was excellent and his precocity and joy in learning delighted his parents and his teachers.

## *Summary*

The analysis of this behavior disorder reveals in specific ways how the aggressive and destructive behavior was employed in the service of defense.

In tracing the motive for a destructive act, we saw very early in the analysis how a fantasy in which the child was in extreme danger was translated into an action in which the content of the fantasy was reproduced and the ego spared itself anxiety through identification with the aggressor and through a shift from passive to active. (As in the first dream reported by Roger, the fear of castration by the faceless man was immediately translated into an action in which the child performed the symbolic destructive act upon objects in the room.) This defense served painful memories as well as fantasies. When primal-scene material emerged in the analysis, the memory of an act perceived as destructive and as "fighting," was translated into aggressive acting in which destruction of objects and fighting was re-enacted and that which was passively experienced through observing and overhearing was transformed into action. Ultimately, the great danger against which the ego defended itself was loss of identity. The extreme negativism and obstinacy that characterized another aspect of Roger's behavior disorder was seen as a fear of surrender to the object, the fear of becoming one with the object (A. Freud, 1952).

The connections between the masturbatory fantasies and impulsive acting provided insights both into certain forms of erratic conduct and the role of isolation of affects in the behavior disorder. Anna Freud (1949, p. 203) has brought our attention to a form of social maladjustment that can be traced back to the complete suppression of phallic masturbation and the consequent acting-out of the masturbation fantasies—". . . the masturbation-fantasy is deprived of all bodily outlet, the libidinal and aggressive energy attached to it is completely blocked and damned up, and eventually is displaced with full force from the realm of the sex-life into the realm of ego-activities." In Roger's analysis it could be demonstrated that he periodically abandoned phallic masturbation under pressure of castration anxiety, and in the erratic and apparently unprovoked periods of acting that followed we could trace a masturbatory fantasy.

But Roger also illuminated for me the process that led to abandonment of masturbation at certain times. On many occasions there was no evidence of a conscious struggle against the urge to masturbate. (The child who fights the urge to masturbate reveals the struggle in defense and resistance in analysis. The argument between the urge and the prohibition is seen in moral ambivalence, self-punishment, self-imposed taboos. He reveals the struggle in transference by identifying the analyst with the repudiated temptations and often behaves toward the analysis as if it were a bad habit that must be broken.) Through Roger I came to understand that at certain times when masturbation was apparently given up he lost "the good feelings" in his penis. His own description of this, in a period of the analysis that I have not included in this report, went as follows—"But my penis doesn't feel good when I touch it. It doesn't feel not nice, either. Not good and not bad. Nothing." In other words, anesthesia took place, probably on a hysterical basis, and masturbation could no longer evoke phallic sensations. Masturbation was then given up, not as the result of a struggle, but because of the loss of feeling and the inability to have sensations in the penis. The fantasies which had lost their connections with masturbation were now acted out, following the pattern described by Anna Freud.

One further connection is suggested in the acting-out of the masturbation fantasy. In the earlier association of the fantasy with the act of masturbation, the fantasy was "made real" by the accompanying phallic excitations. (Another child once said to me, "The stories are more realer when I'm playing with myself.") I have wondered, then, if one of the elements in the acting-out of the masturbatory fantasy is the attempt to make the story real through enactment, to recover the lost excitement, and to animate the fantasy gone dead with the penis. And since the fantasy had once served to excite the penis, is acting-out also a magical device to bring back the lost feelings in the penis?

The most important part of the analytic work was that which dealt with the defenses against affects, and it was here that analysis encountered its strongest resistance. The absence of anxiety and guilt which distorted the early picture of the behavior disorder was seen finally as the achievement of the most elaborate defenses against affect. By identifying with the aggressor and by switching from passive to active, the ego escaped both anxiety and self-reproach. The simultaneous acting-out of libidinal and aggressive fantasies and the provocation of punishment spared the ego the necessity of experiencing guilt. The isolation of affect which proved to be the most formidable resistance of all, served many purposes in the mental economy. The barely disguised oedipal fantasies and castration fantasies were rendered less dangerous by depriving them of affect, making them "not real." Further, by maintaining guilt and anxiety in isolation, Roger was able to enjoy masturbation and its attendant fantasies. We saw that each time analysis re-established the connections between fantasies and affects the anxiety experienced by the child was nearly intolerable.

The analysis of the transference resistance in the last period of treatment shed further light on both the libidinal and ego aspects of the active–passive conflicts in which the behavior disorder had been rooted. Both the passive longings for the father and the defenses against these wishes were revived along with anal masturbation. The fight with mother over bowel training which had extended well into the fourth year was re-enacted in transference along with castration dread. The negativism which had been one of the primary defenses and one that had served resistance throughout the analysis was seen as a defense against the danger of passive surrender to the mother, the "fear of loss of personality" as Anna Freud put it.

# The Ego's Participation in the Therapeutic Alliance

LISELOTTE FRANKL
AND ILSE HELLMAN

Certain aspects of the problem of the ego's participation in the therapeutic alliance have recently been discussed in regard to adult patients at a panel of the American Psychoanalytic Association on criteria for analyzability (1960). On this occasion Elizabeth Zetzel discussed the criteria integral to the analytic situation: the motivation for more than symptomatic relief, the capacity to tolerate anxiety and frustration, the ability to maintain a stable relationship and to sustain secondary-process thinking. All these enable the patient to remain in the analytic situation despite the anxieties experienced in the transference neurosis. For a successful analysis the patient must be able to maintain some mature ego attributes in the analytic situation in spite of anxieties engendered by the analytic process. Also, the patient requires sufficient flexibility to mobilize unresolved conflicts in a regressive transference neurosis. Loewenstein (1954) has contributed several valuable papers to the problem of the therapeutic alliance.

It seemed important to us to study the therapeutic alliance in child patients, as it manifests itself in the treatment of children of various ages. Closer scrutiny of the various aspects of ego development and the part they play in promoting or hindering our therapeutic endeavors is needed. This can further elucidate certain difficulties in the treatment of adult patients which arise from arrest of certain aspects of ego development, from regression, or from certain ego defects.

Analytic work is based on our access to and understanding of the unconscious content and the communications reaching us through transference. The therapeutic process rests on the communications we make to the patient of what we have understood and felt about his inner world. The communication we have chosen to make is in the first place made to his ego, and it is via the ego that communication becomes effective. It is, therefore, essential for favorable progress in treatment to be aware of the important role the ego plays in transmitting to and assimilating into the personality the analyst's communications.

The analyst who is aware of this considers it his task to evaluate carefully the ego's relations both to the inner and outer world. Problems of choice of interpretations, including what Freud referred to as tact, as well as timing and formulation, must play a constant part in the analyst's thinking. One of the considerations in making this choice is determined by our evaluation and anticipation of the child's capacity to take in and assimilate what we are communicating to him at any given time. Our own way of conveying to the child that we keep in touch with his feelings of the moment, for example his anxiety or sadness and the relief he experiences through this, paves the way for a relationship which gradually enables him to feel that he wants to share with his analyst more of his fantasy life, as well as his day-to-day experiences.

Experience of the analyst's empathy and the feeling that the analyst understands the child's need to defend himself further help the child to develop this relationship. On this basis he can stand up to the first experiences of having to face anxiety and guilt, resulting from defense interpretations, as well as phases, even of intense resistance and negative transference. By conveying to the child that we are in touch with his rapidly changing feelings, and essentially through verbalization, we simultaneously help the self-observing function of the child's ego to become operative and gradually to become the valuable ally needed for successful analytic work.

It is, however, not only essential to be in touch with the child's fantasies and feelings and to put them into words. In doing so we must remain aware of the ego's changing capacity to make use of words and keep in touch with the nature of the child's thought processes as they develop. In work with very young patients, of two to two-and-one-half years, it is especially important to realize that causal thinking only develops slowly. The formulation of complicated interpretations which rest on the understanding of causality can therefore obviously not be made full use of.

Though awareness of the developmental level reached by the young child appears to be a basic requirement of which every analyst is aware, we find in practice that children's capacities to take in and assimilate interpretations tend to be overrated. They may, therefore, be faced with formulations well beyond their grasp through the use of concepts and abstract thinking which are not meaningful to them yet and which tend to add to the child's confusion and his misconceptions. The differentiation between the child who has not yet reached the state when he is able to make the specific causal links and the blocking of this capacity depends on our intimate knowledge of details of the development of this ego function.

This approach, based on developmental factors, is not equally taken into consideration where the analyst makes contact with the child patient by directly confronting him with ego-alien id contents. Such an approach contains serious dangers: immediate confrontation which largely bypasses the defensive organization of the ego may result in panic-like reactions and make the analyst into a magic person. The child's initial fantasies about the analyst's magic and omnipotent qualities are thereby confirmed. In this way the analyst counteracts rather than facilitates the child's capacity to feel that, alongside his projected fantasies, there exists a person whose aim it is to help him to differentiate between fantasy and reality within and outside himself.

A further reason why it is essential to keep in touch with the patient's ego lies in the fact that direct confrontation with the unconscious impulses rather than with their derivatives which are closer to consciousness may have an immediate seductive effect. Especially in the very young patient who offers us access to his unconscious comparatively easily, the temptation to take a line of direct approach is great. Through this he is easily precipitated into anxiety outbursts which make him flee the threatening interpretations or driven into defensive measures more intense than those established in him before entering treatment.

The developmental trend of latency to ward off the intensity of earlier oedipal and preoedipal wishes and the conflicts arising from them is reached by the strengthening of the ego's defensive measures. Analytic work can consequently be experienced as a threat to the equilibrium which is in the process of becoming established. Another important tendency in latency, however, leads to establishing the link with external reality more firmly. For this reason the child can accept the analyst's role as a representative of reality and as an ally on the way to clearer distinction between reality and fantasy, between contradictory feelings, opposing forces, and his inner and outer world. As Elisabeth Geleerd (1957) has made clear, one aspect of the analyst's role is always that of representative of reality. Awareness of this aspect is a basic requirement for successful analytic work, even though it may become temporarily submerged during certain phases of treatment. The latency child's growing need to differentiate between fantasy and reality makes him wish to use the analyst also in his capacity to bring this clarification, and this contributes to the bond which helps him through stressful phases of his treatment.

Specific problems shown by latency children in the course of analytic treatment have been fully discussed by Berta Bornstein (1951). In her paper on latency, as in her contribution to the panel on technique related to development (Bornstein, Falstein, & Rank, 1951), she has drawn attention to the obstacles to treatment which arise from the trends inherent in the development during this phase. We have found these confirmed in those of our cases of school age in which age-adequate developmental features were already present initially, while it was of great interest to meet with these typical resistances to treatment only late in analysis of those children whose development had been arrested and who reached an age-adequate stage only as the result of the analytic work which had preceded it. Although latency children bring to treatment certain features which permit them to form a treatment alliance, we also meet with cases in this age group who show no wish to enter into contact with the analyst. From these we can learn how, step by step, a careful approach via affect and defense interpretation can open up the capacity to establish a relationship, to communicate, and finally to actively take part in the analytic work.

If we meet a patient in this age group who shows no signs of a wish to make contact, to communicate anything about himself, and certainly no wish for help, various ways of approach can be chosen. The initial aim is common to all, namely to reduce anxiety sufficiently to allow the child to enter into a relationship and make use of the analyst for therapeutic purposes. Close observation of behavior and of nonverbal communications, knowledge of details of present and past circumstances, and the consistent support of at least one of the parents can lead to establishing a therapeutic relationship purely on the basis of interpretative work also in children who initially meet us with violent hostility.

In the case of a girl of ten years, initially brought against her will, it was possible to follow the steps in detail which led to a "treatment alliance" and to a favorable result followed up into adult life.

Following a prolonged separation from her mother at eighteen months, Angela's personality had shown a marked change after the mother's return. Intense pleasure in inflicting pain on her mother had soon spread to tormenting animals and later her baby brother, who was born when she was six years old. She seemed compelled to make sudden sadistic attacks, and her excitement and pleasure while inflicting pain were freely shown. The absence of manifest guilt and of the wish to make good what she had done made it extremely difficult for adults around her to deal with her sympathetically. Both her parents, but especially her father, had breakthroughs of violent temper; the marriage had brought constant quarrels which the child had witnessed. Later her sadism had turned against the baby brother, but her pleasure in tormenting animals had started long before and remained unchanged after his birth. At the age of ten, her cruelty seemed at times to reach dangerous proportions; animals and small children had escaped serious harm repeatedly only by some chance intervention of an adult. Open hostility to her father and a serious learning inhibition, which hindered normal school progress in spite of an IQ of 167, had convinced the mother of the need for analytic treatment, while the father remained doubtful.

Angela treated the analyst as a dangerous enemy from the moment she saw her and concentrated on her all her hate and aggression. She refused to enter the room, to take off her hat and coat, and she did not talk. She kept an eye on every one of her analyst's movements with a tense expression and a panic-like state, ready to escape or to attack. She did both in turn, sometimes running away after the first few minutes, sometimes approaching the analyst and suddenly attacking her by treading on her foot or pinching her from the back. Her first words were swear words in response to the analyst's first communications. The latter were aimed at reducing the hostile attacks by showing Angela the defensive aspect from which their intensity derived. The analyst consistently interpreted her behavior, as derived from her identification with a fantasied aggressor, and thereby brought about the first verbal communications, through which Angela revealed the content of her own sadistic fantasies and activities, which she had immediately projected onto the unknown analyst. Soon after, she revealed her fear of her father's violent outbursts. The first interpretations which had confronted her with the fantasied nature of the attacks she expected from the analyst led to the recognition of the two main sources of her approach to the analyst as to a dangerous enemy, viz., the projection of her own sadistic wishes and the precursors of transference in which the danger situation made the analyst into the dangerous father at once.

The phase of direct bodily attack and verbal abuse was followed by a treatment phase in which she was tempted to force the analyst completely into her control, prescribing every gesture she was to make, every word to say, severely threatening her for any signs that she had a will or power of her own. Any unexpected movement or word brought a shocklike reaction, as if she were expecting to be hurt. In this way she made the analyst experience her own fears and simultaneously warded off her anxiety that arose from the projection of her own impulse to do harm. The analyst continued to deal consistently with the defensive measures, only confining herself to those areas where the affect was most immediate. She avoided entering into the content of the terrifying fantasies and their deeply unconscious meaning. This led step by step to the decrease of the projections which had made it impossible, at first, for Angela to see or feel the reality of the analyst and her real intentions, alongside her fantasies. Angela came to understand her need to reverse the roles and to control every one of the analyst's movements. This began to open the way for her to test the analyst as a real object of trust, who remains unscathed and unaltered in spite of the manifold aspects transferred on her.

An extreme case of this kind is instructive from many points of view. With regard to our attempt to differentiate the therapeutic alliance from transference phenomena, we can see here that in the large majority of cases we do not experience negative transference as an obstacle that brings treatment to a prolonged standstill, because one element in the ego keeps in touch with the reality of the analyst and his real role. Such loss of touch with reality or the incapacity to take in and react to real and good features of external objects is usually characteristic of psychotic patients. In certain cases of child patients and especially in adolescents it appears that the anxiety concerning the person and role of the analyst is enormously heightened temporarily through the coincidence of intense projection, a real frightening object in the family whose features are transferred to the analyst and the developmental stage of the object relationship which makes the adult an intruder who has to be warded off.

In the case of Angela, as in others who resist treatment tenaciously, a great amount of work is needed to arrive at a point where the child is able to face the fact that the disturbance and suffering in his life are located within him and not in the external world only. Immediate relapse into attacking behavior followed the analyst's first attempt at showing her that her communications about other people, especially about an abnormal child in the neighborhood, contained aspects of herself. As long as they were not expressly related to her she was able to take in the meaning of interpretations and to participate actively in the analysis by bringing further thoughts and feelings related to them. Again, the need to externalize, to displace, to split off certain intolerable aspects are well known to us in patients of all ages. The tenacious fight against the recognition of defenses can create an obstacle in child treatment unless the analyst remains aware that what is needed is to refrain from making himself into a persecuting figure by dealing too rapidly with defense interpretation and especially with ego-alien content, without giving the patient time to make the process of assimilation at his own pace.

In Angela's treatment the awareness of her intolerance of facing her own cruelty and guilt brought a very productive phase in which the content of her most defended sadistic wishes was entirely dealt with through the neighbor's child, allowing her to express her feelings and fantasies via him without attempting to interpret the displacement. She actively began to look for unconscious motivations in others whose behavior she disapproved of; for instance she said, "Jeremy was so cruel to a bird today, do you think he was afraid of something?" Here she turns to the analyst for help for the first time, links the cruelty to fear, and through her question tells the analyst that she expects help from her to see the true link. Soon after this she can express disapproval, and later her guilt is expressed for the first time in another question to the analyst, inviting her to show disapproval of cruel impulses in the other child. The slow process leading from here to the point when she became able to face her own destructive wishes, the instinctual satisfaction she derived from them, and the relation of these fantasies and actions to her masturbatory activities was made on the basis of her ever greater capacity to participate actively in the analysis. The self-observing function had gained strength and had led to active participation especially when it became allied to the capacity to maintain an object relationship.

Simultaneously, during this early phase of treatment, the slow process with its carefully timed interpretations had gradually freed the child's capacity to feel and maintain the relationship to the real aspect of the analyst in her therapeutic function, alongside the intense feelings arising from the changing aspects experienced in the transference.

In Angela the phase of total distrust and expectation of hostility from the analyst was comparatively short. In her positive reactions to the interpretations of the defensive nature of her fears her basic experience of satisfactory mothering in the earliest phase of her life played an important part. In the course of her analysis it became evident that, in spite of the traumatic separation in the second year and the hate against her mother arising from this, the aspect of her mother as a loving and satisfying person who was able to sense her feelings and bring comfort was well established in her and could therefore come to play its part in the treatment. This found expression in her emerging positive transference feelings derived from the relationship to the mother and simultaneously in her capacity to trust the analyst's willingness and ability to help her. Through this she was able to become an active participant in her treatment.

In cases where the experience of good mothering has been severely interfered with from the start, for instance, by psychotic elements in the mother, the establishment of a treatment alliance with the analyst can only be the result of a far longer phase of work. Only after prolonged work is the child enabled to differentiate between his own feelings of love and hate and to react to the real positive and negative qualities he meets in other people. During this phase the projective aspects of the distrust have to be analyzed, but even when these have been much diminished the child has to test the reality of the analyst's trustworthiness again and again, because throughout his past life and in his current experience with his mother her real impulses and actions tend to confirm his fantasies. For example, in the case of a boy whose mother's destructive and seductive impulses led to severe impairment of her capacity to care for him adequately, especially in the earliest phase, his approach to the analyst was for a long time characterized by the almost complete absence of good expectations from her.

It is well known that the analyst faces a variety of problems when attempting to establish and maintain a treatment alliance with patients in puberty and throughout adolescence. These can be understood in terms of the developmental changes taking place in these phases. The coincidence of the changes within the structure of the personality, with the intensification of id impulses and the simultaneous struggle for freedom from the tie to the infantile love objects, creates a situation in which many elements contained in the analytic process and especially the tie to the analyst are felt as a threat.

Specific problems arising from these developmental factors are encountered at the initial stage with patients who have reached the phase in which one of the many forms of adolescent revolt has set in. Among patients in this age group who are referred for treatment, we meet with a considerable number who come for the very reason that their development has been held up. Analytic work here aims at freeing the forward movement, and only after successful treatment do we experience the typical obstacles to active participation in treatment with the repercussions in the transference of the adolescent's need to loosen the object tie.

## *Summary*

While much thought has been given to problems of interpretation in the treatment of adult patients, they have, as yet, not been studied with all their implications where children are concerned. One aspect of importance is related to the changes taking place in the child's developing ego, the part of the personality to which interpretations are conveyed. It is clear that in the course of development questions relating for instance to the growing capacity to tolerate frustration or to master anxiety must affect the choice, formulations, and timing of interpretations. It must be kept in mind that in many cases which are referred for treatment, different aspects of the ego are not on a level corresponding to the child's age. Attention is drawn to the need to remain aware of this in order to find the optimal conditions for transmission and assimilation of interpretations into the personality of child patients.

# REFERENCES


Bornstein, Berta. On latency. *Psychoanal. Stud. Child,* 1951, **6**, 279–285.

Bornstein, Berta, Falstein, E., and Rank, Beata. Child analysis. *Bull. Amer. Psychoanal. Assoc.,* 1951, **7**, 344–348.

Freud, Anna. Certain types and stages of social maladjustment. In K. R. Eissler (Ed.), *Searchlights on delinquency.* New York: International Univer. Press, 1949.

Freud, Anna. A connection between the states of negativism and of emotional surrender. *Int. J. Psycho-anal.,* 1952, **33**, 265. (Abstract)

Geleerd, Elisabeth R. Some aspects of psychoanalytic technique in adolescence. *Psychoanal. Stud. Child,* 1957, **12**, 263–283.

Loewenstein, R.M. Some remarks on defenses, autonomous ego and psychoanalytic technique. *Int. J. Psycho-anal.,* 1954, **35**, 188–193.

❀ CHAPTER TWELVE

# Countertransference

IN CONSIDERING the various aspects of countertransference in work with children, Bick[1] says the following:

> The intensity of the child's dependence, of his positive and negative transference, the primitive nature of his phantasies, tend to arouse the analyst's own unconscious anxieties. The violent and concrete projections of the child into the analyst may be difficult to contain. Also the child's suffering tends to evoke the analyst's parental feelings, which have to be controlled so that the proper analytic role can be maintained. All these problems tend to obscure the analyst's understanding and to increase in turn his anxiety and guilt about his work.

While client-centered therapists do not think in terms of transference and countertransference, their point of view with regard to complete acceptance of the child by the therapist is somewhat analogous to the analyst's concept of countertransference. Yet there are notable differences: The client-centered approach urges the therapist to suppress any negative feelings he may have toward the child; the analyst strives to bring his own positive *and* negative feelings into conscious awareness and may, in certain instances (as suggested in Colm's selection), use his negative reactions in the therapy session.

The selection from Axline indicates how the beginning

[1] Esther Bick, "Symposium on Child Analysis: I. Child Analysis Today," *International Journal of Psycho-analysis*, XLIII (1962), 328–332, p. 330.

therapist may unwittingly convey his annoyance or rejection to the child and reiterates the need for unqualified acceptance.

Colm considers that it may be a valuable maneuver, especially in latency, to encourage the development of situations in which the therapist can let the child know that his actions are annoying. Such countertransference reactions may help the child gain insight into similar reactions which he elicits from other adults.

One further aspect of countertransference concerns the therapist's negative reaction to the child's parents. Often, the initial staffing of a case emphasizes the child, so that the participants, including the prospective therapist, tend to identify with the child and to regard the parents in negative terms. This point is further elaborated by Ekstein *et al.*[2]

> It has been understood for some time that transference manifestations of children include not only the projection of early repressed relationships but also displacements of the crucial relationships with the living contemporary parents. We suggest that corollary to this, the countertransference potential in work with children embraces the parent–child unit as well, and includes the therapist's responses to the contemporary parents of the child, as well as to the child's transferences and displacements. The child therapist faces countertransferences in relation to the parents which are just as complex as those which involve the child and which can best be understood when considered as part of a unit response to the child and his parents of today and yesterday. . . . This position is supported by the observation regarding the extent to which beginning workers with children commonly invoke fantasies of magically rescuing the child from the wickedness of his parents. Such fantasies can be said to reflect the defense against archaic guilt and anxiety generated in reaction to the fantasied replacement of the child's parents, and "parents" more generically.

The final selection by Rubenstein and Levitt further pursues the effect on the therapist of the parents', and especially the father's, reaction to the treatment situation. The authors

---

[2] Rudolf Ekstein, Judith Wallerstein, and Arthur Mandelbaum, "Countertransference in the Residential Treatment of Children," *Psychoanalytic Study of the Child,* XIV (1959), 186–218, p. 187–188.

point out the subtle interplay of dynamic factors that operate to create barriers between all concerned and which may endanger the therapeutic process and perhaps bring about a premature enforced termination.[3]

# Accepting the Child Completely

VIRGINIA M. AXLINE

Complete acceptance of the child is shown by the therapist's attitude. She maintains a calm, steady, friendly relationship with the child. She is careful never to show any impatience. She guards against any criticism and reproof—either direct or implied. She avoids praise for actions or words. All this calls for vigilance on her part. There are innumerable traps into which the unwary therapist might fall. The child is a very sensitive being and is apt to catch the most veiled rejection of himself on the part of the therapist.

When one stops to consider that the child has been brought into the clinic because the parent is seeking to change him, one concludes (and, it would seem, rightly) that the parent is rejecting some part, if not all, of the child. Thus, complete acceptance of the child seems to be of primary importance to the success of the therapy. How can the child achieve the courage to express his true feelings if he is not completely accepted by the therapist? How can he avoid guilt feelings as a result of what he does if he does not feel accepted by the therapist in spite of anything he might do or say? Acceptance does not imply approval of what he is doing. This cannot be emphasized too strongly. Approval of certain negative feelings which the child might express would be more of a hindrance than a help.

Jean is brought into the clinic by her mother. Jean, aged twelve, is getting completely out of hand. She shows no respect for her mother, quarrels with her younger brother, will not have anything to do with the other children in her class at school. After introductions, Jean goes to the playroom with the therapist. The therapist attempts to structure the situation verbally. "You may play with any of the toys in here any way that you want to, Jean. There are paints, clay, finger paints, puppets." The therapist smiles at Jean, who stares back at the therapist in obvious boredom. The therapist waits for a few moments. Jean sits down and maintains her stony silence. The therapist,

[3] For a discussion of the role of fathers in our present culture and the effects of passivity in fathers on their sons' oedipal struggle and ego development see pages 16 to 25 of Ben O. Rubenstein and Morton Levitt, "Some Observations Regarding the Role of Fathers in Child Psychotherapy," *Bulletin of the Menninger Clinic*, XXI (1957), 16–27.

anxious to get things moving, speaks again. "Don't you know just what to do first? Oh, and there is a family of dolls over in the doll house. Do you like to play with dolls?"

Jean shakes her head negatively. The therapist pursues her quarry. "You don't like to play with dolls. Don't you see anything in here that you would like to play with? You may play with any of these things in here in any way that you want to." Jean still maintains the icy silence. Then the therapist says, "You don't want to play. You just want to sit here." Jean nods agreement. "Very well," says the therapist. She, too, sits down, and silence descends upon both of them. But the therapist is tense. "Would you rather just talk?" she asks hopefully. "No," says Jean. The therapist taps her pencil on her barren notebook. She taps her foot. She looks a little annoyed at Jean. This silence is maddening. There is a silent battle going on between the two, of which Jean is surely aware.

The therapist says, after a long silence, "Jean, do you know why you are here?" Jean stares at her. "You mother brought you up here so that you could get some help with the problems that bother you." Jean looks away. "I don't have any problems," she announces coldly. "Well, you have this hour to use any way you want to," comments the therapist. Jean sulks. The therapist very nearly sulks, too. Several minutes pass. Then—

THERAPIST: Did you go to school today?

JEAN: Yes.

THERAPIST: Did everything go along all right?

JEAN: Yes. (*More silence.*)

THERAPIST: You know, Jean, I'm here to help you. I want you to consider me your friend. I wish you would tell me what bothers you.

JEAN (*Sighing.*): Nothing bothers *me!*

There is no doubt about it. The therapy is blocked. The relationship has not been established. Jean is acutely aware that she is not accepted here, either. Jean is resentful enough of her mother's attempt to change her to resist to the bitter end. What, under the circumstances, could the therapist do?

Sometimes the therapist feels that it might inspire activity if she gets out the clay and begins to roll it around in an inviting fashion. Then, perhaps, comment, "Would you like to do this, too?" The therapist, under the circumstances, might get a polite participation, but it is doubtful if the therapy would ever move out of that polite resistance stage.

In the preceding case, the therapist is attempting to control the activity of the hour. It seems important to her that the girl *do* something. She is suggestive. She tries to push things along. "Don't you know what to do first?" implies a criticism of the lack of participation on the part of Jean. The therapist recognizes Jean's feeling when she says, "You don't want to play. You just want to sit there." But the therapist cannot accept this. She pushes harder. "Would you rather just talk?" "No." That is not accepted, either. That nervous, impatient tapping of pencil and foot! Then the therapist commits the unpardonable error of injecting the element of a threat into the therapy situation. "Do you know *why* you are here?" In other words, "You had better start doing something about yourself. There is plenty wrong with you or you wouldn't be here." She even drags in the word "problem," which Jean denies that she has. But the therapist doesn't accept her denial. She says, "I wish you would tell me what bothers you." She says, "You may use this hour any way you want to." Jean proceeds to use it for resistance and silence. The inconsistent therapist starts to probe again. "Did you go to school today?" And then, adding insult to injury, "I want you to consider me your friend." It just didn't add up. The therapist was neither accepting, nor consistent, nor therapeutic.

The alternative suggestion that the therapist draw the girl into participation by more subtle means is equally as unaccepting. If the girl has been fighting for acceptance outside the clinic, why must she continue here? If it is obvious that she does not want to play or talk, why not be accepting and permissive to the extent of letting her sit there in silence? After explaining the situation clearly enough so that she understands that she might play with any of the things in the playroom or use the hour any way she desires, the accepting therapist would go along with the child and, if silence was the order of the hour, then silence it would be. It would seem well to include in the preliminary explanation to the girl that it is her privilege either to play or not to play as she desires, to talk or not to talk, and, after the girl has made the decision, the therapist should abide by it. The therapist might busy herself with notes or with doodling if she feels that she *must* do something. She should be on the alert to reflect any feeling the girl might express. A deep sigh, a longing glance out the window, might safely be reflected to her—"It is boring to just sit here with me. Perhaps you would rather be outside." At that understanding, Jean might relax a little. If she remained adamant, the therapist should remain equally accepting. . . .

Acceptance of the child goes further than establishing the initial contact or getting the child into the room and functioning. After the therapy is well under way, the therapist must maintain an accepting attitude for all the things the child does and says. The process of nondirective therapy is so interwoven that it is difficult to tell where one principle begins and another ends. They are overlapping and interdependent. For example, the therapist cannot be accepting without being permissive. She cannot be permissive without being accepting. She cannot leave the responsibility to make choices up to the child whom she does not respect. The degree to which the therapist is able to put these principles into practice seems to affect the depth to which the therapy can go. When a child is expressing violent, aggressive feelings, the therapist must be alert to accept those feelings, too. Silence, at such a time, might be construed by the child to indicate disapproval and lack of acceptance. The tone of voice, the facial expression, even the gestures used by the therapist, either add to or subtract from the degree of acceptance that is being put into the situation.

### *Application to Group Therapy*

To apply this principle in a group situation, the therapist is continually obliged to check responses so that one child in a group does not feel at any time that he is being compared or contrasted with any other member of the group. Such a feeling can be aroused quite unintentionally if the element of praise or criticism, either direct or indirect, is injected by the therapist's responses. Such a statement as, "John knows what to do, he is getting busy right away," could very easily be taken as criticism by the other members of the group if they happen to be enjoying the bliss of a few minutes of sheer idleness while silently evaluating the situation. Or when the child rolls a ball of clay, seemingly without intent to make something, a statement from the therapist such as, "You don't know just what to make, do you, Bill?" verges on criticism of the child's indecisive activity. It seems that the most worthwhile responses from a therapeutic standpoint are reflections of feelings and attitudes expressed rather than content responses. The tone of voice and the impartial scattering of responses does much to eliminate the feeling on the part of the child that he is being criticized by the therapist.

Indications are that the child's feeling of complete acceptance by the therapist is more easily established in the individual therapy contacts than in the group contacts because the element of comparison or implied criticism does not enter into the situation.

# *A Field-Theory Approach to Transference and Its Particular Application to Children*

HANNA COLM

In my work with both children and adults, I have been struck by the fact that the child patient's responses to me and my reactions to him have many similarities to the equivalent phenomena with adult patients. Yet transference and countertransference phenomena, which are regarded as characteristic in analytic work with adults, have never really been acceptable in work with children. Thinking this over in terms of the controversy between

Anna Freud and Melanie Klein, I have felt that something important has been overlooked in the analysis of children and that this can be clarified, not by approaching the matter from the angle of transference–countertransference, but by approaching it from the point of view of field theory. As a matter of fact, through the field approach one can look at adult and child transference–countertransference problems from the same point of view, at the same time seeing clearly the difference between the situation and needs of the child and those of the adult.

## *A Re-examination of the Concept of Transference*

Transference has always been recognized in analysis as *the* important medium with which the analyst has to work. Through transference experience the analyst can help his patient to recognize defenses which made sense in the past, but do not belong realistically in the present. The analyst can also help the patient to become aware of his attempts to re-create old traumatic situations over and over again in each new relationship. The point of view of field theory does not add anything new to the concept of transference.

I think that field theory does, however, throw a new light on the concept of countertransference. A great deal of recent discussion of the phenomenon of countertransference has brought it into sharper focus, although there is a great variety of opinion about its occurrence and handling. While some authors emphasize that countertransference reactions are valuable as tools in understanding the patient's intent, there is general agreement that countertransference should, if possible, be kept a minor factor in the analysis—that it should be recognized by the analyst but should not appear in the relationship with the patient or come to his awareness.

In field theory, there is no place for this approach of, first, accepted and utilized transference and, second, controlled and interdicted countertransference. In the field experience there can be only spontaneous acting and reacting to the situation, and countertransference becomes merely one facet of the common humanity of patient and analyst. From this point of view, the analytic situation is merely a human situation in which both the analyst and the patient have the same human involvement with their pasts in their responses. The difference is that the analyst is better able to distinguish the past from the present involvement and does not react parataxically; or he is undefensively willingly to be open to the patient's suspicions and accusations that he is not realistically involved and to engage in self-scrutiny. Thus the analyst's human responses—his countertransference reactions—need not merely be used privately by him, but can, when it is called for, be put at the patient's disposal in order to clarify with him the interpersonal interaction. The appearance of countertransference in the open thus becomes not a fault of the analytic situation, but a means for the investigation of the mutual interaction.

It might be well at this point to recall the main points of field theory as it applies to the analytic situation. The term "field" is borrowed from modern physics, which discovered that not the characteristics of individual bodies but what happens *between* them determines their behavior, that is, the field—the magnetic or electric field—may be *essential* for understanding events.

Thus field theory, as applied to human events, emphasizes the complexity and continuity of relationships.[a] Every person, looked at from this point of view, exists in a field of inner and outer forces, with center and fringe areas; his field comprises his conscious and unconscious inner actions and reactions, as well as his past and present inner involvement with other people, concepts, ideas, and goals. In the healthy person, the outer and inner forces are in balance, so that his position in the field is firmly established. This is not true of the neurotic person; he is disturbed and buffeted about in his field.

When two people meet, they bring to this meeting their whole realistic as well as parataxic bodies of experience and all the involvements of their lives—and this on a conscious as well as unconscious level. The interhuman field between the partners extends beyond the personal meeting situation. As one human being reaches into the field of another, he may touch center or fringe areas—some areas essential and some unessential to the other, some areas of defensiveness and some areas of undisturbed "being-himself." Each person forms specific fields with other persons when he relates to them. In such a meeting, polarity always develops, in an unconscious way; field tensions and mutual influences begin to appear. Every event in the relationship causes fluctuations in the common field, condensing it at times, loosening it at others, and causing it to reach varying degrees of depth from time to time. Not only the person's conscious *here and now*, but also his potential, his *becoming*, is carried into the field and is experienced in an encounter by the other person. This fact is of great importance in the meeting of two persons in the analytic situation; the analyst must be acutely aware of this *becoming* part of the patient.

In the therapeutic situation the analyst must deal with the patient *in his whole field*, recognizing at the same time that, through the analysis, the analyst's own field and that of his patient begin to interact. As this happens,

[a] I have drawn upon the following sources in my discussion of the application of field theory to the analytic situation: Harry Stack Sullivan, *Conceptions of Modern Psychiatry* (New York: Norton, 1953); *The Contributions of Harry Stack Sullivan*, Patrick Mullahy, ed. (New York: Hermitage House, 1952); Harry Stack Sullivan, *The Psychiatric Interview* (New York: Norton, 1954); Harry Stack Sullivan, "Psychiatry: Introduction to the Study of Interpersonal Relations" (pp. 98–121), "Notes on Investigation, Therapy, and Education in Psychiatry and Their Relations to Schizophrenia" (pp. 193–210), and "Therapeutic Investigations in Schizophrenia" (pp. 446–454) in *A Study of Interpersonal Relations*, Patrick Mullahy, ed. (New York: Hermitage House, 1949); Helen Swick Perry, "Sullivan's Field Theory," unpublished paper given at the Washington Seminar on Religion and Psychiatry, Washington, D.C., spring of 1954; Kurt Lewin, *A Dynamic Theory of Personality* (New York: McGraw-Hill, 1935); Wolfgang Hochheimer, "Contribution to the Analysis of the Therapeutic Field," *Psyche*, VII (1954), 648–675.

both will have new experiences and reactions, show new defenses and spontaneous reach-outs. In this process the communication is to a great extent from unconscious to unconscious; the analyst tries to get in contact with the center area of the field of the patient in order to help him toward "center-area" living in contrast to his defensive "fringe-area" living. Thus analysis becomes field analysis—an examination of the common field between the two people, in the course of which, for each person, the unconscious probably has the more permanent impact and the conscious, the more temporary impact.

. . . It is clear that in such an encounter the analyst brings his awareness of his own inner field to full participation in the common field "between," in order to analyze the inner field of his patient. This does not mean that the analyst constantly interprets his own reactions to the patient—even though he is constantly aware of them. But it does mean that the analyst is free to use with the patient his insight into his own feelings and reactions to re-establish communication whenever he feels that he does not understand the patient or whenever the patient is at a point of resistance. The point at which the analyst can allow himself to be fully spontaneous is dependent on how fast and how deeply he can relate centrally to the patient. If the patient senses the center acceptance behind the spontaneous reactions of the analyst, there is little danger that this spontaneity will interfere with the relationship and the analytic work. In my experience, my spontaneous reactions have indeed *at first* created anxiety, but have always ultimately resulted in a better working relationship, for a great deal of trust is activated in the patient and experienced by him in the course of learning that fringe area upsets do not affect the continuing center relationship. It is this genuine contact in the center areas of both that produces the creative mutual growth which is healing.

Once the analyst feels that such center contact has been reached, he can allow himself a great deal in relation to his patient, bringing his anger and other negative feelings out into the open. What arouses such feelings? Before going into this question, I wish to make it clear that I do not refer to feelings that arise as a result of unrecognized, unresolved inner problems and conflicts and so lead to the analyst's playing a part in the neurosis of the patient. I am speaking rather of feelings that arise against a background of spontaneousness and relatedness, with one's full awareness and with a willingness to scrutinize both sides of the interaction. I have found that there are two situations which bring forth such negative responses in me.

The first such situation occurs when I feel frustrated because of too intensive and prolonged resistance on the part of the patient, either because his anxieties have led him to defeat and defy me, not permitting me to understand, or because a problem of my own has kept me from recognizing what was going on. The mere expression of hostility by the patient, even though it be extreme, does not cause anger in me, provided I understand its parataxic quality. Analysis is not mainly a process of interpretation of the behavior of the patient, but consists largely of, first, breaking ground for the relationship between analyst and patient and then clarifying this relationship. The analyst will not feel angry in the process of this clarification if he understands the patient's involvements with his past.

But a prolonged period when nothing clicks—that is, a long period of possibly intended frustration—does indeed cause anger in me; and then I am likely to meet the reproach from the patient, "How can I ever dare to express hostility if you get angry?" If he insists that he is "scared now," this usually means continued resistance. It is his attempt to control in a frightening spontaneous situation and is the very thing that needs to be worked on. Here it is necessary to show the patient that it is not his hostility, but his refusal to feel understood or to contribute toward being understood—to allow contact and togetherness—that has brought about the situation. Usually he can be convinced that my anger is a reaction to the frustration brought about by his anxious lack of trust and withdrawal from the interaction—that my anger suggests my interest and my longing for renewed togetherness, rather than a rejection of him. Thus my anger usually establishes a greater degree of mutual center contact and pushes us into a more realistic relationship, provided I have been able to accept my own field involvement. He sees that I have enough sureness about my inner contact with him that I can dare to be angry—to be less controlled and more spontaneous. The acknowledgment of the spontaneous reaction of both sides and an understanding of the dynamic interrelatedness of both reactions is, in addition, often important for understanding the realistic or unrealistic nature of the interaction of patient and analyst. In this way, the experience of analysis can be of mutual gain to both patient and analyst, although naturally to different degrees. . . .

The second situation which causes negative reactions in me arises when the patient touches an unresolved conflict of my own. Here I find it useful to ask myself the following questions: "What does the patient's unrealistic way of defensive fringe experiencing of me do to my own field? Is there a relation between my fringe reactions of aggression, irritation, and anger, and my own field experiences with past and present significant persons?" If there is such an unrealistic quality in the analyst's reaction, he must, of course, become aware of it if he is to help the patient toward more realistic living. Yet every countertransference has in it a grain of reality in terms of the current situation with the patient, and it is this grain of reality which needs to be sifted out from the parataxic part of the analyst's reactions by the analyst alone, early in the analysis, and later, *with* his patient. It is in this later process—once center contact has been reached in some area—that the analyst has to be a full partner, offering his conscious experience and, even more, his unconscious experience of the patient. I do not have to wait to reveal my own field until center contact is *fully* established; *my openness establishes center contact.* This is true even though parts of my reaction may come parataxically from my own field; since I know that it never comes only from something parataxic, I can trust that we will be able to disentangle the realistic interaction of our common field. Only the courage of openness on both sides can elucidate the field between the two people and can move the patient from anxious, condemning, defensive fringe-field living to more accepting and more satisfying center-field living. . . .

### *The Field Approach in Child Therapy*

While field theory gives a new dimension to the concept of transference in relation to adult analysis, it is in work with children that field theory has most to offer. In essence, this approach makes it possible to see in a new light certain problems which have long troubled child therapists. Why is it that transference, which is such a universally recognized process in adult analysis, is not supposed to occur with children? If transference is a common human phenomenon, must it not apply to the therapist–child relationship? Here one is thrown into the long continued controversy growing out of the opposing views of Anna Freud and Melanie Klein, particularly in regard to the therapist's role in child analysis and the question of whether a child develops a transference neurosis during the course of therapy.

It is Anna Freud's belief that in analysis the child has to relate to the analyst in terms of the good mother; she concentrates a great deal of time and effort on convincing the child of the analyst's good, trustworthy attributes. She begins interpretations only after she is confident that the child has accepted her in the good-mother role. She feels that no transference neurosis is possible, since the patient is still living with his parents and his problems in relation to them are part of his daily living. Melanie Klein, on the other hand, feels that the child's concept of the bad parent comes first and foremost into the picture, and her approach is to interpret, in a most accepting way and immediately—before anxieties and secret conclusions accumulate—the child's unconscious and hidden hatred for the bad parent. Because young children cannot free-associate, she provides her patients with toys in order to gain access, through their play, to their unconscious.

While many child therapists in this country have taken over the play-therapy technique of Melanie Klein, they have completely left out her concepts of transference and countertransference. Thus the method has become nonanalytic, relying on the good-mother role of the therapist to help the child, through relatedness and acceptance. Interpretation has been rejected as too intellectual, and great reliance has been put on the acceptance of the unconscious without translating it into consciousness. Where interpretation is used, it is only in terms of the most generalized picture of family relations and ambivalence.

There is no doubt that this method has yielded great improvement in many children, particularly those with disturbances of a relatively minor character or of a more-or-less temporary nature having to do with normal difficulties in growing up. It seems to me, however, that awareness of transference and countertransference difficulties and clarity about them, is of decisive importance in the analysis of *neurotic* children. I agree with the play therapists in their refusal to accept the sterility of intellectual interpretations; yet I feel that they have lost an important tool. I make use of transference and countertransference without getting bogged down in overintellectualization, by revealing and interpreting, not the child's behavior, but *my* reaction to it. In this way, the child becomes aware of and understands his feelings, at the same time becoming aware of and understanding the reactions which his defensive patterns arouse in the adult.

From the field point of view, it makes no difference whether the child reacts to the analyst in terms of the good mother or the bad mother; both experiences are in the child's field, as either conscious or unconscious factors. It is important, however, to realize that the neurotic child is afraid to reveal his bad-parent concept and is not able to trust his good-parent ideal.

It is generally agreed that play therapy has great difficulty in overcoming the resistances of a child in the latency period against revealing himself and his feelings toward his parents and substitute adults—a defensiveness which is connected with the developmental necessities of these years. While the child is busy establishing controls for his growing ego, he must, in order to cope with his overwhelming impulses, thwart the therapist's attempts to loosen him up and to unbind those impulses. He does not want to explore himself, for fear of undoing what he has, with the help of his parents and his school, just barely achieved or is still desperately struggling to achieve. He closes up; he does not talk, does not play. The play-therapy approach of merely "bringing things into the open" with an accepting other person fails in the face of the child's suspiciousness and defensiveness, for his self-condemnation makes him distrust the adult's interest in his total self—good and bad—and he "knows" that the adult is out to blame him in the course of this supposedly helpful search. Any discussion of his fear and control and distrust only makes him withhold more; he feels that somebody is trying to break in and that this must be prevented, for nobody could possibly care to see and accept what he is trying to control and cover up.

In this situation, field analysis reaches the child and convinces him that the aim is not to blame and correct him, but to help him. It begins with the attempt to establish center-field contact with him, even though this threatens him *with opening up on the side of the analyst*, who reveals his own side of the "between" field. In the initial hours, each child brings to bear his own particular defenses—defiance, or contempt, or snobbishness, or a cold "I just don't care for this," or embarrassment. The analyst reacts to the different defenses in very different inner ways and reveals his reactions.

I can best explain the way this opening-up begins by describing some of my own experiences. For example, often a very disturbed child's most frequent reaction is one of silent contempt—"Ha, you are not worth a speck to me, you are against me, I know you. Want to help me! There is nothing you can do."

My inner reaction to this may be sympathy; I know the despair of the child—I know my own despair as a child. Some despair comes up in me and also some tension—will I reach him, will I be sensitive enough to reach him? Sometimes I may notice some anger creeping up, because he is so determined not to give me a chance to reach him. Perhaps more comes to me from the child—"You can't help me—it's beyond you, you have no real idea what I am like inside, and if you knew, you wouldn't care at all." When I feel all this coming to me from the child—seldom in words, mostly in silent looks and a cold, stiff air of brushing me off—I first feel it through, and then I myself open up, showing him my reaction, my feeling, my side of the field—"You know, Paul, you make me feel sort of unhappy—no—really sad. I know you are here because your parents think I can help you, but you don't want any help and make me feel I am no good. You'd rather stay all to yourself—all so alone." There may be a long pause and then I may add, "You know what *I* feel? I feel pushed away—that sort of hurts me." This kind of revelation feels convincing to the child. He would love to trust, but doubts. He wonders. He is beginning to hope a tiny bit.

At this point he may smile a very small smile and look at me with a suspicious but faintly warming glance, and then he may begin to *do* something in the room; this is then his first communication and the opening up of his field. On the other hand, he may stiffen and look more intensely contemptuous, even though his look has a slightly different tinge—a little more two-way feeling comes through; and I sense that his contempt is more *self*-contempt now. I may ask him if he knows how it feels when somebody he thinks he could care about gives him the cold-shoulder treatment. He is silent, hesitating. I say, "Well, *I* hate it—it feels *awful* to me." I reveal how he affects me—how I myself *feel*—and he responds with some curiosity and distrust. Sometimes I have to go on, for he is still detached—"You know, when I give the cold shoulder to someone, it's because I am really scared myself that he might not like me." Once at such a point the single word "You?" popped out of one of these children. Sometimes the child still says nothing, but continues to look at me with great and suspicious puzzlement. I don't push at this point, but say, "Well, maybe I have to wait until you see for yourself." Or the child may now ask, "Why should *you* be scared?" To this I may respond, "I don't know; I only know I *am* scared when I give someone the cold shoulder."

While I talk I always begin to work with clay, pounding it when I am angry and tense or stroking it when I feel sadness, despair, and longing to reach the child. And pretty soon the child takes a lump, too—invariably—and looks secretly at me. He begins to stroke the clay and by so doing opens up and tells me something about his longing for caressing in his field and also about his distrust and his fear that he doesn't really deserve love. I say nothing, but we work with the clay together. One boy asked in this situation, while I was pounding my clay, "You are mad?" I replied, looking warmly at him, "Sure I am, and how! Did you think I liked the way you pushed me away?" This implied to the child that *I cared*, but I left it at that, attempting no big talk, no further conversation. At this point he stepped out of his reserve—out of the fringe area into some more central area of his field—for some interaction of our fields had occurred. He began to pound some nails into a piece of wood violently. I said, "You are mad too." "Yeah." "At whom?" Silence from him. And then from me, "Maybe you hate it—that I want you and you feel you aren't any good—that I could not *really* possibly like you." Big eyes toward me—a smile—touched, yet still scared. And a switch from pounding clay to content play that showed me what made him feel so worthless; he took a ball and threw it at an old clown figure painted on a puppet stage. "There! I hate that face!" he said.

"Sure you do—it looks ridiculous and disgusting." At this point I analyzed his side to myself, naturally knowing that he was telling me something about his father. In such a situation, I might ask the child, after only a few hours, and at a time when it seemed to fit, if he ever had had that disgusted and contemptuous feeling toward his father. In this instance, the analysis of the boy was well under way from the time of this conversation, and was established on the basis of my trusting *him* as shown by me revealing my own feelings.

I never do this in the manner of a standard technique, but try to search in every different case for what I feel; and I am always astonished at the number of different feelings and nuances of feeling that come up in response to the outwardly similar behavior of different children. There is not the same stereotyped exchange in each case, but always my feeling responding to his and to what he is busy awakening in me; thus I reveal myself as touched, hurt, sad, frustrated, or angry—all of which mean to him that I care. This has proved to be much more convincing than accepting words, which so often sound phony to children who *hear* a great deal about love without feeling it come to them. Anna Freud reports that she takes a long time before beginning actual analysis to prove to the child that she really cares. In the field approach, in spite of the child's own fear of trusting and his need to hide, he *experiences*, consciously and unconsciously, in an immediate, genuine way, that the analyst cares.

There is another way in which the field approach seems very valuable to me: it permits the child a greater degree of relating on an unconscious level. The play-therapy concept recognizes the need for the child to relate on an unconscious level, but it by no means exhausts the possibilities for such relating. The neurotic child needs to become aware that his defenses are not really useful to him and to others and for that reason needs to *feel* the reaction that they bring about in the adult he cares for. Rational interpretations do not reach the child; he needs experience on a more-or-less nonverbal, unconscious level. Bringing my unconscious reaction to the child's neurotic defenses into my own consciousness and then revealing my reaction to the child brings to his awareness that his defenses do not make sense to the guiding adult. It is usually the first revealing of my unconscious center-area involvement that opens up the analysis; and only when the child has developed center-area contact and cannot become really shaky any more, can the analysis proceed freely, being open on both sides of the field. This never feels intellectual to the child. I drifted into this "method" first, without being fully aware of what was implied, because I had so often to work with children who were used to too many interpretations at home, whose parents were professionally trained in psychiatry or related fields, or who were over-controlled and engaged in much talk without corresponding feeling. Again and again, in working with these overintellectualized children, I have seen a sudden light of relief or deep joy in their eyes and a turn toward health after a genuine outburst of anger on my side—in contrast to their parents' controlled "accepting" interpretations or artificially loving phrases. The child would feel the genuineness of the reaction on my side, at first with some astonishment that our center-field contact remained undisturbed, even though he had just experienced outer-field condemnation. Because my center contact is not disturbed when I express irritation or anger, my reaction has never made a child so anxious that there was a continued loss of trust; we have always been able to work it through together. This working-it-through is naturally an important part of it.

Actually this approach follows the same line and pattern which the basic growth of the child follows in his unconscious relationship to and dependence on the significant adults in his life. At first he depends completely on the mothering adult, communicating with her in an unconscious way. Gradually he includes the father, and his reactions become more conscious. He takes his first steps into life through his inner trusting relationship to the unconscious guiding reactions of his parents, and he will either progress or be thwarted in his growth according to the degree of center-area contact that is established with them. Both in analysis and in life generally, the child is intensely attuned to the unconscious of the adults around him and at the same time dependent on being guided; and he lives and grows not primarily through the words or actions of the adult, but by his unconscious reactions to the feeling behind the words and actions. Thus the analyst's unconscious reactions to the child are of utmost importance.

The child unconsciously knows whether the adult loves him and has made center-field contact with him or whether only outer-field contact is effected by the adult. Disturbed behavior always indicates that center contact is not established or is temporarily out of focus. When this happens, the child tries to force some center contact, be it of positive or negative nature. In the treatment of a disturbed child, even more than in adult treatment, there can be healing only if the analyst has genuine contact with the unconscious of the child—center contact and center acceptance—*in spite* of the defensive behavior of the child. It is important for the neurotic child to *experience* what he creates in the adult. Thus verbalization and interpretation of what the child is doing are not as important as honest clarification of what he contributes to the adult's feeling-reactions. The child comes to see—without interpretations that feel to him artificial and intellectual or like a technique used upon him by the analyst—that he creates fringe-area reactions of anger and irritation, while he obviously wants center-field contact, love, togetherness. The adult therapist offers himself to the child for polarization, for a chance at another, happier interaction. In this process, the child learns to understand how he evokes the therapist's reactions and how he defeats himself with his unconstructive behavior. He participates in an *experience* with an adult and feels what happens to that adult when he acts as he does, that is, he becomes aware of what happens to the person with whom his field fuses, whether it is his therapist or his mother and father. This awareness gives him a chance to grow again—to give up defensive, distorted reactions; as a result of such awareness, he may be able later on—after the latency years—to even give up complete reaction patterns. In this process the child and analyst continually struggle toward center-field contact, with the child experiencing the fact that his fringe-area behavior is not acceptable, yet that he himself is accepted in center contact. At the same time, he learns that the therapist, as the adult in the situation, will prevent his fringe behavior from becoming too overwhelming for him; the child will gradually come to see that his defensive behavior endangers the very center-area contact that he actually seeks. If the analyst's own self-acceptance is shaky and he still hates his own defenses which he meets in the child, the child cannot improve. Moreover, the child cannot improve merely through unlimited acceptance in the hands of an untrained person or of one who feels that this is all that is needed for healing, since this often feels phony to the child. It may relieve him from anxiety for awhile, but in the long run it often serves to create more intense anxieties, since it has not resolved the child's conflicts and his defenses. . . .

A child transference phenomenon which is seldom recognized in its full significance is the role which the mother in the waiting room plays. Therapists are often too quick to assume, when the child seems disturbed about his mother and runs outside the therapy room to see her, that he is merely anxious about leaving her. This is often the case when the child feels loyalty difficulties and actually has made the analyst into the good mother in contrast to a not yet admittedly bad mother in the waiting room. Yet there is another transference operating at times: in the therapy room, the child experiences his relation with the therapist as "Mother and I," and the third person—the actual mother who is in the waiting room—thus becomes the other adult person in the family—the father. This other person, who is *present* but excluded, is very alarming to the child, and causes him to manifest anxiety in various ways. One child will anxiously and compulsively run out to the mother, another will bring the mother into the room at significant times, still another will want the analyst to go out to the waiting room with him. Sometimes a child will become visibly confused when he has to make the transition from one adult to another. Such a child often reassures his mother by reporting to her immediately after the hour that the relationship with the analyst is not satisfactory, even though the child's productions during the hour may belie his report. It becomes evident that the second adult is not yet integrated, and thus the relationship to both adults is full of conflicts. This particular transference manifestation needs to be worked through.

In order to determine which of these sources is responsible for the child's anxiety, it is necessary to conduct a careful inquiry into the dynamics of the child's family situation—the daily interplay between the child and the significant adults; a mere gathering of various facts about the family does not suffice. Here again, the analyst's own reactions may be useful; the analyst must constantly be aware of whether he is feeling bored, scared, depressed, puzzled, ambitious, defeated, and so on and must compare these reactions with what he knows about the mother's conflicts in her relationship to her child. In this collaborative analysis of the interaction, the child learns for himself to distinguish between "defensive, superficial me" and "center me," rather than "good me" and "bad me"; and the child begins to gradually experience the "bad" mother as less bad and more human. Of course, one would never use these terms to a child. In the process of understanding and experiencing the child's difficulties in living, the analyst naturally has to also keep in mind the normal sequences of child development and to distinguish the characteristic picture of neurotic and psychotic disturbances in the different developmental areas from normal growing-up difficulties. . . .

In order to further illustrate the value of this kind of analysis with children, I will describe an experience with a nine-year-old boy.

> Bill was thought by his parents to be deficient because of a brain injury. Although the injury existed, only the motor centers were damaged, so that only his coordination was affected. His mother felt, however, that any child of hers who was not perfect was necessarily a complete failure; thus she could more easily tolerate a situation of no hope than face the effort necessary to bring out Bill's excellent capacities at his own pace and risk the possibility of failure. There was a great deal of center conflict in the mother, so that she was constantly rather defensively hopeless and anxious. Bill found this intolerable, and his response to it was to live with her in such a way that he actively produced anxiety in her. He could not live with her in an open way, taking things as they came; he closed his inner field off and related on an outer-field defensive basis. Thus he cut himself off from whatever inner-field contact she could offer.
>
> I liked Bill and related immediately to him; he related slowly, at first feeling very suspicious of me. I allowed him to experience the distortion and falsity of these suspicions. At first I did little talking, for the most part merely relying on being with him and accepting his distrustful, hostile actions toward me with some casual expression such as, "Gosh, what are you trying to prove?" or, "What do you think I am?" or, "What do you think I feel?" This sort of state-

ment always made him pause momentarily as he thought it over, apparently feeling some doubt about what he was doing. I began to intervene in this way more and more as I felt that his problem was shifting from merely symbolic projective play, or talk, to *behavior* with me—that is, when trust and inner-field contact were established and he was relating to me as he did to his mother. He was trying now to control the situation, since he would rather feel that he was able to produce the "bad" mother than face the fact that the "happy" mother could become unhappy and try to live with the reality.

The culmination of the experience between us occurred when this supposedly deficient child one day brought in a report card of only A's and B's. He threw the report card on the table; I picked it up, looked at it, and dropped it again, saying warmly, "How nice!" He then became furious and shouted at me, "Oh, you old dumbbell!" and began to kick me. I replied angrily and very spontaneously, "What do you *mean?*" Suddenly I understood his anxiety—he could not accept a friendly feeling from me, because he could not be sure that he would always be able to produce praise from me. He took up a long thirty-inch play gun and beat at me with all his power. I felt immediately very anxious, for I had to really fight with him to gain control of what was for me a dangerous situation, since I had at the time a broken toe. There were moments when I did not know whether I would make it, so anxious and violent was the child, and I myself—as one can imagine—had none of the advocated controlled, therapeutic composure. In the noisy fight, which finally ended with both of us on the floor, I screamed with all my force, "Stop this!" When at last I had the gun in my hand, I got up, and he, anxious, ashamed, and self-conscious, got up too. At this point he began to shout defensively that he always knew I was just as mean as everybody else and that I would scream at him even more than anybody else. I knew that he was right—that probably no one had ever screamed like that at him before—*and* I also knew that he was far enough along in his treatment, in center contact with me, that he could work through this anxiety in transference to me. I straightened out my dress and said, "Well, yes, I believe that nobody ever screamed at you before like that, Bill." Then, walking toward him and taking him by the shoulders—reassuring him by touch, by contact—I said, still panting, "Thank God, I know now how you can scare people. Maybe you do that also to your mother?" After I had got my breath and felt more composed, I said, "Let's look at it all. When I felt pretty happy and said 'how nice' to you—you remember, about the report card—you began to kick me. You know, you sure made me mad as anything—and I tell you, scared, too—you know, because of my toe." He smiled at this point—there was a little triumph in the smile. "And anyhow, the gun is pretty big and you are strong." He smiled again, and I went on: "You know what I think? You *like* it when you can make me real scared and angry. Well, sure, you can't make me happy all the time, like with the A's and B's, but goodness, I had an awful time fighting with you and it felt to you as if I was nothing but mean and shouty. And goodness, Bill, I don't really feel mean toward you—I like you!" His eyes filled with tears and he picked up the report card again, which made me feel that for the first time it did not make sense to him to always have to be the stronger one—the one in control.

Thinking it over afterward, I saw that had I let his "you old dumbbell" go unchallenged with mere acceptance and controlled my spontaneous response, we would not have gotten into *experiencing* with each other how he actively created the bad mother for fear that he could not always be sure of producing the good mother. At the same time he had the experience of finding that the relationship was not permanently destroyed on either his side or mine. And these two experiences were what mattered in terms of healing. There was mutual acceptance *in spite of*. At the end he had *experienced* my reaction to him inside our field, and the uselessness of his defense was obvious. He had felt my great anxiety and resulting anger, but at the same time he recognized that he had produced this behavior as a defense because he did not trust the lastingness of our center contact. He had also experienced the continuity of the inner-field relationship, *in spite of*, leaving us as close after my anger as before and even opening the way to a greater and more realistic mutual inner-field contact.

I have attempted to describe certain experiences related to transference and countertransference with children, and have interpreted these experiences in terms of the field approach. I have shown that the same approach with necessary modifications could also shed light on analytic problems with adults. This approach does not imply that the analyst constantly shares his self-awareness with the patient. It does mean, however, that the analyst at times permits situations in which he spontaneously reacts to the patient in terms of what the patient unconsciously intends to provoke in the other person. When the patient is resistant, such an experience may prove particularly helpful in clarifying and overcoming a stalemate in the analysis.

With children, who operate in their general living on a much more unconscious level, this approach has even more advantages. It includes many of the advantages of play therapy, but it also tackles the whole problem of transference and countertransference, which must be worked out in order to cure the more severe neuroses. In addition, this approach makes it possible to reach certain extremely defensive and distrustful children, particularly those in the latency years and adolescence, who are otherwise so difficult to contact. Children are very sensitive to the unconscious feelings of other people, and they sense any insincerity, no matter how well intentioned, in efforts made by therapists in the process of accepting them in therapy. Thus it answers a special need in child therapy, for it provides a means of being utterly sincere with these young patients, in a way that allays rather than causes anxiety, and enables them to trust—often a new and healing experience.

As for the analyst, this approach requires a constant self-awareness, a willingness to question over and over again what has been worked out in his own past life, and the ability to open up to another person, letting him see the unacceptable along with the acceptable, in the trusting belief that the real interrelatedness will last. This is a difficult undertaking. It carries many anxieties with it, but it includes also the deep enjoyment of a mutual relatedness that is never statically sure and secure, because it is between human beings, but is capable of being made secure again and again in spite of its dynamic inner tensions. The aliveness and security of such a relationship is the trust that the mutual center contact, once established, will not be lost.

## *Countertransference*

BEN O. RUBENSTEIN
AND MORTON LEVITT

. . . This may well be the place to examine the effect of the phylogenetic role of the father upon the therapist. We are here referring to countertransference. This phenomenon is somewhat more complicated in therapeutic work with children than in work with adults. The characteristics of the setting as described earlier are especially conducive to strong countertransference reactions, and these must exert a unique effect upon the therapist–father relationship. But countertransference in child analysis is not a private matter between therapist and patient, for it involves both of the parents. Since these reactions between parents and therapist occur outside the therapeutic process in contrast to adult analysis, they cannot be subjected to interpretation. The parents are not our patients and yet are intimately involved in the treatment. Not infrequently do the parents transfer to us those needs and defenses which are represented in the symptomatology of their child. This transfer of feelings tends to make us over into images that are consistent with the psychic economy of the parents.

The direct physical and emotional demands made upon us by our young patients appear to expedite the countertransference.[a] The required empathy with the child in face of such direct requests may evoke unconscious sibling reactions and revive other infantile needs in the therapist. There appears to be a correlation between the intensity of demands and the necessity for narcissistic endowment of the patient by the therapist. For example, in order to maintain empathy with certain disturbed children, we need to call upon ourselves for more narcissistic supplies. We must make these patients part of ourselves, that is, we must accept what our own education has forced us to dislike. Although sublimation comes to our aid, earlier unconscious mechanisms of introjection, reaction formation, and others still must be called into

[a] This one factor must contribute to the constant exodus of analysts from the field of child analysis. A similar point of view was expressed in the *Bulletin of the American Psychoanalytic Association*, VII (1951), No. 2.

play. The partial regression of the analyst brought about by the new economic distribution serves to make his unconscious keenly sensitive to the unconscious hostility of the child's father.

Another powerful element is at work in stimulating countertransference to either of the parents. This factor is an outgrowth of the need for and use of the treatment by both mother and child. We stated earlier that there is a type of mother who sets the scene for the seduction of the therapist. She comes out of her own needs, ripe for positive transference. The husband is often portrayed as a crude man, without understanding, and with no interest in his wife or child. Implicit is the inference that the sympathetic therapist is none of these. Such a hot-house atmosphere plants the seeds for rebirth of the analyst's oedipal strivings. The father's growing hostility and uncooperativeness adds fuel to this pregnant beginning. These feelings, compounded by other paternal reactions enumerated in earlier sections of this paper, complete the oedipal setting. Thus, we have the abused wife, the menacing father, and the analyst–son all contributing to a climate with which the analyst must be prepared to deal.

There can be little doubt that the circular current which has been opened by the negative countertransference must be sensed by the father. There is certainly no doubt that, as in all analytic work, both the analysis and the patient are affected. The character of the analytic material strengthens the negative countertransference to the father. The treatment of the adolescent most graphically demonstrates this problem. The intensified sexuality and the increased proclivity for acting-out on the part of the patient during this period strengthens the unconscious anxieties of the analyst. As the treatment begins to deal with problems of masturbation and direct sexual and aggressive expressions, the therapist, by unconscious identification with his patient's strivings, is thrown into conflict with the boy's father. It is admittedly difficult to assess quantitatively the influence of the analyst's unconscious hostility and guilt upon the already full-blown reaction to the father. We have noted that the relationship of the therapist to the father has become unconsciously affected in instances in which the adolescent has visited a prostitute or carried out a sexual adventure. The following dream related by a colleague took place shortly after a young patient had visited a bordello. The dream is so patently clear that no comment is necessary:

> I am walking with a prostitute. I note that the father of my adolescent patient is across the street in front of a police station. Filled with great anxiety, I hurry in order to avoid discovery.

As can be surmised, certain fathers are quite threatened by the increased genitality of their sons. The symptoms for which the patient entered treatment—intellectual inhibitions, enuresis, phobias, or compulsions—naturally do not threaten the father as much as direct expression of aggressiveness and sexual impulses. The exaggerated paternal reaction, whether directed at the patient or at the therapist, leaves little doubt that it is intended to emasculate both. In reviewing those cases of adolescent patients whose treatment was abruptly terminated by the father at the point of more open impulse expression, we have observed almost undisguised satisfaction on the father's part. Unfortunately, the exact influence of the countertransference cannot be determined, but the reaction of the therapist is known. Narcissistic injury and anxiety are characteristic in such situations.

Thus, it can be seen that while countertransference is a requisite part of adult analysis, it often creates the basis for the foundering of the process in the child analysis. To sum up, countertransference to the father finds its genesis in the character of analytic material which encourages identification with the patient. Since the patient's fantasies fulfill the therapist's unconscious impulses, they serve to revive latent anxiety about the threatening father figure. Freud's comment (S. Freud, 1949) that "the castration complex is the rock bottom of all psychological stratification" bears new fruit. Finally, since the father is not the patient, whatever object he has made of the therapist is not analyzable. This situation maintains the resistance to the end.

From a historical point of view, child analysis has emphasized the importance of the mother–child relationship and has paid little attention to the father. Corroboration for the construct of the inadequate father is substantiated by (1) a study of the role of the father in the culture, (2) an examination of his behavior within the family, and (3) the impressions gathered from the preliminary analytic material obtained from sons. However, clinical material has forced us to recognize the great influence of the father upon both the course and termination of treatment. This problem is elucidated by deeper examination of the unanalyzable transference of the father to the therapist, the countertransference of the therapist to him, and the deeper significance of the young patient's analytic material. Such examination re-establishes and substantiates the father in the phylogenetic role of the castrator.

## REFERENCES

Freud, S. A child is being beaten (1919). *Collected Papers*, Vol. II. London: Hogarth Press, 1949. Pp. 172–201.

CHAPTER THIRTEEN

# Reflections and Interpretations

TO THE NONDIRECTIVIST, the reflections of feelings are considered to be the most therapeutic statements; to the analyst, interpretations are the most important; to the child, the differences in emphasis or intent or meaning are probably less apparent than the therapists of either orientation would like to admit.

Taft[1] has said, "The content is necessary for communication as paint or some other medium is necessary for a picture, but the therapeutic reality is the actual dynamics of the relationship as it develops from hour to hour between the two human beings who enter upon it, the one as a patient, the other as helper." She adds, "It is not so easy as it sounds to learn to ignore content and to go through it to the fundamental attitudes and emotions behind it . . . ." This is the basic problem, regardless of therapeutic orientation. How can one become aware of and respond to the often disguised feelings of anger, fear, jealousy, guilt, shame, and anxiety?

While beginning therapists may tend to feel that often they are not responding—whether by reflections or interpretations—at the most appropriate times and that they are missing many situations in which they could have been therapeutic, it does seem that with children, perhaps more so than with adults, one can be permitted a few tactical "errors." Activities and episodes tend to reappear if they are not adequately handled the first time.

---

1 Jessie Taft, *The Dynamics of Therapy in a Controlled Relationship* (New York: Macmillan, 1933), pp. 106, 108.

To quote from the selection by Ross,[2] " . . . if he [the therapist] fails to recognize a cue in time because of his necessarily sincere involvement in play activity, he can rest assured that if the material expressed is at all significant it will come out again in a different context at a later time, provided the therapist has done nothing to discourage such expression."

Colm[3] also discusses the child's proclivity for repetition of a play sequence until it is recognized.

> Children usually go ahead with a new expressive, feeling-projecting activity when they feel understood. The sequence of their play activity is like a logically connected conversation. If they do not feel understood, they repeat the expression of feeling either in the same way, or they try to express the same feeling by other means. They never become defensive once the relationship with the therapist is established. They never feel judged or accused. They simply feel that they did not express themselves adequately, and need to take another tack.

Nevertheless, we are justified in asking: How many times can the therapist fail to interpret an activity before the child becomes aware of the therapist's insensitivity?

Freud[4] offers some comforting advice when he instructs the neophyte " . . . not to try to understand everything at once, but to give a kind of unbiased attention to every point that arises and to await further developments." This viewpoint is further elaborated by Finch[5] as he emphasizes the accumulative nature of the child's play and points out that interpretations are " . . . most effective when they utilize a series of events or a repetitious type of behavior by the patient. The more material the therapist has from the patient with which to confirm his interpretations, the more meaningful they will be to the patient."

---

[2] See page 122, this book, or Alan O. Ross, *The Practice of Clinical Child Psychology* (New York: Grune & Stratton, 1959), p. 93.

[3] Hanna Colm, "Play as a Means of Communication between Child and Adult—Three Cases," *Journal of Child Psychiatry*, II (1951), 100–112, p. 107.

[4] S. Freud, "The Analysis of a Phobia in a Five-Year-Old Boy" (1909), *Collected Papers* (New York: Basic Books, 1959), Vol. III, p. 207.

[5] Stuart Finch, *Fundamentals of Child Psychiatry* (New York: W. W. Norton, 1959), p. 267.

The nondirective position is presented in Axline's discussion of reflections; the emphasis is on catching the feeling tone beneath the words or play activity and letting the child know that the therapist has "understood."

Little or no attention is given the symbolic aspects of play by the nondirective school, in contrast to such emphasis in the dynamic orientations. Erikson underscores the importance of understanding play symbols as representations of conflict, and he discusses a climactic type of phenomenon in children's symbolic play which he has labeled "play disruption."[6] Such events are particularly crucial; if poorly handled, the progress of therapy may be greatly impeded since the disruption is the result of repressed material coming close to the surface. When meaningful interpretations are offered at this point, genuine therapeutic insights result. We may ask: Do all children experience such episodes of play disruption in the course of their therapy? If a child patient does not appear to show this reaction, could it be that the therapist was not sensitive to its occurrence?

Melanie Klein's views on the interpretive process are well illustrated in the case material included in these selections from one of her articles. She differs from many child analysts in that she advocates making quite deep interpretations very early in the course of therapy and in treating every play act of the child as having symbolic meaning. She sees the configurations in play as equivalent to the dreams and free associations of adults and interprets them in much the same manner. This selection also gives examples of play disruption and her views on the importance of transference and resistance manifestations.

---

[6] For a further example of Erikson's "play disruption" see the case material in the portions of his monograph used in Chapter 5, "The Initial Session," pages 106–110.

# Recognition and Reflection of Feelings

VIRGINIA M. AXLINE

So often during the initial contact, the therapist's responses seem rather wooden and more a response to the content than to the feeling the child is expressing. The therapist and child are feeling their way and striving to establish rapport. The child is exploring the playroom. He picks up a doll. "What is this?" he asks. "A doll," responds the therapist. He points to the paints. "What's this?" "Paints. Children paint on that easel if they want to." "What's this?" and on and on. Some therapists, trying to catch feelings, have responded, "You wonder what that is," but it seems that such a response does more to bog down the therapy than help it along. It seems advisable to answer factual questions with a direct answer. Then the child can go on from there. It is quite often just an attempt on the part of the child to get acquainted with the therapist. What else do they have in common that they could talk about? However, the therapist should be alert to the feelings the child is expressing either through his direct conversation or through his play, which is the child's natural way of expressing his feelings.

Recognition of feeling and interpretation are two different things. However, it is difficult to differentiate between them. The child's play is symbolic of his feelings, and whenever the therapist attempts to translate symbolic behavior into words, she is interpreting because she is saying what she *thinks* the child has expressed in his actions. This seems to be unavoidable and, at times, even seems to be advantageous. A cautious use of interpretation, however, would seem the best policy, with the therapist keeping the interpretation down to a minimum and, when using it, basing it upon the obvious play activity of the child. Even then, the therapist's response should include the *symbol* the child has used.

For example, a six-year-old boy was brought to the clinic for play-therapy contacts because of his exaggerated feelings of fear and anxiety. He played with the family of dolls in the doll house. He took the boy doll out of the house and said to the therapist, "She is sending the boy out here where the quicksand is. The boy is afraid. He cries and tells his mother that he is afraid, but she makes him go anyway. And see! He is sinking down and down and down into the quicksand." The boy, showing much anxiety and fear, buries the doll in the sand. This child is certainly dramatizing his fear and his feeling of insecurity and lack of understanding. How should the therapist respond to this? It is very certain that this child is playing out the basic issue of his problem. If she follows the child she will say, "The *boy* is being sent out of the house and he is afraid. There is quicksand out there. The boy even cries.

He tells his mother he is afraid, but she makes him go out anyway and he gets buried in the sand." The child is talking about "the boy" and the therapist talks about "the boy." She seems to be saying the child's words right back to him. Had the therapist said, "You are afraid and your mother doesn't pay any attention to your fears and that scares you still more," she is getting ahead of the child and interpreting his remarks. Perhaps the interpretation is correct, but there is the danger of thrusting something at the child before he is ready for it. When the child says, "I am afraid, too. And sometimes I cry, but my mother makes me do it anyway," then he is ready for the direct response, "You are afraid," etc. As long as he feels that it is necessary to use the doll as his medium, the therapist should use it, too.

When the therapist catches the feeling that is expressed and recognizes that feeling, the child goes on from there and the therapist can actually see the child gain insight.

This was evident in the first individual contact with Tom . . . . In this contact, Tom was granted the permissiveness to change from what had been set up as counseling contacts to play-therapy contacts. He had the choice of his medium for expression. His feelings were reflected back to him with sufficient clarity so that he gained enough insight to go on from a denial that he had problems to the fact that he thought everybody had them and that he had them, too. The permissiveness of the situation that granted him the right to go or stay, talk or remain silent, seemed to relax him and to reassure him that this was indeed his hour to use as he saw fit. It is interesting to note that, during the latter part of the contact, he once more returned to the original statement that he did not have anything to say, and when this was recognized and the therapist offered him a choice of coming back again or staying away, he took off his hat and coat and decided to stay.

In this case the acceptance of Tom, the permissiveness of the situation, plus the recognition and reflection of his expressed attitudes helped Tom to clarify his thinking and make a positive step toward helping himself. . . .

The therapist is concerned with the *feelings* the child expresses. A child seldom goes into the playroom and straightway plays out his deep feelings. First there is a period of exploration, of testing, of getting acquainted. The child must have a feeling of confidence in the therapist if he is to share his feelings. He must feel so secure in this situation that he can bring forth his "bad" feelings as well as his "good" feelings and not be fearful that this adult will disapprove of him. This confidence in the therapist is built upon the therapist's consistency in applying the basic principles.

It is important that the child does not develop guilt feelings as a result of his use of the play-therapy contacts. Encouragement, approval, and praise are taboo in a nondirective play-therapy session. Such reactions on the part of the therapist have a tendency either to influence the type of activities or to foster feelings of guilt. The same is true of disapproval or negative criticism. The atmosphere must be neutral.

When a child comes into the playroom and begins to paint, the therapist sits there watching him. She takes down a few notes. The child says, "I can't paint so good. This is terrible." Perhaps the picture is really very good. Should the therapist point it out to the child? Should she say, "You don't think your painting is very good, but *I* think it is." What the therapist thinks is of no consequence. Suppose she just says, "You don't think you paint very well." Suppose the child as a result smears the black paint all over the painting. Does that mean that he was so discouraged that he blacked it out? Or is he expressing a feeling of resentment against the therapist for not duly appreciating his work of art? Or is it the child's reaction against his lack of acceptance? If the therapist follows along with the child, he will bring his feelings out into the open in a recognizable form. It is important that the therapist does not get ahead of the child, also that she does not read into the situation something that isn't there at all.

The permissiveness that is most conducive to successful therapy is in direct proportion to the acceptance of the child. When he feels so securely accepted by the therapist that he can beat up the mother doll, or bury the baby in the sand, or lie down on the floor and drink from a nursing bottle even though he is nine, ten, or eleven years old and yet can do these things without a feeling of shame or guilt, then the therapist has established a feeling of permissiveness. The child is free to express his feelings. He gives vent to his most aggressive and destructive impulses. He screams, yells, throws the sand all over the place, spits water on the floor. He gets rid of his tensions. He becomes emotionally relaxed. Then, it seems, the groundwork for more constructive behavior has been laid. He has gotten rid of the old feelings; he is ready for new ones. The experience brings to the child insight into his behavior. He understands himself a little better. He has gained confidence in himself. He is more capable of solving his own problems. He knows by experience that he can work things out for himself. . . .

# *Clinical Observation of Play Disruption in Young Children*

ERIK H. ERIKSON

. . . As we shall demonstrate, however, the phenomenon of transference in the work with the playing child, as well as with the verbalizing adult, marks the point where simple measures fail, namely, when an emotion of such intensity as to defeat playfulness forces an immediate and only thinly veiled discharge into the play and into the relationship to the play observer. The failure is characterized by what is to be described in this monograph as "play disruption," i.e., the sudden and complete or diffused and slowly spreading inability to play.

Recent work in this country has emphasized the alternatives of "passivity" or "activity" on the part of the play observer, the extreme passive attitude representing a certain seductive lifelessness, a kind of play-hostess attitude, the extreme active one, animated encouragement of the child to "release aggression" against toys named after members of the child's family. Where a child can follow this latter suggestion without immediate or delayed play disruption we have no reason to be worried about the child, although the "release" theory implied in such procedures seems tenable only in clearly "traumatic" cases and there only theoretically, as the thorough analysis of such cases shows. The clinical problem seems to be solved only by the establishment of permanent and sufficient everyday release channels and not by a momentary release under special conditions. Much of this "release" ideology, as well as certain forms of purely symbolic and purely sexual interpretation, seems to be a revival of the most primitive techniques of the early psychoanalysis of adults—now transferred to the new field of play therapy.

Those children who transfer not the solution but the insolvability of their problems into the play situation and onto the person of the observer need to be induced by systematic interpretation to reconsider, on a more verbal level, the constellations which have overwhelmed them in the past and are apt to overwhelm them when reoccurring. Where *this* goal is given, child psychoanalysis begins.

Child analysis proper, in the cases which are its domain, seeks to provide the child with opportunity for catharsis only in the frame of an intimate therapeutic contact in which repeated interpretation furthers the verbal communication of inner dangers and the establishment of a supremacy of conscious judgment over unmanageable or incompletely repressed tendencies. To interpret means to reveal to the patient, at a dynamically specific moment, meanings which he can fully admit to himself only under the guidance of the therapist. Such interpretation is impossible without a technique which systematically and consistently reveals the dynamics of the developing therapeutic situation, especially the forces of transference and resistance. Its application is useless or dangerous where there is not time enough to follow the patient and to give new interpretations until a lasting ability is secured to express in a more conscious and social, more humorous and more useful manner that which he first could only admit to verbalization under the guidance of a therapist. Interpretation waits for a specific moment; it needs preparation and after-treatment; it does not claim success until a general and lasting increase of constructive vitality seems secured.

As the treatment proceeds and as the child's verbal powers increase, play observation loses much if not most of its exclusive importance. For the age group reported, however, the investigation of the child's play is a natural first step which coincides with the first step of a variety of treatments; while it can be abandoned or deferred without damage, it can also be pursued and developed without break. . . .

## *Destruction and Restitution in an "Epileptic" Boy of Four*

With the following description, we merely introduce the second phase of treatment, namely, the period following the decision to proceed with the psychoanalytic procedure proper, and the time of the first interpretations.

Fred was entering the disquieting period of locomotor and sexual development usually associated with the age of four somewhat prematurely before his third birthday; we have tried to characterize this period briefly above. Mentally, his development ratio was 125; he was especially advanced in his verbal expression. Physically excellently developed and well nourished, he was easy to handle—especially if, as was often the case, he was given his own way. Certain sadistic characteristics mainly expressed in teasing and occasional tempers had been outspoken for years; but nothing would have induced either his parents or his pediatrician to suspect the clinical syndrome which now suddenly emerged, namely, "epilepsy."

For some time Fred had seemed to try in provocative games and social experiments to see how far he could go in playfully hurting others and in suffering their reactions. Although he enjoyed exploring by play and error the outer limits for the manifestation of an obviously pressing aggressiveness, he had a low tolerance for situations in which he actually hurt somebody or was actually hurt by somebody. As his silent paleness seemed to indicate, such events forced him to suppress in too short a time and to turn against himself the overwhelming aggression for which he was trying to find a social form.

The tension created by these manifestations which were neither in quantity nor in quality really abnormal, was heightened when one day his grandmother arrived in town for a long visit. She was even more anxious than his mother lest he hurt himself or get hurt; and special restraint was put on Fred's activity because she was afflicted with a heart disease. Fred tried his best, but soon increasing complaints from the neighborhood indicated that he had found a new field of activity. When he hit a boy with a shovel, he was ostracized in the neighborhood. It was shortly after this social trauma that he again went too far in his teasing attacks on his mother and, finally, on his grandmother.

One morning, in the presence only of the grandmother, he climbed on a windowsill and threatened to jump out of the window. Startled, the grandmother tried to reach him but fell on the floor, for the first time in his presence suffering one of her frequent heart attacks; she spent several months in bed, seemed to recover, but suddenly died. "When I saw him standing there, something hurt in here," she had kept repeating over and over.

A few days after the old lady's death, Fred's mother saw him pile up his pillows before going to sleep, in a way which his grandmother had done in order to feel more comfortable. In the morning, at the exact hour he had been awakened five days before by his mother's crying over the grandmother's death, he was heard making strange noises and found in a terrifying attack. His face was white, his eyes glassy; he frothed at the mouth and gagged. Finally, he shook all over and lost consciousness. To his mother he looked like her dying mother, but the hurriedly called physician diagnosed his symptoms as convulsions, ascribed them tentatively to bad tonsils, and administered an injection.

Soon two further attacks (usually beginning with the twitching of the face and subsequent clonic convulsions on the right side) followed at intervals of four weeks and six weeks respectively. The first attack lasted twenty minutes, the second forty-five. Immediately after the third, which lasted more than two hours, Fred was admitted to the hospital where he was diagnosed as an "idiopathic epileptic." However, neurological examinations were entirely negative except immediately after the attack. Fred, they emphasized, was an excellently developed and well nourished boy of above average intelligence and remarkable sociability. Dismissed after a few days of rest and observation, Fred was free of attacks for several months until, after two relatively less violent seizures, he again had to be hospitalized because of an attack at the time of the anniversary of the grandmother's death. The diagnosis appeared gradually modified as "idiopathic epilepsy with psychic stimulus as precipitating factor" and the patient was recommended to the Department of Psychiatry and Mental Hygiene where he received treatment first from Dr. Felice Emery and then from this writer. During these treatments there were many minor (mostly staring) spells; major attacks occurred only five days after his psychiatrist "had gone on a long trip," i.e., had moved to another town, and again, a year later, five days after the present writer had "gone to the Indians," i.e., on a field trip.

I shall first report on the psychological development of the case and then quote a neurologist's interpretation of the medical data in the light of our study.

Fred's parents had tried to explain the grandmother's disappearance by saying she had gone on a long trip. The boy, in spite of having seen the coffin and having witnessed the family's mourning, accepted and clung to the version that the grandmother had not died at all. But children betray their knowledge of such over-eagerly accepted adult lies with an uncanny sense of humor. Thus, one day when his mother asked him for an object which he had mislaid he said, "I guess it has gone on a long trip." During the same period in his nursery school he was noticed building coffin-shaped houses whose openings he would barricade in a way corresponding to a death configuration, generally observable in play and in rituals of primitive people. It seemed clear that the boy "knew" and that this knowledge (or what he tried to do to it) was the "psychic stimulus" the physicians were looking for.

Before every major or minor attack, Fred's aggressiveness would increase. An object would fly out of his hands, sometimes creditably "without his being aware of it" and strike somebody's head. The usually affectionate and reverent boy at such times would indulge in violent attacks against parents and against God. "Did grandmother have a good heart when she was a child?" "The whole world is full of skunks." "I don't like you, mother." "I hate God." "I want to beat God." "I want to beat heaven." After the attack the boy would indicate that he had experienced his unconsciousness as death. He behaved as if he had been reborn, smiling, loving, obedient, and reverent—an angelic child.

I shall first present excerpts from Dr. Felice Emery's notes in order to contrast the transferences which the boy established to this woman psychiatrist and then to me. The following development in play of two dominant ideas, namely, "burning and attacking psychiatrist" and "building a castle," reflect, it seems, the destructive restitutive conflict in the boy's mind.[7]. . .

Fred's treatment was not completed when his first psychoanalyst left the city. She had been able to bring back to his memory the details of his grandmother's death and to discuss with him the phallic-locomotor tension of his maturational stage, which had made him associate aggressive and phallic intentions as characterizing a bad boy. However, it was obvious that other sources of tension of the period in question had not been verbalized. Also, as the psychiatrist suggests, it may be that the playful aggression allowed to this child in analysis made the transference too realistic and permitted the accumulation in Fred of guilt feelings concerning the psychiatrist similar to those concerning the grandmother. In any event, after the psychiatrist had left town, Fred began to speak of her with the same words which he had always used to characterize his relationship to his grandmother ("Why has 'my friend' gone away?") and had a severe epileptic attack (the first one since the beginning of the treatment) five days after the departure, thus repeating the pattern "dying five days after a beloved person whom one had attacked goes on a long journey."

After this attack, I took Fred over for treatment. The difference in the transference became obvious soon. Fred had a period of what one might call an infantile homosexual panic. After the first hour with me, he insisted in retrospect that at the time of his latest hospitalization men nurses had taken his temperature all night and didn't let him sleep. This, of course, did not correspond to the facts since he had been taken care of entirely by female nurses who had taken his temperature only once during the night. But to this fantasy there corresponded the first game he played with me during my first contact with him. Out of plasticine he formed "snakes" or "worms" and tried to get behind me so that they could bite my buttocks. (Remember how,

---

[7] Since the main purpose in presenting the case material from the present selection is to describe the phenomenon of play disruption which occurred in the later sessions, the notes from the first portion of therapy have been omitted at this point. For the entire case presentation the reader is referred to the original monograph.

in his play with the woman psychiatrist in a similar two-fold representation he had jailed the old lady, then fantasied that an old lady was going to jail him.) Correspondingly, at home, his relationship to his father changed. He would without provocation repeat, "Don't touch me, Daddy," and especially when awakening from his nap he would experience and express moments of depersonalization—"I don't want you to come near me, Daddy. Where am I? Where is our home? I don't see well. Is everything all right? Everything looks bigger. Something is hanging from the walls awfully big and crooked." He also began to look intently at his father, remarking, "Grandmother looked just like Daddy." (We see that the man therapist not only attracted another [homosexual] transference but by his very existence brought about the manifestation of the corresponding [previously latent] conflicts at home.)

In the meantime, I questioned the mother again about the weeks preceding the first attack, because it seemed that Fred's guilt feeling was not entirely covered by the explanation of the crime which he felt he had committed against the grandmother. Only against severe emotional resistance did the mother reveal an incident which had occurred about one week before the grandmother's dramatic heart attack. A toy had "inadvertently" flown from Fred's hand, hit his mother in the face, and loosened one of her front teeth. Irritable as she may have been because of the special pressure which the grandmother's visit exerted on the home and also worried for the precious front tooth, the mother had punished Fred corporally for the first time in his life. As she described this, Fred's transference to both the woman psychiatrist and to me appeared in a new light—the crime complex established in connection with the grandmother's death obviously had irradiated, in retrospect and prospect, to include guilt feelings toward both father and mother and expectations of danger for and from the side of both. (It will be remembered that against his father he never had dared to express aggression as he had so liberally done with women.)

I shall report here the way in which the transference of one of these irradiations manifested itself in his first epileptic (minor) spell in our offices.

During the first weeks of his treatment with me, we had in accordance with his wish played dominoes. The possession of the double black, so he had decided, determined who had the first move. If he were not in possession of it and whenever he lost a game, he became angry and pale. I tried (as far as he, a good player, let me) to increase the number of his defeats gradually, in the hope of being able to observe the coming and going of an attack under emotional conditions approximately known to me. One day the threshold seemed reached. Fred had lost again and at a time during the hour when he could not hope to make up for it. Suddenly he got up, took a rubber Popeye doll and hit me in the face with it; then he stiffened, got pale, his eyes stared for a fraction of a second, and he vomited. He had briefly recovered when he said in a most pathetically urgent tone of voice, "Let's go on playing." He hurriedly built up his domino figures in front of him in a rectangle and in such a way that the signs pointed inward; he, their possessor, would have to lie inside of his configuration (like a dead person in a coffin) in order to read them. Fully conscious, he now recognized the queer configuration and gave me the look of a cornered animal. I pointed out to him that every time he hit somebody he felt that he must die. He confirmed this by asking breathlessly, "Must I?" I explained to him the historical connection between these feelings and the death of his grandmother, whose coffin he had seen. "Yes," he said, a little embarrassed because up to now, in spite of the mourning episode, he had insisted that the grandmother had gone on a trip. I furthermore pointed to the similarity between his attack on my face during a game and the attack on his mother's face a week before the grandmother's fatal attack. It appeared that he could not remember the attack on his mother while he seemed never to have forgotten the episodes relating to his grandmother. That the mother, too, might die as a consequence of the (earlier) aggressive acts and fantasies was obviously the deepest danger threatening him. This, too, was pointed out.

Beginning with this episode a series of interpretations used *specific moments* to bring his fear of death into relation with his strong impulses and his low anxiety threshold.

The effect of such interpretational steps can best be illustrated by an episode which occurred a few days after the interpretation reported above. In the afternoon Fred's mother, fatigued, was lying on a couch. Fred stood in the doorway and looked at her. Suddenly he said slowly, "Only a very bad boy would like now to jump on you and step on you, only a very bad boy would want that, isn't that so, mummy?" The mother, to whom I had explained some of the boy's problems, laughed and replied, "Oh no, quite a good boy might *think* that, but, of course, he would know that he did not *really want to do it.*" This conversation established a relationship between mother and son which made it increasingly possible for him to tell her, especially when he felt as if an attack were approaching, of his aggressions, anxieties, and religious scruples, all of which she learned to handle as well as her own attitude toward death permitted. At the same time she could apply in such instances certain preventive measures recommended by pediatricians.

We see what the interpretation had done. It had used the highly *affective moment* (namely the repetition in transference of a scene which the memory resisted) to verbalize for him his impulses against the protecting mother—impulses derived from the same source as those which had "killed" the grandmother and thus might bring about the mother's death. These impulses could now be admitted to consciousness, faced with the superior intelligence of his increased age, understood as more magic than real, and even admitted to the mother, who far from either wildly punishing or lightly approving, understood and offered help. Such experiences are an inducement to further transferences, confessions, and conversations, which of course included Fred's aggressions against his father which consequently were most consistently transferred to the therapist, not without leading to a major attack five days after this therapist, too, had gone on a trip (from which he returned, however). Thus, while historical reality had emphasized the grandmother's death as the trigger stimulus mobilizing Fred's epileptic reaction, analysis proved Fred's sadistic wishes against his mother and death wishes against his father to be the psychological reality of his maturational stage which had made him susceptible for the traumatic event of the grandmother's death. This misunderstanding of the causal connection of what had happened to the grandmother and what he had done to her was transferred and interpreted first; what he was afraid might happen to the mother because of his deeds and wishes, next; while the most dreaded and most deeply repressed aggression against the providers, father and God (the latter now united in heaven with the revengeful grandmother), could be approached only later. . . .

In the course of these events, Fred's attacks became fewer and better predictable, drug applications could be reduced to a minimum and to well circumscribed critical moments, and Fred recovered from minor spells more quickly and with less after-effect. We shall not predict that he will not have a minor attack now and again; but he may be spared major ones especially if the medical suspicion of a progressive lesion of the central nervous system proves unfounded. In any event, we have reason to consider it probable that psychosomatic vigilance can help such a patient to lead a normal life in which possible rare attacks are well isolated and for the most part predictable events.

Fred's case . . . combined dramatic brevity with all the ordinary attributes of a situation in which an interpretation is warranted: The play has failed; the child is about to be overwhelmed by the guilt and the danger of the situation which he wants most to forget or to avoid. All defenses have proved inadequate, all attempts at restitution and atonement futile. The therapeutic situation has become the pathogenic situation, the therapist only one more evil. What seems needed is more cruel self-suppression, deeper regression, more radical repression. At this point the patient suddenly finds his experience put into words. The most human way (which always had seemed most completely impossible), namely, communication, now proves to be open.

However, once the first interpretation is given and its startling effects lived through, the child is conscious of the fact that the therapist understands or wants to understand more than he has been told, and that the patient is expected to cooperate in the verbalization of his suffering and what lies behind it. This brings with it complications and new resistances. . . .

## *Conclusion*[8]

The psychoanalytic attributes of our material are on the whole the mechanisms first described by Freud as resistance, transference, and regression. They appear in the interplay of social, verbal, spatial, and bodily forms of expression.

[8] Erikson's concluding section recapitulates his previous discussion of four cases; only that of "Fred" has been included in the present excerpts. It is felt the reader can derive much of value from these summary notes even without having read the cases, but for complete material in each case, see *Genetic Psychology Monographs,* XXII (1940), 557–671.

To begin with the verbal, the very first words spoken by our patients on meeting us betrayed their dominant system of defense.

John, we remember, appeared armed to the teeth. Asked whom he was going to kill, he answered, "Me"—with one monosyllable betraying this "turning against himself" of all the hate which his secret and other, less conscious reasons prevented him from expressing directly. Mary, however, did not say anything to the therapist until she had regained all her stubborn superiority. She only talked to her mother, in lisping, whining baby talk. We would not be surprised to find her using deliberate regression paired with stubbornness as a defense even in riper years. Dick's greeting—"Are your eyes all right?" makes the therapist the patient and the patient the therapist. It represents what Anna Freud calls "the identification with the (here potential) aggressor" and contains the projective–introjective mechanisms which prove so strong during later observations—Fred's first words are not recorded.

Robbed or about to be robbed of the protective aura of maternal presence, how do our patients *act in space?*

John's mother is nowhere near. While his eyes are evasive, his skin pale, he moves with unafraid strides. But he has surrounded himself with a layer of weapons. (He is the delinquent, afraid of further castration. His recent circumcision had been explained to him as a consequence of the fact that he had "played with himself," a fact which will have to be analyzed immediately after the resistance nearest to consciousness; namely, the secret, is worked through.) Mary, on entering with her mother, throws one mischievous glance across the room toward the therapist, then closes eyes and ears and almost disappears in the maternal skirt, holding the mother near the door. (She acts with hysterical dramatization and phobic avoidance. Ambivalent flight to her mother after a play disturbance with the father and with boys in a play group will prove to be her problem.) Dick, however, with hurried determination leaves his mother and passes by the therapist as if not interested in her. (Interest in the female body will immediately begin to dominate his play.) Fred, finally after some diffused handling of the toys, goes right for the psychiatrist's body. (Playful attack, in his case, will prove to be the defense against his fear of being attacked and of suffering an "internalized" [epileptic] attack.)

It is in the metaphoric and symbolic use of toys that all these defenses are first caught off guard; in the *microsphere* the child does what he does not dare to do in reality.

John, in the macrosphere armed against doctors and police, in playing "delivers" his secret, although only in metaphoric allusion. Mary, the bashful one, has a moment of mischievous hilarity in pushing the toys and finally the toy train, although using a protective extension in doing so. Dick, so indifferent toward mother and psychiatrist, has many urgent questions about the toy cars, in which he plainly alludes to the female body. Fred, the killer, passionately wants to build a house—to restore a body, as we were able to translate the symbolism of his play.

Each one of these *indirect admissions* in the microsphere is an element in a personal transference.

John, in delivering his secret metaphorically, gives the therapist what in reality is the father's. Mary betrays her playful interest in her father and in boys and (during the second contact) takes revenge on the therapist for a scene in which her father had reacted with irritability to her interest in him. Dick takes a little longer to express the more regressive wish to bite the mother's body, in the words, "I want to bite your buttons." Fred, after having "hurt" the therapist, wants her to "walk with a creepy walk" like the grandmother.

It is a question, partly only of words, which of the tricks of play language we are to call symbolic or metaphoric, which to consider analogies or allusions. A symbol, it seems, should be definitiely of a higher order, very condensed and abstracted in its form, superindividual in its meaning and treated with a high degree of affectual inhibition and sublimation.

Mary, who suffered a play disruption when overturning the toy train, develops a raptured admiration for shining locomotives. Her first question on seeing me weeks later concerns the locomotive of the train which took me south. Her [father] in the meantime had regained her friendship by joint visits to trainyards. "Shining locomotive" has become a symbol of admired paternal power.

It will take some careful study to denote how early true symbols appear in play and what their forerunners are. "Metaphoric" is an appealing parallel to "transference" (*metapherein*—to transfer); "allusion" has "play" in it (*alludere*—to play with). At the moment I would say that the play acts reported are analogies to conflict situations. The children unconsciously allude to them by transferring their ambivalence toward their parents onto the therapist and by representing other aspects of the conflict metaphorically in play.

But a child seems to be able to solve a problem in play or other activities only insofar as the traumatic event alluded to mainly consisted of an *enforced passivity*, a violation by a superior force.

Mary, whose indignation with her irritable father and fear of operation are greater than her guilt, can "solve" her problem on the second day, at least enough to meet constructively an improved home situation.

Insofar as the trauma involves "blood guilt," the primitive feeling of having magically violated an ambivalently loved person, only a conscious, verbally communicated "Yes, yes—no, no" can bring relief. This need, becoming urgent with the successful although first unconscious allusion to the conflict, drives some patients from the treacherous play back into symptom and regression. At this point, we offer *interpretation* as a help toward communication.

> John, asked to name the uncles, answers with his symptom (defecation) and reasserts his defense—"Me." Mary becomes stiff, blind, and dumb with anxiety when the toy train overturns. Dick, after having confessed that he wanted to bite the therapist's buttons, appears wrapped in clothes, in silence and in apathy. Fred gives me the first opportunity to observe one of his minor epileptic spells after having hit me in the face as he had done to his mother.

The play, we see, indicates the need which is both intensified ("ready to have its correlative feelings aroused") and in a state of suppression; the form of the disruption alludes to the danger which would follow the fulfillment of the need.

> John's "Me" indicates that, once his secret was revealed, something terrible would happen and that he preferred to be the victim. Mary dramatizes that, if she is too much of a tomboy and dares to envy the male his anatomical share, something similar to what already has happened to foot and genitals will, on the occasion of the threatened operation, happen to other parts of her body. Dick indicates that according to "an eye for an eye" he will be what his oral jealousy makes him wish his sister to be, namely, an unborn nothing. Fred in his arrangement of dominoes, confesses his expectation of death as a punishment or atonement for aggression.

All of this, of course, gives us only a first impression and allows only for tentative conclusions in regard to the degree of emotional arrest, the depth of regression, the weakness of the defenses, the rigidity of conscience, etc. On the one hand, we weigh these impressions against the obstacles and weaknesses in the environment as transmitted by the parents; on the other hand, we have to reconstruct the degree of development attained when the arrest and the regression occurred and weigh this positive aspect against the chances for our getting the environment ready to help the child beyond arrest and fixation, when we succeed in making him set his face again toward the future.

The goal of this description was a presentation of empirical data which (1) would allow the therapist and his study group to account for some of their diagnostic habits, and (2) could be of didactic-comparative use for nontherapeutic psychologists. However, clinical description, even where more skillfully handled, can only approximate such goals; and once such approximation is attempted, the focus shifts from the larger theoretical implications to the details of observation on which first conceptual steps can be based.

It seems advisable in conclusion to point to some of the practical and therapeutic aspects of our material.

Our "short stories" may have given the reader the impression that the psychoanalysis of a child is characterized throughout by high tension and by a rapid succession of dramatic insights. This is not the case. After our interpretations have led to relieving communication and to promising improvement, long periods follow which are quiet, peaceful, even dull. The child plays, builds, paints, writes, and discusses whatever he pleases as long as his guilt and anxiety allow him to do so. Such periods mean recovery for the child, more intimate and slowly growing insight to the therapist. But the therapist by no means accompanies the child's acts with running interpretative commentary. Interpretations to children are rare and on the whole underlie the following guiding principles. They point out symptoms of disruption throughout the patient's life and sum up the problem behind them as it has been reconstructed on the basis of recent observation. However, they do not translate to the child the meaning of any playfully or skillfully accomplished act. Verbal self-consciousness in conditioning connection with playful activities is not desired; for these very activities must help the child later to contact the fields of cultural value, in which alone he can really find a recovery without self-consciousness. There are also no attempts at arguing for an interpretation by transmitting to the child the details of its derivation. The interpretation will be accepted by the child if both the child and the therapist are intellectually and emotionally ready for it; which means, for the therapist, if he is in the right mood and frame of mind to put his insight into coherent, constructive, and understandable words.

This point deserves emphasis in conclusion. Throughout a tedious piece of writing I have paid compulsive attention to details of clinical reasoning. An analytical instrument was to be demonstrated. But to learn to know the properties and the range of an instrument is one thing; to learn to use it unselfconsciously and firmly, another. It is good to be explicit for the sake of training; for the sake of therapy, it is necessary to act with intuitive regard for implied probabilities and possibilities. The scientific world wants to know *why* we are so sure to be on the right track; the patients only *that* we are sure. Few patients (and they are apt to argue and doubt) want to know whether or not our interpretations are scientifically true; most patients are satisfied that they feel true and that they *give meaning to suffering*. Except where the parent already has learned to expect this meaning from elaborate analysis and synthesis, increased scientific conscientiousness on the part of the therapist by no means necessarily conveys a feeling of security to him. Some groups of parents and adult patients, it is true, share the specialist's delight in new terminological, experimental, statistical rituals. The majority are bewildered by them. The conceptual frames of therapeutic habits, it must often seem to them, are like the microsphere in play, into which we project complex reality in order to have our wishes for omnipotence come true according to the less refractory microcosmic law and language. By reprojecting our interpretation into the macrosphere of social reality we are able to observe whether or not it provided constructive meaning within the patient's culture. By correlating it with those of other conceptual microspheres which have been longer and more consistently corrected by systematic experimental reprojection into physical reality we may see how scientific we are. But only if and where science will prove dominant over other sources of psychological strength will the scientific attitude in therapy also necessarily be the efficient one.

It is an intriguing idea that even where nobody sees it or does anything about it children proceed to express their vital problems in the metaphoric language of play—more consistently and less self-consciously than they are able or willing to in words.

To be observed when playing is natural for children; it does not have to wait for the family's clinical surrender. If we can establish the language of play with its various cultural and age dialects, we may be able to approach the problem of why it is that certain children live undamaged through what seem to be neurotic episodes and how early neurotic children may indicate that they have reached a deadlock.

This objective becomes important at a time when there is increasing awareness of both the extent of mental suffering and the impracticability and social deficiency of the alleviating techniques. Their results point to childhood as the possibly more economic time of correction.

The neurotic adult has usually made his choice of vocation and marriage companion on the basis of his neurosis. Both are endangered when that basis is reconsidered. The child's choices (except for that of his parents) are still preliminary; the changes we effect only replace changes which would occur with less planning. Furthermore, the adult patient usually develops a therapeutic dependency on his therapist, a dependency which every observing person will agree, often persists in the cured, and especially the much more frequent half-cured neurotic, in a form which differs from a neurosis only in the degree of terminological rationalization. One reason for this embarrassing fact undoubtedly is the impossibility, after one's analysis, of settling one's grievances with the childhood parents and of beginning life again, where the old road to isolation branched off. One has only one childhood. That which was merely repressed from consciousness, after having been reasonably developed and experienced, one may hope to liberate through analysis; but emotional impoverishment in childhood is incurable in later life, and to face the fact that one is crippled to the extent of having had the wrong childhood and to gain spiritually and intellectually from this fact is, after all, open to few.

The child's dependence, however, is his natural state. Transference in childhood has a different connotation; it is of shorter duration and less consistent, and what is transferred can usually be retransferred to the parents. The parents, in turn, are more accessible to correction and advice as long as they and the child are young, and small changes in the parents are often gratefully responded to by the child with obvious and far-reaching improvements. Thus, what is delegated to the therapist can be returned to the home before the child's personality development is completed and before all chances have been exhausted of identifying thoroughly with parents who are enlightened and live up to their capacity to love.

# ❀ *The Psychoanalytic Play Technique*

MELANIE KLEIN

In this paper, I shall briefly outline the steps by which the psychoanalytic play technique developed. In 1919, when I started my first case, some psychoanalytic work with children had already been done, particularly by Dr. Hug-Hellmuth. However, she did not undertake the psychoanalysis of children under six, and although she used drawings and occasionally play as material she did not develop this into a specific technique.

At the time I began to work, it was an established principle that interpretations should be given very sparingly, and although psychoanalysts were endeavoring to explore the unconscious, with few exceptions they did not penetrate deeply into it. All this applied particularly to children. Moreover, at that time, and for some years to come, only children from the latency period onward were regarded as suitable for psychoanalysis.

My first patient was a five-year-old boy. I referred to him under the name Fritz in my first published paper (Klein, 1923). To begin with, I thought it would be sufficient to influence the mother's attitude. I suggested that she should encourage the child to freely discuss with her the many unspoken questions which were obviously at the back of his mind and impeding his intellectual development. This had a good effect, but his neurotic difficulties were not sufficiently alleviated, and it was soon decided that I should psychoanalyze him. In doing so, I deviated from some of the rules so far established, for I interpreted what I thought to be most urgent in the material the child presented to me and found my interest focusing on his anxieties and the defenses against them.

The treatment was carried out in the child's home with his own toys. This analysis was the beginning of the psychoanalytic play technique, for Fritz expressed fantasies, anxieties, and defenses mainly by play, and I consistently interpreted its preconscious and unconscious meaning to him, with the result that additional material came up in his play. That is to say that I already used with this patient, in essence, the method of interpretation which became characteristic of my technique. This approach corresponds to a fundamental principle of psychoanalysis—free association. In interpreting not only the child's words but also his activities with his toys, I applied this basic principle to the mind of the child, whose play and varied activities, in fact his whole behavior, are means of expressing what the adult expresses predominantly by words. I was also guided from the beginning by two other tenets of psychoanalysis: the exploration of the unconscious as the main task of the psychoanalytic procedure and the analysis of the transference as the means of achieving this. I am here referring to one of the fundamental discoveries of

Freud, that the patient transfers his early experiences and his feelings and thoughts in relation first to his parents and then to other people to the psychoanalyst and that it is by analyzing this transference that the past as well as the unconscious part of the mind can be explored.

Between 1920 and 1923, I gained further experience with other child cases, but a definite step in the development of play technique was the treatment of a child of two years and nine months, whom I psychoanalyzed in 1923. I have given some details of this child's case under the name Rita in my book *The Psycho-Analysis of Children* (Klein, 1932). Rita suffered from night terrors and animal phobias, was very ambivalent toward her mother, at the same time clinging to her to such an extent that she could hardly be left alone. She had a marked obsessional neurosis and was at times very depressed. Her play was inhibited, and her inability to tolerate frustrations made her upbringing increasingly difficult. I was very doubtful how to tackle this case since the analysis of so young a child was an entirely new experiment. The first session seemed to confirm my misgivings. Rita, when left alone with me in her nursery, at once showed signs of what I took to be negative transference: she was anxious and silent and very soon asked to go out in the garden. I agreed and went with her—I may add, under the watchful eyes of her mother and aunt, who took this as a sign of failure. They were very surprised to see that Rita was quite friendly toward me when we returned to the nursery some ten to fifteen minutes later. The explanation of this change was that while we were outside I had been interpreting her negative transference (this again being against the usual practice). From a few things she said and the fact that she was less frightened when we were in the open, I concluded that she was particularly afraid of something which I might do to her when she was alone with me in the room. I interpreted this and, referring to her night terrors, I linked her suspicion of me as a hostile stranger with her fear that a bad woman would attack her when she was by herself at night. When, a few minutes after this interpretation, I suggested that we should return to the nursery, she readily agreed. As I said, Rita's inhibition in playing was marked and, to begin with, she did hardly anything but obsessionally dress and undress her doll. But soon I came to understand the anxieties underlying her obsessions and interpreted them. This case strengthened my growing conviction that a precondition for the psychoanalysis of a child is to understand and to interpret the fantasies, feelings, anxieties, and experiences expressed by play or, if play activities are inhibited, the causes of the inhibition.

As with Fritz, I undertook this analysis in the child's home and with her own toys; but during this treatment, which lasted only a few months, I came to the conclusion that psychoanalysis should not be carried out in the child's home. For I found that, although the child was in great need of help and the parents had decided that I should try psychoanalysis, the mother's attitude toward me was very ambivalent and the atmosphere was on the whole hostile to the treatment. More important still, I found that the transference situation

—the backbone of the psychoanalytic procedure—can only be established and maintained if the patient can feel that the consulting room or the playroom, indeed the whole analysis, is something separate from his ordinary home life. For only under such conditions is he able to overcome his own resistances against experiencing and expressing thoughts, feelings, and desires which are incompatible with convention and, in the case of children, felt to be in contrast to much of what they have been taught.

I made further significant observations in the psychoanalysis of a girl of seven, also in 1923. Her neurotic difficulties were apparently not serious, but her parents had for some time been concerned about her intellectual development. Although quite intelligent she did not keep up with her age group, she disliked school and sometimes played truant. The relation to her mother, which had been affectionate and trustful, had changed since she had started school: she had become reserved and silent. I spent a few sessions with her without achieving much contact. It had become clear that she disliked school, and from what she diffidently said about it, as well as from other remarks, I had been able to make a few interpretations which produced some material. But my impression was that I would not get much further in that way. In a session in which I again found the child unresponsive and withdrawn I left her, saying that I would return in a moment. I went into my own children's nursery, collected a few toys—cars, little figures, a few bricks, a train—put them into a box, and returned to the patient. The child, who had not taken to drawing or other activities, was interested in the small toys and at once began to play. From this play, I gathered that two of the toys represented herself and a little boy, a schoolmate about whom I had heard before. It appeared that there was something secret about the activities of these two figures and that other toy people were resented as interfering or watching and were put aside. The activities of the two toys led to catastrophes, such as their falling down or colliding with cars. This was repeated with signs of mounting anxiety. At this point I interpreted, with reference to the details of her play, that some sexual activity seemed to have occurred between herself and her friend and that this had made her very frightened of being found out and therefore distrustful of other people. I pointed out that while playing she had become anxious and seemed on the point of stopping her play. I reminded her that she disliked school and that this might be connected with the fear that the teacher would find out about her relation with her schoolmate and punish her. Above all, she was frightened and therefore distrustful of her mother, and she might feel the same way about me. The effect of this interpretation on the child was striking: her anxiety and distrust first increased, but very soon gave way to obvious relief. Her facial expression changed, and although she neither admitted nor denied what I had interpreted, she subsequently showed her agreement by producing new material and by becoming much freer in her play and speech; also her attitude toward me became much more friendly and less suspicious. Of course the negative transference, alternating with the positive one, came up again and again; but from this session onward the analysis progressed well. Concurrently there were favorable changes, as I was informed, in her relation to her family, in particular to her mother. Her dislike of school diminished, and she became more interested in her lessons; but her inhibition in learning, which was rooted in deep anxieties, was only gradually resolved in the course of her treatment. . . .

I shall now give a few more detailed illustrations of the psychoanalytic play technique. Here is a typical instance: a little boy in the first analytic session may put up a few toy figures and surround them, let us say, by bricks. I would conclude and interpret that the child shows a room and that the figures symbolize people. Such an interpretation effects a first contact with the child's unconscious. For, through the interpretation, he comes to realize that the toys stand in his mind for people and therefore that the feelings he expresses toward the toys relate to people; also that preceding the interpretation he had not been aware of this. He is beginning to gain insight into the fact that one part of his mind is unknown to him, in other words, that the unconscious exists. Moreover, it becomes clearer to him what the analyst is doing with him. All this implies that the analytic situation is being established. This does not, however, mean that the child would necessarily be able to express in intellectual terms what he is experiencing.

To return to my instance of the little figures representing people in a room. Next the psychoanalyst would try to find out who these people are meant to be, what their relation to each other is, and what they are supposed to be doing in that room. Let us assume that the child picks out as many toy figures as there are people in his family, which in this instance would be four. I would point out to him that the figures represent himself with his parents and his younger brother. The child may then take one of these figures and put it outside the space he had enclosed by bricks. Assuming that he has shown that this figure represents his younger brother, this gives an opening for the next step, namely, to understand why he makes him leave the room at that moment. Having been informed before the start of the psychoanalysis about the symptoms and difficulties of the child, as well as about his history, I might already know something about the relation between the patient and his brother. If I gathered from the play that the three people remaining in the room are father, mother, and the patient, I would interpret that at times he wanted his younger brother out of the way, wishing to remain alone with his parents and to be an only child as he had been before the birth of his brother. This might lead to his putting another of the toy people out of the supposed room—a figure standing for his father—which would lead me to interpret that there are times when he feels his father to be in the way and wants his mother all to himself. I might also have grounds to interpret that in this situation the analyst represented his mother whom he wished to devote herself exclusively to him. At any point in this sequence, even perhaps quite clearly, we might observe on the child's face that telling look, so convincing to the psychoanalyst, which shows clearly that the child has understood something about himself and that he feels this insight to be helpful and valuable.

It is very likely that the child, while playing, has said something which substantiates the conclusions the analyst drew from play. He may also have expressed his disagreement. He may even have pushed away the toys and stopped playing, particularly in response to the interpretation dealing with his aggressiveness toward his brother or father. But by then the psychoanalyst has already gathered the content of the anxiety stirred up, and he would interpret the reasons why the child interrupted the play; he would also interpret the negative transference, according to which the psychoanalyst may have come to represent, for example, the angry father or the disappointing mother. Should the child, as often happens, resume his play after such an interpretation, he might produce the same material in a different way; this can be taken as a confirmation of the correctness of the interpretation now given. The child might, for instance, begin to build with bricks; now the bricks represent people while the room is indicated by fences or other objects. Or he plays with cars or any other toys which in the context of the play can be seen to stand for people. He may also start a game in which he symbolically allots to the psychoanalyst the role of one of his family, thereby transferring his feelings from them into the relation with the analyst. In the course of his play, he possibly refers to some happenings from his everyday life, which again throw light on the former play with the figures. All these activities and associations may present the same material by different means. But the anxiety and feelings of guilt, which in some cases lead to an interruption of the play or a change in it, sometimes introduce what appears to be an entirely different situation. Perhaps the child searches in his drawer for a toy which is soiled or damaged and cleans it thoroughly at the washbasin. In that context, the analyst would gather and interpret that the child is expressing his anxious need to clean and restore his little brother whom he feels he has soiled and damaged by his hostile impulses.

These instances do not, of course, exhaust the range of the situations and experiences which a child may show by his play. Feelings of frustration and being rejected, jealousy of both father and mother, or of brothers and sisters, the aggressiveness accompanying such jealousy, the pleasure in having a playmate or ally against the parents, the feelings of love and hatred toward a newborn baby or one who is expected, as well as the ensuing anxiety, guilt, and urge to make reparation are some of the many emotional situations which may be expressed. We also find in the child's play the repetition of actual experiences and details of everyday life, often interwoven with his fantasies. It is revealing that sometimes very important actual events in his life fail to enter either into his play or into his associations, and that the whole emphasis at times lies on apparently minor happenings. But these minor happenings are of great importance to him because they have stirred up his emotions and fantasies.

I have already discussed the problem of children whose play is inhibited. Such inhibition does not always completely prevent them from playing but may soon interrupt their activities. For instance, a little boy was brought to me for one interview only (there was a prospect of an analysis in the future, but at the time the parents were going abroad with him). I had some toys on my table, and he sat down and began to play, which soon led to accidents, collisions, people falling down whom he tried to stand up again. In all this he showed a good deal of anxiety, but since no treatment was yet intended, I refrained from interpreting. After a few minutes he quietly slipped out of his chair and saying "Enough of playing," went out. I believe from my experience that if this had been the beginning of treatment and I had interpreted the anxiety shown in his actions with the toys and the corresponding negative transference toward me, I should have been able to resolve his anxiety sufficiently for him to continue playing.

The next instance may help me to show some of the causes of a play inhibition. A boy aged three years and nine months, whom I described under the name Peter (Klein, 1932), was very neurotic. To mention some of his difficulties: he seemed unable to play, could not tolerate any frustration, was timid, plaintive, and unboyish, yet at times aggressive and overbearing, very ambivalent toward his family, and strongly fixated on his mother. She told me that Peter had greatly changed for the worse after a summer holiday during which, at the age of eighteen months, he shared the parents' bedroom and had the opportunity to observe their sexual intercourse. On that holiday he had become very difficult to manage, slept badly, and relapsed into soiling his bed at night, which he had not done for some months. He had been playing freely until then, but from that summer onward he stopped playing and became very destructive toward his toys; he could do nothing with them but break them. Soon afterward his brother was born, and this increased all his difficulties.

In the first session Peter started to play; he soon made two horses bump into each other and repeated the same action with different toys. He also mentioned that he had a little brother. I interpreted to him that the horses and the other things bumping together represented people—an interpretation which he first rejected and then accepted. He again bumped the horses together, saying that they were going to sleep, covered them up with bricks, and added, "Now they're quite dead; I've buried them." He put the motorcars front to rear, in a row, which, as became clear later in the analysis, symbolized his father's penis, and made them run along, then suddenly lost his temper and threw them about the room, saying, "We always smash our Christmas presents straight away; we don't want any." Smashing his toys thus stood in his unconscious for smashing his father's genitals; in fact, during this first hour he broke several toys.

In the second session, Peter repeated some of the material of the first hour, in particular the bumping together of cars, horses, etc., speaking again of his little brother, whereupon I interpreted that he was showing me how his mummy and daddy bumped their genitals together (using of course his word for genitals) and that he thought that their doing so caused his brother to be born. This interpretation produced more material, throwing light on his very ambivalent relation toward his little brother and toward his father. He laid a toy man on a brick which he called a "bed," threw him down, and said he was "dead and done for." He then re-enacted the same thing with two toy men, choosing figures he had already damaged. I interpreted that the first toy man stood for his father whom he wanted to throw out of his mother's bed and kill and that one of the two toy men was again the father and the other himself to whom his father would do the same. The reason he had chosen two damaged figures was that he felt that both his father and himself would be damaged if he attacked his father.

This material illustrates a number of points of which I shall mention only one or two. Because witnessing the sexual intercourse of his parents had made a great impact on his mind and roused strong emotions such as jealousy, aggressiveness, and anxiety, this was almost the first thing which Peter expressed in his play. There is no doubt that he no longer had any conscious knowledge of this experience, that it was repressed, and that only the symbolical expression of it was possible for him. I have reasons to believe that if I had not interpreted that the toys bumping together were people, he might not have produced the material which came up in the second hour. Furthermore, had I not, in the second hour, been able to show him some of the reasons for his inhibition in play by interpreting the damage done to the toys, he would very likely—as he did in ordinary life—have stopped playing after breaking the toys.

There are children who at the beginning of the treatment may not even play in the way Peter did, or the little boy who came for only one interview. But it is very rare for a child completely to ignore the toys laid out on the table. Even if he turns away from them, he often gives the analyst some insight into his motives for not wishing to play. In other ways, too, the child analyst can gather material for interpretations. Any activity, such as using paper to scribble on or to cut out, every detail of behavior, such as changes in posture or in facial expression, can give a clue to what is going on in the child's mind, possibly in connection with what the psychoanalyst has heard from the parents about his difficulties.

I have said much about the importance of interpretations for the play technique and have given some instances to illustrate their contents. This brings me to a question which I have often been asked: Are young children intellectually able to understand such interpretations? My experience and that of my colleagues has been that, if the interpretations relate to the salient points in the material, they are fully understood. Of course the child analyst must give his interpretations as succinctly and as clearly as possible and should also use the child's expressions in doing so. But if he translates into simple words the essential points of the material presented to him, he gets into touch with those emotions and anxieties which are most operative at the moment; the child's conscious and intellectual understanding is often a subsequent process. One of the many interesting and surprising experiences of the beginner in child analysis is to find in even very young children a capacity for insight which is often far greater than that of adults. To some extent this is explained by the fact that the connections between conscious and unconscious are closer in young children than in adults, and that infantile repressions are less powerful. I also believe that the infant's intellectual capacities are often underrated and that, in fact, he understands more than he is credited with.

I shall now illustrate what I have said by a young child's response to interpretations. Peter, of whose analysis I have given a few details, had strongly objected to my interpretation that the toy man he had thrown down from the "bed" and who was "dead and done for" represented his father. (The interpretation of death wishes against a loved person usually arouses great resistance in children as well as in adults.) In the third hour, Peter again brought similar material, but now accepted my interpretation and said thoughtfully, "And if I were a daddy and someone wanted to throw me down behind the bed and make me dead and done for, what would I think of it?" This shows that he had not only worked through, understood, and accepted my interpretation, but that he had also recognized a good deal more. He understood that his own aggressive feelings toward his father contributed to his fear of him and also that he had projected his own impulses onto his father.

The next instance was told me by one of my students. A little boy aged four had strongly objected in one analytic session to some of the analyst's interpretations of his play. At the beginning of the following session, he again presented play material identical with that of the previous day. Then he said to the analyst, "Now let's talk." To her question what they should talk about, he replied, "What you were telling about yesterday." The psychoanalyst went over her material of the previous day, repeating and elaborating her interpretations, to which he now listened with great attention and which he obviously accepted. The same child, in a later session, after some interpretations of his anxiety which had clearly produced much relief, coined a new term for his fears by saying in a thoughtful way, "What can you do with my 'afraidynesses'?"

It has already been pointed out in the introduction to this paper that my attention from the beginning focused on the child's anxieties and that it was by means of interpreting their contents that I found myself able to diminish anxiety. In order to do this, I made full use of the archaic language of symbolism which I recognized to be an essential part of the child's mode of expression. As we have seen, the brick, the little figure, the car, not only represent things which interest the child in themselves, but in his play with them they always have a variety of symbolical meanings as well, which are bound up with his fantasies, wishes, and actual experiences. This archaic mode of expression is also the language with which we are familiar in dreams, and it was by approaching the play of the child in a way similar to Freud's interpretations of dreams that I could get access to the child's unconscious. But we have to consider each child's use of symbols in connection with his own particular emotions and anxieties and in relation to the whole situation which is presented in the analysis; mere generalized translations of symbols are meaningless.

The importance I attributed to symbolism led me—as time went on—to theoretical conclusions about the process of symbol formation. Play analysis had shown that the capacity to use symbols enables the child to transfer not only interests but also fantasies, anxieties, and guilt to objects other than people. Thus a great deal of relief is experienced in play, and this is one of the factors which make it so essential for the child. For instance, little Peter, to whom I referred earlier, pointed out to me, when I interpreted his damaging a toy figure as representing attacks on his brother, that he would not do that to his *real* brother—he would only do it to the *toy* brother. My interpretation of course made it clear to him that it was really his brother whom he *wished* to attack; but the instance shows that only by symbolic means was he able to *express* his destructive tendencies in the analysis.

I have also arrived at the view that in children a severe inhibition of the capacity to form and use symbols, and so to develop fantasy life, is a sign of serious disturbance. I suggested that such inhibitions and the resulting disturbance in the relation to the external world and to reality are characteristic of schizophrenia (Klein, 1930, 1952). This conclusion has since influenced the understanding of the schizophrenic's mode of communication and has found its place in the treatment of schizophrenia.

One of the important points in my technique has always been the analysis of the transference. It is my experience that we are able to help the patient fundamentally by taking his desires and anxieties in our transference interpretations back to where they originated, namely, in infancy and in relation to his first objects. For, by re-experiencing early emotions and fantasies and understanding them in connection with his primal relationships—to his mother and father—he can, as it were, revise these early relations at their root and thus effectively diminish his anxieties.

It has been mentioned above how, since my earliest case, my interest has been centered on anxieties and the defenses against them. This emphasis on anxiety led me deeper and deeper into the unconscious and into the fantasy life of the child. My approach was also in contrast to the psychoanalytic point of view prevailing at that time—and for quite a long time to come—that interpretations should not be given frequently. This approach, therefore, involved a radical change in technique. I also ventured into new territory from another angle; the contents of fantasies and anxieties and the defenses against them which I found in young children and interpreted to them were at that time still largely undiscovered. In using this new technique I was faced with serious problems. The anxieties encountered when analyzing my first case were very acute, and, although I was strengthened in my belief that I was working on the right lines by the relief which the interpretations again and again produced, the intensity of the anxieties which were being brought into the open was at times perturbing. At one such moment I sought advice from Dr. Karl Abraham. He replied that since my interpretations up to then had often produced relief and the analysis was obviously progressing, he saw no reason for changing my method of approach. I felt encouraged by his support, and, as it happened, in the next few days the child's anxiety which had come to a head greatly diminished, and this led to further improvement. The conviction gained in this analysis strongly influenced the whole course of my analytic work. . . .

## REFERENCES


Klein, Melanie. The development of a child. *Int. J. Psycho-anal.*, 1923, **4**, 419–474.

Klein, Melanie. The importance of symbol formation in the development of the ego. *Int. J. Psycho-anal.* 1930, **11**, 24–39.

Klein, Melanie. *The psycho-analysis of children*. London: Hogarth Press, 1932.

Klein, Melanie. Notes on some schizoid mechanisms. *Int. J. Psycho-anal.*, 1946, **27**, 99–110.

❀ CHAPTER FOURTEEN

# Termination

THERE ARE very few discussions of termination in the literature, and this lacuna is particularly evident in the writings with an analytic orientation. Certainly many questions can be posed in this area, from both the theoretical and practical standpoints.

The primary problem, of course, concerns the possible guidelines to use in determining whether termination should be anticipated and the signs which indicate that the termination process has spontaneously begun. Also, how can one be sure that progress is genuine rather than a premature "flight into health" as a defense against releasing threatening content?

How is the actual decision to terminate made? Who makes the decision—child or therapist? To what extent should the parents be involved, and at what point? Should termination be definite and final, or might the intervals between sessions be gradually increased? What are the advantages and disadvantages in scheduling the child to return once every month or two for a time?

What can the therapist anticipate in terms of his own possible reactions to "giving up" the child? What may be the effect of termination on the parents, and what help will they need?

What reactions may the child exhibit as termination draws near? How are these to be handled? For instance, the child may become aggressive to the therapist. Should this regression be viewed as a signal that he is not ready to leave after all? Or is he angry because he hates the thought of leaving?

Is it, as Taft suggests, easier to leave someone if you can manage to dislike him? Will it help the child to point out the possible origin of these feelings?

What about giving or receiving parting gifts, or not giving and not accepting, in terms of the dynamic significance to both parties? If the child begs for mementos, is this bona fide interest or is he expecting to be denied and so attempting to establish justification to feel hurt? How can this situation, if it arises, be used to further the child's growth toward independence?

Often, in the last session or two, the child may recapitulate the main themes and sequences of all his previous sessions; how can this be used therapeutically?

What if the child leaves at the end of his last session with just a casual good-by—no closing "paragraph" of farewell, no obvious regrets or spoken amenities? Should the therapist structure any more definite form of leave-taking?

The termination behavior of an eight-year-old boy is outlined below to illustrate both the child's awareness that therapy was nearing its conclusion and his reluctance to leave. Only that content of the last seven sessions which related to termination is presented; the therapist's reactions are given in parentheses where necessary to maintain continuity; the reader is invited to invent his own responses to the other sequences.

(1) Seemed bored, complained of nothing to do. (Therapist suggested he may be tired of coming, and maybe this is his way of saying he thinks he doesn't need to come much longer.)—Started a clay object which would take two sessions to complete.—More than usual interest in the clock, frequently remarked on number of minutes remaining.—Asked what becomes of all the things children make here, "Would you keep them for two years, even?"

(2) Recapitulated many earlier play themes.

(3) Hid from therapist, rather than going directly to the playroom.—Complained of nothing interesting to play with.

(4) Said he'd wanted to stay home and play with his friends today. (Therapist pointed out his ambivalence and suggested they talk about setting a definite termination date.) —Said he was having trouble deciding and was afraid he might need to come again and therapist might not be there.—Said he used to *need* to come, and now he *wanted* to come because it was fun.—Reluctant to leave at end of hour.

(5) (Therapist asked if he'd decided how many more times he would come, pointed out that both she and he felt he didn't really need to come; this is a place to come when you have problems, he could have his fun with his friends and the Cub Scouts. Pointed out she knew it was hard for him to decide to leave, that there are many times when it's hard to give up something you like.)—Decided to come two more times.—Crushed up his favorite plaster-of-Paris dog, said this was his way of saying "good-by."—Subtle attempts to splash water on therapist.—Begged to take three balloons home, rather than the two usually allowed.

(6) Made a "man" out of balloons, incorporating features which had often appeared in previous drawn figures and "hung" it from a chair.—Begged to take home some string and a dried-up glue tube.—Kicked football; said it was funny but he could always kick it better here.

(7) (Final Session.) Wandered around room, real trouble finding an activity. (Therapist, "I guess you're wondering what a person is supposed to do on their last day.")—Asked, "How long have I been coming?"—Ran hand through sand and said he wished it would get cut on a knife so he would need a bandaid. (Therapist reflected his wish to be hurt, so therapist could take care of him.)—Looked at all the craft objects he had made.—Had therapist write out a list for him, while he dictated, of items he would need for his Cub Scout first-aid kit.—With one minute left, started to throw Bobo at the therapist.—Hurried about, finding things to do.—Grabbed the football for "one good kick."— Lingered over handing the "Occupied" sign back to the therapist and said, "Good-by."

The selection from Ross considers the handling of vacation periods and other necessary cancellations and interruptions, as well as various aspects of termination. Both Ross and Allen discuss therapeutic goals and criteria for determining when these goals have been reached; both call attention to the assistance the parents will need in accepting the fact of termination.

Allen answers many procedural questions which arise in conjunction with termination, and he points out the various ways in which the child may react as the final hour approaches.

Taft's selection presents that part of her discussion of a therapy case which illustrates the process of termination. Both Allen and Taft stress their view of all terminations and endings as vital aspects of the total life process.

# Interruptions and Termination of Treatment

ALAN O. ROSS

. . . For a field of endeavor as unpredictable as therapy, it is impossible to prepare a comprehensive list of every situation which can conceivably arise, but two issues deserve separate discussion. One of these occurs frequently, the other inevitably in treatment situations: interruptions and termination. These events are psychologically related inasmuch as both may be seen as rejections, both being situations where the therapist withdraws from the relationship at what, to the child, must seem an arbitrary point in time. Where unilateral parental decisions are responsible for interruption or termination the problem is only slightly modified since the child will often blame his therapist for his failure to oppose the move successfully. Wherever possible, the child should receive adequate prior notice of an impending interruption or termination so that he can be prepared for it and have the therapist's help in handling the feelings this experience will arouse. Depending on the child's concept of the future, which is, of course, partly a function of his age, preparation should start, at the very least, two sessions before the event is to take place. In the case of an interruption, a frank statement of the reason for it (the therapist going on vacation, for example) should be given, together with the date when child and therapist will meet again. Some children seem to find it reassuring to be permitted to mark the date of their return on the therapist's calendar. Where the child is particularly dependent on the therapist, or is especially concerned about being rejected and forgotten, a promise of a postcard (which must be kept!) can be helpful. We are, unfortunately, not always in a position to predict necessary interruptions ahead of time. Illness can strike a day before the next treatment session, making preparation of the child impossible. Knowing one's patient's needs, one can try to help matters by a personal telephone call or, again, a postcard, which, being more concrete, is often preferable with younger patients. At the same time, one should not view oneself as so absolutely indispensable as to assume that every patient is going to be traumatized by the therapist's absence. Whether it is possible to prepare the patient for the therapist's absence beforehand or not, it is important to bring the matter up during the first session after his return, encouraging the child to express whatever feelings were aroused by the interruption.

Because mental health is so difficult to define in tangible terms and improvement as a result of treatment is largely a relative matter, it is often difficult to decide when to terminate therapy. Because the child is an organism in the process of development, he can probably always "use more help." An adult in a relatively stable situation, who has had therapeutic assistance in overcoming a specific problem, can usually be expected to continue to function adequately unless unforeseen environmental complications are introduced. A child, on the other hand, who was helped around an acute difficulty in accepting a new sibling, for example, continues to face developmental crises and may require the therapist's help when entering school, going to camp, experiencing pubescence, or making dates with members of the opposite sex. Since it is not possible to predict with any degree of certainty how a child is going to react at various developmental stages, many insecure parents, having found therapeutic support helpful, will desire to continue the contact indefinitely. Another crisis always seems to be just around the corner. Needless to say, a therapist must guard against becoming a child's permanent crutch. Though it can be made clear that, should a difficulty arise later on, the therapeutic contact may be resumed, a clear-cut termination is highly desirable. The decision of when to terminate should be closely linked to the therapeutic goal set when treatment was originally undertaken and related to the general philosophy of treatment subscribed to by the therapist or the institution within which he functions. A community child-guidance clinic with the responsibility of giving optimal treatment to the greatest number of children must avoid carrying a case beyond the point which was originally viewed as the goal, just as it must abstain from continuing treatment attempts when reasonable expectations no longer promise material improvement. Remembering that child-guidance treatment is largely ego supportive, a case should be terminated when the presenting difficulty has been dealt with successfully, even when, as is often the case, one has not been able to gain true insight into the underlying dynamics and thus had to leave the basic conflicts unresolved. If the latter is essential before the child can be helped, he should be referred for more intensive analytic treatment as soon as the need becomes apparent.

Anna Freud delivered a highly stimulating but as yet unpublished paper on the termination of treatment at Worcester, Massachusetts in September 1957. Though the paper concerned itself principally with psychoanalytic treatment, some of the points Miss Freud made are relevant to our present discussion. Both psychoanalysts and other psychotherapists have to face the questions of how "deep" one should go and whether there is ever an end to treatment. The answer Anna Freud proposed was that one need not take a child further than the position in which all children are at that developmental stage. Any form of therapy must be content to follow a disturbance only to the level at which it has arisen, and when progressive development once again takes place, treatment should be discontinued. We cannot safeguard a child against future dangers and must be willing, in Miss Freud's words, to let him take a chance. Anna Freud doubts the prophylactic effect even of child analysis, feeling (if the writer's notes serve him correctly) that an emotional illness leaves scars and that a recovered patient is no safer from the vicissitudes of life than the person who was never ill.

In a clinic, the decision to terminate is made in a staff conference on the basis of the reports of the therapists involved in the case. In determining whether termination is indicated, it is useful to ask, "Would the parents have brought the child for treatment if his condition at that time had been what it is today?" If the answer is in the negative, it is well to bring treatment to a conclusion. Parents will often need considerable help in accepting termination. They must be assured that the therapist considers them capable of carrying on without the support of treatment; they must be given an opportunity to express their feelings and warned to expect some exacerbation of the child's difficulty around the time of termination.

As in the case of treatment interruption, the child must be prepared for termination as far in advance as possible. It is well to remind him of the original reason for his coming for treatment and to ask him whether he thinks this reason still exists. One must point out to him that his coming for treatment cannot continue "forever" and that, since his therapist knows that he is much improved, it is time to think about when he might stop coming. The child should not be expected to set his own terminal date, since this is not only placing an unfair responsibility on him but may also lead to an impasse, should the child set a date in the distant future. It is best for the therapist to suggest a date, say a month hence, and to seek the child's approval, making the decision, as far as possible, a joint undertaking. As usual, the child must be helped to verbalize his feelings, not only at the time the topic is first broached but repeatedly thereafter when the child is reminded of how many more times he and his therapist will be meeting. During the last session, most children will need an explicit assurance that the therapist likes them and that he has enjoyed the times they had together. A casual remark to the effect that the therapist will be happy to have the child visit him occasionally should he so desire can help make the departure somewhat less final and irrevocable. Still, most children will display some emotional reaction to leaving, a reaction which, being appropriate, must be considered healthy. . . .

# *The Ending Phase of Therapy*

FREDERICK H. ALLEN

The values of the therapeutic experience in which a child and therapist are engaged emerge in part around the fact that this relationship is begun with the goal of its eventual termination. From the first hour, this is the basic orientation of the therapist. Each move the therapist makes that helps the child to be a participant in his own change is one that helps that child to assume responsibility for a self which he can accept as uniquely his and which is the very core of his living. With this orientation, the ending phase of therapy becomes a process of affirming or reaffirming the difference a child perceives in himself as he develops within the steady framework of a relationship made possible by a therapist and child together.

From the outset, the therapist has no desire other than to use his relationship to assist the child to be free finally of the need for this specialized help. The child's feelings are at the center of the experience, and the therapist is in a position to encourage the child to use him in whatever ways he can to grow toward a clearer awareness and acceptance of his own child's self with all that is involved in living with parents, siblings, and companions. The child may use the therapist to symbolize the good or bad parent, the benevolent or the tyrannical despot, or the possessor of magic to cure. These shifting roles, which the child assigns to the therapist, who holds steadily to his real role, spring from the heart of the child's turmoil and represent his efforts to find a solution for his difficulties. The therapist does not need the child to satisfy his own needs and, in the midst of the changing demands of the child, is able to maintain his own integrity. The therapist who is free to be himself[a] can respond to the child's feelings in terms of their meaning to the child. Then he can be ready to assist the child through the differentiating steps of therapy which lead gradually into and through the ending phase, the essence of which is the child's affirmation of himself as an individual, not in isolation but in relation to others.

When the emphasis is placed on the word "ending," it is necessary to keep in mind that this is not a one-sided concept. Actually it describes only half of a life process. Designating the final culmination scene of an educational experience as "commencement day" is not the incongruity it has seemed to many people. This phrase incorporates the positive aspects that belong to every ending experience. The emphasis is not merely on the ending of something already past, but on the new which is being ushered in. The leaving of the old and the beginning of the new constitute the ever-recurring shifting of the scenes in human development. The old is terminated with full regard for the values and satisfactions that have accrued from it. If these values must, however, be measured and felt only in the circumstances in which they were experienced originally, then they cease to be growth-inducing influences and lose their positive meaning. Values from any life experience retain their positive meaning only as the individual is free to use them in the ever-recurring newness of living. This is not forgetting and repressing the old, but it is using the old to provide the structure of the new. Thus, there is the con-

[a] I want to emphasize again that this statement implies a human quality of warmth and understanding that invests the professionally disciplined maturity of a therapist with a quality a child or adult can feel related to. A ten-year-old boy in constant conflict with authority came for his first hour evidently expecting a heavy handed disciplinarian. After his first, he described his puzzle about this person by saying, "That man is a little touched but I like that guy." This boy couldn't quite understand this new person but he knew how he felt about him.

tinuum so essential, not only for individuals, but for the cultures in which they move and live.

An essential quality of the neurotic individual is his inability to be free from a past he will not or cannot part with. When an individual is rooted in a "past present" and fears to loosen the anchorage to which he clings, he will not be able to use the satisfactions which he can legitimately carry over from the past to give meaning to the new. The new becomes a threat to be avoided. The neurotic is the person who has difficulty in ending any phase of living and constantly has his vision fastened on a past[b] that can neither be recaptured nor relinquished. This is the intolerable life dilemma described so vividly by Matthew Arnold in the individual "wandering between two worlds—the one dead, the other powerless to be born."[c]

A typical life situation of parent and child presented to a child guidance clinic is one in which parent and child are mired in a relationship which no longer works, but which neither one has the power to end. Such individuals are held together by an apparently insoluble struggle which must find some solution if the individuals involved are to gain any separate sense of their own values. A fifteen-year-old girl described the dilemma of this deadlock when she said: "My mother and I are closer to each other when we quarrel; otherwise we don't have anything to say." In the everyday life about us we constantly see individuals trying to effect these separations in behavior patterns incompatible with healthy development. The escape into sickness, the explosive running away of the child and adolescent, the breaking up of families through its members' failure to find harmonious ways of being individuals within the family group are extremes to which individuals go in their efforts to destroy and escape from the deadlocks that occur in human relationships.

When a parent makes a move to seek the help a therapist and caseworker can offer for a problem in his child, he is taking a step away from clinging to the untenable past in his relationship with a child and toward finding a better way of living with the child. The therapist enters this picture at the point where a parent and child may be reaching out toward ending this long-standing struggle. When viewed in this way, the entire therapeutic experience is one of ending and becomes symbolic of the new for which a parent and child are reaching. In itself a new experience, it, too, will have its own ending and become another past. This is achieved around the affirmation of the new qualities which gradually came into being through therapy, but which remain when the therapeutic relationship itself is relinquished. It is this emphasis which helps us to understand the ending phase as a process and an integral part of the whole therapeutic experience.

Ending is, as I have said, an integral part of the growth process initiated in

---

[b] A facetious description of the "woofus bird" as one who has eyes in the back of his head to see where he came from because he does not like to see where he is going is a good description of neurotic behavior.

[c] From the stanzas of the Grande Chartreuse in "Poems of Matthew Arnold, 1840–1866" (J. M. Dent and Sons, London, and E. P. Dutton & Co., New York), page 258.

the first hours of a therapeutic experience. In order that this phase of therapy shall acquire its full meaning for the child, it must be brought into relation with a plan that gives clearer definition of what the child is ready to do. When the child has reached a point where both he and the therapist are aware of his readiness to bring their relationship to a close, a plan for effecting this is discussed between them. The child is helped to be an active participant in making the plan. There are no clear-cut signals for a therapist to follow in knowing when a child is ready to make such a plan. The best guides are those supplied by the child, and are recognizable if the therapist maintains an orientation to the whole growth experience and remains sensitive to the changes he has helped the child to bring about.

The changes in the feeling-tone of the hour, the changes in the verbal content, the changes a parent and child describe in their day-to-day relationship, the dream material which children bring, all these and others have great meaning not as isolated bits of behavior, but as parts that fit into a new whole which the child is helping to bring about. These responses become the indicators of the child's readiness to end, indicators which the therapist, sensitive to their meaning, can recognize and bring into the open.

Since therapy terminates as a new separation experience, the child needs opportunity to live through some of the conflicting feelings which are aroused by this step. The relationship to the therapist has come to have great meaning to the child. For many children this has been the means of gaining a new perspective about themselves and their relationships to others. When the ending phase approaches, the child feels he is leaving behind an important support and that he may be risking loss of what he has gained. There is anxiety in this separation just as there was anxiety in the separations at the beginning. The child needed a period of time in the beginning to find what he could be in this new relationship. And, in the ending phase, he will need to have a planned period in order to learn the meaning of this anxiety that is aroused by the prospect of assuming fuller responsibility for the changes he has effected through the help of the therapist.

The ending plan grows from the child's readiness to participate in making that plan. It becomes the more open and organized recognition by child and therapist of the progress made thus far. In the interviews . . . which lead up to the final hour of treatment, the child has opportunity to experience what it means, in feeling, to end a significant phase of living. The parent takes an active part in making an ending plan, and in their living through the final series of interviews many reactions appear which give evidence of the fact that this is a stirring period for both child and parent. Some children swing from such extremes as wanting to come a thousand more times to asserting, "This is my last time." The first extreme represents the determination never to end, and the other swing of the pendulum indicates the child's determination to end entirely on his own terms and thus to avoid the anxieties that are necessarily awakened.

The plan of ending upon which the child and therapist agree now becomes a positive affirmation of the child's readiness to affirm the new in himself. The interviews that follow permit fuller expression of both the satisfactions and the anxieties and struggles the child feels around a plan he has helped to make. . . .

Around ending, the child may and frequently does experience anew some of the disturbance that characterized the beginning. . . . Some of the symptoms which have disappeared during the course of the therapeutic process may temporarily reappear as the child begins to assume responsibility for ending. These reactions of the ending phase frequently are mistaken as evidence that the child needs more help, rather than as partial efforts of the child to cling to a source of help which, in reality, he no longer needs or wants. To postpone the ending and fail to sense the meaning of these responses is a major error which may jeopardize the values that have emerged in the therapy by forcing the child to end negatively.

The child who can say, in his final hours of therapy, "I don't want to stop coming," yet can go ahead with his plans to end the treatment is giving to his feelings the partial expression so essential in normal living. This represents a constructive ending experience since the child is not using one feeling to deny another; instead both exist simultaneously, as partial expressions of feeling. It is the total withholding of a feeling expression in an individual that enables him to maintain an isolation that prevents the therapist from gaining any significant connection with him. The same totality of a possessively positive reaction can enable the child to avoid the dangers of separate and responsible living by trying to hold to the therapist as a symbol of his undifferentiated self. The child who in the course of therapy has found he can be a person in himself and have, at the same time, a relation with another, has broken up this unreal totality. Such a child is ready to end. He has found that he can be a whole in himself and still be a part of a larger whole. These partial feeling expressions in the ending phase become important indicators of this movement and bring out the extent of the child's differentiation. Ending the old and beginning the new stand in natural relation to each other. The child can act on his impulse to live, which the ending of therapy represents in its creative meaning. However, associated with this impulse is some reluctance to let the old die. It is the balance between these aspects of feeling which is a part of each life experience in which the old and the new meet. The child may find this balance for the first time in this particular ending experience he has with his therapist.

Ending, therefore, does arouse some anxiety in children. The therapeutic relationship has come to have great meaning for a child, and it would be unreal for the ending to be accomplished without any feeling. The important support the child needs from the therapist is help to express the feeling that is awakened and not to have these responses interpreted as his need for further treatment. Such an interpretation of these responses would be like investing the original symptom with the control it had had previously and a vicious cycle would be established. If the anxiety aroused in ending is accepted as the evidence of the child's needing more help, this being held for further treatment rouses the child's real anxiety at feeling trapped in a relationship which the therapist cannot or will not help him to end.[d] This vicious cycle more frequently occurs in adult therapy or in child therapy which goes on without the participation of a parent.

The final phase of a therapeutic growth experience presents the therapist with a real test of his convictions and philosophy. The therapist knows that his relation to a patient is an important episode in that person's life, but that it is not, nor should it be, all of the patient's life. Thus the therapist's major interest from the beginning must be in helping the patient eventually to finish with this particular episode in his life. Only in that way can this unique relationship have any value. If a therapist adopts a protective role by trying to become a parent substitute in order to make sure before he "lets him go" that the patient will have no further difficulties, he cannot help the child to end. No therapeutic experience can provide a patient with a paid-up insurance policy against future difficulties although the anxiety centering about ending may activate the patient's need to have such assurance. This may be and frequently is a natural part of the ending process. The therapist can meet it, however, in a way that allows it to be a part and not the whole it becomes where the orientation is focused only on the anxiety. In that case, treatment would go on and on.

The freedom the therapist has to help a patient end carries with it the patient's freedom to return if the future brings the need and desire for further help. When ending is understood as a process it does not have to carry the finality which the patient's anxiety may give it. Around ending many children bring up the question of a future visit. It is important for the therapist to let the child know he would be glad to have him come back to tell or show the therapist how he is getting along. Frequently children never act on this, but it is the immediate feeling that they can be free to act on it in the future which gives the necessary support which enables them to end. It is quite common to have a child come back after a lapse of time to prove to himself he is really through.[e] A single visit may be all that is necessary. . . .

---

[d] For a poignant example of the value of helping a child give outward expression to feeling, see W. S. White, "Journey for Margaret," as condensed in the *Reader's Digest*, November, 1941. This child gained a relation to the new when she was helped to give vent to the surge of feeling aroused by the forceful separation from the old.

[e] Recently a boy who ended treatment nearly ten years ago called his therapist . . . and recalled a number of incidents that happened when he was coming for help, and then said, "I just wanted to tell you I was getting along fine and thought you might like to know."

# Comments on Termination[1]

JESSIE TAFT

. . . The eleventh hour marks the first climax of the love submission, registered in the singing of "Springtime in the Rockies," and this is quickly followed by a marked strengthening of the ego reaction, aggravated by my absence for two consecutive Saturdays. When I remind him, in the fifteenth hour (Thursday) that he won't see me for a long time, he only replies, "I'll still be happy" and admits under the sting of desertion that he'd just as soon not come any more. To make leaving a pure getting even is not the most constructive basis for ending a therapeutic relationship, although it is better than nothing and the sense of injury which the therapist's irregularity or absence arouses may be a useful stimulus to the patient's will if he can be tided over the too violent impulse to go in his turn. I do not hesitate, therefore, to suggest at least one more visit to bring back a borrowed key, with the freedom to go then if he wishes. The violence of his rejection is amusingly evidenced in the throwing away of the envelope (mine) on his way to the car as reported by the caseworker, with a "good riddance to bad rubbish" and a destructive stamping. It is not easy to get free of the entanglement with the love object without a little hate and for some individuals, a great deal.

So extreme a denial of the value of the therapeutic relationship as John allowed himself in the eleventh hour is bound to be compensated for by an equally strong swing in the other direction which we find at its height in the complete acceptance of regression, not emotional, but actual, in the seventeenth hour, the Thursday preceding a second omitted Saturday. The marked fear which is aroused by the acute consciousness of being caught in the therapeutic situation without seeing how it will be possible to bear leaving it (a characteristic reaction to any unusual absence or to the approach of the ending) comes to the fore in the dream of robbers with the sense of utter helplessness which is expressed in an hour of feeling sick and lying feebly on the couch like a baby, fingers in mouth, a complete giving up of the autonomous will to lean upon the strength of the other. It is interesting to note that he leaves on this occasion without the usual joyful ceremony of flapping, ringing, and final admonitions. The ceremonial, I take it, is an overcoming of the limitation which I impose in setting a daily ending. It is his creative use of the environmental limit, a working-it-over to his own ends,

---

[1] In previous sections, Taft has given a complete report of each of thirty sessions over a span of three months. The child, a seven-year-old boy, had been placed by his mother with an aunt and then had been transferred to a foster home while awaiting the final placement referred to in these excerpts. The boy was extremely fearful, enuretic, unable to dress himself, and subject to vomiting episodes. Only the portions of two sections which discuss termination are reproduced.

with a sense of control which extends to me, in that I carry it out in his terms according to direction "Say good-by twice." Today he is too sunk to meet reality creatively to exist on his own without the support of the maternal strength. He feels it only as alien and threatening.

After the second Saturday's absence, he has another ego swing (eighteenth hour) but less extreme. He expresses boredom, threatens not to come for a week but takes it back of his own accord and, after an hour of destructive expression, returns with zest to his ceremonial of leave-taking. From this point on Jack struggles with the problem of the final going which is rapidly drawing nearer. He knows he is to move to a new home in a few weeks and, while he will not admit it overtly, assumes that he will not continue to visit me—"You won't see me very long" (twenty-first hour) as a means to gain his end and "That's why I decided to come (on Saturday), 'cause I got only two more" (twenty-fifth hour). Leaving, separation, growth has to be accomplished inside. The other person cannot take it over if he would. Yet the patient feels at times, inevitably, as if too much were being expected of him. He cannot do it himself, the other must be made to assume the burden by refusing to let him go or by forcing him out. A final showdown is demanded before the patient reluctantly assumes responsibility for his own growing will to be free, to be himself. After many ups and downs, explorations and testings of my patience mingled with spurts of angelic behavior and consideration of my wishes, Jack finally forces me to the wall in one last crucial conflict, in the twenty-third hour. It is a terrific struggle, and I am free to confess that it takes all the courage and firmness I can muster to hold out against the irrefutable logic, the winning sweetness, the desperate pleading for just one thing, "just a little thing." "You won't be bad if you give it to me, and you won't be bad if you don't give it to me either." When he is forced to realize that he cannot get anywhere through domination of me, the pain of inevitable separation and separateness breaks over him, and, for the first time, he cries with genuine emotion, although he recovers quickly and soon seeks to turn the tables on me by asking if he can stay away Saturday. "Would it hurt your feelings if I didn't come?" His own hurt feelings make him aware of mine and also are more easily borne projected upon the therapist than in the self.

After this bitter struggle in which limitation is accepted more deeply than ever before, Jack springs into a new creative possession of the situation and maintains it more-or-less consistently to the last visit. The paper airplanes provide a perfect solution for his problem, as they are within his control, do not threaten me or the office furniture, yet command my constant attention better than any play he has discovered. We now see a growing acceptance of going, a taking-over of the responsibility as to future visits. He wants to feel free to come but also free to decide whether he will or not, replying to my well meant suggestions with an impatient "*I'll* tell *you*" and yet to the end finding some positive value in every contact. The spot where I come nearest to repeating the pedagogical slip of the first record is when Jack so cheerfully fails to return the borrowed nickel. The moralist almost gets the better of me at that point in the instinctive feeling that no child should get away with such behavior, it isn't honest. But actually, why not? Is it not rather a necessity that in some way, somewhere the child should conquer in concrete terms, just as every patient conquers in finally completing the experience his way, regardless of the therapist. But the child has to act it out, to overcome the therapist by some little trick, to win out where he has had to give in so often. In neglecting to pay his debt, Jack holds out effectively against me and his own fear of disapproval, which, I maintain, in this instance and in this situation, is highly therapeutic for him.

In a growing realization of his own desire to go, like many an adult, Jack becomes insistent on the need for fidelity in the other. "When I move you come back here, because I'm coming to see you. You be sure to come back here and you make it Tuesday and Wednesday and Thursday and all like that." Also, he is anxious to feel that he is the only one, or at least unique in some way—"They don't come much (other boys), not like I do." He is able now to admit that he wants *me* to care and is much surer that I do, since he likes the new self he is beginning to experience. "Say you love me truly," shyly but with real feeling (twenty-eighth hour), and as he leaves—"Be sure" —with deep meaning. The awareness of difference which always follows the acceptance of separation can be detected clearly in the twenty-seventh hour when he remarks on my looking fat when he first came. "Do *I* look fat? Was I fatter?" he inquires. It is his feeling of change in himself and his new sense of me as an outside object. I should interpret his sudden interest in the breast, in the picture and with reference to me (thirtieth hour) as a recognition and acceptance of difference, perhaps sex difference in physiological terms, an admission that the mother has something which he does not, a breaking up of too complete identification which is made possible by this new willingness to be himself.

In the symbolic birth struggle of the twentieth hour, "I'm getting born, I don't get hurt," Jack strikes the keynote of a therapeutic experience with a favorable outcome. He has taken over the birth fear and transformed it into an ego achievement. To give up the therapeutic tie may be painful, but Patsy (the dog) is waiting to kiss him when he gets home. Patsy is part of a healing reality which is even better than what he has left behind. Patsy responds to affection, Patsy really does care, and Uncle W. needs his help on the farm; perhaps he (Jack) will "be too busy to come," after vacation. This is as it should be, the patient goes on to a new world which needs him as he needs it. It is the therapist who is abandoned, who, like the scapegoat, takes upon himself the death aspects of the birth process, and becomes the repository of the outworn self. . . .

There remains, then, one further experience to be gained from the therapeutic relationship, without which it becomes a trap as truly as the previous life experiences of the patient, and that is a constructive, creative leaving of the therapist and the therapeutic situation which will diminish the fear of individuation, since to leave convincingly is to find that one can bear both the pain and the fear of withdrawal from a depth of union never risked since birth or weaning and to discover within the self a substitute for the lost wholeness. No particular therapeutic relationship presents such a clear positive picture, since it always has in it all the uniqueness, unexpectedness, and ambivalence of real experience which is lost the second it is abstracted. The interaction between the will to unite and the will to separate is continuous from the first moment to the last. In every hour, there will be minor yieldings and minor withdrawals. Underneath these shorter surface movements, the patient as well as the therapist feels a deeper current which flows with a different time span but with the same interplay of conflicting tendencies. The week has its own ebb and flow, just like the hour, and yet there is a general trend in terms of a still longer span, which carries the love impulse to its climax of acceptance and brings the ego striving to the final point of rejection of the supporting relationship and assertion of the independent self. The hours and weeks which are dominated by the growing power of the transference emotion are never without resistances and rejections on the part of the ego, nevertheless as this is lessened, the total character of the separate parts changes also. The twentieth hour does not feel like the fifth or the tenth. The union which has been attained through hours and weeks of minor destructions and re-creations is fairly strong and elastic enough to contain considerable difference without shattering. Therefore, when the sense of wholeness in the transference emotion is most complete, it is also most able to bear the already included and tolerated impulses to separation. It is at this point of greatest security that the second trend in the relationship can begin to make itself felt and gradually, as the ending becomes a reality which is more and more accepted in terms of the need of the patient to be free, to exercise his own strength, the hours and weeks take on a different coloring under the now frankly enjoyed assertion of the growing ego, which, by living through the therapeutic relationship, has come into possession of its own strength as well as its weakness.

Time, then, as arbitrarily utilized to limit the therapeutic situation, is nothing more than the external symbol, the tangible carrier, of the inevitable limitation in all relationship, which becomes tolerable here for the first time, only because the patient is allowed to discover it one-sidedly, in himself, in terms of his own will and nature. This discovery, which he makes and accepts in greater-or-lesser degree within a comparatively brief period, has no more final, fixed, guaranteed quality than any other growth experience. No therapeutic relationship, however valuable, can make up for years of refusal to live. The more the individual has been able to accept life before he comes to the therapist, the deeper and richer will be his experience in this particular relationship and the more effectively will he be able to connect it with the reality outside. . . .

PART FOUR

# SYMBOLISM AND PLAY THEMES

CHAPTER FIFTEEN

# Symbolism in Nonverbal Activities

PART FOUR has been planned to highlight the symbolic aspects and dynamic implications of certain areas and modes of play. The child may verbalize as he plays, but he may also communicate via body movements, attitudes, and activity level and through various art media, toys, and games. His manner of approach will be as important to observe as his actual use of materials.

Analogies can be drawn between the symbolism inherent in children's play and that which Freud points out as characteristic of the hysterical attack[1] and of the dreams[2] of adults. The chief distortions he notes are the "condensation" of several fantasies into one "act"; "multiple identifications" (i.e., playing the parts of both antagonists at the same time); "inversion" of an element into its opposite; reversal of the sequence of events; and displacement or substitution of seemingly harmless elements for the meaningful one.

If the child's play is seen as representing an ongoing symbolic process, it becomes necessary for the therapist to allow himself some time to think over the events of the previous hour, to consider the sequence in which they occurred, and to engage in some free associations as to the possible dynamic implications underlying the specific play acts or themes. Succeeding activities may then be recognized as varied repetitions or further extensions of earlier episodes. As these play

[1] S. Freud, *The Interpretation of Dreams* (1900) (New York: Basic Books, 1959).

[2] S. Freud, "General Remarks on Hysterical Attacks" (1909), in *Collected Papers* (New York: Basic Books, 1959), Vol. II.

acts accumulate, their impact becomes clearer; then interpretations come easily for the therapist and are accepted readily by the child.

Smolen, in his article, points out the threat that a nonverbal child presents to a beginning therapist. He also discusses the manifestations of defense mechanisms and resistances in children's play and gives illustrations and practical suggestions for handling and interpreting various play situations.

The play patterns often employed by disturbed children are discussed by Jackson and Todd, with emphasis on destructive and regressive modes. They also describe characteristics of the play of obsessive and hyperactive children.

Woltmann considers the diagnostic and symbolic meaning of various nonverbal play activities. After outlining developmental aspects of children's play, he points out the projective possibilities of various play materials. He also suggests that the therapist should develop a "third eye" in order to understand and interpret children's play communications.

When food is provided during play sessions, it too can serve therapeutic and symbolic purposes. Haworth and Keller point out the implications of the offer of food; the child's nonverbal, as well as verbal, reactions; and the measurement of progress in therapy by means of the successive changes in response to food.

# *Nonverbal Aspects of Therapy with Children*

ELWYN M. SMOLEN

For the past several years we have been increasingly impressed with the fact that a large number of children have apparently been helped to a significant degree in a process of individual therapy which did not include any extensive amount of verbal interchange between the therapist and the child patient. Upon first consideration we tended to dismiss this as a beneficial result of the relationship between the patient and the therapist, in short, a situation somewhat analogous to a "transference cure." However, when we began to examine this explanation, we found that things were not quite that simple. It was at this point that we began to examine some of the nonverbal aspects of therapy with children in greater detail.

Further confirmation of the need for emphasis on this area of psychotherapy with children came from our experience with supervision and training. We found, regardless of professional discipline, whether it was psychiatry, psychology, or social work, that the greatest single obstacle which had to be overcome by the trainee was the preconception that therapy could be effective only if it took place within a framework of active verbalization. In fact, one of the intermediate goals of therapy frequently formulated by the trainee, was to get the child to talk about his problems. In examining this attitude further, it soon became apparent that it was determined primarily by the needs of the therapist. These trainees, inexperienced in working with children, felt quite uncomfortable when confined to a room with a child to whom they were expected to do something therapeutic. They sought reassurance for themselves and mastery of the situation by concentrating on getting the child to talk and usually viewed the play aspects of the therapy as a means of pleasantly diverting the child while his oedipal rivalry or castration fears or oral deprivation could be talked over.

This picture is, of course, somewhat exaggerated. However, the fact remains that preconceptions concerning psychotherapy as being limited to "the talking cure"—to quote a truism—did require considerable attention and working-through before the therapist could be completely and appropriately responsive to the behavior of the child and able to recognize the fact that it was the total and not just the verbal behavior of the child which was available for therapeutic intervention.

In analyzing this situation further, we came to the rather obvious conclusion that "the talking cure" was effective only insofar as it represented an adequate substitute for an "acting cure." That words are not always adequate substitutes for actions, even in the therapy of adults, is indicated by the vast amount of literature which has grown up around the problems of the acting-out patient in therapy. Words, then, as substitutes for and abstractions of behavior can often be quite meaningful to adults who have had many years of experience. But how much less true is this of children who, by virtue of the maturational process alone, have not yet attained a capacity to utilize adequately abstractions or symbolic forms of speech or thinking. This point alone imposes on the therapist the necessity of assuring the consensual validity of the language exchanged with the child. Even though many children may have the vocabulary, they do not have the rich background of experience and associations which would render these words meaningful condensates of emotional experiences in terms of their potential usefulness in therapy. Witness the following excerpt from a diagnostic interview with an eight-year-old boy referred because of poor school performance, facial tic, and enuresis.

EXAMINER: "Do you ever feel nervous?"
BOY: "Sometimes."
EXAMINER: "In school?"
BOY: "No."
EXAMINER: "At home?"
BOY: "Yeah."
EXAMINER: "Is this when you do something bad?"
BOY: "No."
EXAMINER (*After exploring various other of the usual possibilities and eliciting negative replies.*): "When did you last feel nervous?"
BOY: "Easter." [Two weeks previous.]
EXAMINER: "Why?"
BOY: "I wanted to see what I got."
EXAMINER: "What did you get?"
BOY: "Oh, you know—candy and things."
EXAMINER (*Bewildered.*): "Don't you like candy?"
BOY (*Patiently.*): "I wanted to see what I got."
EXAMINER (*Beginning to understand.*): "Is being nervous a good or bad feeling? Do you like being nervous?"
BOY: "Yeah, I guess so."

Further questioning finally clarified the fact that, for this boy, "being nervous" really meant being in a state of pleasant anticipation and that this had none of the overtones of displeasure or dysphoric anxiety attributed to it by the examiner.

Aside from the extremely important maturational aspect as well as the fact that the associated emotional values may be quite different for the child than for the therapist, we must also take into consideration that many of the children with whom we deal have suffered deprivations and traumata which have seriously affected their ability to develop the use of language. Often children who show great passivity or passive aggressiveness will not participate to any significant degree in conversation. Still other children will attempt to use language to deny or cover up the existence of problem areas.

For a long time in therapy, a seven-year-old girl with a severe school phobia and a symbiotic attachment to an extremely dependent and hysterical mother would persistently deny the existence of any difficulties despite the most flagrant self-contradictions as well as confrontation by the therapist. Only after she was continually reassured that the therapist would still like her and see her, even if she were not perfect, did she begin to show changes of behavior in therapy. The mother's defenses of suppression, denial, concealment of all aggressions, and need to please everyone at any cost to herself, had obviously influenced this child to the point where she was unable to put into words and thus give final and unmistakable reality to all of the unacceptable feelings she was very tentatively exposing in her play activities.

A most striking example of the way in which early traumatic experiences can affect the use of speech occurred quite recently in our clinic.

A seven-year-old boy was referred because of poor schoolwork, inability to get along with peers, and withdrawn behavior at home. Home consisted of his father, divorced from the patient's mother prior to his birth, and the father's spinster sister who had assumed the role of mother to this boy. The father had taken custody when the patient was three years old after learning of the mother's neglect and abuse. Prominent in the natural mother's treatment of this child had been taping his mouth shut so as not to be disturbed by his crying. Therefore, it was not unexpected when his aunt informed us, as we prepared to take him into the interview, that "He don't have much to say." The boy himself timidly and passively accompanied us to the playroom, but once there, true to the aunt's prediction, did not have much to say. In fact, he not only had nothing to say, he also passively refused participation in any activity except for a few tentative chalk marks on the blackboard.

Recalling from the history the basic oral trauma involved, the therapist began to toy with two rubber hand-puppets, a whale and a crocodile, each with exaggerated oral features. This immediately attracted the attention of the boy who had remained isolated and aloof in the center of the room. The therapist then silently offered the puppets to him. He seized them eagerly, and then asked the therapist how to put them on. He was helped to do this, whereupon he proceeded to spend most of the hour in very active play, alternately giving preference to the orally aggressive crocodile and to the oral incorporative toothless whale puppet. In a few minutes he had admitted the therapist into the play and quickly became involved in what was obviously an intensely abreactive experience accompanied by a great deal of motor activity, shouts, and shrieks of laughter. Upon leaving, he spontaneously held the therapist's hand. We returned him to the aunt who knowingly said, "He didn't have much to say, did he?"

Literally, the aunt was correct. From the point of view which considers words as the primary means of communication, this boy had had very little to say. And yet, how much more actually had gone on between patient and therapist. We must realize that language is only one aspect of behavior, that usually in therapy it is a substitute form of behavior on an abstract and symbolic level, and that meaningful therapeutic interchange can occur without the use of words.

This point of view, of course, imposes certain demands on the therapist. He must be prepared to understand and react appropriately and quickly to any behavior of the child, either verbal or nonverbal. He must observe it, place it in the context of the immediate session, and relate it to his knowledge of the personality structure and functioning of the child as derived from the history, psychologic tests and possible past contacts with him. He must then determine the significance of this behavior in terms of its psychodynamic implications, decide what the appropriate response should be, and then translate it into appropriate verbal or nonverbal behavior according to the needs of the child. Another difficulty derives from the fact that many therapists find it difficult to function as easily or smoothly on a nonverbal as on a verbal plane. Stripped of the defense of the higher level of abstraction involved in the use of words, they may find themselves having to deal with and control their own affective responses much more openly and directly.

For example, the relatively common use of gun play by children may evoke many feelings in the therapist of a purely private nature and unrelated to the immediate situation or needs of the child. One youngster who was having difficulty in handling his hostile feelings toward his rigid, authoritarian, and demanding policeman father retained for himself the role of the "bad guy" and relegated the role of the "good guy" to the therapist. The "bad guy" would then proceed to outmaneuver and destroy the "good guy" time after time. The therapist, who had previously recognized the boy's needs to act out against the father at staff conference, found himself unable to accept as readily these same needs when they were expressed in this direct and somewhat threatening fashion. Accordingly, he dealt with the situation by premature and rather direct interpretation, relieving his own anxiety by replacing the acting-out with verbalization, but at the same time effectively blocking the child from working this through in play.

In another similar situation, the therapist, recognizing his own feelings, dealt with them by excessive compliance with the boy's need to act out against authority. Having failed to note the true extent of the patient's ambivalence, and overresponding to the aggressive component, he so convincingly permitted himself to be shot that he aroused tremendous anxiety in the child who then turned his gun upon himself and joined the therapist on the floor. The therapist had only succeeded in reinforcing the already established pattern of masochistic self-destruction which the boy had manifested in a number of ways, such as accident proneness.

Another point which should be made is that by joining the child in his activities, the therapist may often get clues as to the meaning and function of the behavior by observing his own response to it. A most striking example of this came, not from a treatment session, but from the father of a six-year-old autistic child. In describing various aspects of the behavior, the father mentioned that at one point the child would spend a great deal of time in the bathroom with his face in the toilet bowl and shouting at the top of his voice. This was quite incomprehensible and anxiety-provoking to the parents until the father decided to try it himself in order to determine why the child was doing this. He then discovered that he heard a rather unusual kind of echo effect. This enabled the parents to understand the child's actions as an experiment with this sound effect. Their anxiety diminished, and within a short time the child gave up that kind of play. In this case, although the change in behavior may well have been purely coincidental, mimicking it enabled the parents to understand and deal with it more appropriately.

Emphasis has frequently been placed on the need to observe the patient's actions. Freud's interpretations of bits of behavior seen during analysis, Wilhelm Reich's (1949) observations on muscle tensions, Bela Mittelmann's (1954, 1957) studies on motility, all relate to the fact that the patient's behavior provides information, on a nonverbal plane, which is useful in the process of therapy. We would like to emphasize that similarly, observation of the child provides significant clues to his total mode of functioning, especially during the period of diagnostic work-up.

The first contact with the child is extremely important. The therapist, being forearmed with some history and possibly psychologic test results, knows generally what to expect and can very quickly evaluate the response of the child to meeting him. He himself must be prepared to respond quickly and appropriately in order to get the interview underway as smoothly as possible. Since this usually involves seeing the child alone, it means separation from the parent who has brought him to the clinic. Parenthetically, we have never ceased to be amazed at the readiness with which most children, obviously emotionally disturbed to a greater-or-lesser extent since they are being seen for psychiatric evaluation, separate themselves from their parents to accompany a total stranger to some unknown part of a large and equally unknown building, often with only minimal preparation for this.

The way in which the child separates himself from the parents offers many clues. Further information is obtained from the way in which he accompanies the therapist: whether he walks alongside, precedes, or follows are indications of some aspects of his general mode of functioning. While going to the office or playroom, the therapist also has an opportunity to observe gait, coordination, and general motor behavior. Such observations are often reinforced by holding the hand of the child, especially if he is very young. On a number of occasions we have observed an unevenness of grip and apparently uncoordinated movements of the small muscles of the hand which aroused suspicion, later confirmed, of the possible existence of an organic component in the illness.

If the way in which the child uses his body is important, we should not forget that this is also true of the therapist. By way of illustration we have found that it is possible to handle easily and effectively almost all but the most severe separation anxieties by maneuvering so that the therapist stands between mother and child, at least partially blocking the child's view of the mother. At the same time, the therapist slowly, reassuringly, and expectantly stretches his hand out toward the child, stopping about a foot away. Most often the child responds instinctively by reaching out to take the proferred hand. Once this is accomplished, there is no longer any problem about separating the child from the mother for the interview. Naturally, this leaves the mother's needs in this situation unsatisfied, but if it is done smoothly and quickly enough, she does not have time to build up a reaction to the separation which would possibly interfere with it.

Incidentally, we have also observed that the technique of the "offered hand" is quite often effective with children who are only in limited contact with reality. They seem able to relate themselves to the hand rather easily and can thus be induced to accompany the therapist, whereas, if merely requested to do so by the therapist or parent, or both, they will often refuse or ignore the request.

Before proceeding further, it might be well to clarify this point. In emphasizing the nonverbal aspects of therapy, we do not mean to imply that there is no interchange of speech. Usually there is a considerable amount of talk going on between the child and the therapist. However, in the instances we have been describing, the subject matter was fairly neutral with no continued relationship to or exploration of the child's problems. Even more frequently the therapist responds verbally to the behaviorally expressed need of the child, as in the case of the little girl mentioned above who was reassured concerning the therapist's interest in her. In this situation, as in many others, the impact and validity of the therapist's words could only be determined by a later change in the nonverbal behavior of the child. Actually, in most cases, there is a continuum of behavior, both verbal and nonverbal. Our purpose is merely to focus on and clarify some of the nonverbal aspects.

One frequent misconception is that play therapy consists primarily of making it possible for the child to act out problems in a controlled and accepting setting. Just as the adult patient is told he may say whatever he wishes in the session, but that he cannot expect to do this in everyday life, so the child is often told he may do what he wishes, with the addition of a few simple rules establishing limits and protecting the child, the therapist, and the premises from undue injury. Even this is sometimes too threatening. One little girl of seven, very shy and frightened, asked, "May I really do anything I want?" The therapist grandiosely assured her that she might. Whereupon the girl promptly said, "I want to go home."

Observation will soon reveal that the child's behavior in the play session is much more than merely acting-out and actually represents the same range of resistances and defenses one finds in the verbalizations of adult patients. Mechanisms such as displacement and substitution are frequently seen, as are behavioral defenses against acting-out. Some examples will clarify what we mean.

> One severely deprived and rejected ten-year-old boy was delighted with the clinic. It seemed he could never get enough. He constantly refused to accept the time limits of the interview, would explode with hostility when denied any special privileges, would steal toys and other objects from the clinic, and, in short, was extremely difficult to handle. All of these problems were effectively dealt with when the therapist recognized this behavior to be a carryover of the patient's basic oral frustration. Bypassing the substitutes the child was seeking, he began terminating each session with some candy. The boy responded immediately to this maneuver, and all the previous difficulties in getting him to accept limits were shortly dissipated.
>
> Another extremely passive, restricted youngster suffered from intense sibling rivalry which the parents had never been able to recognize or accept. All aggressive outlets were denied him, even a toy gun with which to play cowboy. His

face was emotionless, his movements were extremely slow and limited, and he showed a complete lack of spontaneity. The reason for referral was failure in school, although he was described as a model child at home. With the understanding that his psychological and behavioral restriction was a defense against aggression, he was gradually introduced to aggressive play. When finally induced to try the darts, his hand became frozen in mid-air, and he could not complete the throw. With much coaxing, persuasion, and support from the therapist, he was finally able to throw one into the target. Following this breaking-through of the motor inhibition, and with continued support, he began to move in therapy.

However, such breaking-through needs to be well-timed and done in such a manner as to provide adequate support for the child. As an example of an ill-timed move in this regard, we cite the instance of a similar problem with sibling rivalry and aggressiveness in an older boy of thirteen, whose sole activity in therapy for a long time consisted of solitary model building in a very meticulous and compulsive manner. He would frequently say no more than five or six words during the entire hour. Finally, the therapist, wearying of his own inactivity and the apparent lack of progress, coaxed the boy into a game of darts. As the boy threw them accurately and forcefully, the therapist overenthusiastically encouraged him and began discussing his difficulties in getting along with his sibling. The boy threw with increasing force and finally drove the point of one dart completely through the brass door knob. Whereupon he looked at the therapist and silently returned to his model building. He then terminated early and missed the next session. Obviously he had not needed to express his hostility so directly. He was fully aware of it and had been attempting to build up his defenses against it in order that he might function more effectively in other areas. The therapist should have realized this from other information which was available to him.

The need to support defenses and help the child control acting-out rather than promote it appears quite often. In this connection it is sometimes helpful to provide more rigid limits and less permissiveness. One very infantile, narcissistic nine-year-old would constantly make unreasonable demands upon the therapist and when these were refused would fly into outbursts of uncontrollable rage, on one occasion even throwing a hammer at him. At the same time, he never missed an appointment, always came early, and in other ways showed that treatment was very important to him. Finally we realized that rather than working-through his unmet and insatiable infantile needs, we should be helping him develop more adequate defenses and controls. The first thing we did was to remove his sessions from a rather large and cluttered playroom to a very small vacant office set up with only a few table games and activities. Within the security provided by the new setting, with the closeness of the walls and minimal stimulation of the activities available, he became much more relaxed and manageable and began to make significant gains in therapy.

In conclusion, in working with children, the therapist must deal with the total behavior of the child in the same way that the therapist of the adult deals with the total verbal productions of his patient. Resistances must be recognized and overcome, defenses worked through, repressions uncovered, and dreams and fantasies—usually manifested in drawings or play with dolls, toy animals, and the like—deciphered. They must be dealt with in a manner most appropriate to the needs of the particular child patient, which often means via nonverbal behavior. In so doing, the therapist must determine his response with the same considered thoughtfulness as if he were responding verbally to an equivalent verbal statement. This requires a high degree of ingenuity, flexibility, self-acceptance, and self-awareness, but it can also be the most challenging, pleasing, and rewarding part of working with children.

# *Play as Expression of Conflict*

LYDIA JACKSON
AND KATHLEEN M. TODD

Freud's observation of a young child who played persistently with a toy tied to a string, which he threw out of his cot, then pulled in again, may have been the starting point of a realization that play can have symbolical meaning and be used diagnostically (S. Freud, 1922, p. 13). The throwing-out of the toy was accompanied by the word "Gone!" uttered in a somewhat alarmed, startled fashion, while the pulling in was done with an exclamation of triumph. The obvious comment, of course, would be that play of this type is so common among young children, that to ascribe to it any symbolic meaning is to distort simple reality in order to make it fit complicated, far-fetched theories. This criticism may hold with regard to this type of play in children under one year of age, in whom it is probably no more than a part of a developmental process and who display no emotion in connection with the act of throwing, except satisfaction at having achieved it and impatience when the object is not handed back to them promptly so that they may throw it again. The child observed by Freud, however, was eighteen months old and was known to be subjected to frequent and prolonged absences on the part of his mother; the emotions he displayed as he threw out and pulled in the toy were clearly those of alarm, followed by relief. In these circumstances, it was justifiable to seek for symbolic meaning, which Freud interpreted as a dramatization of the mother's periodic disappearances and subsequent joyful returns. The child was thus using play as a means of getting rid of his inner conflict (of love and fear) by projecting it into action, and as remedy against his anxiety, by reassuring himself with regard to his mother's ultimate return—a pretty illustration of the double aspect of play, diagnostic and curative. . . .

The fact that play is the most natural means of expression for a young child should be so obvious as to scarcely need further elaboration. . . . Its functions are several; . . . we will examine those that are, for therapeutic purposes, the most important.

## *Play as Help to Diagnosis*

We take for granted that a person who is physically ill will behave differently from one who is in good health—his looks also will betray his ill health. A person suffering from nervous illness, however, may show nothing in his outward appearance, but his manner, his whole demeanor, will reveal his mental state to the experienced observer. So it is with the play of a neurotic child; it differs from that of a normal child in many well-defined ways—his approach to toys, his behavior during play, and the emotions which accompany the play all deserve close observation. His play may indicate both the type and extent of his mental disturbance.

Play may be studied both from the point of view of the choice of materials and from the nature and type of the play. Is it lively and freely expressed or oversolemn and inhibited? Is it at a level appropriate to the child's age, or is it immature and babyish, or perhaps oversophisticated and dominated by grown-up standards? One can decide from the type of play whether a child is comparatively normal or disturbed, whether his disturbance is due to over-anxiety, excessive unresolved aggression for which he cannot find an outlet, or to inferiority and guilt which creep even into his play life. A child with obsessional characteristics reveals such qualities in his pattern of play; an excited impulsive child, whose emotions run away with him and who shows a "pressure of talk," will exhibit this same pressure in the tempo and variety of his play, which is characterized as a rule by an admixture of tension, restlessness, and lack of control.

A strong interest in certain play materials is common to both normal and disturbed children. Water, sand, clay or plasticine, hammer, and paints were constantly in demand at the Raleigh school (Boyce, 1938, pp. 31–32).

> Many of them, especially the girls, insisted on water play for weeks at a time. Dishes, wooden utensils, plates, tea sets, and bedclothes all provided excuses to wash.
>
> Water had enormous attraction for them all, not only for washing but for water play without a purpose. They enjoyed just pouring and dabbling. . . .
>
> Sand was never out of use. Castles were made with the purpose of "bashing them down." "Puddly pools" were beloved, and the messier the mixture the more they delighted in it.

These same materials are used in the clinic and, in addition, dolls, dolls' furniture, including beds and cradles, bathroom sets, soldiers, and all the smaller figures which can stand symbolically for members of the family and playmates. The selection and rejection of particular play materials, the choice or refusal of certain types of play are of significance in the diagnosis of the disorder from which the child is suffering.

### *Inhibition*

One of the most striking characteristics of the anxious child is a strong inhibition of play activity; we may find that such a child is unable to play at all. Placed in a room full of toys, he remains tense and rigid, seemingly incapable of touching any of them, or if he touches them, unable to do anything with them. The inhibition of play activity, needless to say, is not always a neurotic symptom; E. R. Boyce (1938) found it in a considerable proportion of her nursery school children, who came from very poor homes and had never had any toys. Yet the very factors which had deprived these children materially may have starved them emotionally as well, causing a degree of superadded neurosis.

### *Destructiveness*

Another characteristic of a neurotic child's play is the absence of constructiveness and the frequent presence of the opposite impulse, sometimes very powerful, an impulse to destroy. This again, within limits, is not abnormal; the same observer (Boyce, 1938, p. 31) remarks that when, at her nursery school, the children were given freedom to do as they liked, "there was at first an exceptional amount of destruction and aggressive behavior." In fact, as might be expected, the same general trends would appear in the play of all children, but certain particular trends would be more intense and persistent in the play of mentally ill children. Destructive and aggressive play is likely to continue indefinitely in a certain type of neurotic child, unless he is helped by the understanding reassurance and sympathy of his therapist. In the normal child there is a spontaneous gradual transition to creative play. . . .

Such spontaneous recovery can take place even in disturbed children . . . if their mental disturbance is not too profound and their feelings of guilt and insecurity not too acute, but recovery will be both more complete and more quickly attained by psychotherapy and, in the young child, preferably by play treatment.

### *Immaturity*

The neurotic child often plays as if he were much younger than he really is. A child of six or seven, for instance, would repeatedly put things in a box and empty them out again or spend a whole hour filling receptacles with sand or water, as a little child of three to four years likes to do, pouring it out and filling up ad infinitum. In this, again, "normal" children, who had been deprived of opportunities for "normal" play, resembled the neurotic. Miss Boyce (1938, pp. 31–32) found that at her school "children of six and seven played the games usually associated with three- and four-year-olds."

Thus, neither the level of play, nor the material the child uses, nor the nature of his play can be taken as a sure indicator of neurosis or normality. Environmental factors—poverty, cramped living conditions, lack of opportunity and toys—may affect the child's play activities in such a way that the resulting picture very closely resembles the behavior produced by mental conflict. Reversion to an earlier level and eagerness to use materials charged with emotional, primitive, symbolic significance—such as sand, clay, water, and fire—are features common to all children whenever freedom in the choice and use of playthings is given them. Yet even when they play alike and with the same things, the differences in play behavior between the "normal" and the mentally disturbed become quickly obvious with practice and experience.

## *Regressive Play*

A normal child, who had never had the opportunity or been allowed to handle earth, or sand and water, would gleefully make sand castles and mud pies at the seaside, and if, in addition, his early training in toilet habits had been overstrict, he might play with these materials with more than usual interest and absorption. A neurotic child, who has had some especially disturbing experiences in connection with toilet training, if given opportunity for playing with sand and water, might be unable to interest himself in other toys or materials for a long period of treatment.

A case in point is that of Lionel W., a child of five, of high average intelligence. Lionel was a rather unusual-looking child, very fair, with large dark-brown eyes and a pale, somewhat pinched little face. His small body was rather overtopped by a large head. He had, however, a charming smile when his sense of humor was aroused, and he certainly had a sense of humor, although his usual expression was rather solemn and gravely watchful. He came from a working-class family and was the younger of two boys. His outstanding symptoms were aggressive and spiteful behavior to other children, but later interviews with the mother brought out some further facts of his early history.

He had been severely rebuked and punished for an interest—common in infants—in the products of his bowels, his mother's reactions being anger, horror, and disgust. This interest, suppressed by the mother, was transferred to water which Lionel drank "wherever he could find it," including the lavatory pan! At school his behavior changed and he developed a spiteful, bullying attitude to other children.

At the clinic, with the exception of a short period of aggressive play and truculence toward the therapist, Lionel occupied himself entirely with water and sand during the whole of every interview lasting for three-quarters of an hour, for a long phase in the early part of his treatment. He showed little curiosity and next to no interest in other toys, a number of which were to be seen lying about the playroom. Occasionally, he would pick up one or two of them, examine them, place them on the table, move them about, but after a few minutes would invariably return to his sand and water play.

He took little notice of the therapist's presence and behaved almost as if she were not there, differing from the "well" child of this age who likes to share his play, at least intermittently.

Regressive play may be expressed not only in the materials used but in the type of play—the child in fantasy takes over the role of others and constitutes herself the mother, the teacher, or the small baby in scenes in which for the moment she lives, disclosing, as she plays, her individual conflict.

Pamela, aged five-and-one-half, was a graceful, attractive little girl, delightful, imaginative, and with a sense of wonder about life. She spoke in a carefully modulated voice with exact phraseology and clear enunciation. She had been excluded from school for destructiveness, tearing up books, hitting and scratching teachers and companions. She could not mix with children of her own age and preferred the company of grownups.

At home, fits of temper began to dominate the scene and Pamela changed from "a little saint" to a difficult small girl. She was an only child of anxious parents who foolishly discussed her upbringing and their differences of policy in her presence. She had had earlier gastrointestinal illnesses with alternating constipation and diarrhea, and habit training had been accompanied with many tears on both the mother's and the child's part.

In her play during treatment, after a phase of very correct, grownup, realistic play in which she was the teacher—cross, intolerant, insisting upon high standards—and the therapist, the child, subjected to autocratic government, her mood changed; she wished no longer to be the master and took over the role of the little baby, dependent, trusting, and affectionate. The high-pitched sharp voice disappeared, the crisp bell-like tones changed to a babyish wheedling note and a long phase of "regressive" play was lived through. She would say, "I'm just a tiny baby at the kicky stage." She lay on the floor, rolling about as an infant does, she made crooning noises, sang to herself, and tried out baby words with missed consonants. She took the therapist's hand and attempted to walk—she liked to be wheeled in a baby chair. It is only when a child has sufficient confidence in her therapist that she can revert in play to an earlier phase of existence as this little girl did; it is a sign of progress in treatment and indicates that the small patient has been forced to expect too much of herself and has been unconsciously imposing adult standards on a mind and personality which are still those of a child. The price of this forced maturity is neurosis; regressive play was one of the many roads to cure.

The destructiveness of the disturbed child differs from the destructive behavior of a normal child not only in degree but also in quality and has a special meaning for the individual child himself. A normal child would break his toys, pluck off heads of flowers, smash sand castles he had built, hammer and bang. He would do all that with some satisfaction, but there is no evidence that he exults over his acts of destruction or is emotionally much aroused by them. Besides, he does not destroy persistently; within a short period, he would turn to constructive or imaginative play: make a tunnel, a bridge, build a house, sail a boat, or take tin soldiers for a drive on a lorry. He would break things up in order to "see what's inside them" or because he is momentarily impatient or at a loss what to do next; often he breaks them experimentally, but hardly ever for the sole purpose of destroying them. If he shows regret at having destroyed them or fear of punishment, these emotions are not exaggerated out of all proportion to the magnitude of the loss or of the transgression.

The neurotic child, if destructive, tends to destroy extensively and gets caught up in his urge to destroy, seemingly unable to stop or to control it, or he may show no surface emotion in connection with his behavior, but underneath this apparent indifference there is evidence of strong feelings of guilt and fear expressed in tension, overexcitement, and sometimes rapid fatigue in play.

Pamela frequently expressed this off and on in her treatment. Whenever she scolded the therapist in the teacher–child play, although outwardly in command of the situation, she shivered, stretched herself, and would flush and pale alternately. She described these "attacks" as "my excitements" and herself volunteered that they were of two kinds, nice and nasty; the young child cannot verbalize his feelings accurately but this could hardly have been more clearly put. All adults know these two feelings—one a pleasurable excitement, the other an unpleasant state of tension, a borderline awareness of excitement spilling over readily into anxiety or apprehension. It was not until she was free of this apprehension and sense of danger that she could allow herself to destroy in play and, later on, to construct in keeping with her age and intelligence.

Often, however, the neurotic child destroys in order to test his parents' or the therapist's forbearance, not to see how far he may go, but as an appeal for help from an adult, as if to say, "How can I deal with my disorderly and frightening impulses?"; or he may be asking for punishment which serves a double purpose: of allaying his feelings of guilt and of assuring himself that retribution is not as dreadful as he had feared it might be. One boy remarked, "You ought to punish me when I am angry, my mother always does; I like it better if I'm smacked when I'm naughty," with a look at the therapist which was at the same time appealing and anxious. Needless to say, often both these motives underlie the behavior of the same child. . . .

To summarize, a child who regresses to the level of play characteristic of a much younger child and remains for a long time on that level, a child who attacks or destroys persistently with concealed signs of emotion or with a display of real wildness in destruction, and a child who cannot play at all reveal by their behavior that something in their mental development is seriously wrong.

The character of the play itself may, in addition, indicate the type of mental disturbance and give some clue to the conflict which lies behind it. Several examples follow.

### *Obsessional Play*

We all know the type of adult whose life is ordered by routine, who plans his day and allows nothing to disturb this plan: the meticulously clean housewife to whom order comes before comfort, the business man who is more interested in his card index than in the needs of his firm. Young children with these characteristics in the making avoid "dirty" or messy play; they look anxiously for soap and water when sand play is suggested; they arrange toys in neat patterns, for example, half a dozen carefully fenced-in fields, each containing one father, one mother, and one baby animal. They dislike painting, and their drawings are dominated by the ruler, compass, and rubber. They may play silently or keep up a chatter of polite conventional conversation which acts as a screen to hide their deeper and truer feelings. Excessive fixity or rigidity is sometimes characteristic of their play behavior. Such a child seems unable to leave off playing with the same toys or repeating the same pattern of play. He may spend the whole interview making sand castles and destroying them or mixing sand and water and putting it on plates; and he may return to these toys and these activities for many interviews on end.

Fantasy is sedulously avoided by such children at the beginning of treatment; they often look longingly at the doll's house and the family of dolls, then pass a remark that, of course, only small children play with these. One little boy of five told his therapist that he liked playing with dolls but "only when he was a child!"

### *Scatterbrain Play*

The child who is temperamentally unstable tends to go to the other extreme and within the first quarter of an hour during an interview may handle practically every toy in the playroom and initiate half a dozen games. He will start this game or that only to drop it a couple of minutes later; he is constantly besieged by new ideas, but never carrying them through, beginning, but never finishing.

Alfred, age eight, was referred to the clinic for being "beyond control," restless, jumpy, unable to concentrate, and domineering with other children. Here is a typical interview at the beginning of his treatment.

> All over the playroom all the time, talking and acting without a moment of indecision or repose. Shot sticks from a gun at first. On hearing voices outside, went toward the door to shoot at a worker outside. Got out all the tea things. Minced some clay for sugar and tea. Made tea and selected the best cup for the therapist. Drank some clayey water despite warning. Pretended he was a cowboy and was going "murdering"; then said he was shooting rabbits. Said he loved school and his teacher was the best teacher in the world. Showed the therapist a purse he had knitted for his brother. Tried to shoot down a pile of bricks which would not collapse. Resisted leaving the playroom; knocked the bricks down violently with the butt of the gun, rushed to the crockery, and was about to sweep it off into a pail of sandy water. Had to be escorted to his mother in the waiting room.

Such play is characteristic of unstable children, but also of children in an acute state of anxiety. In the unstable it inclines to be more incoherent and purposeless. If a child is unstable and at the same time anxious, he may need to go on playing in this haphazard fashion for some time before he can be helped to attain greater security and a relief from inner conflict. The change becomes evident in his capacity to settle down to more coherent and creative play. In the case just described, the boy had attended the clinic for several weeks before he was able to concentrate on anything for any length of time, but finally, on his own initiative, he would spend a consecutive half-hour on painting a picture or writing a letter to his father in the Forces.

## *Hyperactive Play*

A similar type of play which is always accompanied by excessive and pent-up excitement can be described as "manic." The excitement tends to increase as the play goes on, until the child will be on the point of losing control altogether. He may start by making "a nice picture" in bright colors, then continue by mixing more and more colors, piling them on top of one another, splashing them over the table, and finally spreading paint all around him. Or he may begin by building "a fine high tower," using up all the bricks he can find, then add anything he can lay his hands on, until the whole edifice threatens to collapse, and still he would go on adding and piling up. All this would be done with tremendous gusto, with laughter, squeals, and excited noises, but little realization of the possible consequences of his actions. It is at this point that the therapist brings her experience to bear in helping the child to understand his high-pressure impulses and the compulsive drive behind them. . . .

# Diagnostic and Therapeutic Considerations of Nonverbal Projective Activities with Children

ADOLF G. WOLTMANN

I would like to begin with a clarification of the title of this paper. Consideration of nonverbal projective activities in children implies that such considerations can also be applied to adults. We commonly regard psychoanalysis as a verbal method which utilizes "free association." Yet, the observant analyst will detect numerous manifestations of a nonverbal nature such as involuntary movements of arms or legs, shifting of body position, blushing, periods of silence accompanied by heavy breathing and perhaps profuse sweating, and so on. These body reactions are definite nonverbal expressions for which the mind either has no language or which the mind tries to repress. This paper is not concerned about such nonverbal expressions in children.

We live in a language-centered culture, yet we use many nonverbal means of expression. A wave of the hand may express a welcome or a "good-by." A handshake or a pat on the shoulder may denote more of an empathy with sorrow than words could possibly convey. The orchestra conductor uses his hands, so does a traffic policeman. A shrug of the shoulder brings across a message of "not knowing" or "not having" more comprehensively than a verbal reply.

This paper does not deal with such nonverbal expressions. Instead, an attempt is made to examine those nonverbal modes of representation through which we can understand a child's thinking and feeling. Naturally, not all nonverbal activities of children contain meaningful self references. We are concerned here primarily with those nonverbal communications where the child substitutes lines, form, color, and activity or play patterns for the spoken word. We call this "projection." Projection, in the definition of Lawrence Frank (1948), takes place when a person reacts to a stimulus not the way he is expected to react but by endowing his response with his own idiosyncrasies. Frank stated that each individual lives in his own "private world." This private world is not apart from reality, but rather is each person's own perception of himself and the world around him, the physical environment as well as his social and cultural world, as he has learned and felt about it.

The title of this paper mentions "children." "Childhood" covers a period of ten or twelve years. It is not a homogenous designation. The private world mentioned above differs from child to child and changes from year to year. The newborn infant has no language, no motor control, and no locomotion. These essentials have to be learned through cycles of maturation. The three-year-old child, for instance, perceives and reacts to the world differently than does a six-year-old or a ten-year-old child. In order to properly evaluate nonverbal projective activities of children, one must keep in mind two factors: (1) Children do not express themselves in terms of cultural or social stereotypes, but endow their activities with their own idiosyncratic meanings. (2) Children do not perceive and react alike. Their ability to express themselves verbally and nonverbally depends on maturational factors.

Something else has to be considered. Many of the child's nonverbal activities are his mode of expression, his special language through which he communicates. Instead of using vocabulary, grammar, and syntax, the child uses lines, forms, color, movement, acoustics, selection of play patterns, intensity and duration of play patterns, groupings, repetitions, and many other modes of expression, depending on his maturational growth. They are the media through which the child brings to tangible levels his ideas, concepts, modes of action, perceptions, and levels of understanding, as well as his fears, his anxieties, and also his reaching-out for love and acceptance. In order to properly evaluate these various means of communication, one must learn to decipher and to understand this "nonverbal language" of children.

Different nonverbal activities yield different data. Therefore, before embarking on diagnostic and therapeutic inferences, a few words are in order to consider certain basic characteristics of nonverbal activities of children. When a child wants to draw a picture, he is given only the tools such as pencils, crayons, charcoal, paint, and brushes and the materials such as paper, canvas, or a blackboard on which his graphic communication can unfold. Provided we deal with a spontaneous activity, the child is not told what to draw or to paint. He is free to express through lines and color whatever he wants. The only limitations he runs into are those imposed by his motor maturation, his intellectual, social, and emotional growth. He is not bothered by reality limits such as the law of gravity. He can draw objects suspended in mid-air. Graphic art gives the child the widest possible opportunity to express himself nonverbally.

When the child handles plastic materials such as mud, clay, play-dough, or plasticine, he adds a three-dimensional value to his creation. Again, he is given only the tools, the plastic matter. Here the plastic material becomes at once the tool and the carrier of a meaning, in contrast to graphic art where the tools and the agent on which to draw are necessary for the final product. Again it is up to the child to create whatever he wants. On the one hand, plastic material has the advantage of not presenting problems in perspective because it is three-dimensional and can be viewed from all sides. On the other hand, it also represents a serious drawback. Plastic material is physical matter and as such subject to the laws of gravity. Clay cannot be suspended in mid-air. It falls down. What both graphic and plastic art have in common is the fact that only the tools are given to the child. He selects whatever he wants to communicate through lines, color, and form.

Blocks are somewhat halfway between unstructured and structured material. They are structured because they have geometrical shapes. They are unstructured because the block per se does not represent anything. It takes several blocks in order to build something. Whereas anything can be portrayed in graphic arts and where in plastic arts only physical laws may interfere, in block play elements of length, width, and height, of support and balance enter. Blocks impose a minimum of reality elements and are sufficiently unstructured to allow for the expression of a wide variety of configurations.

When toys are offered to the child the mode of communication changes. Toys are structured miniature representations of reality objects. There is nothing for the child to create. A tree is a tree, a soldier is a soldier, and a car is a car. This fact alone imposes serious limitations. A girl cannot play "house" when only toys such as soldiers, cannons, airplanes, and cars are available. The boy cannot play "cowboys and Indians" with only doll-house furniture and dolls at his disposal. In order to serve as projective nonverbal communications, other modes of expression have to be used. These nonverbal activities utilize selection of toys, their groupings and movements or absence of movements. Other equally important aspects have to do with the intensity and duration of play patterns. Elements of construction, destruction, and repetition also play a vital role. I mention only some of the more important elements of toy play to point out that nonverbal aspects of such activities are as equally important for a full understanding as may be the child's verbalizations about his creation.

Puppets occupy a special place in the play activities of children. Since they represent people, animals, and fantasy figures, they are structured. Like clay, blocks, and toys, they constitute real objects and are subject to the law of gravity. Like toys, they portray specific characters. This imposes limitations, because a child cannot let a puppet crocodile attack other puppets if there is no puppet crocodile available. Furthermore, the specific characteristic of each puppet calls for specific actions. This can also be a limitation. Whereas in toy play a child may utilize the whole room for his performance, puppet play is usually limited to the confines of the stage. Yet, in spite of these restrictions, which are more stringent than those for toy play, puppet play makes possible the interchange of reality and fantasy worlds by using "make-believe" characters like the witch or the devil. Puppet play is a mixture of nonverbal activity and verbalization. It is not an exclusive activity for children like the other nonverbal modes of action, because an adult may perform a puppet show for a group of children.

After this brief survey of some of the basic characteristics of the child's nonverbal modes of projection, let us now consider their diagnostic and therapeutic aspects.

The psychoanalyst listens to the patient's free associations with the "third ear." The child therapist, whether he looks at a child's drawing, plastic creation, block or toy play, has to develop the "third eye" in order to bring his understanding into proper focus. These basic considerations also allow us to deduce that the less structured a nonverbal activity is, the greater are the potentials for projective communication.

Once the therapist has mastered the real meaning of the child's nonverbal language, he can then use it both diagnostically and therapeutically. It is not always easy to draw a rigid line between diagnosis and therapy. Often, both are closely interwoven. For practical purposes we might call a diagnostic clue any information gained from a child's activity when such knowledge is obtained while trying to get a comprehensive picture of a child's personality. For example, as part of a test battery the child might be asked to draw a human figure. If the child produces a small figure that covers about one-tenth of the sheet of paper, he usually communicates to us his own feeling of smallness, or perhaps his fear of being overwhelmed by the large world, or his fear of reaching-out, or his sense of nothingness, of not being important or worthwhile. He may feel this way but he has no verbal language to say it. He projects his feelings into what he draws because he, like all of us, expresses not what he sees, but rather what he knows and feels. The smallness of the figure drawing then becomes a diagnostic clue that adds to our knowledge about the child.

Diagnostic testing is a sampling of bits of information which are combined into a personality composite. This is a comparatively brief process. Therapy, on the other hand, is a learning process aimed at the uncovering of hidden springs of motivation. This takes time. Some patterns may have to be discarded and replaced by more wholesome ones. Other patterns may have to be strengthened. Since the child, especially the younger one, does not have fully developed language facilities at his command and since he may not have verbal expressions for his emotional involvements, these nonverbal modes of expressions are the means through which he tells us something.

I have to insert a word of caution here. All children, at one time or another, draw pictures, work with clay, play with blocks and toys. These activities, among others, are the child's natural mode of expression. If a child engages in any of these activities, this does not mean that the child has problems and communicates to us his plea for help. On the contrary, through the microcosm of these various nonverbal activities the child learns to handle and to master the macrocosm of the grownup world, using Erikson's (1937) terms. These activities become important only when we want to gain a better understanding of the child's world and allow the child to communicate with us by letting him use those media best suited for such a sharing. But unless we can look at these activities with a "third eye," we will miss many and important clues.

Something else applies here. Not all children perform equally well on all of these nonverbal projective activities. Some children may engage in elaborate play patterns and do hardly anything with clay or with crayons. I do not regard this as a diagnostic sign. The fact that a musician plays a horn or drum instead of the first violin does not make him a less skilled member of a symphony orchestra.

Drawings of children have been studied, analyzed, and described by Machover (1949, 1951), Hammer (1958), and others. Therefore, no attempt toward further elaboration is made here.

What diagnostic clues can be gained by watching children handle plastic material? The younger child, below the age of five years, does not create reality objects, because his motor apparatus has not sufficiently developed to allow for fine and coordinated hand and finger movement. His handling of clay is primarily an experimental approach. He soon discovers that clay can be divided into small parts which then can be put together again. He learns that clay can be squeezed, hit, stepped on, bitten into, and thrown. Clay can become a substitute for aggressive outlets. It can also become a very primitive agent for developing social ties: children may enjoy the same activity, or they may admire or perhaps reject the actions of a single child. We readily accept this kind of handling in the preschool child, but when an older child, instead of creating something out of clay, just handles it, one may assume that such a child either is seriously mentally retarded or is exhibiting an autistic withdrawal from reality. Now and then, one runs into children who absolutely refuse to play with plastic material. These children are also prone to reject finger painting as being "too messy." These children usually come from homes where cleanliness is at a premium. To force such children into handling clay or using finger paints will merely produce in the child the conflicts between obeying and defying maternal authority. It is best if one lets such children select other, "cleaner" activities. These children often play with blocks because blocks are clean, do not dirty the child's hands and clothes, and they do not bring the child into conflict with parental standards about things clean and dirty.

The drawing produces a two-dimensional picture. For instance, if the child draws a human figure he can portray only one dimension, either a front view or a profile picture. How does such a person look from the back, from above, or from below? Different views of the same figure call for additional drawings. Furthermore, the picture of a man standing cannot be changed into a person walking or sitting, without destroying the original drawing by erasing and redrawing it. These problems do not exist when a child creates a man out of clay. The clay man can be seen from all sides. Pressure of the hand can change a standing posture into a sitting position. Plastic material, therefore, is an excellent medium through which body images and body ideologies can be studied and experimented with by the child. I have seen a clay man with six testicles or an anus which stretched from the hips to the neck. I have seen clay figures with big heads and small bodies and vice versa. Reddish brown plasticine may easily uncover anal problems. Problems centering around elimination can also be elicited through the use of finger painting. In therapy, the child utilizes plastic material to create situations which, in their configurations and spatial relationships, are much more comprehensive than the spoken word. Examples of such plastic creations are reported by Woltmann (1950).

Important diagnostic clues can be gained from watching children using blocks. A child may be a "lone wolf" when he builds alone or keeps all the blocks to himself. The young child who has not been properly weaned from mother's apron strings may build a cubicle in which he can hide and avoid contact with children around him. Covered-up aggression is evidenced when a child continuously knocks down structures built by other children. Overt aggression is recognized when the child uses blocks as weapons, either to attack other children or the teacher or as a means of defense. Additional factors inherent in block play by children are described by Hartley, Frank, and Goldenson (1952).

What can we learn about the child when he plays with toys? It is customary to divide toy play into large groups. A doll-house play is eminently suited for the exploration of family ideologies and family constellations. The use of environmental toys such as houses, trees, cars, airplanes, people and animals, etc. directs the child's attention toward the environment. Family set-ups and community configurations are produced alike by both boys and girls. The fact that a boy plays with girls' toys and vice versa, in and by itself, is not a diagnostic sign. Only when there are endless repetitions of the same play content, then such an activity becomes significant both diagnostically as well as therapeutically. The grouping of toys in itself can reveal important diagnostic clues. Schizophrenic children may not always create play patterns. Toy houses may be piled on top of each other, and the final creation might be labeled "a house." Or such children may line up toys in rows, disregarding the individual characteristics of each toy so that, for example, a bed, a car, a chair, a stove, a tree, and a horse form a line. An obsessive-compulsive child may spend a whole hour setting up toys in rigid geometric patterns, moving a toy here and removing one there until all the toys are placed in such a way that no matter from where the child views his creation, they form straight lines like a group of soldiers on a parade field. These children do not play by letting the toys interact with each other. They resist any attempt on the part of the therapist to change the pattern. Other children will build very good play set-ups, but refuse to introduce movement and action into their play. These are the children who very often impress one as being shy, inhibited, and afraid of expressing aggression. They want to please. It is almost as if these children, through their neat play patterns, want to show that they are "good" children who do not attack and who do not mess around.

Some children are confused about living patterns. Years ago I worked with a seven-year-old boy who lived with his mother in a loft building. There was no father because the parents were divorced when the boy was an infant.

The huge loft had no separate rooms; only curtains fenced off the various compartments. This boy built a house where the kitchen, the bathroom, and the living room were all in the same enclosure. The bedroom was placed on the second floor with street traffic going right through it. As a compensation, this boy had acquired a tremendous amount of information about outer space of the science fiction type. In his fantasies he was living "out of this world," because the reality of day-by-day living was too unsatisfactory and confusing, especially since his mother did not allow him to play with other children after school hours.

In talking about therapeutic considerations of toy play, I am here primarily concerned with the nonverbal aspects of projection. The verbalizations of the child, of course, are important, but the therapist should not overlook the fact that nonverbal patterns are also a kind of language through which the child communicates. Therapists are adults and as such geared to the word-centeredness of our culture. They look at play patterns, or for that reason, at all activities of children, from the adult point of view and evaluate accordingly. The adult is not always aware of the fact that the nonverbal projective activities are a part of the child's pattern of communication, supplementing the spoken word.

The utilization of such nonverbal projective activities in therapy will be illustrated by a few examples.

Billy, an eight-year-old intelligent boy, was referred for therapy because he was regarded as being a bully, frequently beating up his five-year-old brother, and as being aggressive toward mother, grandmother, teachers, and school children. I soon learned that his mother and grandmother ran the house. The father was meek and passive. The mother openly preferred the younger boy and punished my patient severely for small misdeeds. When Billy first came for therapy, he greeted me with a sullen, hostile look and refused to talk. He kicked several of the toys with his foot and made it quite clear that he did not want to be bothered. The first therapy session was more-or-less spent in silence. When he returned the second time, he dumped all the toys on the floor, watching me very carefully out of the corner of his eye. When I did not react, he turned to the toys, selected a jeep, and then proceeded to ram this jeep through the pile of toys, sending them flying in all directions. After all the toys were "run over" and scattered throughout the room, he silently collected them, put them again into a huge pile in the middle of the room and started his play all over again. This went on for ten sessions. In the beginning, I made a few feeble attempts to become part of his play activity, but he pushed me aside and made it clear through gestures that he did not want to be disturbed. I watched silently. At the start of the eleventh session he told me that the jeep was without a driver and that he, Billy, was moving it by remote control. The pile of toys represented the world. The jeep, at Billy's command, was destroying the world, thus giving Billy an elated feeling of mastery and power. After he talked to me, his play activities changed. He created villages, engaged in war games, and he also played with the doll-house set-up. He responded well to therapy and was discharged five months later.

Billy felt hemmed in, sat upon, and misunderstood. His weak father was of no help to him and his mother clearly rejected him. Billy felt that he was beset by hostile forces against which he had to defend himself as best he could. He had no verbal language for expressing his conflicting feelings toward a hostile world. He projected his emotional reactions into a nonverbal activity. This enabled him to successfully defy the hostile world and to achieve a satisfactory solution where he had the upper hand. Only after he had experienced these repeated mass destructions and consequent victorious conquests, did he become ready for therapy.

Henry came to me at the age of seven. His parents were separated. Henry lived in town with his father, while his nine-year-old sister stayed with the mother in the country. The boy was placed in a private school, but after a few weeks the school refused to keep him because Henry was too aggressive and destructive. Both parents bitterly accused and blamed each other for the failure of their marriage, using vile language. Henry's toy play was full of aggression and destruction. One day Henry, using blocks, made a river boat. He placed toy soldiers on this boat and pushed it around the room, making believe that the soldiers were looking for Indians. Suddenly he turned around half of the soldiers so that they were facing the other soldiers and said, "Look now, they are shooting at each other." I replied quietly, "That's exactly what is going on in your family. Like the soldiers, you all are in the same boat, and you should belong together; instead, fighting is going on." Henry nodded his head. He had understood.

From then on it was comparatively easy to work through the feelings he had for his parents and sister. Whereas formerly he had only repeated what he had heard, he now was able to express, in words and play, his own feelings.

Charles, a six-year-old boy, was referred to me because he was suffering from nocturnal choking spells. A thorough medical examination had been negative for physical causes, and the mother was advised to place her son in therapy. Charles' parents were divorced. His father remained in the Middle West while Charles, with his mother and younger sister, came to live in New York. The mother remarried, giving these two children a most perceptive, sensitive, and loving stepfather.

Right from the beginning Charles played beautifully with an American Revolutionary War toy set, containing American and British soldiers, Indians, rocks, trees, and houses. He never spoke much while playing, but built elaborate play patterns and engaged his toys in lively warfare. I had asked Charles in the beginning about sleep disturbances, but when he vehemently denied having choking attacks, I dropped the matter. After two months of intensive play activities Charles built a road, lined on both sides with rocks and trees. One end of the road was open while the other end was closed off with rocks and trees. American soldiers and Indians were placed behind the trees and rocks. A contingent of British soldiers marched along the road. Charles said, "They [British] don't know it, but soon they find that the road is closed, and then the

Americans and Indians will come out and fight, and the British will fight back and there will be a great battle." When I asked, "Who will win?" Charles shrugged his shoulders and said, "I don't know." I then explained to him that his play pattern demonstrated what goes on inside the body. The road was like the windpipe. Thoughts want to come out through the mouth but other thoughts do not want these thoughts to escape, so they fight with each other, just as the Americans and British were about to fight in his play. While conflicting thoughts fight with each other, the windpipe and the mouth become tense, breathing becomes heavy and irregular, and the person has choking spells. Charles listened silently, as if in a trance. Then he began to talk so fast that the words gushed from his mouth. He readily admitted that he would long for his real father and then feel guilty because his stepfather was so kind and good to him. He also wanted mother to stay with him instead of being with his stepfather and again he would feel guilty toward his kind and loving stepfather. The choking spells disappeared, and Charles was discharged shortly after this session.

The diagnostic and therapeutic clues to be observed in puppet play have been described by Woltmann and are therefore not elucidated here (1951, 1955, 1960).

In summing up, the following points are briefly restated: (1) Nonverbal projective activities are the child's special language where lines, forms, color, grouping, action, repetition, intensity, and duration take the place of vocabulary, grammar, and syntax. (2) The less structured a nonverbal projective activity is, the greater are the potentials for projective communication. (3) Children do not handle all nonverbal projections with the same degree of skill. (4) Effective use of nonverbal projective activities depends on developmental cycles pertaining to motor maturation, intellectual, social, and emotional growth. (5) Each nonverbal projective activity has its own advantages and limitations.

Hope is expressed that nonverbal projective activities will be included more and more in the diagnostic and therapeutic appraisal of children.

## *The Use of Food in Therapy*

MARY R. HAWORTH
AND MARY JANE KELLER

The use of food in the playroom has not been widely discussed in reports of play therapy. Most well equipped playrooms probably provide baby bottles for regressive play, but this discussion refers to cookies (such as vanilla wafers) or hard candies which are made available to the child. Occasionally, real milk has been provided in the baby bottles for autistic children and for others known to have suffered severe infantile deprivations. Ice cream or cokes are especially liked by preadolescents. Children respond in a variety of ways to these oral supplies. The child's eagerness for treats or his refusal of them are pertinent aspects for therapeutic handling, while his spontaneous offer to share the food with his therapist adds yet another dimension.

The present authors have elsewhere reviewed (Haworth and Keller, 1962) the literature on the symbolic meanings attached to food and eating, as well as the significance of various types of reactions to food in the diagnostic setting and in psychotherapy.

The early association of pleasant experiences surrounding food and feeding with feelings of love, comfort, and security has been frequently pointed out in the psychoanalytic literature. Therapists such as Sechehaye (1951, 1956), Federn (1952), Rosen (1953), and Schwing (1954) have reported the introduction of feeding situations as a vital part of therapy with seriously disturbed adult patients in an attempt to re-create the initial mother–child relationship and to work through early affectional deprivations.

Probably the earliest report of the use of food in therapy with children is to be found in Slavson's (1943) descriptions of therapy sessions with groups of boys. He points out rather definite stages in the boys' attitudes to the snack times which were provided toward the close of each session. First there was a stage of shyness and tentative holding back, then overreactions of horseplay and messiness, until finally the refreshment period became a time for relaxation and mutual social interchange.

Reports of therapy with young autistic children, such as Waal (1955) and Alpert (1959), describe the child's reactions when food has been offered. These may include gorging on the food or hoarding of crumbs and pieces, as well as leading to further exploration of his own, and the therapist's, mouth and teeth. Kaufman *et al.* (1957) briefly discuss the values inherent in the use of food with the psychotic child as a means of building up the ability to accept gratification and of reassuring the child that his oral needs are not dangerous.

Only quite recently has the meaning of the patient's offer of food to the therapist been treated at any length. In a paper by Anthony (1961) and its discussion by Kramer (1961), two opposing theories are proposed to explain the meaning of this act. In discussing his analysis of an eighteen-year-old girl, Anthony describes her bringing him a cookie which she had baked, and at the end of each hour she would take it home, only to bring it back the next day. " . . . Both in real life and in her dreams, she was haunted by the anxiety that what she offered would prove unacceptable. If I ate what she produced, it would be proof that I was accepting her since I would be assimilating her products. Something from her would have gotten right inside me" (Anthony, 1961, p. 213). Kramer (1961, p. 249) presents an alternate hypothesis: "I wonder, though, whether the act of feeding the analyst is not also an attempt to . . . assert a degree of independence from him." Kramer proceeds to describe the usual infant's attempts to stuff food into his mother's mouth and interprets such behavior "as one of the earliest efforts at establishing the child's identity separate from his mother. There is a display of purposeful activity where only passivity was present before." He suggests that Anthony's patient was demonstrating "both the wish to merge with him and the wish to become free and 'grow up.'"

The material to be presented here represents the authors' experiences in work with neurotic children. The general types of reactions these children exhibit toward food will be discussed, as well as a more detailed description of food behavior from one child's therapy.

In providing food for the child the therapist is, in effect, presenting herself as the all-giving, good and nurturant parent. But the child may experience such a situation as very threatening, since it may dramatize his conflict between wanting to receive such nurturance and his feeling that this food is somehow forbidden or potentially dangerous. It may be too difficult an act to spontaneously reach out to take a bite of food in the presence of an adult. If the therapist points out the availability of the food or specifically offers it to the child, he may withdraw even more. The therapist's exact role, beyond making certain that the cookies are at hand for each session, cannot be specified in advance, but must be adapted to the child's idiosyncratic reactions to the situation.

While he may not refuse a bite outright, the child may take only one, and this when the therapist's back is turned. Even then, he may not eat it, but slip it into his pocket. Guilt and shame reactions, as well as fearfulness, may have become associated with the child's earlier experiences with food, and these will be reflected in his present pattern of denial and inhibition. Negative feelings related to infantile oral deprivations may now be transferred from the mother to the therapist and become manifest in this tangible eating situation.

As children come to feel more at ease in the playroom, they may help themselves more openly to the contents of the cookie jar, but they are apt to want to wrap the cookies in a paper towel to take with them when they leave. As therapy progresses in all areas, changes will also be noticed in such secretive food reactions. The child will gradually take more than one piece, eat these in front of the therapist, and count out fewer to take home. When the constricted child spontaneously offers cookies to his therapist at the same time that he is eating freely and with enjoyment, definite gains in other aspects of therapy as well can probably be observed.

Suspicious, paranoid children may have fantasies that the food is bad, or dirty, or poisonous.[a] They may refuse food for long periods of time. When they do finally "give in," they have been observed to hold a cookie between their teeth for several seconds before chewing it. One boy, who was sensitive to being watched, would close his eyes as he reached for the cookie jar.

---

[a] Rosen (1953) relates poison fantasies to infantile reactions to the "perverse mother" who was not attuned to her child and failed to meet his oral needs.

In contrast to the inhibited child, others, who still bear sensitive scars of earlier deprivations, are apt to gorge themselves with cookies or candies, at first seeming to never get enough. They will notice at once if the jar is not in its accustomed place and be in near panic until it is produced. As they gradually come to feel secure and satisfied, if not actually satiated, the number of cookies wil be reduced and the sense of urgency toned down to reasonable proportions. Again, after many weeks, such a child may suddenly wish to share his treasure with his therapist .

Once the initial reactions to the food have been worked through, regressive feeding behaviors are often observed. The child may pretend to be a baby and ask the therapist to feed him, piece by piece. Others will take a handful of cookies to a play shelf, crawl up in a fetal position, possibly covering the opening with a blanket or towel, and "indulge" in cozy solitude. Food has also been noted to serve a comforting role as the child progresses to more normal functioning. One ten-year-old boy engaged in many target shooting contests with his therapist and always took a cookie whenever he lost a bout. Children who may not ordinarily take cookies have been observed to do so the last session before a vacation period.

Aggressive reactions toward food also occur, sometimes as an initial behavior, but always as an expression of hostility. Rather than eating the cookies, the child may crush them to bits or throw them across the room. This may represent an aggressive act directed toward the therapist and her "gift," or reluctance to admit to strong oral hungers, or a form of self-punishment and denial. One boy offered a cookie to his therapist after first concealing a thumbtack in the bottom of it. Other children have shot at the cookie jar with water pistols, with or without first making sure the lid was tightly in place. A quite hostile and jealous youngster emptied the cookie jar each week so there would be none left for "the other children who come here." Diminution of such aggressive acts with time, along with an increase in pleasurable eating, represent indications of therapeutic gains.

One further behavior frequently noted pertains to parental reactions. Once they are aware that their children are being given food, some mothers have developed a routine of stopping on the way to the therapy session, to buy the child a coke or ice cream cone, thus beating the therapist at his own game! A healthier reaction was noted in one case when, after six months of therapy and when real gains were becoming evident in all areas, the child announced that his mother had started buying him a treat on their way home from their concurrent sessions.

Some procedural aspects should be pointed out with respect to the use of food in the therapy hour. It is important to determine whether the child has any allergies that would prevent his being able to eat certain foods. It does not seem sufficient to merely have the food available. To be therapeutic one should verbalize the permissiveness of the situation and stress over and over again, "How nice it is to be able to have all the cookies you want" or "It feels good to be able to have them all," etc. In this connection, the number of cookies in the jar becomes quite important. Some therapists feel they can demonstrate their all-givingness best by filling the jar but, ironically, this makes it practically impossible for the child to eat them all and so to experience the joy that comes with feeling they can *all* be his. On the other hand, too few cookies may be regarded as niggardliness on the part of the therapist in spite of his protestations of magnanimity.

It should go without saying that as the various meanings of food to the child and his reactions to the situation become evident, the therapist should reflect and/or interpret as he would in any other play situation.

The therapist wisely lets the child set the pace as to when he offers cookies to the therapist and how many he wishes to share. As discussed earlier, Kramer (1961) points out the possible dual aspects of such offerings—either the desire to be incorporated by the therapist or a demonstration of separateness and independence. The latter explanation has seemed more relevant in the authors' experience. When children reach this "giving" stage it seems to represent a real milestone; it is as if they have achieved a new maturity in now being able to give, where formerly they have been preoccupied with receiving. The therapist is then viewed in a new perspective, as an individual in her own right, rather than just a familiar fixture in the playroom.

Excerpts from the therapy of a seven-year-old boy have been selected to demonstrate many of the symbolic and supportive uses to which cookies were put during a year and one-half of therapy.

During the first session, Billy did not appear to notice the cookies until time to leave. He then asked if he could "have a few" and took two, saying, "Two is a few." Halfway through the second session he ate one cookie. Later in this hour, he sucked water out of two bottles at once and said, "These are the mother's." In the next four sessions he continued taking only one or two cookies, while his play themes during this time were concerned with symbolic birth fantasies and much interest in sucking activities.

In the seventh session he displayed more anxiety than usual and played out various representations of his guilt and fears concerned with looking and seeing. He accompanied these activities with constant eating of cookies and also offered one to the therapist for the first time.

In the ninth session he drew several pictures of "statues of eagles." At one point he got up to get a cookie, but, due to an oversight, none were available that day. He said he really didn't mind since he hadn't gotten used to them, and so he didn't miss them. Later in this same hour he reported the following dream:

> He had shot a mother eagle and brought back the babies—they were almost starved to death; he had fed the babies and sold the mother for a lot of money.

When the therapist suggested that the babies were starving because the mother had not fed them or taken good care of them, he denied this vigorously and blamed it on himself (in the dream) for shooting the mother bird.

(While he can immobilize the depriving mother eagle in his drawings and shoot her in his dream-fantasy, on the conscious level he must stoically deny his oral needs and take the blame for the infants being deprived.)

Sessions ten to fourteen were occupied with activities symbolically representing comparison of size, strength, and virility in phallic rivalry with his father. It is interesting to note that he did not eat any cookies in these sessions.

The next twelve sessions were marked by much oral emphasis as he struggled with his fears of eating and his desires to be fed. First he set up situations in which he would beg for toys and objects which he knew the therapist could not let him have, thus putting her in the role of the depriving mother. In the following session, he mixed plaster-of-Paris with water to form a thin milky substance which he poured into the baby bottles to "fool the baby." Then he fashioned three oral receptacles out of clay—a canteen bottle, a cup, and a bowl. He saw the cookie jar and announced he was "going to eat cookies today." He held his first one in his teeth a long time before chewing it, while he drew a target and shot at darts. Once he started eating, he made repeated trips, finally asking the therapist to bring the jar over to him and hold it for him. His desire to be given *all* he wanted, especially of food, was repeatedly pointed out. He made quite a point of leaving two cookies in the jar and said he'd get sick if he ate them. The therapist remarked that he seemed to be afraid that something bad might happen if he took all he wanted of anything. He immediately became unusually spontaneous and quite daring in his play, as if a great load had been removed.

The following session Billy took the cookie jar to his play area and ate many of them. He offered one to the therapist, but refused to accept any that she offered to him, preferring to pick out his own. He commented he was saving the *last* cookie for her and again she reflected that he didn't ever seem to want the last ones, that maybe he felt it's bad to take all he wants, or that he might get sick, or something bad might happen to him. Toward the end of this session he had been mixing red paint with sand, then he suddenly darted to the shelf for two small bottles. He filled them with red and green paint and specified that these were "poison" for the therapist. (The paranoid attitude to food is clearly evident with the fear of getting sick and so not taking *all* of the food; then he expresses the wish to poison the agent of his food deprivations—the mother-therapist—by first giving her the last, bad cookies and then by mixing up a concoction for her which he labels directly as "poison.")

The next session he inspected the cookie jar at once and said, "Oh, you got a lot because you knew I was coming." He ate many as he played and once the therapist put one up to his mouth which he opened so wide that he engulfed the whole cookie and managed to suck momentarily on her fingers. (Only after having "poisoned" the therapist can he let himself actually be fed by her.) He avoided further opportunities to be fed, kept the jar close and helped himself often, and again made a point of giving the last cookie to the therapist. He denied her reflection of his fears about eating or taking all of anything.

The following five or six sessions were marked by much regressive play with sand and finger paints, accompanied by baby talk and gross eating of cookies. He would stuff several in his mouth at a time, completely emptying the jar and often getting still more from the supply box. At the close of one of these sessions he took two cookies with him "for me and mama." Another time he set up a "tea party" of cookies and water, giving the therapist more cookies than himself because he wanted to see her get fat. He crushed some of his cookies, later asking if he could also crush pieces of chalk and expressing concern about wasting the chalk or the water when he let it run for a long time. It also became obvious, during this period, that whenever he was told his hour would soon be over, he would go at once for more cookies.

An eventful session (the twenty-sixth) occurred the day before he was to go on a long summer vacation. He was engaged in cleaning out the sink with soap flakes and brought the cookie jar to the sink so the therapist could put cookies in his mouth as he worked. She deliberately fed him in steady succession, and he seemed to settle into a comfortable, relaxed regression—wallowing in cookies, soap, and water. When the therapist once did not observe that his mouth was empty, he said, "Cookie, please. No, *not* please." The therapist commented that he seemed to feel she should know when he was hungry without his having to beg, to which he agreed. She then discussed his great need to be given things, that children have a right to feel their mothers will feed them good things without their having to ask, it's fun to be given all you want, etc.

He ate cookies throughout the first session following the vacation, but from then on he largely ignored the cookie jar or ate only a single cookie at the end of the hour. The last session before the Christmas holiday he again showed interest in the cookies, eating throughout the hour, asking the therapist to feed him, and offering one to her.

During the next four months his general play themes were becoming less symbolic and more creative and constructive in nature. Cookies held little interest for him. Only when termination plans were being discussed did he return to the cookie jar at one point when he was verbalizing some of his concerns and questions about the future.

Three weeks before his final session he brought a bag of hard candies to the playroom and offered some to the therapist. She pointed out that before this time he was *getting* things in the hour while now he was able to *give* and that this was a real change, to which he agreed. In his next to last session he once more stuffed his mouth with cookies, but did not seem to notice them in his final hour.

In summary, Billy's use of food can be divided into several stages. At first he was very constricted, denied his desires for food, or allowed himself only one or two cookies in an hour. Only after he acted out his fears of the bad food and retaliated against the bad mother could he then permit the therapist to feed him. This rapidly led to much regression in play and gorging of cookies as he played out pleasurable infantile feeding situations. As gains were noted in all areas of his play, his need for cookies also diminished, and he used them only when he needed extra support, for example, at the close of an hour or before a long vacation. Finally, he brought in food to give the therapist which signified a newly achieved stage of maturity for him.

## REFERENCES


ALPERT, AUGUSTA. Reversibility of pathological fixations associated with maternal deprivation in infancy. *Psychoanal. Stud. Child,* 1959, **14,** 169–185.

ANTHONY, E.S. A study of "screen sensations." *Psychoanal. Stud. Child,* 1961, **16,** 211–245.

BOYCE, ELLA R. *Play in the infants' school.* London: Methuen & Co., Ltd., 1938.

ERIKSON, E. H. Configurations in play. *Psychoanal. Quart.,* 1937, **6,** 138–214.

FEDERN, P. *Ego psychology and the psychoses.* New York: Basic Books, 1952.

FRANK, L. K. *Projective methods.* Springfield, Ill.: Charles C Thomas, 1948.

FREUD, S. *Beyond the pleasure principle.* London: Hogarth Press, 1922.

HAMMER, E. F. *The clinical application of projective drawings.* Springfield, Ill.: Charles C Thomas, 1958.

HARTLEY, RUTH E., FRANK, L. K., and GOLDENSON, R. M. *Understanding children's play.* New York: Columbia Univer. Press, 1952.

HAWORTH, MARY R., and KELLER, MARY JANE. The use of food in the diagnosis and therapy of emotionally disturbed children. *J. Amer. Acad. Child Psychiat.,* 1962, **1,** 548–563.

JUNG, C. G. *Collected papers in analytical psychology.* London: Baillière, Tindall, & Cox, 1916.

KAUFMAN, I., ROSENBLUM, ELEANOR, HEIMS, LORA, and WILLER, L. Childhood schizophrenia: treatment of children and parents. *Amer. J. Orthopsychiat.,* 1957, **27,** 683–690.

KLEIN, MELANIE. *The psycho-analysis of children.* New York: Norton, 1932.

KRAMER, P. Discussion of Dr. Anthony's paper—a study of "screen sensations." *Psychoanal. Stud. Child,* 1961, **16,** 246–250.

MACHOVER, KAREN. *Personality projection in the drawing of the human figure.* Springfield, Ill.: Charles C Thomas, 1949.

MACHOVER, KAREN. Drawing of the human figure: a method of personality investigation. In H. H. ANDERSON and GLADYS L. ANDERSON (Eds.), *An introduction to projective techniques.* New York: Prentice-Hall, 1951. Pp. 341–369.

MITTELMANN, B. Motility in infants, children, and adults. *Psychoanal. Stud. Child,* 1954, **9,** 142–177.

MITTELMANN, B. Motility in the therapy of children and adults. *Psychoanal. Stud. Child,* 1957, **12,** 284–319.

REICH, W. *Character analysis.* New York: Orgone Institute Press, 1949.

ROSEN, J. *Direct analysis.* New York: Grune & Stratton, 1953.

SCHWING, GERTRUD. *A way to the soul of the mentally ill.* New York: International Univer. Press, 1954.

SECHEHAYE, MARGUERITE A. *Autobiography of a schizophrenic girl.* New York: Grune & Stratton, 1951.

SECHEHAYE, MARGUERITE A. *A new psychotherapy in schizophrenia.* New York: Grune & Stratton, 1956.

SLAVSON, S. R. *An introduction to group therapy.* New York: Commonwealth Fund, 1943.

WAAL, N. A special technique of psychotherapy with an autistic child. In G. CAPLAN (Ed.), *Emotional problems of* early childhood. New York: Basic Books, 1955. Pp. 431–449.

WOLTMANN, A. G. Mud and clay. *Personality symposium*, No. 2. New York: Grune & Stratton, 1950.

WOLTMANN, A. G. The use of puppetry as a projective method in therapy. In H. H. ANDERSON and GLADYS L. ANDERSON (Eds.), *An introduction to projective techniques*. New York: Prentice-Hall, 1951. Pp. 606–638.

WOLTMANN, A. G. Concepts of play therapy techniques. *Amer. J. Orthopsychiat.*, 1955, **25**, 771–783.

WOLTMANN, A. G. Spontaneous puppetry by children as a projective method. In A. I. RABIN and MARY R. HAWORTH (Eds.), *Projective techniques with children*. New York: Grune & Stratton, 1960. Pp. 305–312.

CHAPTER SIXTEEN

# Graphic and Plastic Materials

GRAPHIC AND PLASTIC media are easily adapted by children to serve different purposes at successive stages of development and at various levels of communication. The materials can be used in a grossly regressive fashion or in a highly imaginative and creative manner. Speech may accompany the manipulations or be used to describe the product. At other times, or for other children, painting, drawing, or modeling may be completely nonverbal activities.

Rambert discusses drawings as symbolic representations of conflicts, while Woltmann demonstrates the therapeutic aspects of clay.[1]

The consideration of water play by Hartley *et al.* calls attention to the variety of possibilities for therapeutic interaction with a very commonplace medium. The excerpt from Jackson and Todd's book traces the progressive changes in the use of sand and water by one little boy, pointing out the changes in the symbolic purposes served by the same "raw" materials in different periods of therapy.

One might well ask whether meaningful therapy could not be conducted with only sand, water, paint, and balloons as play material?

---

[1] See *also* Woltmann's discussions of both drawing and modeling in Chapter 15.

# The Use of Drawings as a Method of Child Psychoanalysis

MADELEINE L. RAMBERT

Drawing pictures is a child's spontaneous means of expression. . . . Many children up to eleven years of age—even those who play with the puppets—like to express themselves by drawing pictures.

These drawings are not only a means of expression but facilitate the conscious realization of conflicts. They allow one to penetrate deeply into the child's unconscious; they encourage the abreaction of the emotion and permit a surprising catharsis; they also indicate the attempts at the sublimation of instinctive tendencies.

To understand the child's drawings, it is necessary to be initiated not only into his logic but also into his symbolism as in the case of his puppet games. As observed in the child's fairy stories, one again finds general symbols, but each child has a language of his own and expressions peculiar to him as seen in his dreams. We attempt to decipher them as we would riddles, until little by little the child himself gives us the key to them.

In the same way as in his games, the more the conflict has been repressed, the more obscure are the symbols. We would never be able to understand a child's drawings if he did not explain them. On his side he would very quickly cease to draw his pictures for us if he once realized that we did not understand what he was expressing by these pictures. To encourage him to guide us into the deep layers of his personality, we must know how to follow him. A Chinese would very soon cease to bare his soul to us in his own language if our replies remained incomprehensible to him.

It is as necessary here, therefore, as in all other methods of psychoanalytic therapy to establish an understanding, a collaboration between the child and the psychoanalyst.

There are, however, some stereotypic elements which enable us to understand this picture language: (1) transposition or projection of the emotional conflict into exterior objects, example: "a frightened mountain, a fir tree which is afraid," etc; (2) the identification of the child with stars or with very strong animals or giants as Gulliver in the land of the Lilliputians; (3) the overdetermination of certain details which indicate the importance the child attaches to them, for example, seven or eight fingers on one hand, the fantastic number of weapons carried by one soldier, the power, quite out of proportion, of a car's headlights; (4) condensation into one picture of a crowd of details which reveal different traits of character or which recall numerous memories.

It is interesting to observe the dimensions of objects in a child's pictures. A knife as large as the child himself is an indication that the knife is an emotional symbol of the utmost importance to him. The disproportion of the human body or of animals carries the same meaning.

The manner in which stars and people appear in the drawing often indicates the depth of a conflict. Finally the atmosphere of the picture reveals much of the gravity of the neurotic disorders.

Very often the child starts to draw a house or a castle without a single soul in the picture. The door is closed. We ask him, therefore to tell us the story of the little girl or the little boy who lives in this house. This is a point of contact; the next time the child will explain himself more freely; he will open the door of the house.

The first part of a drawing represents a child ill in bed, and the second a child sitting at a table. The painter of this picture, a little girl of eight, explains to me, "My brother is sick and he's going to die." She is delighted and says, "No, he only has infantile paralysis and can't move. Here [second part of the drawing] he is sitting on a chair, he is a little better but he can't run about."

This is a jealousy conflict. The little brother takes up too much attention in the household, the mother is constantly occupied with him. The little girl would like to make him disappear or at least reduce the field of his activities. The compromise is ingenious, paralysis keeps him alive which avoids too violent guilt feelings, but he no longer bothers his sister! The little girl's ambivalence shows itself in the agreeable atmosphere of the drawing. The little boy is well looked after—there are flowers on the table.

Again a jealousy conflict of a boy of seven [is indicated.] It is a drawing, in three parts; the child explains it as follows: "Once upon a time there was a little girl who went off for a walk in the field. It was a magic field and all of a sudden it transformed itself into a pond and the little girl was drowned. The parents looked all over for her but couldn't find her." He tells all this with a happy smile and yet adds, "The parents were sad."

Drawings which express fear are very frequent and resemble nightmares. A little boy of seven draws a giant who is going to kill "us" and eat "us" up. "He has a big knife to cut off the head," says the child. The expression of the eyes and mouth is hardly reassuring. . . .

The boy of eleven who drew a battle of a cowboy and his weapons, expresses his fear rather than any martial instincts. He tells us that he is always terrified at night in bed in case he may eventually be attacked, and in his many nightmares he is always beaten and often cut into little pieces. In the picture, no enemy is seen but only weapons. The child explains, "The enemy thinks he is aiming at his heart but he misses. The cowboy has two revolvers, an automatic pistol and a saber. He is about to fire his revolver and draw his sword." The function of the drawing is to reassure the child, to help him convince himself that he will be victorious in spite of his nightmares.

The boy between seven and eight years who drew a great battle explains to us, "I'm going to kill Hitler!" He makes use of all imaginable weapons, even avalanches of stones. In times of war, it is often the case that aggression is transferred to enemy leaders; this child has, in reality, violent negative feelings in regard to his father and older brother. It is less dangerous to vent them upon a person who is far away than upon someone near at hand; this displacement which facilitates exteriorization reduces tension in the child. It is also a compensation for his inferiority feelings to imagine himself more powerful than the most powerful leaders of the times. The atmosphere of the drawing and the overdetermination of details show the child's state of excitement.

The following drawings (See figures 16-1 and 16-2.) express the fear a little boy nurtures of his mother's remarriage.

FIGURE 16–1

Indeed, the atmosphere of this drawing (See Figure 16-1.) representing an avalanche of stones is completely different from that of the preceding [battle] picture. This boy of eight years expresses his presentiment of an imminent catastrophe. Everything is going to be overthrown and crushed: the fir trees, the dog, the cat, the bull. At best the white bear (upper middle part of the picture) might escape. The sun itself is frightened and seems to want to escape on its thousand legs. What is it that the little boy deep down inside himself fears? He tells us and his drawing expresses his fear very precisely; a man is advancing toward the house. The child is fearful that his mother, who is a widow, may remarry.

This drawing is interesting, both through the overdetermination of the details which express his anguish and the power of projection of his feelings upon exterior things.

"It is the new animal in the Zoological Gardens," is explained to us by a little boy of eight. (See Figure 16-2.) "The head is as large as the body. It has awful eyes, almost like windows. It eats up all little children." We are aware that the child's mother has recently remarried. This terrible animal is the image of his stepfather who is always scolding and who sees all his naughtiness with those terrible eyes like windows! The image of the eyes, a condensed and symbolical drawing, is most revealing, the expression of the mouth and the claws very characteristic. The child lives in terror of his stepfather.

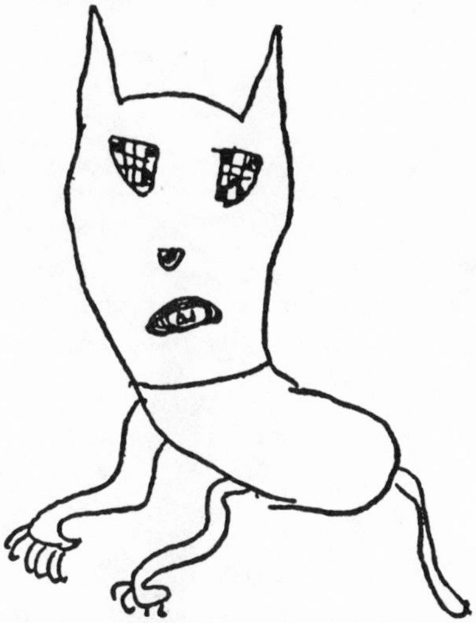

FIGURE 16–2

A little girl of twelve years drew a picture of a castle, expressing something other than fear, but nevertheless profound and poignant preoccupations. One day, she suddenly told me that she was perfectly all right and absolutely refused to speak. I asked her to draw me a picture and her comments were as follows: "To the left, on one side, there's a little girl playing ball with her friend while the nurse watches them. There's a good dog who is playing with the girls. On the other side of the castle to the right, two little girls are playing with a bad dog—or perhaps it is a pig."

The drawing . . . is very characteristic of the little girl's state of mind. The good dog and the two children attended by the nurse are on the road leading to the castle. It was like this in the little girl's infancy. She was rich, lived in a large house rather like a castle and had a nurse to shield her from any vulgar contacts. She would like to live again in those times. Unfortunately, the little girl is actually on the other side of the castle with the pig. I ask her quite simply, "What bad things were you told by some friend?" She was extremely surprised to have been found out so easily and proceeds to tell me about the conversations she has had with some of her friends on sexual matters, which greatly tormented her. . . .

We have previously stated that some children through the whole course of their treatment are able to express themselves more easily by drawing than by playing. The following three series of drawings show the different stages of the treatment.

The drawings of Louis, aged seven, are illustrations of his fear of castration. . . . Louis is a child who seldom speaks or laughs. He is so cold and reserved that never has he spontaneously kissed his mother. He is one of the last in his class and his teacher wonders if he may not be backward.

FIGURE 16–3

His first picture (See Figure 16-3.) is a humorous scene where everyone loses his cane. He relaxes and starts to laugh in telling me this. From there he draws me a number of pictures in which the same symbol always reappears: his mother loses her cane, as do his grandmother and little sister. At that time I did not know what was troubling him, but the atmosphere of the drawing and the overdetermination of the "cane" symbol already showed me that his conflict was deeprooted and troubled him greatly. It is not until after he has drawn a great number of pictures that Louis becomes consciously aware of their significance. The cane is for him the masculine organ. It is necessary to undergo many more months of treatment before Louis draws his second picture of this series, and he finally explains what is tormenting his innerself without his having known it. His little friend had been circumcised, and he has a terrible fear of having to undergo the same operation. . . . This fear is aggravated and sustained by Louis' feelings toward his father.

FIGURE 16–4

In order to understand what the drawing of the sun and the Eiffel Tower (See Figure 16-4.) expresses, it is first necessary to understand Louis' own particular symbols. I finally ended in deciphering them as if they were hieroglyphics and, as soon as I was in possession of the key to his picture language, everything became clear. This sun is the symbol of the father, and the Eiffel Tower the child's own masculine organ. This sun wears a terrifying and menacing expression, and the child explains to me, "He wants to eat the Eiffel Tower which is stopping him from passing. He would like to bite the Tower there (up high) but would be even more pleased if it were cut off further down." This drawing is a most striking image of the castration complex as it was as spontaneous as it was unexpected. It is still another proof that this complex is a heritage of the oedipus complex.

The conscious realization of his fears, my explanations as well as those of his parents, appease Louis, and at the end of the treatment he draws this charming picture (See Figure 16-5.): Two little boys took their tent and went camping the shores of a lake under the sun's amiable and paternal eye. The smiling expression of the sun indicates clearly that Louis' fears have been dissipated.

The child, in fact, is so relieved that he is full of spirit and gaiety. He has become very affectionate and both talkative and demonstrative. He makes very rapid progress at school and is an excellent pupil as he is a remarkably talented and intelligent child.

FIGURE 16–5

Arthur represents a naughty boy of nine years who has been rude to his mother. (See Figure 16-6.) She sends him to bed and Arthur calls her an "old cow" and a "dirty pig." This violent oral aggression is not surprising because Arthur stammers. He is terrified of being cut into pieces and is afraid of castration and death. Nevertheless he has strong guilt feelings all of which are expressed in his numerous drawings.

The horizonal lines (See Figure 16-7.) represent large knives which cut Arthur. They cut off "everything which sticks out" as the children say.

Arthur is now in little pieces. (See Figure 16-8.)

Finally (See Figure 16-9.), Arthur is on the table of the devil all ready to be eaten; he is actually on the fork itself.

This succession of drawings has above all a cathartic value for the child. In drawing such pictures, he releases a part of his aggression and guilt feelings.

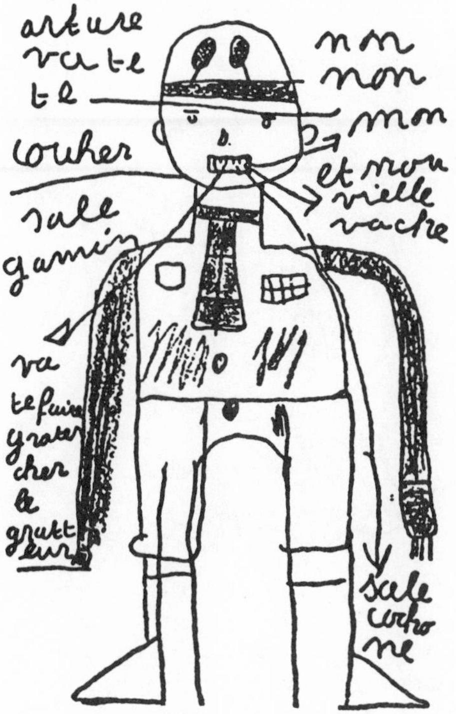


FIGURE 16–6

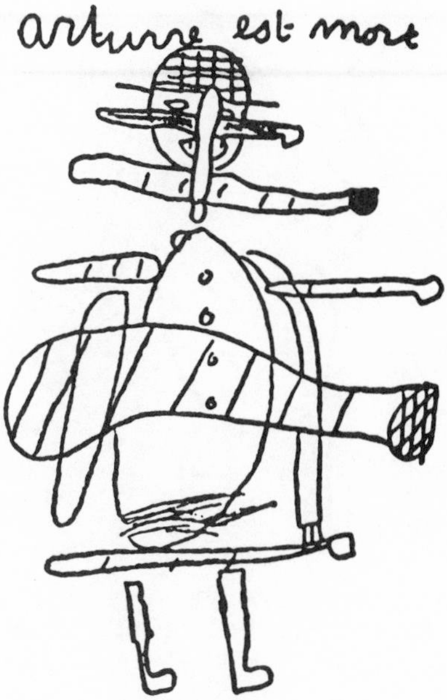


FIGURE 16–7

The last series of pictures are those of a little boy between seven and eight called Peter. During the course of his treatment he has drawn about forty pictures all told, the most characteristic of which allow us to follow him through the decisive phases of his analysis. He is a child who suffers from nightmares.

The first picture is taut and concentrated but the further the treatment advances, the clearer and simpler become the drawings. The first one, as in the child's first puppet story, reveals essential elements pertaining to his psychological problem. As it is impossible to coordinate these elements, we limit ourselves to enumerating them: There is the father in his officer's uniform, a house, an automobile, a cat with a long tail, endless roads, and large spirals of smoke in the house. The father is the principal figure and indeed the analysis revolves around the oedipal conflict.

The second drawing is more precise although still overdetermined: we find the same symbols all through the treatment; it is this fact which gives the picture such a disturbed atmosphere. It is in this house, in the attic, that we find the old man who is the object of Peter's fears as every night he dreams that this old man will kill him with his big knife. Peter knows very well that the old man does not exist except in his dreams, but his nightmares are so

FIGURE 16–8

FIGURE 16–9

frequent that the thought of them torments him during the day. In the drawing, the wicked old man has the most terrifying mouth and pair of eyes.

During the next few sessions, the child speaks of his father for whom he has a great admiration. He depicts him in his drawing as someone of great power, "more powerful than General MacArthur," he says. But at the end of several weeks, Peter starts to express negative feelings; his aggression is also shown in his drawings.

The father is caricatured [in one drawing]. Peter degrades him, makes him a lieutenant although in reality he has the rank of major. He gives his father a long, pointed nose and overly long hair. Peter thinks of himself as tiny beside his father who is very big, but in the drawing he represents him as being hardly taller than a blade of grass.

The picture of a tree expresses the same idea while taking reality into consideration. "Beside a fir tree my father is very small," he says, "All the trees are bigger than he is and the houses too."

Oedipal aggression breaks through with hardly any camouflage in the picture of a cart drawn by a very young horse. Peter explains it thus: "The one in the cage is the older. He is going to be slaughtered. It is the father of the other one. The younger is the bigger and the stronger of the two."

[In another drawing] Peter ventures to express his feelings of rivalry. He can thus think and speak without fear of the terrible punishment he would like to administer to his father. He depicts himself as the Colonel. The only thing one can say is that he has a very erect carriage!

We have arrived at Peter's marriage. [In a later drawing] he has a top hat, is upright, has an important looking nose and a cigar which emits a long trail of smoke: he certainly has all the attributes of masculinity!

A few more weeks go by in organizing Peter's emotional life. He has to find his rightful place among his brothers and sisters but things are easier as, since he is now able to live amicably with his father and does not expect his mother's all-absorbing love to the exclusion of others, he no longer suffers from nightmares.

## *Conclusion*

Drawing—a child's method of expression—reveals him to us in the same way as the stories he tells us, the games he invents, and the dreams he has. In drawing pictures, the child can express certain inner attitudes which he would find difficult to exteriorize in playing a game. In certain cases it is the most direct method to reach an understanding of not only the conflicts which trouble the child but also of his character and personal reactions.

As in all psychoanalytic technique, it is necessary to explain to the child what is going on inside him and his struggles between contradictory tendencies. He must be appeased; he must be shown a new outlet to his emotions and be encouraged along these lines. The drawings of both Peter and Louis and even of Arthur clearly show the work accomplished during our sessions. Our comments on conscious realization, liquidation and re-education prove here their full value. We usually employ drawing as an auxiliary technique, except in certain cases where children express themselves more clearly by this method.

# *Mud and Clay, Their Functions as Developmental Aids and as Media of Projection*

ADOLF G. WOLTMANN

The child's handling of form and color through the use of pencils, crayons, or water colors has been the subject of extensive studies. Comparatively little attention has been paid to the factors involved in the processes through which the child learns to master three-dimensional materials and to employ them as means of projecting his drives, feelings, and desires. An attempt is being made in this paper to roughly trace the maturation factors which lead the child from the undifferentiated approach to creative structuring of pliable three-dimensional materials and to their use as a means of projection.

The term "plastic" will be used throughout this paper. This word should not be confused with the more modern meaning of this term which is given to a variety of chemical products which are now used for the manufacturing of diverse utensils. The term "plastic," as used in this paper, is employed as a collective term for mud, clay, and plasticine. It denotes pliable, three-dimensional materials which can be structured and which offer to the child different creative outlets than the so-called "graphic" or two-dimensional media.

Nearly every infant, at one time or another, discovers the plasticity of his own feces. Mashed vegetables and similar baby food offer endless varieties of play patterns which, in a large measure, are determined by tactile stimulation. As the child grows older he learns to play with sand, water, and mud. Sand lends itself to a variety of play patterns. Through a combination of elevation and indentation the child can build tunnels, hills, rivers, and numerous landscape and geological formations. Sand is stable and gives support to the child's body and to the things which he places in it. Any object that is placed in the sand remains there. Water, on the other hand, is a fluid medium which does not allow for the creation of permanent structures. It is unstable and does not give body support. Objects placed in the water either swim, float, or sink.

> In playing with both media the child quickly realizes that sand makes things dirty, but that water cleans them. This results in a play pattern which can roughly be called "washing." Children seem to enjoy cleaning things as well as dirtying them. Once or several times during the day he experiences the transition from dirty to clean on his own body. Water and sand as play media enable him to experiment with things around him as "wet" and "dry," thus reviving earlier infantile experiences. By mixing water with sand a new plastic medium—mud—is created. By varying the proportion between water and sand, all kinds of consistencies from dirty water to a plastic mass can be made and played with. By throwing sand or mud or by squirting water, the child has in these three media excellent weapons of aggression and defense. The child also sees in them potential threats to his own welfare. There is the danger of catching cold, drowning, or choking. Sand, water, and mud adapt themselves particularly well to group activities (Bender and Woltmann, 1941–1942, p. 31).

These raw media are important developmental aids, because through them the child learns a great deal about the physical properties of his environment. He becomes aware of basic physical laws. Things are experienced as solid and liquid, as warm and cold, as dry and wet, as stable and unstable. Play with mud offers an excellent substitute for an early inhibited play with feces. At the same time, socializing factors appear when several children play together with sand, water, or mud.

The so-called normal child will learn to handle clay or plastic materials between the ages of four to five years. Sometimes other children revert back to the above-mentioned primitive play media. This happens if the child in question either has a very immature ego, if he suffers from a developmental retardation, or if the child is emotionally blocked and unable to compete with children of his own age group. The same applies to children with inadequate language development or with poor language facilities. Before any intensive therapeutic work can be started with such children, one should let them slide back, so to speak, to a more primitive developmental level of playing with sand or mud.

As the child grows older, sand, water, and mud play patterns slowly diminish in importance and are taken over by clay and plasticine. Plasticine is preferred because it does not harden and can be used over and over again. By the time the child comes in contact with plastic material, he usually has had some experiences with graphic media. A comparison between graphic and plastic media reveals that both have advantages and disadvantages. Graphic creative work is carried out with the use of one hand whereas plastic creative work calls for the coordination of both hands. In graphic creative work, forms are created through the use of lines and of color. Once a picture has been drawn or painted its contents remain stationary. The finished picture cannot be changed unless one erases, paints over, or destroys the original painting and makes another one. By using clay or plasticine, a constant change takes place because the medium is responsive to the slightest touch or impression. The consequent changes do not destroy the medium as happens if one erases or tears up paper. Graphic art is a two-dimensional medium and an indication of perspective is nothing but an optical illusion. Plastic material is three-dimensional and as such comes much closer to the representation of real objects. If a human figure is drawn from the front view, one can never see the sides or the back of this figure. A human clay figure automatically is three-dimensional and offers exploration as well as experimentation with all sides.

Graphic creative art allows for a defiance of physical laws, especially of the law of gravity. If one draws falling objects such as bombs dropping from an airplane or a person diving into the water, such drawn objects always remain suspended in mid-air. Plastic materials, on the other hand, are subject to physical laws. A combination of line and color offers more opportunities for realistic representation, but even at its best each portrayed action is but a frozen segment comparable to the individual photograph in a motion picture. Clay and plasticine usually are unicolored materials but the pliability somehow compensates for the lack of color. One should mention here that both graphic and plastic creative work very often are accompanied by acoustics. If children draw an airplane or make one out of clay, they like to imitate the noise of this object. This acoustic forms an integral part of all play patterns of children because the noise supplies a very necessary and realistic aspect in the child's attempt to master his environment.

A brief restatement of the factors cited above shows that plastic material has certain advantages over graphic material. Instead of handling one medium (pencil, crayon, or brush) with one hand and using it on the second medium (paper), the child handles the plastic material directly with both hands. This leads to early bilateral coordination of arms, hands, and fingers.

Both graphic and plastic materials are eminently suited for projective processes because both media are unstructured. They constitute the tools. The child, in creating something with both media, is free to select the content.

> The child learns how to master plastic material through maturation cycles, which are initiated by the sheer love of motor activity directed at the material offered. The early stages of this cycle, during which creative intentions are absent, may be called the kneading period or stage of nonspecific treatment which corresponds to the scribbling period in drawing. It is an investigation of the external world by rhythmic movements out of which patterns are built. An accidentally gained form or shape may be given a name and may become the carrier of a meaning. A more integrated rhythmic rolling seems to be characteristic for the next higher level of maturation during which attempts in object representation appear. The first real form mastered by a small child is usually a rolled cylinder which is comparable to the loop, whirl, and circle which form the primitive units of visual motor *gestalten* in graphic work. Through handling and turning, the cylinder can easily be changed into an arc, a ring, or a spiral. Out of these primitive geometrical forms more complex entities can be created. Rolled balls to which cylinders are attached, are usually the first attempt to create a "man." The plastic creative work of the child is no longer sheer motor exercise, but the representation of real objects to which meaning and emotional values are attached. This, in turn, stimulates the child's fantasy life and leads to the expression of problems which the child may have.
>
> This is one of the reasons why plastic creative work is of such great value in the observation and treatment of behavior problems in children: because it enables the child to clarify more freely and bring to conscious, tangible levels his own phantasies, which are thus accessible to therapeutic procedures.
>
> Aside from the quicker maturation cycles, plasticine offers other advantages. It lends itself extremely well to the repetitive-aggressive-destructive-constructive modes of behavior which seem to characterize the normal development of children and which are so evident in their play patterns and verbalizations. (Woltman, 1943, p. 299.)

One may therefore consider the plastic creative work of the child as an expression of his own motility, as his aggressive investigation into the world of reality, as his drive to produce patterns on the receptive material with which he can express his emotional and social problems and his tendency to solve many of his problems through these experiences. These latter parts take place as soon as the child has reached the stage of object representation. Object representation may occur in the following stages (Bender and Woltmann, 1937, p. 285):

(1) Form as produced by motor impulses.
(2) Form reproduced as seen or in imitation of other children.
(3) Form which arises from the body image or postural model of the body and its manifold sensory and conceptional experience.
(4) Form as an expression of phantasy, emotional and social problems.

Before more attention is given to the stage of object representation, an account of the preceding stage of nonspecific handling is included because it shows that even before the child is developmentally ready for the creation of objects, unstructured clay or plasticine offers many valuable outlets for the small child. The following observations were made of nursery children from two to five years of age and also of older children who were either mentally retarded or emotionally blocked, so that they were unable to make the proper motor, intellectual, emotional or social adjustments of the child above the nursery level.

Their approach to plastic material is that of an experimental investigation. They examine the plasticine by looking at it, smelling it, poking and hitting it, by putting it into their mouths, trying to chew and swallow it. They might drop it on the floor, throw it away, or watch the other children. One or two children will begin to hit the plastic material. Soon the others will follow. First each child will hit the clay in some kind of "individual" rhythm. Before long, the children will coordinate their "individual" rhythms into one steady group beat. While this goes on, new discoveries are made. Because of the repeated hitting, the plasticine lumps will take on a flat shape. One child will suddenly stop and exclaim, "Look what I made! I made a cake!" These activities are repeated over and over again. Once the children have released their undifferentiated motor drives, they soon become interested in the plastic material itself. They take it apart and put it together again. Other children might push holes into the plasticine or even use their fingernails or teeth to make indentations. Various forms and shapes are thus made. A flat piece of plasticine will be called a "cake." A polymorphous lump of clay with a little piece protruding from it is identified as a mouse. The children are happy about their discoveries, show them around, and enjoy having their creations admired by the group. On one occasion, a six-year-old colored girl attached a piece of clay to one end of the armature stem.[a] On top of this, she put another piece of plasticine in the form of a rolled cylinder. She called her creation a "baby." She showed it to a three-year-old white boy and said, "You can't hit my baby." No sooner had she said this than the boy took the armature stem and began to hit the baby. Instead of being angry or upset, the girl laughed and screamed with joy whenever the boy

[a] An armature consists of a square-shaped board 6 x 6 with a hole in the middle. Into this hole is inserted a round dowel.

> touched or hit the clay baby. After it was completely destroyed, she made another one, and this play activity was repeated over and over again.
>
> The emotional implications in this instance are especially interesting because this little colored girl was on the observation ward together with her eighteen-month-old brother. The two children were rejected by their mother and showed clear signs of sibling rivalry for the scant bit of maternal affection that the mother had to share between them.
>
> At this stage we also notice the possessive nature of the child. It seems that the children are never satisfied with the amount of plasticine given to them and try to get as much as possible from the other children. They do not work in social groups yet although working alongside of each other and observing the activities of each other is not only important insofar as their own activities are concerned but this also points toward socializing factors which, at the next higher level, lead to the formation of social groups. (Bender and Woltmann, 1937, p. 286 f.)

Since the preschool child usually handles both graphic and plastic media, one might expect overlappings in their creative endeavors. It is not at all uncommon that a young child will create a solid human figure out of clay. Instead of adding to it a solid hat, the child might form the outline of a hat by rolling clay into a thin, snake-like cylinder and bending this form into the proper shape. This sort of hat, in contrast to the three-dimensional body, has a definite two-dimensional appearance. Other children might attach the clay outline of a torso to a three-dimensional head.

The stage of preoccupation with investigation into the body image and postural model of the body is very well known in graphic art and has been used as a maturation test by Goodenough. The development of the same processes in plastic art has not been standardized. However, the so-called tadpole stage (*Kopffüssler*) in graphic arts has its equivalent in plastic creative work. Many young children leave out the body and attach the clay arms and legs directly to the head.

It was pointed out above that feces are among the earliest plastic materials with which the child comes in contact. Plastic material, due to its softness and pliability bears, for many children, a striking resemblance to fecal matter. Whereas the play with feces is usually strictly inhibited and curbed, clay and plasticine become a socially accepted symbolic substitute for feces. It is not surprising, therefore, that preoccupation with the anal region and elimination is common in the child's handling of plastic material. The child does not always adhere to the anal content but combines it with allied problems such as the proper body posture maintained during the process of elimination and also with larger social issues. Children sometimes are puzzled over the fact that the intake of food is a social occasion in which the whole family participates. The elimination of food, however, is a purely individual and private activity from which others are excluded. In an earlier publication Dr. Bender and this author (1937) refer to several plastic creations which deal with toilets. One seven-year-old boy built an individual toilet for every member of the family. Another boy, slightly younger, created a "community toilet" by pushing five holes into a piece of clay. He placed five round sticks of clay on each hole and called them "father, mother, two sisters, and the baby." The top ends of these so-called human figures were slightly twisted because, using his own words, "they turn their heads away while they sit down there." We have on record other plastic creations of this sort in which anal and sexual content are symbolically expressed. One seven-year-old boy created a bathroom scene in which two toilet bowls looked like doughnuts. He rolled another piece of clay into a round cylinder, bent down one end and used his creation as a gun. For a few minutes he ran around in the playroom, shooting at everybody present. Then he examined his gun very carefully and said, "This looks like something you use in the toilet when you pull the thing. I am going to make a toilet now. I am going to make a big toilet, a fat toilet." He straightened out the gun and placed the elongated clay piece between the two doughnut-shaped toilets. He added two round clay balls to the upright structure and referred to his whole creation as "This is a frankfurter with two meatballs and two doughnuts on each side." He was highly amused by his creation and showed it around to the other children in the room. The other children, too, laughed. When he finally presented his creation to this author, he had a serious expression on his face and maintained with an artificial air of sincerity that he only had been joking and that his real intentions had been to build a toilet.

Psychoanalysis has taught us that the anal contents and references in folklore, slang, and dreams very often carry a decided note of contempt. The following brief case history is included here to demonstrate that cathartic release of contemptuous feelings can be obtained through a very primitive, unspecified handling of plastic material alone. Richard, a nine-year-old boy, was referred for psychotherapy because his mother found it impossible to handle him. The family owned a home in a small community. Richard refused to conform. He had broken several windows, destroyed property, and on one occasion had even tried to set the house on fire. Occasionally he truanted from school and was extremely aggressive toward his younger brother. This boy was seen three times a week in hourly sessions for a period of two years. Treatment attempts were extremely difficult in the beginning because Richard was mean, negative, and aggressive. Several times he sneaked up behind this author and hit and kicked him. Puppets were introduced which from then on received the full fury of his aggressive contempt. After a year and one-half of stormy sessions, during which Richard enacted many family scenes, he suddenly became interested in dollhouse furniture and in animals. Richard identified himself with the snake. He surrounded the snake with other animals who were away from home and who would come at nighttime and try to break in and destroy the house while his father, mother, and younger brother were asleep. One day he suddenly discovered a large play toilet which orginally had served, thanks to the inventiveness of fun-loving manufacturers, as a dispenser of cigarettes. Richard immediately turned this play object into a flying feces factory. He attached two clay hoses to the toilet and made believe that one squirted out urine and that the other shot out feces. After building a bedroom, living room, kitchen, and bathroom, he would hold the toilet in his hand and make believe that the whole house was thoroughly drenched with urine and feces. Not satisfied with this, he allowed the snake to sneak into the house at nighttime and to deposit lumps of clay throughout the whole apartment. Richard had a fiendish glee on his face when this "fecal matter" was placed in the stove and in the coffeepot. He danced around and shouted, "Tomorrow morning, when the mother starts the stove going, this will stink up the whole house and they will drink shit instead of coffee for breakfast." His preoccupation with fecal matters increased from one session to the next. He was no longer satisfied with placing feces into the apartment, but began to bombard his house with huge lumps of clay. He rejoiced when during this process the whole apartment was reduced to shambles. Since it did not occur to him that his parents and brother might fight back, this writer took the initiative by attaching a clay penis to the father figure and by making believe that the father tried to urinate against the flying feces factory as a measure of defense. Richard fixed that. During the night the snake came into the house, castrated the father and touched the genital region of the mother figure. Then Richard said, "They won't be able to make piss at me any more. From now on they always will have to run to the toilet, but only water will come out. The piss will stay inside of them and before long they will get sick and will have to go to the doctor. Now I can throw all the piss and shit at them and they can't fight back."

This intense fecal play lasted for approximately three months. Whereas formerly the boy had been aggressive toward the therapist, he now devoted all of his time and effort to annihilating his family by choking them with and drowning them in urine and feces. Richard was so preoccupied with this play that it was impossible to suggest other play patterns or to engage him into a discussion about the meaning of this play. I therefore took this boy one day to the zoo. While we watched the chimpanzees, one of these primates suddenly began to poke a finger into his anus and to extract fecal matter by force. In true monkey fashion he cleaned his hand by inserting it into the mouth. Richard had watched all of this with great fascination. Then he turned around and said, "Let's go. This is disgusting. Whoever heard of a monkey sticking his finger in his behind and then into his mouth." I explained to him that fecal play is very common among animals and young babies and that he probably, as an infant, had acted like the monkey. Richard flew into a rage. He denied ever having had an interest in fecal matters. He stormed into the hotel lobby where his mother was waiting for him and shouted, "Mother, did I play with shit when I was a baby?" After the thoroughly embarrassed mother and this writer had brought Richard to the privacy of the therapist's office, the mother explained to her son that he had played with his own feces from the age of six months till he was nearly two years old. This unexpected revelation came as a shock and a surprise to the youngster. He was quiet and pensive. When he returned for the next session, he again built an apartment for his parents and younger brother but refused to play with the toilet and clay. Instead he sent over the elephant to the house to ask whether the snake and the other animals could come for a visit. As soon as permission was granted, all of the animals moved into the house and were cordially received by the family. During the following play sessions all of the animals went to school during the day and came back to the house in the evening with very good marks. The mother reported spontaneously that a complete change of behavior had taken place in her son after the incident at the zoo. Shortly after this Richard was discharged from treatment because he no longer was mean and aggressive. Although Richard had never once modeled objects out of clay, he had used plastic material in its primitive, unstructured form for the release of his pent-up aggression and for the working-through of numerous problems on a developmental level which was far below his chronological age.

Problems connected with the size, shape, and functions of the genital regions can likewise be investigated and experimented with through plastic media. Interestingly enough, genital preoccupation, as evidenced through plastic creative work, seems to be much more prevalent among boys than girls. Boys very often endow their clay figures with penises of various sizes and shapes. We have on record the creation of an eleven-year-old boy who attached six clay testicles around the clay penis. Sometimes the clay penis is left out but the nose of the clayman might become the object of experimentation. It also happens that a human clay figure is endowed with a penis and an anus. Experimentation with such concepts might lead to an enlargement of both areas so that, for instance, the anus may reach all the way up to the nape of the neck.

The release of sexual fantasies in experimentation with clay was observed by the author in group activities of five boys between the ages of seven to ten. Ordinarily, sexual knowledge is inhibited, but the uninhibited expressions of one member of the group quickly removes the thin veneer of custom and education from the rest of the group. It is as if the group activity sanctions the collective thoughts of all those who comprise such a gathering. It was of interest to note that all of these activities were carried out with a total absence of fear, guilt, shame, or modesty. At the same time interesting mechanisms of projection were observed. Several of the clay objects were destroyed because they did something bad (sexual activities). In other words it was not the ideations of these boys that was at fault, but the blame was shifted and projected onto the clay objects which these boys themselves had created. The permissive attitude of the therapist, who allowed the boys to act out their repressed and inhibited problems, greatly helped toward bringing this material to a tangible level, so that later on it could be handled therapeutically.

Masturbatory activities which might give rise to castration fears are occasionally encountered. A seven-year-old boy made a human figure out of clay which was devoid of arms but had a penis. He told this writer that his clay boy had been playing with his "dicky" and that God had punished him by cutting off his arms. "The boy knows that it is wrong to play with his dicky, but he cannot stop it. He tries to use his feet, but God will punish him and also cut off his feet. Then the little boy will have no arms and no legs, and he cannot walk no more, and his mother will have to feed him and he cannot play with his dicky no more."

Only once, during several years of daily contacts with groups of children, suffering from a variety of behavior problems, did this writer encounter a plastic creation in which fellatio was the theme. This boy was over twelve years of age. He produced a man, kneeling behind a machine gun. His real intentions were obvious to a group of boys who had been watching him work with clay. After much giggling and snickering the boy finally admitted that the so-called machine gun was in reality a huge penis which the kneeling figure tried to insert into his mouth.

Anyone who observes children and their handling of plastic materials will be struck by the fact that a snake-like figure occurs very frequently in the plastic creative work of children.

> This constant appearance of the snake in the clay work can partly be explained as follows: As mentioned before, the rolled cylinder constitutes the first basic, elementary form the child masters once he has reached the stage of object representation. By rolling a piece of clay with his hands, an oblong, snake-like object is the inevitable result. This explanation covers only the formal aspect but not the emotional contents which point toward a diversified use of one symbol. (Bender and Woltmann, 1937, p. 295.)

Most of the children who produce snakes in their clay work have never seen a real living snake. In some instances, the snake is a phallic symbol. In other cases, the snake might represent aggressive parents or siblings. Very often the snake is the protector or a punishing agent who kills "bad" people. We also have seen plastic creations in which the snake appears as a tame friend of people. An individual study should be made in each case to determine what the snake means to the child and what it supposedly represents.

Among the many plastic creations of children which include snakes, the following one is singled out because the mechanisms of projection are especially clear. What this twelve-year-old colored girl worked out in her plastic creation constituted a great deal of her own personal experiences. Gwendolin made many tall and small snakes out of clay which she put together into some sort of a community. She identified her objects as father snake, stepmother snake, dead mother snake, a snake minister, a snake sitting on the toilet, snake children, and as a lake with a fish in it. She called her creation a "garden of snakes" and told the following story about her clay work:

> Adam and Eve have sinned in the garden because of the snake. God put all the snakes in this garden because the snakes had started the first sin in the world. The snakes have to stay in the garden for a whole year. They were

hidden away from the rest of the world. In this garden there was only one fish. The snake that did the most work should get the fish. So these two lazy snakes started to fight for it. One snake killed the other snake and ate up the fish. After this, God comes and says, "A woman should tread on every man's head because the man snake killed the lady snake." The wife of the snake is dead. He killed her. You see, they were lazy. They didn't want to do the work. There was only one fish in there and the wife said she should have it because she is the lady. He said he should have it because he is a male. So they started fighting and he bit her near the heart and she died.

Gwendolin was asked if the snake would be punished for killing the wife. She answered,

Not yet. He doesn't know that his new wife has a temper. She will beat him up. See these little snakes here? She is their stepmother.

How does the stepmother treat the little children?

Pretty good as long as she is only engaged to the man. After she is married to the man for a couple of days, she gets very nasty. She makes the kids sweep the floor. . . . The stepmother wants presents from the children so she is good to them for one day because it is her birthday. The children give her a present, a big ball. She thinks it is a chocolate ball, but it is made out of rock. She puts it into her mouth and breaks all her teeth. She goes around teethless. She can't eat. All she can take is soup and water.

Will she punish the children for this?

No, because they tell her that the preacher has sent the candy. So she goes and hits the preacher over the head. The father can't do nothing. She hits him over the head with a rolling pin.

Gwendolin had a stepmother with whom she could not get along at all. Many of her behavior adjustment failures are related to a very unsatisfactory home situation. Her story contains many of the unpleasant home episodes and also a simple but very effective plan of revenge in which the hated stepmother is deprived of her oral aggression, of her strength and her vitality. Instead of bossing the children around, she has to live on soup and water. The symbolism involved does not require further comment. It is of interest to note how the biblical content in the beginning of her story is twisted around. The biblical animosity between man and snake is changed to hostility between male and female.

It would be erroneous to assume that the plastic creative work of children deals primarily with oral, anal, and genital content. They are experimented with if the child encounters disturbing problems in this areas. For the greater part children use plastic material as a medium into which they project their own ideologies and curiosities and use it for working-out their own specific problems. It should be mentioned here that a child should be allowed to create freely. Any attempt toward formal instruction and teaching children to create objects such as cups, ashtrays or vases automatically inhibits spontaneous expression. If a group of children is left alone in a permissive atmosphere, an amazing variety of plastic creations will be the result. It is possible that one child might borrow an idea from another child. This is perfectly permissible because the borrowing child will change the idea according to his degree of motor development and maturation, the intensity of his own problems, and his degree of socialization.

One should never be satisfied with looking at the finished creation, but should try to learn from the child what his creative intentions were and what his creation means to him. The child should be encouraged to speak freely about his finished clay work. The above-mentioned snake story gave real meaning and an understanding of Gwendolin's problems to the otherwise well made but static "garden of snakes." The plastic creative work of a child does not bring forth all of his problems and should therefore not be used as a single criterion. Its chief value lies in the fact that the child brings to a tangible level some of his problems which can be seen, discussed, experimented with, and changed. To create a permissive attitude and to allow children to express themselves in plastic creative work is an activity which teachers, settlementhouse workers, recreation workers, and nurses can and should carry out. The evaluation and interpretation of such creations should be left to the specially trained therapist.

A brief description of other plastic creations made by children is given in an attempt to show the range and variety of problems which children bring to a realistic level. An eight-year-old boy showed a great deal of preoccupation with the figure of what he called "a good man." First he referred to a piece of clay as a house and that a good man lived in the house selling vegetables. Then he changed the story and said that the house was full of candy and that all of the candy belonged to the man inside the house. Finally he made a clay face of a man which he covered completely with little bits of clay. He said, "The man is good because his whole face is covered with candy." This boy came from a broken home which the father had deserted. His preoccupation with the good man obviously was an attempt to create an ideal image of the father figure and the wish to have the father come back. It also turned out that this boy, who could not accept the harsh reality of the irresponsible father, had to convince himself over and over again that there was such a thing as a good father.

Fred came to the hospital at the age of seven. His father deserted when he learned that his wife was pregnant. Shortly after the desertion Fred began to stay out late and, on several occasions, was picked up by the police during the wee-hours of the morning and returned home. Finally the mother's condition made it impossible for her to care for this boy and he was therefore recommended to the hospital for a period of observation. At first, this boy was very shy and taciturn. He participated little in the group activities and stayed more-or-less on the fringe of things. Little by little he became interested in working with clay and began to make crude household utensils. Among his creations were a basket full of eggs and a rolling pin which his mother used when baking bread. Fred received intensive individual psychotherapy during which the attention was focused on the fact that before long there would be another baby in the family. His mother visited him regularly at the hospital and, at our suggestion, discussed with him the changes that would take place in the family and the adjustments which would necessitate living in a family with two children and without a father. Fred understood, because before long he began to make mother figures out of clay. Soon he added little babies to the mother figure. Most of the time the clay mother would be holding the clay baby in her arms. He was very glad when he finally learned that he had a baby sister and eagerly looked forward to going home in order to resume a new life with his mother and sibling. He adjusted very well to the new situation.

A number of the clay creations which have come to this writer's attention clearly deal with feelings of loneliness and being deserted. A nine-year-old boy created a clay scene in which a clay boy stands under a lamp post. Nearby is a fence on which a cat is walking. The boy, according to his story, ran away from an orphanage because he didn't like it there.

> The cops go after the boy. They will get him and bring him back to the orphanage. He now will like it there because he had no right to run away. He should have stayed there. This all happens at night time.
>
> What is the cat doing there?
>
> Oh, nothing, the cat just happened to walk by.

This boy had a history of truancy and of running away from home. His clay scene depicts a boy who is out on the street in the middle of the night. He is all alone, has no bed to sleep in, no money with which to buy food. Instead of meeting with excitement and adventure, he finds himself devoid of human contacts and is glad when the police returns him to his environment. It is one thing when a child speaks about being lonely. It is quite another thing when he gives creative expression to his feelings, because the desolateness of a few pieces of clay put together gives spatial dimension to the feeling of being all alone.

Here and there in this paper reference has been made to the fact that clay and plasticine are very good outlets for aggression on several developmental levels. The following observations are included because they reveal children's attempts to experiment with and to repeat various forms of aggression.

Richard and Walter, two seven-year-old boys, made airplanes out of clay and played with them. Both planes had a machine gun and were shooting at each other. After some flying around and shooting both planes collided in mid-air. These collisions were repeated a few times during which the boys held the clay models in their hands. Then they decided to let them crash and dropped the clay figures on the floor after each collision. After this had been carried out a few times, the airplanes lost their shape and became lumps of clay. Instead of letting them drop again, the clay was picked up and thrown down. Richard would leave his piece of clay on the floor and Walter would try to hit it with his piece of clay and vice versa. The boys would say, "He's hitting my airplane" or "He's killing my airplane." After these repeated acts, both boys hurled their pieces through space in projectile-like fashion trying to hit other objects. When class was over, Walter begged us to let him stay saying, "Let me take another shot at that," pointing to a chair.

These play activities which lasted approximately twenty-five minutes showed some of the characteristics inherent in child's play. I would call it repeated experimentation in aggression. Each aggressive act is repeated over and over again. As the child grows older, his problems of aggression become infused with general social problems. It is, therefore, not surprising that quite a number of the plastic creations of older children have to do with social scenes in which bad people murder good people and then are apprehended by the proper authorities and brought to justice.

Aggression may not always be directed toward the outside world but may also take on forms of defense, as is illustrated in the clay work of a thirteen-year-old boy who had below average intelligence and who was physically handicapped. He created a monster out of clay and had the following to say about his plastic creation:

> I was thinking the other day what I'll do when I was big. I decided to get rich. It is easier to get gold than it is to get money. But all the gold mines are discovered already and guarded, so when I get big I want to go to Africa. There is some dynamite that hasn't been discovered. If I go to Africa I need protection. It costs money to have a guard, so I make my own guard. I get tusks from a lot of elephants and make one great big tusk. Then I get all the feet of the gorillas and make two big feet out of them. Then I put the eyes of an eagle in the front and the eyes of a hawk in the back. Then I get the horns of all the rhinoceroses and make great big horns out of those things. Then I give it the brain of a dead human being. Then I cut the head, the tusks and the feet of an elephant so that just its belly is left. Then I put all the things together in the belly and fill it with the blood of a vicious animal. Then I put a tube down his heart and pump it and then it will become alive. Before I do that I put him into a steel cage so he can't hurt anybody. Then I train him that he likes me and do what I say. Then I take him to Africa. If the savages or animals start out with me, he protects me. I give him the skin of a crocodile, so that bullets wouldn't hurt him. I give him the voice of a lion. With his mouth he can swallow a couple of million guys in one gobble. With each horn he can stick through twelve thousand men at once. If a herd of elephants attacks me he can swallow seven or eight elephants at a time. His tail can wrap around seven

thousand men at one time, choke them to death and throw them away. He stays up all night and if a crook comes he will kill him. I will get all the diamonds. In the jungles he can kill plenty of animals but it costs plenty of money to feed him in the city. I know what I do. I give him the scent of a bloodhound so he can follow after the crooks and kick up the house with one foot and kill all the crooks.

Frankenstein seems to be an ineffective amateur next to this clay creation. The interesting part of this clay work lies in the fact that this boy surrounds himself with an all-powerful fantastic monster which keeps away from him injury and ridicule. This boy suffered from a speech defect and was partially paralyzed. A long period of hospitalization had interfered with his educational development. He could compete neither intellectually nor physically with children of his own age group. His speech impediment often made him the target of other children's fun. The creation of the clay monster must therefore be taken as an attempt to retaliate and to express his hidden aggression.

It is impossible to comment on every type of plastic creative work which children may produce. The few examples cited in this chapter may suffice to point out that plastic materials play just as important a role in the development of the child as do graphic media.

When a child works with plastic material, a definite intention to create specific objects is not always present. The activities based upon motor patterns may lead to forms which suggest definite objects which might be elaborated with secondary intent. When a plastic object is created it is not merely considered as an image with more or less similarity to the object, but it is also endowed with function. This function might be a passive one and the object might be merely played with. It might also take over the role of aggressiveness; it may talk and act. In this way, the plastic figure becomes an object of importance in the child's life. The child is given a chance to "create" his conception of the world in a real, visible and tangible form. Consequently, all these activities constitute a great emotional release for the child. (Bender and Woltmann, 1937, p. 299.)

The combination of a child's creative work and his own story are as revealing as Rorschach responses and stories told to the pictures of the Thematic Apperception Test. Plastic creative work is a projective technique in the true sense of the word because, in the words of Lawrence K. Frank, the child, when given plastic material, does not create what the therapist arbitrarily has decided the child should make. The child is confronted with an unstructured, polymorphous, pliable, three-dimensional material, which he must structure and endow with this own meanings, desires and idiosyncrasies.[b]

[b] The author is greatly indebted to Dr. Lauretta Bender, Senior Psychiatrist, Psychiatric Division of Bellevue Hospital, New York, for her help and encouragement in many of the original studies and for giving valuable information which greatly enhanced this selection.

# The Benefits of Water Play[2]

RUTH E. HARTLEY, LAWRENCE K. FRANK,
AND ROBERT M. GOLDENSON

Anyone who has watched a three-year-old zestfully wash and rinse and squeeze a pair of doll socks cannot doubt the irresistible attraction that water holds for the very young. The child's utter absorption in this rhythmic activity and the almost hypnotic effect it has upon him inevitably calls to mind the fascination of a waterfall or of waves rising and falling on a beach.

In view of this fascination, one would expect that water would be given a conspicuous place in programs designed for preschool and kindergarten children. It certainly is easily obtainable and little expense is involved. It is one of the few basic substances still easily available for exploration by urban children. It lends itself to a variety of activities and offers a wide range of manipulation and learning. But it has not merely learning values to recommend it; it has something even more valuable—the absorbed delight and joyous enthusiasm of the children as they play with it. Yet, in spite of the fact that contemporary psychology tends to accept the child himself as the best indicator of his needs and regards need fulfillment as a necessary precursor to healthful advances in development, strangely enough, the child's apparent urge for free and uninterrupted experimentation and exploration with water seems to have been almost completely overlooked. . . .

It might be appropriate at this point to consider the contributions of water play to child development from a more theoretical point of view. Most children in the preschool age range have not yet completed the adjustment tasks set by society in relation to the control of body processes—oral, anal, and urethral. Although their experience is still largely in terms of sensation, their urge to explore is constantly being curbed. Food is to be eaten, not played with, and feces and urine, which have a very intimate connection with their selfhood, are never to be handled at all. In the child's view, body products are as legitimate as any other substance, and his desire to learn about them is particularly urgent since they have been part of himself. To deny him this right is, in a sense, to alienate him from part of his being. Now, we know from

---

[2] This chapter was originally written specifically for teachers of very young children—nursery school and kindergarten—and reports observations and experiences in the use of water play as part of a research project of the Caroline Zachary Institute. It is included in this volume since it is the only extensive treatment of this play medium in the literature. It is felt the same implications for the use of water obtain for the somewhat older, but emotionally immature and disturbed child, as for the younger "normal" child described in these pages. Most of the illustrative cases have been deleted, as well as portions more specifically addressed to the teachers of young children.

recognized studies in genetic psychology that children are able to accept substitutes for activities that are denied them and often seek them in proportion to the degree of deprivation. We know, too, that they frequently equate water with urine. In view of all these related facts, it therefore seems logical to assume that free access to water will give children an opportunity to satisfy in substitute fashion legitimate needs which our child-rearing practices usually frustrate. . . .

## *The Feeling of Mastery*

In addition to the wealth of sensory pleasures and learning experiences offered by water, it is a basic material through which a child can early experience the satisfactions of mastery and achievement. For some youngsters, particularly those with few adjustment problems, the primary gratification found in water play seems to be connected with the control of a fluid medium. . . .

For uncertain children who are generally constricted in movement and show little or no initiative in attempting new activities, blowing soap bubbles seems to offer tremendous opportunities for ego building. Children not only are avid for the activity and participate for long periods at a time, but also talk about it with unmistakable satisfaction. . . .

## *Satisfactions for the Immature*

In many ways water appeared to be the royal road to the hearts of children who were behind others in social development, attention span, and initiative. They seemed most avid for all kinds of play with water, concentrated much longer on it than on any other activity, and seemed to derive the keenest pleasure from handling it as they wished. For these youngsters—whatever their actual age—it seemed to minister to two general types of needs: oral and tactile pleasure and the expression of aggressive impulses. It was therefore especially important to include such accessories as bottles and nipples, small cups, soft cloths, and sponges. Their play was usually extremely simple, repetitive, and organized around one theme, but the expressions of delight, the jealousy with which they guarded the implements, and the tenacity with which they returned to the activity in spite of interruptions and distractions testified to its importance for them. . . .

## *Outlet for Aggression*

In addition to the pleasure it affords, water play offers inviting channels through which aggressive impulses can be released. But we generally need running comments of the children themselves to prove that they are covertly expressing sentiments they dare not express more openly—sentiments such as resentment, defiance, and hostility. . . .

[An] instance of the close connection between water and very primitive hostile impulses is found in the behavior of Bud. A study of his play also illustrates the necessity of making numerous observations before the full intent or meaning can be discovered. For, in his case, we first noticed only indiscriminate delight in playing with water, but as we continued our observations we began to understand that water meant much more to him. For example, in his first session with miniature life toys he splashed some water on the floor and explained that the toy horse he was playing with had urinated. And another time, he used water to obliterate a male figure which he had molded of clay during a series of hostile fantasies....

### *Relaxation and Absorption*

In contrast to some of the statements cited above, other teachers emphasized the soothing and absorbing qualities of water for children ordinarily rather scattered and explosive in their play. For example, one teacher of very young children in a guidance nursery said

> Water is a relaxing kind of thing; it is good in that very few aggressive feelings are expressed there. A very disturbed child, Beth, would be happy at water and retreat to it and play for a long time. We have used water-play to relax a child when he was disturbed. When the kids were hectic and wild we would take a group to the water, especially on rainy days. We could accommodate about seven children at one time. Outside we used water for painting and for scrubbing with soap. The children had a lot of tea parties, pouring the water; they used water in the sandbox too. This would make a noticeable difference in them.

... It would be a mistake, therefore, to believe that ministering to oral and aggressive needs is the only advantage of water play. It seems outstandingly fruitful in these directions for very young or very immature children. But for older children and for other kinds of children it seems to offer additional benefits. Many aggressive children are definitely soothed, relaxed, and quieted by a chance to play freely with water while other children, who are ordinarily extremely inhibited, become stimulated, gay, and free, even inviting social contacts that they cannot ordinarily undertake....

### *Liberating Effects*

Teachers who recognize the release and stimulation derived from water play are often particularly impressed with its catalytic effect on youngsters who are ordinarily solitary and lost. Not only do they mingle with other children during the activity, but afterward they freely approach materials which they had been hesitant to use. An uninterrupted session with water will often prove the "open sesame" to activities with clay, finger paints, or the easel....

### *The Versatility of Water*

Viewed in perspective, the observations of teachers and special observers present a challenge on theoretical grounds. Why should this simple substance have such varied effects? No other material, not even clay or finger paint, has its protean quality to the same degree. For one thing, the repetitious and somewhat monotonous nature of water play, together with the soft and yielding quality of the material, may account for its relaxing effect on tense and anxious children. The fact that it demands no special skills and involves no achievement goals may explain why it neither threatens nor thwarts the anxious child who cannot take the pressure of social contacts or the adult-directed use of other materials. Again, its mild yet pleasurable sensory qualities afford withdrawn, constricted youngsters stimulation without excitement. Likewise, the chance to pour and splash and mess offers these children, as well as more active and outgoing ones, not only a means of expressing aggression but also a way of escaping the pressures of growing up and of regaining the privileges of infancy. Moreover, clinical reports on inhibited children often reveal that they have responded to parental prohibitions by a generalized lack of interest and venturesomeness. They retreat into safe and "good" behavior—but free play with water gives them a chance to explore and experiment with a medium that has been denied to them. Time and again we have seen water play lift the burden of anxiety and release hidden resources of interest and vitality.

But what of the possibility of arousing guilt reactions which might block any benefits that water play could hold for the child? We can only report that not one of the hundred and more children we observed seemed to suffer sufficient anxiety to interfere with enjoyment. In only two cases was some tension reported. In one, the child simply refused to play with water at first, but after a period of observation came to accept it fully. In the other, a three-year-old was reported to need assurance after pouring water over miniature life furniture. Close contact with the teacher and assurance that it was all right to play with water at a special time and with special toys were enough to relieve this child's mind.

The neutral quality of water is another reason for its enormous flexibility and varied effects. Because it offers so little resistance and makes so few demands on the children, yet lends itself to so many satisfactions, the range of its appeal is unlimited. As we have pointed out, the very young child finds in it a substance that he can manipulate and master more easily than any other—provided adults do not interfere. He can transform it into almost anything and use it to experiment with his own powers and with the qualities of other materials. . . .

We have not discussed the contribution of water play to a sense of participation in the adult world. Cleaning-up offers an apportunity for identification with grownups. Unfortunately, however, some teachers regard water play as largely a girl's activity and limit it almost completely to cleaning dishes, bathing dolls, or washing doll's clothes. But in centers where water is freely used as a substitute for paint—water painting—as well as for washing surfaces such as tables and walls, for blowing masses of bubbles, and pouring from vessel to vessel, boys are just as eager to participate and frequently remain at the activity longer than girls do. It may very well be that in the cleaning-up function boys can find an acceptable channel for identification with a mother figure which they need at the preschool level, but cannot find in other activities because of cultural taboos against male interest in "women's work."

## *Conclusion*

To sum up, water play has many values and can be used for many purposes in the preschool and kindergarten program. To the development of sensation and feeling it offers more varied experience and a keener pleasure than any other material except finger paint; to intellectual development it contributes its great flexibility and vast opportunities for experimentation and exploration. It stimulates the inhibited child and soothes the explosive. Scattered, disorganized youngsters are able to concentrate on it for long periods of time. Those who are uncertain of themselves gain a sense of achievement and find in it a channel for expressing emotions not condoned in their primitive forms. Many children who have had trouble in the group situation begin their adjustment through water play. Others who are tense, fearful, withdrawn, and inhibited indicate a general loosening-up and growth in spontaneity by their acceptance of water as a medium and by their increased freedom in using it. . . .

A few words of caution seem appropriate here. Because of the striking and varied advantages of water play, there has been a tendency among educators to expect it to be a universal panacea. This we must guard against. We have no evidence that it is effective in every kind of developmental problem or personality difficulty. Our evidence simply indicates that it is particularly valuable where there is a question of overactivity or constriction of interest or movement. We have reason to suggest, too, that the child who "gets stuck" with water play and who uses it repetitively in the same patterns or around the same theme needs special help in finding other avenues of expression and special encouragement to grow beyond the joys of infancy.

# ❀ Changes in Meaning of Play

LYDIA JACKSON
AND KATHLEEN M. TODD

Many young children talk little, but make use of primitive material, often the same material to express more than one conflict, similar play taking on different meanings as treatment progresses. Lionel's phases of treatment demonstrated this. As mentioned previously,[3] Lionel, aged five, spent the whole of each interview at the clinic, week after week, playing with sand and water. At the first few interviews, he showed extreme eagerness to come to the playroom. This changed to pronounced hostility; when fetched from the waiting room, he refused to come, gazed sulkily at the therapist, and raised his hand as if to strike her. A few more weeks passed, and his attitude, although still hostile, became also playful; he smiled as he shook his head, refusing to come, and the threatening gesture was obviously meant as a joke. He would say to the therapist, "You go first!" and, as soon as she was out of sight, would follow her at a run. Finally, after a fairly long period of treatment, he seemed to accept the therapist as a friend, and signs of hostility vanished completely.

His mother was an intelligent woman of fiery disposition who had a grudge against life, for she had been lame from childhood as a result of a T.B. hip. Lionel resembled her in temperament. She loved him deeply, but in her training of him had been impatient and sometimes violent; early in life he had been severely rebuked and punished for showing what is common in infancy, an interest in the product of his bladder and bowels. Children who are uninhibited ask many questions and show a natural curiosity about both bodily excreta and functions; they take a certain personal pride in what "their bodies can do," and this natural curiosity should not be frowned upon. Lionel's sand-and-water play in the first stage of his treatment . . . was mainly an expression of the repressed earlier excretory interest which he, for the first time, could satisfy fully, although in a symbolic form. His eagerness to greet the therapist was, at that time, merely gratitude for being allowed to play out his forbidden theme. Yet the unconscious memory of his mother's punishment and scoldings for such behavior in the past stimulated feelings of guilt and caused a conflict between the primitive impulse to satisfy these interests and the fear that it was wicked to do so. The mechanism of the crude super-ego, the unconscious controlling factor, came into play; the condemnation of himself for indulging in "dirty" play was projected on to the therapist—she was the wicked person who allowed, nay, even encouraged, him to do wrong

[3] For further discussion of this child see Jackson and Todd's selection, "Play as Expression of Conflict," reproduced in Chapter 15 of this volume.

things. Hence his hostility toward her, which also served as a vehicle for his resentment against the mother who had checked him so sternly in the past.

When Lionel was about halfway through his treatment, an important change occurred in his family situation; his mother, who had been pregnant for some months, fell ill again with T.B. and had to be removed to hospital. The father, a laborer of good character but poor intelligence, was unable to look after the two children (Lionel had an elder brother, aged nine), and they were placed in institutions. The Home where Lionel went was not a good one; the children were too subdued and had no toys to play with, the food was not plentiful, and affectionate attention was completely absent.

After his transfer to this Home, Lionel had to stay away from the clinic because he developed skin trouble. When he came back, he showed neither his former enthusiasm nor antagonism. He began by playing with sand and water as before. He mixed the wet sand carefully, ladled the mixture out on plates, calling it "porridge," "potatoes," or "pudding." Much of it was presented to the therapist, the rest was set upon a tray which had to be put on a high shelf, inaccessible to other children, who, Lionel knew, would come to the playroom after him. This variation in play, with its emphasis on the accumulation and preservation of food, seemed to have arisen directly from his feelings of loss when he was separated from his parents and, perhaps, in a more complex way from his earlier feeding deprivations, for his mother had had difficulties in breast feeding. In the infant's mind food and affection are inextricably connected; deprived of affection, Lionel felt himself deprived of food. Giving "food" to the therapist therefore was prompted by an unconscious desire to propitiate her; he wished to restore to one adult, the therapist, what he longed to take forcibly from another—his mother—that is, her withheld affection.

Lionel's mother remained in hospital for several months. During that time he gradually relinquished play with sand and transferred his interest to water, to which he sometimes added some paint, and sometimes a few grains of sand. He called these concoctions "medicine" and pretended to drink them, usually insisting that the therapist also should do so "to make her better."

Young children often attribute illness in parents to their own hostile and antagonistic feelings toward them. This—his need for restitution to his mother—he demonstrated in his play with the therapist. He played at giving "medicine" to the therapist to reassure himself that he could make her—and his mother—better, that he was no longer a destructive, hateful child, but someone who had the power to "make" and heal.

Granted that some of Lionel's play might have been stimulated by what he saw around him at the institution—the food and medicines being distributed to children—it still remains extremely significant that he played so persistently with the same materials when a considerable choice of playthings was offered him and when at the Home he had no opportunity of playing with toys at all. Owing to his early experiences, this material—sand and water—was to him the most significant and symbolic of several important things; hence he used it to express his numerous conflicts as well as his changing attitudes toward the therapist. The meaning of this later phase of his play had to be communicated to him in different terms; this illustrates how necessary it is to base our understanding of the child's problem, not on play interviews alone, but on the whole situation as it is known at the time, that is, the reality situation, as well as the child's imaginative apprehension of it. . . .

## REFERENCES

BENDER, LAURETTA, and WOLTMANN, A. G. The use of plastic material as a psychiatric approach to emotional problems in children. *Amer. J. Orthopsychiat.*, 1937, **7**, 283–299.

BENDER, LAURETTA, and WOLTMANN, A. G. Play and psychotherapy. *Nerv. Child*, 1941–1942, **1**, 17–42.

WOLTMANN, A. G. Plastic materials as a psychotherapeutic medium. In R. B. WINN (Ed.), *Encyclopedia of child guidance*. New York: Philosophical Library, 1943.

❀ CHAPTER SEVENTEEN

# Symbolic Aspects of Verbal Communication

WHEN THE CHILD verbalizes his fantasies while he is acting them out in his play, the therapist has two media to work with, and the symbolic meanings may stand out more clearly. The therapist's basic orientation will determine the use he makes of this fantasy material and the level of interpretation he employs. In order to fully understand the story or play themes, the therapist needs to share the child's fantasies, to take the roles assigned him by the child, or to sense that a certain role is waiting to be assumed.

Gondor, in her article, stresses not only the importance of understanding the fantasy communications of the child, but the necessity for the therapist to maintain a firm hold on reality.

Many of the children's imaginative productions and fantasies are adapted from fairy tales. Consequently, insight into the universal symbols inherent in myths and folklore aids in understanding the play themes which children are very apt to employ as a means of representing their own conflicts. Schwartz's selection analyzes certain basic symbols, common themes, typical heroes, and interactions frequently encountered in the fairy tale. He points out the similarities to dream material, the recurrent emphasis on magic and omnipotence, and the structural patterning around developmental events.

For further exploration and interpretation of one specific theme found in many folk tales, the reader is referred to

Fraiberg's[1] analysis of tales of the discovery of buried treasure. In summarizing the oedipal symbolism in such tales as "Aladdin," "Ali Baba," and "The Tinder Box," she states,

> These tales of the buried treasure and the discovery of great wealth are among the oldest daydreams of the race. These are the longings of childhood which live on in the unconscious memory of the grown man. Their ageless appeal derives from the universal and perennial mystery which confounds the child in his first investigations of origins. In every life there is this momentous discovery of the secret through an accidental touching or an observation, a revelation of the "magic" of the genitals. And always there has been a magician with greater powers and a secret knowledge which is denied to a poor boy. There is the childhood mystery of "the place" where the treasure is hidden, the mysterious cavern which has no door, the hidden place deep under ground. And there is the unwavering belief of the child that if he should have the magician's lamp, the pirate's map, the key to the treasure, the knowledge of "the place," he could win for himself this treasure of treasures. In this ageless daydream of childhood, the poor boy who has nothing steals the magician's secret, the pirate's map, and outwits the powerful opponent who stands between him and the treasure.

Puppets are frequently used by children in spontaneous dramatizations that partake of the quality of fairy tales. It is often less threatening to express anxieties, fantasies, and hostilities via puppet characters than in more direct play constructions or in face-to-face communications. Woltmann's article is included to alert the therapist to the symbolism with which the different puppet types have been associated in the folklore of the ages.

---

[1] Selma Fraiberg, "Tales of the Discovery of the Secret Treasure," *Psychoanalytic Study of the Child*, IX (1954), 218–241, p. 241.

# *Use of Fantasy Communications in Child Psychotherapy*

LILY H. GONDOR

The field of child psychotherapy is still a young and unexplored territory in which the therapist is engaged in a kind of pioneer work. Often he must grope his way through areas not trodden upon before. He must be alert, inventive, and flexible, and frequently he must make his own discoveries.

This paper deals with the use of fantasy communications in child psychotherapy. To gain understanding of the "private world" of a person who seeks help by psychotherapy we must explore all available avenues. Modern psychotherapeutic techniques make use of the patient's verbal and nonverbal communications, dreams, fantasies, free association, and various transference materials.

In contrast to most adults who come for treatment on their own, the child is frequently referred for therapy as a result of the pressure exerted on him by the family, school, or some other authority. Although his symptoms or difficulties may be bothersome enough to motivate him to seek and accept help, he frequently sees in it either a kind of magic or some sort of learning process in which the therapist plays the role of an omnipotent magician or an authoritarian teacher. In some instances, the child may conceive of therapy as a sort of punishment inflicted upon him by an authority; at other times, he may see it as a more-or-less pleasurable period of play which, because of its weekly recurrence, may or may not interfere with other more pleasurable and more desirable activities. This does not mean that there are not many children for whom the relationship with the therapist becomes so meaningful that this visit constitutes the most important event of the week. The direct verbal communication of the child in therapy will greatly depend on his age, his ability to express himself verbally, his relationship with the therapist, and the interaction between him, the therapist, and the home environment.

We all know that in therapy with children we have to rely upon communications which are in part more subtle and in part more direct than those of adults. In fact, we have to sensitize ourselves to a very wide scale of expressions, from overt acting-out in play and reality to the slightest nuances of nonverbal communication. It is as if the child psychotherapist had to learn a new language and to acquire the art of "listening with the third ear," as Reik puts it. Yet, it is an ear which has to become sensitive to stimuli of a range far wider than those used in ordinary life. It is the understanding and the use of some of the expressions of this "new language" or mode of communication which will be discussed in this paper. It mainly refers to children between six and twelve years who constitute the bulk of the patients at the Children's Clinic of the Postgraduate Center for Psychotherapy. This age span which, in Freudian terms, is described as the latency period, is accepted by all psychological theories as the time of life in which the child makes decisive steps away from the family into the world. It is a time in which he has to learn to conform, to work, to accept limitations, to develop skills and working habits, and to get integrated into the group. It seems that these first steps toward greater independence bring out many disturbances that may have been dormant before and either had not been noticed or were ignored by the family. It is also a period the needs of which may often prove too hard to comply with for a child whose emotional growth has not kept pace with his cultural development. The average child of this age has usually grasped and accepted the fact that there are rules set by the world of adults which prevent him from participating in certain specific activities. He also has become increasingly aware of the fact that his parents are not omnipotent and cannot avert many of life's dangers.

Apart from these anxiety-arousing factors, there are other anxieties emanating from deeper emotional layers. They have a dark, nightmarish quality. They are images which the child finds difficult to express, to explain, or to talk about. When he attempts to do so, he frequently does not elicit an appropriate response from the adults, and often his attempts at communicating are met with smiles or even open ridicule. Thus the child learns that he might be better off keeping them to himself. After all, if he mentions his fear of "witches," "the bad man," "the monster," or "the ghost," figures once introduced into the child's fantasies by the adults themselves (via fairy tales), the benevolent adults then maintain reassuringly that "such things do not exist." Such explanations, logical as they seem, do not alleviate the child's anxiety. They only make him aware that he does not gain much by talking about such fears with adults. Once a nine-year-old, very intelligent boy said to his therapist—and it must be added that he had never heard of Freud and the Oedipus complex—"At night, when the room is dark, I often hear a creaking of the floor. I become terribly afraid and pull the blanket over my head. My heart beats loud and fast. I almost can't breathe. Then the terrible idea comes into my mind that my parents are coming into the room. Father has a knife in his hand." When the boy was asked what he expected to happen, he said, after some hesitation, "I know that this is silly, but I am afraid he will do the same to me that was done to our Mitsoo!" (Mitsoo was the name of the tomcat that had been altered some time before.) After having gotten this off his chest, the boy said, "You see, I know that this is impossible and that my parents would never do that. I also know that there are no monsters and ghosts, but still I am afraid."

There is also another realm of fantasies about which the child hesitates to talk with adults, in which, however, he usually permits participation within the framework of his play. This is the realm in which he is the hero, the all-powerful superman who triumphs over anxiety, weakness, and insecurity. Whereas he rarely permits others to peek into the eery world of spirits and forbidden impulses, he is ready to share these lighter spheres, at least to some extent.

In dealing with children who show such signs of emotional disturbance and who are referred for psychotherapy, it is of paramount importance that the therapist be able to evaluate, understand and utilize the fantasy-communications of the child. Here is one of the factors that help us arrive at a diagnosis. The quality and structure of communication of the fantasy material differ markedly for the psychotic and the neurotic child. It is one of the characteristics of the psychotic child with his feeble anchorage in the world of reality that the slightest stimulation stirs up a flow of fantasies which are usually of a perseverative, obsessive nature and which show elements of bizarreness. The way in which the borderline psychotic and the neurotic child will bring up his fantasies as well as their content can then help us in estimating the depth of the disturbance and indicate the specific emotional phase he is undergoing within the process of psychotherapy.

Some cases which were selected for this purpose may serve as an illustration. The author wishes at this point to emphasize that fantasy material can be used in a similar way as dream material is used in the therapy of adults. We know that dreams have manifest and latent contents, that they operate with general and private symbols, that their content may be indicative of increasing or decreasing ego strength, and that they may inform us about the stage and progress of therapy (Gutheil, 1951). We become acquainted with the patient's private symbolism by having him bring out his associations to his dreams. We become acquainted with the child's private symbolism as it is expressed in his fantasies, we discuss with him these fantasies and accept them as a legitimate means of communication. By doing so, however, we must never ourselves empathize with the child so far as to leave the ground of reality. This would make the child suspicious and anxious.

The therapist has to remain an adult with all his responses rooted in reality, yet an adult who is *with* the child in any situation, even in his world of fantasy—an adult who understands, accepts, and, if he wishes, can converse in the language of this world. It is this ability of the therapist that renders the relationship between child and therapist so unique and special. It frequently becomes the only real experience for the child. Adults have talked and played with him before. Oh yes, they have built and run trains with him. But rarely have they accepted a role in the "make-believe game," taken this role seriously and acted it out the way the child expected them to. It seems to me that, frequently, in the course of such a game, the child begins to feel really understood by the therapist for the first time.

A little six-year-five-months-old boy was referred to therapy because of a severe anxiety state and various obsessive-compulsive traits. He seemed to manifest all the classical features which are characteristic of the obsessive-compulsive syndrome: obsessive fears, meticulousness, reaction formations, isolation, sadomasochism, and intellectualization. At the time of referral, the main objects of his fears were prehistoric animals which he had seen at the Museum of Natural History. He was aware of the fact that these animals did not exist any more and could not again come to life. As it turned out, he was afraid also of ghosts, skeletons, and goats. Yet, as he later brought out, it was the gigantic size of the dinosaur that made him feel as though it could crush him. He was able to give up his obsessive ruminations about these animals, and his fears diminished somewhat, when he started to play with a dinosaur family cut out of paper for him. This activity not only gave him a feeling of mastery over this frightening animal, but it started him on the communication of fantasies of being swallowed up. These, in turn, led to others of a more secretive nature dealing with defecation, fear of contamination and of injury. The little boy, let us call him Peter, who up to the time of therapy indulged almost exclusively in solitary games, had suddenly met a person who was willing to play with him, to listen without being frightened, and to accept him in the double role which mirrored his conflict, namely, the victim and the attacker, the clumsy giant and a superman in the shape of a mouse, which he called significantly "Petey Mouse."

The mother's complaints were that Peter was overly conforming, was very much afraid of aggression and injury, that he had a marked aversion to anything that was "messy" and that—he feared—might contain germs. Apart from his obsessive fears of animals mentioned before, he had marked difficulty in forming relationships. He could play with one child at a time, and even this not too frequently. Although he was liked by the group he kept apart from it. He was an excellent student, very intelligent and alert. He was very good in verbal expression and liked to draw. Thus it was not too difficult for him to communicate both in words and drawings. After the obsessive preoccupation with the dinosaur had somewhat abated, Peter was able to let the therapist into fantasies which were less repetitive and which, eventually, brought out his aggressive impulses and fear of retaliation.

In an early phase of therapy, Peter lived in his fantasies all by himself. His house was underground and had a secret entrance. He had a servant who was, however, not a human being but a robot, a machine. He had no desire for any other company. When his therapist voiced concern about what would happen if Peter got sick or needed some help, while all by himself, he said that he could take a magic potion that would keep him in good health.

As therapy went on, the pattern of fantasies showed marked changes, as did his relationship to the therapist. There came a time in which he identified himself with the "Supermouse" conquering giants, beasts, and bandits. He opened houses by explosions and could make them whole again.

Then came a period of fantasies featuring the fear of being hurt by one's own weapons. It reflected his fear of retaliation in case he permitted himself to give vent to aggressive impulses. He then made drawings of animals—an elephant and a squirrel. In this concept, too, the pattern of the "giant versus the small, helpless one" prevails. He associated to the pictures—"The bullets shot by the elephant come back against him. The greater the bullet the more he gets hurt." The same happened when a bandit (by the name of Peter) fired at a good man. At this time, Peter frequently used the word "back-firing" and acted it out in various games in which explosions and shootings were involved.

Subsequent fantasy patterns showed marked sadomasochistic features. Fear of suffering injury as well as of inflicting injury was a theme with endless variations. Whatever we may call it, be it castration anxiety or feelings of helplessness, it probably could be translated into the terminology of any school of psychology. His fantasies started to deal with punishment meted out upon giants—animals and people. They were executed by cutting out tongues, cutting off noses, and most of all by falling into fire or hot oil. The latter occurred invariably in connection with a bowl which contained the fire or the boiling hot oil and bore marked resemblance to a toilet seat. While acting this out with puppets and drawings, Peter suddenly turned to the therapist, who was given the role of a policeman, and asked her if she knew how people were punished in hell. He then confessed to her that this thought had been bothering him for quite some time, because a little friend of his had told him all about it. In hell people who had done "bad things" were either burned in a fire or cooked in hot oil. After telling this story, Peter responded very strongly to the therapist's interpretation that he seemed to be quite concerned about what sort of punishment was awaiting him. It was about this time that anxiety started to decrease considerably to the extent that Peter was no longer afraid of going to school. He started to play with children and to form closer relationships. He also became more aggressive and less clean at home.

Then periods followed in which his games dealt predominantly with real people. Occasionally, when he played with animals, he considered them circus animals on which he could ride. He played competitive games and enjoyed group activities.

In the last session of therapy he made a picture for his therapist. It represented a caveman with a little baby dinosaur behind him, which was his pet. I don't know whether at that point Peter remembered the picture that he had drawn in one of his initial sessions about two years earlier. He had invented a little story to it. At that time, he depicted a gigantic dinosaur and a baby (little Peter) who was resisting the dinosaur by attempting to frighten it away by crying. Of course, this might suggest the idea that we are dealing here with a reaction formation, a defense mechanism used by the child in dealing with threatening impulses. By this communication we also learned that if therapy could have proceeded, the next goal might have been to bring about in the child an understanding that in reality there were neither cavemen nor dinosaurs which had to be tamed by him.

This case was selected because here the fantasies reflected so clearly the psychodynamics at the various stages of therapy. Moreover, there is a follow-up study on this patient for the next two years. He happens to be one of those patients with whom therapy proved very successful. Soon after it was terminated, Peter got a baby brother, an event for which he had been properly prepared and which he took very well. His first follow-up visit was about one year later, and there were several interviews with the mother within the next two years. The mother had been in therapy simultaneously with the boy. She reported that Peter was happy at home and seemed to be getting along well with the baby. He was good at school, had many friends, and was even a leader of the group.

Of course, Peter was one of those children who expressed himself with ease, which may lead to the following question: What about those children who are withdrawn and who have difficulty in expressing themselves? The author believes that even in such cases it is possible to help the patients in establishing a good rapport with the therapist when they are ready for it, i.e., when the relationship has reached a point of real trust. The important thing is that the therapist should be able to understand the pertinent signs and respond to them appropriately.

The following is an example of such a case, namely, a very withdrawn ten-year-old girl who had difficulty in communicating. It required a great deal of patience and understanding on the part of the therapist not to expect anything too soon from the child. The girl could have easily been threatened and even overwhelmed by any premature insistence on verbalization or on activities other than those solitary games which she herself selected and in which she persevered for a long time.

She had come to her sessions for a few weeks and had talked very little, except about a house across the street which was in the process of being torn down and which she could see from the window of the therapy room. She then selected a box of building bricks which could be interlocked and played with them. She started out by building a rather wide base for a house which she asked the therapist to keep for her until the next session. She seemed pleased when the next time she found the little structure intact, and she continued her work without any remark, seemingly quite detached. She built a wall which consumed the greatest part of the bricks and only when it was about three inches high she inserted a window—but there was no door. The building looked like a miniature prison. Suddenly she became aware that there was no door. She put in a door against the wall and said, "The door is trapped." The therapist remarked on that and asked the child why this was so—"was it because nobody was supposed to get in, because she wanted to be by herself." Then the little girl stuck one of her fingers out of the window as if waving. At this point the therapist started a conversation with the person living in this "house without a door" to which full response was given.

It seems that there is always some means by which a child is able to express himself, and it depends on the motivation and ingenuity of the therapist to help the child find that medium. The same little girl who was building the house and who had such difficulty in verbalizing directly, started to write a story which she continued whenever she felt like it. What had happened to this child within a year can be best illustrated by reading two chapters of the story, one written a year ago and one exactly one year later. The patient was ten years old when she came to therapy. In her early childhood she had shown all the symptoms of infantile autism and, for a time, had given up speech altogether. She had an IQ of 116 on her last test. She went to school and did quite well, yet she was withdrawn and isolated.

The patient started to dictate the story eight months after onset of therapy. Although she originally planned its heroine to be a girl (one of a pair of twins), she concentrated completely on the figure of a boy who until the present time has remained in the focus of the action. She identified with this boy whom she called "Junior." This boy committed all sorts of mischief and had been acting out the patient's fantasies. His pranks were directed against either the father or the mother depending on the transference situation as well as on the course of events at home. Junior displayed all the cravings for omnipotence which the patient desired herself. The story showed stereotyped patterns in its initial phases. As time and therapy proceeded its action has become livelier.

The following is a chapter written on June 21st, 1955. It deals with Junior's mother "Peg," who at that time was the leading figure of the story. She had decided to buy and run a pastry shop.

> Then Peg bought some more chocolate pudding for chocolate cream pies. She bought a package of vanilla pudding which Junior liked on top of chocolate cake because she wanted to try vanilla pudding instead of chocolate for the cream pies. Her customer bought the vanilla cream pie. It was so delicious that the pie was gone by noon. Then, her customer went back into the store and told Peg that the vanilla cream pie was delicious. Then she knew that it was O.K. to have vanilla cream pie. She went back to the market and bought some more packages of vanilla and some packages of butterscotch pudding. Then she started baking more pies with the pudding. When the pies were done she put some in the window and some on the counter. These pies went fast too. Pretty soon there was only one vanilla cream pie left; so she went and bought more stuff for the pies. She made four dozen vanilla cream pies, four dozen chocolate cream pies, and four dozen butterscotch cream pies. Then she put some in the window and some on the counter and the customers were in the pie shop again. The other men in the bakeries were jealous of Peg because she had taken their customers away and was making lots of money. That's why they were so mad at Peg. Nevertheless, they knew that being mad wouldn't help bring back the customers and more came pouring into her shop. She made

> $50.00 this time. Pretty soon it was time to go home and fix dinner. She went to the supermarket and bought a package of vanilla pudding. Then she got out her little pudding mold and started making some vanilla pudding for Junior.

The content of this story mirrors, among other things, the ungratified oral cravings of the child. It evidences an obsessive preoccupation with food purchased and prepared by the mother. However, almost all the delicious sweets are for the customers. In addition to that, the mother had left the home in her husband's absence in order to earn some money. Junior was left on his own. This reflects one of the major problems in the early relationship between this child and her mother. At that time the father seemed to be entirely out of the picture, just as Junior's father was absent.

However, it is the bland, perseverative manner in which this story was told which is of utmost significance. It was completely lacking in any feeling tone. The main content was a more-or-less repetitive enumeration of the edibles that were bought and sold. This pattern had been continued throughout many chapters succeeding the one quoted above.

Another part of the same story, dictated on June 6th, 1956, exactly one year later, follows:

> It was a rainy day. Junior came running to his mother, "Where shall I put these flowers, Mom, they were in the vase that used to be on the table." "Used to be?" said his mother. "These rainy days will be the death of me." "Why, you are not getting wet," said Junior.
>
> ". . . Didn't you hear this vase crash," Peg said to her husband. "Oh, that's what it was. I am so used to crashes," answered Mr. O'Reilly. So Peg said, "Why don't you do something." Mr. O'Reilly said, "O.K. I will do some shopping while I leave Junior at the boys' club." Then he said to Junior, "Do you know that the club is celebrating its 50th anniversary?" "No kidding," said Junior, "that's pretty old for boys. Me and Egbert have a club too." "Is that so?" said the father. "What do you call it?" "We call it 'The Me and Egbert's Club.' " When they came into the Boys Club Mr. O'Reilly said, "How's the club going?" "Just fine, Mr. O'Reilly." Then Mr. O'Reilly said, "I have to do some shopping, would you please take care of Junior?" Junior noticed two boys playing checkers. He said "What do those guys do in there?" "They are playing checkers but that's too old for you." Junior went closer to see the boys better. He said, "I can play this good! Watch, Wow, I got you!" Now that the game of checkers was in ruins, a player said, "Let's have a game of pool."

Comparing this chapter with the previous one written one year ago marked changes can be noted. The entire family is in the picture. There is more emphasis on the figure of the father than on that of the mother. The oral motive has given way to anal trends. Junior outsmarts the parents. The content evidences activity, aggression, and some sense of humor. The plot consists mainly of role playing, indicating that we are dealing here with a pseudoemotional tone rather than genuine emotional expression. However, in spite of that it contains elements of humor and shows action, something which is entirely missing in the chapter of a year ago.

The pattern of fantasy in psychotic children can be one of the best tools in measuring in the course of treatment increasing or decreasing ego strength. Of course, it can be observed only in a long-term treatment. The author had been working for about three years with a boy who was six years eight months old when he came for help. At times he seemed to be completely out of contact with the outside world, people as well as objects. From a very early age on, he had been preoccupied with his inner world which was described as quasilistening to his own inner promptings. There were periods in which he used to lie down on the floor rolling a globe in his hands and readily dropping or breaking one toy after another. His father was an artist, and the little boy showed considerable skill in drawing. His drawings, although executed in a very interesting and skillful way, reflected the bizarre thinking of the child.

During therapy, fantasies emerged which divided the treatment into various stages. At first he talked only about ships; then came a period when he was preoccupied with trains, having them bump together and fall off cliffs. Then followed a stage in which his main topic was wild animals. The peak of this quite long period was when one specific animal, a "rhinoceros," became the focus of his stories. He identified with the rhino, and it became so much an obsession with him that on Thanksgiving Day he insisted that the parents cook and serve a rhinoceros instead of a turkey. This went on for a few months, and then came the first of a sequence of stories in which human beings were included, namely, the therapist and an imaginary "bad man." He drew pictures and made a story about himself allied with the therapist and their fight against the bad man who wanted to intrude. In this session, he asked for food which he ate with good appetite, embraced the therapist, and was far more relaxed than usual.

Following the patterns of fantasy, we were able to see that they led from a preoccupation with inanimate objects over to animals and then to human beings and thus are indicative of stages of ego functioning. At the beginning, the fantasy world of this child did not include people. He did not emerge as a living being, but identified with "moving objects," which were subject to dangers and catastrophe. His anxiety was rooted in his inability to deal with dangerous impulses from within as well as with a dangerous outside world. In the second stage, the inanimate object—the machine—is replaced by a living being, an animal. The child attempts to master his anxiety and to concretize and differentiate some of his impulses. His insatiable oral cravings and aggression as well as his fear of being swallowed up come to the fore. He tries to master some of his anxiety by identification with and incorporation of the rhinoceros, an animal which he described as being his favorite because it is "so fierce and strong."

The third stage shows his acceptance of his therapist as a sort of mother figure which helps him to emerge as a human being. It also brings out some oedipal fantasies in which he unites with the mother figure against the "intruding bad man." It was about this time that the child frequently mentioned that he wanted to live with the therapist in one house and have her all for himself.

To summarize, in the current paper the attempt was made to point out the importance of understanding and using fantasy material in child psychotherapy for the purpose of investigation, evaluation, as well as an indication of the course therapy is taking at the present time. Fantasy material can be dealt with in similar ways as dream material. It can give us some information about increasing or decreasing ego strength. The weaker the ego the vaguer the boundaries between the world of fantasy and reality will become. Another sign of ego weakness is the obsessive preservation of specific fantasies as well as their bizarre content.

For the child, fantasy is a legitimate means of communication which the therapist has to learn to understand and to use.

# *A Psychoanalytic Study of the Fairy Tale*

EMANUEL K. SCHWARTZ

## *Introduction*

Early man did not draw correct conclusions concerning the world about him. At least two conditions were responsible for this: ignorance and unbridled imagination. It is not very hard to see how the lack of knowledge of nature and of the laws of causality makes it difficult for man to understand the world around him. An example of unchecked imagination is the belief, found among all peoples and all cultures, that what takes place in the dream is happening in reality (Frazer, 1923, pp. 180 f.). Among the Arabs of the Middle Ages, for instance, the relationship between dream and life was worked out in a carefully defined system. Many superstitions and misconceived actions grew out of the imperfect understanding of the events taking place in the universe and the inability to consciously think about them. In his struggle for survival, in order to cope with the environment, to perpetuate the group, and to improve himself and those he loved, man needed to be able to control nature and influence people. To achieve this goal with the limited means at his disposal, man used allegorical elaboration and symbolization giving rise to magic, superstition, myth, and folktale.

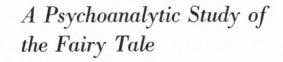

It is not my intention to examine the entire field of magic, prescientific thinking, or of folklore. I wish to devote myself specifically to a very small segment of the products of man's growth, namely, the fairy tale. The fairy tale is found in all cultures and at all times. Its essential nature is didactic and instructional. Its conscious or unconscious intent is working through some of the problems of growing up. Looking at it from a psychological point of view, we can recognize in the symbols of the fairy tale the child's struggle with nature and with parents (giants), idealization of parents, coping with sexuality, and the problems of aggression against the "big people." . . .

## *The Fairy Tale and Reality*

The very young child who tells stories is in the age of myth because he does not yet have enough knowledge of reality and the laws of nature to disregard them, he has no disbelief to suspend. An older child, carried away by play or absorbed in a fairy tale, believes in it until he stops to think, or until he is given the facts with which he can think and with which he can compare the material provided in fairy tales. The suspension of disbelief regarding the story presented in the comics, films, and television, however, becomes more and more difficult. They require, almost demand, that one's beliefs about the nature of reality be suspended, because reality is so different from the fiction of these media that one is almost led to believe that here is the "real" reality, rather than the reality in which we live.[a]

It is true that the fairy tale is not only the product of imagination but that it also stimulates imagination. Those who listen may read into it meanings it did not have for its original creators or meanings of which they could not have been conscious. Our imagination sometimes seeks out the implicit significance of the original and enlarges upon it, drawing upon the experiences of our subsequent development. Nevertheless, the conflict between belief drawn from myths and belief drawn from reality is more critical today than it has ever been.

One of the most obvious characteristics of the fairy tale is its contradiction of reality. The heroes of the fairy tale are human beings, as a rule, ordinary human beings in an ordinary world; but these ordinary human beings are surrounded by and become involved with magic, which stands in opposition to reality. The manner and action of the protagonists are exaggerated and supernatural. The commonplace events of life are cloaked in the supernatural. The birth of the hero is strange (Rank, 1952). He is born because his mother has eaten a particular food or drunk a certain water; he has fallen from heaven in a golden box or is pulled out of the river; he is made

[a] These factors may have some bearing upon the etiology of behavior disorders and even more severe pathology in children. See Heinz Hartmann, "Psychoanalysis and Sociology," in *Psychoanalysis Today*, Sandor Lorand, ed. (New York: International Universities Press, 1944).

of iron by the blacksmith or of wood by the carpenter. Then he may be suckled and reared by an animal. He develops extraordinary powers, usually physical characteristics, such as superhuman strength, speed, and acuteness of the senses, so that he can see and hear at a distance, and even hear the dead under the earth. The fairy tale hero is, in the physical sense, a primitive counterpart of the modern Superman. But he is not distinguished by greater intelligence or education, except for his incredible cleverness—sometimes even cleverness at stealing ("The Turnip"). The hero frequently falls into strange states, such as death-like sleep, or is changed into strange animals, flowers, or stones. Changing form is a typical experience of the fairy tale hero. In death, too, which is rare, he may have a strange fate; he may change into a bird and fly away or sit on top of a mantel and tell the story of his death, or he may grow as a flower or tree out of the grave.

Fairy tales in which the hero is a woman are less common; but these, too, deal with the problem of finding a mate. Here, however, the problem is not so much "getting a man" as getting a husband of royal blood—a prince or king. Sometimes, she gets her just deserts; her efforts may be frustrated, she may be slandered and even punished (for example, the two stepsisters of Cinderella; each had one eye plucked out by a dove).

Most of the heroes and heroines are of marriageable age, in the full bloom of youth. Only those fairy tales which deal specifically with children are exceptions. Usually not more than two generations are included in the fairy tale which begins with the birth of the hero and continues through marriage. The parents play secondary roles. The stepmother, on the other hand, appears prominently in many of these stories, especially as the antagonist of the heroine. Any member of the family, any relation except the father and the mother may be represented as evil and may oppose the hero.

In every way, the fairy tale reflects the culture in which it arises. The high value placed upon the child and the low esteem in which women were held, can be seen in the German fairy tale. A woman who produces boy babies (economically prized higher than girl babies) is, nevertheless, held in low regard even when the pivot of the plot is the baby.

The heroes of the fairy tale come from two opposite social strata: the royalty and the poor. If the hero is of the lower social class, he is usually the son of a peasant, fisherman, shepherd, forester, shoemaker, broommaker, or tailor. Almost exclusively in the German fairy tale (sometimes also in the Persian or Oriental tale), being a soldier is the hero's calling.

One of the most preferred themes is the rise of the lowborn to royal position. Much less frequently does the son of a king, against all opposition, take a lower-class girl for a wife, and only in the fairy tale does she thereby gain the highest rank in the land.

As stated above, the fairy tale is not concerned with reality, for it has a reality all its own. Its causality is not of reality or of science; it is the causality of magic and a world of activity in which everything is possible, anything goes, and no holds are barred. The logic of the fairy tale is not logic in our sense, nor is it real in our sense; it has a logic and reality of its own. . . .

The dramatis personae of the fairy tale may also include the sorcerer, the magician, and the witch. Often they appear in human guise, but are always ugly and old—symbols of the bad parental figures. They have magical knowledge and power and can change into animals at will. Sometimes dwarfs, elves, nymphs, spirits, fairies, goblins, banshees, leprechauns, and other types of spirits play a role in the fairy tale. These are the little people of the forest, earth, air, and water. Often they are annoying and unfriendly to people; sometimes even dangerous, as e.g., giants, especially the man-eating variety. Creatures like the dragon, griffin, and phoenix, and some of the natural phenomena, such as sun, moon, wind, or rain, in highly personalized form may also put in an appearance in the fairy tale. Characters associated with Christianity may be found among Christian peoples, including the devil (who steals unbaptized babies from their cribs), angels, and saints. Very occasionally, even God makes a personal appearance in the fairy tale.

## *Language and Form of the Fairy Tale*

The language and form of the fairy tale are interesting. There is a triadic rhythm, for example, the psychological significance of which will be discussed later. The "sacred" number three is most common in all fairy tales of all lands (and in the Bible). Persons and things appear in threes: three kings, three giants, three glasses of wine, three nights and three days, three years. The hero must overcome three older daughters to win his bride. An obstacle is overcome only on the third trial and then by the third son, usually the youngest. The action may involve getting three wishes, facing three dangers, or solving three tasks of increasing difficulty and intensity. Less frequently, the "lucky" number seven occurs: seven dwarfs, seven ravens, seven sons, seven goats, seven days. Certain clichés have become attached to the fairy tale, such as, "once upon a time," "and they lived happily ever after." Generally, verse is absent in the fairy tale, although occasionally a few lines of poetry may be found at the beginning or end, or on special occasion during the course of the story ("Snow White," "The Fisherman and His Wife," and others). . . .

There is the story of a king who discovered a girl in his land who could spin straw into gold. She was commanded to give an example of her art, but it was impossible for her to do so unless a gremlin came to her assistance. For the third command performance, the magical little man demanded a high price—herself or her first child. She would not have to pay the reward only if she could divine his name in three guesses. The happy ending is known. This tale is to be found in many languages, but its name varies: "Tom-Tit-Tot," in English; "Furti-Furton," in French; "Rumpelstilschen" or "Hoppetinken," in German.

Characteristically, the fairy tale takes place in no specific time or clime. Most begin with "Once upon a time . . . ," "Many, many years ago . . . ," or some other formula referring to the indefinite past, such as, "Long, long ago, even longer than the memory of the oldest man now living, there lived. . . ." The locale is some distant, unknown place, and if a place is specified, it is usually the fantastic and faraway, such as Spain, or the Orient, or the other side of the Nile, or the like. Most of the people remain anonymous. When names are used, they are usually very commonplace, such as Joseph, John, Hans, Gretel, Alice, Mary, and Rose. Some names reflect personal characteristics, as Cinderella, Little Red Riding Hood, Snow White and Rose Red.

## Contents of Thoughts of the Fairy Tale

At first glance, it may seem that the aforementioned fairy tale is intended only for entertainment, but it has a more serious foundation. There is a widespread belief that a person's name is a vital part of him, that his name stands in an indissoluble relationship to his very existence. Power over a human being can be exercised, if you have power over his or her name. This belief has a great tradition in magical, cabalistic (The Golem), and religious thinking (Yahweh). We say, "Speak of the devil" when somebody appears whose name has just been mentioned.

In our fairy tale, the kobold becomes impotent when his real name is discovered and uttered. The name, which is a mishmash of meaningful word-stems describing characteristics of the demon, has such a strange sound because of the old belief that the gods spoke their own peculiar language which was not understandable to mere mortals.[b] The wife or daughter of a king may spin because spinning was one of the most important crafts of olden times; spinning is often the way to win a prince or a king ("The Three Spinning Fairies"). The figure of the gnome who helps her to spin has ancient roots, because dwarfs were supposed to be good spinners. All the essential elements of this fairy tale rest firmly upon early beliefs and cultural developments.

Totemistic thinking, too, is reflected in the fairy tale. A Bear-Son is born to a bear and his human wife. This motif is often masked when the hero is only fed by a female bear, a she-wolf, or another animal. Totemistic ideas are found in food preferences and taboos; they are connected with animals that are spared because their flesh is not to be touched. The hero can be a descendant of animals, or he is conceived when his mother has eaten of a specific animal, such as the fish. Sometimes we find cannibalism expressed in the fairy tale ("The Robber Bridegroom").

In the fairy tale we may also find the belief (quite common among less developed peoples) that certain persons possess secret powers, especially those

[b] Compare here the "secret languages" children often invent in their games.

who practice the art of healing (medicine) or who otherwise deal with illness or sorcery and alchemy. Such power is based upon the possession of specific secret information ("The Devil and the Three Golden Hairs," "The Sorcerer's Apprentice"). . . .

An analytic examination of the material of the fairy tale might seek to uncover its latent meaning and to integrate it with our knowledge of psychodynamics, the culture development and the life styles in which it arises. Or one might gather the type of human problems and the solutions offered. Or the fairy tale might be studied for characteristics of mental functioning. In doing so we find that, like the dream, the fairy tale (1) deals in opposites, in contrasts; (2) is illogical; (3) has manifest and latent meaning; (4) uses symbolism. (In the concrete representation of verbal images abstract ideas are conveyed, such as seven-league boots.) Furthermore, the fairy tale (5) expounds and expands the concept of reality; (6) is a dramatized form of expression; (7) contains sexual elements; (8) contains cultural elements; (9) expresses wishes; (10) is not rational or realistic; (11) has humor, e.g., word play and puns; (12) employs mechanisms of condensation, substitution, displacement, devaluation, and overevaluation. These may well be the characteristics of all forms of human thought, dreams, art, the psychopathology of everyday life, neurosis, and psychosis.

The fairy tale, as we have seen, is timeless and spaceless and operates beyond the limits of objective reality, where nothing that man can imagine is impossible. It is incorrect to assume that, therefore, the fairy tale is an expression of the unconscious which is directed to the unconscious of the child, and that this is its didactic function. There is no unconscious-to-unconscious communication in the fairy tale.

Symbols, to be accepted, must accord somewhere with reason and life's experience. . . . As is the case in other areas where symbols are found, the fairy tale deals with deep perceptions, anticipations, longings, and fears. It is an integration of sensations, intuitions, feelings, and thoughts combined in such a way as to provide symbols to the child in the form of concrete images. To the child it is, therefore, more understandable than other forms of communication. The symbols are used in exhortatory and instructional fashion, in the hope that they will be incorporated in the developing ego.

Sullivan (1953, pp. 329–343) relates the power motif to magic. The child seeks to master the world, and his magical maneuvers, such as reaching for the moon, help develop security and, ultimately, actual mastery of the real world. In this connection, the fairy tale also carries with it some of this magic in that it provides examples or models to be emulated in striving to master the real world, especially the emotional world of human relations, as exemplified in its manifest and latent communications. Sullivan's analysis of dreams and myths also holds true, in part, for the fairy tale, especially where he indicates that the dream, like the myth, represents a valid though distorted operation for the relief of insoluble problems of living. The problems dealt with in the myth, he says, concern many people, and this fact keeps the myth circulating, refined and polished as the generations roll it around.

The dream functions specifically for one person, in an immediate situation, but insofar as the dreamer remembers and communicates it, he seeks validation with somebody else. The fairy tale, on the other hand, is not validated by the culture in which it lives; the educational message (implicit and explicit attitudes and values encouraged or devalued) may be fostered by the consensus of the culture in which the child develops. In this sense, the fairy tale reflects the problem-solving mechanisms, typical of many of the most creative acts of mankind.

## *The Number Three*

In connection with the question of symbolism and magic, I wish to discuss the number three in greater detail. In olden days, numbers have been thought to be of magical quality. Many numbers, such as, one, three, five, seven, eleven, twelve, thirteen, twenty-one, thirty-nine, seventy-seven, have special significance. Those who play dice, cards, or roulette know the magical meaning of some numbers. In religious thought, cabalistic lore, and magical practices the number three is of particular importance. This is the case in Oriental as well as in Western cultures. The number three is significant not so much, as Freud put it, because it is a symbol of the male genitals,[c] but, it seems to me, because it is the actual number of what constitutes the smallest basic human unit, namely, the family. A family consists of a father, a mother, and a child. This is one of the basic human experiences. Of course, my position is as undemonstrable a notion as the idea that the number three symbolizes the male genitals. Hence, number three is sacred (Freud, 1943, pp. 137 f.).

Abraham (1923) makes an interesting analysis of the meaning of threeness. He feels the number three in myths and fairy tales has deep psychological significance, a significance which can be confirmed by individual fantasies in psychoanalysis. One of the most interesting insights arises from the analysis of the fairy tale, "Tischlein, deck' Dich!" in English, "The Table, the Ass and the Stick." A father sends his three sons out into the wide, wide world. Each has learned a trade and has received a gift from his master at the end of his apprenticeship. The oldest son gets a small table which, upon command, will cover itself with the most delectable foods. The second is given an ass out of whose anus, upon command, gold pieces fall. The third receives a sack in which there is a stick. Upon command of its possessor, the stick comes out of the sack, routs all enemies and, again upon command, returns to the sack.

[c] Ovid offers many examples of the importance of three in love-making; success is guaranteed, for instance, if you put three pinches of incense into a mouse-hole under the threshold.

According to Abraham, the first gift, the table, indicates a wish-fulfillment in the area of orality. Every child, he says, through the omnipotence of his thoughts, wants to be able to have, at all times, any food that he may desire. The second gift is related to anality. Prizing the feces and equating them with gold is easily seen in the development of the child. The second gift, the ass, represents, then, the realization of the wish to be able to create hoped-for riches by way of anal production. The significance of the third gift—the stick in the sack—is not so immediately apparent, says Abraham. It would be difficult to understand it if we did not recognize the symbolic significance of the stick. The sack and the stick and the commands "out of the sack" and "into the sack," clearly represent erection and sexual intercourse. The third son, therefore, receives the gift of unlimited potency which obeys his will, unconditionally and unreservedly.

The tale contains three wish-fulfillments involving the three erogenous zones: the mouth, the anus, and the phallus. Abraham points out that the wish series follows Freud's levels of psychosexual development.

It is interesting that the two older brothers in the beginning ridicule the youngest brother. The oldest, however, very soon loses his wonderful table to a fraudulent innkeeper with whom he had spent the night; he thinks he has his magic table but, instead brings home an ordinary one. His father laughs at him as, in vain, he tries to make the table produce the desired delicacies. The second brother fares no better with his ass; he, too, is deceived by an innkeeper and scoffed at by the father. That the innkeeper and the father both symbolize the jealous father can be guessed, says Abraham, without further psychoanalytic investigation. Only the youngest son conquers the innkeeper by his manliness, symbolized in the stick, and he is, therefore, also recognized as such by the father at home. Abraham feels that this fairy tale confirms real experience, that not the infantile fantasies of oral or anal origin, but rather the successful primacy of the genitality of man is the goal to be prized.

The Roumanian tale, "Fairy of Fairies,"[d] also points in this direction. The hero woos the beautiful maiden, a nymph, and is held off. "Until you have accomplished what no man has ever accomplished, you shall not touch me." He begins adventures that take him "through undreamt-of regions to the ends of the world, where no bird has ever flown, where the spaces are filled with unearthly voices and with far unearthly silences, devoid even of a breath of wind." Soaring winged horses appear; golden palaces spring up in the manner of baffling mirages; there are "strange forests of which the boughs resound like so many strings of music; airy, creeping and wild-rambling things endowed with human speech." Our hero conquers all but wins his true love only by a ruse, typical of these stories. He comes upon two brothers who

[d] Adapted from Marcu Beza, *Paganism in Roumanian Folklore* (London: J. M. Dent & Sons, 1928), pp. 84 ff.

ask him to settle a fight over who shall get a magical leather cap and a magical brass rod, given them by their father. "Whoever puts the cap on his head is concealed from the eyes of all people; as for the rod, whoever possesses it and strikes the ground with it obtains command and authority over seven tribes of Jinns." The rest of the story is obvious. Our hero throws a stone and says, whoever reaches it first gets the rod. They go chasing the stone, as our hero dons the cap and grabs the rod. With the acquisition of aggressive genitality, he has the wherewithal to win the fair maiden. . . .

## *The Fairy Tale and the Development of Man*

It is especially interesting to attempt to relate the development of the fairy tale to the development of man. We can thus see the effects of growing horizons and changing cultures upon the fairy tale, as upon other forms of art, dance, and literature. The most widespread form of early folk literature is the fairy tale and the myth. Wundt (1900) suggests that fairy tales fall into two general classifications: the "heavenly" or "celestial fairy tales" and the "fairy tales of fortune." Celestial fairy tales appeared quite early in man's history and were later displaced or assimilated by celestial mythology, so that mythology may be viewed as fairy tales about the gods. The fairy tales of fortune, on the other hand, have remained as a permanent kind of fiction, by which all other forms of narrative writing have been influenced. These fairy tales trace the fortunes of man through all the trials and tribulations of living and all the struggles with the forces around him, with society, nature, and himself. In a sense, the Horatio Alger stories, so popular with young men of two generations ago and, to some extent, even of the last generation, are tales of fortune or of adventure. Fairies do not have to appear in a fairy tale, although in some cultures they (or other little people) always do (*Fairy Legends*, 1825). In these we get the beginnings of a personal hero who gradually becomes somewhat more differentiated.

The fairy tale hero is often a child who gradually approximates the form of a hero. He goes forth into the world and meets with adventures. In these adventures he is aided by powers of magic which either he possesses himself or which are given to him by friendly supernatural forces. Opposed to him are the hostile demoniacal beings who seek his destruction (frustration). The plot usually ends with their overthrow. Good fortune comes, in part, from the actions of the hero and, in part, from the use of greater skill or magic, which derives from without. Magic plays a decisive role in the hero's destiny. His own cunning and skill are additional assets, but they rarely determine the victory (conquest). In the outcome of the fairy tale, the "good" always triumphs over the "evil." This is the manifest message, the moral of the fairy tale. (There is no choice, no compromise, no middle ground. It is always a matter of extremes.) . . .

Magnitude is an important dimension of the fairy tale. It has special psychological significance for children and, of course, also for neurotics and psychotics for whom the size of the "self," of the body and body parts, has a significant emotional cathexis. It is sometimes related also to competitive strivings with regard to the value of the "self" and its attributes. In all human beings, size is part of reality and is related to our understanding of it. Children, in fantasy and play activities, express desire for being big and doing what the big people do (Freud, 1922). Changing size is related to growth and sexuality. The fairy tale reveals these strivings.

In the fairy tale everything seems to grow to supernatural proportions. It is peopled with giants and small folk. Even animals increase in nature and stature; but they act in very human ways; they speak, show friendship and gratitude, hostility and hatred. Sometimes they represent the hero's "other self" and are his constant companions and aides. They help transport him with the speed of the wind, chop down a forest, carry away mountains, or dam up rivers. They save him from all kinds of danger and recover lost objects. But they are always exaggerated; they appear, for example, as a bird with golden feathers or as a fish who fulfills all wishes; the flesh of an animal, when eaten, makes one rich, or powerful, or able to speak the language of birds. Animals are married to human beings. Many change into human beings and then back into animals. One of the most common motifs of the fairy tale is the prince charming who, as an animal, seeks to win the love of the fair young maid and then changes again into human form to marry the princess.

In this sense of exaggeration, trees and flowers, stones and objects also have magic powers—for example, hats and clocks that make one invisible; seven-league boots; swords that, upon command, make all heads fall off; bugles that call forth an entire army; cure-all ointments and potions that make one invulnerable; dew that makes the blind see; food and drink that guarantee eternal youth, health, or life; ships that travel over land and sea. These superservices, suggestive of a brave new world in the twenty-fifth century, are given as gifts to the human hero of the fairy tale by friendly supernatural beings. On the other hand, the hero must sometimes do battle with unfriendly demons in order to extract from them these magical instrumentalities. . . .

Psychoanalytic theory describes the psychosocial development of the child through the individual stages. It deals with different kinds of experiences with regard to orality, anality, genitality, latency, puberty, adolescence, and maturity. In trying to understand the dynamics of a person's current adaptation, one seeks to reconstruct his past positive and negative experiences which may account for his present functioning. Freud looked for the multidimensional historical forces determinating the adult personality. Sullivan, too, stressed the detailed elucidation of the dynamic development of the human being from infancy onward.

There is a parallel in structure, content, and action of a fairy tale, as it follows the development of a human being. In this sense, the fairy tale may be seen as a biography, a study of the development of a man or woman, from conception to maturity. It tells about the birth of the child: in what kind of a family it was brought up; what kind of endowment it had; the ways it was educated and trained; how it went through various struggles to grow into maturity and into marriage. This is generally where the fairy tale ends.

Snow White is born out of the magic wish of her mother, the queen, who dies at her birth. The story of her growing sexuality involves her (projected or real!) struggle with the competitive, phallic stepmother, who is threatened by the beauty of the seven-year-old girl and will not allow her to be sexually more desirable than herself. She wants to eat Snow White's heart. We are told about Snow White's amazing companions, the seven dwarfs, from whom she gets training in keeping house; about animism and magic. The stepmother in disguise laces her bodice up till she's breathless (swaddling? suppression? the breasts?); combs her hair with poison (seduction? false love?) to no avail. The third time, Snow White shares the poisonous apple (sexual knowledge? the mouth?). She succumbs (enters latency?) and is put under glass until the prince comes along and awakens her (arouses her sexually?); at last they marry. So the story ends, but not without first telling about the stepmother's punishment.

True adventure fairy tales lack the aforementioned biographical construction, and the plot revolves about a hero with a certain characteristic already formed, which is the key to the action. It can be, for example, unusual smallness or great strength—"Tom Thumb," "The Young Giant."[e]. . .

The element of magic in the fairy tale is of considerable interest to the psychoanalyst who sees it also in some pathologic manifestations, such as obsessive-compulsive neuroses or some types of pychotic thinking and behavior. Magic, as already indicated, is very closely related to omnipotence feelings of childhood and plays a part in the child's struggle to cope with his environment, to understand and control sources of security and gratification.

Magic is used by the child not only in relation to parents, to gain their love or to secure a love object, but also in relation to the siblings; for example, in "Cinderella," sibling rivalry is the source of the difficulty, and magic is used by Cinderella to overcome the resistance of the siblings to her acquisition of the love object, the prince. Sometimes it is a factor in deciding the mother–daughter struggle, where the mother (or her surrogate) is seen in the framework of the Electra complex as the person who thwarts the daughter from achieving her love object ("Snow White").

But the heart of the fairy tale is not magic nor the supernatural. The plot, the action situation, for the psychologist, is the life story, the story of growing up. One of the most frequent motifs is the extremely masculine hero in pursuit of a wife. The story really consists of details of overcoming inordinate

---

[e] For a discussion of the fairy tale of adventure see Selma Fraiberg, "Tales of the Discovery of the Secret Treasure," *Psychoanalytic Study of the Child,* IX (1954), 218–241.

obstacles in order to acquire a wife, and the fairy tale usually ends in marriage. The bride may be lost several times in the course of the action but, in the end, she is his for ever, evermore.

Wife-getting may be of two general kinds. The first may be called the "heroic liberation." By his own strength and fortitude, the hero frees the young girl from evil monsters into whose power she has fallen. The second, a less violent method, may be described as a "demonstration of power." The hero must perform tasks or solve problems which he can do only through magical intervention. In the first, he uses his own resources; in the second, he needs supernatural help.

## *Fairy Tale and Ethics*

The fairy tale sponsors very few ethical values as such. Love or deep feeling almost never arises. Pure sensual desire for the physical beauty of the princess drives the hero to acquire her. They have no relationship to each other; sometimes they have never spoken a word to each other. If it is not to possess her physically, he may wish to possess the treasure that is hers or the empire of her father. Sympathy is the most common feeling.

Nevertheless, some ethical lesson may be derived from a formulation in black-and-white terms; no matter how triumphant evil may seem in the beginning, it will meet complete destruction in the end. But negative ethical values prevail, at least temporarily, such as, lust, cruelty, and brutal punishment. Sometimes stealing, clever misrepresentation, and fraud are looked upon with great delight and favor ("Puss-in-Boots"). As in many folk songs, some kind of criminality pervades most of the fairy tales. One might say they are id dominated with some (but all too little) ego or superego involvement.

The struggle between what is perceived as the "good parent" and the "bad parent" is one of the big problems of childhood. In the fairy tale, the bad mother is commonly seen as the witch (phallic mother). The great man, the father figure (Oedipus), represents the hero, or the hero-to-be, the prototype, for the young protagonist of the fairy tale. The process of social and psychological change, characteristic of the fairy tale, is childishly pursued, and magic is used to effect the changes. On the other hand, experience with having to struggle for the gratification and the fulfillment of wishes results in a social adherence to and the development of an understanding of social norms and social conformities. This does not mean, however, that the reinforcement of an awareness of socialization results in submissiveness; but a certain amount of common sense, which goes into conforming with the social mores, is a realistic necessity for children and adults alike.

All folklore, says Jones (1951, pp. 13 f.), relates to real concerns of people and to "the themes of birth, love and death. These are the springs of life, and psychoanalysis would go so far as to maintain that all our manifold imaginative interests originate there and consist only in ramifications of these themes modified by the influence of two other factors, the defensive reactions against certain dangers inherent in them (the moral superego) and contact with outer reality." Moreover, all characters in the fairy tale, for example, "represent immediate blood relatives: parents, siblings, and children. Attitudes and feelings about other people are developed by either transforming or directly transferring those belonging to the relatives." . . .

### *Summary*

The fairy tale, which, like psychoanalysis, views human behavior as conflict, is a biography told for the purpose of educating by means of the promise of gratification in the future as a premium for growing up. It is an assurance of sexual fulfillment, a union with a handsome prince or a beautiful princess. Often there is a suggestion that the lovers are actually familial figures. The child is expected consciously or unconsciously to emulate the symbolic process of the fairy tale and thus be motivated to enjoy (in anticipation) the struggle of growing-up. The fairy tale escorts the child through the stages of childhood to a satisfactory heterosexual adaptation, and, in fantasy, helps him resolve some of the significant conflicts he might have. It inspires him with the promise of heterosexual fulfillment in maturity and marriage. It reflects the timeless, spaceless, magical quality of childhood and the wonders of living. It appeals to the imagination and stimulates the possibilities of struggling with resistances in the surrounding world and in the self which make growing up so difficult. The fairly tale depicts the growth of the individual and the culture as an historic and dynamic process, an expression of the creative genius of man.

## *Psychological Rationale of Puppetry*

ADOLF G. WOLTMANN

. . . The following remarks are pertinent to a fuller understanding of the therapeutic application of puppetry. . . . Puppetry, like the folk song, the folk dance, the arts, and architecture, had its origin in religious rituals. It is not an artifact like the radio or the movies. Together with the other mentioned cultural manifestations, it has survived the rise and fall of nations and races. It has been modified by divergent cultural streams but has never been flooded out of existence; its survival to the present day testifies well for its inherent strength and general appeal.

Throughout its long existence, hand puppetry has retained a very important trait that has been lost by the marionette: hand puppetry still employs *types*, rather than *characters* created for a specific play. These types developed in various cultures and were modified by changes within those cultures, so that today the type remains although the original archetype may have disappeared. . . .

The hero of all the puppet shows that were used in the therapeutic puppet shows at Bellevue Hospital (Bender and Woltmann, 1936; Woltmann, 1940) is a boy by the name of Casper. His pointed cap and multicolored costume render him ageless, so that he can easily portray youngsters between the ages of six and twelve. The origins of this type go back to about 5000 B.C., when it appeared on the East Indian shadow stage as a servant to a rich master. Basically, he is a comedian who causes his master to become involved in all sorts of compromising situations. The same type is also noted on the Greek and Roman stage, either as a living actor or as a puppet. He has become world-famous as the English "Punch," having been introduced into Great Britain by Italian showmen during the time of Queen Elizabeth. In France, he has thrived under the name of "Guignol," in Russia, as "Petrushka," and he entertained German children first as "Hanswurst" and later on as "Kasper." The Turkish shadow puppet, "Karagöz," belongs to the same family. Basically, this type represents the man on the street with all his ambitions, strivings, and desires. He stresses primarily the earthy and material things in life. Like all of us, he oscillates between courage and cowardice. He seldom is at a loss for words, but more often than not, he uses physical force to defend himself and to settle an argument. He is both clever and naïve, full of hope and in deep despair, trusting and rejecting. Since he is only a puppet, he can act out his audience's innermost wishes and desires.

This type was used in the Bellevue puppet shows as the main character. The nature of the therapeutic aims and the age distribution of the audiences made it necessary to change him from a man into a boy. Right from the start, we noted the great popularity that he enjoyed among the children of the ward. An investigation into the children's responses and reactions over a period of several years gave us pertinent clues to his popularity. We learned that most children identified themselves very closely with him. He seemed to express their wishes and desires, and his combination of words with actions was a real demonstration for them of how problems could be handled and settled.

> Casper and his fellow puppets cannot simply be defined in psychoanalytical terms, but there is no question that the various sides of the total psychic structure are reflected differently in the various puppets. Casper is the expression of strong infantile desires which demand satisfaction. He knows that he must adapt his drives to the demands of reality. This satisfies the demands of the super-ego. We must therefore see in Casper something of the Freudian "idealized ego" which reaches for reality without being in conflict with the "id" or pleasure principle. The monkey, which plays an important part in some of the shows, gets his gratifications easily and corresponds in many ways to the "id"

> which has not been restricted. . . . Casper's parents take over the role of the super-ego. We believe that the child sees his parents as dual personalities. The Good father and the Good mother love and protect the child, feed him and show him affection. The Bad father and the Bad mother inhibit the pleasurable impulses of the child and train him in a manner not always agreeable to him. (Woltmann, 1940, p. 447.)

In order to underline the superego function of the father, we made him appear as a plainclothes detective, connected with the police department. He thus not only represents authority in the family setting, but also personifies the controlling force through which law and order are maintained in the community. The bad mother in the puppet shows is portrayed by the witch. She is the product of folklore and fairy tales. As such, she does not need any specific introduction because the children immediately sense what Casper or any other puppet might expect from her. In one of our shows, she denies food and rest to Casper, makes him work hard, and belittles all of his attempts to please her by being orally aggressive to him. In another show, she helps Casper to get rid of his baby sister.

> The part of the Bad father is portrayed by the giant, the magician, and also partly by the cannibals. The giant, through his enormous body, is a physical threat to Casper. The magician, through his magic and clever scheming, is intellectually superior to Casper. (Woltmann, 1940, p. 447.)

The cannibals show hostility to Casper and threaten him with oral aggression. They would like to cook and eat him. Cannibals appeared on the European puppet stage about two hundred years ago, probably as a result of mercantilism and colonization, which brought Europe in contact with primitive cultures.

The crocodile or alligator plays a very important part in a good puppet show. This animal represents oral aggression in a twofold way. Those children who like the crocodile identify their own oral aggression with the big mouth and sharp teeth. The child's oral aggression against the world is frequently met by counteraggression, directed by the environment against the child. Therefore, those children who are greatly afraid of the crocodile usually express their own fears of counteraggression. This probably appears to them as punishment and as fear of the harsh, forbidding forces in the world about them. Occasionally, children become overwhelmed by their own aggression. Fear of the crocodile might then be expressed in the words of an eight-year-old boy who said during a group discussion about a puppet show, "I am afraid of the crocodile. It might eat me up myself." The crocodile or alligator made its appearance on the European puppet stage with the cannibals.

The figure of the devil is another puppet character of long standing. Like the witch, he is a product of folklore and fairy tales, to which have been added theological identifications. He needs no special introduction, because every child immediately knows what he stands for. How intense the projection of youngsters into a puppet show can become is best illustrated by the example of a six-year-old boy. When the devil suddenly and without any prior warning popped up on the stage, this boy bolted from the room shouting, "Casper, pray for Jesus Christ. The devil is here."

Added to these major actors are minor characters that serve to round out any specific plot. In one of our shows, Billy, the bad boy, and his mother appear. Billy is the negative Casper in the sense that he completely rejects authority, sasses and hates his mother, beats up Casper, and is very demanding and overbearing. The contrast between the good Casper and the bad Billy has served for many illuminating discussions about various family constellations, attitudes toward parents, and the consequences that might ensue if the balance of power were shifted toward the child. Another character type, General "Hitt-'em-and-kick-'em from bang-'em-and-slang-'em," serves as Casper's Prime Minister and Chief Executor when Casper tries to build up a government for children and finds it expedient to eliminate adult control and authority.

This enumeration of puppet types may suffice to stress that puppets are capable of representing specific personalities, either directly or indirectly, or specific sides or aspects of personalities. With such an array of types, there is hardly any limit to the portrayal of problems.

Over and above the flexibility that is provided through the grouping of these various puppet types, there are other psychological factors that make hand puppetry an ideal medium for tackling and solving problems.

## *Puppetry Is a Make-Believe Affair*

A puppet consists only of a head and a costume. The hand and the voice of the puppeteer give it a pseudolife. A puppet might be beaten, but it does not feel real pain. It might be killed, but since it consists of inanimate material to begin with, killing is never real but only simulated. Situations may be very threatening, but puppetry carries with it the reassurance that everything on the stage is only a make-believe affair. This by no means detracts from the realness with which the children follow the actions, identify themselves with this or that character, and project their own wishes into the show. The make-believe nature of puppetry allows it to go beyond the limits of biological life. It is perfectly normal that a bad character like the crocodile is killed, comes back to life, is again killed, and so on. Children are not concerned about the killing, but clamor for the reassurance that takes place each time the bad and threatening character is killed. Solutions to problems have to be experienced again and again before complete mastery is achieved. However, should severely neurotic or psychotic children feel threatened by the show, one can easily reassure them by taking them backstage, where they can see for themselves that the puppets are not really alive, but are only doll-like characters guided by the puppeteer.

This make-believe nature of puppetry is further expressed by the combination of puppets used. A puppet show in which only realistic characters appear is too logical and does not allow for fantasy digressions. A puppet show in which only fantasy characters act is too unreal and fantastic and does not allow for identifications on a reality level. A good puppet show, like a good fairy tale, should therefore combine both realistic and fantasy factors. This mixture of reality and fantasy makes it easier for the child to enter into the spirit of the problem presented and aids in the identification. Since parts of the show or some of the puppets (witch, devil, giant, and so on) are symbolic expressions of attitudes, the child himself feels free to project his own attitudes into the show.

Children, by and large, enter quickly into the make-believe nature of the puppet show. Yet it will happen that very disturbed and psychotic children object to a puppet show because their own main problem consists of a severe struggle between maintaining a reality appreciation and giving in to their own delusions. One psychotic youngster felt compelled to wash not only the puppets, but also the stage. He claimed that the puppets and everything connected with them were dirty and had to be cleaned. Dirt, to this child, represented the threat of insanity, whereas clean and white stood for reality. Another one of our young patients objected to the puppet show as being too mechanical and called me the "mechanical man." This little girl went through a rapid phase of deterioration toward the end of her stay in the ward and always went into hiding when a puppet show was given. These and similar experiences taught us that severely psychotic children might conceive the puppet show as a threat to their endeavor to hang on to reality. These children were much more aware of the make-believe nature of the puppet shows and therefore reacted in very marked fashion. They felt threatened and had a strong desire of defending themselves against such make-believe. . . .

## REFERENCES


Abraham, K. Zwei Beiträge zur Symbolforschung. *Imago,* 1923, **9,** 122–126.

Bender, Lauretta, and Woltmann, A. G. The use of puppet shows as a psychotherapeutic method for behavior problems in children. *Amer. J. Orthopsychiat.,* 1936, **6,** 341–354.

*Fairy legends and traditions of the south of Ireland.* London, 1825.

Frazer, J. G. *The golden bough.* New York: Macmillan, 1923.

Freud, S. *Beyond the pleasure principle.* London: Hogarth Press, 1922.

Freud, S. *A general introduction to psychoanalysis.* Garden City: Garden City Publishing Co., 1943.

Gutheil, E. A. *The handbook of dream analysis.* New York: Liveright Publishing Corp., 1951.

Jones, E. *Essays in applied psychoanalysis.* London: Hogarth Press, 1951.

Rank, O. *The myth of the birth of the hero: a psychological interpretation of mythology.* New York: Robert Brunner, 1952.

Sullivan, H. S. *The interpersonal theory of psychiatry.* New York: W. W. Norton, 1953.

Woltmann, A. G. The use of puppets in understanding children. *Mental Hygiene,* 1940, **24,** 445–458.

Wundt, W. *Völkerpsychologie.* Leipzig, 1900.

CHAPTER EIGHTEEN

# Latency Games

WITH PROGRESSION through the latency period, active fantasies are less easily elicited. As the ego increases in strength and defenses become more firmly established, the child is generally more reality oriented. Rules and regulations assume added importance, and organized games take precedence over more imaginative forms of play. The beginning therapist may find himself at a loss in imputing any "meaning" into endless hours spent in checkers, ball throwing, or competitive dart games. He may also find himself curiously impelled to win over his young opponent and may want to explore with his supervisor, "Why do I react in this way?" and "What is it doing to the child?"

Davidson and Fay trace the transformations of early childhood fantasies, rivalries, and fears that can be found to underlie secret gangs, sports, games of chance, hobbies, collections, and other more formalized activities and learning situations.

The game of checkers is used by Loomis to illustrate the resistances and conflicts that may be evoked and then resolved by means of skillful interpretations. The dynamic implications of winning and losing are discussed as well as the values in using a game as a medium of interaction with shy, silent children.

In connection with the material covered in this chapter, the reader should also refer back to Peller's article in Chapter 9, in which she points out symbolic aspects of the structured games which are such a prominent part of the latency period.

Once the meaning of the game behavior becomes clear, the therapist is better able to respond to the feelings and defenses underlying the rather prosaic play activity.

# ❀ *Fantasy in Middle Childhood*

AUDREY DAVIDSON
AND JUDITH FAY

As children grow older, we notice gradual but none the less striking changes in their interests, attitudes, and behavior. The eight- or nine-year-old is largely concerned with activities that have definite, concrete results, with the exact ways in which things really work, and with rules, conventions, and accepted codes of behavior—that is, with the world around him as it actually is. Bob, nine, staying on a farm, was engrossed in watching and helping the men with their work, his conversation centering in the workings of agricultural machinery and details of farm management; Norman, eight, was absorbed in making the practical arrangements for a secret society; while his sister Catherine, eleven, devoted all her energy to the acquiring of Girl Guide badges and the planning of what she would need at camp.

Although at all ages the amount of fantasy expressed will depend to a considerable extent upon the environment, at this age it seems in general to be much less in evidence. This is partly due to some modification of it, as the child grows older, by increasing knowledge and experience of the real external world. The tiny child who screams with excitement and fear when a train passes cannot know that the engine is not something alive like himself—noisy, violent, and powerful as he would like to be, but is at the same time afraid of being—a creature whose behavior is frighteningly unpredictable. The older boy, who makes lists of train numbers or sets out his model railway, knows more of the true nature of trains; he has learned that they are under control and can only behave in certain ways. The dressing-gown which, to Harry, was a frightening object with a life of its own, jumping up and down in the night, the waste-pipe which seems to suck and gulp down the water like a greedy animal, and the coalman with his black face all lose their terror as the child discovers and is able to understand more of their real quality; and as they become less terrifying, they in their turn serve to modify the fantasy figures and objects which they represent.

In addition, there is in middle childhood an unconscious drive toward the repression of fantasy. At this stage, there are often great efforts to overcome masturbation, largely in an attempt to escape from the guilt and fear arising from the underlying fantasies—the dangerous and painful unfulfilled wishes to possess, displace, and separate the parents, which reached their height and were fully experienced at about three to four years. The child now deals with them by a gradual denial of the whole situation, which is seen in his growing reserve about emotional matters and his marked decrease in dependence on his parents, with some tendency to distrust them. Children of this age will often show embarrassment, contempt, or boredom over anything savoring of romantic or tender feeling. . . .

The feelings of love and hate which in early childhood were expressed vividly and directly toward the parents are now canalized and socialized and seen in relation to other adults, as for instance in admiration of famous men and women, real or fictional, and later of Scoutmasters and games mistresses, and in contempt for villains, unsuccessful schoolteachers, and all people on "the wrong side." The external world, with its comparatively stable limits, its emphasis on control and conformity, and its recognized moral standards, offers safety and reassurance against the incalculable, uncontrollable, and often overwhelming inner world of fantasy.

From this it might look as if, in middle childhood, fantasy is no longer an integral part of the child's personality. There is, however, evidence that it is not only operative, but is, in fact, finding expression in reality terms. Many of the interests of seven- to eleven-year-old children, although strongly tied to reality, can be seen to be deeply rooted in fantasy. For instance, Paul, eight, would periodically spend days digging in the garden to find buried treasure—"jewels" and "olden-day things." He dug up several pieces of china, which he carefully washed and tried to fit together, convinced that they were fragments of ancient pottery and probably of great value and eager to present them to a museum; he also found a ring, which he insisted should be taken to a jeweler to be valued and was delighted to find worth thirty shillings. At other times, he was busy digging a tunnel in an attempt to find a secret passage into the house and tapping walls and exploring the boxroom to try to find the other end of it, certain that it must exist. . . . In trying to find his lost mouth organ he thought of digging in the garden for it in case it had got buried, and insofar as this object seemed to stand for some good thing belonging to his mother, one might take his repeated searches for hidden valuables to express a fantasy of digging into her body ("Mother Earth"), "jewels" and "treasure" perhaps representing the penises and babies he expected to find inside her, and "olden-day things," the good breast which he had long ago possessed and now like the mouth organ had lost. Similarly, his many efforts to find an underground passage into the house could be seen as the acting-out of a fantasy of seeking a secret way into the mother—secret insofar as it was not known consciously by Paul himself and possibly, too, because he felt it to belong to someone else. Other material, which will be discussed later, pointed to Paul's deep interest in the contents of the human body, to his desire, combined with horror, to look inside it, and to his equation of all acts of inquiry and investigation with an aggressive penetration of the mother and a displacing of the father.

This element of secrecy and its relation to underlying fantasy is seen particularly in the organization of gangs, with their secret languages, signs, and meeting places, and exploits and activities which must be hidden from the adults even if, in reality, they would be approved of and permitted. Here the tables are turned; the child himself has an exciting alliance with other children from which his parents are debarred. In the secret society organized by Norman, there was some evidence of the underlying sexual meaning of that alliance. Each child who wished to become a member had to walk along a high wall without falling off, to refrain from crying when salt was rubbed into a pinprick made in the arm, and to show that he or she possessed at least one pubic hair. While the third condition clearly showed the desirability in Norman's mind of being sexually mature, the other two, signifying active physical prowess and passive endurance of pain, may possibly have expressed fantasies of masculine and feminine roles in intercourse. Here, as in the case of Paul, the disguise of fantasy certainly did not lead to a less graphic expression of it.

Apart from giving powerful support against the adults and the gratification of a rival alliance, a gang allows a child opportunity to express primitive feelings of love and hate in the approved and more socialized sphere of trusty comrades and sworn enemies—feelings which, basically, belong to his parents and brothers and sisters. In the same way, games and activities of all kinds in which there is rivalry give legitimate outlet to aggressive and exhibitionistic impulses which, at this age, can generally no longer be brought out into the open and expressed directly.

For instance, in the popular games of chance which are played with such tireless enthusiasm, the child can in winning be enacting his wishes to steal and displace, exploit and triumph, while in losing he can feel robbed, cheated, and punished, yet all the time with the reassuring knowledge that the result has been achieved solely by the rules and luck of the game. Athletics and games involving physical activity serve as proofs of what the individual can do with his body, thus reassuring the child that he is whole and strong and potent; they, too, allow expression of aggressive impulses and, in permitting effortful use of the body to its full extent, must give particular relief from the fight against masturbation, with its demand for rigid control and inactivity. Some activities, such as wrestling, boxing, pillowfights, tickling games, and horseplay of all kinds give direct gratification of the wish for physical contact, which was expressed in early childhood in cuddling, riding on the parent's knee, and being given pick-a-back rides. . . .

Many fantasies are expressed by children in the middle years in terms of their possessions. In some children there is an exaggerated dependence on external objects, as in the case of Tony, who, because he could never face grief at having destroyed something, had either to turn from the damaged object and quickly make reparation in relation to something or someone else or to direct his attention to some longed-for, idealized object, unable to rest until he had gained possession of it . . . . [A] favorite story of his was "The Tinder Box"; he never seemed to tire of discussing what one could obtain by means of such a box and was full of admiration for the soldier's ruthless acquiring of it. But in practice he seemed so deeply convinced that to possess anything was to destroy it, that as soon as he obtained the object he had set his heart on he seemed compelled to break it. . . .

In general, however, great importance is attached at this age to possessions, collections of all kinds being constantly added to, reorganized, and improved; carelessly lost, spoiled, or exposed to dangers; anxiously retrieved and repaired or mourned over; and eventually abandoned for something unquestionably better.

As in collecting, so in making and doing, much satisfaction is experienced at this age. In being practical and constructive, a child can give expression to his good impulses and gain reassurance as to their power. . . .

Learning and schoolwork too, have their underlying fantasy meanings as well as their conscious significance. . . . The figures of speech used about learning suggest that it is a taking-in process which is related, among other things, to the early feeding situation. Generally in the case of young children, learning centers in the teacher–pupil relationship, a teacher's ability to give out good material and to stimulate and satisfy the children under her care being as unconsciously meaningful to her as to the children themselves. At the same time, the relationship of the child with his work has the significance of a feeding situation, quite apart from his relationship with his teacher, the learner always feeling that he is taking from and giving to somebody, even when working independently. We know how adults can feel that work thrusts itself upon them, reproaching them if left unfinished and rewarding them if they have given time and energy to it, implying the existence of a give-and-take relationship. In its deepest meaning, this is a relationship with inner fantasy figures, which are projected onto the work so that the problems of love and hate are enacted in it. As we have seen, the basis of a satisfactory feeding situation is the child's feeling that in taking in good things in a loving way he makes his mother good and that with what he is given he is able to create something of value. Learning can in many ways be a means of reparation; on the other hand, it may be invested with meanings of attack and destruction, often resulting in inhibition and failure. Some children are receptive and creative and take an active part in the learning process; in others, interest and curiosity do not lead to gain in knowledge or skill in spite of normal intelligence, facts being confused with each other or quickly forgotten, explanations half-heard or interrupted with irrelevant remarks; while yet others may appear to take in knowledge and to accept facts and principles, but are not able to make use of them, often with the hopeless attitude that no work they produce can ever be any good. . . .

In Paul we get some indication of the complexity of fantasy which underlies the learning of school subjects—an activity which might, on the surface, appear to be entirely governed by reality values. In his case, anxiety about sadistic wishes led to his being unable to learn, although he had a lively conscious wish to know; in others the inhibition of curiosity leads to boredom and apathy. But to the majority of children learning is, on the whole, a positive activity, expressing constructive fantasies. As a rule, a child feels that schoolwork well done is something good, and so is reassured about his own potency and power to repair, while many anxieties are allayed by knowledge about real things. Moreover, all children make use of the school situation in itself, as a setting outside home in which they can express fantasies in terms of parent-figures who are not parents and other children who are not brothers and sisters.

Above all, fantasy is expressed in imaginative play, although in middle childhood this tends to be less free than in early years, when it occurs spontaneously with whatever material comes to hand. Although children of this age do many constructive things on their own, their imaginative play usually occurs in groups. Whereas the little child makes much use of toys and other materials to play out his fantasies, as he grows older he depends more and more in his imaginative games on the cooperation of other children playing different roles and acting as a support to him in expressing fantasies more directly and overtly than in other forms of activity. The imaginative games of an older child are generally formalized to some extent and are often carefully planned in advance, while there is frequently an insistence that they should be played with real materials and that the setting should be true to life. But in spite of this limiting of imagination by adherence to reality, which must surely be partly due to a fear of underlying fantasies, these are expressed both in the situations the children choose to depict and the way they carry them out. In the school and hospital games, for instance, generally played by girls, the relationship between teacher and pupil, nurse and patient, must often represent the child's fantasy of a mother–child relationship. In boys' games of pirates, Indians, cowboys, gangsters, or simply "good 'uns and bad 'uns," the implied if not actual presence of an enemy is an essential part of the game, and plotting ways to outwit them, overhearing their plans, stealing their ammunition or supplies, shooting or capturing them can be seen to symbolize the child's wish to overpower and replace his father. The very strict teacher with her favorites, the rude and cheating pupil, the dominating, overattentive nurse, the patient in extreme pain, the angry, retributive enemy, and the numerous other roles that are played are all representatives of the child's fantasy figures.

Many fantasies of putting right, restoring, and repairing are expressed in imaginative play. Bob, eight, was genuinely worried by his habit of lying, saying hopefully, "I'm getting a bit better about telling lies, aren't I?" One day he built what he called "a church in the garden" and put his Bible in it, saying that only people who spoke the truth could be admitted. One of his games was called "Swallows and Amazons," based on the book by Arthur Ransome in which he had been particularly interested. With one or two younger children, to whom he behaved in a kindly, parental way, he would build and equip a boat in which they were to sail to an unknown island. They never reached the stage of setting sail, however, the whole point of the game lying in the preparations and the loading up of the boat with every conceivable object which might be needed on the journey and for camping. It seems likely that both the church and the boat stood for his mother (cf. the term "Mother Church" and the fact that boats are always referred to in feminine terms and are often given female names). The putting of the Bible in the church and the equipping of the boat could mean restoring the mother by putting good things inside her and by preventing the entrance of bad things—people who tell lies. Also, the fact that Bob played the part of a mother to the younger children would suggest that he was at the same time building up himself and that in incorporating the Bible, he was taking in something strong and good which could control his bad impulses, represented by his lying. Many imaginative games of hospitals with sick patients and careful, devoted nurses, and of mothers and babies express this wish to make reparation, and much satisfaction is gained from dressing the patient's wounds and making him comfortable, feeding and changing the baby, and being the good person on whom people depend. Shop games can express many different fantasies, the shopkeeper sometimes having everything in stock and taking pleasure in pleasing his customers, like the mother overflowing with good things, and sometimes frustrating them by repeatedly not having what is wanted. Bob was always most polite to the people in his shop, but would tell them with a beaming smile that he was very sorry that the shop had "wasted out of" what they asked for. . . .

The inner life of fantasy never loses its meaning; the child who develops well grows to be less at the mercy of it and more closely in contact with reality, but throughout life it underlies all his activities and is the core of his existence.

# The Use of Checkers in Handling Certain Resistances in Child Therapy and Child Analysis

EARL A. LOOMIS, JR.

Resistance has been defined by Freud as "anything that interferes with the course of analysis." While the rediscovery of lost memories and the disclosure of the contents of the repressed constitute indispensable aspects of the analytic process, this disclosure will be facilitated and the analysis will be enhanced if the resistances are concurrently analyzed and overcome. In fact, the more emphasis we place upon character and ego problems, the more we are concerned with resistance analysis.

In this brief communication I will attempt to demonstrate some of the types of resistances and character problems uncovered in checker play with children in analysis or psychotherapy. In addition, examples will be given from some uses of checkers as a means of disclosing content, handling resistances, and introducing interpretations.

An eight-year-old boy had from the beginning seemed entirely too comfortable and symptom-free in his relations with the therapist, too blissfully agreeable to participation in therapy, and apparently possessed of too little anxiety to motivate his really being willing and able to think about his troubles. Treatment proceeded several months without significant change. The patient's parents acknowledged no alteration in his symptoms at home (anxiety, enuresis, shyness, and mild school phobia). When checkers were casually introduced, the patient accepted the possibility of playing without obviously being threatened. He proceeded to lose every game, however, despite his prior experience with checkers. His losses were neither simply accidental nor careless, but seemed calculated to defeat the analyst's attempts to play as an appropriate opponent of an eight-year-old. When the therapist and the patient became aware of what was going on, the patient could express for the first time his fear of winning, of triumphing, or of successfully competing in anything. His passive, agreeable veneer began to crack, and the underlying aggressive needs and competitive drives became apparent as the therapeutic situation—more particularly the checker games—provided a neutral and safe context of acceptance and understanding in which could be worked out in microsphere some of his fears of his drive to strive successfully.

"But I don't need to win." "I mean, I don't want to win." "I don't care if all boys want to win at least part of the time!" "What do you mean I'm too good a player to lose?" "You mean I try to lose?" "What do you mean I use my head to lose rather than to win?" "No, I don't think you'll be mad if I would beat you." "I don't care if some boys do fear people will get mad sometimes when they beat people." "I just don't want to beat people." "Let's play checkers." (The interpretations between these remarks here telescoped are probably obvious.)

The next step for the therapist was to reintroduce the subjects of ambivalence and internal conflict as ways in which the lad's self-defeat came about. He got what I meant when I suggested that he was fighting the checker game inside his head rather than on the checkerboard and that not I but rather he himself was his opponent. The final and crucial tying-up with reality experiences of past and current life situation and behavior was an essential stage of the boy's therapy, but is not relevant to the topic of this paper.

Here checkers offered a boy an opportunity to see his resistances and character defenses, to play with leaving behind one or another aspect of them in miniature, to retreat into the play *with* checkers rather than to talk about them, but in so doing to give himself and the therapist a convenient and useful symbol to summarize and communicate a complicated intrapsychic conflict. Hence, again and again in this boy's analysis, he could turn off painful material by saying, "Let's play checkers," to which the analyst could acquiesce by saying, "Perhaps the game will make the checker feelings less hard to talk about" or "Perhaps today we talk less with words and more with checkers."

In another eight-year-old the fear of losing so dominated that he devised his own checker game, "Larry-checkers." This consisted of rules which he created somewhat as follows:

> Red checkers on red squares, black on black. Checkers move on an angle, staying on their own color, but jumping straight ahead onto another square of their own color. They may, however, jump over the end and back to their position in taking a man on an end row, or they may jump in a diamond pattern around a man and return to their own square or any square of the diamond. You get "kings" by jumping a lot or by bringing a man on top of another man close to him. If a king wants to, he can move two squares on an angle or can jump two squares of his own color forward. Another way to take men is to pass by them as the king moves his two squares forward.

Usually by reserving the right to move first and through launching an attack from the start, he could win overwhelmingly. When on occasion I managed to beat him at his own game, he would usually anticipate this and change the rules abruptly before the last move, only to trap and defeat my nearly victorious army. Rarely, he would actually allow me to win. In these cases, he insisted that alongside the score which was religiously kept be recorded, "Dr.

Loomis won only because Larry let him." Interpretations of his fear of losing, his dread of not having everything under control, and his displacement and projection of fears reinforced material and experiences from other areas including the school, the home, and the history. Larry is still fighting the battle of his fears of inner anarchy, inner insanity, and inner aggression, but he has learned to see sometimes that his foes are as often inside as out, and Larry-checkers has helped him to see this. In fact, a leading remark of his led me to predict to him that "Sometime you will let me teach you 'Earl-checkers.'" His answer, "O.K., when I get Larry-checkers out of my system," led me to believe my prediction would be fulfilled.

Fears of winning and losing, of dominating or being dominated, are not the only resistance creators which checkers may disclose. A more serious paranoid distrust with ill-concealed hostility first made its appearance to the therapist in the course of highly competitive games compulsively played and competitively scored by a fourteen-year-old boy. At first I felt that he was "merely" eager to win, normally competitive for adolescence, and busily attaining to the state where he could teach his elders. (He did in fact teach me most of what I know about competitive checker playing.) Yet as we went along from game to game and from tournament to tournament, it became evident that Will was not just trying to keep me in my place; he was trying to humiliate me—more, to destroy me. In the course of the checker games he would allude to "strangleholds," "head-locks," "jujitsu," "bayonet practice," "judo," "hand-to-hand combat," and "ambush or attacks from the rear." The anxiety warnings which had much earlier left me puzzled now fitted together to justify concern for this boy's reality judgments, defenses against homosexuality, and ego integrity. Attention to the threatened fragmentation of civilized veneer disclosed through checker games (and no other discernible place at first) led me to take more appropriate steps in his handling. Checkers here served as catalyst to delusional and hostile breakthrough —again, thank fortune, on the level of "only a game!"

Awkward silences may or may not constitute resistances. Usually, I think they do. Techniques that work with adults too seldom yield results with young children or adolescents. Checkers offers a communication medium that can continue through the verbal blackout both to reassure the patient that the therapist is still "in there pitching" and also to keep the therapist in touch with possible changes in the meanings of the silences.

Naomi, a thirteen-year-old girl with a tic-like compulsion, talked freely with the therapist one hour out of twelve, sparsely one hour out of six, and maintained all but total silence on more than one occasion. During these periods of affective and communicational inertia, checkers frequently broke the vicious circle of silence begetting silence and question begetting monosyllable. Throughout the game the eyes flashed with excitement, the muscles tensed with expectancy, and the dry and occasionally caustic wit appeared. On occasion mercy would be implored through tender, longing glances, and on others grace would be gratuitously proffered. I did not play silently, and Naomi did not speak often. Yet we communicated: I through words and she through checkers—sometimes, both of us through checkers. Naomi's fears partly stemmed from the sex difference of the therapist; yet even after she had been transferred to a woman physician, checkers served to provide an occasion for conversation—at least by the doctor. For example, Naomi is sitting, staring straight ahead. "Would you like to play checkers?" "I really can't be sure if you are silent, perhaps we won't go far wrong if we assume that silence gives consent." Medium smile from Naomi. "I guess this means you are glad." Broader smile. "But I can understand smiles only a little and shrugs even less. Sometime when you can tell me in words how you think and feel, we can understand together even better." And so on into the game. . . .

For another boy, Pat, eleven, asthmatic, and shy, checkers revealed content, history, feeling, and transference in a fascinating manner. I knew that he was lonely, that his real father died when he was three, that his stepfather frightened him. I knew that his mother was overprotective, almost parasitic upon him, and that his grandmother fought to get in on the act too. Yet I never had been able to help him voice just how he felt when in the middle of the night he would choke up and feel he was going to die. He could never bring himself to relate how he felt then and after his mother came to his bed. Usually as he sat talking of trivia he would be comfortable. As his associations led him into tension areas, he would gradually tighten up verbally, become anxious, and begin to wheeze. He lost his ability to talk at this point and only gradually regained it. In time we both learned that if at a moment when he first began to choke up he would ask for a checker game, the attack would pass.

One day he said, when I had asked him again what checkers meant, "Checkers feels like it does when I'm going to have an attack at night and mother comes to me and brings me a drink of water and my medicine and puts a cool cloth on my forehead and lies down beside me and stays with me till I fall asleep." From then on his request "Let's play checkers!" became more meaningful to both of us and we grew to use the phrase "the checkers feeling" as shorthand for the cravings to be protected and loved.

As his confidence and insight grew, he came to use checkers in other ways, and as each stage of meaning developed and was clarified, a new understanding of his character, his life situation, and the transference emerged. Only resistance aspects of this symptom have been considered here.

From these five examples the role of checkers in disclosing the presence of resistances, aiding in analyzing them, and helping to discover their inner meaning is illustrated. The advantages of the game to the child analyst and child therapist are its flexibility, variety of personal meanings (as projective technique), and its wide range of therapeutic applicabilities. Thus it can be seen that checkers is flexible far beyond the obvious form of the medium (a competitive game).[a]

## *Summary*

Five clinical examples of ways in which checkers illuminated or facilitated therapy and analysis of children have been presented. While I personally find checkers particularly valuable in the uncovering and analysis of resistances and character problems, I am sure that similar applications are being made with many other games and modalities. The advantages of checkers are the facts that it is widely known, is familiar to most latency children and adolescents, and is unusually appropriate as a game between adult and child which does not require any condescension on the part of the adult. This paper covers only a few of the special attributes and possibilities of checkers. It is hoped that it will stimulate the uncovering and sharing of other uses of the game, together with the examination of other types of therapist–child activities from similar points of view.

---

[a] It should not be necessary to remind the experienced child analyst that while checkers or any other game or device of this type may be valuable as an adjuvant in child analysis, none of these techniques is considered a treatment in itself nor can any of them replace the faithful searching out of the unconscious forms and content which arise in the context of the therapeutic relationship and transference, as Peter B. Neubauer reminded us in his discussion of this brief communication.

PART FIVE

# EVALUATION

❀ CHAPTER NINETEEN

# Assessment of Individual Progress

IF THE THERAPEUTIC process involves moving through more-or-less recognizable steps or stages, it should be possible to develop objective means of assessing the child's current treatment status by comparing his present play behavior with that of earlier sessions. Alhough every therapist engages in some sort of evaluative process, very little research consideration has been given to this problem, probably because of the difficulty in setting up general criteria that could be applied to large samples. Nevertheless, it does seem feasible to set up individual criteria for each child on the basis of his particular problems and predetermined therapeutic goals.

Dorfman[1] suggests that more consideration be given to specific changes in play when she states:

> Thus far, there has been no attempt to test rather specific hypotheses in a study which would include playroom actions. For example, as therapy progresses, is there a trend from "accidental" to "purposeful" actions? That is, does a child who begins therapy with, "The Daddy fell over," increasingly come to state, "I knocked over the Daddy"?

In addition to changes in play patterns, progress can be noted in other areas such as interpersonal relations, self-acceptance, frustration tolerance, fewer repetitive activities, mastery of fears, reduction of guilt feelings and/or aggression. Specific criteria may need to be tailor-made to suit the

[1] Elaine Dorfman, "Play Therapy," in *Client-Centered Therapy*, Carl R. Rogers, ed. (New York: Houghton Mifflin, 1951), pp. 235–277, p. 274.

individual child. At least some of the following guides may be pertinent in any particular case:

Is there less dependence on the therapist?

Is there less concern about other children using the room or seeing his therapist?

Can he now see and accept both good and bad in the same person?

Have there been changes in his attitude toward time, in terms of awareness, interest, or acceptance?

Has there been a change in his reactions to cleaning up the room: less concern if he formerly had been meticulous or interest in cleaning up as contrasted to earlier messiness?

Does he now accept himself and his own sex?

Are there evidences of insight and self-evaluation; does he compare his former actions or feelings with those of the present?

Is there a change in the quality or amount of verbalization?

Is there less aggression toward, or with, toys?

Does he accept limits more readily?

Have his forms of art expression changed?

Is there less need to engage in infantile (e.g., bottle) or regressive (e.g., water) play?

Is there less gorging on cookies? Does he now offer some to the therapist?

Is there less fantasy and symbolic play and more creative-constructive play?

Has there been a diminution in the number and intensity of fears?

The unanswered questions, at least with the techniques presently available, pertain to how much of the observed progress or improvement in the child can be attributed to the effects of psychotherapy and how much would have occurred anyway as a concomitant of the ongoing growth process.

Moustakas' selection is concerned with the stages in the manifestations of anger and anxiety throughout the therapy process. Moustakas[2] subsequently employed his hypotheses in a comparative study of normal and disturbed children.

---

[2] Clark Moustakas, "The Frequency and Intensity of Negative Attitudes Expressed in Play Therapy: A Comparison of Well-Adjusted and Disturbed Young Children," *Journal of Genetic Psychology*, LXXXVI (1955), 309–325.

With only four therapy sessions per child there was no opportunity to measure changes over time, but he did find that negative attitudes were more frequent and more intense in the disturbed group and were expressed in more diffuse and pervasive ways.

## The Therapeutic Process

CLARK E. MOUSTAKAS

. . . The therapeutic process itself seems to follow a regular pattern. It is perhaps more clearly observable with disturbed children than with normal children. However, certain aspects of the process are evident in therapy sessions with well-adjusted children, too, usually in milder form and of shorter duration.

The picture seems to be as follows: The emotions of disturbed children and troubled children to a large degree, at the beginning of therapy, are diffuse and undifferentiated. The feelings are generally negative. Children have apparently lost contact with the people and the situations that originally aroused frustration, anger, fear, and guilt. Their emotions, in other words, are no longer tied to reality. They are magnified, generalized, and easily stimulated and evoked.

Attitudes of hostility, anxiety, and regression are pervasive in their expression in the playroom. Children are frightened, angry, or immature without definitely focusing their feelings on any particular person or persons or emotional experiences. They are often afraid of almost everything and everybody and sometimes feel like destroying all people, or merely wish they would be left completely alone, or wish to regress to a simpler, less demanding level of adjustment. The basic attitudes of anxiety and hostility in the child motivating his behavior are used here to illustrate the process. Anger, for example, may express itself by direct attacks on the toys, by smashing, pounding, breaking, by tearing, crushing, and a variety of other actions. These attacks seem to be without purpose. Apparently, there is nothing in the therapy situation which provokes them. The child is left free with his own impulses, and the level of the relationship with the therapist to a great degree determines the amount and quality of the hostility expressed. The greater the child's trust in the therapist and the greater his feeling of acceptance and respect, the more focused his anger may be.

As the relationship between the child and the therapist is clarified and strengthened, the attitude of hostility becomes gradually sharpened and more specific. Anger now is expressed more directly and often is related to particular persons or experiences. Pounding and smashing, even the expression of the desire to kill, may still be present, but in this second stage of the therapeutic process it is a parent, or a sibling, or perhaps the entire family that is attacked. The threapist or any other person may be attacked or denounced or threatened in the child's play. As the child expresses and releases more and more of these negative feelings in direct ways toward the people in his life who aroused them and made him feel inadequate and as these expressions are accepted by the therapist, the feelings become less intense and affect the child less in his total experiences. The child begins to feel that he is a worthy person.

A third level of the process now begins to appear. The child is no longer so completely negative in his expressions of feelings. Anger is still specific, but he shows a variety of ambivalences toward particular people in his life. For example, the child's anger toward his baby brother or sister may fluctuate in his play between feeding and caring for the baby and spanking the baby or mistreating him in other ways. These ambivalent reactions may be severe in intensity at first, but as they are expressed again and again in the therapeutic relationship, they become less tense. In the final stage of this process, positive feelings begin to emerge. The child now sees himself and his relationships with people more as they really are. He may still resent the baby, but he no longer hates the baby merely because he is the baby. As a four-year-old once put it in one of her final sessions. "I'm going to have a big party and invite everybody, even my baby brother." The process of anger may be summarized in these four stages. First, it appears diffuse and pervasive. Next, it becomes focused in the form of hostility toward parents, siblings, other children, the therapist, relatives, or other people in the child's life. Third, anger remains specific and becomes mixed with positive attitudes not yet completely differentiated. Finally, positive attitudes and negative attitudes become separated and more consistent with the reality that motivates them. The intensity of feelings accompanying these stages also seems to change. First the feelings of anger are severe in nature. Then they become less intense in their expression, and finally they appear to be more moderate.

Anxiety may be looked at in the same way. In the beginning of child therapy, anxiety may be diffuse and the child may be generally withdrawn and frightened, tense and garrulous, or overanxious about being clean, neat, or orderly. This attitude is often so pervasive that the child is immobilized and unable to start anything, or complete anything, or even to think clearly and attack problems logically. He does not seem to know how to go about doing what he really wants to do. Fears also may take other forms, such as regular night terrors or bizarre fears of animals and things. In the first stage of the therapeutic process, fears seem to obsess the child. At the next level, they take on more specific aspects. Fears of the father or the mother or some other particular person are expressed again and again. Fear then becomes mixed with positive attitudes, becomes milder in its expression. Finally positive and negative attitudes toward particular people become separated and more in line with the actual situation. Here again, negative feeling tones change from severe to moderate.

The child's emotional problems and symptoms are reflections of his attitudes, and as the attitudes change the problems and symptoms disappear. It must be remembered that these levels of the process and the changes in feeling tones are not distinct entities or even always definitely observable. They occur in the child's play and in his emotional behavior, not step by step, but in individually varying sequences. The levels overlap at many points, as do the children's attitudes themselves. On the other hand, they are definite sequences of the process which can be seen and analyzed.

The therapeutic process does not automatically occur in a play situation. It becomes possible in a therapeutic relationship where the therapist responds in constant sensitivity to the child's feelings, accepts the child's attitudes, and conveys a consistent and sincere belief in the child and respect for him.

❀ CHAPTER TWENTY

# Research

THE DIFFICULTIES encountered in designing and carrying out a research project in the field of child psychotherapy are readily apparent and no doubt help explain the relatively small number of efforts in this field. Most of the research that has been reported has been done by the client-centered school; the analysts' writings are largely directed to case presentations and discussions of theoretical problems.

Lebo's summary article was written in 1953 and provides a comprehensive review of research prior to that date. For a review of the few additional research studies since 1953, the reader is referred to the earlier portions of Ginott's chapter, "Research in Play Therapy,"[1] which are not included in the present volume. The section of his chapter which is reproduced here poses questions for which research answers are needed, suggests hypotheses for investigation, points out the numerous variables that must be considered and, if possible, controlled, and gives some positive suggestions of methods for the study of the actual process of therapy.

It is hoped the presentations in this and the previous chapter will highlight the research needs, point to some possible approaches, and stimulate further explorations and significant research efforts.

---

[1] Haim G. Ginott, *Group Psychotherapy with Children* (New York: McGraw-Hill, 1961).

# *The Present Status of Research on Nondirective Play Therapy*

DELL LEBO

To many persons nondirective play therapy has seemed easy to learn, pleasant to undertake, and gratifying in results. Much of the attention attracted to play therapy has resulted from its apparent ease as well as from the concept that play is the natural medium of expression of the child. Play has come to be recognized as the most satisfactory way of understanding the nonverbal child. Because of the current widespread interest in child psychology, child training, education, and mental hygiene, recent years have seen a great deal of concomitant activity in nondirective play therapy. Much of the activity has resulted in emotional articles lauding nondirective play therapy. These articles generally explain the efficacy of nondirective play therapy on the basis of philosophical constructs arising from the growth principle developed from nondirective counseling with adults.

Research in nondirective therapy with adults is sound and extensive. Research in nondirective play therapy with children is still meager, unsound, and frequently of a cheerful, persuasive nature. It has seemed to the present writer that such articles could be more correctly classified as propaganda than as research.

The present paper is an attempt to review current research in nondirective play therapy. With one exception, studies involving more than one child have been reported here. The report giving only a single case history has been avoided. Also, only studies concerned with nondirective play therapy are reported. There is no doubt that play therapy has a considerable history. It may be said to extend back to Rousseau (1925) who studied the play of the child to understand his psychology. However, nondirective play therapy developed from the work of Carl Rogers (1942, 1951) and his associates. One of them, Virginia Axline (1947b), was the first to successfully apply nondirective methods to play therapy with children. Axline's book, while widely read, is more suggestive than it is factual. It seems to have been the forerunner of much of the persuasive material to be found in studies of nondirective play therapy.

A recent example of the continuing propagandistic tendencies in nondirective play-therapy research papers is to be seen in an article titled, "An Experiment in Play Therapy" (Bloomberg, 1948). The stated purpose was to help children who semed unable to adjust to the school situation. The children were selected on the basis of Rorschach tests, their teacher's impression, and the therapist's observations. Two groups of five children each were selected for nondirective play therapy. The majority of children selected had problems of sibling rivalry. The groups met once a week for play therapy. Much verbatim material from the therapy notes was presented to enable the reader to partake of the emotional flavor of the situation.

The shortcomings of the "experiment" are serious. First, it lacks a clear hypothesis and a control group. Second, the results seem to indicate a lack of rigorous method. For it is the conclusion of the research (Bloomberg, 1948, p. 180) that "through group work they [the children] learned that they were not alone in having 'bad feelings.' Other children had them too." Further that ". . . their natural healthy drive toward maturity, which had been retarded, could once more assert itself." Such conclusions would seem to savor more of a desire to support nondirective play therapy than they do of experimental procedure.

*What Takes Place in Nondirective Play Therapy?* With the philosophy of the love of children and the idyllic purposefulness of many of the typical articles stripped off, nondirective play therapy seems to be left a rather thin framework. A determination of the process of play therapy, as contrasted with the results of play therapy, has been subject matter for only three known research studies.

The first such study was the work of Landisberg and Snyder (1946). They attempted to analyze what actually took place in client-centered play therapy by an objective approach. Their procedure was to study the protocols of three successful and one incomplete case. Each statement made by the counselor was categorized as to its content. Statements made by the children were categorized as to content, emotion expressed, and activity. Although the children ranged in age from five to six years, the categories used had been developed for employment with adult cases.

They reported finding an increase in the child's physical activity during the last three-fifths of therapy. The children were found to have released much feeling during therapy. About 50 per cent of their actions and statements during the first two-fifths of treatment were devoted to emotional release. This percentage rose to seventy for the last three-fifths of the process. It was noticed that negative feelings particularly increased in frequency. The major part of the children's feelings were directed toward others and not to themselves or to the counselor. No insightful statements were made by the children whose records were studied.

Finke (1947) did not use adult categories in analyzing children's nondirective play-therapy protocols, but derived her categories from an analysis of children's statements. Expressions of feeling were emphasized as it was believed such expressions would mirror the child's changing emotional reactions resulting from the play therapy.

She selected complete protocols from six play therapists concerning six different children referred for behavior problems. The children ranged in age from five to eleven years. The possibility of bias resulting from one person's categorizing all the cases was avoided by having five students recategorize one or more interviews chosen at random. Their results corresponded adequately with the original categorization.

It was found that different children undergoing therapy with different therapists showed similar trends which tended to divide play therapy into three stages:

> (1) Child is either reticent or extremely talkative. He explores the playroom. If he is to show aggression at any time during therapy, a great deal of it will be exhibited in this stage.
>
> (2) If aggression has been shown, it is now lessened. This child tests the limitations of the playroom. Imaginative play is frequently indulged in here.
>
> (3) Most of the child's efforts are now expanded into attempted relationship with counselor. The child tries to draw the therapist into his games and play.

Like Landisberg and Snyder (1946), Finke (1947) found no trends for positive statements. Unlike them, she found no trends for negative statements. The verbal characteristics of adult counseling sessions did not appear. Finke concluded that nondirective play therapy had its own characteristic pattern which was repeated in case after case.

Both studies indicated that children's attitudes changed during therapy and that the changes could be quantitatively reported. There seem to be serious limitations in both studies. Landisberg and Snyder used adult categories. Finke found fault with this. She indicated that differences in the age and sophistication of the adults and the children would affect the degree and type of verbalization made. Consequently, she felt it was not justifiable to evaluate children's comments on the basis of categories derived from adults.

Finke seemed to have failed to recognize the possibility that just as the wide age discrepancies between adults and children might influence the character of their verbalizations, so might children's categories vary significantly from one level of maturity to another.

The present writer (Lebo, 1952) undertook a study of the possible relationship between chronological age and the types of statements made by children in play therapy. He used Finke's (1947) categories.

> Twenty children were given three play-therapy sessions by the same therapist in the same playroom. The children were reasonably equated for intelligence and social adjustment. Five age stages were represented with two boys and two girls in each stage. Children were selected who were four, six, eight, ten, and twelve years of age.
>
> Fifteen pages of verbatim style notes were selected by a table of random numbers from the 166 pages of protocol. These fifteen pages were then categorized by three experienced play therapists. Their percentages of agreement were adequately similar to one another. All of the protocols were then analyzed by the writer.

> It was found that maturation, as represented by chronological age, did seem to account for some definite trends in the types of statements made by children in the play-therapy situation.
>
> As the children became older, they told the therapist fewer of their decisions. They spent less time on exploring the limitations. They made fewer attempts to draw the therapist into their play and they expressed more of their likes and dislikes.

The three studies, while not strictly comparable, would seem to indicate that nondirective play therapy is an objectively measurable process, that children's emotional expressions are altered in a discernible manner, and that maturation appears to be related to the type of expression of therapeutic change. Beyond such statements the studies substantiate few of the philosophical aspects of play therapy.

## *The Successfulness of Nondirective Play Therapy*

*The Outcome of Play Therapy in Various Types of Cases.* Nondirective play therapy has been used in the study and treatment of such seemingly diverse problems as allergy, mental deficiency, personality problems, physically handicapped children, race conflicts, and reading difficulties. From the published reports one receives the impression that it has usually been either successful or incomplete. The children are seemingly relieved of their presenting symptoms or the therapy is unavoidably interrupted in a promising but unfinished phase.

*Nondirective Play Therapy in the Treatment of Allergy.* Miller and Baruch (1948), following a successful preliminary psychotherapeutic treatment of allergy (Baruch and Miller, 1946), undertook to treat six children under eleven years of age by play therapy. All their subjects had classical allergic symptoms confirmed by positive skin reactions to various allergens. Prior to nondirective play therapy all the subjects had been unsuccessfully treated medically.

They cite as a representative case a five-year-old asthmatic boy who used attacks of asthma to gain contact with his mother. Whenever she left him, the asthma would express his hostile feelings. His asthmatic attacks cleared after five months of play therapy. Unfortunately, for purpose of this investigation, sixteen allergic adults were included in the results. As a result, it can only be said that of the twenty-two patients (including the six children), twenty-one showed improvement while one was unchanged.

*Nondirective Play Therapy in the Study of Mental Deficiency.* Exploratory material suggestive of the emotional factors in mental deficiency is presented by Axline (1949a). In a report of an examination of selected play-therapy protocols, evidence is offered which indicates marked improvement in some IQ scores after completing play therapy.

The verbatim stenographic reports of fifteen six- and seven-year-old children referred for behavior problems were studied. Each child had been seen individually by the same therapist for eight to twenty contacts. The reports were selected and analyzed at some time after therapy on the basis of Stanford-Binet IQ ratings and the age of the children. The records were then grouped as follows:

(1) Children who showed no appreciable change in IQ scores after therapy. Pre- and posttesting indicated low intelligence.

(2) Children who showed a gain in IQ scores after therapy. Pretests were low; posttests were indicative of normal intelligence.

(3) Children with average intelligence both before and after play therapy. Children from this group had play therapy in a children's home.

In every case of those children whose IQ stayed low, their mother had indicated shame, disapproval, and rejection. It was felt that the children's difficulty lay in their daily lives. "They were not able to communicate clearly to others the things that were uppermost in their lives" (Axline, 1949a, p. 528). The therapist felt that each of the cases in the first category was incomplete. However, it was impossible to finish therapy.

In the case material presented, it is evident that both the children whose IQ's did not improve and those whose IQ's became normal initiated play activity. Both groups freely expressed negative feelings and destructive play which was followed by outgoing and more positive behavior. The only difference would seem to be that the children whose IQ's were raised had completed their therapy.

The same behavior was shown by the children of average intelligence whose IQ's did not change. This group was included to indicate that mental deficiency was not the cause of behavior problems for these children.

Axline (1949a) did not claim that nondirective play therapy raised the IQ of the children of group two. She explained the increase in IQ scores by saying the child was freed from emotional constraint and could thus more adequately express his true capacities.

*Nondirective Play Therapy in the Treatment of Personality Disorders.* While most of the work in play therapy has been done in the area of personality, there is a dearth of research material. This can be explained by the client-centered philosophy from which nondirective play therapy sprung. Play therapy is oriented around the needs of the client and not around the demands of research. For this reason there are "cases" offered to prove that play therapy works, but there are still few research studies undertaken to see how well it works. Bloomberg's (1948) work, already discussed, represents the research aspects of proselytizing for play therapy. Instead of presenting one case, she presents ten. But she presents these ten cases in a manner in keeping with the philosophy of nondirective play therapy. That is to say, the experiment was not designed to stimulate research, it was designed to help children. Consequently, her material merely indicates that play therapy works—a fact which no one disputes.

An experiment that deserves to be a model for future play-therapy work is available in this area. Fleming and Snyder (1947) endeavored to determine if measurable changes in social and personal adjustment resulted from non-directive play therapy.

> They had three simple personality tests administered to forty-six children. Seven children who ranged in age from eight to eleven years were selected for play therapy on the basis of poor results in these tests. After a lapse of twelve weeks, thirty of the forty-six children were available for retesting.
>
> Fleming and Snyder (1947) found the three girls had improved their adjustment with a greater amount of positive feelings. The least amount of improvement for the girls was in the social area. Save for one individual who fared worse, the four boys made no significant changes. The control group posttest score was the same as their pretest score.
>
> From an analysis of the group scores as well as from individual data, they concluded the greatest change for the subjects was in personal feelings toward the self and in daydreaming. Hence, the theory is offered that personal changes in adjustment must precede social change. The therapy experience had created more positive feeling among the subjects but it did not cause the control group to like them any better.

Since this was the first study of its kind, it was to be expected that certain of their findings should contradict some of Axline's (1947b) early observations. Although Fleming and Snyder did not indicate it, the following contradictions of Axline's observations were suggested:

> (1) The therapist's sex was an important factor in establishing rapport. They found ten-year-old boys would not respond well to a female therapist. Axline (1947b, p. 65) had said, "Nor does the sex of the therapist seem to be important [for successful play therapy]."
>
> (2) A housemother who was not given therapy prevented successful therapy with the boys' group. Previously, Axline (1947b, p. 68) had stressed that, "It is not necessary for the adults to be helped in order to insure successful play-therapy results."
>
> (3) The best therapeutic results seem to be achieved when the children in the group have the same degree of maladjustment. Axline (1948a, pp. 269 f.) had said, "Experiments in groupings indicate that there are no . . . rules to govern them: Successful groupings have included both sexes, siblings, and wide age ranges." In another place (Axline, 1948a, p. 27) she noted, "A handicapped child can be treated in a group with normal children."

Axline's statements would seem to warrant additional experimental investigation.

*Nondirective Play Therapy in the Treatment of Children with Physical Handicaps.* Axline (1947b) included cases of handicapped children in her pioneer work. Cowen and Cruickshank (1948) and Cruickshank and Cowen (1948) undertook the only other known research study to supplement her reports. They set themselves the problem of determining whether or not nondirective group play therapy could be applied to physically handicapped children.

> They held thirteen meetings with five physically handicapped children all of whom had at least one emotional problem. The children's teachers and parents made an essay-type report on the child's problems at the start of the program. At the last meeting similar reports were filled out again.
>
> In a verbatim account the authors recount the play of a hemophiliac child. This boy would pretend to cut the therapist's fingers to cause him to bleed to death. The imaginary blood was collected in glass jars placed around the therapist.
>
> The investigators found three of the children showed considerable observed improvement in both the home and the school. One child made slight reported gains, and one showed no improvement. They concluded (Cruickshank and Cowen, 1948, p. 214) that "the nondirective play group offers an ideal setting for the self-solution for a particular type of emotional problem, namely, those stemming from the specific disability of the physically handicapped child."

The investigators themselves realize their work has been conducted at a very gross level. They point out several weaknesses of the project. Among these weaknesses are the lack of quantitative material. There were no pre- and posttherapy tests. There was no follow-up study to see if the indicated gains were temporary or cyclical in nature. Nor was a control group utilized to demonstrate more clearly that the play situation was the critical factor.

The recognition of such lacks is a healthy sign. It suggests an awareness of the possibility of improving future research work in play therapy by more rigorous procedure.

*Nondirective Play Therapy in the Handling of Race Conflicts.* The effectiveness of play therapy for small groups of children who had difficulty adjusting to other children was the primary purpose of an investigation by Axline (1948a), "Play Therapy and Race Conflict in Young Children." She selected four groups of four children, two boys and two girls, who were either withdrawn or aggressively antisocial.

> Each group met once a week for ten meetings. After the tenth meeting the children were mixed for five additional meetings. Axline (1948a, pp. 309 f.) found that Negro girls were accepted by the group after the seventh meeting. This new acceptance was carried over into the classroom. In all groups, "There was a tendency to participate in the group meetings with an awareness of the rights of others." The race problem was never an issue during the five mixed meetings.

This study is more provocative than it is definitive. The children selected were antisocial and not racially bigoted. It is quite possible that the figure of an habitual intergroup improvement in social relations was dressed in the false whiskers of lessening social antagonism. In that case Axline has given an old phenomenon a new name.

*Nondirective Play Therapy in the Treatment of Reading Disabilities.* Since reading difficulty is frequently associated with emotional disturbances, it is not unexpected to find several research articles on the effectiveness of a therapeutic approach designed to relax and better adjust children who are retarded readers.

> Axline (1947a) reported a study of fifty second-graders, listed as poor readers by their teachers, who were given a reading test. The thirty-seven who received the lowest scores were placed in a special class. At the end of the semester, three and one-half months later, intelligence and reading tests were administered.
>
> There were eight girls and twenty-nine boys in the groups with Stanford-Binet IQ's ranging from 80 to 148. Unlike most remedial reading classes, these children had all their schoolwork in one room with the same teacher. The reading problems (Axline, 1947a, p. 65) were considered to be part of the whole child. "The children came first. The reading, writing, and arithmetic came secondly." The children were given the opportunity for ample emotional expression. In accordance with the techniques of nondirective play therapy their feelings and attitudes were not only accepted but were also clarified. No remedial reading instruction per se was given.
>
> Axline (1947a) found that twenty-one children gained more than the maturationally expected 3.5 in words. In the case of four subjects there was a noteworthy difference in the first and second IQ score. One subject's score was increased from 83 to 119.

This study would seem to indicate that nondirective therapeutic procedures are effective in building up a readiness to read in children.

In a later and briefer report Axline (1949b) studied three problem readers. Interestingly enough, only two of the children were poor readers, while the third child read too much. This child used books as a substitute for friends. All the children were above average in intelligence.

It was found that the feelings expressed in play brought out emotional problems that could easily account for the reading difficulties. Axline (1949b, p. 161) concluded, "Given the opportunity the child can and does help himself."

Neither of Axline's (1947a, 1949b) reports included experimental controls. Bills (1950a), working with twenty-two slow learners in the third grade utilized three thirty-day periods of study. The first period was a control period in which all the children were tested with oral reading, silent reading, and Stanford-Binet tests. At the end of that period all the children were retested. They were also retested at the end of the second and third periods.

> The second period was the therapy period. The four children with the largest discrepancy between mental age and reading age were given nondirective play therapy. These children all had high IQ's. Four other children were selected whose IQ's were approximately average.
>
> The third period was used as a follow-up period in which the children were tested again.
>
> During the experiment, reading instruction was not remedial in nature and it was kept constant for all members of the class. Thus, a single group was compared with itself for three thirty-day periods. Each child was his own control as the three periods were comparable in regard to reading experiences.
>
> The therapy group made a significantly greater gain in the therapy period than it did in the control period. The gains of the therapy group during both the second and third periods of the study were significantly greater than the gains during the first period of study.
>
> The gains in reading ability appeared immediately after therapy for some children and after a short period following therapy for others. The gains were found to be present six weeks (thirty schooldays) after therapy had ended.
>
> Three judges agreed that five of the children had gained in emotional adjustment following play therapy. However, the design of the study did not permit conclusions as to the effect of maladjustment on children's reading ability.

To answer the question as to whether improved reading ability was due to improved personal adjustment Bills (1950b) conducted play therapy with well-adjusted readers. The design of the second study was similar to that of the first save that children were now selected for good adjustment by projective and objective personality tests.

He found reading gains were not significantly greater during the therapy period. So, it would appear that nondirective play therapy may improve reading in those children where emotional adjustment exists with the retardation. Consequently, play therapy is not necessarily the method of choice for all retarded readers as the reports of Axline (1947a, 1946b) might suggest.

*Follow-up Studies of Nondirective Play Therapy.* While it seems to have been demonstrated that play therapy is productive of personality improvement, it has not been shown whether the effects of therapy are permanent or temporary. Consequently, the value of follow-up studies cannot be denied.

Bills (1950a) found improved reading ability present six weeks after therapy. Axline (1948b) reports on an interesting study of a boy whose IQ was 65; upon retest it was 68. Six months after play therapy his IQ was 96. A year later it had gone up to 105. Part of this gain may be ascribed to test familiarization. However, the lasting effects of play therapy are again suggested.

In a long-range follow-up, Axline (1950) selected thirty successful play-therapy case records. Of these, twenty-two subjects were available for follow-up study. Nineteen of the subjects were still successfully adjusted a year later, two were successfully adjusted three years later, and one five years after the original contacts. A follow-up of twenty-four of the thirty-seven children used in previous research (Axline, 1947a) was made five years later. Of this group originally designated as poor readers five were honor-roll students and four others had reading skills adequate for their grade placement.

The effects of play therapy then would seem to be lasting, particularly in the area of personality adjustment.

## *Summary and Critique*

The principles and methods of nondirective play therapy are frequently presented as though they were firmly established. The assured manner of writing of many of the authors and the large-scale possibilities held before the reader, tend to make one believe that, at long last, "the way" has been found. Actually, this is not so. Indeed, it may not be the specific procedures of play therapy per se that effect the rather remarkable personality changes. The children may be benefiting from having someone constantly and consistently interested in their welfare. Those with experience in hospitals and institutions involving the mentally ill have noticed the unusually high percentage of cures attending any new treatment. They have reported that it is not the treatment method that effects the improvement, rather it is the increased interest taken in the patient. So, too, may it be with nondirective play therapy.

Axline (1947b) presented no experimental evidence to prove the worth of play therapy. A search of the literature reveals fewer than twenty published articles on the therapeutic uses of play therapy. To be admitted to the ranks of approved therapeutic methods nondirective play therapy needs more than enthusiasm, belief, and the shibboleth, "It works, if you only try it."

The greatest weakness of nondirective play therapy lies in this impetuous overlooking of the real need for a foundation in research. The most pressing need is for the employment of controls in play therapy. The personal adjustment of two equated groups should be assessed before therapy. The children in the group should then be randomly assigned to experimental and control groups. Upon termination of therapy all the children should be retested to determine the quantitative effectiveness of the play therapy technique in "helping children attain maturity."

Nondirective play therapy, while promising when evaluated subjectively, has been seen to have rather serious methodological lacks. One cannot concur with Kanner (1940) that play work with children, while still in its beginning stages, "has come to stay," until play therapy has been established by objective means. In the long run, nondirective play therapy should stand or fall on the results of experimental studies investigating its effectiveness in relation to other procedures.

# Research in Play Therapy

HAIM G. GINOTT

. . . The studies cited in this chapter, interesting and significant as they may be, have left unanswered the most important questions about play therapy: What is the process of play therapy? What variables critically affect this process? What are the behavioral changes that follow play therapy? How does the effectiveness of play therapy compare with that of other treatment methods? Thus far, research has not provided verified answers to these questions; moreover, most of these questions have not been put to controlled experimental study.

Most of the studies in play therapy have attempted to show that the method is effective in treating various problems. While it is gratifying to believe that play therapy can alleviate children's symptoms, the validity of the method cannot rest on the disappearance of symptoms. On the basis of available research, it is impossible to know whether or not the beneficial outcomes of play therapy are directly related to its practical procedures and theoretical rationales. Experience in mental hospitals has indicated that cures occur with any treatment (placebos included); this suggests that cures stem not only from the potency of a particular procedure but from the increased attention paid to patients. This pattern may also occur in play therapy. Some children may improve because they enjoy a weekly ride to the clinic, or because they experience increased concern from mother, or because an adult attends to their play and conversation. The therapist's theoretical orientation and his therapeutic techniques may have little relevance to the treatment results.

The accumulating evidence that patients improve regardless of the treatment approach cannot be ignored; apparent "successes" are scored with various (and often weird) healing methods, such as suggestions, prayers, confessions, group singing, hypnosis, electric shock, and tepid baths. If psychotherapy is to achieve scientific status, research-minded practitioners must provide convincing proof of the worth of their methods. Experimental confirmation is needed of the effectiveness of play therapy in treating personality problems. Thus far, for example, there is no evidence to indicate the superiority of play therapy over dancing lessons in the treatment of shyness or its superiority over boxing lessons in the treatment of aggressiveness.

In determining the value of play therapy, researchers must show (1) that desirable changes in personality and behavior come about concomitantly with play therapy and (2) that such changes would not have occurred in the absence of therapy.

On the surface, the design of such a study is simple: the personal adjustment of two equated groups of children can be assessed by tests and reported behavior and the children randomly assigned to a therapy group and a control group. Upon termination of therapy and at follow-up periods, all the children can be re-evaluated and the quantitative effects of play therapy established.

However, the hypothetical study becomes very complex when the researcher attempts to control the many factors that may affect therapy results, such as age, sex, intelligence, socioeconomic status, parents' attitudes to therapy, environmental influences, and the type, severity, and duration of the disturbance. Scientific procedure requires that, with the exception of the experimental variable, the control and experimental groups be treated as nearly alike as possible. A truly rigorous study would require a comparison of a therapy group not only with a no-therapy group but also with a placebo group. This means that children who come to a clinic for play therapy should be compared with children who come to the clinic for play sessions without a therapist, with a researcher observing the children through a one-way-vision glass.

The hypothesis of such a study would state that personality and behavioral changes occur in an experimental group concomitantly with a series of therapy sessions but do not occur in a control group concomitantly with a series of play sessions and do not occur in a no-therapy group concomitantly with the passage of time. The "own-control" method could be used to test several related hypotheses: (1) personality and behavioral changes do not occur in a child after a period of play sessions but do occur in the same child after a period of therapy sessions; (2) personality and behavioral changes do not occur in a child after a "wait period" but do occur in the same child after a period of therapy sessions. To minimize bias, it is desirable that the researcher who measures posttherapy results be unaware of the pretherapy test scores and predictions.

Another variable that needs to be controlled in a study of child therapy is the means of getting the children to the clinic. Some children are brought to the clinic by their parents, others are brought by maids, and still others come by themselves. Transportation provided by the clinic may control this variable and also ensure more regular attendance.

Some comments are also necessary about process studies. Hobbs (1955, p. 37) states, "The most important studies of [play] therapy are those which illuminate the process . . . but so far we have little illumination." Thus far there has not been even a single large-scale, objective investigation of the play-therapy process; consequently there is very little verified, systematic knowledge in this area. On the basis of research, it is impossible as yet to answer the fundamental question: How is improved adjustment attained in play therapy? There is an obvious need for an integrated series of investigations focused on the internal dimensions of play therapy; first and foremost, the process itself needs to be scrutinized and its lawfulness discovered (Rogers, 1958).

The main obstacle to process studies in play therapy is a technical one:

the complexity and cost of recording and transcribing play-therapy sessions. Rogers (Rogers and Dymond, 1954, p. 416) estimated that "over five hundred man-hours of effort were necessary to collect and transcribe the data from one typical [adult] client [thirty interviews] and the matched control individual." Similar expenditure of time may also be involved in play-therapy research. It is clear than an individual researcher cannot afford the time and money required in obtaining raw data for process studies. There is, therefore, a definite need for a central library of complete typescripts (words and activities) of play-therapy sessions. These typescripts could be made available to interested researchers and could serve as the basic data for studying the process of play therapy.

Two recent studies of adult psychotherapy may serve as models for research in child psychotherapy. They are the Psychotherapy Research Project of the Menninger Foundation (Luborsky *et al.*, 1958) and Coordinated Research Studies in the Client-Centered Approach (Rogers and Dymond, 1958). These studies test coordinated sets of sophisticated hypotheses derived from two different personality theories: the psychoanalytic and the client-centered. The hypotheses and their rationales are clearly articulated so that "the empirical support of a hypothesis tends to confirm a whole body of theory; the disproof of such a hypothesis tends to cast doubt upon the related theoretical system" (Rogers and Dymond, 1958, p. 7). Clinicians planning research in child therapy will do well to consult these two studies. Many of the hypotheses and procedures of these studies may, with some modifications, be employed in play-therapy research. Thus, in studying the process of analytic play therapy, a researcher may want to know (Luborsky *et al.*, 1958, pp. 137 f.):

> (1) What were the major *themes* of the patient's material as to content and defense and in what sequential order did they unfold? What was the therapist's response to each of these, and how did the patient then react? How did the nature of the therapist–patient interaction affect the patterns of development of the material? Were particular themes encouraged or discouraged in their unfolding?
>
> (2) What were the major *transference* patterns as they unfolded, and in what sequence? How were transference phenomena worked with? To what extent were they explicitly brought into focus and made the object of transference interpretations? To what extent did a full-fledged "transference neurosis" develop in psychoanalytic treatment? To what extent, and in relation to which manifestations, and in what ways, were particular aspects of the transference deliberately fostered? To what extent were transference phenomena resolved before termination, and to what extent were they deliberately left unresolved?

In studying the process of client-centered play therapy, an investigation may test the following hypotheses (Rogers, 1951, p. 137) that have already received support in the research of client-centered adult therapy:

There is a trend toward an increasing number and proportion of positively toned self-references and self-regarding attitudes as therapy progresses.

There is a trend toward a decreasing number and proportion of self-references and self-regarding attitudes which are negative in emotional tone.

Attitudes of ambivalence toward the self, in which positive and negative feelings are expressed together, tend to increase slightly until somewhat beyond the midpoint of therapy and then to decrease slightly.

At the conclusion of therapy there are more positively toned self-references than negative.

These trends are not found, or are found in lesser degrees, in cases regarded as unsuccessful.

In the initial phases of therapy, self-references tend to be negative expressions, emotional in tone or objectively negative; at the conclusion of therapy the self-references tend to be either objective expressions, neutral in emotional tone, or objectively positive expressions.

It should be pointed out that in play-therapy research investigators frequently fail to utilize useful tools that are readily available. Dorfman (1951) mentions the fact that the Vineland Social Maturity Scale has never been employed with mothers to quantitatively assess their children's therapy and that no attempt has been made to apply the Q technique to play-therapy research. A useful research instrument for studying the play-therapy process is available in the literature; it is the Helene Borke Categories for Quantifying the Play-Therapy Process.[a] It gives a quantitative picture of the change in the child's emotions while in the process of play therapy. Although the scale was originally designed to quantify the process of client-centered play therapy, it may also be employed in studying play-therapy protocols of other orientations. Borke's scale makes it possible to compare the therapy process found in the content analysis of consecutive client-centered play-therapy sessions with the therapy process of other treatment schools. It is evident that even with the imperfect techniques and tools available to us at the present much significant research can be accomplished; the need in play-therapy research is not just for new techniques of testing but for meaningful ideas to test. . . .

## REFERENCES

Axline, Virginia. Nondirective therapy for poor readers. *J. consult. Psychol.*, 1947a, **11**, 61–69.

Axline, Virginia. *Play therapy*. Boston: Hougton-Mifflin, 1947b.

Axline, Virginia. Play therapy and race

[a] Lebo revised Helene Finke's categories for quantifying the play-therapy process and published them under Finke's married name, Borke. See D. Lebo, "Quantification of the Nondirective Play Therapy Process," *Journal of Genetic Psychology*, *LXXXVI* (1955), 375–378; and Helene Finke, "Changes in the Expression of Emotionalized Attitudes in Six Cases of Play Therapy," unpublished master's thesis, University of Chicago, 1947.

conflict in young children. *J. abnorm. soc. Psychol.*, 1948a, **43,** 300–310.

AXLINE, VIRGINIA. Some observations of play therapy. *J. consult. Psychol.*, 1948b, **12,** 209–216.

AXLINE, VIRGINIA. Mental deficiency—symptom or disease? *J. consult. Psychol.*, 1949a, **13,** 313–327.

AXLINE, VIRGINIA. Play therapy—a way of understanding and helping reading problems. *Childh. Educ.*, 1949b, **26,** 156–161.

AXLINE, VIRGINIA. Play therapy experiences as described by child participants. *J. consult. Psychol.*, 1950, **14,** 53–63.

BARUCH, DOROTHY W., and MILLER, H. Group and individual psychotherapy as an adjustment in the treatment of allergy. *J. consult. Psychol.*, 1946, **10,** 281–284.

BILLS, R. E. Nondirective play therapy with retarded readers. *J. consult. Psychol.*, 1950a, **14,** 140–149.

BILLS, R. E. Play therapy with well-adjusted readers. *J. consult. Psychol.*, 1950b, **14,** 246–249.

BLOOMBERG, CLAIRE M. An experiment in play therapy. *Childh. Educ.*, 1948, **25,** 177–130.

COWEN, E. L., and CRUICKSHANK, W. M. Group therapy with physically handicapped children: II. Evaluation. *J. educ. Psychol.*, 1948, **39,** 281–297.

CRUICKSHANK, W. M., and COWEN, E. L. Group therapy with physically handicapped children: I. Report of study. *J. educ. Psychol.*, 1948, **39,** 193–215.

DORFMAN, ELAINE. Play therapy. In C. R. ROGERS, *Client-centered therapy*. Boston: Houghton Mifflin, 1951. Pp. 235–277.

FINKE, HELENE. Changes in the expression of emotionalized attitudes in six cases of play therapy. Unpublished master's thesis, Univer. of Chicago, 1947.

FLEMING, LOUISE, and SNYDER, W. U. Social and personal changes following nondirective group play therapy. *Amer. J. Orthopsychiat.*, 1947, **17,** 101–116.

HOBBS, N. Client-centered psychotherapy. In J. L. MCCARY (Ed.), *Six approaches to psychotherapy*. New York: Dryden Press, 1955.

KANNER, L. Play investigation and play treatment of children's behavior disorders. *J. Pediat.*, 1940, **17,** 533–546.

LANDISBERG, SELMA, and SNYDER, W. U. Nondirective play therapy. *J. clin. Psychol.*, 1946, **2,** 203–214.

LEBO, D. The relationship of response categories in play therapy to chronological age. *Child Psychiat.*, 1952, **2,** 330–336.

LUBORSKY, L., *et al.* Treatment variables. *Bull. Menninger Clinic*, 1958, **22,** 126–147.

MILLER, H., and BARUCH, DOROTHY W. Psychological dynamics in allergic patients as shown in group and individual psychotherapy. *J. consult. Psychol.*, 1948, **12,** 111–115.

ROGERS, C. R. *Counseling and psychotherapy*. Boston: Houghton Mifflin, 1942.

ROGERS, C. R. *Client-centered therapy*. Boston: Houghton Mifflin, 1951.

ROGERS, C. R. A process conception of psychotherapy. *Amer. Psychologist*, 1958, **13,** 142–149.

ROGERS, C. R., and DYMOND, ROSALIND F. (Eds.), *Psychotherapy and personality*. Chicago: Univer. Chicago Press, 1954.

ROUSSEAU, J.-J. *Emile*. New York: Dutton, 1925.

❀ CHAPTER TWENTY-ONE

# The Learning of Psychotherapy

ANY CONSIDERATION of the evaluation of the therapeutic process would not be complete without some attention to the impact of the experience on the therapist himself. While Ekstein and Wallerstein are addressing their remarks more specifically to therapists who are working with adults, their point of view can be applied equally well to the learning situation of child therapists. In fact, the affective reactions when working with children may be even more intense as the therapist finds himself reliving, with the child, various episodes similar to those from his own childhood.

To relate such learning problems more specifically to situations often encountered in work with children, the following examples are presented as typical of experiences which tend to intensify the therapist's own subjective reactions:

(1) The therapist finds himself impelled to win over the child in dart games or checkers, perhaps even rationalizing that the child would be offended if he suspected that the adult was deliberately trying not to win.

(2) When the child patient is working through problems relating to castration anxieties, the therapist may unwittingly inflict further injury on the child by accidentally nicking the child with the scissors, breaking something he has made, or throwing a ball close enough to hit the child's arm.

(3) The therapist takes the initiative in getting out the fingerpaints, wetting the paper, etc. or both mixes and pours the plaster-of-Paris molds under the guise of being helpful; another therapist may resent a child's dependency and repeated calls for assistance.

(4) Sometimes messy activities are dreaded or limited outright.

(5) Silences are felt as embarrassing.

(6) The therapist feels hurt if excluded from the child's play, or uneasy if the child asks personal questions.

(7) The therapist is unable to set definite limits, as if he must prove to the child (and himself) that he cannot be hurt; others may be genuinely fearful of any expression of aggression by the child.

(8) Some therapists tend to align themselves with the child (and, in effect, against the supervisor) with comments such as, "We boys had better not do that" or "We shouldn't get too much water on the floor."

For the beginning therapist, especially, the conscious focusing on his interactional processes and the increased awareness of his own dynamics may be a totally new experience which needs to be explored in the supervisory relationship.

# *Therapist and Patient—Learning Problems*

RUDOLF EKSTEIN
AND ROBERT S. WALLERSTEIN

The "learning problem," the problem the therapist has in responding appropriately and helpfully to his patient, is the final justification of the entire supervisory and training structure. The student comes to his supervisor in order to acquire psychotherapeutic skills. He discovers in his work with his patients that at times he acts and responds within the psychotherapy situation in ways that are determined, not by the objectively demonstrated needs of the patient, but by characteristic, automatic, and inappropriate patterns within himself. These he discovers to be his learning problems.

[Elsewhere], these problems [have been] projected into the student's relationship with his supervisors as problems about learning.[1] [Here] they emerge in the psychotherapy situation with the patient, and are brought from there—

[1] See R. Ekstein and R. W. Wallerstein, *The Teaching and Learning of Psychotherapy* (New York: Basic Books, 1958), Chapter 9.

as learning problems—for discussion with the supervisor. All this could convey the impression that these "problems" are to be regarded as impedimenta to true learning, neurotically based obstacles to be gotten rid of so that proper learning can proceed with optimum efficiency. Actually any process involving personal change is impossible without affective components and the consideration of these components—inevitable in the most "normal" of interpersonal relationships—is what is meant by working with the learning problems. Put another way, working-out and solving the learning problems (and the problems about learning as well) is the very process of learning—it is itself the learning that is sought, and not just the necessary preliminary.

Such a view differs, of course, from the many attempts to consider as learning problems (and hence appropriate to the supervisory process) only "intellectual" problems—problems where the difficulties are presumably lack of knowledge of either theory or technique—whereas "emotional" problems which carry charges of affective and therefore drive-influenced behavior are to be excluded from supervision and to be considered necessarily analytic problems or therapy problems. We feel that learning is not just conveying the technical tricks of the trade, any more than it is just the removal of blind spots that impair the therapist's objectivity in his relationship with his patient. The skill that is acquired consists essentially of the capacity to integrate factual knowledge with appropriate emotional responses. True learning therefore combines cognitive and affective levels of experience into new and enduring integrations. Learning that results in the acquisition of skill and that therefore requires change, necessarily involves strongly charged affective components. This is especially so when the vehicle of the learning is the interpersonal process between the supervisor and the student, wherein the student reports what transpires between himself and his patient and gradually becomes aware of the characteristic patterns of his relationships, to his supervisor on the one hand and to the patient on the other. Where these characteristic patterns determine and limit the manner of professional performance and the level of professional competence, they are focused upon as learning problems within the supervisory context.

Perhaps this can best be illustrated by the learning problem common to many beginning therapists, the problem of the therapist's overidentification with the patient expressed in the formula, "I can't treat this patient because I am too much like him. He has the same problems that I have and I'm not sure that I can solve mine. How can I help him solve his?" The problem here [is one] of establishing a real *difference* between the therapist and his patient—between the help-giver and the help-seeker—and using this difference to promote the psychotherapeutic process. . . .

One kind of learning problem . . . is the automatic assumption of the role of a well-intentioned, controlling father who with greater wisdom can rechannel the patient's life into more satisfying molds. An example of this can be drawn from a sample of Dr. S's work with Dr. Field, in which the student came to the supervisory hour with material that he was at a loss to understand. For example, the patient presented her therapist with a reality event and tried to obtain a change in her appointment arrangements involving the missing of some hours—she said she wanted to go with her boy friend to the funeral of a distant relative of his. Dr. S felt that, regardless of the reality (which need not have forced so large a shift in appointment arrangements as the patient asked), the request was an overdetermined one. A number of possible meanings occurred to him. The patient might be expressing her feelings about how unimportant the therapy hours really were to her. Or she might be probing Dr. S to see how important *he* thought them. Or it might be a reactive hostile impulse ("You're about to take off and miss an hour—I can miss hours, too"). Whichever it was, Dr. S felt peculiarly helpless to determine. He said, "I can't just guess at what goes on. I have to be able to take this up with her and explore all these possible meanings."

Dr. S was asked then where he felt all the difficulty in doing this resided. He was not sure. He felt, though, that it was a function of his own "poor timing" in the therapeutic interviews. He said, "All these things came up right there in a big rush at the end of the hour. They were so jumbled that I did not have time to deal with them at all." Dr. Field asked, if this were so, why then had Dr. S waited literally to the very last minutes of the hour to bring up such an important matter to the patient as the fact that he would have to be away and would miss the next appointment—which released counterfeelings with no time left to handle them. Dr. S said that that was just it. That was an example of how he had gotten all mixed up on timing. He was going to tell her about the session he would have to miss. The hour with the patient turned out to be such a desultory one and there were so many fruitless interchanges that he was quite surprised when she "suddenly opened up" after forty minutes had gone by and began to talk quite volubly about her family. Dr. S had thought that he was going to draw another blank with his question about the family, but instead she did what she *shouldn't have*. She opened up. Dr. Field at this point questioned the words "shouldn't have." He asked, "Do you really mean that you decide what she should and should not talk about?" Dr. S became flustered. He said that he had had ten minutes allotted to this matter of his necessary absence at this time, but the patient had encroached on this allocation. When asked whether he really felt that he could control the interchanges and manipulate the hour that way, Dr. S was indeed embarrassed. He suddenly said that that was the same thing that they had been talking about again and again in the supervision, that he always did with the patient—like constantly outguessing her or putting her thoughts in for her. It was just another way of trying to control her. He had seen that he did it in the other interviews when it had been previously pointed out. But here it was startling, it was so clear. He was *really* learning about it, he said.

And yet, though he was *really* learning about it, Dr. S's problem of control —of making the patient into a predictable mechanical doll to which he had the key—was by no means worked out as much as he thought, and it is instructive perhaps to see it in another manifestation in the subsequent supervisory session. The following week Dr. S came in much troubled. The patient had spent a whole hour talking about her family and, with an unusual degree of vehemence, complained of their hostility and rejection, their interest in her only for her pension check, etc. Yet Dr. S had felt at a loss as to how to enter helpfully into any of this. If he would try to relate to any of these themes, she would constantly slip away to another example rather than face more fully the impact of any one. He said, "So then I tried a short cut and brought it to her direct and told her I felt she must be depressed today. But it didn't work. She couldn't make the connection to all the material she had been dealing with and just denied the feeling." Dr. Field said that he felt that this was quite right; the patient couldn't make such a connection, it was much too remote from the manifest material. Dr. S said that he had done this deliberately. He had been getting nowhere following all her complaining material. So he had in effect deliberately changed the subject completely. At this point Dr. Field asked did he mean that, as a result of feeling that he was making little contact with the patient on her themes, Dr. S had felt that this ought best be handled by changing the subject completely—to *his* theme. Wasn't this more of the very control they had been talking of? At this point Dr. S was again embarrassed. Yes, it certainly was. He could see all that now.

This problem of the need to control can, of course, reveal itself in a variety of ways, as we can see from a contrasting example from the work of another student, Dr. R, where the control was differently manifested—in the intellectual realm of control by knowing rather than in the active realm of control by doing, as with Dr. S. Dr. R had a need to constantly "know" the whole structure of the unfolding psychological terrain—and to know it in advance. He tried each time to reformulate the "structure of the case" and to predict ahead the development of the therapeutic process. He came to the supervisor, Dr. Daniels, as to a compendium of greater knowledge and experience, to fill in gaps where his own knowledge was insufficient. His questions of the supervisor were usually requests for further elaborations of the dynamics of the patient. And in his hours with the patient he very carefully selected all of his questions and chose the themes that he would respond to, in terms of selecting pathways that promised to lead to the preconceived theoretical formulations. This all came up most clearly when, in response to some speculations during the supervisory hour about what the patient may have intended by a particular kind of behavior, the supervisor asked why Dr. R had not asked the patient. Dr. R was suddenly at a loss. It had not occurred to him to ask the patient—it was the kind of thing that he counted on figuring out during the supervisory hour. It would have made him uneasy to ask the patient, since he himself had no idea what it meant or where it would all lead or how to deal with what might come next in response to his question. And around this issue Dr. R was able to see for the first time his avoidance of open-ended questions, where he would really be asking things that he didn't know and wanted to find out about and have clarified. He said somewhat lamely, "I guess I only really ask questions where I feel I already know what kind of answer to expect." The need to "control" the therapeutic situation—and one's own anxiety—by always "knowing" in advance had prompted this student to ask questions only where he already knew the answers!

A very different learning problem characterized the work of the action-oriented Dr. Q who, with his patients, constantly fell into the role of the "therapeutic acter-outer." A sensitive and gifted individual, Dr. Q demonstrated a quick and intuitive grasp of his patient's material, which he tended to react to by acting to thwart the neurotic expectation, without, however, helping to expose the mechanism involved or to bring the insight that would enlarge the patient's own effective area of control. For example, his patient once came to him complaining of her difficulty in getting a friend, whom she had allowed to share her apartment for a while, to move out. The patient complained of the friend's stubborn passivity in the face of which she felt helpless. She had no idea as to what to do, and in her helplessness turned to her therapist for advice as to what would be the best way to handle this situation—to rid herself of her undesirable tenant. Dr. Q empathically grasping that his patient was turning to him with the same stubborn passivity of which she complained when she was its victim, indicated that, no, he would not advise her in this situation. It was best that she figure out the alternatives in such a dilemma herself. The patient was frustrated and angry. She called her therapist unhelpful. What had Dr. Q done? He had felt his patient imposing the selfsame demand on him that she correctly felt as an unwelcome "neurotic" demand when it was made on her by her roommate. Feeling this as his patient's neurotic demand, he had avoided gratifying it —and hence perpetuating the neurotic interaction—by taking a strong counteractive stand. In so doing, however, he had failed to help his patient see that what she was describing as her roommate's passive-hostile behavior likewise characterized her very own behavior and represented her own inappropriate expectation and frustration in the therapy. Rather than interpreting in this way, Dr. Q had reacted.

Useful as such techniques may be at times with many categories of patients, they are singularly limited when applied to classically neurotic patients, candidates for truly insight-aiming therapies. And it was with the difficulties created in work with just such patients (of which this was one), with the many opportunities for therapeutic progress that were not fully consolidated, that Dr. Q, our therapeutic acter-outer, could himself come to see the inappropriateness of his own response patterns and to institute delay mechanisms between impulse and action. Somewhat further along in his work with the same patient he reported to the supervisor that his patient, a teacher, had maneuvered herself into a position where she would have a teaching relationship to her therapist's young son. Mindful of how the patient's previous therapy had disrupted shortly after the patient secured professional contact with her then therapist's child, Dr. Q's immediate impulses were to one of two actions. One was to forbid his patient to take on this new position. The second was to withdraw his son from the school. This time he undertook neither action, but brought the whole matter to his supervisor to be discussed as a technical problem in the therapy. At this moment, Dr. Q's learning problem has—for the moment at least—matured into a technical-skill problem.

Still another kind of learning problem is operative in the student who cloaks his dilemmas behind stated theoretical and research interests. Such an individual was Dr. Z, a psychologist with a research-oriented and academic background, who came to the clinical setting primarily, he stated, with an eye to the introduction of objective, quantifiable and hence "scientific" methods to the subjective and up-to-now unprecise data of psychotherapeutic processes. He had a research interest in comparing theoretical "systems of psychotherapy" and in validating one against another. An interest was stated in "proving" that psychotherapy is "scientific"—or at least in establishing just how scientific it is or can be made to be. One can certainly postulate that this is usually not an unambivalent wish. It may cover another and deeper need to prove that no system is effective, that none is scientific and that, therefore, one can spare oneself the need for empathic closeness and emotional involvement that real psychotherapeutic work demands.

Approaching psychotherapeutic work from an opposite direction (but one equally embedded in research objectives) was Dr. P, an earnest and intellectual individual who also described his would-be role in psychiatry as that of the "objective scientist." He had come from a primary interest in the physical sciences and was much preoccupied with the "data of psychiatry" and with validating the scientific nature of its methodology to his friends who remained in other medical disciplines. As one might expect, a major kind of learning problem that served to block his fullest usefulness in his chosen role as a psychotherapist (as it also blocked his research-psychologist colleague, Dr. Z) was his need to keep uninvolved in the emotional world of his patient, lest his position, which he conceived to be that of the "scientific observer" of the clinical interaction, be undermined. In turn, Dr. P's patient was a timid and inhibited young lady, recently recovered from an overt psychotic illness and wondering now whether in her interpersonal relationships she could dare allow herself to be more spontaneous and more emotionally involved. A main technical issue in her psychotherapy rested in the problem of helping her perceive that interpersonal involvements need not be hurtful and anxiety-arousing. It was this very technical problem in the therapy which was met, however, by the therapist's learning problem—his own need to take a detached and uninvolved stance—and it was only as this learning problem was somewhat resolved that attention could be effectively paid to the technical issues posed by the patient and constructive therapeutic solutions worked out.

This brings us to the point that it is only through unraveling the learning problems that he experiences with his patient that the therapist can come to see the other side of the therapeutic interaction—the technical-skill problems posed by the disturbed mental processes in the patient. This will be a rather late achievement in the training process of the young therapist. It may even seem that this achievement is not a part of the process of learning, but rather is the end-product of successful learning. The therapist can now use himself with so much freedom that he can decide on therapeutic interventions entirely in terms of the patient's needs, revealed through the structure of his personality and of his illness and through the strategic situation of the therapeutic process as influenced by the current transference position and by the current social reality.

This hard-won achievement on the part of the therapist is, however, also a part of the training process, just as the patient's new-found capacity for insight may represent both the cause and the effect of change. The psychotherapist, when he has arrived at this advanced stage of the training process, will use the supervisor not only as a source of greater experience and knowledge, but also as a teacher who can help him to become this very source himself. The therapist will then test his own ideas, play with various models of therapeutic strategy, and slowly take hold of the training process in an increasingly active way. He will put forth his own suggestions and permit himself a process of discovering which will lead him to independent learning. Articles on the process of supervision usually contain very little concerning this part of learning. Actually, however, one may turn to the rich clinical literature concerned with case studies for a description of that part of learning in which the performance of the therapist or the supervisor recedes in the background and the focus is brought onto the technical (and theoretical) problems in the therapeutic process.

However, even the experienced therapist who has acquired his mature capacity will not always be able to maintain this position. From time to time he will fall back on positions which have been previously described as learning problems and as problems about learning. This should not be considered a form of retreat, but rather as a peculiar aspect of any emotional growth process which—like a spiral—climbs higher and higher, but returns again and again to similar relative positions. As the therapist becomes more fully aware of his own automatic response tendencies in the therapeutic situation, he will also become increasingly able to modify these responses in terms of the objectively determined needs of his patient—to acquire, that is, increased therapeutic skill. As his skill increases, his need to fall back on outmoded automatic responses will diminish or will reach different, more subtle levels of automatization and require of him and his teacher a more subtle, a more involved, but also a more deeply enriching way of working together.

At this point, rather than catalogue an increasing variety of learning problems, it may be well to turn to a specific problem that arises in this kind of supervised work with learning problems, with its inquiry into so many affective, drive-determined aspects of functionings, and that is the need for exposure of the self in order to learn. Though as compared with psychotherapy, for example, the sector of total functioning surveyed in supervision is but a narrow one, the problems uncovered and the resolutions sought may at times be equally deep. One student expressed his great fear of this process by his concern that, if he were really open and free in his discussions of the many dilemmas he experienced in trying to carry out psychotherapeutic work, he would be placing himself in a very dangerous position where he could be "stabbed in the back," if not by the supervisor, then by the administrator who might have access to this material.

Certainly the knowledge revealed in discussions on problems in doing psychotherapy can be extremely intimate and private. Much of the material that emerges in the process of supervision exposes significantly the infantile aspects of the individual's functioning, at times almost equally so as in psychotherapy. Teachers can well ruin the confidence of their students by betrayal of such intimate material and have, moreover, a clear ethical duty to avoid doing so. A guidepost might be that the process itself be understood to remain quite confidential. The final evaluation, however, which is a series of derivative judgments based, to be sure, on that process, is, as fully as possible, a mutual understanding and a shared conclusion. This material, including its judgments and prognoses about the effectiveness of the learner's work, should be, in a fully responsible organization, shared with the administration. It is shared and known equally to all the participants—student, supervisor, and administrator.

It is also, and over and again, one of the core resistances to learning that one must expose his weaknesses and dilemmas in order to learn and to do this in the face of so many possible consequences to job, status, salary, professional training, and advancement. Analogously with the patient who comes to psychotherapy seeking help, the therapist coming to supervision must display his weakness for which he desires the help. Just as one tries to teach the therapist to do with his patient, so the supervisor must *demonstrate* to the therapist his realization that the weaknesses displayed are *not* all there is to his total professional functioning. It can even be said paradoxically that in displaying their weakness the patient and therapist, respectively, show us a side of their strength, which consists in their ability to focus on their weaknesses and bring them to another person, rather than to deny or conceal them. This self-exposure, then, despite the fear of possible consequences, is in itself a considerable forward step. It must be emphasized and seen by each participant that in each case the aim is not to "infantilize"—what is seen at any one time is merely a phase of a larger process. In subsequent stages of the process we can be sure that the therapist will come to relate with different facets of his personality functioning.

In this entire consideration . . . of what constitutes a proper "problem about learning" and a proper "learning problem," questions both of separateness and of interrelatedness with personal (and therefore therapy) problems, on the one hand, and with technical (and therefore skill) problems, on the other, insistently require definition. The conviction that they can be clearly defined and helpfully worked with is the rationale for a system of supervision that is neither personal therapy nor just a conveying of didactic information on theory and technique. Since these various kinds of problems ramify into one another so widely, however, and are separately perceived largely in terms of the frame of reference within which they are viewed and the purposes to which these perceptions are to be put, it cannot be denied that help in any one area can result in overlapping effects on another. For instance, the kind of change that stems from the resolution of troubling personal problems through therapy cannot fail to facilitate the tackling of problems about learning and learning problems in supervision. In some cases (and one object of beginning supervision would be to help detect these early) supervised therapeutic work should not be carried out at all until a measure of personal help is attained through therapy. But no matter what the extent of resolution of personal problems through therapy, this does not solve or substitute for, but will merely facilitate, the working with the learning difficulties—the core of the supervisory process. And this, the psychoanalytic institutes whose students have been the recipients of such an intensive help-giving process (their personal analyses) specifically acknowledge in the requirement that ultimately learning comes from doing—and doing under supervision geared to focus on the problems in doing and in learning.

## Acknowledgments

Frederick H. Allen, M.D., *Psychotherapy with Children* (New York: W. W. Norton & Company, Inc., 1942). Copyright 1942 by W. W. Norton & Company, Inc. Reprinted from chapters 4 and 9 by permission of the author and the publisher. — Pages 101–105, 292–297

Fanny Amster, "Differential Uses of Play in Treatment of Young Children," *American Journal of Orthopsychiatry*, XIII (1943), 62–68. Reprinted by permission of the author and the publisher. — Pages 11–19

Virginia M. Axline, *Play Therapy* (Boston: Houghton Mifflin Company, 1947). Reprinted from chapters 2 and 7 through 11 by permission of the author and the publisher. — Pages 34–39, 93–101, 239–242, 262–264

Ray H. Bixler, "Limits Are Therapy," *Journal of Consulting Psychology*, XIII (1949), 1–11. Reprinted by permission of the author and the American Psychological Association. — Pages 134–147

Dorothy T. Burlingham, "Child Analysis and the Mother," *Psychoanalytic Quarterly*, IV (1935), 69–92. Reprinted by permission of the author and the publisher. — Pages 70–76

Hanna Colm, "A Field-Theory Approach to Transference and Its Particular Application to Children," *Psychiatry*, XVIII (1955), 329–352. Copyright 1955 by William Alanson White Psychiatric Foundation, Inc. Reprinted by special permission of the author and the William Alanson White Psychiatric Foundation, Inc. — Pages 242–256

Audrey Davidson and Judith Fay, *Phantasy in Childhood* (New York: Philosophical Library, Inc., 1952). Reprinted from chapter 6 by permission of the authors and the publisher. — Pages 401–406

J. Louise Despert, "Play Therapy: Remarks on Some of Its Aspects," *Nervous Child*, VII (1948), 287–295. Reprinted by permission of the author. — Pages 87–90, 110–114

Rudolf Ekstein and Robert S. Wallerstein, *The Teaching and Learning of Psychotherapy* (New York: Basic Books Publishers, Inc., 1958). Copyright © 1958 by Basic Books Publishers, Inc. Reprinted from chapter 10 by permission of the authors and the publisher. — Pages 437–445

Erik H. Erikson, "Studies in the Interpretation of Play: I. Clinical Observation of Play Disruption in Young Children," *Genetic Psychology Monographs*, XXII (1940), 557–671. Reprinted by permission of the author and The Journal Press. — Pages 106–110, 264–276

Erik H. Erikson, *Childhood and Society* (New York: W. W. Norton & Company, Inc., 1950). Copyright 1950 by W. W. Norton & Company, Inc. Reprinted from chapter 6 by permission of the author and the publisher. — Pages 3–11

Sibylle Escalona, "Some Considerations Regarding Psychotherapy with Psychotic Children," *Bulletin of the Menninger Clinic*, XII

(1948), 126–134. Reprinted by permission of the author and the publisher. Pages 50–58

SELMA FRAIBERG, "Technical Aspects of the Analysis of a Child with a Severe Behavior Disorder," *Journal of the American Psychoanalytic Association,* X(1962), 338–367. Reprinted by permission of the author and the publisher. Pages 207–228

LISELOTTE FRANKL and ILSE HELLMAN, "Symposium on Child Analysis: II. The Ego's Participation in the Therapeutic Alliance," *International Journal of Psycho-analysis,* XLIII (1962), 333–337. Reprinted by permission of the authors and the publisher. Pages 229–235

ANNA FREUD, *The Ego and the Mechanisms of Defence* (New York: International Universities Press, Inc., 1946). Chapter 3 reprinted by permission of the author and the publisher. Pages 193–200

HAIM G. GINOTT, "The Theory and Practice of 'Therapeutic Intervention' in Child Treatment," *Journal of Consulting Psychology,* XXIII (1959), 160–166. Reprinted by permission of the author and the American Psychological Association. Pages 148–157

HAIM G. GINOTT, *Group Psychotherapy with Children* (New York: McGraw-Hill Book Company, Inc., 1961). Copyright 1961 by McGraw-Hill Book Company, Inc. Reprinted from chapters 7 and 10 by permission of the author and the publisher. Pages 125–130, 431–434

LILY H. GONDOR, "Use of Fantasy Communications in Child Psychotherapy," *American Journal of Psychotherapy,* XI (1957), 323–335. Reprinted without illustrations and by permission of the author and the publisher. Pages 374–383

RUTH E. HARTLEY, LAWRENCE K. FRANK, and ROBERT M. GOLDENSON, *Understanding Children's Play* (New York: Columbia University Press, 1952). Pages 364–368

ELISABETH F. HELLERSBERG, "Child's Growth in Play Therapy," *American Journal of Psychotherapy,* IX(1955), 484–502. Reprinted by permission of the author and the publisher. Pages 168–176

LYDIA JACKSON and KATHLEEN M. TODD, *Child Treatment and the Therapy of Play* (London: Methuen Co., Ltd., 1947). Reprinted from chapters 5 through 7 by permission of the authors and the publisher. Pages 76–80, 314–321, 369–371

MELANIE KLEIN, "The Psychoanalytic Play Technique," *American Journal of Orthopsychiatry,* XXV (1955), 223–237. Copyright 1955 by the American Orthopsychiatric Association, Inc. Reprinted by permission of the publisher. Pages 119–121, 277–286

DELL LEBO, "The Present Status of Research on Nondirective Play Therapy," *Journal of Consulting Psychology,* XVII(1953), 177–183. Reprinted by permission of the author and the American Psychological Association. Pages 421–430

EARL A. LOOMIS, JR., "The Use of Checkers in Handling Certain Resistances in Child Therapy and Child Analysis," *Journal of the American Psychoanalytic Association,* V (1957), 130–135. Reprinted by permission of the author and the publisher. Pages 407–411

JOEL MARKOWITZ, "The Nature of the Child's Initial Resistances to Psychotherapy," *Social Work,* IV(1959), No. 3, pp. 46–51. Reprinted by permission of the author and the National Association of Social Workers. Pages 186–193

Agnes G. McClure, "Reaction Types in Maladjusted Children," *British Journal of Medical Psychology*, XX(1945–1946), 389–392. Reprinted by permission of the publisher. Pages 45–50

Clark E. Moustakas, *Children in Play Therapy* (New York: McGraw-Hill Book Company, Inc., 1953). Copyright 1953 by McGraw-Hill Book Company, Inc. Reprinted from chapter 1 by permission of the author and the publisher. Pages 417–419

Clark E. Moustakas, *Psychotherapy with Children* (New York: Harper & Row, Publishers, Inc., 1959). Reprinted from chapter 1 by permission of the author and the publisher. Page 105

Lili E. Peller, "Libidinal Development as Reflected in Play," *Psychoanalysis*, III(Spring 1955), No. 3, pp. 3–11. Reprinted through the courtesy of the author and the editors and publisher, National Psychological Association for Psychoanalysis, Inc. Pages 176–183

Ralph D. Rabinovitch, "An Evaluation of Present Trends in Psychotherapy with Children," *Journal of Psychiatric Social Work*, XXIV (October 1954), No. 1, pp. 11–19. Reprinted by permission of the author and the National Association of Social Workers. Pages 39–45

Madeleine L. Rambert, *Children in Conflict* (New York: International Universities Press, Inc., 1949). Reprinted from chapter 4 of Part III by permission of the publisher. Pages 340–349

Eveoleen N. Rexford, "Antisocial Young Children and Their Families," in *Dynamic Psychopathology in Childhood*, Lucie Jessner and Eleanor Pavenstedt, eds. (New York: Grune & Stratton, Inc., 1959), pp. 186–200. Reprinted by permission of the author and the publisher. Pages 58–62

Alan O. Ross, "Confidentiality in Child Guidance Treatment," *Mental Hygiene*, XLII(1958), 60–66. Reprinted by permission of the author and the publisher. Pages 80–87

Alan O. Ross, *The Practice of Clinical Child Psychology* (New York: Grune & Stratton, Inc., 1959). Reprinted from chapter 5 by permission of the author and the publisher. Pages 121–125, 290–292

Ben O. Rubenstein and Morton Levitt, "Some Observations Regarding the Role of Fathers in Child Psychotherapy," *Bulletin of the Menninger Clinic*, XXI(1957), 16–27. Reprinted by permission of the authors and the publisher. Pages 256–258

Emanuel K. Schwartz, "A Psychoanalytic Study of the Fairy Tale," *American Journal of Psychotherapy*, X(1956), 740–762. Reprinted by permission of the author and the publisher. Pages 383–395

Elwyn M. Smolen, "Nonverbal Aspects of Therapy with Children," *American Journal of Psychotherapy*, XIII(1959), 872–881. Reprinted by permission of the author and the publisher. Pages 306–314

Jessie Taft, *The Dynamics of Therapy in a Controlled Relationship* [1933] (New York: Dover Publications, Inc., 1962). Reprinted from Part I; chapter 3, Part II; chapter 4, Part III; and the Conclusion. Pages 160–163, 200–205, 298–301

Adolf G. Woltmann, "Mud and Clay, Their Functions as Developmental Aids and as Media of Projection," in *Personality—Symposium on Topical Issues*, W. Wolff, ed. (New York: Grune & Stratton, 1950), No. 2, pp. 35–50. Reprinted by permission of the author and the publisher. Pages 349–363

Adolf G. Woltmann, "The Use of Puppetry as a Projective Method in Therapy," in *An Introduction to Projective Techniques and Other Devices for Understanding the Dynamics of Human Behavior*, Harold

H. Anderson and Gladys L. Anderson, eds. (New York: Prentice-Hall, Inc., 1951), pp. 606–638. Copyright © 1951 by Prentice-Hall, Inc. Reprinted by permission of the author and the publisher. Pages 395–399

Adolf G. Woltmann, "Concepts of Play Therapy Techniques," *American Journal of Orthopsychiatry*, XXV(1955), 771–783. Reprinted by permission of the author and the publisher. Pages 20–32

Adolf G. Woltmann, paper presented at the annual meeting of the New York Chapter of the Society for Projective Techniques, April 27, 1963, New York Medical College, New York City. Printed by permission of the author. Pages 322–330

# Index